JavaBeans

Dr. Donald Doherty and Rick Leinecker

SAMS

Unleashed

JavaBeans Unleashed

Copyright ©2000 by Sams Publishing

International Standard Book Number: 0-672-31424-x

Library of Congress Catalog Card Number: 98-87578

Printed in the United States of America

First Printing: December 1999

01   00   99   4   3   2   1

Trademarks

Warning and Disclaimer

ASSOCIATE PUBLISHER
Michael Stephens

ACQUISITIONS EDITOR
Don Roche

DEVELOPMENT EDITOR
Bryan Morgan

MANAGING EDITOR
Charlotte Clapp

PROJECT EDITOR
Carol Bowers

COPY EDITORS
Pat Kinyon
Heather Urschell
Jeff Riley

INDEXER
Heather McNeill
Erika Millen
Greg Pearson

PROOFREADERS
Candice Hightower
Linda Morris
Beth Rago
Tony Reitz
Mary Ellen Stephenson

TECHNICAL EDITOR
Eric Wolfe

TEAM COORDINATOR
Pamalee Nelson

MEDIA DEVELOPER
John Warriner

INTERIOR DESIGNER
Gary Adair

COVER DESIGNER
Aren Howell

COPY WRITER
Eric Bogert

LAYOUT TECHNICIANS
Stacey DeRome
Ayanna Lacey
Heather Hiatt Miller

Contents at a Glance

Contents

About the Authors

Tom Archer is a veteran developer with more than 15 years of experience. Many programmers know him from his tutorials and advice on the popular developer resource CodeGuru and the new SourceDNA, where Tom provides answers to development questions from around the world. In addition to building large-scale Windows DNA applications, Tom has contributed to several successful software products including PeachTree Office Accounting and the IBM/World Book Multimedia Encyclopedia. Tom has been an author on several books including *Visual C++ 5 Bible*, *Visual C++ 6 Bible*, *Windows 98 Programming Bible*, *Visual J++ Bible*, and *Sams Teach Yourself Visual InterDev 6 in 24 Hours*.

Dr. Donald Doherty is a neuroscientist and a computer expert. He received his Ph.D. from the Department of Psychobiology at University of California, Irvine. Don's computer experience includes programming large-scale computer models of brain systems. He's written on a wide range of computer topics. His books include *Sams Teach Yourself JavaBeans in 21 Days*. Don is a Technical Architect at Actium (`http://www.actium.com`). Visit his personal Web site at `http://ourworld.compuserve.com/homepages/brainstage/`.

Rick Leinecker was born and raised in Miami, Florida. He attended college at Western Carolina University, University of Cincinnati, Ohio University, and University of Miami. He was awarded bachelors and masters degrees and earned a number of credits towards a doctorate.

Rick has held a number of positions including Director of Programming and online services at COMPUTE Publications; Senior Programmer and later Director of Technology at IntraCorp, Inc.; Senior Software Engineer at MCI's Digital Imaging Division; Senior Software Engineer at Landmark Communications; and professor of Computer Science at Rockingham Community College.

Rick has a number of achievements outside of his jobs. He's written twelve books on the subject of programming and over a hundred magazine articles in publications such as *COMPUTE*, *Dr. Dobbs*, and *Byte*. Some of his software can be found on the shelves of retail outlets, such as CompuSA, and include Championship Chess and Bicycle Bridge.

When he's not writing software or books, he's probably rollerblading with his children, singing in a contemporary Christian group named Gentle Healer, or acting as musical director for the Rockingham County Theater Guild.

Bryan Morgan is a software developer with TASC, Inc. in Fort Walton Beach, FL where he develops custom client/server and Web-based applications for a variety of commercial and government customers. He also works as a freelance editor and writer and lives in Pensacola, FL with his wife, Becky, and his daughter, Emma.

Dedication

My work in this book is dedicated to Jane, Judy, and Beth: three wonderful daughters—Rick

Acknowledgments

I'd like to thank Don Roche, Bryan Morgan, and Carol Bowers—they are world-class editors and great to work with—Rick

Tell Us What You Think!

As the reader of this book, *you* are our most important critic and commentator. We value your opinion and want to know what we're doing right, what we could do better, what areas you'd like to see us publish in, and any other words of wisdom you're willing to pass our way.

I welcome your comments. You can fax, email, or write me directly to let me know what you did or didn't like about this book—as well as what we can do to make our books stronger.

Please note that I cannot help you with technical problems related to the topic of this book, and that due to the high volume of mail I receive, I might not be able to reply to every message.

When you write, please be sure to include this book's title and author as well as your name and phone or fax number. I will carefully review your comments and share them with the author and editors who worked on the book.

Fax: 317-581-4770

Email: mstephens@mcp.com

Mail: Michael Stephens
        Associate Publisher
        Sams Publishing
        201 West 103rd Street
        Indianapolis, IN 46290 USA

Introduction

With Java fast on its way to becoming the standard programming language and runtime environment of choice for the Internet, many have wondered what's next for Java. JavaSoft, the creators of Java, apparently had similar thoughts after the incredible success of Java. They realized that Java clearly had lots of potential in terms of the Internet, but also started realizing that Java's benefits extended far beyond online applications. Instead of standing around waiting to see what other people could do with Java, JavaSoft seized the opportunity to assess the weaknesses of Java and beef it up with new technologies to make it a well-rounded software technology. One of these new Java-related technologies is JavaBeans, which is Java's answer to component software.

If you aren't familiar with component software, it is a type of software that is designed heavily around the idea of code reuse and compartmentalization. Component software is a very popular and powerful concept that is rapidly being used throughout the software industry to increase development efficiency. Software components are designed and built so they can be accessed and used in a variety of different development and runtime scenarios. The JavaBeans component software technology is based on Java and provides a means of creating and using Java classes as software components. JavaBeans is very significant to the future of Java because many viewed the lack of a component software technology as a big weakness in Java.

JavaSoft saw the need as well and quickly made JavaBeans a high priority on its list. When assessing the initial goals of JavaBeans, the architects at JavaSoft managed to come up with a very simple mission statement that cuts right to the point of what the JavaBeans technology is to accomplish. This mission statement follows:

"Write once, run anywhere, reuse everywhere."

This statement expresses the goals of JavaBeans in a very simple, concise, and elegant set of requirements. The first of these requirements, "write once," refers to the need for JavaBeans code to be written once and not require rewrites to add or improve functionality. The second requirement, "run anywhere," refers to the need for JavaBeans components to be able to run on a wide range of operating system platforms. The final requirement, "reuse everywhere," refers to the need for JavaBeans components to be reusable in a variety of different applications and in different types of development environments.

Although the requirements of the JavaBeans mission statement are admittedly a little vague, they nevertheless paint a general picture of what the technology is to accomplish. This book is devoted to exploring the JavaBeans technology and shedding light on how this mission statement is met throughout the various parts of JavaBeans. Throughout this book you learn all about JavaBeans at a conceptual level by addressing each fundamental area of the technology. You also learn a great deal about JavaBeans from a very practical perspective by building your own JavaBeans components that can be reused in your own Java applets or applications.

You'll be pleasantly surprised by the depth in which JavaBeans is covered. Even so, we make every effort to keep you on a level footing by balancing technical details with practical concepts. When all is said and done, we think you'll agree that JavaBeans is quite possibly the most exciting technology to come about since Java itself. We had a lot of fun working with JavaBeans during the development of this book, and we truly look forward to putting it to work in our own projects.

Who Should Read This Book?

This book covers the JavaBeans technology from a few different angles. As such, the book targets a variety of different readers with different technical backgrounds and expertise. From a conceptual perspective, this book requires little more than a basic understanding of the Java programming language and runtime system. To follow the topics about JavaBeans component creation requires a definite knowledge of Java programming. If you are a Java programmer, you will find yourself right at home with this book. On the other hand, if you are interested only in learning about the conceptual aspects of the JavaBeans technology, you will still find a great deal of the book useful and insightful.

Regardless of your technical knowledge or reason for wanting to learn about JavaBeans, keep in mind that at least a general knowledge of Java is required to fully appreciate the coverage of JavaBeans. This is due to the fact that JavaBeans is itself an extension of the Java technology. We encourage you to refer to one of the many books that cover the Java programming language and runtime system if you have no prior knowledge of Java.

Conventions Used in This Book

The following typographic conventions are used in this book:

- Code lines, commands, statements, variables, and any text you type or see onscreen appear in a `computer` typeface. When lines of input and output are shown, **`bold computer`** typeface is often used to show the user's input.

- Placeholders in syntax description appear in an *`italic computer`* typeface. Replace the placeholder with the actual filename, parameter, or whatever element it represents.

- *Italics* highlight technical terms when they first appear in the text and are being defined.

- A special icon (➥) is used before a line of code that is really a continuation of the preceding line. Sometimes a line of code is too long to fit as a single line in the book, given the book's limited width. If you see an ➥ before a line of code, remember that you should interpret that "line" as part of the line immediately before it.

Getting Started

PART

I

IN THIS PART

Introducing JavaBeans and the Enterprise

CHAPTER 1

Over the past 30 years or so, computers have gradually begun to dominate every facet of life. From day-to-day tasks in businesses, to making airline reservations for your vacation, to checking out at the grocery store, nearly every action you take every day is analyzed, recorded, and tracked by an information system of some sort. However, as you unwittingly move from system to system, all of this data is stored using a mind-boggling array of various methods. Some of these systems may be 30 years old and operate on large mainframe computers ("Big Iron") centrally located at a corporate headquarters. Other systems, such as a ticket purchase you make over the Internet, may reside in the form of a collection of relational databases, Windows NT and UNIX servers, CGI scripts, and middleware.

Somewhere in this vast assortment of new and old technologies stands you: the professional programmer. While it was common ten years ago to find developers who, for instance, only wrote COBOL code and knew nothing about relational databases, it is very rare today to find a programmer who only utilizes one skill. Instead, the typical job description can consist of multiple operating systems, multiple programming languages, multiple databases, and multiple network management packages. Because of this complexity, the Holy Grail of computer programming has long been a language that was distributed, object-oriented (and therefore more modular and reusable), cross-platform, and easy to learn and use. Industry veterans have seen "hot" languages come and go (remember Eiffel? Dylan? Ada?), but the vast testbed that is the business enterprise has always quickly found problems that prevented these languages from reaching widespread acceptance.

And Then Came the Web

While the Internet backbone and related applications (ftp, telnet, email) had existed for quite some time, the first glimpse our industry ever saw of an opportunity to grasp the Holy Grail previously mentioned was the introduction of the World Wide Web in 1994. Suddenly, documents, queries, and transactions could be made available to a large number of users without worrying about client platforms or computing horsepower.

It was shortly after this lightning bolt hit the computing industry, that Sun Microsystems (www.sun.com) introduced the Java programming language and subsequent runtime environment they termed the Java Virtual Machine or JVM. Although it was still very much a

1

rch product, Java purported to be fully "buzzword-
rords used by Java's lead engineer, James Gosling, at
said to be

inications (developer of the then-ubiquitous Netscape
hat they would include Java support in a future
er. I still remember the day when I downloaded the
actual (although tiny) application dynamically within
my Web browser. At that moment, the computing industry changed in monumental fashion and continues to change to this day.

The Java Programming Language: A Brief Overview

Java as a programming language is very similar in syntax to C++; therefore, if you know
C++, you will find Java very, very easy to learn. If you have ever written in any object-
oriented programming language (such as SmallTalk, ObjectPascal/Delphi, Ada, and so
on) you are also a step ahead of the game. In this section, we will briefly highlight the
key features and concepts of the Java programming language before diving into specifics
of the JavaBeans Component Architecture.

Note

In Chapter 2, "Tools for Getting Started," we will download, install, and test out
a variety of Java development tools and technologies. Of course, the remainder
of the book will focus heavily on JavaBeans development specifics. In this chapter, however, let's concentrate on understanding the overarching concepts of
Java programming and why the JavaBeans Component Architecture is important to you as a developer.

In its infancy, Java programming consisted solely of either applet or application development. However, the Java platform currently has dramatically expanded to include the development of the following items (and much more!):

- *Applets*—GUI programs that run within an HTML page.

- *Applications*—Standalone programs that can be either text-mode or consist of a modern graphical user interface.

- *JavaBeans*—Components used to "compartmentalize" code into a reusable, re-distributable object. JavaBeans are the Java equivalent of ActiveX components for those readers familiar with Microsoft's ActiveX component technology.

- *Servlets*—Java scripts that run on a Web server that can access other Java objects, databases, messaging queues, or any other Java technology.

- *Enterprise JavaBeans*—Enterprise components that will be discussed in more detail in Chapter 23, "Using Enterprise JavaBeans." EJBs are run within an EJB "container" and provide for transaction management, among other things.

- *JDBC Drivers*—Java Database Connectivity drivers are the Java equivalent of Microsoft's ODBC database access architecture. JDBC provides a standardized methodology for performing database access in Java.

- *JavaIDL*—A CORBA 2.0-compliant ORB supplied with the Java2 SDK Enterprise Edition. Using CORBA, Java objects can interoperate with objects written in a variety of other languages including C++, Delphi, COBOL, and Smalltalk.

- *Java Message Service (JMS)*—As part of the effort to allow Java to succeed at the enterprise level, JMS is an API that supports the construction of message queuing applications in Java.

Other interesting uses for Java also available include electronic commerce capabilities using JavaCard and JavaCheck, Web services via the Java WebServer, more enterprise functionality using the Java Transaction Service and Java Naming and Directory Interface, and Sun's own Java Web browser: HotJava. To see a complete listing of Java products currently underway from Sun alone, visit http://www.javasoft.com/products/products.a-z.html.

Object-Oriented Programming in Java

As stated earlier, Java is an object-oriented programming (OOP) language. If you are completely unfamiliar with OOP or Java, I'd suggest getting another reference text that provides a thorough introduction to Java. This book will focus primarily on Java *component* programming, in other words, JavaBeans, so some basic understanding of Java is assumed. At this point, we'll spend a little time reviewing Java programming without dropping down to the lowest syntactical levels (explaining *if* statements, comments, loops, and so on).

The three essential features that must exist for any language to be considered fully object-oriented are

- Encapsulation
- Inheritance
- Polymorphism

Encapsulation

Java code consists of *variables* that are used to hold data and *methods* that are used to perform operations on that data. Unlike C++, all variables and methods are declared inside (and are members) of a *class*. This process of grouping related properties and methods within a single object is known as *encapsulation*, therefore we can see that Java clearly meets the first tenet of OOP.

Inheritance

The second tenet, *inheritance*, is also fulfilled as well. A class can inherit from a parent class (known as the *superclass*) and can also choose to implement any number of *interfaces*.

> **Note**
>
> A primary difference between Java and C++ is this issue of inheritance. In Java, a class can only inherit from one class (known as *single inheritance*) whereas multiple inheritance is supported in C++. However, Java does support the concept of the *interface*, which is essentially a "contract" between classes. When you design a class that says it will implement an interface, this means that your class will implement *all* of the methods of that interface. Java does allow for the implementation of multiple interfaces. As you gain experience with the Java programming language, you will find that this idea of single class inheritance/multiple interface implementation is a much cleaner way to build objects (and it also makes the compiler writer's job **much** simpler...a primary goal of any language that seeks to be cross-platform!).

Inheritance allows child objects to be derived from parent objects, which ultimately means that programmers can reuse code without having to reinvent the wheel on each project. The issue of inheritance is what clearly sets object-based languages, such as Visual Basic, apart from object-oriented languages like Java. Visual Basic allows the reuse of objects (in the form of Visual Basic classes, ActiveX controls, or COM objects), however, existing objects cannot be inherited from.

Polymorphism

The concept of polymorphism allows the programmer to build an object that can be reused within an application or across multiple applications. In other words, a class can appear to be several different things to different callers. For instance, examine the following three method declarations:

```
Integer DriveTheCar(String s)
Integer DriveTheCar(int x)
Integer DriveTheCar(Object o)
```

As you can see, there are three methods named `DriveTheCar()` and all three can exist inside a single class. However, all three methods take different arguments and perform different operations inside. Still, all three methods (hopefully) perform similar operations—they drive the car—they just all take different inputs. This allows a class to be extremely flexible.

Information Hiding and OOP

One final object-oriented feature that Java supports is the ability to "hide" methods and variables from other objects through the process known as *information hiding*. You can restrict access to an object by using keywords such as `public`, `private`, and `protected`. The meanings of these restrictions are as follows:

- `public`   A variable or method defined as `public` is freely available to other objects.
- `protected`   A variable or method defined as `protected` can be accessed only by members of this object or objects derived from this object.
- `private`   A variable or method defined as `private` can be accessed only by members within this object.

Objects Versus Components

This brief introduction to the basic concepts of encapsulation, inheritance, polymorphism, and access restrictions was provided to give you an overview of Java's object-oriented capabilities. Large-scale Java projects are currently in production now that use literally thousands of classes. These classes do everything from accessing relational databases to operating robotic equipment to analyzing real-time operational data from manufacturing floors. If Java provides the ability to logically group and distribute code in the form of classes, you may find yourself asking what value lies in the JavaBeans Component Architecture?

The term *component* differs from the term *object* in several subtle ways. An object is generally thought of as being the runtime incarnation of a class within a larger system. Once a class has been instantiated and exists in memory, it is then referred as an `object` in the Java vernacular. Therefore, note that a single version of a class may exist, but multiple instances of objects of that class may exist in a system at runtime.

Components are generally referred to as specific objects that are packaged and intended for reuse. Components can exist in the form of Java RMI objects sitting on a middle-tier server, CORBA components that interact with existing transaction-processing systems, or graphical user interface components such as spreadsheets, image utilities, and widgets such as buttons, list boxes, and so on. An item, such as a spreadsheet component, is designed to specifically meet a certain demand: the need to perform routine spreadsheet calculations within applications. It is much simpler and more cost-efficient to simply purchase a pre-built spreadsheet component that has all the features you need (and more!) than to build it yourself.

What Exactly Is a Java Bean?

To gain an understanding of the importance of the JavaBeans Component Architecture, consider this hypothetical situation for a moment. Referring back to the spreadsheet example we just discussed, imagine that you're working with the JDK, version 1.0 (circa 1995) and that you have decided that on your latest project you will use a Java Integrated Development Environment (IDE) such as Symantec Visual Café Version 1.0. You go to several Web sites and download several evaluation copies of some popular Java spreadsheet components. You don't have any documentation (hey, they were free evaluations after all!).

Coming from the Visual Basic programming world, you're very familiar with the process of simply adding a component to the toolbar at design time, and then dragging and dropping that component onto a form. You then graphically set all the properties for the spreadsheet component at design-time such as color, fonts, number of columns, column headings, spreadsheet size, and so on. You also graphically set the filename of an Excel spreadsheet to be read in at runtime. At this point, you click the Run button and up pops a screen with your spreadsheet loaded, all properties set, and ready for use! The whole process took about 10 minutes, approximately seven of which were spent on downloading the files from the Web site.

Now, back to the fictional Java example. The spreadsheet class files are now downloaded, but there's no simple way to simply load them onto your Visual Café toolbar and perform a drag-and-drop operation onto an existing form. Why? Because Visual Café has no standardized way of looking into the class files and understanding what methods and properties they support. In addition, it doesn't understand how to display these components at design time. This leaves you with a lengthy manual process of building the Java code from scratch to instantiate a new form, add the spreadsheet to it, and then set all of the desired properties one line of Java code at a time. If you're a component developer, you could write the hooks that would allow your component to work well with Visual Café, but what about IBM Visual Age, Borland JBuilder, and other popular development tools that might be released at some point in the future?

As you can see, after Java 1.0 was released, it became quickly apparent that Java sorely needed a standardized component architecture that would support the compartmentalization and redistribution of Java components. The JavaBeans model supports three fundamental aspects of every component: events, properties, and methods.

Key Capabilities of JavaBeans

All Java beans conform to a broad specification (see `java.sun.com/beans/docs/spec.html` for the specification) that defines the complete set of features supported by the JavaBeans Component Architecture. Among these features are a complete event model, serialization, and introspection.

A JavaBean component has the ability to notify its environment of specific events (mouse-downs, errors, data retrievals, and so on) and changes in state (list box selections, text changes, and so on). Events are useful because they allow the parent application to customize its reaction to specific notifications fired off by the bean. A Java bean can also register itself as the target for other events as well, which allows it to react at runtime to changing conditions and actions around it. The compartmentalization of the code within the bean allows this event-trapping to be completely self-contained inside a well-defined component.

The term *serialization* refers to a component's capability to save its state and restore it at a later time or location. For example, suppose you are working within Visual Café and you download a far superior JavaBeans version of that spreadsheet component we discussed earlier. You add it to your form, set all the properties, and then run your application. Everything looks great! However, how does Visual Café know how to restore all your properties tomorrow when you return to work and reopen your project?

Serialization allows the bean (through its implementation of the `java.io.Serializable` interface) to restore its state. As you will see in later chapters, serialization is a particularly powerful concept that also allows Java objects to be passed across a network to support distributed computing via Java Remote Method Invocation (RMI).

Java beans also provide public interfaces through properties and methods. Any public properties defined by the bean according to the JavaBeans specification allows a design-time environment such as Visual Café or JBuilder (as in our earlier example) to "look inside" the bean and identify the properties and their data types.

> **Note**
>
> This process of discovering an object's characteristics is known as *introspection*, and a Java bean supports introspection through the Java Reflection API found in the `java.lang.reflect` package. This Reflection API supports the low-level examination of objects' characteristics and is an essential part of the JavaBeans Component Architecture.

Java bean properties are identified through a very simple convention. All properties must be accessed via a pair of `get()` and `set()` methods. The JavaBeans specification says that properties should be identified by using the following syntax: `getXXX()` to get property *XXX* and `setXXX()` to set property *XXX*. As an example, the two following method definitions would provide for the getting and setting of a `String` property named `ObjectName`:

```
public void setObjectName(String name);
public String getObjectName(void);
```

Among other interesting features that will be discussed throughout this book is the ability of a bean to provide its own custom property editor. This means that when you add a bean with a custom property editor to your form and select the feature that allows you to edit that bean's design-time properties, a custom dialog box built by the bean manufacturer will appear. This type of functionality is common to those developers with Windows programming experience in environments such as Delphi, Visual Basic, and PowerBuilder, and Java now stands on equal footing with those environments (actually, as you'll see in this book, you might say that Java is superior to these environments!).

Summary

The purpose of this chapter was to provide the reader with a good introduction to Java programming in general, as well as give you a glimpse of the power and usefulness of JavaBeans components. In this book, you will reuse existing JavaBeans components to construct small applications. In addition, you will use the JavaBeans API to construct our own JavaBeans. In the next chapter, we will make sure your development environment is set up correctly and prepared to work through the remainder of this book. We will also discuss the wide variety of tools and technologies that are available for your use.

Tools for Getting Started

CHAPTER 2

A wide variety of tools from leading software companies such as IBM, Sun, Microsoft, Oracle, and Borland exist for the JavaBeans developer. These tools range from the freely downloadable Java2 SDK to high-end application servers from companies such as BEA, Novera, and IBM. In this chapter, we'll focus on a more general set of tools that will be of use to all JavaBeans developers—from the beginner all the way to the advanced programmer. The key thing to remember is that with the portability and standardization of Java, you are not locking yourself into a vendor's toolset when you write pure Java code. Of course, this does not hold true if you were to use vendor-specific features (Oracle database access classes within Oracle JDeveloper, for instance). All of the tools covered in this chapter include support for JavaBeans design and development with some tools even including reusable code templates and wizards to help speed the development process.

The Java2 Software Development Kit (SDK)

The Java2 Software Development Kit Version 1.2.2 represents the latest (at the time of this writing) version of Sun's own Java toolset. From the Sun Web site (see the "Download Instructions" later in this chapter), users can freely download both Windows and Solaris versions of the SDK.

> **Note**
>
> Although Sun only provides support for the Windows and Solaris SDKs, the Java2 SDK is also available on a wide range of platforms from other vendors. Visit the Sun site at `http://java.sun.com/cgi-bin/java-ports.cgi` to see a complete list of Java licensees.

The Java2 SDK (formerly called the Java Development Kit, or JDK, for versions 1.1 and earlier) contains a full set of command-line tools such as a compiler, interpreter, debugger, applet viewer, compression utility, and distributed object registry among other things. Along with this set of tools, the Java Runtime Environment (JRE) is provided. The JRE represents the minimum "image" required to produce a working runtime environment for redistribution purposes. Also included is a comprehensive set of example applications that can be used as learning aids for various aspects of Java technology. All

of these tools (and much more) will be discussed and used in various examples throughout the remainder of this book. The purpose of this chapter is to make sure that you understand the different capabilities of the toolsets, where to get them, and how to set them up properly on your development machine.

Download Instructions

To begin with, download the Java2 SDK starting at the following URL: `http://java.sun.com/products/jdk/1.2/`. From this page, you have the choice to either download the Solaris or Windows products. If you select the Windows version, you will be given the option of downloading one large file (approximately 20MB) or fifteen smaller files (approximately 1.4MB each). Once downloaded, you are ready to proceed with the installation.

Installation Instructions

Installing the Java2 SDK is a straightforward process that essentially consists of three steps:

1. Running the installation program to copy the appropriate files to your disk and register all the components
2. Setting your system PATH to the .\bin subdirectory of the Java SDK installation so that all its Java executable tools will be accessible from the command line
3. Setting the system CLASSPATH to the appropriate Java class libraries

The first step is extremely simple. Run the executable that you downloaded and select where you want to install the SDK (see Figure 2.1), what features you would like to install (see Figure 2.2), and, finally, where you would like to install the Java Runtime Environment (see Figure 2.3).

FIGURE 2.1

Select the installation directory.

FIGURE 2.2

Select the appropriate installation options.

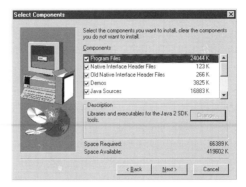

FIGURE 2.3

Select the Java Runtime Environment installation directory.

After the SDK has been installed, you need to set the PATH environment variable to point to the .\bin subdirectory. For example, if you installed the SDK to the c:\java directory, you would add "c:\java\bin¦ to your PATH environment variable. This is necessary to run the various tools such as the compiler, debugger, and interpreter from the command line (without typing in a complete path to the executable).

Following this, your final step will be to set the CLASSPATH environment variable. The Java interpreter uses this variable as a "search path" for classes. One new feature of the Java2 platform is that CLASSPATH is no longer a requirement. However, if you have an older version of the JDK (1.1.x or earlier), you will need to set this environment variable.

Your First Test Drive

Now that the SDK is installed, test things out with that ageless application: HelloWorld! This application is perhaps the simplest Java application possible. It simply prints out the words "Hello, World!" on the command line. While it doesn't do much, it will enable you to determine if your compiler and interpreter are set up and installed correctly.

To compile and run this example, type the code in Listing 2.1 into a text editor and save the file as `HelloWorld.java`.

LISTING 2.1   The "HelloWorld" Program in Java

```
import java.lang.*;
class HelloWorld
{
        public static void main (String[] args)
        {
                System.out.println("Hello, World!");
        }
}
```

Now compile the `HelloWorld` class using the following command-line operation:

```
javac HelloWorld.java
```

Run the application using the Java interpreter:

```
java HelloWorld
```

You should see the following text output on the command line:

```
Hello, World!
```

If this was successful, you are now ready to compile and run Java applications on your machine.

The Java Plug-In

The Java Plug-In is a very important tool provided by Sun, however it is not nearly as well-known or widely used as the Java SDK. The purpose of the Java Plug-In is to provide a certified Java runtime environment for applets running within Web browsers. At the time of this writing, Netscape Navigator 4.5 and Microsoft Internet Explorer 5.0 both included Java support. However, this support is buggy at best and downright lacking in some areas in both Web browsers. Developers have found that it is extremely difficult to get any Java applet of even moderate complexity to work correctly in both these browsers due to JVM problems with both products. Meanwhile, however, both browsers support a "plug-in" model that works very well.

> **Tip**
>
> A plug-in is a separate software product that is installed on your machine separate from your Web browser. Due to special HTML tags, however, the plug-in can be loaded and act as a "helper" application in conjunction with the browser for specified data types. Other common plug-ins include those for the Adobe Acrobat Reader and the Apple QuickTime Movie Player.

To solve this problem of inconsistent browser JVM support, Sun has developed the Java Plug-In. The advantage to the plug-in is, of course, that applets will run correctly in any browser. The disadvantage to using the Java Plug-In, however, is that the Plug-In must be loaded separately on the user's machine before he or she can view your applet. Using the Plug-In is a design decision that you, the developer, will have to make. Generally speaking, if you have a site on the Internet that will be used by large volumes of users (the vast majority of whom will not have the Plug-In loaded), it's probably best to either find a way to get the applet working in both browsers or find another way to present your solution. It should be noted that if your browser detects that the Plug-In is not installed, it will redirect to the Sun site to "silently" download it. However, this process can take several minutes and valuable users may simply cancel out of the process to avoid the wait. In an intranet setting where you can identify the operating systems and user base beforehand, the Java Plug-In provides an excellent solution.

Download and Installation

To download the Java Plug-In for either Windows, Solaris, or HP-UX, go to `http://java.sun.com/products/plugin/index.html`. The Java Plug-In is now included as part of the Java Runtime Environment, so you must download the standard JRE (totaling approximately 6MB) to install the Plug-In.

> **Note**
>
> Recall that earlier, in the discussion of the Java2 SDK, we mentioned that the SDK also included the Java 1.2.2 Runtime Environment (JRE). The JRE also includes the Java Plug-In, so if you have already downloaded and installed the Java2 SDK, the Java Plug-In is already installed on your machine.

Java applets are typically included in HTML files using the `<APPLET>` tag. For instance, Listing 2.2 shows the source for a simple HTML file that contains the fictional `Example1` Java applet.

LISTING 2.2 The <APPLET> Tag in HTML

```
<html>
<title>Example 2.1<title>
<body background="images/fdotback.jpg">
<applet code="Example1.class" Name="Example1" width="400" height="200"
➥align="center">
<param name="PARAM1" value="125">
<param name="PARAM2" value="250">
<param name="PARAM3" value="375">
</applet>
</body>
</html>
```

To briefly review, the <APPLET> tag tells the browser to load the Java applet whose class file is specified in the code parameter. The <PARAM> tags inside the <APPLET> tag specify parameters that are "passed" to the applet (and are usually read in within the applet's start() or init() methods). This is standard HTML syntax used by both Netscape Navigator and Microsoft Internet Explorer.

Things change just a bit when you use the Java Plug-In because you have to "override" the browser's default Java Virtual Machine and use the Java Plug-In instead. Using Internet Explorer, you make use of ActiveX/COM technology and use the <OBJECT></OBJECT> tags to load the Plug-In using that object's ClassID. Using Netscape Navigator, you make use of the Netscape plug-in architecture and use the <EMBED></EMBED> tags. To ease this process, Sun also provides one more nifty tool: the Java Plug-In HTML Converter, also freely downloadable from http://java.sun.com/products/plugin/1.2/converter.html. Listing 2.3 shows the appearance of Listing 2.2's HTML after being run through the Java Plug-In HTML Converter.

LISTING 2.3 HTML for the Java Plug-In

```
<html>
<title>Example 2.1<title>
<body background="images/fdotback.jpg">
<!--"CONVERTED_APPLET"-->
<!-- CONVERTER VERSION 1.0 -->
<OBJECT classid="clsid:8AD9C840-044E-11D1-B3E9-00805F499D93"
WIDTH = "400" HEIGHT = "200" NAME = "Example1" ALIGN = "center"
codebase="http://java.sun.com/products/plugin/1.2/jinstall-12-
➥win32.cab#Version=1,2,0,0">
<PARAM NAME = CODE VALUE = "Example1.class" >
<PARAM NAME = NAME VALUE = "Example1" >
```

continues

2

TOOLS FOR GETTING STARTED

LISTING 2.3 continued

```
<PARAM NAME="type" VALUE="application/x-java-applet;version=1.2">
<PARAM NAME = "PARAM1" VALUE ="125">
<PARAM NAME = "PARAM2" VALUE ="250">
<PARAM NAME = "PARAM3" VALUE ="375">
<COMMENT>
<EMBED type="application/x-java-applet;version=1.2" java_CODE =
"Example1.class" NAME = "Example1" WIDTH = "400" HEIGHT = "200"
ALIGN = "center"  PARAM1 = "125" PARAM2 = "250" PARAM3 = "375"
pluginspage="http://java.sun.com/products/plugin/1.2/plugin-
➥install.html"><NOEMBED></COMMENT>

</NOEMBED></EMBED>
</OBJECT>
<!--"END_CONVERTED_APPLET"-->

</body>
</html>
```

Using the Java Plug-In in your own development and testing will allow you to more quickly identify and fix problems. It is very frustrating to work on a bug for several hours (or even days) only to finally determine that the bug lies within the Web browser software itself.

Now that you have the Java2 SDK and Java2 Plug-In successfully downloaded and installed, we will take a look at the JavaBeans Development Kit for the development and testing JavaBeans components.

The JavaBeans Development Kit (BDK) 1.1

From Sun documentation, the JavaBeans Development Kit (or BDK) is "intended to support the development of JavaBeans components and to act as a standard reference base for both component developers and tool vendors." It can be used as a standalone development tool (similar to the command-line tools provided by the Java2 SDK) or as a testing tool to verify that your components work as you intended. Recall the Java Plug-In discussion and the problems developers routinely find with browser JVM implementations. To verify that your bean is, in fact, working correctly, the BDK provides an excellent "sanity check." Included with the BDK are the following:

• *The BeanBox*—The BeanBox is the JavaBeans reference container and it also acts as an excellent example of how to build your own bean container (should the need ever arise).

- *Example Beans*—Included with the BDK are 15 example beans that demonstrate concepts such as customization, serialization, properties, custom property editors, and events.
- *Reference Source Code*—The complete source code for the BeanBox container is provided and can be freely recycled and reused "at your own risk."
- *Tutorial*—Also included is The JavaBeans Tutorial which steps through the main JavaBeans 1.0 concepts.

To download the BDK, go to the following site: `http://java.sun.com/beans/software/ bdk download.html`. Versions for both Windows and Solaris are available from Sun.

> **Note**
>
> The Java2 Standard Edition is required to successfully run BDK, Version 1.1. If you haven't downloaded the Java2 SDK (as described earlier in this chapter), you should do so before downloading and installing the BDK 1.1.

Installation of the BDK requires a series of steps. After accepting the license conditions, you will be prompted to select the installation directory (see Figure 2.4).

FIGURE 2.4

Select the BDK installation directory.

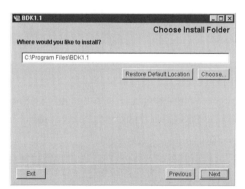

You will then be prompted to select a default Java Virtual Machine. This JVM will be used to run the BeanBox, which is itself a Java application. As you can see from Figure 2.5, I have quite a few different VMs installed (including that of the Java2 SDK, Java2 Runtime Environment, and the Microsoft VM). For your purposes, select the Java2 SDK version, which is located in the `C:\jdk1.2.2\bin` directory.

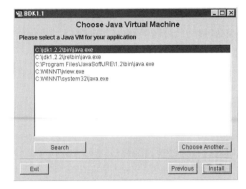

Following this, the BDK will be installed to your hard drive. When installation has completed, you will be prompted (as shown in Figure 2.6).

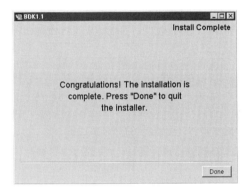

To make sure that the application was installed successfully and that your environment is also set up correctly, run one of the BDK examples here. For complete information on the BDK and the example programs provided with it, view the README.HTML file located in the root of the BDK installation directory (C:\Program Files\BDK1.1 on my machine).

Using the BeanBox

To use the BeanBox as a testbed container for a Java bean, change to the /beanbox subdirectory (where stands for the BDK installation directory). In that subdirectory, you'll see a run.bat file (for Windows users) or a run.sh script (for Solaris users). Depending on your operating system, run one of these files to start up the BeanBox (by either typing **run** on Windows or **run.sh** on Solaris). The BeanBox will appear as shown in Figure 2.7.

FIGURE 2.7

*The BDK 1.1
BeanBox container.*

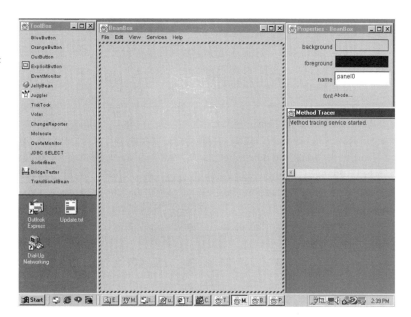

Three windows are of immediate interest: the Properties window (used to show the properties for the current bean), the ToolBox palette (used to select which bean to add to the container by first selecting it in the toolbox and then clicking the BeanBox), and the main BeanBox composition window (used to host the Java beans to be examined). To load a bean into the BeanBox, select it in the ToolBox palette, and then drag it over to the main BeanBox window. Figure 2.8 shows the Molecule bean loaded in the BeanBox.

FIGURE 2.8

*The Molecule bean
loaded in the
BeanBox.*

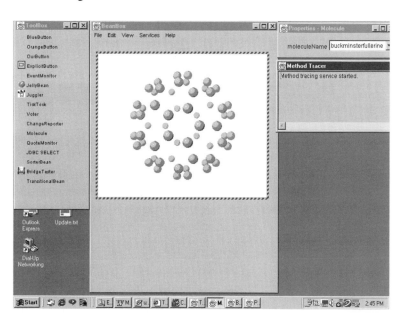

Connecting Event Handlers

In addition to simply viewing a running bean and setting its properties, you can also con-nect events fired by one bean to event handlers on other beans. Doing this, you can both verify that the event communication is working properly and also that your event handler is working properly as well. To do this, add two Java beans to the BeanBox. Select one of the beans and then go to the Edit/Events menu item. You will see several selections that represent the events that this bean fires. Select any of the events off the menu option and you will notice that a "rubber band" will be drawn out from the bean. This allows you to graphically connect events being fired to methods on the objects that you want to handle the events. When you click the border of the target bean, a list of methods that accept the same EventObject will be listed. Select one of these methods and then wait a short while for the BeanBox to build and compile the adapter class for the handler.

Adding Your Own Beans to the BeanBox

You can add your own beans to the BeanBox toolbox using one of two methods. As you will learn later in the book, all Java beans must be stored in a compressed archive known as a JAR file. This file uses the standard ZIP compression format but ends with the .jar extension. To add you own bean to the BeanBox toolbox, either add the JAR file to the jars subdirectory underneath the BDK installation directory or select the LoadJar menu item from the File menu.

The BDK is a good tool for testing beans on a reference toolset. However, obviously, it's not good for much besides that. There is no editing window for modifying and compiling code on-the-fly, and there's also no graphical design environment for building new beans from existing components. In the next section, we will discuss several popular Java IDEs that provide all these features and much, much more.

Integrated Development Environments

An Integrated Development Environment, or IDE, is a development tool (or set of tools) whose graphical user interface allows the user to fully design, develop, compile, debug, and run his/her project without ever leaving the environment. Typically, nearly all mod-ern IDEs include things like graphical debuggers (with graphical breakpoints, watch win-dows, and code stepping capabilities), user interface designers, code wizards for automating routine tasks, and event connectors for connecting the senders of events with event receivers.

In this section, we'll quickly examine some of the more popular Java IDEs. If you are undecided on which tool to purchase, visit all of their Web sites, download evaluation versions, and experiment with them using the examples throughout the remainder of this book. There's nothing better for familiarizing yourself with a software development tool than actually sitting down and using it to develop software.

Borland JBuilder/Oracle JDeveloper

The first tool we'll examine (in no particular order other than alphabetical vendor order) is Borland's JBuilder. Note that the previous heading also refers to Oracle JDeveloper. This is because Oracle Corporation has licensed JBuilder, added some specific Oracle database access functionality to it, and resells the product under the name JDeveloper (see Figure 2.9).

FIGURE 2.9

Oracle JDeveloper.

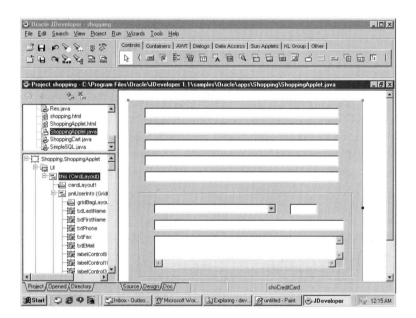

JBuilder comes in three versions: Standard, Professional, and Enterprise. The product includes comprehensive support for the Java 2 platform, so programmers can rapidly deliver reliable and scalable Java applications written entirely in the Java language; visual tools and reusable components for rapidly creating platform-independent applications, servlets, and applets; integrated and automated CORBA support for dramatically reducing the time and effort required to develop and deploy robust, high-availability CORBA clients, servers, and servlets; and Wizards and Visual Designers for creating reusable Java beans and Enterprise JavaBeans. Borland has announced support for the 3.0 version of JBuilder on the Windows, Solaris, and Linux platforms. For more information, visit the JBuilder Web site at `http://www.borland.com/jbuilder`.

IBM Visual Age for Java

Visual Age for Java is the name of IBM's entry into the competitive Java IDE market (IBM also markets Visual Age products for the Visual Basic, COBOL, C++, and SmallTalk languages). This product comes in two versions: Professional and Enterprise on the OS/2, Windows, AIX, and OS/390 platforms. A release for the Linux platform is scheduled after the publication of this book. Visual Age for Java includes Data Access Beans for JDBC database access, source code management tool integration (for TeamConnection, ClearCase, and PVCS), Enterprise JavaBean tool creation and deployment (Enterprise version), server-side development for AS/400 and S/390 (Enterprise version), and the Enterprise Access Builder for CICS (ECI, EPI), TXSeries, SAP R/3 and CORBA (Enterprise version). For more information, visit the Visual Age for Java Web site at `http://www.software.ibm.com/ad/vajava/`.

Symantec Visual Café

Symantec's Visual Café was the original Java IDE (originally simply titled "Café") and is still the most popular Java development environment. Visual Café is available in four different "models:" Standard, Professional, Database, and Enterprise. Basically, if you're planning to do any serious programming at all, the Professional version (and probably the Database version) is the minimal purchase you'll want to make. The Enterprise version is new to this product suite and contains support for n-tier development using RMI and CORBA, a UML designer, and numerous wizards and components for the construction of Java beans and database applications. For more information, visit the Visual Café Web site at `http://www.symantec.com/domain/cafe/index.html`.

Summary

In this chapter, we covered a wide variety of tools that will be of interest to the Java beans developer. Beginning with the Java2 SDK and ending with a brief look at popular Java IDEs, you should have a good idea at this point as to the current state of the Java development tools market. In the next chapter, we will begin to look at the actual process of developing Java classes and components.

Creating Beans

IN THIS PART

CHAPTER 3

Building Java Components

In This Chapter

All source code for this chapter can be found on the Sams Publishing Website at `http://www.mcp.com/info/0-672/0-672-31424-x`.

You can build and use Java components, known as *beans*, with two development kits provided free of charge from Sun; the Java Development Kit (JDK) and the Beans Development Kit (BDK). This chapter describes the parts of these development kits essential to your JavaBeans development efforts. You will learn the skills that you will need to compile and test example beans throughout this book.

Using the Java Development Kit (JDK)

The Java Development Kit (JDK) is the fundamental development tool that underlies all JavaBeans development even if you use an integrated development environment. In fact, the JDK is essential to all Java programming. JavaBeans programming, the programming of Java software components, is a special subset. The JDK includes many JavaBeans-specific packages and utilities demonstrating the central part that the JavaBeans specification plays in Java application development.

JDK Packages

The JDK provides the `java.beans` and `java.beans.beancontext` packages for JavaBeans-specific classes and interfaces. However, you're not limited to just these packages when you're programming beans. All of the packages in the JDK are JavaBeans-compatible, and all of the classes in the packages are designed following the JavaBeans specification. Many classes provided by the JDK are beans, especially classes that form graphic user interface controls such as most of the classes in the Abstract Windowing Toolkit (the `java.awt` package) and Swing (the `javax.swing` package). In this book, you will learn about and use most of the packages in the JDK while creating JavaBeans.

JDK Tools

The Java Developer's Kit (JDK) is freely available. You can download it from `http://java.sun.com/products/jdk/1.2/`. This download is version 2, which is recommended as you work through this book. The Bean Development Kit (BDK) can also be freely downloaded. Just go to `http://java.sun.com/beans/software/bdk`, and you can get the latest version.

The full range of tools provided by the JDK can be used while developing Java beans. Just like with all Java programs, you use the `javac` tool provided with the JDK to compile your beans, and you use the `jar` tool to create Java archive (JAR) files. There are other tools that aren't always as useful, such as the `appletviewer` tool, unless you're using the bean inside an applet. Finally, there are some tools, such as the java tool, that are only useful in certain circumstances. The following sections describe some of the useful tools provided with the JDK and how they should be used.

The java Tool

You can use the java tool to run a bean only if you transform the bean into a program by adding a main() method. In this book, the beans typically don't include main() methods. Instead, you run and test the beans in the BeanBox tool included in the Beans Development Kit (BDK) described in the "Using the Beans Development Kit (BDK)" section later in this chapter. However, you can easily add a main() method to most of your beans so that they can be self testing and easy to debug.

Adding main() Methods to Bean Classes

You can add a main() method to many of your bean classes so that you can run them using the java tool provided by the JDK. In this section, you're shown an example of a simple bean, the Hello bean, and how to add a main() method to the bean. The Hello bean source code, contained in the Hello.java file, is shown in Listing 3.1.

LISTING 3.1   Source Code for Hello.java

```
package sams.components;

import java.awt.Canvas;
import java.awt.Dimension;
import java.awt.Graphics;

public class Hello extends Canvas {
  public Hello( ) {
    setSize( 75, 40 );
  }

  public void paint( Graphics g ) {
    Dimension dimension = getSize( );
    g.drawString( "Hello", dimension.width/3, dimension.height/2 );
  }
}
```

Place the Hello.java file in the sams\components\ directory inside your root class directory. Then compile the code using the javac tool. The resulting class file can be run as a Java bean, but it can't be run as a Java application using the java tool. You must add a main() method to the bean to be able to do that. Listing 3.2 shows the source code for a Hello bean that includes a main() method. The bold type code is newly added to the code shown in Listing 3.1.

LISTING 3.2   Source Code for `Hello.java` (with the `main()` Method Added)

```java
package sams.components;

import java.awt.Canvas;
import java.awt.Dimension;
import java.awt.Graphics;
import javax.swing.JFrame;
import javax.swing.WindowConstants;

public class Hello extends Canvas {
  public Hello( ) {
    setSize( 75, 40 );
  }

  public void paint( Graphics g ) {
    Dimension dimension = getSize( );
    g.drawString( "Hello", dimension.width/3, dimension.height/2 );
  }

  public static void main( String[] args ) {
    JFrame window = new JFrame( "Bean Tester" );
    window.setDefaultCloseOperation( WindowConstants.DISPOSE_ON_CLOSE );
    Hello myBean = new Hello( );
    window.getContentPane( ).add( myBean );
    window.setSize( new Dimension( 175, 100 ) );
    window.setVisible( true );
  }
}
```

The `main()` method uses one new class and one new interface both from the `javax.swing` package. The `javax.swing.JFrame` class and `javax.swing.WindowConstants` interface are used to create a window in which to display the bean. Use the `javax.swing.JFrame` class to create the window and use the `DISPOSE_ON_CLOSE` integer constant defined in the `javax.swing.WindowConstants` interface to set the window's default close operation so that it completely kills the application on closing the window. When you run the bean as an application, you should see a window displaying the `Hello` bean (see Figure 3.1). You can use a similar `main()` method to display any bean that acts as a visual component.

FIGURE 3.1

The `Hello` *bean displayed in a window created by its own* `main()` *method.*

To compile a .java file, simply enter javac and the filename. For example, if you wanted to compile Hello.java, you'd use the following command line:

```
java Hello.java
```

To execute a Java program, you can use the Java interpreter. The following command line runs Hello.class from the sams/component directory:

```
java sams/components/Hello
```

The jar Tool

The standard way to deploy JavaBeans is to store them into JAR files. You store the bean's class file along with the class files of its supporting classes, if any, into one file with the .jar extension. You can also store supporting resource files in the JAR, such as image and sound files. You use the jar tool provided with the JDK to create JAR files.

Creating JAR Files

Create JAR files using the jar tool. For example, you can put the Hello bean you created from Listing 3.1 into a JAR file named hello.jar. First, you must create a manifest file that names all of the classes and resources that will be contained in the JAR file. The manifest file for the Hello bean is shown in Listing 3.3.

Listing 3.3 Source code for hello.man

```
Name: sams/components/Hello.class
Java-Bean: True
```

The complete path and filename is listed next to a name field for each class or resource file in the JAR. A Java-Bean field that is set to true or false, depending on if the class is a bean, follows the name field. The Java-Bean field of resource files is always set to false. Throughout this book, a bean's manifest file is presented shortly after presenting the bean's source code. Type the following command at the prompt of a command or DOS window opened to your Java root class directory to create the hello.jar file:

```
jar -cmf hello.man hello.jar sams\components
```

The c flag tells the jar tool to create a new archive file. The m flag tells the jar tool to include manifest information in the JAR archive from a specified pre-existing manifest file, in this case the hello.man file. The f flag tells the jar tool the name of the JAR file to create, in this case hello.jar. Finally, you can specify the folder or folders where the files to be included in the JAR file reside. In this case, the Hello.class file resides in the sams\components folder. After the command is executed, you should find a new JAR file in your root class directory.

Using the Beans Development Kit (BDK)

The Beans Development Kit (BDK) includes example beans and the BeanBox tool. The BDK is optional; you can create beans without it. However, the BeanBox tool is extremely useful and is used throughout this book.

The BeanBox Tool

JavaSoft's Beans Development Kit provides a simple application named the BeanBox tool for testing your beans and simple applications composed of beans. The BeanBox tool is itself a composite JavaBean application. The BeanBox tool displays a form (the BeanBox window) where you place and arrange beans. You then connect the beans together so that they can communicate. The resulting application can be saved and reloaded through the BeanBox tool.

Running the BeanBox Tool

The beanbox folder inside your Bdk folder contains the run.bat file for running the BeanBox tool on a Windows platform, and it contains the run.sh file for running it on a UNIX platform. Execute the run command on a Windows platform or a run.sh com-mand on a UNIX platform. The BeanBox tool appears in design mode displaying three windows—the ToolBox, BeanBox, and Properties windows (see Figure 3.2).

FIGURE 3.2

The three windows displayed by BeanBox during design time.

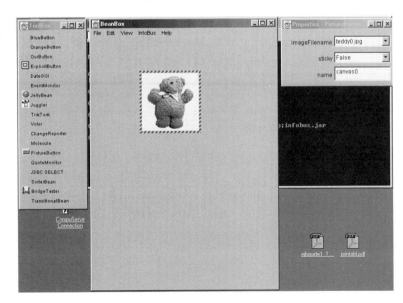

The ToolBox window displays all of the beans currently available to the BeanBox tool. These are the beans packaged in JAR files and placed in the `jars` folder found inside the `Bdk` folder.

The BeanBox window is a kind of form that you drop beans onto and arrange into an application. The BeanBox window in Figure 3.2 displays a `PictureButton` bean. Only the BeanBox window remains displayed when you turn off the BeanBox tool design mode by selecting the `Disable Design Mode` command from the View menu. The result is your visually designed application like the one shown in Figure 3.3.

FIGURE 3.3

The BeanBox tool displays only the BeanBox window during runtime.

The Properties window displays the properties of the bean selected in the BeanBox window. The properties and their values are displayed with the appropriate property editors so users can edit property values.

Some beans provide a customizer, a separate user interface that can allow you to edit aspects of the bean that are not properties displayed in the BeanBox Properties window. A customizer can also provide assistance in configuring complex aspects of a bean. Beans that provide customizers activate the `Customize` command on the BeanBox tool's Edit menu when they are selected in the BeanBox window.

Creating an Application

Create an animated application in this section to test some of the BeanBox tool's capabilities. The application will consist of three beans that are supplied with the BeanBox tool: a `Juggler` bean and two `OurButton` beans.

Adding a `Juggler` Bean

Start creating your animated program by adding the `Juggler` bean to the BeanBox window. The `Juggler` bean is an animation bean that displays a little man named Duke, the Java mascot, juggling coffee beans.

To add the `Juggler` bean to the BeanBox window, first point to the Juggler label in the ToolBox window or to the Juggler icon to the left of the label and then click your left mouse button. Your mouse cursor should change from an arrow into a crosshair. You've selected the `Juggler` bean from the ToolBox window.

Move your mouse cursor to the BeanBox window. Point to the general location where you want to place the `Juggler` bean in the window and then click your left mouse button. A `Juggler` bean with Duke juggling should be displayed in the BeanBox window (see in Figure 3.4).

FIGURE 3.4

The `Juggler` *bean animation runs by default.*

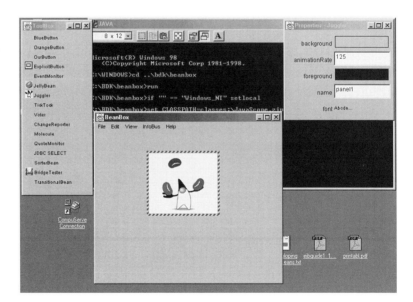

Newly added beans display a striped boundary. The striped boundary indicates that the bean that has the focus or, in other words, it is the currently selected bean. The Properties window displays the properties of the currently selected bean. If your `Juggler` bean is still selected, you should see the `animationRate` property listed in the Properties window along with other `Juggler` bean properties.

Adding a Button Bean

Now that your program displays animation, you want a way to start and stop the animation. Add a Start button and a Stop button. Use the OurButton bean for your buttons.

Point to the OurButton bean in the ToolBox window and click your left mouse button. Then point to the approximate location in the BeanBox window where you want to place the button and click your left mouse button. An OurButton bean should be added to your BeanBox window (see Figure 3.5).

FIGURE 3.5

The OurButton bean displays the press *label by default.*

Use this first button to stop the animation running because it is running by default. Make sure that the OurButton bean you just added is still selected. You should see the bean's properties listed in the Properties window, including the label property.

The current value for the label property, press, is displayed in an editable text box to the right of the property name. Highlight press in the label property text box and type **Stop** in its place. Your BeanBox window should look like Figure 3.6.

The application looks good so far. However, clicking the Stop button doesn't do anything. You must connect the Stop button with the Juggler bean.

FIGURE 3.6

The new Stop label displays across the face of OurButton *bean's graphic representation of a button.*

Connecting Beans

Connect or "wire up" the Stop button with the Juggler bean. That way, when an event occurs at the button, it can be communicated to the Juggler bean. Make sure that the Stop button remains selected and then look at the kinds of events that the button can signal by opening the Events submenu in BeanBox tool's Edit menu (see Figure 3.7).

FIGURE 3.7

The Events submenu lists all of the kinds of events to which the selected bean responds.

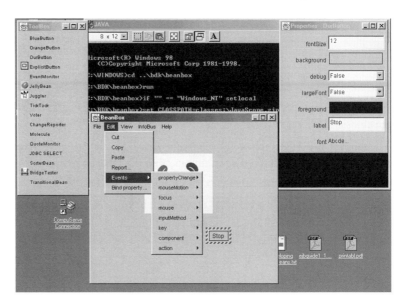

A `Button` bean produces an action event notification when the button is pressed. Button pressing can be accomplished through a mouse click or by selecting the button using the Tab key and then pressing the spacebar.

> **Note**
>
> Learn all about events and the Java event model in Chapter 6, "Event Model."

Connect the Stop button to the `Juggler` bean through action event notifications. Select `action` from the Events submenu, and then select the `actionPerformed` command from the action submenu. A red line should appear connected from the Stop button to the tip of your mouse cursor arrow.

Point to the `Juggler` bean and click anywhere inside the bean's graphic interface. The EventTargetDialog dialog box should appear (see Figure 3.8).

FIGURE 3.8

The target bean displays a list of available methods in the EventTargetDialog dialog box.

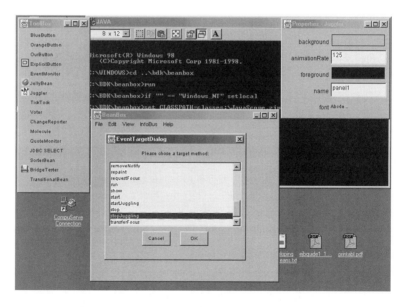

The EventTargetDialog dialog box displays a list of Juggler bean methods that an event, an action event in this case, can trigger. You want the `Juggler` bean animation to stop when you click the Stop button. Therefore, select the `stopJuggling` method from the scrolling list, and then click the OK button.

The BeanBox tool takes a moment to wire the components up for you. It generates the source code for an adapter class and then compiles the adapter class into bytecode. The adapter class is registered as a listener to action events that are generated in the Stop button. When an action event occurs, the `Juggler` bean `stopJuggling()` method is executed.

> **Note**
>
> Learn all about events, the Java event model, and adapter classes in Chapter 6.

When the BeanBox tool is finished, click the Stop button. The animation stops!

Adding Another Button

Your animation program isn't finished. You need to be able to start the animation running again! In this section, you go through similar procedures to add a Start button and then wire it up with the `Juggler` bean.

Add another `OurButton` bean to the BeanBox window. Point to the OurButton bean in the ToolBox window and click your left mouse button. Point to the approximate location where you want the button in the BeanBox window and then click your left mouse button. You just added another `OurButton` bean to the BeanBox window.

Make sure that the new `OurButton` bean, with the `press` label, remains selected. In the Properties window, change the label property by typing **Start** in its property editor. Rearrange the beans by dragging them with your mouse so that the application looks just the way you want it. Your BeanBox window should look similar to Figure 3.9.

Finally, wire the Start button up with the `Juggler` bean. Make sure that the Start button has the focus, and then select `Events` from the Edit menu. Then, from the Events submenu, select `action` to open the action submenu. Finally, select the `actionPerformed` command from the action submenu. The red line connecting the Start button and the tip of your mouse cursor appears.

Point to the `Juggler` bean and click anywhere within its graphic interface. The EventTargetDialog dialog box appears. This time select the `startJuggling` method from the scrolling list and click the OK button. Once the BeanBox tool is finished wiring the components up, click on the Start button. The animation starts back up. You've finished the application!

FIGURE 3.9

The animation program with both the Start and Stop buttons.

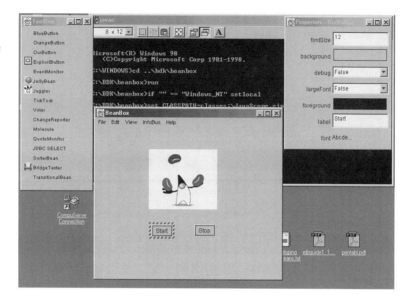

Running in Runtime Mode

You design applications in the BeanBox tool while it is in design-time mode. The BeanBox tool opens in design-time mode by default. Switch to runtime mode by disabling the BeanBox tool's design-time mode. Selecting the Disable Design Mode command from the View menu and the ToolBox and Properties windows disappear leaving the BeanBox window displayed. You cannot move or edit the beans displayed by the BeanBox Window in any way while it's in runtime mode. Switch back to design-time mode by selecting the Enable Design Mode command from the View menu.

Saving and Restoring an Application

The BeanBox tool lets you save applications that you wire together in the BeanBox window. For instance, you can save the animation program you created in previous sections by selecting the Save command from the File menu. The Save BeanBox File dialog box appears (see Figure 3.10).

> **Note**
>
> The BeanBox tool's Save command from the File menu is available in both design-time and runtime modes.

3

BUILDING JAVA COMPONENTS

FIGURE 3.10

Save your creations through the Save BeanBox File dialog box.

Type in the name of a program, **duke.bnb**, for instance, to the File Name text box and click the Save button. The animation program is saved to disk. The BeanBox tool is not very good in that it really doesn't enforce or suggest a default extension. It is a good idea for users to adopt a common extension and .bnb should be used.

Once you've saved an application created in the BeanBox tool, you can reload it through the Load command on the File menu. For example, after you've saved the animation program to disk, clear it from the BeanBox window by selecting the Clear command from the File menu. Now load the animation program. Select the Load command from the File menu and the Load saved BeanBox dialog box appears (see Figure 3.11).

FIGURE 3.11

Restore your creations through the Load saved BeanBox dialog box.

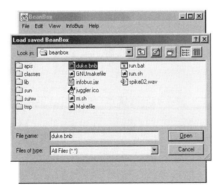

Note

The BeanBox tool's Load command from the File menu is available in both design-time and runtime modes.

Select the application you want to load, `duke.bnb` for example (if you've created an application with this name), and then click the Open button. The application loads in the same state as you saved it.

Adding New Beans to the ToolBox Window

The BeanBox tool provides two ways for you to add new beans to the ToolBox window. All of the beans used by the BeanBox tool must be packaged in a JAR file. If you want the new bean to be available in the ToolBox window every time you start up the BeanBox tool, place the bean's JAR file to in the `jars` folder found inside the `Bdk` folder.

Otherwise, you can add a bean to the ToolBox window for as long as your current session using the BeanBox tool through the LoadJar command on the File menu. Select the LoadJar command on the BeanBox tool's File menu and the Load Beans From JAR File dialog box appears (see Figure 3.12).

FIGURE 3.12

Temporarily display a bean in the ToolBox window by selecting its JAR file in the Load Beans From JAR File dialog box.

> **Note**
>
> The BeanBox tool's LoadJar command on the File menu is available in both design-time and runtime modes. However, because the bean is added to the ToolBox window, you will only be able to see the newly loaded bean in design-time mode.

Type the name of the JAR file into the File Name text box or select the JAR file and then click on the Open button. The BeanBox tool analyzes the JAR file and adds all the beans found inside it to the ToolBox window. The beans remain available until you exit the BeanBox tool.

Summary

In this chapter, you learned about the Java Development Kit (JDK) and the Beans Development Kit (BDK) and how to use them. Some tools are essential to all Java program development, such as the `javac` compiler, while other tools, such as the BeanBox tool, are not mandatory but are very useful. You will be able to work through most of the example programs in this book using the packages and tools in these two kits. When exceptions arise, the appropriate tools will be described. All of the tools used in this book are available for free from the Sun Microsystems' Java Web site located at `http://java.sun.com`.

The JavaBeans Component Architecture

All source code for this chapter can be found on the Sams Publishing Website at
`http://www.mcp.com/info/0-672/0-672-31424-x`.

Java components, known as beans, can be distinguished from simple Java objects that don't earn bean status because they don't adhere to the Java component architecture known as JavaBeans. JavaBeans components are written in the Java language and run in the Java Virtual Machine (JVM). One of the biggest advantages of the JavaBeans component architecture over other component architectures is that Java components are easy to write. The Java language and the JVM already impose most of the JavaBeans design specifications on Java objects. By following simple design rules, it's only a small step from creating Java objects to creating Java components.

When an Object's a Bean

A simple Java object becomes a Java bean when all of the object's data fields are private and are only accessible through methods, known as *accessor methods*. That's it! These requirements should be followed in object-oriented programming anyway. It's just that JavaBeans forces you to use proper object-oriented programming techniques.

There are also mutator methods, which change the values. The following example shows something that many of us have encountered:

```
Frame f = new Frame();
f.setVisible( true );
boolean visible = f.isVisible();
```

The incredibly simple migration from writing Java objects to writing Java beans is no accident. The JavaBeans component architecture is designed so that nearly all of the complexities of implementing a component model are hidden from the component writer and the component user. This was accomplished by letting Java and the JVM or application builder environment take care of those complexities automatically. Of course, as a programmer you can override many of the automatic mechanisms to build advanced or customized solutions. You learn how throughout this book.

Definition of a Bean

The ease of changing a Java object into a bean makes the JavaBeans component specification look deceptively simple. Although you can create beans by simply creating Java objects with private data fields accessed through special public accessor methods, a bean must support all five of the following features:

- *Properties* or private data fields
- *Events* or the ability of the bean to send event notifications of internal property changes to other beans, applications, or scripting languages

- *Introspection* or the ability of objects, external to a bean, to analyze how the bean works

- *Customization* or the ability of objects, external to a bean, to customize the appearance or behavior of the bean

- *Persistence* or mechanisms that result in saving a bean to disk or other storage device until it can be reloaded

Java and the JVM provide automatic support for most of the five features most of the time. That's why you could easily modify a Java object to make it a bean. As long as you follow the JavaBeans design pattern, the JVM or rapid application development environment automatically handles most of the computational overhead to carry out or enable the bean features.

Bean Properties

Bean properties are equivalent to the data fields in a Java object, except that bean properties must be declared as private data fields, and they must be accessible through special public methods known as accessor methods. Properties are discrete chunks of named data that are like attributes of physical objects such as color, temperature, and size. Add a property to a bean by adding a private data field and at least one accessor method. As the creator, you have to decide if a private data field is what you want. If you make it private, you give up some of the benefits of inheritance. This is not the case if you make it a protected property.

Private Data Fields

Use descriptive variable names for your property's private data field. It's important that the variable name be human readable and specify the variable's associated property. This is part of the JavaBeans design pattern. When an application builder environment analyzes your bean through introspection, the variable name is taken as the name of one of the bean's properties. For instance, you can add a background color property to a bean by adding the following declaration to the bean's class.

```
private Color backgroundColor;
```

The bean now has a background color property. An application builder environment displays `backgroundColor` as one of your bean's properties. As mentioned previously, this is done automatically by your bean testing tool, such as the BeanBox, or by application builders through introspection when you follow the JavaBeans design pattern.

A bean's properties must be accessible to other beans or they would cease to be properties of that bean. For instance, a rock has color, temperature, and size properties. If no one can see, the rock ceases to have a color property, or, at least, color becomes unimportant. If no other object can access a bean's data field, it ceases to exist as a property of that bean. Because properties are private data fields, there must be an accessor method to act as an indirect way to publicly access that data fields.

Accessor Methods

The JavaBeans design pattern specifies special methods called accessor methods for accessing property data fields. You can either set a property or you can get a property. That is, you can set your bean's background color or you can get its current background color. These two accessor method types are known as *accessor* and *mutator* methods. As long as you provide public access to a private data field by using accessor and mutator methods, introspection automatically knows what data fields are the properties of a bean.

Accessor Methods

Accessor methods are public methods used to get the value of a bean's property. All accessor method names must start with the get prefix. Typically, the get prefix is followed by the property name. For instance, a simple accessor method for your backgroundColor property should look like the following.

```
public Color getBackgroundColor() {
  return backgroundColor;
}
```

Accessor methods have return values of the same data type as the property that they get, and they take no parameters.

There is a special accessor method design pattern for Boolean properties. For instance, you might have a Boolean property named visible, declared in the following line, whose state determines whether the bean is visible or not.

```
private boolean visible;
```

The isVisible property accessor method should look like the following.

```
public boolean isVisible( ) {
  return visible;
}
```

Using the Boolean property design pattern is optional. You can use the standard accessor method design pattern if you prefer.

Mutator Methods

Mutator methods are public methods used to set the value of a bean's property. All mutator method names must start with the `set` prefix. Generally, the `set` prefix is followed by the property name. For instance, a simple mutator method for your `backgroundColor` property should look like the following.

```
public void setBackgroundColor( Color color ) {
  backgroundColor = color;
  repaint();
}
```

Mutator methods use the `void` return value, and they take a parameter of the same data type as the property they set. Naturally, when a property changes, the bean should reflect that change. In this case, the bean is repainted so that the new background color is displayed. This example is a minimal implementation of a mutator method. Typically, mutator methods check new values to make sure they're appropriate before a property is changed, and they fire an event that can notify other beans or applications of the change in a bean's property.

Bound Properties

A *bound property* is a property that fires an event when its value changes. The firing of an event results in the creation of an event object that notifies beans, applets, scripts, or other applications about the occurrence of a particular event, in this case a change in a property value.

> **Note**
>
> See Chapter 6, "Event Model," to learn more about bound properties and how to create them.

Constrained Properties

A *constrained property* is a property that fires an event when a new value being applied to the property does not fall within specified constraints. The firing of an event results in the creation of an event object that notifies beans, applets, scripts, or other applications about the occurrence of a particular event, in this case, an attempt to set a property to an invalid value. For example, you could specify that one of your bean's properties can only hold a value from 0 to 100. If a person, object, or script tries to set that property to 101, the property generates a notification that an attempt has been made to set the property to

4

THE JAVABEANS
COMPONENT
ARCHITECTURE

an invalid number. All constrained properties are also bound properties, so they also send out notifications when their values change within the constraints placed on them. This is similar to throwing an exception except that the application doesn't have to handle it.

> **Note**
>
> See Chapter 6 to learn more about constrained properties and how to create them.

Indexed Properties

A bean property is sometimes held in an array of values. For instance, you might create a color palette property. The colors on the palette, named `paletteColors`, form an array of `Color` objects. Properties that are an array of values are known as *indexed properties*.

Indexed properties get their name from the manner in which you get or set individual values in the private data field's array. You use accessor and mutator methods to access indexed property values like you do for all JavaBeans property types. However, indexed properties require an integer index value to specify which value in the property's array you want to get or set.

Indexed Accessor Methods

In this section, you're going to use the following declaration for the discussion:

```
Color[] paletteColors = new Color[10]; // create 10 Color objects
```

Indexed property accessor methods are written just like the single-valued property accessor method, except they have an integer index parameter, as shown in the following example accessor method for the `paletteColors` property.

```
public Color getPaletteColors( int index ) {
  return paletteColors[index];
}
```

The integer value passed to the `index` parameter is used in the usual way to access a particular value in an array. For instance, if the `paletteColors` array holds 10 colors and you want to get the third color in the array, you would make the following call to the `getPaletteColors()` accessor method.

```
thirdPaletteColor = paletteColors.getPaletteColors( 2 );
```

> **Note**
>
> Recall that the Java language uses zero-based indexing. This means that the index of the first value in an array is 0, the second value is 1, and so on.

Indexed Mutator Methods

Indexed property mutator methods are written just like the single-valued property mutator method, except they have an integer index parameter, as shown in the following example mutator method for the `paletteColors` property.

```
public void setPaletteColors( int index, Color color ) {
  paletteColors[index] = color;
}
```

The integer value passed to the `index` parameter is used as the index to the property's array variable so that a value can be assigned to that particular position in the array. For instance, if the `paletteColors` array holds 10 colors and you want to set the third color in the array, you make the following call to the `setPaletteColors()` accessor method.

```
PaletteColors.setPaletteColors( 2, someColor );
```

Getting and Setting Whole Arrays

Two additional accessor methods provided by the JavaBeans design pattern let you get and set whole indexed property arrays. This type of accessor method is just like the single-valued property accessor method, except that it returns the indexed property's array data type. For instance, the accessor method shown next returns the whole array of palette colors from the `paletteColors` property.

```
public Color[] getPaletteColors( ) {
  return paletteColors;
}
```

The mutator method for setting a whole indexed property array is just like the single-valued property mutator method, except that its parameter is the indexed property's array data type. For example, the mutator method shown next sets the whole array of palette colors in the `paletteColors` property to a new array.

```
public void setPaletteColors( Color colors[] ) {
  paletteColors = colors;
}
```

These two methods provide the only way you can change the size of an indexed property.

Bean Events

Internally, beans use the Java event model just like any Java application, but they also use events to communicate with other beans. It's communication through events that gives you the ability to wire beans into applications. You have already seen two occasions for beans to fire events: when a property value changes and when an attempt is made to change a property to an invalid value. There are many other standard events that a bean can fire, and you can define your own event objects. The Java language provides an event model to use when creating components and applications known as the *delegation event model*.

Delegation Event Model

Java's delegation event model provides a simple, logical mechanism for implementing communication between beans. The model is built on three concepts: event sources, event objects, and event listeners. *Event sources* produce event objects; *events* are encapsulated in event objects; and *event listeners* listen for, receive, and process event objects. A Java bean must be defined as an event source for any occurrence, such as a change in property value, that you want the bean to communicate to other beans or applications. The other beans or applications that listen for notification of a change in property value or other occurrences, must be defined as event listeners for the particular event. When something happens in a bean that is a source for the particular event, the bean creates an event object that encapsulates information about the event and sends it to all of the beans and applications that are listeners for the particular event.

> **Note**
>
> See Chapter 6 to learn more about the delegation event model and how to create Java beans that use events.

Bean Methods

Other than accessor methods, there is nothing special about a Java bean method. However, keep in mind that any public method is visible to users through application builders and other JavaBeans containers like the BeanBox. Only make methods public if you really do want them public. And when you do write a public method, give it a human readable name that makes it obvious for what the method should be used.

Introspection

You learn about a bean through introspection. *Introspection* is the process of analyzing a bean to expose its properties, public methods, and the events that it can produce. You don't carry out the analysis yourself. Typically, your visual bean-testing tool or your application builder carries out introspection. In fact, you don't need to worry about the gritty details of how introspection is carried out unless you're writing a program similar to the BeanBox, or you're writing a rapid application development (RAD) program. Except for these special cases, introspection is carried out automatically as long as you design your beans' properties, events, and methods in the way outlined earlier in this chapter.

Introspection can be carried out on two levels. On one level it can be used to expose a bean's properties, public methods, and events as mentioned previously. This information is exposed by using high-level introspection mechanisms. Because beans are self-contained objects, you must ask a bean about itself, like an employer asks a potential employee about himself or herself during a job interview. The results of a high-level introspection are usually displayed to a user in property sheets, menus, or dialog boxes. The BeanBox provided with the Beans Development Kit (BDK) uses high-level introspection and displays the results in each of the three ways just listed.

The BeanBox's Properties window displays a bean's property sheet that lists the bean's properties and property editors. For instance, the Properties window in Figure 4.1 shows all five of the Juggler bean properties. The property labels, such as `foreground` and `animationRate` are listed down the left, and the property editors are listed down the right side of the window. A *property editor* is the place where you customize or change the value of a property. It can be as simple as a text box or as sophisticated as a dialog box or wizard. You learn more about property editors later in this chapter in the section titled "Property Editors."

FIGURE 4.1

The Juggler bean's properties and property editors are listed in BeanBox's PropertySheet window.

The Events submenu in the BeanBox's Edit menu displays the results of a high-level introspection on the events a bean produces. For example, you can see in Figure 4.2 that the Juggler bean can signal many different kinds of events. These include various mouse and keyboard interactions with the Juggler bean's graphic user interface. The actual event types are listed in submenus derived from the Events submenu, such as the `componentAdded` and the `componentRemoved` events shown in Figure 4.2.

FIGURE 4.2

BeanBox's container events are listed in the container Events submenu.

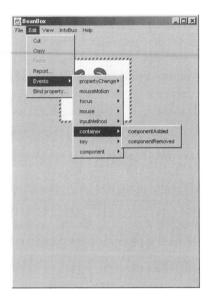

The BeanBox displays the results of a high-level introspection of a bean's public methods, other than accessor methods, in a different context. You need to know a bean's public methods when you want another bean to do something to the bean. For instance, the Juggler bean displays a continuous animation by default. You could wire up an application that presents the Juggler bean and two buttons, perhaps two `OurButton` beans. Users would click one `OurButton` bean to start up the Juggler bean animation and one to stop it. When you connect the Juggler bean to an `OurButton` event, the BeanBox displays the EventTargetDialog dialog box listing all of Juggler bean's public methods (see Figure 4.3). You select the public method that you want to call in the dialog box and the beans are wired up. You have to select the `OurButton` object, and then select Edit, Events, Mouse, MouseClicked. Now the pointer becomes a drawing line. If you move the line so that it connects the `OurButton` object and the `Juggler` object, the EventTargetDialog box in Figure 4.3 is displayed.

This isn't cool because you can link actions and objects, but instead, the tool reads how the `Juggler` bean reacts to a `mouseclick` and adds it to the list in the EventTargetDialog box automatically. The seemingly unrelated objects can be quickly linked and understood in relationship terms.

FIGURE 4.3

The BeanBox's EventTargetDialog dialog box lists a bean's public methods detected through introspection.

In some situations, you need more detailed internal information about a bean that is typically kept hidden, just like the information your bank asks you for when you open an account or apply for a loan. JavaBeans provides a low-level introspection mechanism for gathering this more detailed information when it is appropriate, such as in application builders. High-level and low-level introspection is carried out automatically by your visual bean testing or application builder tools, so you usually get reap the benefits of introspection without doing anything beyond following the JavaBean design patterns.

Customization

You change a bean's properties through customization. There are two ways to customize a bean—through property editors and through direct calls to mutator methods.

Property Editors

Earlier in this chapter you learned that a bean's properties are exposed through introspection and are listed in a property sheet along with property editors. You change a bean's property through its property editor. There are many different types of property editors. One of the simplest is the text box where you delete the old value and type in a new one. For example, the default value of OurButton bean's label property is press. You can delete press and type **Start Animation** into the label text box to change the label property (see Figure 4.4). The result is that you customized the OurButton bean.

The OurButton bean property sheet lists properties with other kinds of property editors. The foreground property holds the bean's foreground color, which is black by default. The foreground color is the color used for displaying the label and other parts of the OurButton bean. The foreground property editor is a Color Editor dialog box, shown in Figure 4.5. This dialog box displays when you click in the foreground property editor area showing the current foreground color.

4

THE JAVABEANS
COMPONENT
ARCHITECTURE

FIGURE 4.4

Customize the
OurButton *bean by*
typing new text
into the label
property editor.

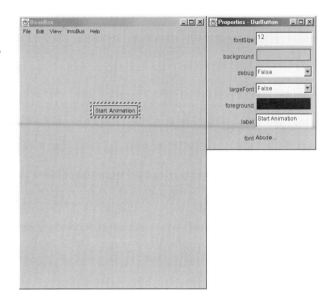

FIGURE 4.5

Customize
OurButton *bean's*
foreground prop-
erty through the
Color Editor dia-
log box.

The Color Editor is also used by the OurButton bean background property. Similarly, you edit the font property through the Font Editor dialog box, shown in Figure 4.6.

FIGURE 4.6

Customize
OurButton *bean's*
font property
through the Font
Editor dialog box.

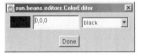

Finally, the largeFont and debug properties use Boolean property editors. These editors consist of a drop-down list containing the True and False entries. These are some of the built-in property editors that are automatically displayed when you use their correspond-ing data types to declare a property's data field. When you create properties using custom data types, you need to write your own custom property editor to go with it.

> **Note**
>
> See Chapter 25, "Customization," to learn more about customization and how to write your own custom property editor.

Calls to Mutator Methods

You can program the old fashioned way using beans rather than visual application builder tools. That is, you can write code and never see the property sheets, menus, and dialog boxes that result from introspection in a visual application builder. To do this, you need to know the bean's available properties and mutator methods through documentation provided with the bean. Then you customize the bean by making calls to mutator methods and passing new values to the bean's properties.

Persistence

Bean properties should remain the same until they are explicitly changed through a customization mechanism. For instance, once you change the OurButton bean's label property from press to Start Animation, you expect its value to remain as Start Animation unless you decide to change it again. This is known as *persistence*. JavaBeans make implementing persistent beans easy. It's mostly done for you. However, you'll need to be alert for those moments when you need to help out the JavaBeans automatic persistence mechanisms a little bit. Usually when this happens, you need to add some serialization code, which is code that saves or retrieves data from some permanent storage device.

> **Note**
>
> See Chapter 5, "Persistent Storage," to learn more about persistence and how to add serialization code when you need it.

Transforming an Applet into a Bean

Now you've gone over the design patterns you follow to create a bean, but what about all of those applets that you already wrote? Do you need to throw all of that work out and start all over to create beans? No! Java provides support for converting all of those Java applets into JavaBeans-compatible components. In this section, you convert a Java applet into a bean. Once you're finished you can convert all of your applets into beans.

You will convert a Java applet named LogoApplet (see Listing 4.1). LogoApplet displays business or company logos. In this case, it displays the Sams logo found in the samslogo.jpg file.

LISTING 4.1 Source Code for LogoApplet.java

```
package sams.applet;

import java.awt.Graphics;
import java.awt.Image;

public class LogoApplet extends java.applet.Applet {
   private Image logo;
   public void init() {
     logo = getImage(getCodeBase( ), "sams/applet/samslogo.jpg");
   }
   public void paint(Graphics g) {
     g.drawImage(logo, 0, 0, this);
   }
}
```

LogoApplet loads the image from the samslogo.jpg file through a simple call to the Applet class getImage() method. Recall that an applet's window size is set in the applet tag in the HTML code that display's the applet, like the HTML code shown in Listing 4.2.

LISTING 4.2 Source Code for teddyapplet.html

```
<html>
<head>
<title>Logo Applet</title>
</head>
</html>
<body>
<applet code="sams.applet.LogoApplet.class" width=160 height=60></applet>
</body>
```

You need to do two things to convert the LogoApplet applet into a bean; set up its getImage() method parameters so that they read the image file from a JAR, and package the revised LogoApplet class named LogoBean and the samslogo.jpg file into a JAR.

Revising the `LogoApplet` Class

Revise the `LogoApplet` class and rename it the `LogoBean` class, as shown in Listing 4.3.
The only change involves loading the Sams logo. There are two lines of code in the
`LogoBean` class's `init()` method rather than one call to the `Applet` class's `getImage()`
method. First, the `init()` method creates an `URL` object encapsulating the URL of the
Sams logo with the following statement:

```
URL url = new URL(getCodeBase( ), "sams/applet/samslogo.jpg" );
```

Create a URL of a file held in a JAR by passing the return value of the `getCodeBase()`
method to `URL` class's first parameter and passing the package path and name of the logo
file that will reside inside the JAR to the second parameter.

Once you have the file's URL, you simply pass it to the `getImage()` method, as shown in
the following:

```
logo = getImage( url );
```

You've now converted your `LogoApplet` applet into a bean named `LogoBean`. Everything
else is already done for you. The `Applet` class is completely bean compatible. In fact,
you are able to run `LogoBean` as an applet or a bean. You can display `LogoBean` in a Web
browser or the appletviewer utility now (see Figure 4.7). However, to use the bean in the
BeanBox, you first need to package `LogoBean` and the Sams logo file into a JAR. If you
run the program on a UNIX system, the filenames will all be lowercase.

LISTING 4.3 Source Code for `LogoBean.java`

```
package sams.applet;

import java.awt.Graphics;
import java.awt.Image;
import java.net.URL;

public class LogoBean extends java.applet.Applet {
   private Image logo;
   public void init( ) {
    try {
     URL url = new URL( getCodeBase( ), "sams/applet/samslogo.jpg" );
     logo = getImage( url );
    }
    catch( Exception e ) {
    }
   }
   public void paint( Graphics g ) {
     g.drawImage( logo, 0, 0, this );
   }
}
```

4

THE JAVABEANS
COMPONENT
ARCHITECTURE

FIGURE 4.7

LogoBean *displays as an applet.*

Creating the `logobean.jar` File

You must create a Java Archive or JAR file containing your bean if you want the bean to appear in the BeanBox. Even if you don't use the BeanBox, it's a good idea to create a JAR file. JAR files bring together all of the files that your bean needs and compresses them into one so they are easy to keep track of and take the minimum amount of disk space and Internet band width possible.

After you compile `LogoBean` and create the `LogoBean.class` file, you are ready to create the `logobean.jar` file. The `LogoBean.class` and `samslogo.jpg` files should be in the `sams.applet` package folder `..\sams\applet\`. You should find these folders in your root class folder.

Create a temporary manifest file to tell the `jar` utility which files are beans. Listing 4.4 shows a temporary manifest file, named `manifest.tmp`, for LogoBean. It tells the `jar` utility that the `LogoBean.class` file is a bean and that the `samslogo.jpg` file is not a bean. Place the `manifest.tmp` file in your root class folder.

> **Note**
>
> There must be an empty line between the listings of the different files, or the JAR file isn't created correctly.

LISTING 4.4 Source Code for `manifest.tmp`

```
Name: sams/applet/LogoBean.class
Java-Bean: True

Name: sams/applet/samslogo.jpg
Java-Bean: False
```

Open your DOS window or console window and change the prompt so that it's opened at your root class folder. Then use the `jar` utility to create the `logobean.jar` file by typing the following command at the prompt.

```
jar cf logobean.jar sams
```

> **Note**
>
> The appletviewer utility is part of the JDK. You find appletviewer in the
> `c:\jdk1.2\bin` directory. You should be able to run the appletviewer from any
> directory, as long as you add the `c:\jdk1.2\bin` directory to your PATH variable.

The c directive tells the `jar` utility to create a new JAR file, and the f directive tells the utility that you are providing the name of the new JAR file. After the two directives, you provide the name of the new JAR file, `logobean.jar`, which is followed by the root name of the bean's package. After you run the jar utility, the JAR file is created and the `LogoBean` can be viewed using a Web browser (or the appletviewer utility) or in any JavaBeans container.

Writing the `logobean.html` File

Displaying beans or applets packaged in JAR files in Web pages is nearly identical to displaying them when they aren't packaged. The `logobean.html` file, shown in Listing 4.5, displays `LogoBean` as an applet as shown in Figure 4.7, except that the source files are packaged in a JAR file. Everything should look familiar in this HTML file, except a new parameter added to the applet tag.

The new applet tag parameter is `archive`. Set the `archive` parameter equal to the name of the archive file, or JAR file. In this case, archive is equal to `logobean.jar`. Be sure to set the code parameter equal to the full package path. For the `LogoBean` class, it should read `sams.applet.LogoBean.class`. Now you're ready to view `LogoBean`.

LISTING 4.5 Source Code for `logobean.html`

```html
<html>
<head>
<title>Logo Applet</title>
</head>
</html>
<body>
<applet code="sams.applet.LogoBean.class" archive=logobean.jar
 width=160 height=60></applet>
</body>
```

Testing LogoBean in BeanBox

View LogoBean as an applet or a bean from the logobean.jar file. To view LogoBean as an applet, place the logobean.jar file and the logobean.html file into the same folder. Change your DOS window directory to the same folder. Type the following line at your DOS prompt and press Enter.

```
appletviewer logobean.html
```

Your LogoBean should appear in an appletviewer window. Alternatively, double-click the logobean.html file and your Web browser should load and display LogoBean.

Display LogoBean as a bean by placing the logobean.jar file in the jars folder inside the Bdk folder and then running the BeanBox, placing a LogoBean bean into the BeanBox window (see Figure 4.8).

FIGURE 4.8

LogoBean *displays as a bean in the BeanBox window.*

Summary

In this chapter, you learned the difference and the similarities between plain old Java objects and Java beans. The central difference is that classes written to create beans must follow the JavaBeans design patterns. Typically, that means implementing properties and events correctly using accessor methods and bound or constrained events. You also learned how easy it is to convert an applet into a bean. In fact, classes extended from the Applet class are already beans and can be viewed as applets or beans.

Persistent Storage

All source code for this chapter can be found on the Sams Publishing Website at http://www.mcp.com/info/0-672/0-672-31424-x.

Something that is persistent sticks around, and that's exactly what beans do when they're in persistent storage. Beans brought out of persistent storage are the same as they were before being stored. Storing beans is known as *serialization,* and restoring beans is sometimes called *deserialization.* Java does most of the work of serializing and restoring beans for you, but there are times when you need to do some of the work yourself. Java also takes care of keeping track of the version of each saved bean, but you need to do some work to make sure that your new version of a bean is compatible with the old versions. Serialization means to be able to write to file the state of the object at the given time. You can serialize all Java objects, not just beans, by implementing the `Serializable` interface.

JavaBeans Serialization

Beans have properties, and those properties define what a bean is like—for instance, the color of a bean or the message it displays. Users customize beans to their own liking by setting bean properties. If a user customizes a bean so that it's red, he or she expects it to stay red. Beans maintain their properties, such as being red, through serialization.

Much of the time, you can leave the work of serialization to Java. However, there are times when you need to add serialization code manually. There usually isn't much that you need to add to your code in these cases, but you must know when the modifications are needed. You just need to make sure that your bean and all of the objects in your bean implement the `Serializable` interface.

Using Object Streams

Java uses object streams to save data to persistent storage media and restore data back from the media. A *stream* is a path of communication between a data source and its destination. The object sending data through the stream is the *producer* and the item receiving data is the *consumer.* The Java Virtual Machine (JVM) requires that an object reads or writes its own state. A Java bean must implement the `Serializable` or `Externalizable` interface from Java's `java.io` package for it to be serialized properly.

Using Java's `Serializable` Interface

Java beans implementing the `Serializable` interface from Java's `java.io` package can save or retrieve their state. The Serialization interface does not define any methods or data fields, it simply marks the class as serializable. When you write a class that implements the `Serializable` interface, either directly or through inheritance, you are promising the JVM that objects instantiated from the class can be successfully saved and restored through the virtual machine's serialization mechanisms. It is up to you to make sure that the class does, in fact, keep its promise. This means making sure that any transient or static variables are properly accounted for and taken care of. In this section, you learn about transient and static variables, and you work through examples of making a properly persistent bean using the `Serializable` interface. The source code for the Seriablizable interface is as follows:

```
public interface Serializable
{
  private void writeObject(java.io.ObjectOutputStream out) throws
    IOException private void readObject( java.io.ObjectInputStream in )
      throws IOException, ClassNotFoundException;
}
```

Most of Java's Abstract Windowing Toolkit (AWT) classes implement the `Serializable` interface so JavaBeans classes simply inherit it. For instance, all of the classes you extend from Java's `Canvas` class inherit the `Serializable` interface and are, therefore, automatically serialized during persistent storage.

Some beans aren't extended from a class already implementing the `Serializable` interface. For instance, you could write a bean that doesn't have a graphic interface; it's invisible during runtime. Such a bean wouldn't implement the `Serializable` interface unless you explicitly added one. A good example of a bean without a graphic interface is the `Timer` bean, which you can create and learn more about in Chapter 9, "Invisible Runtime Beans."

Use the `Timer` bean, along with the `TestTimer` bean, to see how the `Serializable` interface is used. Place the `timer.jar` file in the appropriate folder so you can use the beans that it contains in the BeanBox (there will be two beans in the jar). The `timer.jar` file contains the `Timer` and `TestTimer` beans. The `TestTimer` bean is created exactly the same way as in Chapter 9. However, the `Timer` bean in the JAR file is created from source code with the serialization features taken out, as shown in Listing 5.1.

Listing 5.1   Source Code for `Timer.java`

```
package sams.time;

import java.awt.AWTEventMulticaster;
import java.awt.event.ActionEvent;
import java.awt.event.ActionListener;

public class Timer implements Runnable {
 Thread thread = null;
 private boolean running = false;
```

continues

Listing 5.1   continued

```
private long time = 0;
private long timeInterval = 1000;
private ActionListener actionListener = null;

public boolean isRunning( ) {
 return running;
}

public void setRunning( boolean running ) {
 this.running = running;
 if( running && thread == null ) {
   thread = new Thread( this );
   thread.start( );
   time = System.currentTimeMillis( );
   time += timeInterval;
 }
 else if( !running && thread != null ) {
   thread = null;
 }
}

public long getTimeInterval( ) {
 return timeInterval;
}

public void setTimeInterval( long interval  ) {
 if( interval >= 100 )
     timeInterval = interval;
}

public void run( ) {
 while ( thread != null) {
   long currentTime = System.currentTimeMillis( );
   if( currentTime >= time ) {
    time += timeInterval;
    processActionEvent( new ActionEvent( this, ActionEvent.ACTION_PERFORMED,
null ) );
   }
   try {
     Thread.sleep( timeInterval/10 );
   }
   catch ( InterruptedException e ) {
     break;
   }
 }
}

public synchronized void addActionListener( ActionListener act ) {
   actionListener = AWTEventMulticaster.add( actionListener, act );
```

```
    }

    public synchronized void removeActionListener( ActionListener act ) {
      actionListener = AWTEventMulticaster.remove( actionListener, act);
    }

    protected void processActionEvent( ActionEvent e ) {
      if ( actionListener != null )
        actionListener.actionPerformed( e );
    }
}
```

The `Timer` bean in the `timer.jar` file included for this chapter does not implement the `Serializable` interface (see Listing 5.1). The `Timer` class declaration looks like the following:

```
public class Timer implements Runnable
```

Run the BeanBox and place a `Timer` bean along with a `TestTimer` bean into the BeanBox window. Wire the `Timer` bean's `actionPerformed` event to the `TestTimer` bean's `incrementCounter()` target method. Also, change the `Timer` bean's `timeInterval` property to 500 milliseconds in the `timeInterval` property editor in the BeanBox Properties window. This way, you can test to see whether serialization leads to the persistent storage of the `Timer` bean's properties.

When you change the property from `true` to `false`, it doesn't stop running. That's because it only detects the change in property but doesn't have support for stopping the action.

> **Note**
>
> See Chapter 9 for more information on wiring up the `Timer` and `TestTimer` beans.

Save the new `Timer` and `TestTimer` bean layout by selecting Save from BeanBox's File menu. The Save As dialog box appears. Type in a file name, **timertest**, for example, into the File Name text box. Click the Save button. An Error dialog box should appear, as shown in Figure 5.1.

5

FIGURE 5.1

*Beanbox's Error
dialog box
appears with a*
NotSerializable
Exception *message when a bean
doesn't implement
the* Serializable
interface.

The Error dialog box says that the Timer object threw a NotSerializableException when the BeanBox tried to save it. Click Continue and then exit the BeanBox.

Fix the Timer bean so that it can be serialized. Simply modify the Timer class so that it implements the Serializable interface, as shown in the Timer class declaration that follows:

```
public class Timer implements Runnable, java.io.Serializable\par
```

Note

The Timer bean in Chapter 9 implements the Serializable interface. Objects that are not persistent, that don't serialize properly, cannot be called a bean. Persistence is one of the five features that define a bean (see Chapter 4, "The JavaBeans Component Architecture").

Recompile the class and repackage it into a JAR file with the TestTimer bean. Try wiring up the Timer and TestTimer beans just as you did before. Set the timeInterval property to 500 milliseconds and save the layout to the timertest file. It should work this time.

Clear the BeanBox by selecting Clear from the File menu. Next, load the serialized beans. Select Load from File menu and the Load Saved BeanBox dialog box appears. Select the timertest file you saved and click the Open button. The whole layout should appear in the BeanBox window just as you saved it, including the same property values.

Now start the Timer bean by changing its running property to True. Save the layout again by selecting the Save command from the File menu. Save the beans to the timertest file again. The BeanBox asks you if you want to overwrite the old timertest file. Say yes by clicking on the OK button. The Error dialog box reappears!

The Error dialog box says almost the same thing as before except this time it's the `Thread` object that threw a `NotSerializableException` object. Click the Continue button and then exit the BeanBox. This time the error is due to a transient variable in the `Timer` class that wasn't declared as transient with the `transient` keyword.

Using Java's `transient` Keyword

Transient variables are those variables that are assigned values that are necessarily different each time the object containing the variables is instantiated. Variables assigned references to objects are in this category.

A *reference to an object* is the address in computer memory where that object is found. Each time an object is created, it is likely to be placed at a different memory address. You can't count on the address being the same each time the object is instantiated. This is true when a bean is restored from persistent storage. The objects making up the bean are newly created and placed in your computer's memory. You can't depend on a saved object reference value to point to the right place in your computer's memory. In fact, the JVM doesn't allow the deserialization of object reference values. That is why, in the last section, the `thread` variable that is assigned a reference to a `Thread` object caused an exception to be thrown. The JVM is telling you that you can't deserialize that variable.

> **Note**
>
> Objects assigned to a variable must be instantiated from a class that implements the `Serializable` interface or the variable is transient. The `Thread` class does not implement the `Serializable` interface and neither does the `Object` class from which it's extended. Always look up the class defining a variable's data type to see if it, or one of its parent classes, implements the `Serializable` interface. If it doesn't, the class should be defined as transient.

Avoid saving transient variables and attempting to deserialize them by including the `transient` keyword in their declaration. Change the `thread` variable declaration by adding the `transient` keyword so it looks like the following.

```
transient Thread thread = null;
```

The `transient` keyword tells the JVM not to serialize the variable. When the object encapsulating the variable is reserialized, the transient variable hasn't been save, so the JVM doesn't try to restore it and no exception is thrown. However, the `Timer` bean still has a problem.

There are other uses for the transient keyword. For example, you might have an application that reads encrypted credit card numbers from a file or network and stores them in an unencrypted string. You wouldn't want that to be serialized to a file; therefore, you could make that String transient.

Compile the new Timer class, package it in the timer.jar file, and wire up the Timer and TestTimer beans in the BeanBox. Run the Timer bean by setting its running property to True and save the BeanBox layout. Clear the BeanBox and then load the Timer and TestTimer beans you just saved. No exception is thrown. This is good, but the timer isn't running anymore. Notice that the displayed number is static and the same as when you saved the beans.

Select the Timer bean in the BeanBox window and look at the Properties window. The running property remains set to True. This is how it should be because the bean's state should be the same as when you saved it. The problem is that its running property is set to True but, in fact, the bean isn't running. The root of the problem is that the restored bean has no Thread object because the Thread object wasn't serialized. Java provides a way to solve this problem, you can override the serialization mechanism's readObject() method.

Using Java's readObject() Method

The readObject() method is called automatically by Java objects implementing the Serializable interface when they are deserialized. This provides a place for you to reassign values to transient variables. The readObject() method is where you put all of your code for restoring variables that aren't automatically serialized: all of a class's transient variables.

The Timer class has the one transient variable, thread. When a Timer object is deserialized, the thread variable is either assigned a new Thread object or null, depending on the state of the runnable property, which is saved when the object is serialized. If the runnable property is true, a new Thread object is instantiated and assigned to the thread variable, and then the thread is started by calling its start() method. Otherwise, when the runnable property is set to false, the thread variable is assigned null. The Timer class setRunning() method already does all of this. Add the following readObject() method to your Timer class.

```
private void readObject( ObjectInputStream stream )
  throws IOException, ClassNotFoundException {
  stream.defaultReadObject( );
  setRunning( running );
}
```

> **Note**
>
> You need to import the `ClassNotFoundException` and `IOException` classes from the `java.io` package into the `PictureButton` class when you add the `readObject()` method. The complete source code for the `Timer` bean is shown in Listing 9.7 in Chapter 9.

The `readObject()` method is called on reloading the serialized `Timer` bean. The `Timer` bean's `ObjectInputStream` object is passed to the `readObject()` method and assigned to the `stream` variable. The first statement in the method calls the `ObjectInputStream` class's `defaultReadObject()` method so that all of the usual automatic loading of the serialized bean is carried out. It is essential that you always add this line of code to the overridden `readObject()` methods so that non-transient and non-static variables are properly reserialized. Next, a call is made to the `Timer` class's `setRunning()` method, which is passed the running variable.

Recompile the `Timer` class, package it in the `timer.jar` file, and wire up the `Timer` and `TestTimer` beans in the BeanBox. Once again, run the `Timer` bean by setting its running property to `True` and save the BeanBox layout. Clear the BeanBox and then load the `Timer` and `TestTimer` beans you just saved. No exception is thrown and the timer is counting. This is very good. The `Timer` bean is now persistent in whatever state you save it. Only now can you call the `Timer` component a true bean.

> **Note**
>
> Recall that one of the five required features that define a bean is persistence. To be a bean, a software component must be able to be properly serialized and deserialized in all of its possible states. See Chapter 4 for more information on the five features that define a Java bean.

Looking at Another Example

The `PictureButton` bean, created in Listing 7.4 in Chapter 7, "JavaBeans as Graphical User Interface Components," is another example of a bean with transient variables and an implementation of the `readObject()` method. The `currentImage` variable, which can be assigned an `Image` object, is a transient variable. The `Image` class, which is part of the `java.awt` package, does not implement the `Serializable` interface.

The currently displayed image doesn't need to be saved because the image files displayed by the PictureButton bean are stored in the same JAR file as the bean itself. The name of the image file is assigned to the String, imageFilename, which is automatically serialized by the JVM because the String class—the variable's data type—implements the Serializable interface. The PictureButton bean is properly reserialized through a call to the readObject() method, as shown in the following:

```
private void readObject(ObjectInputStream stream)
  throws IOException, ClassNotFoundException {
  stream.defaultReadObject( );
  loadImage( );
  repaint( );
}
```

After the usual call to the input stream's defaultReadObject() method, the loadImage() method is called. The loadImage() method is the same method that the image filename setter method calls to load the image file once the file's name is assigned to the imageFilename variable. After the image is properly loaded, the repaint() method is called to repaint the bean's graphic interface and display the image.

Using Java's writeObject() Method

You can serialize objects that aren't automatically serialized in your bean by adding the writeObject() method to the bean's class. The class must implement the Serializable interface. When you add the writeObject() method to a bean, it is run automatically when a container object or visual application builder environment tries to save the bean. The writeObject() method, shown next in skeletal form, is where you put all of your code for storing objects that aren't automatically serialized.

```
private void writeObject( ObjectOutputStream out ) throws IOException {
  out.defaultWriteObject( );
  // your code here
}
```

> **Note**
>
> You need to import the IOException class from the java.io package into classes to which you add the writeObject() method.

The principles of using the writeObject() method are the same as when you use the readObject() method except that code you add to the writeObject() method should write out or save objects, such as images, rather than read or deserialize them as in the readObject() method.

Versioning Beans

At some point, you will have created a useful bean that people will want to use. Suppose that you decide that the PictureButton bean you considered in the "Looking at Another Example" section earlier in this chapter is ready for prime time. You package the PictureButton bean up into a JAR file and distribute it around the world through the Internet to many happy users.

> **Note**
>
> The source code for the PictureButton bean is shown in Listing 7.4 in Chapter 7. Alternatively, you can use the picturebutton.jar file that includes the PictureButton bean.

One day you get an email from a user of your bean who prefers programming in Java with a text-based editor to using rapid application development techniques. The programmer is unable to use the PictureButton bean effectively because he can't set its properties through a constructor. In other words, he wants to create PictureButton objects using the new keyword.

You decide that it's a good idea to add a constructor that gives users the ability to set the PictureButton bean's image filename and sticky properties when it's created. But there is a problem.

Pretend that you are a person out there that is using your first distributed PictureButton bean. Assume that the bean was distributed in the picturebutton.jar file. Add this JAR file with the PictureButton bean to your BeanBox jars folder. Run the BeanBox and add a PictureButton bean to the BeanBox window. Load an image into the PictureButton bean, the teddy0.jpg image for instance. Now save the bean in the picturebuttontest file using the Save command on the BeanBox's File menu. Exit the BeanBox.

Create a new version of the `PictureButton` bean by adding an additional constructor to it. Add the following constructor to the `PictureButton` class, right after the default constructor.

```
public PictureButton( String imageFilename, boolean sticky ) {
   super( );
   setImageFilename( imageFilename );
   setSticky( sticky );
}
```

Note

Add the new constructor to the source code for the `PictureButton` bean found in Listing 7.4 in Chapter 7. Or you can use the `PictureButton.java` file that includes the `PictureButton` bean source code with the new constructor already added.

Recompile the `PictureButton` class and package it up in a new JAR file using the same name, `picturebutton.jar`. Replace the old `picturebutton.jar` file in the BeanBox `jars` directory with the new `picturebutton.jar` file holding the new version of the `PictureButton` bean.

Start up the BeanBox again and load the `picturebuttontest` file by selecting Load from BeanBox's File menu. This should generate an `InvalidClassException` resulting in the display of an Error dialog box (see Figure 5.2).

FIGURE 5.2

Beanbox's Error dialog box appears telling you that it could not read the serialized BeanBox data from the JAR file.

Tip

The error message may exceed the available room on the dialog box. You can resize the Error dialog box by dragging its edges.

The `PictureButton` bean that was serialized isn't compatible with the new version of the `PictureButton` bean with the extra constructor. This could spell disaster to all of the people across the globe using your `PictureButton` bean in their applications. You need a mechanism for Java class versioning so that your new bean versions can be backward-compatible with earlier versions. Java provides mechanisms for versioning beans.

Design Considerations

There are some simple rules that you need to follow when you design your beans so new versions of a Java class are backward-compatible with old versions of the same class. When you make changes to a class, do not

- Delete a data field or change its declaration so that it's transient or static or uses a different data type

- Delete a public method or change the method's parameters

- Change access—`private`, `protected`, and `public`

To keep a class backward-compatible, you need to retain the old interface while you add new interface items or change encapsulated data fields, methods, or procedures inside public methods. You followed these rules with the new version of the `PictureButton` bean. You added a new constructor to `PictureButton` class's interface without changing anything else.

Tracking Class Versions

You might wonder how the JVM detected the relatively minor difference between the old and new versions of the `PictureButton` class. It does it by assigning each object a unique identifier known as the `serialVersionUID`. A `serialVersionUID` is a long number computed by the JVM by looking at the structure of an object including its class name, interface names, method names, and data field names. Each object is unique in its combination of these structural attributes, so the computation always results in a unique identification number.

> **Note**
>
> The error message displayed by the Error dialog box in Figure 5.2 showed the `serialVersionUID`s calculated for both the new and old versions of the `PictureButton` bean.

An object's `serialVersionUID` is stored with the object when it is serialized. When the object is restored, the saved `serialVersionUID` is verified against the actual object loaded from the installed component. When the `serialVersionUID` between the saved and loaded objects are different, the JVM knows that they used different versions of the same class, and it generates an `InvalidClassException` object. Java's class versioning support provides a way to let you use new versions of a bean when you restore objects serialized using the older versions of the bean.

Reading a `serialVersionUID`

You can read an object's `serialVersionUID` by using the `serialver` tool provided with the Java Development Kit. Read the `serialVersionUID` of the original serializable version of the `PictureButton` class by typing the following command at your DOS or command window prompt when it is set to your root class directory.

```
serialver sams.controls.PictureButton
```

> **Note**
>
> If your `PictureButton` class file is currently the newer version with the second constructor, you can easily make the old version again by marking out the new constructor and recompiling.

> **Note**
>
> Be aware that when you run the BeanBox, it resets your CLASSPATH variable in the window that you run it. Open separate windows: one for running BeanBox and another for running other Java tools such as `serialver`.

The `serialver` tool should return something like the following:

```
sams.controls.PictureButton: static final long serialVersionUID =
    7766077034699316914L;
```

The first serializable version of the `PictureButton` object has a `serialVersionUID` of `7766077034699316914L`.

You can also use a graphic user interface version of the `serialver` tool by typing in the following command at the DOS prompt:

```
serialver -show
```

The Serial Version Inspector window opens(see Figure 5.3). Type the full class name into the Full Class Name text box and press the Show button. The same `serialVersionUID` should be displayed.

Recompile your `PictureButton` class with the new constructor and then recheck the class's `serialVersionUID`. You should get something like the following:

```
sams.controls.PictureButton: static final long serialVersionUID =
    -6846617395331759799L;
```

Making New Classes Compatible with Old Classes

You can make the new `PictureButton` class compatible with the older version by adding the old version's `serialVersionUID` as a static final long declaration to the new version. Add the following declaration to the declaration area of the new version of your `PictureButton` class.

```
static final long serialVersionUID = 7766077034699316914L;
```

Recompile the new `PictureButton` class and package it into a `picturebutton.jar` file. The old `PictureButton` object serialized into the `picturebuttontest` file should load without any problems when you use this new version of the `PictureButton` bean.

Summary

In this chapter, you learned how to create your own serialization capabilities. You learned when you need to implement the `Serializable` interface. When that wasn't enough, you learned to add methods that are called automatically by the JVM when a bean is being stored or loaded. Finally, you learned how to make old versions of your bean compatible with new version by utilizing Java's `serialVersionUID`.

Event Model

All source code for this chapter can be found on the Sams Publishing Website at
`http://www.mcp.com/info/0-672/0-672-31424-x.`

A useful bean communicates with other beans, scripting languages, or components derived from other component models. One of the ways that beans communicate is by sending and receiving event objects. When something happens to a bean, such as when a user clicks his or her mouse in the bean's window, it creates an event object that encapsulates information about what happened. The bean sends the new event object to other components to read and, possibly, act on. Bean events are central to creating beans for Web page interactivity and programming using rapid application development (RAD). Java's delegation event model provides the mechanisms you need to make JavaBeans components useful. In this chapter, you will learn about Java's delegation event model, and will also learn to use events in your Java beans.

Using Java's Delegation Event Model

Bean event communication depends on Java's delegation event model. The delegation event model (introduced with Java 1.1) supplants the old Java 1.0 event model. Three concepts, each associated with an abstract Java class, form the basis of the model:

- The event source
- The event object
- The event listener

> **Note**
>
> Java's delegation event model gets its name from the fact that event sources are delegated out (assigned) to specific event listeners. The result is an efficient event communication system.

Event Sources

Java objects that "fire" events and create event objects are known as *event sources*. For instance, each graphic user interface component in Java's Abstract Windowing Toolkit is an event source.

Event sources can send event objects to one or many event listeners. All of Java's Abstract Windowing Toolkit graphic user interface components can send each event object to many event listeners. An event source's ability to send an event object to more than one event listener is known as *multicasting* and is made possible by a *multicasting model.* Some event sources can only send an event object to one event listener. This is known as *single-casting* and is based on a *single-casting model.*

Note

Java implements efficient multi-cast event dispatching of Abstract Windowing Toolkit events using the `java.awt.AWTEventMulticaster` class.

Event Objects

Event objects represent the events themselves. Each event object is an instance of an event class derived from the `java.util.EventObject` class. The Java API provides 45 subclasses of the `java.util.EventObject` class, listed in Table 6.1.

There are three categories of classes extended from the `java.util.EventObject` class:

- Abstract Windowing Toolkit Events (AWT Events)
- Swing Events
- JavaBeans Events

Most events occur at a Java bean's user interface. These include the events signaled by the event object classes in the Abstract Windowing Toolkit and Swing packages. The other important bean events occur when a bean's properties change. The event object classes in the JavaBeans package signal bean property changes.

TABLE 6.1 `java.util.EventObject` Subclasses

Class	Description
	AWT Events
`java.awt.event.ActionEvent`	The action semantic event relays the message that a particular action was performed.
`java.awt.event.AdjustmentEvent`	The adjustment semantic event emitted by Adjustable objects relays the message that a value was adjusted.
`java.awt.AWTEvent`	The root event class for all Abstract Windowing Toolkit events.
`java.awt.event.ComponentEvent`	The root event class for all component-level events relays the message that a component was resized, moved, and so on.

continues

TABLE 6.1 continued

Class	Description
	AWT Events
java.awt.event.ContainerEvent	The class for container-level events. Indicates that a component was added or removed.
java.awt.dnd.DragGestureEvent	Indicates that a drag-and-drop gesture has occurred on the component that is being tracked.
java.awt.dnd.DragSourceDragEvent	Contains the current state of the operation to enable the operations initiator to provide the end user with the appropriate drag over feedback.
java.awt.dnd.DragSourceDropEvent	Contains information for the originator of the operation that allows appropriate feedback to the end user when the operation completes.
java.awt.dnd.DropTargetDragEvent	The class that's delivered to a DropTargetListener via its dragEnter(), dragOver(), and dragScroll() methods.
java.awt.dnd.DropTargetDropEvent	The class that's delivered via the DropTargetListener drop() method.
java.awt.dnd.DropTargetEvent	The base class for the drop target event classes.
java.awt.event.FocusEvent	The component-level focus event relays the message that a component got focus or lost focus.
java.awt.event.InputEvent	The root event class for all component-level input events.
java.awt.event.InputMethodEvent	Contains information about text that is being composed using an input method.
java.awt.event.InvocationEvent	Executes the run() method on a Runnable object when dispatched by the AWT event dispatcher thread.
java.awt.event.ItemEvent	The item semantic event emitted by ItemSelectable objects relays the message that an item state has changed.
java.awt.event.KeyEvent	The component-level keyboard event relays the message that a component got key-press, key-release, and so on.
java.awt.event.MouseEvent	The mouse event relays the message that a component got mouse-down, mouse-move, and so on.
java.awt.event.PaintEvent	The component-level paint event.

6

Class	Description
	AWT Events
java.awt.event.TextEvent	The text semantic event emitted by TextComponents relays the message that the value of the text object changed.
java.awt.event.WindowEvent	The window-level event.
	Swing Events
javax.swing.event.AncestorEvent	The class that can be used to find ancestors.
javax.swing.event.CaretEvent	Notifies listeners that the text caret has changed in the event source.
javax.swing.event.ChangeEvent	Notifies listeners that the state has changed in the event source.
javax.swing.event.HyperlinkEvent	Notifies listeners that something has happened with respect to a hypertext link.
javax.swing.event. InternalFrameEvent	An AWTEvent that adds support for JInternalFrame objects as the event source.
javax.swing.event.ListDataEvent	The class that notifies of data changes.
javax.swing.event. ListSelectionEvent	Characterizes a change in the current selection.
javax.swing.event. MenuDragMouseEvent	Notifies listeners that the menu element has received a MouseEvent object forwarded to it under drag conditions.
javax.swing.event.MenuEvent	Notifies listeners that the menu that is the event source has been posted, selected, or canceled.
javax.swing.event.MenuKeyEvent	Notifies listeners that the menu element has received a KeyEvent object forwarded to it in a menu tree.
javax.swing.event.PopupMenuEvent	Contains the source of the event that is the JPopupMenu sending the event.
javax.swing.event. TableColumnModelEvent	Notifies listeners that a table column model has changed, such as a column was added, removed, or moved.
javax.swing.event.TableModelEvent	Notifies listeners that a table model has changed.
javax.swing.event. TreeExpansionEvent	Identifies a single path in a tree.

continues

TABLE 6.1 continued

Class	Description
Swing Events	
`javax.swing.event.TreeModelEvent`	Encapsulates information describing changes to a tree model, and used to notify tree model listeners of the change.
`javax.swing.event.TreeSelectionEvent`	Characterizes a change in the current selection.
`javax.swing.event.UndoableEditEvent`	Indicates that an undoable operation has happened.
JavaBeans Events	
`java.beans.beancontext.BeanContextEvent`	The abstract root event class for all events emitted from a bean context.
`java.beans.beancontext.BeanContextMembershipEvent`	The event fired by a bean context when the state of one or more of its child's objects changes.
`java.beans.beancontext.BeanContextRemovedEvent`	The event fired by a bean context when one or more new child's objects are added to its set of children.
`java.beans.beancontext.BeanContextServiceAvailableEvent`	Identifies the service being registered.
`java.beans.beancontext.BeanContextServiceRevokedEvent`	Identifies the service being revoked.
`java.beans.PropertyChangeEvent`	The JavaBean event delivered when a bean's bound or constrained property changes.

AWT Event Objects

Use Java's Abstract Windowing Toolkit event objects to signal user interactions with a bean's graphic user interface. The AWT includes two broad types of event objects: those created when users interact and use graphic interface controls, such as text or button controls, and those created while users perform drag-and-drop operations. The event classes in the former category are part of the `java.awt.event` package, while the event classes included in the Drag-and-Drop API are part of the `java.awt.dnd` package. The `java.awt.AWTEvent` class is inherited by all of the AWT event classes found in the `java.awt.event` package.

Note

See Chapter 12, "Drag-and-Drop," for more information on the Drag-and-Drop API and the `java.awt.dnd` package, which are part of the Java Foundation Classes (JFC).

Each event class represents a group of event types. For instance, the `java.awt.event.MouseEvent` class represents all event types related to mouse activity including mouse button pressed events, mouse button released events, mouse click events, and so on.

Note

A mouse pressed event occurs when a mouse button is pressed down, and a mouse released event happens when the button pops back up because you released it. A mouse click event is the combination of these two; it's when a mouse button is pressed and then released rapidly in succession on one component.

Event objects pass class constants, also known as field indexes, which represent the individual event type that occurred among the group of event types represented by a particular event class. When you point to a component and click your left mouse button, the component creates a `java.awt.event.MouseEvent` object that carries a type class variable assigned the `MOUSE_CLICKED` integer constant. `MOUSE_CLICKED` is the `java.awt.event.MouseEvent` class constant that represents a mouse click event.

Four of the AWT event classes (`java.awt.event.ActionEvent`, `java.awt.event.AdjustmentEvent`, `java.awt.event.ItemEvent`, and `java.awt.event.TextEvent` classes) represent a special category of events known as *semantic events*. Most of the event classes, such as the `java.awt.event.MouseEvent` class, encapsulate event types that represent events specific to the tool used to interact with a bean. For instance, the `java.awt.event.MouseEvent` class encapsulates events related to various movements of a mouse's buttons such as the pressed, released, and click events. In contrast, semantic events are abstract events whose relations to specific tool manipulations depend on the particular event source object that produced it. For instance, `java.awt.event.ActionEvent` objects are produced when a `java.awt.Button` object is pressed, a `java.awt.List` object is double-clicked, or a `java.awt.MenuItem` object is selected.

Swing Event Objects

Use Swing event objects to signal user interactions with a bean's graphic user interface when the interface is created from a Swing component. Swing is a graphic user interface toolkit that simplifies your visual software component development efforts. The Swing toolkit, which is part of the Java Foundation Classes (JFC), extends the Abstract Windowing Toolkit (AWT). Swing components are endowed with many features and capabilities that the AWT components don't have. The Swing event package, `javax.swing.event`, contains Swing specific event classes.

JavaBeans Event Objects

Use JavaBeans event objects when you want to signal bean property, state, or context changes. Beans signal property changes using the `java.beans.PropertyChangeEvent` class. The rest of the JavaBeans event classes, all part of the `java.beans.beancontext` package, signal changes in bean context.

Event Listeners

Event listeners are Java objects that listen for and process Java events. All event listener objects implement an extension of the `java.util.EventListener` interface. Java includes several interfaces, listed in Table 6.2, that are specially designed to listen for and process objects instantiated from the `java.util.EventObject` subclasses listed in Table 6.1. There's one event listener interface available for each AWT and Swing event class included in the `java.awt.event` and `javax.swing.event` packages. Two event listener interfaces are available for the `java.beans.PropertyChangeEvent` object, the `java.beans.PropertyChangeListener` and `java.beans.VetoableChangeListener` interfaces.

> **Note**
>
> There are no event listener interfaces for the `java.awt.AWTEvent` and `java.awt.event.InputEvent` superclasses.

Each event listener interface provides an abstract method for every event type encapsulated by its corresponding event object. For instance, the `java.awt.event.MouseListener` interface provides a `mousePressed()` abstract method for processing the mouse button pressed event, a `mouseReleased()` abstract method for processing the mouse button released event, a `mouseClicked()` abstract method for processing the mouse click event, and so on.

TABLE 6.2 `java.util.EventListener` Interface Subclasses

Interface	*Description*
AWT Listeners	
`java.awt.event.ActionListener`	The listener interface for receiving action events.
`java.awt.event.AdjustmentListener`	The listener interface for receiving adjustment events.
`java.awt.event.ComponentListener`	The listener interface for receiving component events.
`java.awt.event.ContainerListener`	The listener interface for receiving container events.
`java.awt.event.EventQueueListener`	The listener interface for receiving notification of events posted to the event queue.
`java.awt.event.FocusListener`	The listener interface for receiving keyboard focus events on a component.
`java.awt.event.InputMethodListener`	The listener interface for receiving input method events.
`java.awt.event.ItemListener`	The listener interface for receiving item events.
`java.awt.event.KeyListener`	The listener interface for receiving keyboard events.
`java.awt.event.MouseListener`	The listener interface for receiving mouse events on a component.
`java.awt.event.MouseMotionListener`	The listener interface for receiving mouse motion events on a component.
`java.awt.event.TextListener`	The listener interface for receiving adjustment events.
`java.awt.event.WindowListener`	The listener interface for receiving window events.
Swing Listeners	
`javax.swing.event.AncestorListener`	Supports notification when changes occur to a `javax.swing.JComponent` object or one of its ancestors.
`javax.swing.event.CaretListener`	Listener for changes in the caret position of a text component.
`javax.swing.event.CellEditorListener`	Defines the interface for an object that listens to changes in a cell editor.
`javax.swing.event.ChangeListener`	Changes a listener object.
`javax.swing.event.DocumentListener`	Interface for an observer to register to receive notifications of changes to a text document.

continues

TABLE 6.2   continued

Interface	Description
Swing Listeners	
`javax.swing.event.HyperlinkListener`	A hyperlink listener.
`javax.swing.event.InternalFrameListener`	The listener interface for receiving internal frame events.
`javax.swing.event.ListDataListener`	Listens for data changes.
`javax.swing.event.ListSelectionListener`	The listener that's notified when a list's selection value changes.
`javax.swing.event.MenuDragMouseListener`	Defines a menu mouse-drag listener.
`javax.swing.event.MenuKeyListener`	Defines a menu key listener.
`javax.swing.event.MenuListener`	Defines a menu listener.
`javax.swing.event.MouseInputListener`	A listener implementing all the methods in both the `java.awt.event.MouseListener` and `java.awt.event.MouseMotionListener` interfaces.
`javax.swing.event.PopupMenuListener`	A popup menu listener.
`javax.swing.event.TableColumnModelListener`	Defines the interface for an object that listens to changes in a table column model object.
`javax.swing.event.TableModelListener`	Defines the interface for an object that listens to changes in a table model object.
`javax.swing.event.TreeExpansionListener`	The listener that's notified when a tree expands or collapses a node.
`javax.swing.event.TreeModelListener`	Defines the interface for an object that listens to changes in a tree model object.
`javax.swing.event.TreeSelectionListener`	The listener that's notified when the selection in a tree selection model object changes.
`javax.swing.event.TreeWillExpandListener`	The listener that's notified when a tree expands or collapses a node.
`javax.swing.event.UndoableEditListener`	Interface implemented by a class interested in hearing about undoable operations.
JavaBeans Listeners	
`java.beans.beancontext.BeanContextMembershipListener`	Compliant bean context objects fire events on this interface when the state of the membership of the bean context changes.

Interface	Description
JavaBeans Listeners	
`java.beans.beancontext.` `BeanContextServiceRevokedListener`	Listens for revoked context services.
`java.beans.beancontext.` `BeanContextServicesListener`	Listens for context services.
`java.beans.PropertyChangeListener`	The listener interface for receiving changed bean bound property events.
`java.beans.VetoableChangeListener`	The listener interface for receiving changed bean constrained property events.

Communicating Events

Java provides discrete objects for the event source, the event itself, and the event listener. Communicating events in Java isn't unlike the way you communicate events.

Think of yourself as an event source and a friend as an event object. Someone kicks you and you say, "Ouch!" You, the event source, produced a sound event object containing the "Ouch!" event. The "Ouch!" event travels through the air to the event listener, your friend. Your friend has an event listener object specific for picking up sounds—ears. The sound event listener receives the "Ouch!" event through the sound event object.

This example can even demonstrate event-casting models roughly similar to Java's single-casting and multicasting models mentioned earlier in the "Event Sources" section. You may create your sound event object by whispering it, so that only your friend's sound event listener picks up the "Ouch!" This is similar to a single-casting model. On the other hand, you might say "Ouch!" at a normal volume so that a small group of people nearby can pick up the sound event object. This is similar to a multicasting model. Finally, you may just scream out "Ouch!" so that everyone hears the event object. This is a broadcasting model. Java doesn't implement a broadcasting model, but notice how this model fits in with the rest.

Note

News broadcasts, radio broadcasts, television broadcasts, and so on all get their names from the fact that they use the broadcasting model. They cast their signals broadly—to many listeners.

Communicating Events Created by Java Components

Users talk to a bean through event objects created by interacting with the bean's graphic user interface. JavaBeans graphic user interfaces are typically composed of components from the AWT or Swing. In this section, you learn how to register event listeners with AWT or Swing components. Afterwards, you'll use your new knowledge to write beans that respond to user interactions.

Registering Event Listeners

Each Java AWT and Swing component can create event objects in response to all sorts of user interactions. For instance, a java.awt.Button object can produce java.awt.event. ActionEvent, java.awt.event.ComponentEvent, java.awt.event.FocusEvent, java.awt.event.KeyEvent, java.awt.event.MouseEvent, and java.awt.event. MouseMotionEvent objects. Java programs containing many different AWT or Swing components can quickly become inundated with a lot of event objects that they never need to process. Java's delegation event model solves this problem by only producing event objects that are registered by a component.

A Java event source only creates event objects that can be received by the source's registered event listeners. An event source can register the appropriate event listener interface for each type of event object the source can produce.

The following series of tables, Table 6.3 through Table 6.11, list the AWT and Swing classes that produce events with the event registration methods that they implement. Each table, except Tables 6.6 and 6.11, contains event sources extended from a particular class—listed first in the table—with all of the event registration methods that that class implements. The other classes that follow implement all of the event registration methods of the base class, plus any methods listed specifically for the subclass.

For instance, Table 6.3 lists all of the AWT event sources extended from the java.awt.Component class. The java.awt.Component class is listed first with the class's event registration methods. The java.awt.Button class is one of the classes extended from the java.awt.Component class. The java.awt.Button class inherits all eight event registration methods from the java.awt.Component class, plus it implements one event registration method of its own: the addActionListener() method. The java.awt.Canvas class also inherits all eight event registration methods from the java.awt.Component class, but it doesn't implement any event registration methods of its own.

Note

The classes listed in Table 6.3 are graphic interface components when they are instantiated.

TABLE 6.3 AWT Event Sources Extended from `java.awt.Component`

Class	Methods
java.awt.Component	addComponentListener(ComponentListener)
	addFocusListener(FocusListener)
	addInputMethodListener(InputMethodListener)
	addKeyListener(KeyListener)
	addMouseListener(MouseListener)
	addMouseMotionListener(MouseMotionListener)
	addPropertyChangeListener(PropertyChangeListener)
	addPropertyChangeListener(String, PropertyChangeListener)
java.awt.Button	addActionListener(ActionListener)
java.awt.Canvas	
java.awt.Checkbox	addItemListener(ItemListener)
java.awt.Choice	addItemListener(ItemListener)
java.awt.Container	addContainerListener(ContainerListener)
java.awt.Label	
java.awt.List	addActionListener(ActionListener)
	addItemListener(ItemListener)
java.awt.Scrollbar	addAdjustmentListener(AdjustmentListener)
java.awt.ScrollPane	
java.awt.TextArea	addTextListener(TextListener)
java.awt.TextComponent	addTextListener(TextListener)
java.awt.TextField	addActionListener(ActionListener)
	addTextListener(TextListener)

The classes listed in Table 6.4, when instantiated, are all AWT container components. Container components are able to hold any number of other components. The `java.awt.Container` class is extended from the `java.awt.Component` class (see Table 6.3), so the `java.awt.Container` class implements all eight of the `java.awt.Component` class event registration methods, plus the one method that it implements itself.

TABLE 6.4 AWT Event Sources Extended from `java.awt.Container`

Class	Methods
`java.awt.Container`	`addComponentListener( ComponentListener )`
	`addContainerListener( ContainerListener )`
	`addFocusListener( FocusListener )`
	`addInputMethodListener( InputMethodListener )`
	`addKeyListener( KeyListener )`
	`addMouseListener( MouseListener )`
	`addMouseMotionListener( MouseMotionListener )`
	`addPropertyChangeListener( PropertyChangeListener )`
	`addPropertyChangeListener( String, PropertyChangeListener )`
`java.awt.Panel`	
`java.awt.Window`	`addWindowListener( WindowListener )`

The classes listed in Table 6.5, when instantiated, are all AWT window components. Window components display a window graphic interface and are able to hold any number of other components. The `java.awt.Window` class is extended from the `java.awt.Container` class (see Table 6.4), which is extended from the `java.awt.Component` class (see Table 6.3). The `java.awt.Window` class implements all nine of the `java.awt.Container` class event registration methods, plus the one method that it implements itself.

TABLE 6.5 AWT Event Sources Extended from `java.awt.Window`

Class	Methods
`java.awt.Window`	`addComponentListener( ComponentListener )`
	`addContainerListener( ContainerListener )`
	`addFocusListener( FocusListener )`
	`addInputMethodListener( InputMethodListener )`
	`addKeyListener( KeyListener )`
	`addMouseListener( MouseListener )`
	`addMouseMotionListener( MouseMotionListener )`
	`addPropertyChangeListener( PropertyChangeListener )`

Class	Methods
java.awt.Window	addPropertyChangeListener(String, PropertyChangeListener)
	addWindowListener(WindowListener)
java.awt.Dialog	
java.awt.FileDialog	
java.awt.Frame	

The objects created from the classes listed in Table 6.6 are all AWT event sources, but none of them are AWT components—they are not extended from the java.awt.Component class. Most of the classes in this table are used in menus. The other two classes, java.awt.EventQueue and java.awt.Toolkit, are used to create event queuing objects and for communication between platform specific code and the AWT platform independent classes, respectively.

TABLE 6.6 AWT Event Sources Not Extended from java.awt.Component

Class	Methods
java.awt.CheckboxMenuItem	addActionListener(ActionListener)
	addItemListener(ItemListener)
java.awt.EventQueue	addEventQueueListener(EventQueueListener)
java.awt.Menu	addActionListener(ActionListener)
java.awt.MenuItem	addActionListener(ActionListener)
java.awt.PopupMenu	addActionListener(ActionListener)
java.awt.Toolkit	addPropertyChangeListener(String, PropertyChangeListener)

The class listed in Table 6.7, javax.swing.Box.Filler, provides a way to fill in a box-shaped area in a graphic interface, but it doesn't provide its own view. Because it doesn't provide its own view, an object created using the javax.swing.Box.Filler class can't contain any components and is the exception to the rule that all Swing components are also containers. The javax.swing.Box.Filler class is extended from the java.awt.Component class, which is listed with its event registration methods at the top of the table.

TABLE 6.7 Swing Event Sources Extended from `java.awt.Component`

Class	Methods
`java.awt.Component`	`addComponentListener( ComponentListener )`
	`addFocusListener( FocusListener )`
	`addInputMethodListener( InputMethodListener )`
	`addKeyListener( KeyListener )`
	`addMouseListener( MouseListener )`
	`addMouseMotionListener( MouseMotionListener )`
	`addPropertyChangeListener( PropertyChangeListener )`
	`addPropertyChangeListener( String, PropertyChangeListener )`
`javax.swing.Box.Filler`	

The classes listed in Table 6.8, when instantiated, are all Swing components extended from the `java.awt.Container` class. All Swing components, except one (see Table 6.7), are either included in or extended from the classes in this table. They all are able to hold other Swing or AWT components.

TABLE 6.8 Swing Event Sources Extended from `java.awt.Container`

Class	Methods
`java.awt.Container`	`addComponentListener( ComponentListener )`
	`addContainerListener( ContainerListener )`
	`addFocusListener( FocusListener )`
	`addInputMethodListener( InputMethodListener )`
	`addKeyListener( KeyListener )`
	`addMouseListener( MouseListener )`
	`addMouseMotionListener( MouseMotionListener )`
	`addPropertyChangeListener( PropertyChangeListener )`
	`addPropertyChangeListener( String, PropertyChangeListener )`
`javax.swing.Box`	
`javax.swing.CellRendererPane`	
`javax.swing.JApplet`	

Class	Methods
javax.swing.JComponent	addAncestorListener(AncestorListener)
addPropertyChangeListener (PropertyChangeListener)	
	addVetoableChangeListener(VetoableChangeListener)

The classes listed in Table 6.9, when instantiated, are all Swing window components. Swing window components, like their AWT counterparts (see Table 6.5), display window graphic interfaces and are able to hold any number of other components.

TABLE 6.9 Swing Event Sources Extended from `java.awt.Window`

Class	Methods
java.awt.Window	addComponentListener(ComponentListener)
	addContainerListener(ContainerListener)
	addFocusListener(FocusListener)
	addInputMethodListener(InputMethodListener)
	addKeyListener(KeyListener)
	addMouseListener(MouseListener)
	addMouseMotionListener(MouseMotionListener)
	addPropertyChangeListener(PropertyChangeListener)
	addPropertyChangeListener (String, PropertyChangeListener)
	addWindowListener(WindowListener)
javax.swing.JDialog	
javax.swing.JFrame	
javax.swing.JWindow	

The classes listed in Table 6.10, when instantiated, are all Swing components extended from the `javax.swing.JComponent` class. Nearly all Swing components are extended from the `javax.swing.JComponent` class, which is itself extended from the `java.awt.Container` class (see Table 6.8). The Swing components are all are able to hold other Swing or AWT components.

TABLE 6.10 Swing Event Sources Extended from `javax.swing.JComponent`

Class	Methods
javax.swing.JComponent	addAncestorListener(AncestorListener)
	addComponentListener(ComponentListener)
	addContainerListener(ContainerListener)
	addFocusListener(FocusListener)
	addInputMethodListener(InputMethodListener)
	addKeyListener(KeyListener)
	addMouseListener(MouseListener)
	addMouseMotionListener(MouseMotionListener)
	addPropertyChangeListener(PropertyChangeListener)
	addPropertyChangeListener(String, PropertyChangeListener)
	addVetoableChangeListener(VetoableChangeListener)
javax.swing.AbstractButton	addActionListener(ActionListener)
	addChangeListener(ChangeListener)
	addItemListener(ItemListener)
javax.swing. DefaultListCellRenderer	
javax.swing. DefaultListCellRenderer. UIResource	
javax.swing.JButton	addActionListener(ActionListener)
	addChangeListener(ChangeListener)
	addItemListener(ItemListener)
javax.swing.JCheckBox	addActionListener(ActionListener)
	addChangeListener(ChangeListener)
	addItemListener(ItemListener)
javax.swing.JCheckBoxMenuItem	addActionListener(ActionListener)
	addChangeListener(ChangeListener)
	addItemListener(ItemListener)
	addMenuDragMouseListener(MenuDragMouseListener)
	addMenuKeyListener(MenuKeyListener)

6

Class	*Methods*
javax.swing.JColorChooser	
javax.swing.JComboBox	addActionListener(ActionListener)
	addItemListener(ItemListener)
javax.swing.JDesktopPane	
javax.swing.JEditorPane	addCaretListener(CaretListener)
	addHyperlinkListener(HyperlinkListener)
javax.swing.JFileChooser	addActionListener(ActionListener)
javax.swing.JInternalFrame	addInternalFrameListener(InternalFrameListener)
javax.swing.JInternalFrame.JDesktopIcon	
javax.swing.JLabel	
javax.swing.JLayeredPane	
javax.swing.JList	addListSelectionListener(ListSelectionListener)
javax.swing.JMenu	addActionListener(ActionListener)
	addChangeListener(ChangeListener)
	addItemListener(ItemListener)
	addMenuDragMouseListener(MenuDragMouseListener)
	addMenuKeyListener(MenuKeyListener)
	addMenuListener(MenuListener)
javax.swing.JMenuBar	
javax.swing.JMenuItem	addActionListener(ActionListener)
	addChangeListener(ChangeListener)
	addItemListener(ItemListener)
	addMenuDragMouseListener(MenuDragMouseListener)
	addMenuKeyListener(MenuKeyListener)
javax.swing.JOptionPane	
javax.swing.JPanel	
javax.swing.JPasswordField	addActionListener(ActionListener)
	addCaretListener(CaretListener)
javax.swing.JPopupMenu	addPopupMenuListener(PopupMenuListener)
javax.swing.JPopupMenu.Separator	

continues

TABLE 6.10 continued

Class	Methods
javax.swing.JProgressBar	addChangeListener(ChangeListener)
javax.swing.JRadioButton	addActionListener(ActionListener)
	addChangeListener(ChangeListener)
	addItemListener(ItemListener)
javax.swing. JRadioButtonMenuItem	addActionListener(ActionListener)
	addChangeListener(ChangeListener)
	addItemListener(ItemListener)
	addMenuDragMouseListener(MenuDragMouseListener)
	addMenuKeyListener(MenuKeyListener)
javax.swing.JRootPane	
javax.swing.JScrollBar	addAdjustmentListener(AdjustmentListener)
javax.swing.JScrollPane	
javax.swing.JSeparator	
javax.swing.JSlider	addChangeListener(ChangeListener)
javax.swing.JSplitPane	
javax.swing.JTabbedPane	addChangeListener(ChangeListener)
javax.swing.JTable	
javax.swing.JTextArea	addCaretListener(CaretListener)
javax.swing.JTextField	addActionListener(ActionListener)
	addCaretListener(CaretListener)
javax.swing.JTextPane	addCaretListener(CaretListener)
	addHyperlinkListener(HyperlinkListener)
javax.swing.JToggleButton	addActionListener(ActionListener)
	addChangeListener(ChangeListener)
	addItemListener(ItemListener)
javax.swing.JToolBar	
javax.swing.JToolBar. Separator	
javax.swing.JToolTip	

Class	Methods
javax.swing.JTree	addTreeExpansionListener(TreeExpansionListener)
	addTreeSelectionListener(TreeSelectionListener)
	addTreeWillExpandListener(TreeWillExpandListener)
javax.swing.JViewPort	addChangeListener(ChangeListener)

The objects created from the classes listed in Table 6.11 are all Swing event sources, but none of them are Swing components. They are not extended from the javax.swing.JComponent class or even the java.awt.Component class. Most of the classes in this table are used as default models for various component behaviors.

TABLE 6.11 Swing Event Sources Not Extended from javax.swing.JComponent or java.awt.Component

Class	Methods
javax.swing.AbstractAction	addPropertyChangeListener(PropertyChangeListener)
javax.swing.AbstractListModel	addListDataListener(ListDataListener)
javax.swing.DefaultBoundedRangeModel	addChangeListener(ChangeListener)
javax.swing.DefaultButtonModel	addActionListener(ActionListener)
	addChangeListener(ChangeListener)
	addItemListener(ItemListener)
javax.swing.DefaultCellEditor	addCellEditorListener(CellEditorListener)
javax.swing.DefaultComboBoxModel	addListDataListener(ListDataListener)
javax.swing.DefaultListModel	addListDataListener(ListDataListener)
javax.swing.DefaultListSelectionModel	addListSelectionListener(ListSelectionListener)
javax.swing.DefaultSingleSelectionModel	addChangeListener(ChangeListener)
javax.swing.JToggleButton.ToggleButtonModel	addActionListener(ActionListener)
	addChangeListener(ChangeListener)
	addItemListener(ItemListener)
javax.swing.JTree.EmptySelectionModel	addPropertyChangeListener (PropertyChangeListener)
	addTreeSelectionListener(TreeSelectionListener)

continues

Table **6.11**   continued

Class	Methods
javax.swing.JMenuSelectionManager	addChangeListener(ChangeListener)
javax.swing.Timer	addActionListener(ActionListener)
javax.swing.UIDefaults	addPropertyChangeListener (PropertyChangeListener)
javax.swing.UIManager	addPropertyChangeListener (PropertyChangeListener)

Writing Java Beans with Event Listeners

Creating Java beans with graphic user interfaces that do something requires that user interactions with the interface's Swing or AWT components create events, and that those events cause the bean to carry out methods. There are three steps to using the delegation event model in your Java bean:

1. Create an event listener class.
2. Create event listener objects in your Java bean.
3. Register the event listener objects with the Swing or AWT components that will produce the events.

In this section you will write a Java bean named `Signal` that presents three buttons all sitting in a panel. The buttons are labeled Green, Yellow, and Red. When you click a button, the background color of the panel containing the buttons changes. Refer to Listing 6.2 frequently while writing the `Signal` Java bean in the following sections.

Create an Event Listener Class

The `Signal` bean reacts to mouse click events in one of three ways: The background color of the button's container object, a panel, changes to green, yellow, or red.

Because you want the Java bean to respond to a mouse click, you must create an event listener class that implements the `java.awt.event.MouseListener` interface. The example bean, `Signal`, uses the `sams.events.PanelButtonCommands` class shown in Listing 6.1.

`sams.events.PanelButtonCommands` objects listen for mouse events and process mouse click events. When a `sams.events.PanelButtonCommands` object detects a mouse click event, it checks to see which of three possible commands the mouse click represents—change the color of the `java.awt.Panel` object containing the button to green, yellow, or red. A `sams.events.PanelButtonCommands` class constant—GREEN, YELLOW, or RED—represents each command.

LISTING 6.1   Source Code for `PanelButtonCommands.java`

```java
package sams.events;

import java.awt.Color;
import java.awt.Panel;
import java.awt.event.MouseEvent;

public class PanelButtonCommands implements java.awt.event.MouseListener {
  public static final int GREEN = 0;
  public static final int YELLOW = 1;
  public static final int RED = 2;

  int command;
  Panel panel;

  public PanelButtonCommands( int command, Panel panel ) {
    this.command = command;
    this.panel = panel;
  }

  public void mouseClicked( MouseEvent e ) {
    switch( command ) {
      case GREEN:
        panel.setBackground( Color.green );
        break;
      case YELLOW:
        panel.setBackground( Color.yellow );
        break;
      case RED:
        panel.setBackground( Color.red );
        break;
    }
  }

  public void mouseEntered( MouseEvent e ) {
  }

  public void mouseExited( MouseEvent e ) {
  }

  public void mousePressed( MouseEvent e ) {
  }

  public void mouseReleased( MouseEvent e ) {
  }
}
```

You must override all five of the `java.awt.event.MouseListener` interface methods, even though you're only interested in mouse click events, because they're all declared abstract—as they must be. (Recall that all interface methods are abstract.) Simply leave the methods you don't use empty.

> **Note**
>
> Java provides adapter classes that make it easier for you to use the component-level event listener interfaces. These classes provide empty methods for all of the event listener abstract classes, so all you need to do is override the particular methods that you need. For instance, you can extend the `sams.events.PanelButtonCommands` class from the `java.awt.event.MouseAdapter` class instead of implementing the `java.awt.event.MouseListener` interface. The rest of the code would be the same, except that you wouldn't need to add the four empty methods. We're implementing the interface for example purposes. Because of Java's single inheritance limitation, the user might be prevented from inheriting from `MouseAdapter`.

Create Event Listener Objects

Create `sams.events.PanelButtonCommands` objects that carry out specific commands when they receive button click events. The `sams.events.PanelButtonCommands` class constructor, shown next, takes two parameters: the `command` and `panel` parameters.

```
public PanelButtonCommands( int command, Panel panel )
    this.command = command;
    this.panel = panel;
}
```

Pass the `command` parameter one of the three `sams.events.PanelButtonCommands` class constants, `GREEN`, `YELLOW`, or `RED`, described in the previous section, and pass the `panel` parameter the `java.awt.Panel` object that contains the `java.awt.Button` object. `sams.events.PanelButtonCommands` objects need the `java.awt.Panel` object to carry out each of the three commands. They need access to `java.awt.Panel` object's `setBackground()` method, inherited from the `java.awt.Component` class.

The `Signal` bean creates one `sams.events.PanelButtonCommands` object for each of the `sams.events.PanelButtonCommands` class constants and assigns them to the `greenCommand`, `yellowCommand`, and `redCommand` variables through the following statements:

```
greenCommand = new PanelButtonCommands( PanelButtonCommands.GREEN, this );
yellowCommand = new PanelButtonCommands( PanelButtonCommands.YELLOW, this );
redCommand = new PanelButtonCommands( PanelButtonCommands.RED, this );
```

These statements are found in the `initializeCommands()` method, the same place where the command objects are registered.

Note

Recall that the command objects assigned to the `greenCommand`, `yellowCommand`, and `redCommand` variables implement the `java.awt.event.MouseListener` interface. Variables assigned listener objects registered with event sources are transient and must be indicated as transient by the `transient` keyword. See Chapter 5, "Persistent Storage," for more information on transient variables, the `transient` keyword, and persistence in Java beans.

Register the Event Listener Objects

Connect each `java.awt.Button` object in the `Signal` bean to a specific `sams.events.PanelButtonCommands` object through registration. Use the `java.awt.Panel` class's `addMouseListener()` method, inherited from the `java.awt.Component` class, to register a `sams.events.PanelButtonCommands` object with a `java.awt.Button` object.

The `Signal` bean registers a `sams.events.PanelButtonCommands` object to each of the three buttons in the `initializeCommands()` method. The `initializeCommands()` method is called from the `sams.events.Signal` class constructor after the three buttons are added to the `java.awt.Panel` object by using a `java.awt.Panel` class `add()` method inherited from the `java.awt.Container` class. The `initializeCommands()` method is also called from the `readObject()` method when a `Signal` bean is being deserialized. The `initializeCommands()` method from the `Signal` bean is shown next:

```
private void initializeCommands( ) {
    greenCommand = new PanelButtonCommands( PanelButtonCommands.GREEN, this );
    greenButton.addMouseListener( greenCommand );
    yellowCommand = new PanelButtonCommands( PanelButtonCommands.YELLOW, this );
    yellowButton.addMouseListener( yellowCommand );
    redCommand = new PanelButtonCommands( PanelButtonCommands.RED, this );
    redButton.addMouseListener( redCommand );
}
```

In the `sams.events.Signal` class constructor, each `java.awt.Button` object is created, assigned to one of three variables (the `greenButton`, `yellowButton`, or `redButton` variable), and added to the `java.awt.Panel` object. Then the `initializeCommands()` method is called to create objects implementing the `java.awt.event.MouseListener` interface, `sams.events.PanelButtonCommands` objects, which are registered with the java.awt.Button objects through the addMouseListener() method. This is done separately in the initializeCommands() method, so it can be carried out both on the creation of the Java bean and on its deserialization.

Add the java.awt.Panel class's setVisible() method as the last line in the sams.events.Signal class constructor, as shown in the following:

```
setVisible( true );
```

> **Note**
>
> The java.awt.Panel class inherits the setVisible() method from the java.awt.Component class.

Passing true to the setVisible() method makes the java.awt.Panel object, and the components it contains, visible.

LISTING 6.2 Source Code for Signal.java

```
package sams.events;

import java.awt.Button;
import java.io.IOException;
import java.io.ObjectInputStream;

public class Signal extends java.awt.Panel {
  private transient PanelButtonCommands greenCommand = null;
  private transient PanelButtonCommands yellowCommand = null;
  private transient PanelButtonCommands redCommand = null;
  private Button greenButton = null;
  private Button yellowButton = null;
  private Button redButton = null;

  public Signal( ) {
    add( greenButton = new Button( "Green" ) );
    add( yellowButton = new Button( "Yellow" ) );
    add( redButton = new Button( "Red" ) );
   initializeCommands( );
    setVisible( true );
  }

  private void initializeCommands( ) {
    greenCommand = new PanelButtonCommands( PanelButtonCommands.GREEN, this );
    greenButton.addMouseListener( greenCommand );
    yellowCommand = new PanelButtonCommands( PanelButtonCommands.YELLOW, this );
```

```
    yellowButton.addMouseListener( yellowCommand );
    redCommand = new PanelButtonCommands( PanelButtonCommands.RED, this );
    redButton.addMouseListener( redCommand );
  }

  private void readObject( ObjectInputStream stream ) throws IOException,
ClassNotFoundException {
    stream.defaultReadObject( );
    initializeCommands( );
  }
}
```

Use the `Signal` Bean

Your `Signal` bean is complete. Compile the `sams.events.Signal` and `sams.events.PanelButtonCommands` classes, and then package them into a JAR file using the `signal.man` manifest file shown in Listing 6.3.

LISTING 6.3 Source Code for `signal.man`

```
Name: sams/events/Signal.class
Java-Bean: True

Name: sams/events/PanelButtonCommands.class
Java-Bean: False
```

When you try out your `Signal` bean in the BeanBox, you should see something that looks like Figure 6.1.

FIGURE 6.1

Each of the three buttons in the `Signal` *bean carries out a different command.*

Writing JavaBeans with Semantic Event Listeners

The event listener class you wrote in the last section responds to an event specified by the input device and the way the device interacts with a particular AWT component. That is, `sams.events.PanelButtonCommands` objects only respond to events created when a mouse clicks a `java.awt.Button` object. You can register `sams.events.PanelButtonCommands` objects with any AWT or Swing component, not just buttons. However, it's doubtful that you want those commands carried out when, for instance, you click a `java.awt.List` object. Users expect to be able to click once on a `java.awt.List` object and move around a list before carrying out a command by choosing an OK button, pressing an Enter key, or double-clicking a list item. That's the reason why the event listener class is named `sams.events.PanelButtonCommands` rather than `sams.events.PanelCommands`. You probably only want to register it with `java.awt.Button` or `javax.swing.JButton` objects.

Java's semantic events provide you with a higher level of abstraction so you can make more versatile event listener classes. You can modify the `sams.events.PanelButtonCommands` class so that it listens to action events rather than mouse events. Several AWT and Swing components produce `java.awt.event.ActionEvent` objects, and each of them produces a `java.awt.event.ActionEvent` object in a manner of interaction appropriate for the class of component. A mouse click on a `java.awt.Button` object produces a `java.awt.event.ActionEvent` object, but so does a double-click on a `java.awt.List` object. Furthermore, a keyboard focus on a `java.awt.Button` object followed by pressing the spacebar also produces a `java.awt.event.ActionEvent` object.

In the following section you will write a Java bean named `SemanticSignal` that end users won't be able to tell apart from the `Signal` bean you created in the previous section. Nevertheless, internally the new bean uses a semantic event listener class that listens for `java.awt.event.ActionEvent` objects.

Create a Semantic Event Listener Class

`SemanticSignal` bean's `sams.events.PanelCommands` class in Listing 6.4 is the `sams.events.PanelButtonCommands` class, shown in Listing 6.1, modified to act as a semantic event listener class. The most obvious change is that the `sams.events.PanelCommands` class implements the `java.awt.event.ActionListener` interface rather than the `java.awt.event.MouseListener` interface. Also, the `sams.events.PanelCommands` class imports the `java.awt.event.ActionEvent` class rather than the `java.awt.event.MouseEvent` class, because classes that implement the `java.awt.event.ActionListener` interface listen for `java.awt.event.ActionEvent` objects.

Notice that the `sams.events.PanelCommands` class implements only one method, the `actionPerformed()` method. The `java.awt.event.ActionListener` interface declares only one abstract method in contrast to the five declared in the `java.awt.event.MouseListener` interface.

LISTING 6.4   Source Code for `PanelCommands.java`

```java
package sams.events;

import java.awt.Color;
import java.awt.Panel;
import java.awt.event.ActionEvent;

public class PanelCommands implements java.awt.event.ActionListener {
  public static final int GREEN = 0;
  public static final int YELLOW = 1;
  public static final int RED = 2;

  int command;
  Panel panel;

  public PanelCommands( int command, Panel panel ) {
    this.command = command;
    this.panel = panel;
  }

  public void actionPerformed( ActionEvent e ) {
    switch( command ) {
      case GREEN:
        panel.setBackground( Color.green );
        break;
      case YELLOW:
        panel.setBackground( Color.yellow );
        break;
      case RED:
        panel.setBackground( Color.red );
        break;
    }
  }
}
```

Create a Bean Class

Create a Java bean named `SemanticSignal` that, like the `Signal` bean you created earlier, presents three buttons all sitting in a panel. The buttons are labeled Green, Yellow, and Red. When the user clicks a button, the background color of the panel containing the buttons changes. But unlike `Signal` beans, use the semantic event listener that you just wrote: the `sams.events.ButtonCommands` class.

Write the `SemanticSignal` class in Listing 6.5. There are only two differences between the `sams.events.SemanticSignal` class and the `sams.events.Signal` class in Listing 6.2. The `sams.events.SemanticSignal` class uses the `sams.events.PanelCommands` class, rather than the `sams.events.PanelButtonCommands` class, and it registers the event listener objects by using the java.awt.Button class's addActionListener() method, rather than the addMouseListener() method inherited from the java.awt.Component class.

> **Note**
>
> You can use the sams.events.PanelCommands class with any AWT or Swing component class that has an addActionListener() method.

LISTING 6.5 Source Code for SemanticSignal.java

```java
package sams.events;

import java.awt.Button;
import java.io.IOException;
import java.io.ObjectInputStream;

public class SemanticSignal extends java.awt.Panel {
  private transient PanelCommands greenCommand = null;
  private transient PanelCommands yellowCommand = null;
  private transient PanelCommands redCommand = null;
  private Button greenButton = null;
  private Button yellowButton = null;
  private Button redButton = null;

  public SemanticSignal( ) {
    add( greenButton = new Button( "Green" ) );
    add( yellowButton = new Button( "Yellow" ) );
    add( redButton = new Button( "Red" ) );
    initializeCommands( );
    setVisible( true );
  }

  private void initializeCommands( ) {
    greenCommand = new PanelCommands( PanelCommands.GREEN, this );
    greenButton.addActionListener( greenCommand );
    yellowCommand = new PanelCommands( PanelCommands.YELLOW, this );
    yellowButton.addActionListener( yellowCommand );
    redCommand = new PanelCommands( PanelCommands.RED, this );
    redButton.addActionListener( redCommand );
  }

  private void readObject( ObjectInputStream stream ) throws IOException,
ClassNotFoundException {
    stream.defaultReadObject( );
    initializeCommands( );
  }
}
```

Use the `SemanticSignal` Bean

Your `SemanticSignal` bean is complete. Compile the `sams.events.SemanticSignal` and `sams.events.PanelCommands` classes, and then package them into a JAR file using the `semanticsignal.man` manifest file in Listing 6.6. The `SemanticSignal` bean should look and act just like the `Signal` bean in Figure 6.1.

LISTING 6.6   Source Code for `SemanticSignal.man`

```
Name: sams/events/SemanticSignal.class
Java-Bean: True

Name: sams/events/PanelCommands.class
Java-Bean: False
```

Communicating Events Created by JavaBeans

Beans need to talk to other beans. Users talk to a bean through events created by interacting with the bean's graphical user interface. Likewise, a bean talks to other beans through events created when one of its properties changes. In this section, you will write a bean that creates a JavaBeans property change event, and you will write another bean that can receive and process the property change event.

Writing Java Beans That Create Property Change Events

In this section you write a Java bean named `SendEvents` that, like the beans you wrote in the previous sections, presents three buttons all sitting in a panel. The buttons are labeled Green, Yellow, and Red. When the user clicks a button, the background color of the panel containing the buttons changes. Additionally, the `SendEvents` bean presents a text field that displays text reflecting the color of the panel. The text is a bean property named `colorString`. The `colorString` property is a private `java.lang.String` class variable. The `SendEvents` bean creates and sends a property change event when the `java.lang.String` object assigned to the `colorString` property variable changes. Refer to Listing 6.8 frequently while writing the `SendEvents` Java bean in the following sections.

Modify the Semantic Event Listener Class

The `SendEvents` bean uses a semantic event listener class for listening to `java.awt.Button` object click events (the `sams.events.SendEventsCommands` class in

Listing 6.7). It is similar to `Signal` bean's `sams.events.PanelCommands` class in Listing 6.4. Like `sams.events.PanelCommands` objects, a `sams.events.SendEventsCommands` object reacts to mouse click events in one of three ways: The background color of the button's container object, a panel, changes to green, yellow, or red. But the `sams.events.SendEventsCommands` object also changes `sams.events.SendEvents` object's private `java.lang.String` class instance variable `strColor` to green, yellow, or red through the `sams.events.SendEvents` class `setColorString()` accessor method.

> **Note**
>
> The next section describes the `strColor` variable and its accessor method in detail.

A `sams.events.SendEvents` object must be passed to the `sams.events.SendEventsCommands` class constructor, rather than the more general `java.awt.Panel` object, so that the `sams.events.SendEventsCommands` object has access to the `sams.events.SendEvents` class `setColorString()` accessor method. The instance variable, named bean in the `sams.events.SendEventsCommands` class, must be declared as a `sams.events.SendEvents` data type. After you've made these changes, you can add the calls to the `sams.events.SendEvents` class's `setColorString()` accessor method. Each call passes the appropriate string representing the background color of the bean's panel.

LISTING 6.7 Source Code for `SendEventsCommands.java`

```java
package sams.events;

import java.awt.Color;
import java.awt.Panel;
import java.awt.event.ActionEvent;

public class SendEventsCommands implements java.awt.event.ActionListener {
  public static final int GREEN = 0;
  public static final int YELLOW = 1;
  public static final int RED = 2;

  int command;
  SendEvents bean;

  public SendEventsCommands( int command, SendEvents bean ) {
    this.command = command;
```

```
      this.bean = bean;
   }

   public void actionPerformed( ActionEvent e ) {
     switch( command ) {
       case GREEN:
         bean.setBackground( Color.green );
         bean.setColorString( "green" );
         break;
       case YELLOW:
         bean.setBackground( Color.yellow );
         bean.setColorString( "yellow" );
         break;
       case RED:
         bean.setBackground( Color.red );
         bean.setColorString( "red" );
         break;
     }
   }
}
```

Modify the Bean Class

Create a Java bean named `SendEvents` that, like the `SemanticSignal` bean you created earlier, presents three buttons all sitting in a panel. The buttons are labeled Green, Yellow, and Red. When the user clicks a button, the background color of the panel containing the buttons changes. But unlike `SemanticSignal` beans, the `SendEvents` bean uses the event listener that you just wrote—the `sams.events.SendEventsCommands` class. Additionally, it presents the panel's background color as text in a text field.

Write the `sams.events.SendEvents` class in Listing 6.8. There are two general differences between this class and the bean classes you wrote earlier. You create and use a `java.awt.TextField` object, and you implement changes so that the bean produces property change events. There are four steps to creating a Java bean that produces property change events.

1. Create a `java.beans.PropertyChangeSupport` object.
2. Provide methods for registering objects implementing the `java.beans.PropertyChangeListener` interface.
3. Create an accessor method for the property.
4. Add the `java.beans.PropertyChangeSupport` object method for firing a property change event to the accessor method.

All of the JavaBeans property change event classes and interfaces are part of Java's `java.beans` package.

Creating a `java.beans.PropertyChangeSupport` Object

The `java.beans.PropertyChangeSupport` class provides critical support to your JavaBeans class that you want to create property change events. Most importantly, the `java.beans.PropertyChangeSupport` class provides methods for registering objects implementing the `java.beans.PropertyChangeListener` interface and for firing property change events. You can extend the `java.beans.PropertyChangeSupport` `sams.events.SendEvents` class you're writing; it creates a `java.beans.PropertyChangeSupport` object.

> ### Note
>
> The decision to have your class extend the `java.beans.PropertyChangeSupport` class or to create a `java.beans.PropertyChangeSupport` object is usually practical, because Java only supports a single inheritance model. For instance, the `sams.events.SendEvents` class cannot extend both the `java.awt.Panel` and the `java.beans.PropertyChangeSupport` classes.

The `java.beans.PropertyChangeSupport` class provides only one constructor, shown in the following:

```
public PropertyChangeSupport(Object sourceBean)
```

The constructor takes one parameter, the `sourceBean` parameter. When you create a `java.beans.PropertyChangeSupport` object, pass the `sourceBean` parameter a reference to the JavaBeans object that you want to produce property change events. The `sams.events.SendEvents` bean passes a reference to itself through the `this` keyword, as shown in the following line of code:

```
private PropertyChangeSupport changes = new PropertyChangeSupport( this );
```

The `sams.events.SendEvents` class assigns the `java.beans.PropertyChangeSupport` object to the `changes` private class variable.

Registering an Object Implementing `java.beans.PropertyChangeListener`

Once you add code in a bean to instantiate the `java.beans.PropertyChangeSupport` class, you can add support for registering objects implementing the `java.beans.PropertyChangeListener` interface. Java beans, unlike plain Java objects, are registered with event listener objects during design time (which is after programming the bean but before runtime when it's actually used). This is a critical feature of

JavaBeans, because you are creating the beans as standalone components that others can use to plug together into applications. Your bean doesn't know beforehand the exact event listener objects that it will be registered with, only the kinds of objects it supports.

The `java.beans.PropertyChangeSupport` class provides two methods used for design-time registration: the `addPropertyChangeListener()` and `removePropertyChangeListener()` methods. The following is the `addPropertyChangeListener()` method signature:

```
public synchronized void addPropertyChangeListener(PropertyChangeListener
listener)
```

The method's one parameter, the `listener` parameter, takes an object that implements the `java.beans.PropertyChangeListener` interface. The object is passed during design time and adds the event listener to an event listener list. Because the registration is dynamic, the method is synchronized so no threads get crossed.

The other relevant method, the `removePropertyChangeListener()` method, removes objects implementing the `java.beans.PropertyChangeListener` interface from the event listener list. The following is this method's signature:

```
public synchronized void removePropertyChangeListener(PropertyChangeListener
listener)
```

An object implementing the `java.beans.PropertyChangeListener` interface is passed to the `removePropertyChangeListener()` method's `listener` parameter during design time. This results in the removal of the event listener from the object's event listener list.

> **Note**
>
> You will see later in this chapter, after you've created both the `SendEvents` and the `ReceiveEvents` beans, how design-time registration works. Simply put, they're registered when you connect a bean that sends property change events to another bean that listens for property change events. You remove the registered object by implementing the `java.beans.PropertyChangeListener` interface when you disconnect the beans.

If your bean inherited the `java.beans.PropertyChangeSupport` class, you could use the inherited methods and you'd have nothing to do. Your `SendEvents` bean, however, must provide these two methods and pass the class's methods the proper parameters. The following lines of code add addPropertyChangeListener() and removePropertyChangeListener() methods to the sams.events.SendEvents class:

```
public void addPropertyChangeListener( PropertyChangeListener listener ) {
  changes.addPropertyChangeListener( listener );
}

public void removePropertyChangeListener( PropertyChangeListener listener ) {
  changes.removePropertyChangeListener( listener );
}
```

The changes class variable is assigned the java.beans.PropertyChangeSupport object. You can see that the methods have the same signatures as they do in the java.beans.PropertyChangeSupport class. They pass objects implementing the java.beans.PropertyChangeListener interface assigned to the listener variables to java.beans.PropertyChangeSupport class methods.

Creating an Accessor Method

All access to Java bean data fields is restricted to accessor methods. Bean accessor methods must have a set prefix. The sams.events.SendEvents class's strColor private variable, which is declared as a java.lang.String data type, is accessed through the setColorString() accessor method shown next:

```
public void setColorString( String newColorString ) {
  String oldColorString = strColor;
  strColor = newColorString;
  myTextField.setText( strColor );
  changes.firePropertyChange( "colorString", oldColorString, newColorString );
}
```

When an object wants to change the value of the sams.events.SendEvents class strColor variable, it simply passes a new java.lang.String object to the setColorString() method's newColorString parameter. You can see the line that assigns the new java.lang.String object, assigned to the newColorString variable, to the strColor variable. The rest of the code in the setColorString() method relates to the java.beans.PropertyChangeSupport class's firePropertyChange() method.

Using the firePropertyChange() Method

The java.beans.PropertyChangeSupport class firePropertyChange() method, shown next, actually creates the java.beans.PropertyChangeEvent objects that are sent by the SendEvents bean.

```
public void firePropertyChange(String propertyName, Object oldValue, Object
newValue)
```

Pass a java.lang.String object that describes the property being changed to the propertyName parameter. The sams.events.SendEvents class passes "colorString" to the parameter. Pass the property's old value to the oldValue parameter and its new value to the newValue parameter.

Most of the code in the sams.events.SendEvents class setColorString() method is there to hold the old value of the strColor variable while assigning it a new value. There is also a statement that sets SendEvents bean's text field to strColor variable's new value. After the three parameters are passed to the firePropertyChange() method, a java.beans.PropertyChangeEvent object encapsulating all of the information is sent.

LISTING 6.8 Source Code for SendEvents.java

```
package sams.events;

import java.awt.Button;
import java.awt.Color;
import java.awt.TextField;
import java.beans.PropertyChangeEvent;
import java.beans.PropertyChangeListener;
import java.beans.PropertyChangeSupport;
import java.io.IOException;
import java.io.ObjectInputStream;

public class SendEvents extends java.awt.Panel {
  private transient SendEventsCommands greenCommand = null;
  private transient SendEventsCommands yellowCommand = null;
  private transient SendEventsCommands redCommand = null;
  private Button greenButton = null;
  private Button yellowButton = null;
  private Button redButton = null;
  private TextField myTextField = null;
  private String strColor = "default";
  private PropertyChangeSupport changes = new PropertyChangeSupport( this );

  public SendEvents( ) {
    add( greenButton = new Button( "Green" ) );
    add( yellowButton = new Button( "Yellow" ) );
    add( redButton = new Button( "Red" ) );
    add( myTextField = new TextField( strColor ) );
    initializeCommands( );
    myTextField.setBackground( Color.lightGray );
    myTextField.setEditable( false );
    setVisible( true );
  }
```

continues

LISTING 6.8 continued

```
  private void initializeCommands( ) {
    greenCommand = new SendEventsCommands( SendEventsCommands.GREEN, this );
    greenButton.addActionListener( greenCommand );
    yellowCommand = new SendEventsCommands( SendEventsCommands.YELLOW, this );
    yellowButton.addActionListener( yellowCommand );
    redCommand = new SendEventsCommands( SendEventsCommands.RED, this );
    redButton.addActionListener( redCommand );
  }

  private void readObject( ObjectInputStream stream ) throws IOException,
ClassNotFoundException {
    stream.defaultReadObject( );
    initializeCommands( );
  }

  public void setColorString( String newColorString ) {
    String oldColorString = strColor;
    strColor = newColorString;
    myTextField.setText( strColor );
    changes.firePropertyChange( "colorString", oldColorString, newColorString );
  }

  public void addPropertyChangeListener( PropertyChangeListener listener ) {
    changes.addPropertyChangeListener( listener );
  }

  public void removePropertyChangeListener( PropertyChangeListener listener ) {
    changes.removePropertyChangeListener( listener );
  }
}
```

Use the `SendEvents` Bean

Your `SendEvents` bean is complete. Compile the `sams.events.SendEvents` and
`sams.events.SendEventsCommands` classes, and then package them into a JAR file using
the `sendevents.man` makefile in Listing 6.9. The `SendEvents` bean should look like the
one shown in Figure 6.2. However, to see the property change events in action, you need
to write a bean that implements the `java.beans.PropertyChangeListener` interface.

LISTING 6.9 Source Code for `sendevents.man`

```
Name: sams/events/SendEvents.class
Java-Bean: True

Name: sams/events/SendEventsCommands.class
Java-Bean: False
```

FIGURE 6.2

The SendEvents *bean looks similar to the other beans you made in this chapter, except it has a text field.*

Writing Java Beans That Receive Property Change Events

Write a simple bean that implements the java.beans.PropertyChangeListener interface so that it can be registered by the SendEvents bean you wrote in the previous sections. The sams.events.ReceiveEvents class in Listing 6.10 extends the java.awt.Panel class and implements the java.beans.PropertyChangeListener interface. ReceiveEvents beans have a text field that, when registered with a SendEvents bean, displays the content of SendEvents bean's strColor variable.

The java.beans.PropertyChangeListener interface declares only one abstract method, the propertyChange() method shown next:

```
public abstract void propertyChange(PropertyChangeEvent evt)
```

Classes that implement the java.beans.PropertyChangeListener interface must also implement a propertyChange() method. It's where all the work is done.

The sams.events.ReceiveEvent class's propertyChange() method is shown in the following:

```
public void propertyChange(PropertyChangeEvent event) {
  if ( event.getPropertyName( ) == "colorString" ) {
    strColor = (String) event.getNewValue( );
    myTextField.setText( strColor );
  }
}
```

The java.beans.PropertyChangeEvent objects produced by any Java beans attached to the ReceiveEvents bean during design time are passed to the propertyChange() method's event parameter. The if statement checks to see if the property name encapsulated by the java.beans.PropertyChangeEvent object is the colorString property by using the java.beans.PropertyChangeEvent class's getPropertyName() method. Recall that SendEvents beans have colorString properties. If the property that is changed is a colorString property, the java.beans.PropertyChangeEvent class's getNewValue()

method is used to get the property's new value. Notice that the getNewValue() method returns a java.lang.Object object, so you need to cast the return value as a java.lang.String object. You should use casting sparingly, but you can do this with confidence because you know what property you're working with at this point.

LISTING 6.10   Source Code for ReceiveEvents.java

```
package sams.events;

import java.awt.TextField;
import java.beans.PropertyChangeEvent;

public class ReceiveEvents extends java.awt.Panel implements
java.beans.PropertyChangeListener {
  private TextField myTextField = null;
  private String strColor = "default";

  public ReceiveEvents( ) {
    add( myTextField = new TextField( strColor ) );
    myTextField.setEditable( false );
    setVisible( true );
  }

  public void propertyChange(PropertyChangeEvent event) {
    if ( event.getPropertyName( ) == "colorString" ) {
      strColor = (String) event.getNewValue( );
      myTextField.setText( strColor );
    }
  }
}
```

Use the ReceiveEvents Bean

That's all there is to it. Compile your ReceiveEvents bean and package it into a JAR file using the ReceiveEvents.man manifest file shown in Listing 6.11. Your ReceiveEvents bean should look like the one in Figure 6.3 when it's sitting all by itself doing nothing. Take your SendEvents and ReceiveEvents beans for a test-drive in the next section.

FIGURE 6.3

The ReceiveEvents *bean displays* default *in its text field and does nothing until you connect it up with a* SendEvents *bean.*

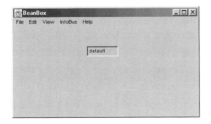

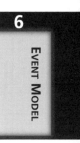

LISTING 6.11   Source Code for ReceiveEvents.man

```
Name: sams/events/ReceiveEvents.class
Java-Bean: True
```

Use the SendEvents and ReceiveEvents Beans

The SendEvents and ReceiveEvents beans are made to work together. You hook them up during design time. Fire up your BeanBox and try them out. Put one SendEvents bean and one ReceiveEvents bean into the BeanBox window. Select the SendEvents bean so that a thick dashed line surrounds its interface. Tell the BeanBox that you want to connect the SendEvents bean's property change events with a method in another bean. Open the Events submenu in BeanBox's Edit menu. From the Events submenu select the propertyChange submenu. Select the propertyChange command from the propertyChange submenu.

A red line should appear from the SendEvents bean to the tip of your mouse cursor. Connect the free end of the "wire" at the tip of your mouse cursor to the ReceiveEvents bean. You need to point to the bean's panel outside of the text field. (This is a thin area.) Then click your left mouse button. BeanBox's EventTargetDialog dialog box appears, as shown in Figure 6.4.

FIGURE 6.4

BeanBox's EventTargetDialog dialog box provides a list of available target methods.

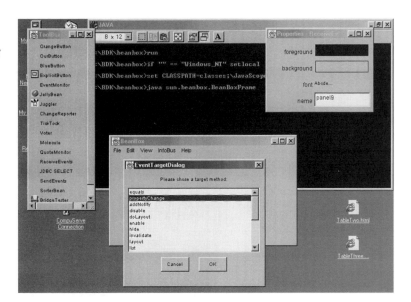

Select ReceiveEvents bean's propertyChange() method. Recall that the propertyChange() method is the method used to process property change event objects. Click the OK button.

The BeanBox creates code that connects the two beans together. It registers the SendEvents bean with an object implementing the java.beans.PropertyChangeListener interface, the ReceiveEvents bean. This is the design-time registration mentioned in previous sections.

Take the BeanBox out of design mode by selecting the Disable Design Mode command from the View menu, and try the beans. Click the buttons in the SendEvents bean. You should see the bean change color and the text field display the color's name, as shown in Figure 6.5. Simultaneously, you should see the ReceiveEvents bean display the current color's name in its text field. The SendEvents bean is sending events to the ReceiveEvents bean when its colorString property changes.

FIGURE 6.5

The SendEvents *bean talks to the* ReceiveEvents *bean in the BeanBox.*

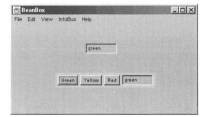

Summary

In this chapter, you learned about Java's delegation event model and the way JavaBeans software components send and receive events. Events are a powerful way to communicate user interactions with a bean's graphical user interface. They also make it possible to create JavaBeans components that can work together as a program or communicate with other objects or scripting languages in a Web page. Now that you understand how to use events in Java beans, you've mastered what is probably the most important and the most difficult part of the JavaBeans specification.

JavaBeans as Graphical User Interface Components

All source code for this chapter can be found on the Sams Publishing Website at
http://www.mcp.com/info/0-672/0-672-31424-x.

Buttons, fuel gauges, and other graphic user interface controls are ideal objects to make into beans. In fact, Java's Abstract Windowing Toolkit (AWT) classes are all JavaBeans controls. Create your own controls by extending classes from the Abstract Windowing Toolkit. After you've done this, you can experiment with applying the same concepts to Swing.

Using Control Beans

Control beans are graphical user interface beans that users interact with to control program execution. Sometimes a control simply displays text or graphics. All control beans are discrete graphic objects that populate JavaBeans containers.

> **Note**
>
> See Chapter 8, "Beans as Containers," to learn more about JavaBeans containers and how to create them.

You can plop a control bean into any container bean. In fact, the BeanBox window that is part of the Beans Development Kit (BDK) is a container bean. Container beans can be windows, frames, or dialog boxes.

You typically write control beans by extending an AWT class derived from the `Component` class.

Extending Java's Canvas Class

The `Canvas` class, which is part of the `java.awt` package, makes an excellent base class for control beans. Creating a JavaBeans control from Java's `Canvas` class is simple. In this section, you write a bean that extends the `Canvas` class and can display any supported image file. Users type the name of the image file into the bean's property sheet, presented by the BeanBox or an application builder program, and the image file is loaded and displayed by the bean. In other words, this bean has an image `filename` property.

The code for the new bean class, named `Picture`, is in Listing 7.1. There are a couple of key elements in the `Picture` class code. All of the code used to load the image is in the `getImageFilename()` accessor method. This accessor method is one of the supporting accessor methods for the `Picture` bean's `imageFilename` property. After the bean loads an image, its graphic interface automatically snaps to the size of the loaded image.

Adding the `imageFilename` Property

Like all bean properties, the `imageFilename` property is a private class variable, this time a `String` variable. The following is the class instance variable declaration:

```
private String imageFilename = "";
```

The `imageFilename` private class variable is assigned an empty string (`""`). To make the private data field a property, you must add at least one accessor method for accessing the data field.

Adding `imageFilename` Accessor Methods

You will add two accessor methods for the `imageFilename` property: a mutator and an accessor method. You will add the `setImageFilename()` method that will set the image filename and the `getImageFilename()` method that will get the filename of the currently loaded image. When you write these two methods following the JavaBeans design patterns, `imageFilename` is automatically designated a bean property. Programs like the BeanBox and other JavaBeans visual editing tools automatically detect the bean's properties through introspection and display their property editors on a property sheet.

Most of the work done by the Picture bean involves properly finding and transferring an image from an image file to the bean. Once transferred, the bean encapsulates the image in an `Image` object assigned to the `currentImage` variable. Add the following declaration and assignment statement right under the `imageFilename` variable declaration:

```
private transient Image currentImage = null;
```

The `currentImage` variable is private and accepts `Image` objects. The `Image` class is part of the `java.awt` package. The `currentImage` variable is initially assigned a `null` value because there is no default image displayed by the bean. The only reason that the `Picture` bean doesn't have a `currentImage` property is that you don't provide public accessor methods for the `currentImage` variable. Indeed, it doesn't make sense to do so because it's the `imageFilename` property that determines the image assigned to the `currentImage` variable. The name of the image file is what is important, not the specific properties of an `Image` object.

The `transient` keyword is added to the `currentImage` variable declaration so the JVM doesn't try to save the `Image` object if the bean is serialized. You must perform this small task and override the Serializable interface `readObject()` method to allow beans encapsulating `Image` objects to serialize properly. Recall that persistence, the proper serialization of a bean, is one of the five requirements for a Java object to be considered a

JavaBean (see Chapter 4, "The JavaBeans Component Architecture"). The `Picture` bean overrides the `readObject()` method, which is shown in Listing 7.1. Nothing more will be said of this method in this chapter. Learn more about persistence, the `transient` keyword, and the Serializable interface and its `readObject()` method in Chapter 5, "Persistent Storage."

> **Note**
>
> The `Picture` class inherits the Serializable interface, which is part of the `java.io` package, from the `Canvas` class. The `Canvas` class itself inherits the Serializable interface from the `Component` class. All objects extended from the `java.awt` package's `Component` class inherit the Serializable interface.

Adding the `setImageFilename()` Method

The `setImageFilename()` method, shown in the following code, gets the image from the file designated by the `imageFilename` property and assigns it to the `currentImage` variable.

```
public void setImageFilename( String imageFilename ) {
  this.imageFilename = imageFilename;
  loadImage();
  Dimension d = getMinimumSize( );
  Component p = getParent();
  if (p != null) {
    p.setSize( d );
  }
}
```

The `setImageFilename()` method itself takes the image filename entered in the bean's property sheet or passed to the method programmatically and assigns the `String` object to the `imageFilename` private class variable. Then it calls the `loadImage()` method, a private method you add later this chapter in the "Loading the Image" section, which actually transfers the content of the image file to the `Picture` bean and assigns it to the `currentImage` variable. After the image is transferred, the rest of the code in the `setImageFilename()` method is executed to resize the bean's graphic interface to fit the size of the new image.

The first statement after execution returns from the `loadImage()` method calls the `Picture` class's `getMininimumSize()` method, a private method you add later this chapter in the "Resizing the Bean" section, which returns a `Dimension` object encapsulating the minimum size of the `Picture` bean's graphic user interface. The next statement gets a reference to `Picture` bean's parent `Component` object through a call to the `getParent()`

method inherited from Java's `Component` class. If the p variable is assigned a `Component` object, the `if` statement calls the `Component` object's `setSize()` method. The minimum dimensions are passed to the `setSize()` method and an event is fired. The result is that the `Picture` bean's graphic user interface automatically snaps to the size of an image on loading.

Loading the Image

The `Picture` bean image loading routines are placed in a separate private method, the `loadImage()` method, so they can be accessed by both the `setImageFilename()` method and the `readObject()` method. The first method provides a way to load an image programmatically or through a property sheet, and the second method is used by the JVM to automatically load an image on deserialization of a bean. (The image loaded by this last method is the same image that was encapsulated by the bean when it was serialized.) The following is the code for the `loadImage()` method:

```
private void loadImage( ) {
  Class myClass = getClass( );
  try {
    URL url = myClass.getResource( imageFilename );
    currentImage = createImage( (ImageProducer) url.getContent( ) );
  }
  catch (Exception ex) {
    return;
  }
}
```

The first line of code gets the canvas runtime class of the `Picture` bean and assigns the `Class` object to the `myClass` variable. The `Picture` class inherits the `getClass()` method from the `Object` class, which is part of the `java.lang` package. All Java objects are ultimately extended from the `Object` class. The `Picture` bean uses the `Class` object returned by the call to the `getClass()` method to access the bean's resources.

The address of the image file that will be transferred is determined using the `Class` class's `getResource()` method. You needed to get the bean's `Class` object so you could use this method. Pass the name of the image file assigned to the `imageFilename` variable to the `getResource()` method, and it returns a Uniform Resource Locator (URL) style address to the image file encapsulated in a `URL` object. The `URL` object, created from the `URL` class that is part of the `java.net` package, is assigned to the `url` variable.

Next, the image is transferred by a call to the `URL` class's `getContent()` method and is passed to the `Component` class's `createImage()` method. The `createImage()` method returns the data encapsulated in an `Image` object, which is assigned to the `currentImage` variable.

At this time, there's support for `.gif` and `.jpg` images. More image types will probably be seen in the near future.

> **Note**
>
> The object returned from the `getContent()` method must be cast to the ImageProducer interface, which is part of the `java.awt.image` package. Each image in the Java environment must be associated with an object implementing the ImageProducer interface, which is used to reconstruct the image whenever it's needed.

Adding the `getImageFilename()` Method

The `imageFilename` property accessor method, shown next, is simple.

```
public String getImageFilename( ) {
  return imageFilename;
}
```

The `getImageFilename()` accessor method simply returns the filename of the currently loaded image file.

Resizing the Bean

The `Picture` bean overrides two `Component` class methods so the bean automatically conforms to the size of the loaded image. Most of the work is done by the `getMinimumSize()` method is shown in the following:

```
public Dimension getMinimumSize( ) {
  int width = 150;
  int height = 150;

  try {
    while ( ( width = currentImage.getWidth( null ) ) != -1 )
      Thread.sleep( 1 );
    while ( ( height = currentImage.getHeight( null ) ) != -1 )
      Thread.sleep( 1 );
  }
  catch ( Exception e ) {
  }
  return new Dimension( width, height );
}
```

Two local variables, `width` and `height`, are declared and assigned default values for when no image is loaded. The code that follows calls the `Image` class's `getWidth()` and `getHeight()` methods to get the width and height of the currently held image. For some reason, these methods are a bit flaky. If you don't keep trying, you get a `-1` returned from the methods, indicating that the width or height isn't known yet. When you use these methods, put them each in a `while` statement and create an infinite loop that includes a call to the `Thread` class's `sleep()` method for a brief sleep. Each loop runs until the method returns a value greater than `-1`.

The other overridden `Component` class method is the `getPreferredSize()` method, shown in the following:

```
public Dimension getPreferredSize( ) {
 return getMinimumSize( );
}
```

The `getPreferredSize()` method simply calls the `getMinimumSize()` method you were just looking at. That way, the size of the `Picture` bean is kept at the same size as the currently loaded image.

Other Features

Another important feature of the `Picture` bean code is the `paint()` method, which paints the image to the bean's graphic interface. As you saw previously, the `currentImage` private class variable is assigned a `null` value until it's assigned an image in the `loadImage()` method. `Picture` bean's `paint()` method, shown in the following code, includes an `if` statement that tests the `currentImage` variable to see if it's assigned a value that is not equal to `null`. The reason you check that the `currentImage` isn't null is so you don't draw before the user of the bean has set the current image.

```
public void paint(Graphics g) {
    if ( currentImage != null )
        g.drawImage(currentImage, 0, 0, this);
}
```

If the value assigned isn't equal to `null`, the `currentImage` property has been assigned an image and the `paint()` method can go ahead and draw the image to the component by calling the `Graphic` class's `drawImage()` method. The code can be seen in Listing 7.1. One thing to note: you should never directly call `paint()`; you should call `repaint()` to place a request upon the JVM.

Listing 7.1 Source Code for `Picture.java`

```
package sams.controls;

import java.awt.Component;
import java.awt.Dimension;
import java.awt.Graphics;
import java.awt.Image;
```

continues

Listing 7.1   continued

```java
import java.awt.image.ImageProducer;
import java.io.IOException;
import java.io.ObjectInputStream;
import java.net.URL;

public class Picture extends java.awt.Canvas {
  private String imageFilename = "";
  private transient Image currentImage = null;

  public void setImageFilename( String imageFilename ) {
    this.imageFilename = imageFilename;
    loadImage( );
    Dimension d = getMinimumSize( );
    Component p = getParent();
    if (p != null) {
      p.setSize( d );
    }
    repaint( );
  }

  public String getImageFilename( ) {
    return imageFilename;
  }

  private void loadImage( ) {
    Class myClass = getClass( );
    try {
      URL url = myClass.getResource( imageFilename );
      currentImage = createImage( (ImageProducer) url.getContent( ) );
    }
    catch (Exception ex) {
    }
  }

  private void readObject(ObjectInputStream stream)
    throws IOException, ClassNotFoundException {
    stream.defaultReadObject( );
    loadImage( );
    repaint( );
  }

  public void paint(Graphics g) {
    if ( currentImage != null )
      g.drawImage(currentImage, 0, 0, this);
  }

  public Dimension getPreferredSize( ) {
    return getMinimumSize( );
```

```
    }

    public Dimension getMinimumSize( ) {
      int width = 150;
      int height = 150;
      try {
        while ( ( width = currentImage.getWidth( null ) ) < 0 )
          Thread.sleep( 1 );
        while ( ( height = currentImage.getHeight( null ) ) < 0 )
          Thread.sleep( 1 );
      }
      catch ( Exception e ) {
      }
      return new Dimension( width, height );
    }
}
```

Compile the `Picture` class and package it into a JAR file along with any image files that you want to be able to load. The `Picture` bean can only load image files that are packaged into the same JAR as the bean itself. For instance, package the `teddy0.jpg` image file into the `Picture` bean's JAR file named `picture1.jar`. Use the `picture1.man` manifest file shown in Listing 7.2 (adding the `m` flag specifies this).

Listing 7.2   Source Code for `picture1.man`

```
Name: sams/controls/Picture.class
Java-Bean: True

Name: sams/controls/teddy0.jpg
Java-Bean: False
```

Open your DOS window or console window and change the prompt so that it's opened at your root class folder. Then use the `jar` utility to create the `picture1.jar` file by typing the following command at the prompt:

```
jar cmf picture1.man picture1.jar sams
```

Place the `picture1.jar` file in the `jars` folder inside the `Bdk` folder and then run the BeanBox.

Add the `Picture` bean to the BeanBox window. You should see the bean displayed with no images and an `imageFilename` property editor displayed as an empty text box in the Properties window because the property currently contains an empty string, as shown in Figure 7.1.

FIGURE 7.1

The Picture bean's `imageFilename` *property is initially empty.*

Type the complete filename of the image that you want the `Picture` bean to display into the `imageFilename` text box in the Properties window. Make sure that the image's file is packaged into the same JAR as the `Picture` bean! The image should appear in the `Picture` bean as soon as you type in the filename, as shown in Figure 7.2.

There is one other item to note. You can't use a `fileDialog` because the file is in the JAR, not on the filesystem. There's really no way to provide a selector such as the `fileDialog` either. Unfortunately, you can't make the code more robust, eliminating the fallibility of typing errors.

FIGURE 7.2

The `Picture` *bean displays the image held in the* `teddy0.jpg` *file.*

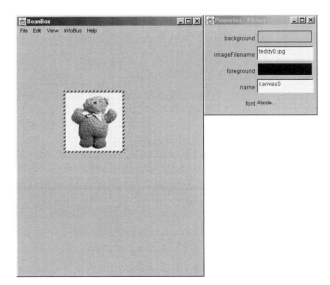

Creating an Image Button Bean

The `Picture` bean is useful, but, with some additional modifications, you can make it even more useful. You can turn it into an image button bean. Image buttons are popular components in toolbars where there's usually no room for text to be displayed. In this section, you modify the `Picture` bean code to transform it into code for an image button bean named `PictureButton`.

Picture Bean as Button

You might be surprised by the amount of "button" functionality already in the `Picture` bean. The `Picture` bean is derived from Java's `Canvas` class, which is derived from the `Component` class. The `Component` class, which is part of the `java.awt` package, already contains most of the event handling mechanisms used by graphic user interface controls. You can already use the `Picture` bean like a button.

Try wiring up two `Picture` beans with the `Juggler` bean in the BeanBox. You can use any image file in the `Picture` bean, but you might want to use the `stop.gif` and `go.gif` files.

Create a new JAR file with the new image files. For instance, you can call the new file `picture2.jar` and use the `picture2.man` manifest file shown in Listing 7.3. Then type the following command at your DOS or console window prompt to create the `picture2.jar` file:

```
jar cmf picture2.man picture2.jar sams
```

Place the `picture2.jar` file in the `jars` folder inside the `Bdk` folder and then run the BeanBox.

Listing 7.3   Source Code for `picture2.man`

```
Name: sams/controls/Picture.class
Java-Bean: True

Name: sams/controls/go.gif
Java-Bean: False

Name: sams/controls/stop.gif
Java-Bean: False
```

> **Note**
>
> You could create one JAR file that holds all three image files, or, for that matter, any number of image files.

First, you will add a `Juggler` bean to the BeanBox window. Select the `Juggler` bean from the ToolBox by pointing to Juggler or the Juggler icon to the left of the label in the ToolBox window and then clicking your left mouse button. Your mouse cursor arrow should change into a crosshair. Move your mouse cursor to the BeanBox window. Point to the general location where you want to place the `Juggler` bean in the BeanBox, and then click your left mouse button. You should see a `Juggler` bean displayed in the BeanBox window with the little man, known as Duke, juggling (see Figure 7.3).

FIGURE 7.3

The `Juggler` bean animation runs by default.

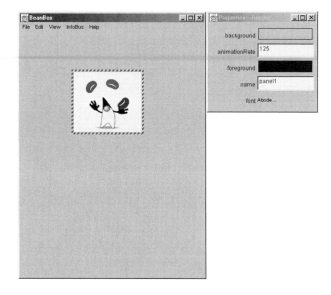

Newly added beans display a striped boundary. The striped boundary indicates the bean that has the focus or, in other words, is the currently selected bean. The Properties window displays the properties of the currently selected bean. If your `Juggler` bean is still selected, you should see the `animationRate` property listed in the Properties window along with other `Juggler` bean properties.

Next you add a Start button and Stop button, each created from the `Picture` bean. Point to the `Picture` bean in the ToolBox window and click your left mouse button. Then point to the approximate location in the BeanBox window where you want to place the button, and click your mouse button again. A `Picture` bean should be added to your BeanBox window. Use this bean as a button that stops the `Juggler` bean animation from running. With this new `Picture` bean selected, type the name of the stop image file, `stop.gif`, into the `imageFilename` property editor and press your Enter key. The BeanBox should display something similar to what is shown in Figure 7.4.

Connect or "wire up" the `Picture` bean displaying the image in the `stop.gif` file to the `Juggler` bean. When you do, an event that occurs at the `Picture` bean can be communicated to the `Juggler` bean. With the `Picture` bean selected, open the Events submenu in

BeanBox's Edit menu. Select `mouse` from the Events submenu, and then select the `mouseClicked` command from the mouse submenu. A red line connected from the `Picture` bean to the arrow tip of your mouse cursor should appear. Point to the `Juggler` bean and click anywhere inside the bean's graphic interface. The EventTargetDialog dialog box should appear, as shown in Figure 7.5.

FIGURE 7.4

The `Picture` *bean's* `imageFilename` *property is set to the* `stop.gif` *image file.*

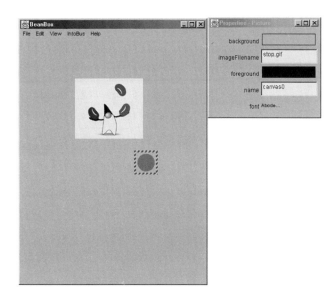

FIGURE 7.5

The target bean displays a list of available methods in the EventTargetDialog dialog box.

The EventTargetDialog dialog box displays a list of Juggler bean methods that an event—a mouse click in this case—can trigger. You want the `Juggler` bean animation to stop when you click the `Picture` bean displaying the image in the `stop.gif` file. Therefore, select the `stopJuggling` method from the scrolling list, and then click the OK button.

The BeanBox takes a moment to wire up the components for you. Now click the new stop button made from a `Picture` bean. The animation stops.

Finally, you will add another `Picture` bean that will act as a start button. Add another `Picture` bean to the BeanBox by pointing to the `Picture` bean in the ToolBox window and clicking your left mouse button. Point to the approximate location where you want the button in the BeanBox window, and then click your left mouse button. With this new `Picture` bean selected, type the name of the start image file, **`go.gif`**, into the `imageFilename` property editor and press your Enter key. The BeanBox should look similar to the one shown in Figure 7.6.

FIGURE 7.6

The `Picture` *bean's* `imageFilename` *property is set to the* `go.gif` *image file.*

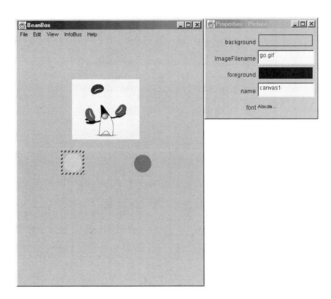

Next, wire up the start button with the `Juggler` bean. Select the recently added `Picture` bean and then select `mouse` from the Events menu. Then click the `clickMouse` command from the mouse submenu. The red line appears connecting the `Picture` bean and the tip of your mouse cursor.

Point to the `Juggler` bean and click anywhere within its graphic interface. The EventTargetDialog dialog box appears. This time, select the `startJuggling` method from the scrolling list and click the OK button. After the BeanBox is finished wiring up the components, click the start button. The animation starts back up.

> **Note**
>
> You can disable BeanBox's design-time mechanisms by selecting the Disable Design Mode command from the View menu. Also, you can save different "programs" that you wire together in the BeanBox. For instance, you can save the animation program you just wrote by selecting the Save command from the File menu. The Save As dialog box appears. Type in the name of the program— **animation**, for instance—and click the Save button. When you want to load the animation program, select the Load command from the File menu, select the animation program, and then click the Open button.

The `PictureButton` Bean

Although the `Picture` bean performs a lot of what you want a button to do, you need to add graphics that make the bean look like a button and show button-like user feedback. It's also handy if a button bean provides an action event. The `Picture` bean doesn't change its appearance by showing a depression when clicked while a `Button` does— it just changes the border.

> **Note**
>
> An *action* event is an event created through the typical or common action that users perform on a particular control. For instance, a typical button event is a mouse click to the button. Learn more about the Java event model and action events in Chapter 6, "Event Model."

In the following sections, you modify the `Picture` bean so it's the `PictureButton` bean shown in Listing 7.4. You add graphics that make the bean look and act like a button, and you add code that lets the `PictureButton` bean register action event listeners and produce `ActionEvent` objects.

Creating the Button Look and Behavior

The look and behavior of a button are closely related. A button isn't a button unless it's three-dimensional and it moves in and out in three dimensions. Movement is a button's response to user interactions, and user interactions are communicated in Java through events and event processing.

When you created the `Picture` bean, you saw that an object created from a subclass of Java's `Component` class receives all of the graphic user interface events and can register those events with event listeners. However, the `PictureButton` bean needs to process some of those events locally so it can react to them with graphics that properly represent the look and behavior of the button.

Note

There's a completely different approach to event handling that's common, especially for programmers who aren't familiar with `enableEvents()`. The alternate method is this: When you want a class to respond to its own events, you set the target to `this`. For example, the following code might be used:

```
this.addActionListener( this );
```

Then you can define the `ActionPerformed` method in the class and implement the interface. This is different from what is shown, but also works well.

Adding `PictureButton` Properties

The `PictureButton` bean has two new properties that the `Picture` bean doesn't have: the `sticky` and the `down` properties. Both are Boolean properties. The `sticky` property setting determines whether or not the `PictureButton` bean is sticky. That is, if the bean is `sticky`, the button stays pressed after you click it, and you must click it again to release the button. The `down` property holds the current state of the button. If the `down` property is `true`, the button is pressed down; otherwise, it's in the released position.

The `sticky` property is set at design time by the application developer using the bean. The `down` property, on the other hand, is used internally by the `PictureButton` bean. As you might expect, the `sticky` property has both accessor and mutator methods, while the `down` property only has an accessor method.

The `down` property is set according to the particular mouse events that are caught and detected by the `PictureButton` bean, and then the state of the `down` property determines how `PictureButton` bean's `paint` method updates the bean's graphic interface.

Enabling Events

The `PictureButton` bean needs to capture mouse events and determine what mouse events occurred to the bean's graphic user interface. The first thing to do to accomplish this is to enable mouse events to be captured by the `PictureButton` bean. To do this, you add the `enableEvents()` method, shown in the following code, to the `PictureButton` code.

```
protected final void enableEvents(long eventsToEnable)
```

Java automatically enables event types in an object when the object registers a listener for that type. In this case, however, the object needs the events for manipulating its graphic interface, not for sending to listeners. You pass the event masks for the particular event objects that you want enabled to enableEvents() method's eventsToEnable parameter. Enable mouse events by adding the following statement to the PictureButton bean constructor.

```
enableEvents( AWTEvent.MOUSE_EVENT_MASK );
```

The event masks are AWTEvent class constants. The AWTEvent class is part of the java.awt package. All of the AWTEvent class event mask constants are listed in Table 7.1. The constants are static final. You only use the masks for the events you need to trigger changes in the PictureButton bean graphic interface. For instance, you don't use the ACTION_EVENT_MASK. The PictureButton bean creates ActionEvent objects, but the bean doesn't need these event objects for triggering graphic interface changes. It's the mouse events, specifically clicking and releasing the mouse button, that the PictureButton needs to trigger changes in its graphic interface.

Table 7.1 AWTEvent Class's Event Masks

Event Mask	Description
ACTION_EVENT_MASK	Selects action events
ADJUSTMENT_EVENT_MASK	Selects adjustment events
COMPONENT_EVENT_MASK	Selects component events
CONTAINER_EVENT_MASK	Selects container events
FOCUS_EVENT_MASK	Selects focus events
INPUT_METHOD_EVENT_MASK	Selects input method events
ITEM_EVENT_MASK	Selects item events
KEY_EVENT_MASK	Selects key events
MOUSE_EVENT_MASK	Selects mouse events
MOUSE_MOTION_EVENT_MASK	Selects mouse motion events
TEXT_EVENT_MASK	Selects text events
WINDOW_EVENT_MASK	Selects window events

Processing Events

Once the PictureButton bean enables mouse events, it needs to process them. Override the Component class's processMouseEvent() method and add code to test for the various mouse events. The following is the overridden method in the PictureButton class:

```
protected void processMouseEvent( MouseEvent e ) {
  switch( e.getID( ) ) {
   case MouseEvent.MOUSE_PRESSED:
     down = !down;
     repaint( );
     break;
   case MouseEvent.MOUSE_RELEASED:
     if ( down && !sticky ) {
       processActionEvent( );
       down = false;
       repaint( );
     }
     break;
  }
  super.processMouseEvent( e );
}
```

MouseEvent class constants represent each particular type of mouse event. Call the MouseEvent class's getID() method, inherited from the AWTEvent class, to get the current mouse event type, and then check it against the constants representing event types for which you're looking. The PictureButton is looking for mouse pressed and mouse released events.

When the bean detects a mouse pressed event, its down property is toggled to the opposite of what it was before the mouse button was clicked. That is, if the down property is true, it is changed to false; or if it is false, it's changed to true. Next, the PictureButton bean's repaint() method executes. The result is the repainting of the graphic interface to reflect the state of the bean's down property.

The PictureButton bean does nothing when it detects a mouse-released event if its sticky property is set to true. Otherwise, if the bean's down property is set to true, the bean calls its processActionEvent() method through the following statement to create and fire off an action event.

```
processActionEvent( new ActionEvent( this,
    ActionEvent.ACTION_PERFORMED, null ) );
```

After firing off an action event, the down property is changed to false, and the repaint() method is called.

PictureButton Bean's down Property and paint Method

There are several differences between the paint() methods of the PictureButton and Picture beans. The differences are due to the addition of the graphic representation of a button in the PictureButton bean. The state of the bean's down property is pivotal in determining how the button's graphic representation is constructed at any one time.

The first statement in the paint() method, shown in the following code, passes a Dimension object containing the current width and height of the bean to the size variable.

```
Dimension size = getSize( );
```

The bean's current width and height are needed for calculations that are carried out to create the button graphic.

The next line of code sets the bean's color using the current background color.

```
g.setColor( getBackground( ) );
```

After the bean's color is set, the paint() method creates the three dimensional button graphic through the following two statements.

```
g.fillRect( 1, 1, size.width - 2, size.height - 2 );
g.draw3DRect( 0, 0, size.width - 1, size.height - 1, !down );
```

The first statement fills in the button's background, and the second statement paints a three-dimensional effect around the edges of the button.

Next, the color is set to a dark gray and, if the button is initially clicked, a dark gray line is drawn at top and left of the button. Otherwise, the dark lines are drawn at bottom and right of the button.

```
g.setColor( Color.darkGray );
if ( down ) {
  g.drawLine( 1, size.height + 1, 1, 1 );
  g.drawLine( 1, 1, size.width + 1, 1 );
}
else {
  g.drawLine( 2, size.height, size.width, size.height );
  g.drawLine( size.width, size.height, size.width, 1 );
}
```

Finally, if the PictureButton bean currently holds an image, the image is drawn down and to the right if the button is pushed down; it's drawn up and to the left if the button is up.

```
if ( currentImage != null ) {
  if ( down )
    g.drawImage(currentImage, 1, 1, this);
  else
    g.drawImage(currentImage, 0, 0, this);
}
```

Enabling `ActionEvent` Objects

Your final task is to add code to the `PictureButton` bean that enables it to register action event listeners and produce `ActionEvent` objects. This step is necessary for enabling visual design tools like the BeanBox to connect the `PictureButton` bean with other beans. Begin by adding the following `addActionListener()` method definition to the `PictureButton` class.

```
public synchronized void addActionListener( ActionListener act ) {
  actionListener = AWTEventMulticaster.add( actionListener, act );
}
```

Adding the `addActionListener()` method enables Java components implementing the ActionListener interface to listen for `ActionEvent` objects created by the `PictureButton` bean. Components implementing the ActionListener interface are passed to the `AWTEventMulticaster` class's `add()` method, which adds the component to a list of action event listener objects. Components added to the list are considered registered action event listeners. The `PictureButton` bean must be able to remove these same objects from the action event listener list when someone disconnects a listener object from the bean. The following `removeActionListener()` method enables the removal of action event listeners.

```
public synchronized void removeActionListener( ActionListener act ){
  actionListener = AWTEventMulticaster.remove( actionListener, act );
}
```

The `PictureButton` bean must create `ActionEvent` objects. It creates `ActionEvent` objects through the `processActionEvent()` method shown in the following:

```
protected void processActionEvent( ActionEvent e ) {
  if ( actionListener != null )
    actionListener.actionPerformed( e );
}
```

The `processActionEvent()` method sends an `ActionEvent` object to any action event listeners that are registered. Otherwise, it doesn't send any events. The source code can be seen in Listing 7.4. For the `processActionEvent()` method to do its work, it must be "fired." It's fired when it is called and passed an `ActionEvent` object. Recall that under certain conditions a call to `processActionEvent()` is made in `PictureButton` bean's `paint()` method.

Listing 7.4   Source Code for `PictureButton.java`

```
package sams.controls;

import java.awt.AWTEvent;
import java.awt.AWTEventMulticaster;
import java.awt.Color;
```

JavaBeans as Graphical User Interface Components

CHAPTER 7

145

7

JAVABEANS AS
GUI
COMPONENTS

```java
import java.awt.Component;
import java.awt.Dimension;
import java.awt.Graphics;
import java.awt.Image;
import java.awt.event.ActionEvent;
import java.awt.event.ActionListener;
import java.awt.event.FocusEvent;
import java.awt.event.MouseEvent;
import java.awt.image.ImageProducer;
import java.net.URL;

public class PictureButton extends java.awt.Canvas {
  private String imageFilename = "";
  private transient Image currentImage = null;
  private boolean sticky = false;
  private boolean down = false;
  private transient ActionListener actionListener = null;

  public PictureButton( ) {
    enableEvents( AWTEvent.MOUSE_EVENT_MASK );
  }

  public boolean isSticky( ) {
    return sticky;
  }

  public void setSticky( boolean sticky ) {
    this.sticky = sticky;
  }

  public boolean isDown( ) {
    return down;
  }

  public void setImageFilename( String imageFilename ) {
    this.imageFilename = imageFilename;
    loadImage( );
    Dimension d = getMinimumSize( );
    Component p = getParent();
    if ( p != null ) {
      p.setSize( d );
    }
  }

  public String getImageFilename( ) {
    return imageFilename;
  }

  private void loadImage( ) {
```

continues

Listing 7.4   continued

```java
    Class myClass = getClass( );
    try {
      URL url = myClass.getResource( imageFilename );
      currentImage = createImage( (ImageProducer) url.getContent( ) );
    }
    catch (Exception ex) {
      return;
    }
  }

  private void readObject(ObjectInputStream stream)
    throws IOException, ClassNotFoundException {
    stream.defaultReadObject( );
    loadImage( );
    repaint( );
  }

  public void paint( Graphics g ) {
    Dimension size = getSize( );
    g.setColor( getBackground( ) );
    g.fillRect( 1, 1, size.width - 2, size.height - 2 );
    g.draw3DRect( 0, 0, size.width - 1, size.height - 1, !down );
    g.setColor( Color.darkGray );
    if ( down ) {
      g.drawLine( 1, size.height + 1, 1, 1 );
      g.drawLine( 1, 1, size.width + 1, 1 );
    }
    else {
      g.drawLine( 2, size.height, size.width, size.height );
      g.drawLine( size.width, size.height, size.width, 1 );
    }
    if ( currentImage != null ) {
      if ( down )
        g.drawImage(currentImage, 1, 1, this);
      else
        g.drawImage(currentImage, 0, 0, this);
    }
  }

  public Dimension getPreferredSize( ) {
    return getMinimumSize( );
  }

  public Dimension getMinimumSize( ) {
    int width = 150;
    int height = 150;
    try {
      while ( ( width = currentImage.getWidth( null ) ) < 0 )
        Thread.sleep( 1 );
```

```
      while ( ( height = currentImage.getHeight( null ) ) < 0 )
        Thread.sleep( 1 );
    }
    catch ( Exception e ) {
    }
    return new Dimension( width + 8, height + 8 );
  }

  protected void processMouseEvent( MouseEvent e ) {
    switch( e.getID( ) ) {
      case MouseEvent.MOUSE_PRESSED:
        down = !down;
        repaint( );
        break;
      case MouseEvent.MOUSE_RELEASED:
        if ( down && !sticky ) {
          processActionEvent( new ActionEvent( this,
            ActionEvent.ACTION_PERFORMED, null ) );
          down = false;
          repaint( );
        }
        break;
    }
    super.processMouseEvent( e );
  }

  public synchronized void addActionListener( ActionListener act ) {
    actionListener = AWTEventMulticaster.add( actionListener, act );
  }

  public synchronized void removeActionListener( ActionListener act ) {
    actionListener = AWTEventMulticaster.remove( actionListener, act );
  }

  protected void processActionEvent( ActionEvent e ) {
    if ( actionListener != null )
      actionListener.actionPerformed( e );
  }
}
```

Package and Test the Bean

You've finished writing the `PictureButton` bean. Package it with some image files, in this case the `go.gif` and `stop.gif` image files, using a manifest file like the one in Listing 7.5. Try wiring up the `Juggler` bean with a pair of `PictureButton` beans in the same way you did with a pair of `Picture` beans earlier in this chapter. The result should look similar to the setup shown in Figure 7.7.

7

JAVABEANS AS
GUI
COMPONENTS

Listing 7.5   Source Code for `picturebutton.man`

```
Name: sams/controls/PictureButton.class
Java-Bean: True

Name: sams/controls/go.gif
Java-Bean: False

Name: sams/controls/stop.gif
Java-Bean: False
```

FIGURE 7.7

Wire up `PictureButton` *beans displaying images in the* `go.gif` *and* `stop.gif` *files to a* `Juggler` *bean.*

Summary

You built full-blown useful JavaBeans components in this chapter. You created a `Picture` bean that loads and displays any image file, and then you modified the `Picture` bean to create a `PictureButton` bean. The `PictureButton` bean is a button that displays any image file on its face. You learned how to use events internally to set various bean properties, and you learned how to add facilities to create event objects in your bean. You will learn how to create container beans that can hold your control beans in Chapter 8, "Beans as Containers."

Beans as
Containers

All source code for this chapter can be found on the
Sams Publishing Website at
http://www.mcp.com/info/0-672/0-672-31424-x.

A container is an environment that beans live in, just like objects that exist within the environment we know as the world around us. A container for beans is known as a bean context, which can be a bean itself. The container or bean context provides various services to its beans including the Java Virtual Machine (JVM). Some containers, such as the BeanBox tool's BeanBox window, may hold any software component that conforms to the JavaBeans specification. Other containers, such as containers in Enterprise JavaBeans servers, hold beans that are specialized to take advantage of their unique services. In this chapter, you learn about containers and how to build them.

Containers

JavaBeans containers hold, or contain, Java beans. The `java.awt.Container` class defines several `add()` methods for adding components to a container. There are also methods for removing components (the `remove()` method), getting the number of components held by the container (the `getComponentCount()` method), and getting an array of all of the components held by the container (the `getComponents()` method). Each bean sits in a container, and each bean can be a container itself.

Containers, by their very nature, need ways to keep track of the components added to them. Computer scientists have been hard at work for decades on algorithms (sequences of operations) that help manage collections of things in computer programs. The core Java platform includes a Collections Framework that provides a set of some of these solutions, which includes algorithms for copying, filling, sorting, binary searches, set operations, finding the minimum or maximum, simple object removal, and collection shuffling. The Java Collections Framework goes beyond providing algorithms; it also provides support for read-only and thread-safe containers.

In the following section, you create a simple container by extending the `java.awt.Panel` class, add beans to the container, and have the beans interact with the container. Next, you learn about bean contexts and how you can structure JavaBeans containers into a useful hierarchy. Finally, you delve into collections and the Java Collections Framework. You learn about the range of algorithms provided by the Java Collections Framework.

Extending the `java.awt.Panel` Class

You create containers all the time when you write Java beans. Any bean that can hold another bean is a container. For instance, all beans extended from an Abstract Windowing Toolkit (AWT) control are containers. In this section, you write a simple `Dot` bean and a container bean, which is extended from the `java.awt.Panel` class, named `MyContainer1`. You add `Dot` beans to the container bean.

The `Dot` bean is extended from the `java.awt.Canvas` class and displays a small red circle. The code is shown in Listing 8.1. The reason for creating the `Dot` bean is to have something for a container bean to hold.

Listing 8.1   Source code for `Dot.java`

```
package sams.containers;

import java.awt.Canvas;
import java.awt.Color;
import java.awt.Graphics;
import java.awt.Rectangle;

public class Dot extends Canvas {
  private int diameter = 20;
  private Rectangle bounds = new Rectangle( diameter, diameter );

  public Dot( ) {
    this( 20 );
  }

  public Dot( int diameter ) {
    this.diameter = diameter;
    setSize( diameter, diameter );
  }

  public void setDiameter( int diameter ) {
    this.diameter = diameter;
    bounds = new Rectangle( diameter, diameter );
  }

  public int getDiameter( ) {
    return diameter;
  }

  public void paint(Graphics g) {
    g.setColor( Color.red );
    g.fillOval( bounds.x, bounds.y, bounds.width, bounds.height );
  }
}
```

One of the simplest ways to build a container bean, at least one that displays a graphic user interface, is to write a class that extends the `java.awt.Panel` class. You do this to write the `MyContainer1` bean, as shown in Listing 8.2.

Listing 8.2   Source code for `MyContainer1.java`

```
package sams.containers;

import java.awt.Color;
import java.awt.Dimension;
import java.awt.Graphics;
import java.awt.Panel;
import java.awt.Point;

public class MyContainer1 extends Panel {
  private int panelWidth = 300;
  private int panelHeight = 175;
  private Dot dot1 = null;
  private Dot dot2 = null;

  public MyContainer1( ) {
    setLayout( null );
    dot1 = ( Dot ) add( new Dot( ) );
    int diameter1 = dot1.getDiameter( );
    dot1.setBounds( 10, 35, diameter1, diameter1 );
    dot2 = ( Dot ) add( new Dot( ) );
    int diameter2 = dot2.getDiameter( );
    dot2.setBounds( 230, 120, diameter2, diameter2 );
  }

  public void paint( Graphics g ) {
    if ( dot1 != null && dot2 != null ) {
      Point point1 = dot1.getLocation( );
      Point point2 = dot2.getLocation( );
      g.setColor( Color.red );
      int diameter1 = dot1.getDiameter( );
      int diameter2 = dot2.getDiameter( );
g.drawLine( point1.x + ( diameter1/2 ),
      point1.y + ( diameter1/2 ), point2.x + ( diameter2/2 ),
      point2.y + ( diameter2/2 ) );
    }
  }

  public Dimension getPreferredSize( ) {
    return getMinimumSize( );
  }

  public Dimension getMinimumSize( ) {
    return new Dimension( panelWidth, panelHeight );
  }
}
```

It's important to note that the `Dot.class` file needs to be in the current directory when compiling the program.

The MyContainer1 bean isn't anything special or exotic. You've probably seen many similar beans. You add two Dot beans to the MyContainer1 bean in its class constructor. The sams.containers.MyContainer1 class's paint() method checks for the Dot beans. If they are present, a red line is drawn between the center of the two beans, as shown in Figure 8.1. Package the Dot and MyContainer1 beans into a JAR file using the mycontainer1.man manifest file shown in Listing 8.3.

FIGURE 8.1

The MyContainer1 *bean is a container holding two* Dot *beans.*

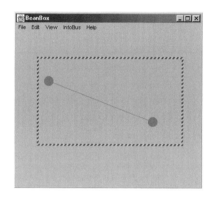

Listing 8.3   Source code for mycontainer1.man

```
Name: sams/containers/MyContainer1.class
Java-Bean: True

Name: sams/containers/Dot.class
Java-Bean: True
```

Bean Contexts

All beans exist within a bean context. A bean is instantiated in a bean context where it exists in relation to other beans until it is killed and eaten up by the JVM's garbage collectors. Services can be added to or removed from the bean context while the bean is running. Beans are able to explore their environment (the bean context) looking for available services. After they find them, beans are able to use the services provided by a bean context. The bean context is formalized by a set of bean context interfaces. Four interfaces form the root of the bean context interface hierarchy: the java.util.Collection, java.beans.DesignMode, java.beans.Visibility, and java.beans.beancontext. BeanContextChild interfaces. Tables 8.1 through 8.3 describe these interfaces.

> **Note**
>
> Learn more about the `java.util.Collection` interface in the "Collections Framework" section later in this chapter.

Table 8.1   The `java.beans.DesignMode` Interface

Field	*Description*
Field Summary	
`static Object globalHierarchyLock`	This global lock is used by both `BeanContext` and `BeanContextServices` implementors to serialize changes in a `BeanContext` hierarchy and any service requests and so on.
Method Summary	
`void addBeanContextMembership Listener(BeanContextMembership Listener bcml)`	Add a `BeanContextMembershipListener`
`URL getResource(String name, BeanContextChild bcc)`	Get a URL resource
`InputStream getResourceAsStream (String name, BeanContextChild bcc)`	Get a resource as a stream of data
`Object instantiateChild(String beanName)`	Instantiate the Java bean named as a child of this `BeanContext`
`void removeBeanContextMembership Listener(BeanContextMembership Listener bcml)`	Remove a `BeanContextMembershipListener`

Table 8.2   The `java.beans.Visibility` Interface

Method	*Description*
Method Summary	
`boolean avoidingGui()`	`true` if the bean is currently avoiding use of the GUI (for example, due to a call on `dontUseGui()`).
`void dontUseGui()`	This method instructs the bean that it should not use the GUI.
`boolean needsGui()`	`true` if the bean absolutely needs a GUI available to get its work done.
`void okToUseGui()`	This method instructs the bean that it is OK to use the GUI.

Table 8.3 The `java.beans.beancontext.BeanContextChild` Interface

Field
Field Summary
protected BeanContext beanContext
BeanContextChild beanContextChildPeer
protected PropertyChangeSupport pcSupport
protected boolean rejectedSetBCOnce
protected VetoableChangeSupport vcSupport

Constructor	*Description*
Constructor Summary	
BeanContextChildSupport()	Construct a `BeanContextChildSupport` where this class has been subclassed to implement the JavaBean component itself.
BeanContextChildSupport (BeanContextChild bcc)	Construct a `BeanContextChildSupport` where the JavaBean component itself implements `BeanContextChild`, and encapsulates this, delegating interface to this implementation.

Method	*Description*
Method Summary	
void addPropertyChangeListener (String name, PropertyChange Listener pcl)	Add a property change listener.
void addVetoableChangeListener (String name, VetoableChange Listener vcl)	Add a vetoable change listener.
void firePropertyChange (String name, Object oldValue, Object newValue)	Fires a `propertyChange` event.
void fireVetoableChange (String name, Object oldValue, Object newValue)	Fires a `vetoableChange` event.
BeanContext getBeanContext()	Gets the bean context.
BeanContextChild getBeanContext	Gets rgw bean context's child `ChildPeer()` peer.

continues

Table 8.3 continued

Method	Description
Method Summary	
`protected void initializeBean` `ContextResources()`	This method may be overridden by subclasses to provide their own initialization behaviors.
`boolean isDelegated()`	Returns true if delegated.
`protected void releaseBean` `ContextResources()`	This method can be overridden by subclasses to provide their own release behaviors.

`void removePropertyChange`
`Listener(String name,`
`PropertyChangeListener pcl)`
	Remove a property change listener.

`void removeVetoableChange`
`Listener(String name,`
`VetoableChangeListener vcl)`
	Remove a vetoable change listener.

`void serviceAvailable(BeanContext` `ServiceAvailableEvent bcsae)`	A new service is available from the nesting `BeanContext`. Subclasses may override this method to implement their own behaviors.
`void serviceRevoked(BeanContext` `ServiceRevokedEvent bcsre)`	A service provided by the nesting `BeanContext` has been revoked. Subclasses can override this method to implement their own behaviors.
`void setBeanContext` `(BeanContext bc)`	Sets the bean context.
`boolean validatePendingSetBean` `Context(BeanContext newValue)`	Called from `setBeanContext` to validate (or otherwise) the pending change in the nesting `BeanContext` property value. Returning `false` will cause `setBeanContext` to throw `PropertyVetoException`.

The `BeanContext` acts a logical hierarchical container for Java beans. Java beans wanting to be nested within and obtain a reference to their execution environment or context, as defined by the `BeanContext` sub-interface, need to implement the `BeanContextChild` interface. Another related interface is the `BeanContextContainer` interface— implemented by `BeanContext`s that have an AWT container associated with them. Compliant `BeanContext`s fire events on this interface when the state of the membership of the `BeanContext` changes. One of the primary functions of a `BeanContext` is to act as a rendezvous between Java beans and `BeanContextServiceProviders`. The `BeanContextServices` interface provides a mechanism for a `BeanContext` to expose generic "services" to the `BeanContextChild` objects within.

Beans that you want to have access to their environment, known as the bean's context, need to implement the `java.beans.beancontext.BeanContextChild` interface. All other interfaces in the bean context interface hierarchy are extended from this interface. The `java.beans.beancontext.BeanContext` interface is extended from the `java.beans.beancontext.BeanContextChild` interface, and the `java.beans.beancontext.BeanContextServices` interface is extended from the `java.beans.beancontext.BeanContext` interface. The code required to implement the methods defined by the `java.beans.beancontext.BeanContextChild` interface can be tricky. The Java platform provides the `java.beans.beancontext.BeanContextChildSupport` class, which implements the `java.beans.BeanContextChild` interface for you.

> **Note**
>
> Instance variables that may be assigned references to nesting instances of classes implementing the `java.beans.beancontext.BeanContext` interface must be declared as transient; otherwise, persistence mechanisms may fail to function properly.

The `java.beans.beancontext.BeanContextChildSupport` Class

Write classes that extend the `java.beans.beancontext.BeanContextChildSupport` class when you want them to implement the `java.beans.BeanContextChild` interface. All of the interface's methods are already written for you, so you can focus on your bean specific code. Listing 8.4 contains the code for an example child bean that extends the `java.beans.beancontext.BeanContextChildSupport` class. When a bean implementing the `java.beans.beancontext.BeanContextChild` interface is added to a container implementing the `java.beans.beancontext.BeanContext` interface, the container passes a reference to itself through the child bean's `setBeanContext()` method. The `ChildBean` bean is added to an instance of the `sams.containers.MyContext` class described in the following section, which implements the `java.beans.beancontext.BeanContext` interface.

Listing 8.4   Source code for `ChildBean.java`

```
package sams.containers;

import java.awt.TextArea;
import java.beans.beancontext.BeanContextChildSupport;
import java.beans.beancontext.BeanContextServiceRevokedEvent;
import java.beans.beancontext.BeanContextServiceRevokedListener;
```

continues

Listing 8.4 continued

```java
import java.beans.beancontext.BeanContextServices;

public class ChildBean extends BeanContextChildSupport
    implements BeanContextServiceRevokedListener {
  private final String MESSAGE = "This message is displayed by a service
➥provided by the bean context.";
  private TextArea textService = new TextArea( );

  public void useContext( ) {
BeanContextServices beanContext =
    ( BeanContextServices ) getBeanContext( );
    if ( beanContext.hasService( textService.getClass( ) ) ) {
      try {
textService = ( TextArea ) beanContext.getService( this,
        this, textService.getClass( ), null, this );
      }
      catch ( Exception ex ) {
        System.out.println( ex.toString( ) );
      }
      textService.setText( MESSAGE );
    }
  }

  public void serviceRevoked( BeanContextServiceRevokedEvent ev ) {
  }
}
```

The `java.beans.beancontext.BeanContext` Interface

Classes implementing the `java.beans.beancontext.BeanContext` interface can partici-
pate in a formal bean hierarchy that enables beans to recognize or interact with their
environment, also known as their context. This interface provides the standard data fields
and methods for Java bean containers and their services. The code required to implement
the methods defined by this interface can be tricky. The Java platform provides the
`java.beans.beancontext.BeanContextSupport` class, which implements the
`java.beans.BeanContextChild` interface for you.

> **Note**
>
> The `java.beans.beancontext.BeanContext` interface extends the
> `java.beans.beancontext.BeanContextChild` interface. This allows beans instan-
> tiated from classes implementing the `java.beans.beancontext.BeanContext`
> interface to act as both a bean context and a child bean.

The `java.beans.beancontext.BeanContextSupport` Class

Write classes that extend the `java.beans.beancontext.BeanContextSupport` class when you want them to implement the `java.beans.BeanContext` interface. All of the interface's methods are already written for you, so you can focus on your bean-specific code.

> **Note**
>
> The `java.beans.beancontext.BeanContextSupport` class extends the `java.beans.beancontext.BeanContextChildSupport` class. This allows beans instantiated from classes extending the `java.beans.beancontext.BeanContextSupport` class to act as both a bean context and a child bean.

The `java.beans.beancontext.BeanContextServices` Interface

Beans instantiated from classes implementing the `java.beans.beancontext.BeanContextServices` interface expose services to their child beans. The code required to implement the methods defined by this interface can be tricky. The Java platform provides the `java.beans.beancontext.BeanContextServicesSupport` class, which implements the `java.beans.BeanContextServices` interface for you.

> **Note**
>
> The `java.beans.beancontext.BeanContextServices` interface extends the `java.beans.beancontext.BeanContext` interface.

The `java.beans.beancontext.BeanContextServicesSupport` Class

Write classes that extend the `java.beans.beancontext.BeanContextServicesSupport` class when you want them to implement the `java.beans.BeanContextServices` interface. All of the interface's methods are already written for you, so you can focus on your bean-specific code. Listing 8.5 contains the code for an example child bean that extends the `java.beans.beancontext.BeanContextServicesSupport` class.

8

BEANS AS CONTAINERS

> **Note**
>
> The java.beans.beancontext.BeanContextServicesSupport class extends the java.beans.beancontext.BeanContextSupport class.

Listing 8.5   Source code for MyContext.java

```java
package sams.containers;

import java.awt.TextArea;
import java.beans.beancontext.BeanContextChild;
import java.beans.beancontext.BeanContextServices;
import java.beans.beancontext.BeanContextServicesSupport;
import java.beans.beancontext.BeanContextServiceProvider;
import java.beans.beancontext.BeanContextServiceRevokedListener;
import java.util.Iterator;
import java.util.TooManyListenersException;

class MyContext extends BeanContextServicesSupport
      implements BeanContextServiceProvider {
  private TextArea textService = null;

  public MyContext( TextArea service ) {
    textService = service;
    addService( textService.getClass( ), this );
  }

public Object getService( BeanContextChild child,
    Object requestor, Class serviceClass, Object serviceSelector,
    BeanContextServiceRevokedListener bcsrl ) throws TooManyListenersException {
    return textService;
  }

public Object getService( BeanContextServices bcs, Object requestor,
    Class serviceClass, Object serviceSelector ) {
    return textService;
  }

public Iterator getCurrentServiceSelectors( BeanContextServices bcs,
    Class serviceClass ) {
    return null;
  }

public void releaseService( BeanContextServices bcs,
    Object requestor, Object service ) {
  }
}
```

Completing the `MyContainer2` Bean

Complete the bean context example in this section by writing the
`sams.containers.MyContainer2` class shown in Listing 8.6 and compiling it along with
the `sams.containers.ChildBean` and `sams.containers.MyContext` classes shown in
Listings 8.4 and 8.5.

Listing 8.6   Source Code for `MyContainer2.java`

```
package sams.containers;

import java.awt.Color;
import java.awt.Dimension;
import java.awt.Graphics;
import java.awt.Panel;
import java.awt.Point;
import java.awt.TextArea;

public class MyContainer2 extends Panel {
  private int panelWidth = 400;
  private int panelHeight = 175;
  public TextArea textService = new TextArea( );
  private MyContext myContext = new MyContext( textService );


  public MyContainer2( ) {
    add( textService );
    ChildBean child = new ChildBean( );
    myContext.add( child );
    child.useContext( );
  }

  public Dimension getPreferredSize( ) {
    return getMinimumSize( );
  }

  public Dimension getMinimumSize( ) {
    return new Dimension( panelWidth, panelHeight );
  }
}
```

8

BEANS AS CONTAINERS

For the previous program you'll need the `ChildBean.class` file in the current directory.

Package the three classes for the bean context example into the `mycontainer2.jar` file
using the `mycontainer2.man` file shown in Listing 8.7. Type the following command at
the prompt in your console or DOS window:

```
jar -cmf mycontainer2.man mycontainer2.jar sams\containers
```

The child bean's message should appear in the text area provided by the text service, as shown in Figure 8.2.

FIGURE 8.2

The MyContainer2 *bean.*

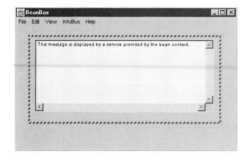

Listing 8.7   Source Code for mycontainer2.man

```
Name: sams/containers/MyContainer2.class
Java-Bean: True

Name: sams/containers/MyContext.class
Java-Bean: False

Name: sams/containers/ChildBean.class
Java-Bean: False
```

Collections

A collection is an object that represents a group of objects. You can use collections to represent relationships among objects. These relationships can be between one object and another object (one-to-one), one object and many other objects (one-to-many), or many objects and many other objects (many-to-many). A simple array can be used to represent a one-to-one relationship. Special collection classes are essential when you want to represent one-to-many and many-to-many relationships.

Collections can be gathered together in many different ways. The way you represent a collection of objects largely depends on the kinds of objects you're collecting and what you want to do with them. There are five types of collections available in Java: arrays, vectors, sets, lists, and maps.

Arrays

Arrays are indexed lists of objects. Each array is a fixed size and each object in its collection of objects is of the same data type. Arrays are a standard part of the Java language and are not part of the Collections Framework.

Vectors

A vector is an array of elements that can grow or shrink through the addition or removal of objects after its initial creation. Each object in a vector can be of a different data type. Vectors remain part of the core Java platform as the `java.util.Vector` class. However, it's recommended that vectors should only be used while writing and maintaining Java 1.0 and 1.1 programs. Vectors are not part of the Collections Framework. What *is* recommended for this type of functionality is the `java.util.ArrayList` class.

Sets

A set is a collection of objects with no duplication. One and only one of each object is allowed. Sets may or may not be ordered, for instance numerically or alphabetically. Sets are part of the Collections Framework.

Lists

A list is an ordered sequence of objects that can include duplicates. You have precise control over where each object is added in a list, and you can access objects by their position in the list. You can also search a list. Lists are part of the Collections Framework.

Maps

A map is an array of key-value pairs. A key maps to one and only one value (one-to-one), and no duplicate keys are allowed. Maps are part of the Collections Framework.

Collections Framework

The Java Collections Framework, also known as the Collections API, is a unified framework for representing and manipulating collections. Through the Collections Framework, you can manipulate collections of objects independently of the particular ways that the objects are implemented. The Collections Framework is composed of four groups of interfaces or classes.

- Collection interfaces
- Implementations of the collection interfaces
- Partial implementations of collection interfaces
- Algorithms

Collection Interfaces

The Collections Framework provides interfaces to two basic types of collections: collections and maps represented by the `java.util.Collection` and `java.util.Map` interfaces, respectively. Collections implementing the `java.util.Collection` interface are composed of any group of objects, whereas those implementing the `java.util.Map` interface are composed of key-value pairs. Two of the basic collection types are extended from the `java.util.Collection` interface. These are the set and list types represented by the `java.util.Set` and `java.util.List` interfaces, respectively. The four basic collection interfaces are listed in Table 8.4.

Table 8.4 Basic Collection Interfaces

Collection Interface	*Description*
`java.util.Collection`	Represents a group of objects that may or may not be ordered. The base collection is duplicate-free and mutable. This class provides the base interface that most of the interfaces in the Collections API extend.
`java.util.Set`	Represents a collection in which no duplicate elements are permitted. Ordering, if any, is typically established at set creation time.
`java.util.List`	Represents a collection that can hold duplicate objects and has specific ordering. This interface provides precise control over the position of each element in the list.
`java.util.Map`	Represents a mapping between keys and values. Each key can map to one value at most. This interface doesn't extend the `java.util.Collection` interface.

There are two more collection interfaces extended from two of the basic interfaces that are listed in Table 8.5. These interfaces specify that their collections are automatically sorted.

Table 8.5 Sorted Collection Interfaces

Collection Interface	*Description*
`java.util.SortedSet`	Represents a set whose elements are automatically sorted
`java.util.SortedMap`	Represents a map whose mappings are automatically sorted by key

Implementations of Collection Interfaces

Each of the three main types of collections represented by the `java.util.Set`, `java.util.List`, and `java.util.Map` interfaces are implemented in classes with names that reflect the type of data structure used to store the collection. These include arrays, linked lists, trees, and hash tables. The implementations of collection interfaces are also known as containers because you are able to view and work with collections of objects through instantiations of these classes. The Collections Framework container classes are listed in Table 8.6. Use these classes directly or subclass them and add additional behavior to the collection interfaces.

Table 8.6 Java Collections Framework Containers

Container	Description
`java.util.HashSet`	Implements the `java.util.Set` interface and backs the implementation with a hash table.
`java.util.TreeSet`	Provides a balanced binary tree implementation of the `java.util.SortedSet` interface, which is extended from the `java.util.Set` interface. Unlike instances of the `java.util.HashSet` class, instances of this class imposes ordering on its elements.
`java.util.ArrayList`	Implements the `java.util.List` interface. Instances of this class provide a resizable array. This class is similar to the `java.util.Vector` class, which is not part of the Collections Framework.
`java.util.LinkedList`	Instances of this class provide a doubly-linked list. Use this class if elements are frequently inserted or deleted within the list. This class is useful for queues and double-ended queues.
`java.util.HashMap`	Implements the `java.util.Map` interface. Instances of this class provide a hash table. This class is similar to the `java.util.Hashtable` class, which is not part of the Collections Framework.
`java.util.TreeMap`	Implements the `java.util.SortedMap` interface, which is extended from the `java.util.Map` interface. Instances of this class provide a balanced binary tree and, unlike instances of the `java.util.HashMap` class, impose ordering on its elements.

8

BEANS AS
CONTAINERS

You have the choice to work with the actual objects through read and write operations or you can work with them through read-only operations so there is no chance of changing the original objects. You also have the choice of working with your collections through thread safe (synchronized) containers. The `java.utils.Collections` class provides several static methods so you can select these options.

The `java.utils.Collections` Class

The `java.utils.Collections` class is a collection of static methods that operate on or return collections. You can perform any arbitrary algorithmic operations on collections using the methods in this class. Two additional important uses of the methods in this class are to get read-only containers and to get thread-safe, or synchronized, containers wrapping collections.

You can instantiate read-only containers for all types of collections except vectors. Call a `java.utils.Collections` class static method with a name that begins with `unmodifiable` and ends in the kind of collection for which you want a read-only container. They are listed in Table 8.7. You pass the collection itself to the method parameter.

Table 8.7   `java.utils.Collections` Class Methods That Invoke Read-Only Containers

Method	*Type of Collection*
`unmodifiableCollection()`	`java.util.Collection`
`unmodifiableList()`	`java.util.List`
`unmodifiableMap()`	`java.util.Map`
`unmodifiableSet()`	`java.util.Set`
`unmodifiableSortedMap()`	`java.util.SortedMap`
`unmodifiableSortedSet()`	`java.util.SortedSet`

You can create thread-safe containers that are synchronized for all types of collections except vectors. Call a `java.utils.Collections` class static method with a name that begins with `synchronized` and ends in the kind of collection for which you want a thread-safe container. They are listed in Table 8.8. You pass the collection itself to the method parameter.

Note

Collections containers are unsynchronized by default. This has performance advantages, but the disadvantage is that unsynchronized containers are not threadsafe.

Table 8.8 `java.utils.Collections` Class Methods That Invoke Thread-Safe (Synchronized) Containers

Method	Type of Collection
synchronizedCollection()	java.util.Collection
synchronizedList()	java.util.List
synchronizedMap()	java.util.Map
synchronizedSet()	java.util.Set
synchronizedSortedMap()	java.util.SortedMap
synchronizedSortedSet()	java.util.SortedSet

Note

Collections containers are unsynchronized by default. In fact, most of the Collections API has an unsynchronized implementation, except for the `java.util.Hashtable` and `java.util.Vector` classes. An unsynchronized implementation has performance advantages, but the disadvantage is that unsynchronized containers are not thread safe.

Partial Implementations of Collection Interfaces

Partial implementations, also known as *abstract implementations*, of collection interfaces provide easy-to-use classes that you can extend to use the collections provided by the core Java platform as shown in Table 8.9.

Table 8.9 Abstract Implementations of Collection Interfaces

Container	Description
java.util.AbstractCollection	Implements the `java.util.Collection` interface. Rather than a set or a list, instances of classes extended from this class are general-purpose collection objects.
java.util.AbstractSet	Implements the `java.util.Set` interface.
java.util.AbstractMap	Implements the `java.util.Map` interface.
java.util.AbstractList	Implements some of the `java.util.List` interface and is backed by a random-access data store.
java.util.Abstract SequentialList	Classes extended from this abstract class represent a list backed by a sequential-access data store such as a linked list.

Algorithms

The Collections API provides algorithms that operate on collections, collection views, and collection wrappers. The algorithms are provided in the `java.util.Collections` class, which has several public static methods that operate on collections or return collections as you can see in Table 8.10.

Table 8.10 Algorithms Provided Through Static Methods in the `java.utils.Collections` Class

Method	Description
`binarySearch()`	Searches for an element in an ordered list using the binary search algorithm.
`copy()`	Copies the source list passed to the method's second parameter to the destination list passed to the method's first parameter.
`fill()`	Overwrites every element in a list passed to the method's first parameter by the value passed to its second parameter.
`max()`	Returns the maximum element in a collection.
`min()`	Returns the minimum element in a collection.
`reverse()`	Reverses the order of the elements in the list passed to the method.
`sort()`	Sorts a list using a merge sort algorithm that provides average-case performance comparable to a high-quality quick-sort, guaranteed $O(n*\log n)$ performance and stability. (A stable sort is one that does not reorder equal elements.)
`shuffle()`	Randomly shuffles the order of the elements in the list passed to the method.

Iterating Through Collections

The Collections Framework includes two interfaces, the `java.util.Iterator` and `java.util.ListIterator` interfaces, which you implement in classes that step through collections of objects one at a time. An object that implements one of these interfaces generates a series of objects, one at a time, as successive calls to the `next()` method return successive objects in a collection.

Write classes that implement the `java.util.Iterator` interface to iterate over collections of objects represented by objects implementing the `java.util.Collection` interface. When you want to iterate over lists, write classes that implement the `java.util.ListIterator` interface, which extends the `java.util.Iterator` interface. This interface provides easier bi-directional iteration over lists.

> **Note**
>
> You may be familiar with the `java.util.Enumeration` interface, which is similar to the `java.util.Iterator` interface but is not part of the Collections Framework. A collection can be modified while it's being iterated over by an object implementing the `java.util.Iterator` interface. In contrast, you cannot modify a collection while it's being iterated over by an object implementing the `java.util.Enumeration` interface.

Summary

In this chapter you learned about containers, the formal JavaBeans container hierarchy implemented through beans contexts, and the Collections Framework used to manipulate objects placed in the JavaBeans containers. Containers, known as bean contexts, are where beans live. You wrote some beans that provided typical and specialized containers, including a bean context that provided a special service. Use the considerable power of the Collections Framework to iterate through and manipulate collections of beans added to your containers.

8

BEANS AS
CONTAINERS

Invisible Runtime Beans

All source code for this chapter can be found on the Sams Publishing Website at
http://www.mcp.com/info/0-672/0-672-31424-x.

A bean doesn't need to be a graphical user interface control to be a bean. In fact, a bean doesn't need to be visible at all to the application user. Only the application builder needs to see some kind of representation of the bean during design time. Popular beans that are invisible during runtime include timer beans and beans that provide database access. In this chapter, you use Java's time-related classes and methods to write an invisible timer bean.

Invisible JavaBeans Components

You can create JavaBeans components that are invisible to the application user. However, you should be able to use all beans effectively in a visual application builder environment. Therefore, beans that are invisible at runtime, while the application user is using the bean, must be represented visually during design time while the application designer is building the application.

> **Note**
>
> Visual application builders mostly take care of the design-time representation of invisible beans. You can, however, customize a bean's designtime look. Learn how in Chapter 25, "Customization."

In this section, you'll write a bean that is invisible during runtime: the popular timer bean. You will write other useful beans along the way while you learn, or review, Java's time facilities.

Time and Timers

Timers naturally need some way to keep time. Your computer's central processing unit is an excellent timekeeper as it cycles up to hundreds of millions of times every second. Java provides classes and methods so you can take advantage of the time-keeping abilities of every computer.

In this section, you'll write a clock bean named ClockOne. ClockOne includes the TimerOne object, which gathers time information from computers through Java's Date class. TimerOne passes the current time, including the date and day, to the ClockOne object that displays the time to ClockOne bean's graphic interface. The TimerOne and ClockOne classes provide the basis upon which you will build a standalone timer bean and a bean for testing the timer bean.

Writing the `TimerOne` Class

The `TimerOne` class is a very simple subclass of Java's `Thread` class, as displayed by the source code in Listing 9.1. A timer must run continuously and check the time periodically, so it's important to run timers as a separate thread.

`TimerOne` has one class instance variable. It's a private variable named `clock` that holds references to `ClockOne` objects. The reference is necessary so that the timer can pass the current time to the `ClockOne` object, the object that displays the time to the `ClockOne` bean graphic interface. The following `TimerOne` constructor takes a single parameter:

```
public TimerOne( ClockOne clock ) {
  this.clock = clock;
}
```

A `ClockOne` object must be passed to the `TimerOne` constructor when a `TimerOne` object is created. The one statement in the constructor assigns the `TimerOne` object, that was passed to the constructor, to `TimerOne` class's `clock` class variable.

Our example, `TimerOne`, has only one method other than its constructor, the `run()` method. The `run()` method automatically executes when a `Thread` subclass's `start()` method is called. `TimerOne` class's `run()` method, shown next, does most of the timer's work.

```
public void run( ) {
  while ( true ) {
    Date date = new Date( );
    clock.setCurrentTime( date.toString( ) );
    try {
      Thread.sleep( 1000 );
    }
    catch ( InterruptedException e ) {
      break;
    }
  }
}
```

The `run()` method goes into an infinite `while` loop. Inside the loop, the first statement gets the current time and date by creating a new `Date` object. The `Date` object, created from Java's `Date` class found in the `java.util` package, encapsulates the computer's date, day, time, and time zone at the moment that the object was created.

A call is made to `Date` class's `toString()` method in the second statement in the `while` loop. The current date and time information encapsulated in the `Date` object is translated into a string and passed to the `ClockOne` object's `setCurrentTime()` method. The `ClockOne` object then displays the information, as you'll see shortly.

The rest of the statements in the while loop make the TimerOne thread sleep for 1000 milliseconds, which is equal to 1 second. The length of time you make the thread sleep is critical, because it sets the approximate sample rate. In other words, the timer's sampling rate is about once every second with the thread set to sleep for 1000 milliseconds every time it loops. The sampling rate would be about two times per second if you set the thread to sleep for 500 milliseconds. If the sleep method throws an exception, it's caught and the while loop is ended. This is clearly shown in the source code in Listing 9.1.

Listing 9.1 Source Code for TimerOne.java

```java
package sams.time;

import java.util.Date;

class TimerOne extends Thread {
 private ClockOne clock = null;

 public TimerOne( ClockOne clock ) {
  this.clock = clock;
 }

 public void run( ) {
  while ( true ) {
    Date date = new Date( );
    clock.setCurrentTime( date.toString( ) );
    try {
      Thread.sleep( 1000 );
    }
    catch ( InterruptedException e ) {
      break;
    }
  }
 }
}
```

Writing the ClockOne Class

The ClockOne class, shown in Listing 9.2, receives a string containing date and time information from a TimerOne object and displays it on the ClockOne graphic interface. The ClockOne window is set to 200 pixels wide by 30 pixels tall by the call to the setSize() method in the ClockOne class constructor.

The ClockOne class has three class instance variables: currentTime, running, and timer. The currentTime variable holds the string containing the date and time that is passed from the TimerOne object. The running Boolean class variable indicates that a TimerOne object is currently running when it's set to true; otherwise, when it's false, there is no TimerOne object running. Finally, the timer variable holds a reference to the currently instantiated `TimerOne` object. Of these three variables, only the `running` variable is a `ClockOne` bean property.

The `ClockOne` bean's `running` property includes both accessor and mutator methods. The Boolean accessor method, shown next, gets the current state of the `running` variable.

```
public boolean isRunning( ) {
 return running;
}
```

The mutator method, on the other hand, is central to the proper functioning of the `ClockOne` bean. The `setRunning()` method, shown next, passes a Boolean setting to the `ClockOne` bean and assigns it to the `ClockOne` class's `running` variable, as you would expect.

```
public void setRunning( boolean running ) {
  this.running = running;

  if( running && timer == null ) {
    timer = new TimerOne( this );
    timer.start( );
  }
  else if( !running && timer != null ) {
    timer.stop( );
    timer = null;
  }
}
```

Then the method checks the `running` and `timer` variables. If the `running` variable is set to `true` and the `timer` variable holds a `null` value, the bean creates a new `TimerOne` object, assigns it to the `timer` variable, and then starts it running by calling the `TimerOne` object's `start` method. Otherwise, if the `running` variable is `false` and there is a currently running `TimerOne` object, the `TimerOne` object is stopped running by a call to the `Thread` class `stop` method. The `timer` variable is set to `null` so that the clock can start running again if the `running` property is set back to `true`.

The rest of `ClockOne` bean's functionality is carried out by the `setCurrentTime()` and `paint()` methods. You saw earlier that `TimerOne` objects pass a string holding the current date and time information to `ClockOne` class's `setCurrentTime()` method, shown in the following:

```
public void setCurrentTime( String currentTime ) {
 this.currentTime = currentTime;
 repaint( );
}
```

The `setCurrrentTime()` method is a public method that passes a string to `ClockOne` class's `currentTime` class instance variable and then calls the `repaint()` method so that the `ClockOne` bean graphic interface displays the latest contents of the `currentTime` variable.

9

INVISIBLE RUNTIME
BEANS

ClockOne class's paint() method, shown next, draws the string held by the currentTime variable to the ClockOne bean graphic interface.

```java
public void paint( Graphics g ) {
  g.drawString( currentTime, 20, 20 );
}
```

Your simple clock bean, built from a timer and an interface object, is finished (see Listing 9.2). Next, package the bean and test it.

Listing 9.2 Source Code for ClockOne.java

```java
package sams.time;

import java.awt.Graphics;

public class ClockOne extends java.awt.Canvas {
 private String currentTime = "";
 private boolean running = false;
 private TimerOne timer = null;

 public ClockOne( ) {
  setSize( 200, 30 );
 }

 public boolean isRunning( ) {
  return running;
 }

 public void setRunning( boolean running ) {
  this.running = running;
  if( running && timer == null ) {
    timer = new TimerOne( this );
    timer.start( );
  }
  else if( !running && timer != null ) {
    timer.stop( );
    timer = null;
  }
 }

 public void setCurrentTime( String currentTime ) {
  this.currentTime = currentTime;
  repaint( );
 }

 public void paint( Graphics g ) {
  g.drawString( currentTime, 20, 20 );
 }
}
```

Packaging and Testing the `ClockOne` Bean

Package your `ClockOne` bean into a JAR file in the usual way by using the `jar` utility and the `clockone.man` manifest file in Listing 9.3. The `ClockOne` bean consists of both the `ClockOne` and `TimerOne` Java objects, so you need to package both objects into the JAR file, but only the `ClockOne` class is designated as a bean. Enter the following command at the DOS or Console prompt:

```
jar cmf clockone.man clockone.jar sams
```

Once you package the class files into a JAR, test the `ClockOne` bean out in the BeanBox. Go to the `ClockOne` bean's running property editor on the property sheet and set it to `true`. Your `ClockOne` bean should display the current date, time, and time zone, as shown in Figure 9.1.

Listing 9.3   Source Code for `clockone.man`

```
Name: sams/time/ClockOne.class
Java-Bean: True

Name: sams/time/TimerOne.class
Java-Bean: False
```

FIGURE 9.1

Set ClockOne *bean's running property to* true, *and the bean displays the current date, time, and time zone.*

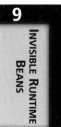

9

INVISIBLE RUNTIME BEANS

System Time and Timers

The ClockOne bean displays the date, time, and time zone, but the representation of time in your computer is a bit different. Java's Date class puts the computer's internal representation of time, the system time, through some transformations and formatting. But when you write a timer bean, you don't need all of the fancy formats. You just need to know every time a certain number of milliseconds, seconds, or other block of time has passed. System time is the ticket.

You can access a computer's system time through Java's System class that forms part of the java.lang package. Make a call to the currentTimeMillis() method, and a long number representing the current system time in the number of milliseconds that have passed since midnight, January 1, 1970 is the output. Yes, it's true. Without going into the why of it, you can see that some calculations need to be done to figure out exactly how many years, days, hours, seconds, and milliseconds have passed since January 1, 1970. But you don't need to do that (and Java's Date class does it for you when you do).

In this section, you'll make minor modifications to the TimerOne and ClockOne classes to create the TimerTwo and ClockTwo classes for the ClockTwo bean. The ClockTwo bean displays system time without any formatting or calculations.

Writing the TimerTwo Class

TimerTwo uses the system time. You make two changes to the TimerOne class to transform it into the TimerTwo class (see Listing 9.4). First, replace occurrences of the ClockOne string with ClockTwo. You need to do this for the clock variable declaration and for the clock parameter in the TimerTwo class constructor.

The second modification you make is to get rid of the statement creating a Date object and change the code so that a String object is passed to the ClockTwo object's setCurrentTime() method. Make a static call to System class's currentTimeMillis() method and pass the long number to a static call to String class's valueOf() method. The resulting statement, shown next, passes a string representation of the current system time in milliseconds to ClockTwo object's setCurrrentTime() method.

```
clock.setCurrentTime( String.valueOf( System.currentTimeMillis( ) ) );
```

That's it. Now you need to make a couple of simple modifications to the ClockOne class, and then you're ready to watch changes in the raw system time (see Listing 9.4).

Listing 9.4   Source Code for `TimerTwo.java`

```
package sams.time;

public class TimerTwo extends Thread {
 private ClockTwo clock = null;

 public TimerTwo( ClockTwo clock ) {
  this.clock = clock;
 }

 public void run( ) {
  while ( true ) {
    clock.setCurrentTime( String.valueOf( System.currentTimeMillis( ) ) );
    try {
      Thread.sleep( 1000 );
    }
    catch ( InterruptedException e ) {
      break;
    }
  }
 }
}
```

Writing the `ClockTwo` Class

There's very little that you need to modify in the `ClockOne` class to create the `ClockTwo` class shown in Listing 9.5. Change all references to `TimerOne` to `TimerTwo` (there are two) and, if you like, make the graphic area of the `ClockTwo` bean smaller by decreasing the width from 200 millimeters to 100 millimeters in `ClockTwo` constructor's `setSize()` method call.

Listing 9.5   Source Code for `ClockTwo.java`

```
package sams.time;

import java.awt.Graphics;

public class ClockTwo extends java.awt.Panel {
 private String currentTime = "";
 private boolean running = false;
 private TimerTwo timer = null;

 public ClockTwo( ) {
  setSize( 100, 30 );
 }

 public boolean isRunning( ) {
```

9

INVISIBLE RUNTIME
BEANS

continues

Listing 9.5   continued

```
  return running;
}

public void setRunning( boolean running ) {
  this.running = running;
  if( running && timer == null ) {
    timer = new TimerTwo( this );
    timer.start( );
  }
  else if( !running && timer != null ) {
    timer.stop( );
    timer = null;
  }
}

public void setCurrentTime( String currentTime ) {
  this.currentTime = currentTime;
  repaint( );
}

public void paint( Graphics g ) {
  g.drawString( currentTime, 20, 20 );
}
}
```

Packaging and Testing the `ClockTwo` Bean

Package your ClockTwo bean into a JAR file in the same way that you did the ClockOne bean, except use the clocktwo.man manifest file in Listing 9.6. The ClockTwo bean consists of both the ClockTwo and TimerTwo Java objects. Package both objects into the JAR file and designate the ClockTwo class as a bean. Enter the following command at the DOS or console prompt:

```
jar cmf clocktwo.man clocktwo.jar sams
```

After you package it into a JAR, test the ClockTwo bean in the BeanBox. Go to the bean's running property editor on the property sheet and set it to true. Your ClockTwo bean should display your computer system's time in milliseconds, as shown in Figure 9.2. It's the system time that your invisible timer bean will use to keep time.

Listing 9.6   Source Code for `clocktwo.man`

```
Name: sams/time/ClockTwo.class
Java-Bean: True

Name: sams/time/TimerTwo.class
Java-Bean: False
```

FIGURE 9.2

Set ClockTwo *bean's running property to* true, *and the bean displays your computer system's current time in milliseconds.*

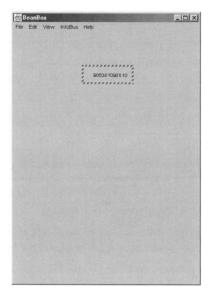

Writing a Timer Bean

Creating an invisible runtime timer bean is a snap now that you know how to work with time using Java and JavaBeans. The Timer bean, created from the Timer class shown in Listing 9.7, is based on the TimerTwo class you wrote in the last section.

To write invisible runtime beans, don't derive the beans from a class that displays a graphic user interface. You don't need to derive an invisible runtime bean from any class. The Timer class isn't derived from another class, but it does implement Java's Runnable interface so that it can run as a separate thread. The Timer bean must run as a separate thread for the same reason that the TimerOne and TimerTwo objects needed to run in separate threads. The Timer bean runs in an infinite loop and periodically checks the system time.

Once you have the invisible runtime bean class that lacks a graphical interface, add properties and events to the Timer bean. Because a bean is an autonomous software object, the Timer bean needs a running property so that it can be started and stopped. The Timer bean should also have a time interval property so users can set the amount of time that elapses between each event fired by the Timer bean. For instance, you should be able to set the Timer bean so that it fires an event every 100 milliseconds or every second.

Invisible beans must create event objects and fire them off themselves. There is no triggering of events through user interaction with a graphical user interface. The passage of time tracked by the Timer bean is a perfect periodic internal event for triggering the production of event objects. The Timer bean fires an action event for every time interval that passes.

Adding Properties

Add two properties to the Timer class: the running and time interval properties. The running property is nearly identical to the running property used in the ClockOne and ClockTwo classes in previous sections. The time interval property is new with the Timer bean.

The running Property

Use the running property to start and stop the Timer bean. The running class variable, its declaration shown next below, holds the Boolean running property value.

```
private boolean running = false;
```

Timer bean's running property accessor methods are similar to the running property methods in the ClockOne and ClockTwo classes. However, the Timer class instantiates itself in its own thread. The Timer bean's running property accessor method, shown next, is named isRunning().

```
public boolean isRunning( ) {
  return running;
}
```

This is the same as this chapter's other running property accessor methods. The isRunning() method returns the Boolean value of the running property.

Timer bean's running property mutator method named setRunning(), shown next, has some modifications because the bean runs in its own thread and reports the passage of time intervals. Recall that the ClockOne and ClockTwo beans present the current time but don't need to keep track of the passage of time.

```
public void setRunning( boolean running ) {
  this.running = running;
  if( running && thread == null ) {
    thread = new Thread( this );
    thread.start( );
    time = System.currentTimeMillis( );
    time += timeInterval;
  }
  else if( !running && thread != null ) {
    thread.stop( );
    thread = null;
  }
}
```

The setRunning() method passes a Boolean value to the Timer bean and assigns it to Timer class's running variable. Then the method checks the running and thread variables. If the running variable is set to true and the thread variable holds a null value, the bean creates a new `Timer` thread, assigns it to the `thread` variable, and then starts it running by calling the `start()` method. Otherwise, if the `running` variable is `false` and there is a thread currently running, the thread is stopped by a call to the `stop()` method. The `thread` variable is set to `null` so that the `Timer` bean can start running again if the `running` property is set back to `true`.

There are two statements in the `setRunning()` method that assign values to the `time` long variable. These statements are closely related to `Timer` bean's time interval property and the way that the bean keeps track of the passage of time. The first statement, shown next, assigns the system time to the `time` class variable when the thread starts running.

```
time = System.currentTimeMillis( );
```

The next statement adds the value of the `timeInterval` property to the system time when the timer was started.

```
time += timeInterval;
```

You'll see, in the "Adding Events" section later in this chapter, that this statement is necessary so that the time interval events fire off accurately.

The `timeInterval` Property

Use the `timeInterval` property to set the period of time represented by each `Timer` bean action event produced. The `timeInterval` class variable, shown next, holds the `long` `timeInterval` property value.

```
private long timeInterval = 1000;
```

The `getTimeInterval()` accessor method, shown next, returns the current value of the `timeInterval` property.

```
public long getTimeInterval( ) {
 return timeInterval;
}
```

The `setTimeInterval()` mutator method, shown next, isn't much more complicated.

```
public void setTimeInterval( long interval ) {
  if( interval >= 100 )
    timeInterval = interval;
}
```

The method passes the length of the time interval in milliseconds to the Timer bean through the `interval` variable. The method checks to see that the interval value is greater than or equal to 100 milliseconds and, if it is, assigns the value to the `timeInterval` class variable.

> **Note**
>
> You'll see when you test the `Timer` bean that the constraint placed on the `timeInterval` property value in the `setTimeInterval()` mutator method is automatically enforced through the `timeInterval` property editor. The `timeInterval` property editor doesn't let you type in a number less than 100.

Adding Events

In this section, you will add action event registration and creation facilities to the `Timer` bean. First, add the code that tracks the passage of time intervals and fires action events when an interval passes. Most of the code for this is included in `Timer` bean's `run()` method. The `run()` method is similar to the `TimerTwo` class `run()` method.

```
public void run( ) {
  while ( true ) {
    long currentTime = System.currentTimeMillis( );
    if( currentTime >= time ) {
      time += timeInterval;
      processActionEvent( new ActionEvent( this, ActionEvent.ACTION_PERFORMED,
null ) );
    }
    try {
      Thread.sleep( timeInterval/10 );
    }
    catch ( InterruptedException e ) {
      break;
    }
  }
}
```

There are two differences. The `if` statement block is new, and the way the thread's sleep interval is passed to the thread's `sleep()` method is changed.

The `if` statement block begins by testing the current system time just gathered to see if it is greater than or equal to the value held by the `time` class variable. Recall from earlier that the `time` variable is initially set equal to the system time when the timer starts running plus the time interval that the timer is tracking. That means that the `if` statement's conditional test is `true` as soon as the duration of the time interval has passed.

For example, if you start the `Timer` bean's timer running at 100,000 milliseconds system time and you set its `timeInterval` property to 1000 milliseconds, the initial value of the `time` variable is 101,000 milliseconds. The `if` statement's conditional will be `true` after 1000 milliseconds have passed and the current system time is 101,000 milliseconds.

> **Note**
>
> The system time of 100,000 milliseconds used here is purely fictional and is used purely for pedagogical purposes. Clearly, many more milliseconds have passed since January 1, 1970. My system currently displays the following system time: 905,382,322,500 milliseconds.

When the `if` statement's conditional is `true`, the value of the `timeInterval` property is added to the value held by the `time` variable. The conditional will be `true` again when the time interval has passed. Then the bean creates an `ActionEvent` object and passes it to the bean's `processActionEvent()` method, as shown in the following:

```
protected void processActionEvent( ActionEvent e ) {
  if ( actionListener != null )
    actionListener.actionPerformed( e );
}
```

This is the same `processActionEvent()` method you added to your image button bean from the previous chapter. If an action event listener is registered, the `processActionEvent()` method sends the listener the `ActionEvent` object just created. This is the firing of an action event that occurs after each `Timer` bean time interval passes.

Action event listeners are registered during design time in the usual way through the `addActionListener()` and `removeActionListener()` methods, shown in the following:

```
public synchronized void addActionListener( ActionListener act ) {
  actionListener = AWTEventMulticaster.add( actionListener, act );
}

public synchronized void removeActionListener( ActionListener act ) {
  actionListener = AWTEventMulticaster.remove( actionListener, act );
}
```

> **Note**
>
> Learn about registering action event listeners and Java's event model in Chapter 6, "Event Model."

Finally, look at the new way the thread's sleep interval is passed to the `sleep()` method. Recall that previously the timer threads were set to sleep for about 1000 milliseconds so that the time would be gathered and displayed approximately once every second. You're able to set the length of tracked time intervals in the Timer bean so it's clear that the thread can't sleep any longer than the particular interval being used (the value held by the timeInterval property).

However, passing the contents of the timeInterval variable to the sleep( ) method isn't enough. To be accurate, the timer should loop several times during a single time interval. Timer accuracy is only as good as the duration between each while loop—for example, if the timer loops only once every second when the timeInterval property is set to 1000 milliseconds and the timer can fire anytime between 1000 and 1999 milliseconds. If the last loop occurred at 999 milliseconds, the timer didn't go off because it still hadn't reached 1000 milliseconds. However, because the timer only loops once every 1000 milliseconds, 1999 milliseconds could pass before the next loop is carried out and the conditional is satisfied.

Increased timer accuracy is achieved by passing to the sleep( ) method the value of the timeInterval variable divided by 10. You can see this in the source code found in Listing 9.7. That way, for instance, time intervals of 1000 milliseconds are detected accurately to about 100 milliseconds or a tenth of a second.

Listing 9.7 Source Code for Timer.java

```
package sams.time;

import java.awt.AWTEventMulticaster;
import java.awt.event.ActionEvent;
import java.awt.event.ActionListener;

public class Timer implements Runnable {
  Thread thread = null;
  private boolean running = false;
  private long time = 0;
  private long timeInterval = 1000;
  private ActionListener actionListener = null;

  public boolean isRunning( ) {
   return running;
  }

  public void setRunning( boolean running ) {
   this.running = running;
   if( running && thread == null ) {
     thread = new Thread( this );
     thread.start( );
     time = System.currentTimeMillis( );
```

```
    time += timeInterval;
  }
  else if( !running && thread != null ) {
    thread.stop( );
    thread = null;
  }
}

public long getTimeInterval( ) {
  return timeInterval;
}

public void setTimeInterval( long interval ) {
  if( interval >= 100 )
     timeInterval = interval;
}

public void run( ) {
  while ( true ) {
    long currentTime = System.currentTimeMillis( );
    if( currentTime >= time ) {
     time += timeInterval;
     processActionEvent( new ActionEvent( this, ActionEvent.ACTION_PERFORMED,
➥null ) );
    }
    try {
      Thread.sleep( timeInterval/10 );
    }
    catch ( InterruptedException e ) {
      break;
    }
  }
}

public synchronized void addActionListener( ActionListener l ) {
    actionListener = AWTEventMulticaster.add( actionListener, l );
}

 public synchronized void removeActionListener( ActionListener l ) {
    actionListener = AWTEventMulticaster.remove( actionListener, l );
 }

 protected void processActionEvent( ActionEvent e ) {
    if ( actionListener != null )
      actionListener.actionPerformed( e );
 }
}
```

Writing a `TestTimer` Bean

You can wire up the `Timer` bean to many different types of beans, but for now you'll write a very simple `TestTimer` bean, shown in Listing 9.8. The `TestTimer` bean is a simple control extended from Java's `Canvas` class that displays the current count. The current count starts at 0 and is held by the `currentCount` variable. The value is incremented by 1 and the bean's display is refreshed with each call to the `incrementCounter()` public method.

Listing 9.8   Source Code for `TestTimer.java`

```
package sams.time;

import java.awt.Graphics;

public class TestTimer extends java.awt.Canvas {
  private int currentCount = 0;

  public TestTimer( ) {
    setSize( 75, 30 );
  }

  public void incrementCounter( ) {
    currentCount += 1;
    repaint( );
  }

  public void paint( Graphics g ) {
    g.drawString( String.valueOf( currentCount ), 20, 20 );
  }
}
```

Packaging and Testing the `Timer` Bean

Package your `Timer` and `TestTimer` beans into a JAR file using the `timer.man` manifest file in Listing 9.9. Enter the following command at the DOS or console prompt:

```
jar cmf timer.man timer.jar sams
```

Once you package the beans into a JAR, test the `Timer` bean in the BeanBox. Add a `Timer` bean and a `TestBean` to a BeanBox window, as shown in Figure 9.3.

Listing 9.9   Source Code for `timer.man`

```
Name: sams/time/Timer.class
Java-Bean: True

Name: sams/time/TestTimer.class
Java-Bean: True
```

FIGURE 9.3

A Timer *bean and a* TestTimer *bean are added to the BeanBox window.*

The BeanBox represents the Timer bean as a box displaying the bean's class name because it has no graphic user interface. The TestTimer bean displays 0 counts.

Select the Timer bean and open the Events submenu from BeanBox's Edit menu. Select action from the Event submenu, and then select the actionPerformed command. A red wire appears. Connect the wire to the TestTimer bean and the EventTargetDialog dialog box appears (see Figure 9.4).

FIGURE 9.4

The EventTargetDialog box lists the various methods and properties available in the TestTimer *bean.*

9

INVISIBLE RUNTIME BEANS

Select the incrementCounter target method from the EventTargetDialog dialog box and click the OK button. Each action event created by the Timer bean now increments TestTimer bean's currentCount variable by one.

Set the Timer bean's timeInterval property in the timeInterval property editor or leave it at the default 1000 milliseconds. Then go to the bean's running property editor and set it to true. You should see TestTimer bean's display increment every time your time interval passes, as shown in Figure 9.5.

Figure 9.5

The TestTimer *bean's counter increments by one after each time interval, set in the* Timer *bean, passes.*

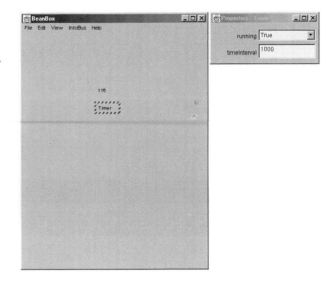

Summary

In this chapter, you wrote an invisible runtime bean, the Timer bean. You learned how to use Java's time and date classes and methods while you developed clocks and timers leading up to the final Timer bean. You also learned that you can write a bean that's invisible during runtime simply by leaving out any graphical user interface code and by not creating your bean from an AWT class.

Bean Security

CHAPTER 10

All source code for this chapter can be found on the Sams Publishing Website at
http://www.mcp.com/info/0-672/0-672-31424-x.

Introduction

Beans distributed over the Internet can potentially pose a serious security risk. The developers of the Java language built several layers of security into the language to isolate downloaded programs from the local computer and keep them trapped in the Java Virtual Machine (JVM). However, these security features compromise the functionality of Java programs, including beans, by restricting access to the local system. You can provide complete functionality with your beans by stamping them with a *security signature*. This is known as *code signing*. The digital signature tells users the person or organization that wrote or distributed the Java bean. If the user decides that he or she trusts the person or organization that signed the bean, the user can run it. The JVM gives trusted beans full access to the user's computer. In this chapter, you will learn about the Java Security API and the `keystore` file, use the `keytool` and `jarsigner` security tools, and digitally sign a bean.

Java Security API

The Java Security API mostly provides cryptography functions and is supplied in the `java.security` package and its subpackages: `java.security.acl`, `java.security.cert`, `java.security.interfaces`, and `java.security.spec`. *Cryptography* literally means the study of secret writing. Modern cryptography forms the basis for computer data encryption, which is the process of making information indecipherable to protect it from unauthorized viewing or use. The Java Security API cryptography functions provide the infrastructure so that you can digitally sign your beans through the process of encryption.

When you create a digital signature, you're using cryptography for *authentication*, which is the verification of a person's or organization's identity. The encryption is carried out using public key cryptography.

Public Key Cryptography

The encryption of information takes a secret code that can only be read by people with the key to the code. You might remember passing encrypted messages between friends when you where in school. Only you and your friends knew the code that enabled you to read the messages. Public key cryptography provides a means to pass around secret messages.

You have two keys to a secret code when you use public key cryptography: one public and one private. Your private key is unique to you; nobody else has it. Your public key is unique also, but you can pass that around to other people. Those people holding your public key can read anything that you encrypt with your private key. Also, they can encrypt messages to you using your public key. Only you can read the messages encrypted with your public key by using your private key.

Public key cryptography is an ideal vehicle for authentication. Because your private key is unique, it follows that only you can encrypt messages with it. So, if you send me a message encrypted with your private key, and I can decipher it with your public key, that's as good as receiving a piece of paper with your signature on it. It must be you, who else could it be? This is the basis for digital signing.

> **Note**
>
> Of course, if someone else gets your private key, anyone can forge your signature. It's essential that you keep your private key private!

Signed Code

Beans can be digitally signed to guarantee the end user that a third party has not modified the file. Users must decide if they trust the author, but at least they know who created the bean. When you digitally sign a bean, you actually add a digital signature to the bean's JAR file, which means you end up digitally signing the whole JAR package.

Creating Digitally Signed JAR Files

Digitally sign your beans by generating your own digital signature and then including the signature in the bean's JAR file. To generate a digital signature, your identity profile must be included in your `keystore` file as a digital certificate along with a pair of encryption keys.

Creating a Keystore and Keys Using `keytool`

The first step to creating your digital signature is to create a keystore database that will hold the keys to your electronic signature. You create the keystore database by creating the public key and associated private key—the key pair—that you will use to sign your JAR files. Use `keytool`, provided with the JDK, to generate the keystore and key pair by using its –genkey command. Type the following at your DOS or Console window prompt:

```
keytool -genkey
```

When you enter the generate a key pair command (`-genkey`) in this way, the `keytool` prompts you for the various information it needs to create a key pair. The following is the first prompt you should see:

```
Enter keystore password:
```

The entire keystore database file is password protected. You are asked by `keytool` to enter a password that you will use every time you open your keystore file. Type in a password, `secret` for instance, press the Enter or Return key, and a prompt appears, like the one shown next, asking for your first and last name. One word of caution: When entering the password, it will be displayed as it is typed.

```
What is your first and last name?
  [Unknown]:
```

The `keytool` is beginning to ask for your identity information. The values between the brackets (`[]`) are the default values if you don't type in your own values. If you simply press Enter or Return, the name value will be `Unknown`. Type in your first and last name, `Donald Doherty` for instance, and press the Enter or Return key. The following prompt appears:

```
What is the name of your organizational unit?
  [Unknown]:
```

An organizational unit is your own department or other unit within a larger organization, such as a company or university. You can leave it unknown if you don't have a small unit within your organization. The following is the next prompt:

```
What is the name of your organization?
  [Unknown]:
```

Enter the name of your organization at the prompt, `Brainstage Research` for instance, and press the Enter or Return key. The next prompt appears:

```
What is the name of your City or Locality?
  [Unknown]:
```

Enter the name of your city or locality at the prompt, `Pittsburgh` for instance, and press the Enter or Return key. The following prompt appears:

```
What is the name of your State or Province?
  [Unknown]:
```

Enter the name of your state or province at the prompt, `PA` for instance, and press the Enter or Return key. The next prompt appears:

```
What is the two-letter country code of this unit?
  [Unknown]:
```

Enter the two-letter country code at the prompt. For instance, US is the two-letter code for the United States. Press the Enter or Return key and a prompt displays all of your selections and asks you if they are correct. Table 10.1 lists all six kinds of identity information and their associated codes. If something in the information at the prompt is incorrect, type **no** and press the Enter or Return key, and you are cycled back through the different prompts so you can correct the error or errors. Otherwise, type **yes** and press the Enter or Return key.

For a complete reference to country codes that Java uses, refer to Table 27.1 in Chapter 26, "International Beans."

TABLE 10.1 Keystore Database Information Codes

Code	Description
CN	First and last name
OU	Organizational unit
O	Organization
L	City or locale
ST	State or province
C	Two-letter country code

The tool computes a pair of keys and prompts you for a key password with a prompt, similar to the one shown next:

```
Enter key password for <mykey>
        <RETURN if same as keystore password>:
```

The name on the first line between the angled brackets (<>), mykey, is the default name given to the new key pair. Type in a unique password for the mykey key pair at the prompt or use the same password you typed in for the entire keystore database by simply pressing the Return or Enter key.

Creating a Keystore Using Codes

You can use the codes in Table 10.1 to bypass many of the keytool prompts when you create a keystore and key pair. For instance, you can create the same database as in the previous section by typing in the following at a DOS or console prompt:

```
keytool -genkey -dname
➥"CN=Donald Doherty, O=Brainstage Research, L=Pittsburgh, S=PA, C=US"
```

10

BEAN SECURITY

The new command, -dname, tells the keytool to associate the values listed between the quotes that follow. The default value is automatically used for any code that you don't enter, such as for OU previously. When you enter the previous command, the keytool prompts you for a keystore password and a key password.

Using Other `keytool` Commands

There are many `keytool` commands available. There are two commands, however, that are particularly useful. One command allows you to name the key created, and the other command allows you to list the contents of your keystore database.

So far, you have been only able to create keys with the default `mykey` name when you create a key using `keytool` with the -genkey command. You can specify a key name in your keystore database by using the -alias command. You can create a keystore and key pair the same as in the previous section, except the name of the key is changed to "don" by typing the following command at your DOS or Console prompt.

```
keytool -genkey -dname
➥"CN=Donald Doherty, O=Brainstage Research, L=Pittsburgh, S=PA, C=US"-alias don
```

> **Note**
>
> The key name you provide to the alias command can have capital letters; however, the -alias command doesn't recognize capital letters and will simply treat them as lowercase. For instance, if you provide the name Don, the key name will be don.

The only difference in the command is the addition of -alias don at the end of the command line. You're prompted for the keystore and key passwords, and then the keystore and don key are created.

Use the -list `keytool` command to list the contents of the keystore database. If you also specify the -v command, the key certificates are printed in human readable form. For instance, you can view the keystore database you just created by typing the following command at the DOS or console window prompt and pressing the Enter or Return key:

```
keytool -list -v
```

You are prompted to enter the keystore password. After you enter the password, the certificate information is printed out as shown in Figure 10.1.

FIGURE **10.1**

The keytool -list *and* -v *commands are used to list the contents of the keystore database.*

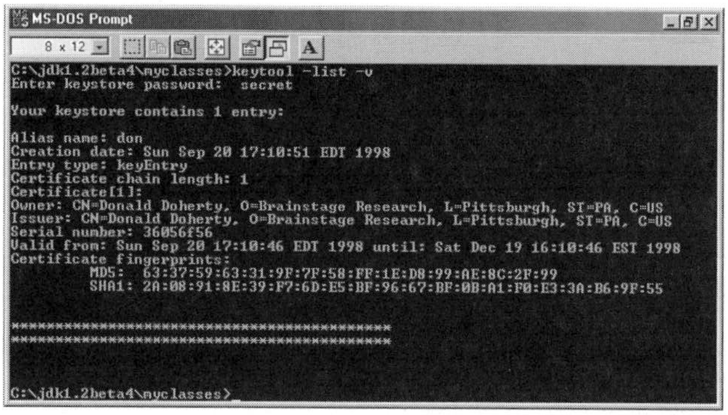

Notice that the Owner and Issuer information in the keystore database are the same. That's because you've created a self-signed certificate. You generated the certificate and key pair yourself. There is no outside agency authorizing the certificate. Typically, you want to use an independent agency to issue a certificate when you are ready to sign and deploy your JavaBeans components. Nevertheless, it's handy to use self-signed certificates while you're learning the electronic signing ropes.

Browsers can all load self-signed certificates just like they can load independently signed certificates. Most browsers allow self-signed certificates to be set independently in the security settings. For instance, users can set to automatically load independently signed certificates while it can still ask to load self-signed certificates. The default browser settings are usually more restrictive on self-signed certificates.

The difference is going to be in the trust a user places in your self-signed certificate versus the trust they place in an independently signed certificate. I won't run a self-signed certificate because of the security risk, and most others won't either.

> **Note**
>
> Learn how to get signed certificates from certification authorities in the "Getting Signed Certificates" section later this chapter.

The keystore database only has one key pair, named don, in the example so far. If your database has more than one key, you can display a specific key by using the -alias command. You specify the display of the don key by typing in the following command.

```
keytool -list -v -alias don
```

10

BEAN SECURITY

The Keystore File

The keystore database is held in a file named `.keystore`. The default location of this secure file depends on your platform, as shown in Table 10.2. The *userName* in the table stands for the current user name.

TABLE 10.2 Location of `.keystore` File

Platform	*Directory*
Single-user Windows 95 and Windows 98	`C:\Windows`
Multi-user Windows 95 and Windows 98	`C:\Windows\Profiles\userName`
Windows NT	`C:\Windows\Profiles\userName`

Signing the JAR File

When you add a digital signature to a JAR file, you are signing all of the files that reside in the JAR. Not only is the bean signed, all of the files that the bean depends on such as image and sound files are signed. In this section, you sign the `PictureButton` bean's JAR file, named `picturebutton.jar`.

> **Note**
>
> You created the `PictureButton` bean if you worked through Chapter 7. Otherwise, you can find a `picturebutton.jar` file containing the `PictureButton` bean and the `teddy0.jpg` image file on the www.mcp.com Web site in the JavaBeans Unleashed section.

Use the `jarsigner` tool provided with the Java Development Kit (JDK) to sign JAR files. Place the `PictureButton` bean packaged in the `picturebutton.jar` file into your root class directory. Any image files can be a part of the JAR. This example includes the `teddy0.jpg` image, as shown in the WinZip view of the `picturebutton.jar` file contents in Figure 10.2.

The `picturebutton.jar` file contains three files: the PictureButton class file, the teddy bear image file, and the JAR's manifest file.

FIGURE 10.2

The contents of the
`picturebutton.jar`
file.

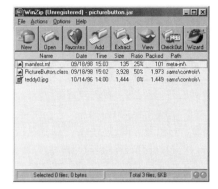

Open a DOS or console window and change the prompt so that it's open to your root
class directory. Sign the `picturebutton.jar` file by typing the following command at
the DOS or console window prompt:

```
jarsigner picturebutton.jar don
```

The `jarsigner` command is followed by the name of the JAR file that you want to sign,
`picturebutton.jar` in this case, and the key that you want to sign it with, `don` for example. When you enter the command, the `jarsigner` tool displays the following prompt:

```
Enter Passphrase for keystore:
```

Type in the password to your keystore database, `secret` for instance, and press the Enter
or Return key. The `jarsigner` tool digitally signs the `picturebutton.jar` file.

You can prove to yourself that the `picturebutton.jar` file was signed by displaying the
file's contents using WinZip, as shown in Figure 10.3.

FIGURE 10.3

The contents of the
digitally signed
`picturebutton.jar`
file.

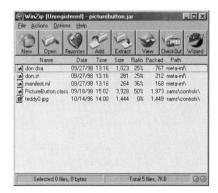

10

BEAN SECURITY

You should see two new files added to the digitally signed JAR file. The files take the name of the key, don in this case, followed by the sf and dsa extensions. The file displaying the sf extension is known as the *signature file*. The file displaying the dsa extension is known as the *signature block file*.

The Signature File

The signature file contains information that enables verification of JAR file contents. It includes three pieces of information for each file in the JAR: the file's name, the name of the digest algorithm used, and the digest algorithm value.

> **Note**
>
> By default, the jarsigner tool uses the SHA-1 digest algorithm.

The Signature Block File

The signature block file contains the actual digital signature and certificate from the keystore database that authenticates the public key associated with the private key used for signing. The extension of the signature block file depends on the algorithm that is used to sign the JAR file. A dsa extension indicates that the Digital Signature Algorithm (DSA) was used.

> **Note**
>
> By default, the jarsigner tool uses the Digital Signature Algorithm (DSA).

Getting Signed Certificates

A certificate is only as good as the signer. If you worked through the example earlier in this chapter, you created a self-signed certificate. JAR files signed with self-signed certificates work fine as long as the user trusts you. Unfortunately, the user probably never heard of you and doesn't know that you're the trustworthy person that you are. Users are more likely to trust your digitally signed JAR files if a well-known certification authority signs them.

Request a digital signature from a certification authority by submitting a Certificate Signing Request (CSR) file. You create a CSR file with keytool included in the JDK. Enter the following command at your DOS or console window prompt:

```
keytool -alias don -certreq -file don.csr
```

The -alias option tells keytool to use the named key pair alias, in this case don, from your keystore database. The -certreq option tells keytool to generate a CSR, and the -file option tells keytool to generate the CSR file with the filename that follows, in this case don.csr.

After you enter the command, keytool prompts you for your keystore file password. Enter your password, and keytool should crunch for a while. When it's finished, you should find a newly created CSR file. Submit the CSR file to a certification authority.

> **Note**
>
> VeriSign is a popular certification authority. The VeriSign Web site is at http://www.verisign.com.

The certification authority authenticates you and then returns a certificate with their digital signature that authenticates your public key.

Verifying Digital Signatures

Use the jarsigner tool, included with the JDK, to verify the digital signature of signed JAR files and to make sure that the JAR files haven't been tampered with. Verify the signature added to the picturebutton.jar file by entering the following command at your DOS or console window prompt:

```
jarsigner -verify picturebutton.jar
```

The -verify option tells the jarsigner tool to verify the signature in the JAR file specified after the option, in this case the picturebutton.jar file. If the verification is successful, the tool displays the jar verified message. Otherwise, it displays the jar is unsigned (signatures missing or not parsable) message.

You can get details about the digital signature in a JAR file by using the jarsigner tool -verbose option in conjunction with the -verify option, as in the following command:

```
jarsigner -verify -verbose picturebutton.jar
```

If you verify your picturebutton.jar file signature with this command, the jarsigner tool should display information similar to that shown in Figure 10.4.

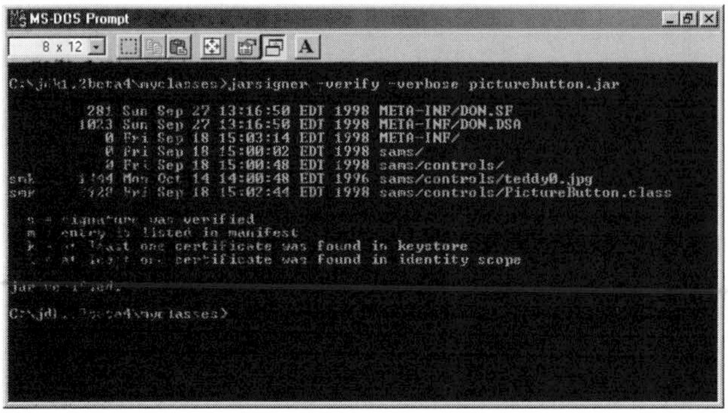

FIGURE 10.4

*The detailed con-
tents of the digital-
ly signed*
`picturebutton.jar`
file shown using the
`-verbose` *option.*

Up to four letters may be displayed to the left of class and resource files listed in the
DOS or console window by the `jarsigner` tool. As you can see in Figure 10.4, these letters tell you if the file is signed (s), if it's listed in the manifest file (m), if its certificate is
part of the keystore database (k), and if its part of the identity scope (i).

You can get details about JAR file certificates by using the `jarsigner` tool `-certs`
option, along with the `-verify` and `-verbose` options. Type in the following command at
your DOS or console window prompt to display details about the `picturebutton.jar`
file's digital signature and certificates:

```
jarsigner -verify -verbose -certs picturebutton.jar
```

The `jarsigner` tool should display information similar to the information shown in
Figure 10.5.

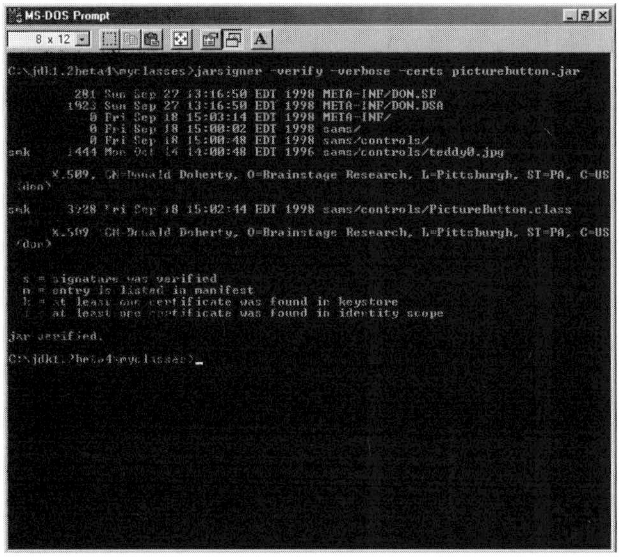

FIGURE 10.5

*The detailed infor-
mation about the
digitally signed*
`picturebutton.
jar` *file including
information about
its certificate.*

The information for the digital certificate(s) associated with the signature for each file is listed under the file listing. In this case, the certificate is the same for both the teddy0.jpg and PictureButton.class files. The first item displayed on the line of certificate information tells you the type of certificate. For instance, the certificate associated with the teddy0.jpg signature is an X.509 certificate. The certificate type information is followed by the identity information, entered into the certificate and listed in Table 10.1. Finally, the alias name for the key is displayed between parentheses.

Deleting Keystore Database Entries

You can delete key pairs from your keystore database file by using keytool. For instance, assume that you added another key pair with an alias of vanessa to your keystore database with the following command:

```
keytool -genkey -dname "CN=Vanessa Keech, O=Duquesne University, L=Pittsburgh,
S=PA, C=US" -alias vanessa
```

You now have two aliases, don and vanessa, in your keystore database. A listing of a keystore database with these two aliases is shown in Figure 10.6.

FIGURE 10.6

The keytool -list *option was used to display the two aliases stored in this keystore database.*

You can delete a key pair entry using the keytool -delete option. For instance, delete the vanessa key pair by entering the following command at your DOS or console window prompt:

```
keytool -delete -alias vanessa
```

The -delete option tells keytool that you want to delete a keystore database entry. The -alias option, in conjunction with the -delete option, indicates that you want the key pair alias that follows, in this case vanessa, to be deleted.

10

BEAN SECURITY

When you enter the command, keytool prompts you to enter your keystore database password. Once you enter the password, keytool deletes the designated key pair. You can check to make sure that the pair was deleted by listing the keystore database information using the keytool -list option.

Using Digitally Signed Beans

You use digitally signed beans from other people and organizations that you trust by registering their trusted certificates with the keystore file managed by the keytool Java security tool.

> **Note**
>
> In Java 1.1, digitally signed beans were registered with an identity database that was managed by the javakey tool. These have been replaced by the keystore architecture and the keytool and jarsigner security tools in Java 1.2. The new digital signing architecture and tools are not backward compatible.

A certificate is a digitally signed statement that provides information about the person or organization that signed the statement. It also provides the value of the signer's public key.

Certificates Authenticating Public Keys

Users that want to run your signed beans need your public key and a certificate that authenticates your public key. Likewise, you need the same information from signers of beans that you want to use. Generate a copy of the certificate authenticating your public key using the keytool -export option. For instance, suppose you want to supply the certificate authenticating the public key for the don key pair. Enter the following command at your DOS or console window prompt:

```
keytool -export -alias don -file don.cer
```

The -export option tells keytool that you want to export certificate information from your keystore database. The -alias option indicates that you want to export the certificate information associated with the key pair alias that follows, in this case don. Finally, the -file option indicates that you want the information exported to the file named right after the option, in this case don.cer.

When you enter this command, keytool prompts you to enter your keystore database password. Enter your password, and keytool displays a message similar to the following:

```
Certificate stored in file <don.cer>
```

This message tells you that the digital certificate was exported and stored in a file with the filename indicated between the angle brackets (<>), don.cer in this case.

Once you've created the .cer file, you will create a keystore to use it to import the certificate into an entry with an alias of something such as "test." A keystore is created whenever you use a keytool command specifying a keystore that doesn't yet exist. Thus, you can create a keystore named testcore and import the certificate via the following command:

```
keytool -import -alias test -file MyTest.cer -keystore testsore
```

Because the keystore doesn't yet exist, it will be created. You will be prompted for a keystore password; type whatever password you want.

Distributing Signed Beans

Signed beans are no different than others as far as deployment. Put them on the server and they'll be served up to client machines. The only difference is if the bean hasn't been previously loaded by the client machine. This is when (depending on the browser security settings) the user might be asked for permission to download.

Summary

In this chapter you created a public and private key pair using keytool, which is provided with the Java Development Kit. Then you digitally signed a bean using the jarsigner tool. The keytool and jarsigner tools together provide an easy way for you to take advantage of the Java Security API to create, manage, and deploy digitally signed Java beans. Signed beans that are trusted have access to the local computer's operating system. This allows beans to provide much more functionality than they would otherwise be able to provide.

Enterprise Through the Desktop GUI

PART
III

Cut-and-Paste

CHAPTER 11

The Need for a Clipboard

One of the most useful tools that modern operating systems have added is the clipboard. While editing a document in a word processor, users can easily cut, copy, and paste pieces of the document within the document or to and from other documents.

The clipboard is a temporary transfer area in the computer that can be used to hold information and then move it or replicate it elsewhere.

Clipboards can contain text, pictures, sound, formatted text, specific data formats and more. Applications can define their own clipboard type if the desired data type isn't explicitly supported. However, all programs cannot interpret all data formats. The data to be placed on the clipboard is selected most of the time by the user.

Data can either be copied or cut out of the running program and placed on the clipboard. Copied data will remain in the original document while cut data will be deleted from the original document. The copied data is then placed back into the same document or into a new document by pasting it from the clipboard. Pasting does not remove the data from the clipboard on most operating systems.

Java provides clipboard support in two ways: clipboards local to a JVM and system clipboards. This functionality has been added in JDK 1.2.

The `java.awt.datatransfer` Package

The `java.awt.datatransfer` package provides interfaces and classes for transferring data to and from the system clipboard. So far the support is relatively simple and many programs don't implement it. Other data types and drag-and-drop will be added later. (This will probably be in response to the requests and needs of programmers and users.)

The `java.awt.datatransfer.Transferable` interface is implemented by classes representing the data to be transferred, such as "plain text." It also includes methods that determine the possible data flavors of the object and retrieve the data itself. A *transferable* object is an object capable of being transferred between or within applications. An object identifies itself as being transferable by implementing the `Transferable` interface.

`java.awt.datatransfer.DataFlavor` is a class that provides a MIME-type–based system for determining the type of data on the clipboard. Examples of flavors include `text/plain`, `charset=unicode`, and `application/x-java-serialized-object`. When you ask a `Transferable` object to return its contents in an incompatible flavor, a `java.awt.datatransfer.UnsupportedFlavorException` is thrown.

In Java, a clipboard is an object that temporarily holds transferable objects. The `java.awt.datatransfer.Clipboard` class allows data to be transferred through cut, copy, and paste operations. There is only one system clipboard; however, your program may create many different Clipboard objects for internal use. For the purpose of synchronization, each clipboard must be the exclusive property of one object, which must implement the `java.awt.datatransfer.ClipboardOwner` interface. This interface declares a single method, `lostOwnership()`, which warns an object that it no longer owns the clipboard.

The one concrete implementation of `Transferable` and `ClipboardOwner` included in Java is the `java.awt.datatransfer.StringSelection` class, which allows you to transfer plain text to and from the clipboard. This is a data type that you can count on regardless of the platform.

Table 11.1 shows an interface summary for the interfaces, classes, and exceptions found in the `datatransfer` package.

TABLE 11.1 Interfaces, Classes, and Exceptions of `datatransfer`

Interface, Class, or Exception	*Description*
`ClipboardOwner`	The interface for classes providing data to a clipboard
`FlavorMap`	An interface to a map that maps platform native type names (strings) to MIME type strings and also to their associated `DataFlavors`
`Transferable`	The interface for classes used in providing data for a transfer operation
Class Summary	
`Clipboard`	Implements the transfer of data using cut, copy, and paste operations
`DataFlavor`	Represents the opaque concept of a data format as it appears on a clipboard, during drag-and-drop, or in a file system
`StringSelection`	Implements the transfer of a simple Java String in plain text formats
`SystemFlavorMap`	An external map configuration that maps platform native type names (strings) to MIME type strings and to their associated `DataFlavors`
Exception Summary	
`UnsupportedFlavorException`	Sends a signal that the requested data is not supported in this flavor

There are a few methods and classes outside the `java.awt.datatransfer` package that are relevant to copy and paste. The `getSystemClipboard()` method of the `java.awt.Toolkit` class returns a `Clipboard` object that represents the system clipboard:

```
public abstract Clipboard getSystemClipboard()
```

Not all operating systems support clipboard operations. In such cases, the `getSystemClipboard()` method will return a null.

The `java.lang.SecurityManager` class includes a `checkSystemClipboardAccess()` method used in determining whether this program is allowed to access the system clipboard. If access is not allowed, the method is void and throws a `SecurityException`. I've found that as a rule Java applications won't throw this exception while Java applets will.

```
public void checkSystemClipboardAccess()
```

One concern is that the clipboard may contain sensitive data that the user would not want revealed to the server. Applets loaded from Web servers will not be allowed to access the client's system clipboard as a general rule. However, this does not apply to private clipboards you create. For example:

```
try
{
  SecurityManager sm = SecurityManager.getSecurityManager();
  if( sm != null ) sm.checkSystemClipboardAccess();
  Clipboard cb = Toolkit.getDefaultToolkit().getSystemClipboard();
  // Perform clipboard operations here.
}
catch( SecurityException e )
{
  System.err.println( "Cannot access the system clipboard" );
}
```

Implementing Copying

There are two ways to implement a clipboard. One method uses a private clipboard that only the applet or application can use. The other is to use the system clipboard and share data with all other applications that can access the clipboard. Both methods are described here.

A private clipboard is probably best if you're just manipulating data within a single application. You won't run the risk of a conflict with another application where the data you expect is gone or altered.

The system clipboard is essential if you're planning to share data between applications.

One thing to remember is that a private `Clipboard` object must remain in scope during the period when you need to retrieve data. A `Clipboard` object that goes out of scope can no longer be used, and any data that was copied into it is gone.

Copying with a Private Clipboard

The following are the steps required to create, copy, and use a private clipboard.

1. Create a `Clipboard` object with the new operator.

2. Create a new object, such as a `StringSelection`, which contains the data you want to copy and implements the `transferable` interface.

3. Using the `setContents()` method, place that object on the clipboard. For example:

```
// This is Example1

Clipboard clipboard; // This object is global to the application.

public void copy(TextField tf)
{

    StringSelection data = new StringSelection(tf.getText());
    clipboard = new Clipboard();
    clipboard.setContents(data, this.Example1);

}
```

The code in Listing 11.1 is an example of what not to do. Notice that the clipboard goes out of scope upon exit of the `copy()` method, and the `paste()` method won't be able to retrieve the data.

LISTING 11.1 Improper Use of Clipboard Scope

```
// This is Example2

public void copy( TextField tf )
{

  Clipboard clipboard; // This object is local to the method.
  clipboard = new Clipboard();
  StringSelection data = new StringSelection( tf.getText() );
  clipboard.setContents( data, this.Example1 );

}
```

continues

LISTING 11.1   continued

```
public void paste(TextField tf)
{

  Clipboard clipboard; // This object is local to the method.
  clipboard = new Clipboard();

  Transferable data = clipboard.getContents(this);
  String s;
  Try
  {
    s = (String) (data.getTransferData(DataFlavor.stringFlavor));
  }
  catch (Exception e)
  {
    s = data.toString();
  }

  tf.setText(s);
```

Copying with the System Clipboard

The following steps are what's required to create, copy, and use the system clipboard.

1. Use the getSystemClipboard() method of the java.awt.Toolkit class to access the system clipboard.

2. Create a new object, such as a StringSelection, which contains the data you want to copy and implements the transferable interface.

3. Using the setContents() method, place that object on the clipboard. For example:

   ```
   // This is Example3

   public void copy(TextField tf)
   {

     StringSelection data = new StringSelection(tf.getText());
     Clipboard clipboard =
       Toolkit().getDefaultToolkit().getSystemClipboard();
     Clipboard.setContents(data, this.Example2);

   }
   ```

Implementing Pasting

Here again, there are two approaches to pasting—one with a private clipboard and the other with the system clipboard.

Pasting with a Private Clipboard

The following steps are necessary to paste from a private clipboard.

1. Use a `Clipboard` object that has stayed in scope since any copy or cut operations and contains data.

2. Use the `getContents()` method of the `Clipboard` class to get the contents of the clipboard.

3. Use `getTransferData()` to get the data in a particular flavor.

4. Cast the object returned to the appropriate type. For example:

```
Clipboard clipboard; // This object was created with the new operator
                     // in the paste() method.

public void paste(TextField tf)
{

  Transferable data = clipboard.getContents(this);
  String s;
  Try
  {
    s = (String) (data.getTransferData(DataFlavor.stringFlavor));
  }
  catch (Exception e)
  {
     s = data.toString();
  }
  tf.setText(s);

}
```

Pasting with the System Clipboard

The following steps are what you need to do to paste from the system clipboard.

1. Use the `getSystemClipboard()` method of the `java.awt.Toolkit` class to access the system clipboard.

2. Use the `getContents()` method of the `Clipboard` class to get the contents of the clipboard.

3. Use `getTransferData()` to get the data in a particular flavor.

4. Cast the object returned to the appropriate type. For example:

```
public void paste(TextField tf)
{

  Clipboard clipboard =
```

```
    Toolkit().getDefaultToolkit().getSystemClipboard();
Transferable data = clipboard.getContents(this);
String s;
Try
{
  s = (String) (data.getTransferData(DataFlavor.stringFlavor));
}
catch (Exception e)
{
  s = data.toString();
}
tf.setText(s);

}
```

Data Flavors

Different applications interpret data differently, even the same kind of data. Most word processors support some form of formatted text with different fonts, styles, sizes, and so on. However, Microsoft Word 6.0 for Macintosh is not able to read formatted text produced by ClarisWorks and vice versa. Another example is Pictures from PhotoShop, which can be copied and pasted into many programs, but the layers tend to get flattened. The clipboard only understands raw bytes; it does not essentially know whether those bytes are text, a picture, a table, or something else. The `java.awt.datatransfer.`
`DataFlavor` class uses MIME types and subtypes to identify the kind of data stored in the clipboard. MIME (Multipurpose Internet Mail Extensions) is an Internet standard defined in RFCs 2045 through 2049 for transferring multimedia, binary data through 7-bit ASCII email. RFC 2046, in particular, specifies the MIME type system and defines the base set of media types. New MIME types are registered with and approved by the Internet Numbers Authority (IANA). A MIME has a type and a subtype. Examples of a MIME are `text/plain`, `application/x-java-serialized-object`, and `image/gif`. There are eight defined types including text, image, audio, video, multipart, message, model, and application. The first seven are self-explanatory and the last one is used for arbitrary binary data. Subtypes beginning with a x, such as `x-java-serialized-object`, are unofficial specific application extensions. There is no guarantee that two different programs will interpret the same x type as representing the same kind of data.

The `java.awt.datatransfer.` `DataFlavor` class

The `java.awt.datatransfer.DataFlavor` class provides interfaces and classes for transferring data between and within applications. It also provides a clipboard device that temporarily holds a transferable object. A *transferable* object is defined as an object capable of being transferred between or within applications and is identified as being transferable by implementing the `Transferable` interface. The `java.awt.datatransfer.DataFlavor` class encapsulates a MIME type to represent the data format of an object stored on the clipboard as raw bytes. Each data flavor has a representation class, a MIME type, and a human presentable name. The representation class is the Java class that approximates the data. For example, the plain text flavor uses the representation class `java.io.InputStream` and the MIME type `text/plain; charset=unicode`. This example indicates that the corresponding file is a plain text file that uses the Unicode character set. By default, the server maps the file extension `UTF` to that MIME type. The human presentable name is just a slightly more reader-friendly variant of the MIME type, such as "JPEG picture" instead of `image/jpeg`. There are two specific data flavors currently defined: `DataFlavor.plainTextFlavor` and `DataFlavor.stringFlavor`. There are two constructors that allow you to create new data flavors:

```
public DataFlavor(Class representationClass, String humanPresentableName)
```

```
public DataFlavor(String mimeType, String humanPresentableName)
```

The first constructor specifies the representation class and the human presentable name; however, the MIME type is normally set to `application/x-java-serialized-object`. The second constructor allows you to set the MIME type, but uses the representation class `InputStream`.

The `java.awt.datatransfer.Clipboard` class

This class represents an object that you can put transferable objects onto and from which you can get transferable objects. There is one constructor that can be used to create private clipboards. However, most of the time you will get the system clipboard instead:

```
public Clipboard(String name)
```

Only one object can be on the clipboard at a time, and there are three methods that can be used to get the name of the object currently on the clipboard. Paste can be used to get the contents of the clipboard and Cut or Copy can be used to set the contents of the clipboard.

The `java.awt.datatransfer.ClipboardOwner` Interface

Each clipboard must be the exclusive property of one object for the purpose of synchronization, and this object must implement the `java.awt.datatransfer.ClipboardOwner` interface. This interface declares a single method, `lostOwnership()`, to warn an object that it no longer owns the clipboard.

The `java.awt.datatransfer.Transferable` Interface

This interface must be implemented by any class representing the data to be cut or pasted. It defines the following three methods:

```
public abstract boolean isDataFlavorSupported(DataFlavor flavor)
public abstract DataFlavor[] getTransferDataFlavors()
public abstract Object getTransferData(DataFlavor flavor)
    throws UnsupportedFlavorException, IOException
```

To ask a `Transferable` object whether it supports a particular data flavor, use `isDataFlavorSupported()`, and to request a list of all data flavors it supports, use `getTransferDataFlavors()`. Notice particularly that one object can support multiple data flavors. Most objects provide a plain text flavor as the lowest common denominator that can be handled by all applications. However, the same data may also be available in an HTML flavor for applications that can handle the additional formatting. To request an object of a particular flavor use `getTransferData()`, and if that flavor is not available, an `UnsupportedFlavorException` is thrown.

The `java.awt.datatransfer.StringSelection` Class

The implementation of the `java.awt.datatransfer.Transferable` interface and the `java.awt.datatransfer.ClipboardOwner` interface is the `java.awt.datatransfer.StringSelection` class. This class allows you to transfer a string in plain text format. To support its interfaces, it has four methods it must implement:

```
public abstract boolean isDataFlavorSupported(DataFlavor flavor)
public abstract DataFlavor[] getTransferDataFlavors()
public abstract Object getTransferData(DataFlavor flavor)
    throws UnsupportedFlavorException, IOException
public void lostOwnership(Clipboard clipboard, Transferable contents)
```

The `java.awt.datatransfer.StringSelection` class also has a constructor that can be used to create a new `StringSelection` object:

```
public StringSelection(String data)
```

Creating an Example Program

It's time to get down to business and create some programs that use the clipboard techniques discussed so far. The first program you'll build uses a private clipboard. It copies or cuts data from a `TextField` object in response to the Copy and Paste buttons. When the user clicks the Paste button, any text in the clipboard is transferred into the read-only `TextField` object.

Listing 11.2 shows you the source code. Take a look at it and then read the explanation that follows.

LISTING 11.2 Source Code for the `PrivateClipboard` Program That Demonstrates Using a Private Clipboard

```
import com.sun.java.swing.*;
import java.awt.*;
import java.awt.datatransfer.*;
import java.awt.event.*;
import javax.swing.*;

public class PrivateClipboard extends JApplet implements ClipboardOwner
{

    Clipboard clipboard = new Clipboard( "FirstClip1" );

    public void init()
    {
      //{{INIT_CONTROLS
      getContentPane().setLayout(null);        setSize(387,160);
      getContentPane().add(textField1);
      textField1.setBounds(12,24,364,24);
      textField2.setEditable(false);
      getContentPane().add(textField2);
      textField2.setBounds(12,72,360,24);
      button1.setLabel("Copy");
      getContentPane().add(button1);
      button1.setBackground(java.awt.Color.lightGray);
      button1.setBounds(60,120,71,30);
      button2.setLabel("Cut");
      getContentPane().add(button2);
      button2.setBackground(java.awt.Color.lightGray);
      button2.setBounds(156,120,71,30);
      button3.setLabel("Paste");
      getContentPane().add(button3);
      button3.setBackground(java.awt.Color.lightGray);
      button3.setBounds(252,120,71,30);
      //}}

      //{{REGISTER_LISTENERS
      button1.addActionListener( new cmdCopyActionListener() );
      button2.addActionListener( new cmdCutActionListener() );
```

continues

LISTING 11.2   continued

```java
    button3.addActionListener( new cmdPasteActionListener() );
    //}}
}

public void lostOwnership( Clipboard clipboard, Transferable transferable )
{
}

//{{DECLARE_CONTROLS
java.awt.TextField textField1 = new java.awt.TextField();
java.awt.TextField textField2 = new java.awt.TextField();
java.awt.Button button1 = new java.awt.Button();
java.awt.Button button2 = new java.awt.Button();
java.awt.Button button3 = new java.awt.Button();
//}}

class cmdCopyActionListener implements ActionListener
{
  public void actionPerformed(ActionEvent event)
  {

    StringSelection fieldContent =
        new StringSelection( textField1.getSelectedText() );
    clipboard.setContents( fieldContent, PrivateClipboard.this );
  }
}

class cmdCutActionListener implements ActionListener
{
  public void actionPerformed(ActionEvent event)
  {

    StringSelection fieldContent =
        new StringSelection( textField1.getSelectedText() );
    clipboard.setContents( fieldContent, PrivateClipboard.this );

    String strText = textField1.getText();
    int nStart = textField1.getSelectionStart();
    int nEnd = textField1.getSelectionEnd();
    int nLength = strText.length();
    if( nLength > 0 )
    {
      String strDest = strText.substring( 0, nStart ) +
        strText.substring( nEnd, nLength );
      textField1.setText( strDest );
    }
  }
}
```

```
class cmdPasteActionListener implements ActionListener
{
  public void actionPerformed(ActionEvent event)
  {

    Transferable clipboardContent = clipboard.getContents( this );

    if( clipboardContent != null )
    {
      if( clipboardContent.isDataFlavorSupported( DataFlavor.stringFlavor )
)
      {
        try
        {
          String tempString;
          tempString =
           (String)
             clipboardContent.getTransferData( DataFlavor.stringFlavor );
          textField2.setText( tempString );
        }
        catch( Exception e )
        {
        }
      }
    }
  }

}
```

The source code, a compiled applet, and HTML code can be found in the *JavaBeans Unleashed* section on the www.mcp.com Web site. You can run the PrivateClipboard.html file from Applet Viewer, or you can create a project for the source code and run it from your development environment. The HTML code for the applet is shown in Listing 11.3.

LISTING 11.3 HTML Code for the PrivateClipboard Program That Demonstrates Using a Private Clipboard

```
<HTML>
  <HEAD>
    <TITLE>Chap 11 - Simple Cut and Paste Example</TITLE>
  </HEAD>
  <BODY>
    <APPLET CODE="PrivateClipboard.class" WIDTH="387" HEIGHT="160">
    </APPLET>
  </BODY>
</HTML>
```

When the program runs, you'll see two text fields and three buttons (see Figure 11.1). The first text field is where you type text, select text, and copy and cut from.

FIGURE 11.1

Once you type some text into the editable text field, you can select any or all of it and Copy or Cut.

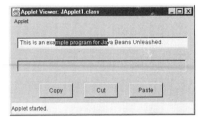

The second text field is read only and will be updated every time you select the Paste button as any text in the clipboard is pasted into it.

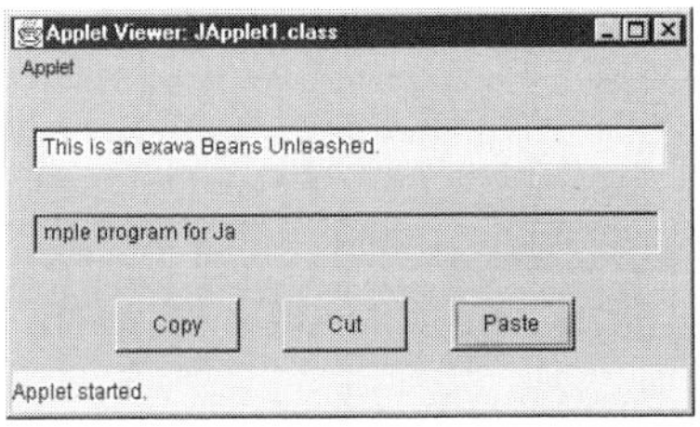

FIGURE 11.2

When you click the Paste button, any text that's in the clipboard will be pasted into the second, read-only text field.

Now to the source code. The first thing you'll see is the declaration and creation of the `Clipboard` object. This object is global to the `PrivateClipboard` class and remains in scope during the life of the applet.

The `init()` Method

The `init()` method simply creates the five objects (two `TextFields` and three `Buttons`), sets the appropriate attributes so that they display correctly, and then adds them to the applet. All of the code in the `init()` method was created by Visual Café in response to adding controls in the design mode.

Three `ActionListeners` were added in the `init()` method. Of course the `ActionListeners` must be added so that we can respond to button selections.

Declaration of Controls

After the `init()` method are the control declarations. There are two `TextField` and three `Button` objects that are declared and then created with the new operator.

If you get the chance, you can add more controls and experiment further with the applet. Any additional controls can be added here.

The `cmdCopyActionListener` Class

This class's `actionPerformed()` method is kicked off when users select the Copy button. (Remember that you added this `ActionListener` in the `init()` method.) Of the three `ActionListeners`, this is the shortest and simplest—two lines do the work. First, a `StringSelection` object is created with the `TextField`'s `getSelectedText()` method as the contructor's argument. This copies whatever text is currently selected in the StringSelection object.

Please note that the `getText()` method was not used. The `getText()` method returns all text in the `TextField`, while the `getSelectedText()` method returns only what's selected.

Then, a call to the `Clipboard` object's `setContents()` method sets the clipboard's contents to whatever is contained in the `StringSelection` object.

Now the `Clipboard` object contains whatever text was selected in the `TextField` object.

The `cmdCutActionListener` Class

The cut operation starts in the same way as the copy operation. It takes the selected text and puts it into the clipboard. What happens next is that the selected text must be removed. This differentiates the Copy and Cut operations.

The first thing that's done is to retrieve the entire text from the `TextField` object and place it into a `String` object. Then, the start and end positions of the text selection are obtained using the `getSelectionStart()` and `getSelectionEnd()` methods. The string length is also obtained because it is needed for the text removal operation.

Finally, a new string is created from the entire string by using the `substring` method. Once the substring is created, it is placed into the `TextField` object, which updates the control, and the user sees a new string minus the selected string.

The `cmdPasteActionListener` Class

This operation bears no resemblance to the Cut and Copy operations. It starts by creating a `Transferable` object from the clipboard's `getContents()` method as follows:

```
Transferable clipboardContent = clipboard.getContents( this );
```

Check for a null `Transferable` object in case nothing has been copied into the clipboard. Then make sure that what you have is a `stringFlavor` data type by using the `isDataFlavorSupported()` method. (This isn't really necessary in this case because it's a private clipboard, and you already know what flavor is there—it's just good practice.)

The next thing that's done is to get the string data from the `Transferable` object as follows:

```
String tempString;
tempString =
  (String) clipboardContent.getTransferData( DataFlavor.stringFlavor );
```

The last thing to do is set the `TextField` object so that the text taken from the clipboard is seen by the user. The `setText()` method is used to carry this out.

Creating Another Example Program

The next step toward a total understanding of the clipboard is to use the system clipboard. The second program does just that and communicates with programs that are independent of the Java program itself.

The first use of the program can be seen in Figure 11.3 where text that was typed into a `TextField` object was copied into the system clipboard. This text was then copied into Notepad with a paste operation.

FIGURE 11.3

Here you can see text that was typed into a Java program, copied into the system clipboard, and then copied into Notepad.

Listing 11.3 is the program source code. One thing to note, though, is that the applet will produce a security exception in some cases. This occurs when the security manager doesn't allow system clipboard access by a Java applet. If you want, you can set your browser's security to allow system clipboard access (both Netscape and Internet Explorer). This security exception won't happen in an application.

LISTING 11.3   Source Code for the `SystemClipboard` Program That Demonstrates Using the System Clipboard

```
import java.awt.*;
import java.applet.*;
import java.awt.event.*;
import java.awt.datatransfer.*;

public class SystemClipboard extends Applet implements ClipboardOwner
{

  Clipboard clipboard;

  public void init()
  {

    clipboard = getToolkit ().getSystemClipboard ();

    //{{INIT_CONTROLS
    setLayout(null);
    setBackground(java.awt.Color.lightGray);
    setSize(426,245);
    add(textField1);
    textField1.setBounds(12,12,396,24);
    add(textArea1);
    textArea1.setBounds(12,48,398,139);
    button1.setLabel("Set System Clipboard");
    add(button1);
    button1.setBackground(java.awt.Color.lightGray);
    button1.setBounds(60,204,132,28);
    button2.setLabel("Get System Clipboard");
    add(button2);
    button2.setBackground(java.awt.Color.lightGray);
    button2.setBounds(216,204,132,28);
    //}}

    //{{REGISTER_LISTENERS
    button1.addActionListener( new cmdToSystemClipboardActionListener() );
    button2.addActionListener( new cmdFromSystemClipboardActionListener() );
    //}}

  }

  public void lostOwnership( Clipboard clipboard, Transferable transferable )
  {
  }

  //{{DECLARE_CONTROLS
```

continues

LISTING 11.3   continued

```java
java.awt.TextField textField1 = new java.awt.TextField();
java.awt.TextArea textArea1 = new java.awt.TextArea();
java.awt.Button button1 = new java.awt.Button();
java.awt.Button button2 = new java.awt.Button();
//}}

class cmdToSystemClipboardActionListener implements ActionListener
{
  public void actionPerformed(ActionEvent event)
  {

    StringSelection fieldContent =
        new StringSelection( textField1.getSelectedText() );
    clipboard.setContents( fieldContent, SystemClipboard.this );
  }
}

class cmdFromSystemClipboardActionListener implements ActionListener
{
  public void actionPerformed(ActionEvent event)
  {

    Transferable clipboardContent = clipboard.getContents( this );

    if( clipboardContent != null )
    {
      if( clipboardContent.isDataFlavorSupported( DataFlavor.stringFlavor ) )
      {
        try{
          String tempString;
          tempString =
            (String) clipboardContent.getTransferData( DataFlavor.stringFlavor
);
          textArea1.setText( tempString );
        }
        catch( Exception e )
        {
        }
      }
    }
  }
}

}
```

The source code, a compiled applet, and HTML code can be found in the JavaBeans section on the www.mcp.com Web site. You can run the SystemClipboard.html file from Netscape or Internet Explorer, or you can create a project for the source code and run it from your development environment.

When the program runs, you'll see one text field, one text area, and two buttons (see Figure 11.4). The first text field is where you type text, select text, and from which you copy. Note: If you run the program from your development environment, everything will be fine—but within a browser you'll probably get a security exception.

FIGURE 11.4

The `SystemClipboard` *program also uses text from other applications, such as here where Notepad copied a block of text from the clipboard that was populated by a Java program.*

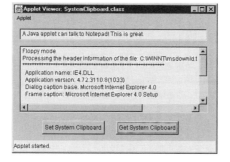

Figure 11.5 shows Microsoft Word interacting with a Java program via the clipboard.

FIGURE 11.5

Even mighty Microsoft Word can now communicate via the clipboard with Java programs.

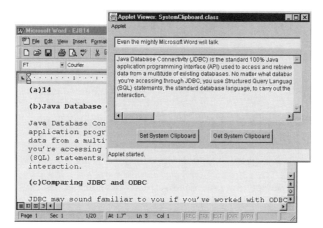

Now to the source code. The first thing you'll see is the declaration and retrieval of the system `Clipboard` object. This object is global to the `SystemClipboard` class and remains in scope during the life of the applet.

The `init()` Method

As with the first program, the `init()` method simply creates the four objects (one `TextField`, one `TextArea`, and two `Buttons`), sets the appropriate attributes so that they display correctly, and then adds them to the applet. All of the code in the `init()` method was created by Visual Café in response to adding controls in the design mode.

Two ActionListeners were added in the init() method. Of course the ActionListeners must be added so that we can respond to button selections.

Note that a method named lostOwnership() was added to the SystemClipboard class. This is required because the class implements the ClipboardOwner interface. This method will handle situations in which the program loses ownership of the clipboard.

Declaration of Controls

After the init() method are the control declarations. There's one TextField, one TextArea, and two Button objects that are declared and then created with the new operator.

As with the last program, you're encouraged to experiment by adding additional controls.

The cmdToSystemClipboardActionListener Class

This class's actionPerformed() method is kicked off when users select the Copy button. (Remember that you added this ActionListener in the init() method.) Of the two ActionListeners, this is the shortest and simplest. Two lines do the work. First, a StringSelection object is created with the TextField's getSelectedText() method as the contructor's argument. This copies whatever text is currently selected in the StringSelection object.

Please note that the getText() method was not used. The getText() method returns all text in the TextField, while the getSelectedText() method returns only what's selected.

Then, a call to the Clipboard object's setContents() method sets the clipboard's contents to whatever is contained in the StringSelection object.

Now the Clipboard object contains whatever text was selected in the TextField object.

This operation starts by creating a Transferable object from the clipboard's getContents() method as follows:

```
Transferable clipboardContent = clipboard.getContents( this );
```

Check for a null Transferable object in case nothing has been copied into the clipboard. Then make sure that what you have is a stringFlavor data type by using the isDataFlavorSupported() method. Unlike the first program, this is necessary because you don't know what flavor of data is in the clipboard.

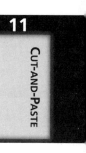

The next thing that's done is to get the string data from the `Transferable` object as follows:

```
String tempString;
tempString =
  (String) clipboardContent.getTransferData( DataFlavor.stringFlavor );
```

The last thing to do is set the `TextArea` object so that the text taken from the clipboard is seen by the user. The `setText()` method is used to carry this out.

Summary

In this chapter, you've learned how to use both a private and a system clipboard in your Java program. It's easy to do and can enhance your program tremendously. The clipboard is a modern device that users have come to expect.

Take these two programs and use them as a basis for your own experiments. It won't be long before you use the clipboard on a regular basis.

For more examples, go to `www.sourcedna.com`. It's a Web site dedicated to all topics in the realm of distributed network architecture (DNA), and Java clipboards is one subtopic that you'll find.

Drag-and-Drop

CHAPTER 12

This chapter covers the techniques necessary to use drag-and-drop in your program. Introduced a number of years ago, this compelling user interface technique has added functionality and ease of use in an impressive dose. I'm now so accustomed to dragging files to the Notepad shortcut on my desktop that I rarely run Notepad and then open a file with the standard file selector. Dragging and dropping on Notepad saves me so much time and effort that I never want to do it any other way.

Programs that support drag-and-drop do several things. First, they say to the user that this is a professional program that uses techniques that make it easier to use. They also provide a way to reduce errors because there's usually less manual typing for users when they drag and drop. And lastly, they save users time and effort because that's what a well-planned user interface can do.

To develop the drag-and-drop metaphor, Java defines several classes in the `java.awt.dnd` package.

First, you'll look at how a GUI component representing the data source of a drag-and-drop operation maintains an association with a `java.awt.dnd.DropSource` object. Second, you'll examine how another GUI component representing the destination of the data of a drag-and-drop operation maintains an association with a `java.awt.dnd.DropTarget` object. Finally, you'll wrap up with an example program that ties both together.

DataFlavors and Actions

Data is made available to `DropTarget` in a variety of `DataFlavor`s through the `Transferable` object. `Transferable` provides an object reference for a local transfer within the same Java Virtual Machine (JVM).

This wouldn't make sense for transfers to another JVM or to the native system, so a `DataFlavor` using `java.io.InputStream` subclass is usually provided.

When implementing drag-and-drop operations, you may request various drag-and-drop actions. The `DnDConstants` class defines the class variables for the supported actions.

- `ACTION_NONE` No action taken.
- `ACTION_COPY` The `DragSource` leaves the data intact.
- `ACTION_MOVE` The `DragSource` deletes the data upon successful completion of the drop.

- `ACTION_COPY` or `ACTION_MOVE`   The `DragSource` will perform either action requested by the `DropTarget`.
- `ACTION_LINK` or `ACTION_REFERENCE`   A data change to either the source or the destination propagates to the other location.

Creating a Draggable Component

For a GUI component to act as the source of a drag-and-drop operation, it must be associated with five objects:

```
java.awt.dnd.DragSource
java.awt.dnd.DragGestureRecognizer
java.awt.dnd.DragGestureListener
java.awt.datatransfer.Transferable
java.awt.dnd.DragSourceListener
```

The `DragSource` Object

There are two ways to obtain a `DragSource` object. One option is to use one instance per JVM where the class method `DragSource.getDefaultDragSource()` will obtain a shared `DragSource` object that is used for the lifetime of the JVM. Another option is to provide one `DragSource` per instance of the `Component` class. If you choose this option, however, you accept responsibility for implementation.

The `DragGestureRecognizer`

The user gesture or set of gestures initiating a drag-and-drop operation will vary per component, platform, and device. A `DragGestureRecognizer` protects you from platform dependencies by enclosing these implementation details. The instance method `dragSource.createDefaultDragGestureRecognizer()` obtains a recognizer and associates it with a component, action, and `DragGestureListener`. This example creates a subclass of a `Swinglabel` (`JLabel`). In its constructor, the necessary classes and associations are made for it to act as a drag source for either a copy or a move operation. Listeners will be discussed next. The code in Listing 12.1 represents the first steps in making any draggable component.

LISTING 12.1   First Steps to Creating a Draggable Component

```
public class DragLabel extends JLabel
{

  public DragLabel( String s )
  {
    this.setText( s );
    this.dragSource = DragSource.getDefaultDragSource();
    this.dgListener = newDGListener();
    this.dsListener = new DSListener();

    //component, action, listener
    this.dragSource.createDefaultDragGestureRecognizer(
this.DnDConstants.ACTION_COPY_OR_MOVE,
      this.dgListener );
  }

  private DragSource dragSource;
  private DragGestureListener dgListener;
  private DragSourceListener dsListener;

}
```

The DragGestureListener

The DragGestureRecognizer associated with the GUI component recognizes a drag-and-drop action and sends a message to the registered DragGestureListener. The DragGestureListener then sends the DragSource a startDrag message to initiate the drag.

```
interface DragGestureListener
{
  public void dragGestureRecognized( DragGestureEvent e );
}
```

After the DragSource receives the startDrag message, it creates a DragSourceContext context object, which tracks the state of the operation by listening to a native DragSourceContextPeer. In a situation like this, the DragSource may be obtained from either the Event object or by an instance variable.

The DragSourceListener that will be informed during the drag-and-drop operation is specified as a formal parameter to dragGestureRecognized. In addition, the initial drag cursor that shows the preliminary state of the drag-and-drop operation is also specified as a parameter. If the draggable component cannot accept drops, the initial cursor should be DragSource.DefaultCopyNoDrop.

You can specify an optional *drag image* to be displayed in addition to the cursors, if your platform allows it. However, Win32 platforms do not support drag images.

A `Transferable` object encapsulates the data that is most likely associated with the `Component` (the label's text) that will be transferred. To start a drag

```
public void dragGestureRecognized( DragGestureEvent e )
{
  //check to see if action is OK…
  try
  {
    Transferable transferable = new StringSelection( getText() );
    //initial cursor, transferable, dsource listener
    e.startDrag( DragSource.DefaultCopyNoDrop, transferable,dsListener );
    //or if dragSource is an instance variable:
    //dragSource.startDrag( e, DragSource.DefaultCopyNoDrop, transferable,
dsListener );
  }
  catch( InvalidDnDOperationException idoe )
  {
    System.err.println( idoe );
  }
}
```

The Transferable Object

The `java.awt.datatransfer.StringSelection` class works well for transfers within the same JVM but experiences a `ClassCastException` when used in inter-JVM cases. To solve this problem, you will have to provide a custom `Transferable` object.

A custom `Transferable` object creates instances of the `DataFlavors` it wants to provide. The `getTransferDataFlavors()` method is directed by the `Transferable` interface to return an array of these flavors. To facilitate the implementation of `isDataFlavorSupported(DataFlavor)`, create a `java.util.List` representation of this array.

This example provides two flavors, and you can use the two predefined `DataFlavor` flavors because you are simply transferring text data. You can use `DataFlavor.stringFlavor` for local transfers that are within the same JVM. However, `DataFlavor.plainTextFlavor` is preferred for nonlocal transfers because its internal representation class is a `java.io.InputStream` and it will transfer faster.

You can also define your own `DataFlavors` to map to MIME types, such as `image/JPEG`, or define custom-text charsets, such as `Latin-1`. The `Transferable` doesn't necessarily have to be a `ClipboardOwner` for drag-and-drop, but enabling this functionality will make it available for clipboard transfers.

Look at the definition of a simple `Transferable` for text data (see Listing 12.2).

LISTING 12.2 A Simple Transferable for Text Data

```
public class StringTransferable implements Transferable, ClipboardOwner
{
  public static final DataFlavor plainTextFlavor = DataFlavor.plainTextFlavor;
  public static final DataFlavor localStringFlavor = DataFlavor.stringFlavor;

  public static final DataFlavor[] flavors = {
    StringTransferable.plainTextFlavor,
    StringTransferable.localStringFlavor
  };

  private static final List flavorList = Arrays.asList( flavors );

  public synchronized DataFlavor[] getTransferDataFlavors()
  {
    return flavors;
  }

  public boolean isDataFlavorSupported( DataFlavor flavor )
  {
    return (flavorList.contains(flavor));
  }

}
```

A subclass of `java.io.InputStream` should be provided for native-to-Java or inter-JVM requests. For `StringTransferable.plainTextFlavor` requests, `get TransferData` returns a `java.io.ByteArrayInputStream`. As specified in the MIME specification, text data may have different character encodings.

The `DataFlavor` should be queried for the encoding requested by the `DropTarget`. Common character encodings are Unicode and Latin-1 (ISO 8859-1). The `Transferable` can provide text data in a variety of formats and encoding, as shown in the following:

```
public synchronized Object getTransferData( DataFlavor flavor )
  throws UnsupportedFlavorException, IOException
{

  if( flavor.equals(StringTransferable.plainTextFlavor ) )
  {
    String charset = flavor.getParameter( "charset" ).trim();
    if( charset.equalsIgnoreCase( "unicode" ) )
    {
      System.out.println( "returning unicode charset" );
      // uppercase U in Unicode here!
```

```
      Return( new ByteArrayInputStream( this.string.getBytes( "Unicode" ) ) );
    }
    else
    {
      System.out.println( "returning latin-1 charset" );
      return( new ByteArrayInputStream( this.string.getBytes("iso8859-1" ) ) );
    }
  }
  else if ( StringTransferable.localStringFlavor.equals( flavor ) )
  {
    return( this.string );
  }
  else
  {
    throw new UnsupportedFlavorException( flavor );
  }
}
```

The DragSourceListener

The DragSourceListener provides *drag over* effects during the drag-and-drop operation. These drag over effects provide visual feedback while the cursor is over a component. However, they do not permanently change the appearance of components.

```
interface DragSourceListener
{
  public void dragEnter( DragSourceDragEvent e );
  public void dragOver( DragSourceDragEvent e );
  public void dragExit( DragSourceEvent e );
  public void dragDropEnd( DragSourceDropEvent e );
  public void dropActionChanged( DragSourceDragEvent e );
}
```

Most of the time, the DragSourceListener displays drag over effects by changing the mouse cursor. Two cursors are available—a drop cursor and a non-drop cursor. The non-drop cursor is displayed when over anything besides a valid target. The DragSource class has several predefined cursors as class variables:

> DefaultCopyDrop
>
> DefaultCopyNoDrop
>
> DefaultMoveDrop
>
> DefaultMoveNoDrop
>
> DefaultLinkDrop
>
> DefaultLinkNoDrop

The `DragSourceListener` object can change the cursor by sending a `setCursor()` message to the `DragSourceContext`, which is obtained from the `DragSourceEvent` parameter. In addition, the definitions of the `dragOver()` and `dropActionChanged()` methods are similar. If the `DropTarget` rejects the operation, these methods aren't invoked.

Enter the following to change the cursor to provide drag over feedback:

```
public void dragEnter( DragSourceDragEvent e )
{
  DragSourceContext context = e.getDragSourceContext();
  // both the users selected action, and the source and target actions
  int myaction = e.getDropAction();
  if( ( myaction & DnDConstants.ACTION_COPY ) != 0 )
  {
    context.setCursor( DragSource.DefaultCopyDrop );
  }
  else
  {
    context.setCursor( DragSource.DefaultCopyNoDrop );
  }
}
```

The `DragSourceListener` receives notification from a `dragDropEnd` message when the operation has ended. After receiving notification, the listener's responsibility is to check the success of the operation and, if successful, perform the requested action. There's nothing for the `DragSourceListener` to do if the operation isn't successful.

In the case of a move action, the listener will also remove the source data. It will be taken out of the hierarchy if it's a component, and it will be erased if it's the text data displayed in a text component.

The following is an example of `dragDropEnd()`. The methods simply return if the operation isn't successful, and the drop action is examined to see if it was a move operation.

```
public void dragDropEnd( DragSourceDropEvent e )
{

  if ( e.getDropSuccess() == false )
  {
    return;
  }

  int dropAction = e.getDropAction();

  if ( dropAction == DnDConstants.ACTION_MOVE )
  {
    // do stuff
  }

}
```

Flow Review

At this point, it would be good to review the flow, because the messages passed among the several objects discussed are so complex.

The `DragGestureRecognizer` recognizes a gesture and notifies the `DragGestureListener`. The `DragGestureListener`, assuming the actions and/or flavors are okay, asks `DragSource` to `startDrag()`.

The `DragSource` creates a `DragSourceContext` and a `DragSourceContextPeer`. The `DragSourceContext` adds itself as a `DragSourceListener` to the `DragSourceContextPeer`. The `DragSourceContextPeer` receives state notifications (component entered/exited/is over) from the native system and delegates them to the `DragSourceContext`.

If the `DropTargetListener` accepts the action, the `DragSourceContext` notifies the `DragSourceListener`, which provides drag over feedback. Typical feedback includes asking the `DragSourceContext` to change the cursor.

The `DragSourceListener` receives a `dragDropEnd` notification message when the drop is complete.

Creating a Droppable Component

For a GUI component to act as the destination of a drag-and-drop, it must be associated with two objects:

```
java.awt.dnd.DropTarget
java.awt.dnd.DropTargetListener
```

The DropTarget

The `DropTarget`'s constructor makes associations with both the `DropTarget` and the `DropTargetListener` objects. Alternatively, the `DropTarget` has `setComponent()` and `addDropTargetListener()` methods. Newly defined `java.awt.Component` methods are used by the `DropTarget`'s constructors to inform the `Component` that it is now associated with the `DropTarget`.

The following are the additions to `java.awt.Component`:

```
public void setDropTarget( DropTarget dt )
Public DropTarget getDropTarget()
```

Let's define a droppable component. After you create a DropTarget in your Component's constructor, the Component associates itself and a DropTargetListener with the DropTarget via the DropTarget's constructor (see Listing 12.3).

LISTING 12.3   Associating a Component with a *DropTarget*

```
public class DropLabel extends JLabel
{

  public DropLabel( String s )
  {
    this.setText( s );
    // not strictly necessary to maintain this reference
    this.dtListener = new DTListener();

    // component, ops, listener, accepting
    this.dropTarget = new DropTarget( this, this.acceptableActions,
      this.dtListener, true );
  }

  private DropTarget dropTarget;
  private DropTargetListener dtListener;
  private int acceptableActions = DnDConstants.ACTION_COPY;

}
```

The DropTargetListener

The DropTargetListener needs a link with the Component so that the Component can notify the DropTargetListener to display *drag under* effects during the operation. This listener can be conveniently created as an inner class, which transfers the data when the drop occurs.

> **Caution**
>
> The Component itself shouldn't be the listener, because this implies its availability for use as some other Component's listener.

The dragEnter(), dragOver(), and dropActionChanged() methods must accept or reject the current operation after inspecting the action and flavor. The DragSourceListener will call its dragEnter() and dragOver() methods only if the operation is accepted.

In addition, the `DropTargetListener` invokes the `dragExit()` method after the user leaves the droppable area. Here the listener may undo any drag effects.

Listing 12.4 is a `DropTargetListener` implementation that provides drag under feedback by displaying a green border if it can handle the transfer and a red border if it cannot. Discussion on how `isDragOk()` determines this will follow.

LISTING 12.4 Providing Drag Under Feedback

```
class DTListener implements DropTargetListener
{

  public void dragEnter( DropTargetDragEvent e )
  {

    if( isDragOk( e ) == false )
    {
      e.rejectDrag();
      return;
    }

    DropLabel.this.borderColor = Color.green;
    showBorder( true );
    e.acceptDrag( DropLabel.this.acceptableActions );
  }

  public void dragOver( DropTargetDragEvent e )
  {

    if( isDragOk( e ) == false )
    {
      e.rejectDrag();
      return;
    }

    e.acceptDrag( DropLabel.this.acceptableActions );

  }

  public void dropActionChanged( DropTargetDragEvent e )
  {

    if( isDragOk( e ) == false )
    {
      e.rejectDrag();
      return;
    }
```

continues

LISTING 12.4 continued

```
    e.acceptDrag( DropLabel.this.acceptableActions );

  }

  public void dragExit(DropTargetEvent e)
  {
    DropLabel.this.borderColor=Color.green;
    showBorder( false );
  }

}
```

The complex flow of these messages remains hidden during action. For the curious, the Event objects maintain a reference to their DropTargetContext, and the DropTargetContext in turn maintains a reference to the native DropTargetContextPeer. When the various accept or reject messages are sent by the listener, they go all the way to the native system.

How can the listener determine the validity of the current drag operation? The dragEnter(), dragOver(), and dropActionChanged() methods use the isDragOk() method to determine whether the DataFlavor being dragged is compatible with the flavors the target component can accept. In this example, any of the flavors defined in StringTransferable will be accepted. Also, a class variable referring to a collection of DataFlavors defined in the drop component might be used.

The DropTargetListener compares the actions supported by the DragSource to the actions acceptable to the DropTarget if the flavor is compatible. Actions specified when the Component created the DragGestureRecognizer could be retrieved through the DropTargetDragEvent's getSourceActions() method. A true value is returned if both the action and the flavor are okay.

In examining the definition of isDragOk(), the DataFlavors and actions offered by the DragSource are inspected.

```
private boolean isDragOk( DropTargetDragEvent e )
{
  DataFlavor[] flavors = StringTransferable.flavors;
  DataFlavor chosen = null;
  for( int i = 0; i < flavors.length; i++ )
  {
    if( e.isDataFlavorSupported( flavors[i] ) )
    {
      chosen = flavors[i];
      break;
    }
```

```
  }

  if( chosen == null )
  {
    return( false );
  }

  // the actions specified when the source
  // created the DragGestureRecognizer
  int sa = e.getSourceActions();

  // we're saying that these actions are necessary
  if( ( sa & DropLabel.this.acceptableActions ) == 0 )
    return( false );

  return( true );

}
```

Data Transfer

The DropTargetListener's drop method is responsible for the data transfer. There are three parts to the drop method:

- Checks validity of the dropped action and DataFlavor; the drop is rejected, if necessary.
- Accepts the drop with a specified action and the Transferable's data object is retrieved.
- Reads and uses the data.

Drop Method Part 1: Validation

The DropTargetListener chooses the DataFlavor and checks the operation before the transfer takes place. The DropTargetListener sends a rejectDrop message to the DropTargetDropEvent if none of the DataFlavors and/or operations is acceptable. The Event object may be queried with isLocalTransfer if the drag source is in the same JVM. If this is so, the DropTargetListener can choose an appropriate DataFlavor.

```
public void drop(DropTargetDropEvent e)
{
  DataFlavor[] flavors = StringTransferable.flavors;
  DataFlavor chosen = null;
  if (e.isLocalTransfer() == false)
  {
    chosen = StringTransferable.plainTextFlavor;
  }
```

```
  else
  {
    for (int i = 0; i < flavors.length; i++ )
    {
      if (e.isDataFlavorSupported(flavors[i]))
      {
        chosen = flavors[i];
        break;
      }

    }
  }

  if (chosen == null)
  {
      e.rejectDrop();
      return;
  }

  // the actions that the source has specified with DragGestureRecognizer
  int sa = e.getSourceActions();
  if ( ( sa & DropLabel.this.acceptableActions ) == 0 )
  {
    e.rejectDrop();
    showBorder( false );
    return;
  }

}
```

Drop Method Part 2: Accepting the Drop

After the drop passes the validation, the DropTargetListener sends an acceptDrop message (with the desired operation specified) to the DragSourceListener in its dragDropEnd() method. After the DropTargetListener accepts the drop, it retrieves the Transferable and requests its data. The following is the continuation of the drop method:

```
Object data=null;

try
{
  e.acceptDrop(DropLabel.this.acceptableActions);
  data = e.getTransferable().getTransferData( chosen );
  if( data == null )
    throw new NullPointerException();
}
catch ( Throwable t )
{
```

```
    t.printStackTrace();
    e.dropComplete( false );
    showBorder(f alse );
    return;
}
```

Drop Method Part 3: Data Transfer

In native-to-Java or inter-JVM transfers, the data's representation class should be a sub-class of `java.io.InputStream`, because references to a Java object only make sense in the JVM.

The `Transferable` returns an object reference for local transfers.

The `DropTargetListener` must send a `dropComplete(false)` message to the `DropTargetDropEvent` if there are any exceptions thrown during data transfer.

Once data has been successfully transferred, the `DropTargetListener` sends the `DropTargetDropEvent` a `dropComplete(true)` message.

> **Note**
>
> Unfortunately, Java 2 still contains a bug that prevents some native-to-Java transfers. Java-to-native transfers, however, do not crash, despite a few inserted garbage characters.

Continuing with the drop method definition, you finally retrieve the data:

```
if (data instanceof String )
{
  String s = (String) data;
  DropLabel.this.setText( s );
}
else if( data instanceof InputStream )
{
  String charset = chosen.getParameter( "charset" ).trim();
  InputStream input = (InputStream) data;
  InputStreamReader isr = null;

  try
  {
    isr = new InputStreamReader( input, charset );
  }
  catch( UnsupportedEncodingException uee )
  {
    isr = new InputStreamReader( input );
```

```
      }

      StringBuffer str = new StringBuffer();
      int in = -1;
      try
      {
        while( ( in = isr.read() ) >= 0 )
        {
          if (in != 0)
            str.append( (char) in );
        }

        DropLabel.this.setText( str.toString() );
      }
      catch( IOException ioe )
      {
        System.err.println( "cannot read" + ioe);
        e.dropComplete(false);
        showBorder(false);
        String message = "Bad drop\n" + ioe.getMessage();
        JOptionPane.showMessageDialog( DropLabel.this, message, "Error",
          JOptionPane.ERROR_MESSAGE );
        return;
      }
    }
    else
    {
      System.out.println( "drop: rejecting");
      e.dropComplete( false );
      showBorder( false );
      return;
    }

    e.dropComplete( true );
    showBorder( false );
```

Path of the Transferable

Listed are the details of the path taken by the `Transferable`:

The `DragGestureListener` gets the `Transferable` (probably from the GUI component) and sends it to the `DragSource` by the `startDrag` message.

The `DragSource` sends the same message to its `DragSourceContext`, which in turn forwards it to its peer (passing itself as a parameter). The native system thus has access to the `Transferable` through the `DragSourceContext`.

The `DropTargetContextPeer` now has access to this `Transferable`. When the `DropTargetContext` receives the `getTransferable` message, it creates and returns a `TransferableProxy` object from the `DropTargetContextPeer`'s `Transferable`.

The TransferableProxy is returned to the DropTargetListener when the DropTargetListener asks the DropTargetEvent for the Transferable. The Event forwards the Listener's getTransferable message to its DropTargetContext.

Creating an Example Program

It's time to take what you've learned and create an example program (see Listing 12.7). This program simply places two controls in a Java application, and then allows the text from one control to be dragged to another.

There are two classes that do the majority of the work. They're named DropLabel (see Listing 12.6) and DragField (see Listing 12.5). The DropLabel class extends a JLabel class and is the target to which the drop operation aims. The DragField class extends a JTextField class and is the source for the drag operation. When the program runs, you'll see that the editable text field says "Drag Me!" and the label says "Drop On Me" (see Figure 12.1). Listing 12.5 shows the source code for the DragField class.

FIGURE 12.1

This program invites you to drag an editable text field onto a label.

LISTING 12.5   Source Code for the *DragField* Class

```
import java.awt.*;
import java.awt.event.*;
import javax.swing.event.*;
import javax.swing.*;
import javax.swing.text.*;
import java.awt.datatransfer.*;
import java.io.*;
import java.awt.dnd.*;

public class DragField extends JTextField
{

    public DragField( String s )
    {
        this.setText( s );
```

continues

LISTING 12.5 continued

```java
        this.dragSource = DragSource.getDefaultDragSource();
        this.dgListener = new DGListener();
        this.dsListener = new DSListener();
        this.dragSource.createDefaultDragGestureRecognizer( this,
          DnDConstants.ACTION_COPY_OR_MOVE, this.dgListener );
    }

    private DragSource dragSource;
    private DragGestureListener dgListener;
    private DragSourceListener dsListener;

    public class DGListener implements DragGestureListener
    {
        public void dragGestureRecognized( DragGestureEvent e )
        {
          try
          {
            Transferable transferable = new StringSelection( getText() );
            e.startDrag( DragSource.DefaultCopyNoDrop, transferable,
                dsListener );
          }
          catch( InvalidDnDOperationException ie )
          {
          }
        }
      }
    }

    public class DSListener implements DragSourceListener
    {
      public void dropActionChanged( DragSourceDragEvent e )
      {
      }
      public void dragOver( DragSourceDragEvent e )
      {
      }
      public void dragExit(  DragSourceEvent e  )
      {
      }
      public void dragEnter(  DragSourceDragEvent e  )
      {
        DragSourceContext context = e.getDragSourceContext();
        int nAction = e.getDropAction();
        if( ( nAction & DnDConstants.ACTION_COPY ) != 0 )
          context.setCursor( DragSource.DefaultCopyDrop );
        else
          context.setCursor( DragSource.DefaultCopyNoDrop );
      }
      public void dragDropEnd( DragSourceDropEvent e )
      {
```

```
        if( e.getDropSuccess() != false )
        {
        }
      }
    }

}
```

The `DragField` Class

The `DragField` class extends the `JTextField` class. The first thing you'll notice is the `DragField` constructor. It allows the control's text to be set and takes care of other initialization details.

The default drag source is obtained with the `getDefaultDragSource()` method. There's a `DragSource` object declared immediately below the `DragField` constructor named `dragSource`. This variable will contain the default drag source.

A new `DGListener` class is created next. This class's `dragGestureRecognized()` method will be called when the drag is ready to start (more on this shortly). A `DragGestureListener` object is declared immediately below the `DragField` constructor named `dgListener`. This variable will contain the newly-created `DGListener()`.

A new `DSListener` class is created next. This class's `dragEnter()` method will be called when the drag is over the droppable object. A `DragSourceListener` object is declared immediately below the `DragField` constructor named `dsListener`. This variable will contain the newly-created `DSListener()`.

The `DGListener` class implements the `DragGestureListener` interface. The `DropTargetListener` interface is the callback interface used by the `DropTarget` class to provide notification of DnD operations that involve the subject `DropTarget`. The method in this interface that does the work is the `dragGestureRecognized()` method. This method is called when a `DragGestureRecognizer` has detected a platform-dependent drag-and-drop action initiating gesture and is notifying this `Listener` for it to initiate the action for the user. Two things happen in this method. First, the text is obtained and assigned to a `Transferable` object. Next, the `startDrag()` method is called.

The `DSListener` class (see Listing 12.6) implements the `DragSourceListener` interface. The `DragSourceListener` defines the event interface for originators of drag-and-drop operations to track the state of the user's gesture to provide the appropriate feedback to the user. The method in this interface that does the work in this program is the `dragEnter()` method. This method is triggered when the hotspot enters a platform-dependent drop site. In this method, you can see that the cursor is changed.

12

DRAG-AND-DROP

LISTING 12.6 Source Code for the `DropLabel` Class

```java
import java.awt.*;
import java.awt.event.*;
import javax.swing.event.*;
import javax.swing.*;
import javax.swing.text.*;
import java.awt.datatransfer.*;
import java.io.*;
import java.awt.dnd.*;

public class DropLabel extends JLabel
{
  public DropLabel( String s )
  {
    this.setText( s );
    this.dtListener = new DTListener();
    this.dropTarget = new DropTarget( this, DnDConstants.ACTION_COPY,
        this.dtListener, true );
  }

  private DropTarget dropTarget;
  private DropTargetListener dtListener;
  private Color borderColor;

  private void showBorder( boolean b )
  {
    if( b )
      this.setBorder( BorderFactory.createLineBorder( this.borderColor, 10 ) );
    else
      this.setBorder( BorderFactory.createEmptyBorder() );

    this.getParent().validate();
    this.repaint();
  }

  class DTListener implements DropTargetListener
  {
    public void dragEnter( DropTargetDragEvent e )
    {
      if( isDragOk( e ) == false )
        e.rejectDrag();
      else
      {
        DropLabel.this.borderColor = Color.green;
        DropLabel.this.showBorder( true );
        e.acceptDrag( DnDConstants.ACTION_COPY );
      }
    }
    public void dragOver( DropTargetDragEvent e )
    {
```

```
    if( isDragOk( e ) == false )
      e.rejectDrag();
    else
      e.acceptDrag( DnDConstants.ACTION_COPY );
  }
  public void dropActionChanged( DropTargetDragEvent e )
  {
    if( isDragOk( e ) )
      e.rejectDrag();
    else
      e.acceptDrag( DnDConstants.ACTION_COPY );
  }
  public void dragExit( DropTargetEvent e )
  {
    DropLabel.this.borderColor = Color.green;
    showBorder( false );
  }
  public void drop( DropTargetDropEvent e )
  {

    Object data = null;
    try
    {
        e.acceptDrop( DnDConstants.ACTION_COPY );
        data =
          e.getTransferable().getTransferData( DataFlavor.stringFlavor );
      if( data == null )
        throw new NullPointerException();
    }
    catch( Throwable t )
    {
      e.dropComplete(false);
      showBorder(false);
        return;
    }

    String s = (String) data;
      DropLabel.this.setText( s );
    e.dropComplete( true );
    showBorder( false );

  }
  private boolean isDragOk( DropTargetDragEvent e )
  {

    boolean bFlavorOk = false;

    if( e.isDataFlavorSupported( DataFlavor.stringFlavor ) )//flavors[i] ) )
      bFlavorOk = true;
```

continues

LISTING 12.6   continued

```
     if( !bFlavorOk )
       return( false );

     if( ( e.getSourceActions() & DnDConstants.ACTION_COPY ) == 0 )
       return( false );

     return( true );
   }
 }

}
```

The `DropLabel` Class

The `DropLabel` class extends the `JLabel` class. The first thing you'll notice is the `DropLabel` constructor. It allows the control's text to be set and takes care of other initialization details.

Note that a `DTListener` object is created in the `DropLabel` constructor. This is then used when creating the `DropTarget` object.

Below the constructor and the declarations, you'll find the `showBorder()` method. This method is used by the class to change the color of the label border. This gives a visual clue for users. When you run the program, you'll see the border of the label turn to green when the text field is dragged over it.

The `DTListener` class implements the `DropTargetListener` interface. The `DropTargetListener` interface is the callback interface used by the `DropTarget` class to provide notification of drag-and-drop operations that involve the subject `DropTarget`. There are a number of methods in this class that are important for the program, so we'll take them one at a time.

The `dragEnter()` method is first used to change the border color to green. This method is triggered when a drag operation has encountered the `DropTarget`. When the dragged object enters the droppable object, the border turns green. The `acceptDrag()` method is also called. This method should be called from a DropTargetListener's `dragEnter()`, `dragOver()`, and `dragActionChanged()` methods if the implementation wants to accept an operation from the `srcActions` other than the one selected by the user as represented by the `dropAction`.

The `dragOver()` and `dropActionChanged()` methods either call the `rejectDrag()` method or the `acceptDrag()` method. The `rejectDrag()` method rejects the drag as a result of examining either the `dropAction` or the available `DataFlavor` types.

The dragExit() method changes the border back to invisible.

The drop() method is where the majority of the work happens. It accepts the drop with the acceptDrop() method, gets the data, sets the label text, and calls the dropComplete() method—this is the method that notifies the DragSource that the drop transfer(s) are completed.

The test program ties it altogether by instantiating both classes, and then allowing user to interact.

LISTING 12.7   Source Code for the Test Class

```
import java.awt.*;
import java.awt.event.*;
import javax.swing.event.*;
import javax.swing.*;
import javax.swing.text.*;
import java.awt.datatransfer.*;
import java.io.*;
import java.awt.dnd.*;

public class Test {

  public Test()
  {
  }

  public static void main( String[] args )
  {
    JFrame frame = new JFrame();
    frame.setTitle( "Drag and Drop Test" );

    Container content = frame.getContentPane();
    content.setLayout( new GridLayout( 6, 1, 5, 5 ) );
    content.add( new DragField( "Drag Me!" ) );
    content.add( new DropLabel( "Drop On Me!" ) );

    frame.addWindowListener( new WindowAdapter() {
      public void windowClosing( WindowEvent e )
      {
          System.exit(0);
      }
      });
    frame.setSize(300,300);
    frame.setVisible(true);
  }
}
```

The editable text field can be changed so that you can easily see the results of each drag-and-drop operation. Figure 12.2 shows the JTextField object after it's been edited.

FIGURE **12.2**

The JTextField *object can be edited.*

The results of a drag-and-drop operation can be seen in Figure 12.3

FIGURE **12.3**

Here you can see the result of a drag-and-drop operation.

Summary

Java now has the long-awaited capability to transfer data using a drag-and-drop metaphor that is available on many platforms. Although it's not entirely easy to implement, it's well worth the effort. I expect that as Java matures, the drag-and-drop API will become easier.

There are several additional examples on www.sourcedna.com that illustrate drag-and-drop techniques. Visit the site and download the examples.

Java Naming and Directory Interface (JNDI)

The Java Naming and Directory Interface (JNDI) is an API that provides naming and directory functionality for Java applications. Because the JDNI is a platform-independent specification that can be used with any directory service implementation, let's take a look at what a "directory service" is and how it can help you. A directory service is much like a telephone directory. However, instead of simply containing telephone numbers and addresses, directories contain information needed to maintain a network. Examples of the type of information included in a directory are device locations, user information, and available network services. What makes a directory service (and hence this chapter) of interest to you is the fact that more and more information is being put into these directories. This is being done so that application developers have a single repository from which to retrieve system-level information.

Having said that, all directory services also include an Application Programming Interface (API) that is used to access this data. This is where the JNDI comes in. The JNDI consists of an API and Service Provider Interface (SPI). The SPI is plugged into the JNDI transparently allowing a variety of different directory systems, such as a file directory or Internet domain names to be accessed using a single API. This chapter explores the main concepts behind JDNI and shows you how to use the interface.

> **Note**
>
> JNDI is a standard extension to the Java platform that can be downloaded from `http://java.sun.com/products/jndi/index.html#download`. You will need to ensure that the `JNDI.JAR` file is in your classpath.

Naming Interface

The Naming Interface provides a way to relate human-readable names with addresses, identifiers, or other objects used by computer systems. This allows you to provide a name, such as a filename in a directory system, and have the corresponding file object returned to you for processing. The naming interface in use determines the form of the name that must be supplied. For instance, a UNIX-based file directory will have names in the form `/usr/bin`, whereas an Internet DNS will have names in the standard `www.sun.com` form. A naming interface can be anything from a local directory service to an entity on the Internet.

To use the naming interface of the JNDI, you will need to import the `javax.naming` package:

```
import javax.naming.Context;
import javax.naming.InitialContext;
import javax.naming.NamingException;
```

Three concepts form the basis of the Naming Interface:

- Context and names
- Bindings
- References

Context and Names

The main function of the naming interface is to map objects to names. Each object in a naming system must have a name that conforms to the naming convention. To look up an object in a naming system, you supply the name of the object in the correct form.

For instance, the naming convention for the UNIX file system demands that each file be named according to its place in the directory tree relative to the root directory. The list of directories, starting at the root directory, that need to be traversed to reach the file are arranged in left-to-right order as a slash (`/`) separated list. Thus, `/usr/bin/install.log` names a file called `install.log` file in the `/usr/bin` directory, which itself is in the `/usr` directory, which is in the root directory.

A context is a set of relationships between names and objects. Each context has a naming convention that determines the form of the name. A context provides a lookup or resolution operation that, when given a name in the correct form, returns the associated object. The context can also provide means to associate an object with a name, remove an association with a name, and list all objects that have names. This association is called a *binding* and will be discussed in the next section.

An object with a name in one context can be bound to a second context with the same naming convention. In this case, the second context is called a *subcontext*. In the UNIX file system, for example, the directory `/usr` is a context, as is the subdirectory `/usr/bin`. As a context, the subdirectory `/usr/bin` becomes a subcontext of the context usr. In terms of a DSN domain, `sun.com` is a subcontext of the `com` context.

To use a context, you will need to create a new `Context` object and set its environment properties. These properties are represented by a `HashTable` object and are used to specify various preferences and properties that define the environment in which the context will operate.

13

JAVA NAMING AND DIRECTORY INTERFACE (JNDI)

The following lines create a context and set the environment properties to use the file system service provider from Sun Microsystems and to use the /java directory:

```
// Create a hashtable
Hashtable env = new Hashtable();
// Fill the hashtable with environment properties
env.put(Context.INITIAL_CONTEXT_FACTORY,
  "com.sun.jndi.fscontext.RefFSContextFactory");
env.put(Context.PROVIDER_URL, "file:/java");

// Create the context
Context ctx = new InitialContext(env);
```

No server needs to be set up to use the local file system, but if you want to use a different server, you would need to ensure that the SPI server software was installed correctly before proceeding. If you wanted to use a Lightweight Directory Access Protocol (LDAP) service provider such as the one at ldap.BigFoot.com, for example, you would need to provide the server URL as well as the username and password:

```
Hashtable env = new Hashtable();
env.put(Context.PROVIDER_URL, "ldap://ldap.Bigfoot.com");
env.put(Context.SECURITY_PRINCIPAL, "username");
env.put(Context.SECURITY_CREDENTIALS, "password");
Context ctx = new InitialContext(env);
```

Once you have a context, you can use it to look up an object as follows:

```
// Lookup the object named "book"
Object obj = ctx.lookup("Book");
```

Notice that the lookup method returns an object. The significance of this is that you can use method to access any business object in your system. The type of object you receive depends on the naming interface and the data associated with each object contained in the context. If the context contains files and directories, you would need to cast the returned object to the correct type before using it:

```
import java.io.File;
...
File f = (File) ctx.lookup(name);
```

An alternative to looking up objects in a context one by one is to list all the objects using a single operation. The Context.list() API returns an enumeration of NameClassPair. Each NameClassPair contains the name and the class name of the object. For example, to list all NameClassPairs in the /java directory, you would do the following:

```
// Obtain an enumerated list of names and class names
NamingEnumeration namelist = ctx.list("java");
// Iterate through the list
while (namelist.hasMore()) {
```

```
NameClassPair nameclass = (NameClassPair) namelist.next();
// do something with nameclass
}
```

Another option is to list all bindings in a context. The `Context.listBindings()` API
returns an enumeration of `Binding`. `Binding` is a subclass of `NameClassPair`, and it contains the object itself, as well as the name and class name of the object. Notice in the following code snippet that this information is returned in the form of a
`NamingEnumeration` interface. For purposes of this conversation, it is enough to understand that the `NamingEnumeration` interface is used to enumerate through lists returned
by methods in the `javax.naming` and `javax.naming.directory` packages. Also note that
this interface extends `Enumeration` to allow exceptions to be thrown during the enumeration.

```
// Obtain an enumerated list of names, class names and objects
NamingEnumeration namelist = ctx.listBindings("java");
// Iterate through the list
while (namelist.hasMore())
{
 Binding b = (Binding) namelist.next();
 // do something with b
}
```

The difference between the two methods is that `list()` will only provide access to the
name and class name of the object, whereas `listBindings` will provide access to the
underlying objects themselves. This makes `list()` suitable for directory listing applications and `listBindings()` suitable for instances where you need to access the entire
contents of a context in one go. As expected, a call to `listbindings()` will be more
expensive than a call to `list()`, so you should choose your method carefully.

Of course you are never guaranteed that the creation of a context or a context operation
will be successful. To check the success or failure of an operation, you must be prepared
to catch `NamingException` or `NameingException`-derived exceptions. With error checking, your context creation and lookup code would look like the following:

```
try
{
 // Create the initial context
 Hashtable env = new Hashtable();
 env.put(Context.INITIAL_CONTEXT_FACTORY,
  "com.sun.jndi.fscontext.RefFSContextFactory");
 env.put(Context.PROVIDER_URL, "file:/java");
 Context ctx = new InitialContext(env);

 // Look up an object
 Object obj = ctx.lookup(name);
}
```

```
catch (AuthenticationException e)
{
 System.err.println("Authentication Error occurred");
}
catch (NamingException e)
{
 System.err.println("Error occurred");
}
```

The javax.naming package contains a number of exceptions classes derived from the NamingException class. The names and descriptions of the exceptions are shown in Table 13.1.

Table 13.1 Exception Classes

Exception Name	*Description*
NamingException	All naming exceptions thrown by Context and DirContext operations are derived from this class.
CannotProceedException	This is thrown when an operation cannot proceed any further.
CommunicationException	Thrown when a client cannot communicate with the directory or naming service.
ConfigurationException	Thrown when there is a configuration problem.
ContextNotEmptyException	Thrown when an attempt is made to remove a non-empty context.
InsufficientResourcesException	Thrown to indicate there are insufficient resources available for the operation.
InterruptedNamingException	Thrown to indicate that an operation has been interrupted.
InvalidNameException	Thrown to indicate that the specified name does not conform to the naming convention of the naming system in use.
LimitExceededException	Thrown when a method terminates due to a user or system limit being reached.
SizeLimitExceededException	Thrown when a method terminates due to a user or system size-limit being reached.
TimeLimitExceededException	Thrown when an operation does not terminate within a specified time.
LinkException	Thrown in response to problems resolving links.
LinkLoopException	Thrown to indicate a circular link reference or a link with too many link counts has been encountered.
MalformedLinkException	Thrown to indicate a malformed link was encountered.

Exception Name	Description
NameAlreadyBoundException	Thrown when an attempt to bind a name that is already bound to another object.
NameNotFoundException	Thrown when an attempt to reference a name that is not bound is made.
NamingSecurityException	All security-related exceptions thrown by operations in the Context and DirContext interfaces are derived from this class.
AuthenticationException	Thrown when an authentication error occurs while accessing the naming or directory service.
AuthenticationNotSupported Exception	Thrown when the requested authentication method is not supported.
NoPermissionException	Thrown when an operation is requested for which the client does not have sufficient permission.
NoInitialContextException	Thrown when an initial context cannot be created.
NotContextException	Thrown when a context is required for an operation but the object is not a context.
OperationNotSupportedException	Thrown when an attempt is made to perform an operation that is not supported by the context.
PartialResultException	Thrown to indicate that the result is only a partial result, and the operation cannot be completed.
ReferralException	An abstract class used to represent referral exceptions.
ServiceUnavailableException	Thrown when an attempt is made to communicate with a directory or naming service that is not available.

13

**JAVA NAMING
AND DIRECTORY
INTERFACE (JNDI)**

Bindings

A binding is the association of a name with an object. The association of a filename with the file object, the association of a machine name with an IP address, and even the association between an email address and the target mailbox are all examples of bindings.

Use the Context.bind() method to add a binding to a context. You need to supply the object and its name. For example, to create an object and bind it to the name "Object 1", you would use the following code:

```
// Create a new object
Object object = new Object("1");
// Bind the object and the name "Object 1"
ctx.bind("Object 1", object)
```

Attempting to bind another object to the name `"Object 1"` will result in a `NameAlreadyBoundException` exception being thrown. To reuse the name `"Object 1"`, you need to use `rebind`:

```
// Create a new object
Object object2 = new Object("2");
// Bind the object and the name "Object 1"
ctx.bind("Object 1", object2)
```

This will replace the object referred to by `"Object 1"` with `object2`.

To remove a binding, simply use `unbind`. This method takes the name of the object to be unbound:

```
ctx.unbind("Object 1");
```

To rename an object, use the `rename()` method. This methods requires that you supply the old name and the new name.

```
ctx.rename("Object 1", "Object 2");
```

This renames `"Object 1"` to `"Object 2"`.

As well as manipulating objects, you can also add and remove subcontexts using the `createSubcontext()` and `destroySubcontext()` methods of `Context`.

```
Context result = ctx.createSubcontext("child");
```

The creates a subcontext that is a child of `ctx` called `"child"`. To remove this subcontext, perform the following:

```
ctx.destroySubcontext("child");
```

The `"child"` subcontext will no longer be contained in `ctx`.

References

It may not be possible to contact an object directly in some naming services. Instead, you use a reference. A reference to an object is an object that contains information allowing you to access that object indirectly.

For example, a file on a hard drive is not usually accessed directly but rather through a file handle. Another example is a printer reference, which may contain only the protocol and server name of the printer but not a means to access the printer directly.

The Directory Interface

A directory interface is an extension of a naming interface. A naming interface allows names and objects to be associated through a binding, whereas a directory interface allows you to associate objects and attributes. Thus, in addition to being able to look up an object through its name, you can also look up its attributes or perform searches for objects that contain certain attributes.

In a typical file directory service, for example, you would not only have names and files associated but also the files' attributes such as size and creation time.

To use the directory interface of the JNDI, you will need to import the following from the `javax.naming` and `javax.naming.directory` packages:

```
import javax.naming.Context;
import javax.naming.directory.InitialDirContext;
import javax.naming.directory.DirContext;
import javax.naming.directory.Attributes;
import javax.naming.NamingException;
```

Four concepts form the basis of the Directory Interface

- Directory Objects and Attributes
- Directory Objects as Naming Contexts
- Searches
- Schema

Directory Objects and Attributes

A directory object is an object in a directory and is sometimes referred to as a *directory entity*. A directory object can represent a directory in a file system, a computer on a remote network, a printer, or even a person. Each directory object contains attributes that describe the object it represents.

An attribute is information that is associated with the directory object. Each attribute consists of a attribute identifier and an attribute value. For example, a directory that represents a printer can have attributes such as paper size and resolution. The paper size, for example, might have an attribute identifier `"Page size"` that contains the value `"A4"`.

Creating a directory object is very similar to creating a name object, except that the context you create is a `DirContext` instead of a `Context`. In the following example, you will create a `DirContext` that uses an LDAP server on your local machine instead of a local file system.

```
try
{
 // Create a hashtable
 Hashtable env = new Hashtable();

 // Fill the hashtable with environment properties
 env.put(Context.INITIAL_CONTEXT_FACTORY,
```

```
  "com.sun.jndi.ldap.LdapCtxFactory");

 env.put(Context.PROVIDER_URL, "ldap://localhost");

 // Create the directory context
 DirContext ctx = new InitialDirContext(env);
}
catch (NamingException e)
{
 System.err.println("Error occurred");
}
```

To read the attributes from an object in a directory, you use
`DirContext.getAttributes()`. This method takes the name of the object for which
you want the attributes and returns an `Attribute` object. If you wanted to retrieve the
attributes of an object named `"MyFile"`, you would do the following:

```
Attributes MyAttr = ctx.getAttributes("MyFile");
```

The `Attribute` object can then have its contents enumerated as such:

```
for (NamingEnumeration attrs = MyAttr.getAll(); attrs.hasMore();)
{
 Attribute attr = (Attribute) attrs.next();
 // The attribute ID is retrieved using attr.getID()
 // Now List all values in the attribute
 for (NamingEnumeration val = attr.getAll(); vals.hasMore();)
  System.out.println("value: " + vals.next());
}
```

Attributes and attribute values in a directory can be easily modified. One way to achieve
this is to create a list of modifications and pass it to the `modifyAttributes()` method of
`DirContext`. Each modification is stored in a `ModificationItem` object, which consists
of a numeric value indicating the type of modification to be made and an `Attribute`
describing the modification to make. There are three types of modifications available:

- `ADD_ATTRIBUTE`
- `REPLACE_ATTRIBUTE`
- `REMOVE_ATTRIBUTE`

Modifications are performed in the order in which they are stored in the list.

Suppose you have an object and you want to change the `"Name"` attribute's value from
`"Tom"` to `"Krista"`. Suppose you also want to add a `"email address"` attribute, and
remove the `"phone number"` attribute. Use the following code to perform such a series of
modifications:

```
// Create the list
ModificationItem[] mods = new ModificationItem[3];
```

```
// Modification 1: Replace a value
mods[0] = new ModificationItem(DirContext.REPLACE_ATTRIBUTE,
 new BasicAttribute("Name", "Krista"));

// Modification 2: Add a value
mods[1] = new ModificationItem(DirContext.ADD_ATTRIBUTE,
 new BasicAttribute("email address", "Tom@codeguru.com"));

// Modification 3: Remove a value
mods[2] = new ModificationItem(DirContext.REMOVE_ATTRIBUTE,
 new BasicAttribute("phone number "));

// Perform the modifications on the object
ctx.modifyAttributes(object, mods);
```

As an alternative, you can specify the type of modification you want to make to an object and the attributes to which the modification should be applied. For example, if you want to change certain attributes of an object with the attributes in an `Attributes` object `attrs`, simply call the following:

```
ctx.modifyAttributes(object, DirContext.REPLACE_ATTRIBUTE, attrs);
```

Any attributes in the object that are not specified in the `attrs` object will remain unchanged. Figure 13.2 shows the list of these attributes and their function.

Table 13.2   Attributes and Their Use

Attribute	*Use*
AttributeInUse Exception	Thrown when an attempt to add an already existing attribute is made
AttributeModification Exception	Thrown when an attempt to modify, add or remove an attribute, its values or its identifier contrary to its definition or state is made
InvalidAttribute IdentifierException	Thrown when an attempt is made to add an attribute using an invalid identifier
InvalidAttributes Exception	Thrown when an attempt to add or modify an attribute set is made, and that attribute set is specified incorrectly or is incomplete
InvalidAttribute ValueException	Thrown when an attempt to add an attribute value is made that is contrary to its definition
InvalidSearch ControlsException	Thrown when the specified `SearchControls` for a search is invalid

continues

Table 13.2   continued

Attribute	Use
InvalidSearch FilterException	Thrown when a specified search filter is invalid
NoSuchAttribute	Thrown when an attempt is made to access a non-existent Exception attribute
SchemaViolation Exception	Thrown when an operation is requested that will violate the schema

The `javax.naming.directory` package also contains a number of exception classes, all derived from `NamingException`.

Directory Objects as Naming Contexts

Directory objects are often arranged in a tree or hierarchical structure. For example, the typical file system has directories and subdirectories arranged in a strict hierarchy. In this case, the file system contains directories of files, which in turn contain files and subdirectories. When directory objects are arranged in this manner, they assume the role of being a naming context in addition to their role of attribute containers.

Searches

As in a naming object, you can look up a directory object by specifying the object's name. However, because a directory object also contains attributes, there is scope to perform a search for an object or objects that contain the attribute or attributes specified. This is called a *search*, and the query specifying the conditions of the search is called the *search filter*. For example, in an LDAP directory context containing information on employees, you may want to search for all employees with the surname "Smith" and an ID with any value. To perform this search, you create a list of required attributes and pass these to the `search()` method:

A simple form of search is where you specify a set of attributes to be matched in the search:

```
// The "true" in the BasicAttributes constructor means the search
// will be case-insensitive
Attributes attrs = new BasicAttributes(true);
attrs.put(new BasicAttribute("sn", "Smith"));
attrs.put(new BasicAttribute("id"));

// Search for objects with those matching attributes
NamingEnumeration matches = ctx.search("ou=Employees", attrs);
```

You can then print the results as follows:

```
while (matches.hasMore())
{
 SearchResult result = (SearchResult) matches.next();
 System.out.println(">>>" + result.getName());
}
```

You can also select the attributes returned by the search by passing the `search()` method an array of attribute identifiers you want to receive from the operation. You simply create an array of attribute identifiers and then call `search()`:

```
String[] attrIDs = {"sn", "id", "cn", "mail"};
NamingEnumeration matches =
 ctx.search("ou=Employees", attrs, attrIDs);
```

An alternate method to specifying a list of desired attributes is to create a search filter. This is analogous to performing a search in a file directory system, such as searching for all files ending in `.txt` using the directory search filter `*.txt`.

The syntax of a search filter for the `DirContext.search()` method is laid out in RFC2254 (`ftp://ftp.isi.edu/in-notes/rfc2254.txt`). To create a search filter equivalent to the previous attribute list example, you would specify the search filter

```
(&(sn=Smith)(id=*))
```

To perform a search, you also need to supply a `SearchControls` object, which will be discussed later in this chapter. For the moment, use a default `SearchControls` object.

To use this filter, use the following code:

```
// Create a search controls object.
SearchControls ctls = new SearchControls();

// Construct the filter
String filter = "(&(sn=Smith)(id=*))";

// Search for objects
NamingEnumeration results =
 ctx.search("ou=Employees", filter, ctls);
```

The `SearchControls` object is used to specify which attributes will be returned by the search. The previous example returned all attributes, but if you want to narrow this down to a select few, use the `SearchControls.setReturningAttributes()` method. To do this, you create an array of attribute identifiers that you want to have returned in the result. For example:

```
// Specify the identifiers of the attributes to return
String[] attrIDs = {"sn", "id", "cn", "mail"};
```

```
// Create a search controls object.
SearchControls ctls = new SearchControls();

// Set the Search control identifier list
ctls.setReturningAttributes(attrIDs);

// Construct the filter
String filter = "(&(sn=Smith)(id=*))";

// Search for objects
NamingEnumeration results =
 ctx.search("ou=Employees", filter, ctls);
```

This is equivalent to the list of string identifiers you used in the example that used a `BasicAttributes` list.

The `SearchControl` object also has a `setSearchScope()` method that allows you to specify the search scope. The available values that can be set are

- `ONELEVEL_SCOPE`
- `SUBTREE_SCOPE`
- `OBJECT_SCOPE`

`ONELEVEL_SCOPE` is the default and searches a single level of the directory. `SUBTREE_SCOPE` allows you to search an object and all its descendants. `OBJECT_SCOPE` searches a single object and is useful in testing whether or not an object has a particular attribute.

For example, to perform the search in the previous example and extend it to all subtrees, you would do the following:

```
// Create a search controls object and set the attribute IDs.
String[] attrIDs = {"sn", "id", "cn", "mail"};
SearchControls ctls = new SearchControls();
ctls.setReturningAttributes(attrIDs);

// Set the search scope
ctls.setSearchScope(SearchControls.SUBTREE_SCOPE);

// Search for objects
String filter = "(&(sn=Smith)(id=*))";

NamingEnumeration results =
 ctx.search("ou=Employees", filter, ctls);
```

Another option is to limit the number of results the search returns. To do this, use the `SearchControls.setCountLimit()` method.

```
// Set search controls to limit count to 1
SearchControls ctls = new SearchControls();
ctls.setCountLimit(100);
```

If the number of results returned would otherwise be larger than the count limit, a `SizeLimitExceededException` exception will be thrown, but only the specified number of objects will be returned.

One final limitation that can be imposed on the search is to set a time limit using the `SearchControls.setTimeLimit()` method. You pass the number of milliseconds to which the search time should be restricted:

```
// Set search controls to limit time to 5 second (5000 ms)
SearchControls ctls = new SearchControls();
ctls.setTimeLimit(5000);
```

If the operation takes longer than the specified number of milliseconds, a `TimeLimitExceededException` exception is thrown and the search is terminated.

Schema

The Schema is used to specify the types of objects a directory may contain and the mandatory and optional attributes that each different type of directory object must have. It can also specify the structure of the namespace and the relationship between different types of objects.

Summary

In this chapter you learned about Java's Naming and Directory Interface (JNDI) and how it can be used with any directory service implementation. The naming interface allows you to store and retrieve objects by associating a human readable name with an object. The directory interface extends this concept to include attributes and provides the means to conduct searches based on search filters and attribute lists.

Now that you understand the concepts and the main interfaces behind JNDI, you can use the techniques on a directory service, be it a local hard drive or an Internet-wide domain.

13

JAVA NAMING AND DIRECTORY INTERFACE (JNDI)

Enterprise and Data

PART

IV

Java Database Connectivity (JDBC)

All source code for this chapter can be found on the Sams Publishing Website at http://www.mcp.com/info/0-672/0-672-31424-x.

This chapter shows you how to use the Java Database Connectivity (JDBC) classes. Besides learning the underlying principles, you'll see some practical examples.

JDBC is the standard 100 percent Java application programming interface (API) used to access and retrieve data from a multitude of existing databases. No matter what database you're accessing through JDBC, you use Structured Query Language (SQL) statements, the standard relational database language, to carry out the interaction.

Comparing JDBC and ODBC

JDBC may sound familiar to you if you've worked with ODBC. ODBC, or Open Database Connectivity, is a Microsoft standard API that provides access to a multitude of existing databases. Like ODBC, JDBC is based on the X/Open SQL Call Level Interface (X/Open SQL CLI). However, ODBC is a C or C++ API, using a lot of pointers, and it is mostly Microsoft Windows-platform specific. In contrast, JDBC is a pure Java API and it works on any platform running the Java Virtual Machine (JVM). JDBC is also an object-oriented API, so it is easier to learn and implement than the ODBC API.

JDBC Supported Drivers

You can access nearly any database through the JDBC API including Microsoft Access, Informix, InterBase, Microsoft SQL Server, Oracle, Paradox, Sybase, and xBase. JDBC provides this broad database support through four types of connectivity:

- *JDBC-ODBC Bridge*—The JDBC-ODBC bridge, a driver provided in the Java Development Kit (JDK), allows existing ODBC drivers to be used through the JDBC API. However, this is not the best solution for using existing databases through the JDBC API because it requires the installation of ODBC drivers and client libraries. ODBC drivers are implemented natively, which compromises cross-platform support. There's a significant maintenance and distribution problem with using the JDBC/ODBC Bridge. Because alternative methods exist, one would most likely not want to roll out and maintain ODBC drivers on the client. Besides, this only works on the Windows platform.

Note

The JDBC-ODBC Bridge is a 32-bit Windows specific driver.

- *Native API to Java*—Native API to Java drivers translate JDBC API calls to database management systems (DBMSs) into native API calls to DBMSs. This type of connectivity requires native code on the client machine. However, if you are developing for a particular platform only, native API to Java drivers may provide some performance enhancements over the other database connection alternatives. Another danger is that this approach may lock you into a proprietary database.

- *Neutral Network Protocol*—Neutral Network Protocol drivers use DBMS-neutral network protocols to translate JDBC API calls into native DBMS API calls. This kind of driver is typically used with middleware, such as CORBA, to facilitate access from pure Java clients to DBMS servers and may be provided as part of the middleware package.

- *Native Network Protocol*—Native Network Protocol drivers translate JDBC API calls into DMBS-proprietary network protocol calls that the DMBS can use directly. This kind of driver is typically used for Intranet access and, being DMBS-proprietary, is obtained from the database vendor. Drivers created using the Native Network Protocol are 100 percent Java.

The Neutral Network and Native Network Protocol driver solutions are recommended as the preferred ways to access databases through the JDBC API. However, the JDBC-ODBC Bridge is probably one of the most commonly used solutions because the bridge is included in the Java Development Kit (JDK) and a large proportion of databases provide ODBC drivers.

Tip

For the latest information from Sun regarding JDBC drivers, connect with `http://java.sun.com/products/jdbc/`.

14

JAVA DATABASE CONNNECTIVITY (JDBC)

Using the JDBC-ODBC Bridge

The JDBC-ODBC Bridge is provided with the Java Development Kit (JDK), so it's readily available to all Java developers. Several products provide the option to install ODBC drivers including most Microsoft applications, such as Microsoft Office and Microsoft Access, and most other major software packages.

> **Tip**
>
> ODBC is most commonly used on Windows client platforms. If you're using another client platform, you might need to use a different connection protocol. Keep in mind that an ODBC Windows client can connect to non-Windows database servers.

After you've installed an ODBC driver on your machine, you can configure the drivers through the ODBC applet available on Windows platforms through the Control Panel, as shown in Figure 14.1.

FIGURE 14.1

The ODBC (32bit) icon displays in the Windows platform Control Panel.

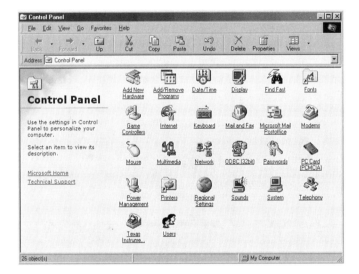

Setting Up an ODBC Driver

Configure your ODBC drivers after you've installed them on your computer. On the Windows platform, open the Control Panel and click (or double-click) the ODBC (32bit) icon to activate the ODBC Data Source Administrator, as shown in Figure 14.2.

> **Tip**
>
> The examples on how to set up ODBC drivers are shown using the Windows platform. The ODBC Data Source Administrator icon is labeled ODBC (32bit) in Windows 95 and Windows 98 and is labeled ODBC in Windows NT. Setup procedures are similar on other platforms.

FIGURE 14.2

Add, remove, and configure ODBC drivers through the User DSN page of the ODBC Data Source Administrator dialog box.

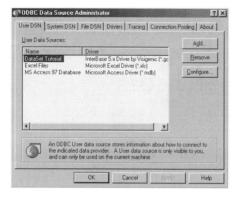

Click the User DSN tab to display the User DSN page of the ODBC Data Source Administrator dialog box if it isn't displayed already. Some ODBC drivers may already appear in the User Data Sources list, depending on the software you've installed on your computer and the options you selected during installation.

In this section, you create a simple text database and use an ODBC driver that accesses databases saved in text files, the Microsoft Text Driver. Click the Add button on the User DSN page of the ODBC Data Source Administrator dialog box. The Create New Data Source dialog box appears, as shown in Figure 14.3.

FIGURE 14.3

Select from the available ODBC drivers through the ODBC New Data Source dialog box.

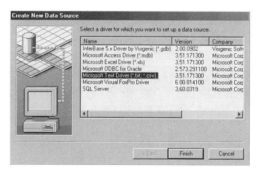

The ODBC drivers available through the ODBC New Data Source dialog box depend on the drivers that you installed on your computer. Select the Microsoft Text Driver, or a similar ODBC text driver, from the driver list and click the Finish button. The ODBC Text Setup dialog box appears, as shown in Figure 14.4.

Configure the text driver to look in a particular folder for text files with specified extensions (for instance, .txt). Type **Text Files** into the Data Source Name to indicate that the driver works with any text file. Then set the driver so that it looks in the folder where

14

JAVA DATABASE
CONNNECTIVITY
(JDBC)

the database text files reside. This example assumes that two database text files, `artists.txt` and `plants.txt`, are in the `database` folder on the C: drive. However, you can use any database text files, any folder, and any disk drive that you want.

Tip

The `artists.txt` and `plants.txt` files can be found in the JavaBeans Unleashed section on www.mcp.com. The `artists.txt` file is a database of 20th century artists listing the artist's name, medium that he worked in, nationality, and date of birth and death. The `plants.txt` file is a database of native plants of North America listing the plant's common name, its native region, and a common visitor to the plant.

Clear the Use Current Directory check box in the Database area of the ODBC Text Setup dialog box to activate the Select Directory button. Then click the Select Directory button and the Select Directory dialog box appears, as shown in Figure 14.5.

Tip

You can select folders on other computers across a network from the Select Directory dialog box by clicking the Network button.

Select the folder containing your database files. Click the OK button to return to the ODBC Text Setup dialog box.

You can define the file extensions so that the text driver recognizes through the ODBC Text Setup dialog box. Click the Options button and the files area appears, as shown in Figure 14.6.

FIGURE 14.6

Add and remove the file extensions that are recognized by the driver through the ODBC Text Setup dialog box.

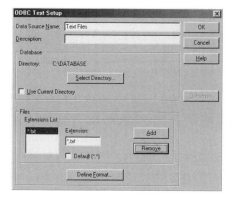

Click the OK button to return to the User DSN page of the ODBC Data Source Administrator dialog box. The Microsoft Text Driver should be added to the User Data Sources list, as shown in Figure 14.7.

FIGURE 14.7

The Microsoft Text Driver is added to the User Data Sources list on the User DSN page of the ODBC Data Source Administrator dialog box.

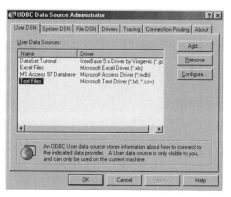

14

JAVA DATABASE CONNNECTIVITY (JDBC)

Click the OK button and the ODBC Data Source Administrator dialog box closes. You're finished configuring the Microsoft Text Driver. You configure other ODBC drivers in much the same way.

Retrieving Data Using JDBC

Retrieve data through the JDBC API by implementing the following three steps:

1. Obtain a driver and establish a connection to a database.

2. Send an SQL statement to the database and retrieve data.

3. Assign the data returned from the database to local variables.

The following sections introduce methods you can use to implement each of the three steps used to retrieve data through the JDBC API while you write an example bean, the DatabaseAccess bean, shown in Listing 14.1.

> **Tip**
>
> The DataAccess bean is hard coded to use a JDBC-ODBC Bridge text driver configured with the directory selected containing the database text files. See the previous section, "Setting Up an ODBC Driver," for more information.

Listing 14.1   Source code for DatabaseAccess.java

```java
package sams.jdbc;

import java.awt.BorderLayout;
import java.awt.Font;
import java.awt.GridLayout;
import java.awt.Label;
import java.awt.Panel;
import java.awt.TextArea;
import java.awt.TextField;
import java.awt.event.ActionEvent;
import java.awt.event.ActionListener;
import java.sql.Connection;
import java.sql.DriverManager;
import java.sql.ResultSet;
import java.sql.ResultSetMetaData;
import java.sql.SQLException;
import java.sql.Statement;

public class DatabaseAccess extends Panel {
  private static final String DATA_SOURCE = "jdbc:odbc:Text Files";
  private TextField query = new TextField( );
  private TextArea result = new TextArea(  );
  private Connection connection = null;

  public DatabaseAccess( ) {
    setLayout( new BorderLayout( ) );
    Panel childPanel = new Panel( );
    add( childPanel, BorderLayout.NORTH );
    add( result, BorderLayout.CENTER );
```

```
    childPanel.setLayout( new GridLayout( 0, 1 ) );
    childPanel.add( new Label( "Query:" ) );
    childPanel.add( query );
    childPanel.add( new Label( "Result:" ) );
    result.setEditable( false );
    Font font = new Font( "Monospaced", Font.PLAIN, 12 );
    query.setFont( font );
    result.setFont( font );
    query.addActionListener( new QueryHandler( ) );
    try {
      Class.forName( "sun.jdbc.odbc.JdbcOdbcDriver" );
      connection = DriverManager.getConnection( DATA_SOURCE );
    }
    catch ( ClassNotFoundException cnfe ) {
      System.out.println( cnfe.toString( ) );
    }
    catch ( SQLException sqle ) {
      System.out.println( sqle.toString( ) );
    }
  }

  class QueryHandler implements ActionListener {
    public void actionPerformed( ActionEvent evt ) {
      try {
        Statement statement = connection.createStatement( );
        ResultSet resultset = statement.executeQuery( query.getText( ) );
        displayResult( resultset );
        statement.close( );
      }
      catch ( SQLException sqle ) {
        System.out.println( sqle.toString( ) );
      }
    }
    public void displayResult( ResultSet resultset ) {
      try {
        ResultSetMetaData resultsetMetaData = resultset.getMetaData( );
        int cols = resultsetMetaData.getColumnCount( );
        result.setText( "" );
        while ( resultset.next( ) ) {
          for ( int i = 1; i <= cols; i++ ) {
            String text = resultset.getString( i );
            if ( text == null )
              text = "";
            result.append( text + ":" );
          }
          result.append( "\n" );
        }
        resultset.close( );
      }
      catch ( SQLException sqle ) {
        System.out.println( sqle.toString( ) );
      }
    }
  }
}
```

14

JAVA DATABASE
CONNECTIVITY
(JDBC)

Package the `DatabaseAccess` bean into a JAR file using the manifest file shown in Listing 14.2. Enter the following command at your console or DOS window prompt:

```
jar -cmf databaseaccess.man databaseaccess.jar sams\jdbc
```

Listing 14.2   Source code for `databaseaccess.man`

```
Name: sams/jdbc/DatabaseAccess.class
Java-Bean: True
```

Type query statements into the `DatabaseAccess` bean's Query text field, such as **Select * From artists.txt**. Individual text files are considered tables when using text file databases. When you enter the query, you should see the result in the Result text area (see Figure 14.8).

FIGURE 14.8

The DatabaseAccess *bean displays a query result.*

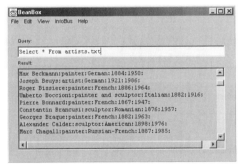

Obtain a Driver and Establish a Connection

Typically, your bean obtains a database driver through the `java.sql.DriverManager` class. This class contains a number of methods for managing, registering, and de-registering drivers. However, most of the time, you only need to call the `getConnection()` method, and the `DriverManager` object automatically loads the appropriate driver for the requested database. Table 14.1 provides a summary of the key methods defined in the `java.sql.DriverManager` class.

Table 14.1   `java.sql.DriverManager` Class Methods

Method Signature	Summary
deregisterDriver (Driver)	Removes the specified object implementing the `java.sql.Driver` interface from the `DriverManager` object's list of registered drivers
getConnection(String)	Returns an object implementing the `java.sql.Connection` interface, which encapsulates a connection to the database located at the URL encapsulated in the `String` object passed to the method

Method Signature	Summary
getConnection (String, Properties)	Returns an object implementing the java.sql.Connection interface that encapsulates a connection to the database located at the URL encapsulated by the String object passed to the method, with the connection properties encapsulated in the Properties object
getConnection(String, String, String)	Returns an object implementing the java.sql.Connection interface that encapsulates a connection to the database located at the URL encapsulated by the first String object passed to the method and logs in using the login encapsulated in the second String object and the password encapsulated in the third String object
getDrivers()	Returns an object implementing the java.util.Enumeration interface that encapsulates a list of the available drivers
registerDriver(Driver)	Adds the object implementing the java.sql.Driver interface that is passed to the method to the DriverManager object's registered drivers list

The registerDriver() and deregisterDriver() methods allow the calling class to add or delete drivers from the class loader's driver object list. The getDrivers() method returns a list of all the drivers available to the calling class.

The overloaded getConnection() method gives you several ways to establish a connection, all three requiring the use of a URL. The URL syntax for accessing databases through JDBC probably looks a bit different than what you're used to seeing. The following is the basic format:

protocol:subprotocol:subname

In a typical URL, the most common protocols are http: and ftp: and subnames usually look like //www.microsoft.com or //www.javasoft.com. A subprotocol isn't normally used. In contrast, when using JDBC, the protocol is jdbc:; a subprotocol is used, which represents a particular type of database mechanism; and the subname is the information actually used to connect to the database. To use the getConnection() method, you pass the appropriate URL as a String object to the method's url parameter.

The DatabaseAccess bean loads the JDBC-ODBC driver, the driver for the JDBC-ODBC bridge, and then opens a connection to the Text Files database. Load the JDBC-ODBC driver using the java.lang.Class class forName() method as shown in the following statement:

```
Class.forName( "sun.jdbc.odbc.JdbcOdbcDriver" );
```

14

JAVA DATABASE CONNECTIVITY (JDBC)

The JDBC-ODBC driver is instantiated from the `sun.jdbc.odbc.JdbcOdbcDriver` class, which is part of the core Java platform. The `java.lang.Class` class `forName()` method throws a `ClassNotFoundException` exception object if the method is unable to find the class passed to it.

After the JDBC-ODBC driver is loaded, the `DatabaseAccess` bean obtains the text file database driver by passing the `DATA_SOURCE` string constant to the `java.sql.DataManager` class's `getConnection()` method, as shown in the following statement:

```
connection = DriverManager.getConnection( DATA_SOURCE );
```

The `DATA_SOURCE` constant value is `"jdbc:odbc:Text Files"`. The `getConnection()` method throws an `SQLException` exception object if it is unable to create a connection with the database. Otherwise, once you've made a successful connection, an object implementing the `java.sql.Connection` interface is returned. In the `DatabaseAccess` bean, this object is assigned to the `connection` variable.

The `java.sql.Connection` Interface

When a bean opens a connection to a database, an object implementing the `java.sql.Connection` interface represents the connection. Classes that implement the `java.sql.Connection` interface can override methods that lock tables, commit and roll back changes, and close connections. Table 14.2 summarizes some of the `java.sql.Connection` interfaces more commonly overridden methods.

Table 14.2 `java.sql.Connection` Interface Methods

Method Signature	Summary
`close()`	Immediately closes a connection and releases JDBC resources.
`commit()`	Permanently updates the table with all modifications made since the last commit or rollback. It also releases connection locks on database.
`createStatement()`	Returns a new object implementing the `java.sql.Statement` interface that is used to send SQL statements to the database.
`getAutoCommit()`	Returns `true` if the connection is in auto-commit mode, otherwise `false` is returned.
`getMetaData()`	Returns an object implementing the `java.sql.DatabaseMetaData` interface that contains information about the tables, stored procedures, and supported SQL grammar for the current connection database.
`isClosed()`	Returns `true` if the connection is closed, otherwise `false` is returned.
`prepareCall (String)`	Returns a new object implementing the `java.sql.CallableStatement` interface. The object encapsulates a precompiled version of the SQL statement passed to this method as a `String` object.

Method Signature	Summary
prepareStatement (String)	Returns a new object implementing the java.sql.PreparedStatement interface. The object encapsulates a precompiled version of the SQL statement passed to this method as a String object.
rollback()	Drops all modifications made since the last commit or rollback. It also releases connection locks.
setAutoCommit (boolean)	Pass the boolean argument true to put the connection into auto-commit mode, otherwise pass false to disable the connection's auto-commit mode.

You can use the isClosed() method to determine whether the connection is still open. If it is, you can use the Close() method to immediately release the connection.

The getMetaData() method returns all the information that is available about the properties of the current connection's database in an object implementing the java.sql.DatabaseMetaData interface. This information can include a list of the database's stored procedures, the SQL grammar that it supports, access rights for table columns, primary and foreign keys, indexes, the database product name and version number, the driver version number, schema, and literally dozens of pieces of information about the database itself.

What comprises a transaction depends on the state of the auto-commit mode. By default, the auto-commit mode is set to true, which means that each statement is a transaction that will get committed as soon as the statement is executed. If the auto-commit mode is set to false, all statements since the last commit or rollback are grouped together into a single transaction.

The getAutoCommit() method tells you whether or not the connection is set to auto-commit mode. To group statements, pass a false value to the setAutoCommit() method and use the commit() and rollback() methods to manage the transactions.

The createStatement() method creates a new object implementing the java.sql.Statement interface. The prepareCall() and prepareStatement() methods create objects implementing the java.sql.CallableStatement and java.sql.PreparedStatement interfaces, respectively. These objects are used to store precompiled SQL statements, which can then be executed through the connection. JDBC statements form the core of database transactions.

Send an SQL Statement and Retrieve Data

When you enter a query into the `DatabaseAccess` bean, it gets compiled and packaged and sent out to the database. This is accomplished through a sequence of events enabled through the registration of the `QueryHandler` inner class as a listener to query text field action events. When you enter a query into the Query text field, the text field creates an `ActionEvent` object. The `QueryHandler` object receives the `ActionEvent` object, which results in the execution of its `actionPerformed()` method.

The `QueryHandler` inner class `actionPerformed()` method includes two statements that create and send SQL statements to the database. The first statement, shown next, calls the `java.sql.Connection` class's `createStatement()` method to create an object that implements the `java.sql.Statement` interface.

```
Statement statement = connection.createStatement( );
```

The object returned from the `createStatement()` method and assigned to the `statement` variable is ready for sending an SQL statement to the database that is connected through the `Connection` object assigned to the `connection` variable. The `createStatement()` method throws an `SQLException` object if a database access error occurs.

The `java.sql.Statement` Interface

You can handle and execute several types of SQL statements through objects that implement the `java.sql.Statement` interface. Table 14.3 summarizes some of this interface's more commonly overridden methods.

> **Note**
>
> An SQL (Structured Query Language) statement is the actual instruction that enables you to communicate with the database.

Table 14.3   `java.sql.Statement` Interface Methods

Method Signature	Summary
cancel()	Cancels this `Statement` object if the DBMS and driver both support aborting an SQL statement.
close()	Provides a way to close the connection and immediately release JDBC resources.

Method Signature	Summary
execute(String)	Executes the SQL statement encapsulated in the String object passed to the method. Returns true if the result is an object implementing the java.sql.ResultSet interface and false if the result is an update count or there is no result.
executeQuery(String)	Executes the SQL statement encapsulated in the String object passed to the method. Returns an object implementing the java.sql.ResultSet interface that encapsulates the query results.
executeUpdate(String)	Executes the SQL UPDATE, INSERT, DELETE, or no-return statement (such as the SQL DDL statements) encapsulated by the String object passed to the method. Returns an int value representing the number of rows that were affected or 0 for no-return statements.
getMoreResults()	Move to the next result in an object implementing the java.sql.Statement interface. Returns a true value if the next result is an object implementing the java.sql.ResultSet interface and false value if it's an update count or there are no more results.
getQueryTimeout()	Returns an integer value representing the number of seconds the object implementing the java.sql.Driver interface (the driver) will wait for a SQL statement to execute.
getResultSet()	Returns an object implementing the java.sql.ResultSet interface if there are current results. Otherwise, if the result is an update count or there are no more results, null is returned.
setCursorName(String)	Sets the identifier of the current row (set by an SQL UPDATE or DELETE statement) to the value encapsulated by String object passed to the method.
setQueryTimeout(int)	Sets the number of seconds the object implementing the java.sql.Driver interface (the driver) will wait for a SQL statement to execute to the integer value passed to the method.

14

JAVA DATABASE
CONNECTIVITY
(JDBC)

In the DatabaseAccess bean, the query typed into the Query text field is retrieved by the TextField object assigned to the query variable by calling the getText() method. The text is passed to the java.sql.Statement class's executeQuery() method, as is shown in the following statement:

```
ResultSet resultset = statement.executeQuery( query.getText( ) );
```

The executeQuery() method returns an object that implements the java.sql.ResultSet interface and encapsulates the results of the database query.

The `java.sql.CallableStatement` and `java.sql.PreparedStatement` Interfaces

In addition to the `java.sql.Statement` interface, there are two other interfaces to be considered when sending an SQL statement to retrieve data from a database: the `java.sql.CallableStatement` and `java.sql.PreparedStatement` interfaces. The `java.sql.CallableStatement` interface extends the `java.sql.PreparedStatement` interface that, in turn, extends the `java.sql.Statement` interface. Each interface provides abstract methods specific to the types of SQL statements that it handles.

The `java.sql.CallableStatement` interface is usually implemented by an object that encapsulates a precompiled stored procedure statement that must be used with stored database procedures containing `OUT` or `INOUT` parameters.

Use an object implementing the `java.sql.PreparedStatement` interface when you want to precompile a simple SQL statement to execute it multiple times or when the SQL statement has `IN` parameters and has to be precompiled. This provides an efficient way of calling the precompiled statement.

Assign the Returned Data

A SQL query to a database results in the return of an object encapsulating the results and implementing the `java.sql.ResultSet` interface. This interface provides several methods for the manipulation and display of returned.

The `java.sql.ResultSet` Interface

The `java.sql.ResultSet` interface provides abstract methods used to control access to row results returned from databases after executing an SQL statement. Table 14.4 summarizes some of the key methods provided by the `java.sql.ResultSet` interface.

Table 14.4   `java.sql.ResultSet` Abstract Methods

Method Signature	Summary
`close()`	Provides a way to immediately close the object's associated database connection and release its JDBC resources.
`findColumn(String)`	Returns an integer value representing the column index corresponding to the column name encapsulated in the `String` object passed to the method.
`getAsciiStream(int)`	Returns an `InputStream` object encapsulating the ASCII values in the `LONGVARCHAR` value from the current row. The `int` value passed to the method represents the column index.

Method Signature	Summary
getAsciiStream (String)	Returns an `InputStream` object encapsulating the ASCII values in the `LONGVARCHAR` value from the current row. The `String` object passed to the method encapsulates the column name.
getBinaryStream(int)	Returns an `InputStream` object encapsulating the ASCII values in the `LONGVARBINARY` value from the current row. The `int` value passed to the method represents the column index.
getBinaryStream (String)	Returns an `InputStream` object containing the ASCII values in the `LONGVARBINARY` value from the current row. The `String` object passed to the method encapsulates the column name.
getCursorName()	Returns a `String` object encapsulating the identifier of the current row (set by a SQL `UPDATE` or `DELETE` statement).
getMetaData()	Returns an object implementing the `java.sql.ResultSetMetaData` interface that encapsulates the number of columns, data types, and other properties of the rows in the current object implementing the `java.sql.ResultSet` interface.
getXxxx(int)	Returns a data type represented by `Xxxx` (for example, `int`, `long`, `java.lang.String`, `java.lang.Object`, and so on) containing the value in the current row. The `int` value passed to the method represents the column index.
getXxxx(String)	Returns a data type represented by `Xxxx` (for example, `int`, `long`, `java.lang.String`, `java.lang.Object`, and so on) containing the value in the current row. The `String` object passed to the method encapsulates the column name.
next()	Returns `true` if the next row is a valid row and `false` if there are no more rows.
wasNull()	Returns `true` if the value just read was `null`, otherwise `false` is returned.

There are two `getXxxx()` methods for each Java type, one that uses a column index and one that uses a column name. For example, to get a `String` object from the second column of the current row, you would use the following statement:

```
getString( 2 );
```

This statement returns the value in that field encapsulated in a `String` object. To get a character value from the column named `Gender`, you would use the following statement:

```
getChar( Gender );
```

The `findColumn()` method returns the column number associated with the specified column name.

> **Caution**
>
> SQL indexes begin at 1, unlike Java indexes that begin at 0. Also unlike Java, SQL column names are not case sensitive. If you use column names to access fields in the current row, there may be more than one column with the same name due to case-insensitivity. If that happens, the first matching column name is used.

The cursor in an object implementing the `java.sql.ResultSet` interface is positioned just before the first row when the object is created. To iterate the cursor through the object, call the `next()` method. Before attempting to read the data in the row, however, you should test the value returned from the `next()` method to see whether you have landed on a valid row or if there are no more rows left to examine.

The `java.sql.ResultSet` interface's `getMetaData()` method returns an object implementing the `java.sql.ResultSetMetaData` interface that encapsulates information about the object implementing the `java.sql.ResultSet` interface. It also returns information about individual columns (fields) such as the name, label (for headers), maximum width, data types, precision (decimal digits), scale (decimal points), and other pertinent information.

The `displayResult()` method in the `QueryHandler` inner class does all of the handling of the `DatabaseAccess` bean's returned data. In the first statement, shown next, the `java.sql.ResultSet` interface's `getMetaData()` method is called to retrieve an object implementing the `java.sql.ResultSetMetaData` interface.

```
ResultSetMetaData resultsetMetaData = resultset.getMetaData( );
```

The object assigned to the `resultsetMetaData` variable encapsulates detailed information about the returned data that you need for display such as the number of columns of data. The next statement, shown next, calls the `java.sql.ResultSetMetaData` interface's `getColumnCount()` method to get a count of the number of columns of data and assign it to the `cols` variable.

```
int cols = resultsetMetaData.getColumnCount( );
```

The remainder of the code, shown next, sends the data to the `TextArea` object assigned to the `result` variable and displays it in a readable format.

```
result.setText( "" );
while ( resultset.next( ) ) {
  for ( int i = 1; i <= cols; i++ ) {
    String text = resultset.getString( i );
    if ( text == null )
      text = "";
    result.append( text + ":" );
  }
```

```
    result.append( "\n" );
}
resultset.close( );
```

The first statement sets the TextArea object's text property to an empty string. Then the code enters a while loop that calls the java.sql.ResultSet interface's next() method to sequentially move through the data returned from the database. The conditional is true as long as there is another row of data in the data set.

Inside the while loop is the for loop. The for loop iterates through the columns in each row. Then each data item is retrieved using the java.sql.ResultSet interface's getString() method and assigned to the text variable. If null is assigned to the text variable, it is reassigned an empty string. The final statement in the for loop adds a colon (:) to the end of the output of a single data field and outputs it to the DatabaseAccess bean's text area. A new line is started with a call to the last statement in the while loop after each row of data is output.

After all of the data returned from the database is displayed, the object implementing the java.sql.ResultSet interface is closed by a call to the close() method.

Mapping Data Types

Data types specific to SQL need to be mapped to Java data types so that your Java component is able to handle them. Mapping between SQL and Java data types falls into three categories:

- *SQL data types that have direct equivalents in Java*—These data types can be directly assigned to Java data types. For example, an SQL INTEGER is a direct equivalent of the Java int data type.

- *SQL data types that can be converted to an equivalent Java data type*—For example, the SQL CHAR, VARCHAR, and LONGVARCHAR data types can all be converted to the Java java.lang.String class data type. It isn't necessary for Java to have a distinct data type for every SQL data type.

- *Unique SQL data types that require the creation of special Java data objects*—Special classes are created to accommodate unique SQL data types. For example, the SQL DATE is converted to an object created from the Java java.sql.Date class, which is defined especially for this purpose.

14

JAVA DATABASE
CONNECTIVITY
(JDBC)

Caution

Don't confuse the java.sql.Date class used for converting SQL DATE information with the java.util.Date class that is typically used in Java to handle dates. A java.util.Date object will *not* accept a SQL DATE field.

The SQL DECIMAL and NUMERIC data types need to be converted using a special class because absolute precision is necessary (as in dealing with currency values). The JDBC API includes the java.sql.Numeric class, which enables you to convert the SQL DECIMAL and NUMERIC values to Java.

The SQL DATE data type consists of day, month, and year; TIME is hours, minutes, and seconds; TIMESTAMP combines DATE and TIME and adds a nanosecond field. The java.sql.Date class handles the SQL DATE and TIME values. The java.sql.Timestamp class handles the SQL TIMESTAMP data type.

Summary

In this chapter, you learned how to use JDBC, a 100 percent Java API, to connect with and use databases from your JavaBeans components. JDBC, part of the core Java platform, enables you to interact with most existing databases using the standard database language, SQL. The Java platform includes the JDBC-ODBC Bridge that allows you to access databases with ODBC drivers through the JDBC API. You learned how to create beans that read and write database tables through the JDBC-ODBC Bridge. You also learned how to access and display result sets. The JDBC API is indispensable for programming database-aware Java beans for the Enterprise.

CHAPTER 15

InfoBus

The InfoBus enables dynamic exchange of data between two or more JavaBeans. It does this by defining a small number of interfaces that are used between cooperating beans. The InfoBus also defines the protocol for use of those interfaces. These protocols are based on a notion of an information bus, hence the name "InfoBus." All components that implement these interfaces can exchange information with any other InfoBus-enabled component in a structured manner. Simple items such as strings and numbers, as well as complex items such as lists, arrays, and tables, can all be passed via the InfoBus.

In this chapter, you will learn about this new and exciting technology and how to use it in an example involving multiple Java beans. To reinforce what you learn, you will also see a demonstration involving three different components (all of which exchange data using the InfoBus).

Overview of the InfoBus Architecture

The InfoBus is itself a Java API, jointly created by Lotus Development Corporation and Sun Microsystems' JavaSoft division, that allows cooperating JavaBeans to communicate data to one another. These Beans can be located in a Java application or even on a Web page. In InfoBus parlance, there are three main terms (and roles) to keep in mind: data producers, data consumers, and data controllers. Here's a brief description of each of these terms:

- *Data producers*—Data producers are Beans whose primary function is to access data from their native store, such as a DBMS, spreadsheet, flat file, Lotus Notes database, and so on, and to offer data onto the InfoBus. These components respond to requests for data from data consumers (explained next).

- *Data consumers*—Data consumers retrieve data from the bus for analysis or visual display. This segregation of producer from consumer is extremely powerful in that it enables applications to be independent of their data; for example, a charting bean need not understand SQL or JDBC in order to access DBMS data. Data consumers are interested in hearing about any new data sets that enters the environment (provided by the data producers).

- *Data controllers*—You can think of the data controller as a kind of InfoBus "traffic cop." A data controller is an *optional component* that regulates or redirects the flow of events between data producers and consumers.

One important fact to mention here is that a JavaBean can be both a consumer and producers. As an example, consider a spreadsheet JavaBean. A spreadsheet might read data from a DBMS (database management system) and expose—or provide—that data to other JavaBeans (such as a chart JavaBean) via the InfoBus.

Therefore, InfoBus interfaces allow application designers to create "data flows" between cooperating components. In contrast to an event/response model where the semantics of an interaction depend on understanding an applet-specific event and responding to that event with applet-specific callbacks, the InfoBus interfaces have very few events and an invariant set of method calls for all applets. The semantics of the data flow are based on interpreting the contents of the data that flows across the InfoBus interfaces as opposed to responding to names of parameters from events or names of callback parameters.

Book Title Search Demo Overview

The demo that you'll see in this chapter involves the capability to search for books written by a specified author. Although it's not overwhelmingly exciting on its face, this demo provides a good example of how three disparate components can exchange data using the InfoBus. Please note that to use the InfoBus technology, you must first download it from `http://java.sun.com/beans/infobus/index.html`.

Because the name of the game with regard to the InfoBus is data, let's look at this application from that vantage point. As mentioned, the application consists of three applets. Each of these applets is connected using HTML statements that identify the names of the data items that each applet handles (see Listing 15.1).

Listing 15.1   This HTML File (`main.htm`) Is Used to Drive, or Host, the Demo

```
1.   <HTML>
2.   <BODY>
3.   <CENTER>
4.
5.   <APPLET codebase=".." CODE="lotus.sheet.Sheet"
➡ARCHIVE="jars/lot_sheet.jar" Width=550 HEIGHT=350>
6.   <PARAM NAME="InfoBusName" VALUE="xyzBus">
7.   <PARAM NAME="DataName"     VALUE="AuthorData">
8.   <PARAM NAME="WIDTH" VALUE="550">
9.   <PARAM NAME="HEIGHT" VALUE="350">
10.  </APPLET>
11.
12.  <APPLET CODE="lotus.jdbc.JdbcSource"
13.   NAME="Jdbc"
14.   CODEBASE=".."
15.   HEIGHT=475
16.   WIDTH=475>
17.
18.  <PARAM NAME="InfoBusName" VALUE="xyzBus">
```

continues

15

INFOBUS

Listing 15.1   continued

```
19. <PARAM NAME="host" VALUE="mydbhost">
20. <PARAM NAME="database"
    ➥VALUE="jdbc:dbaw://%HOST%:8889/Sybase_
    ➥SQLANY/myDB">
21.
22. <PARAM NAME="ID" VALUE="user1">
23. <PARAM NAME="password" VALUE="password1">
24. <PARAM NAME="autoConnect" VALUE="false">
25. <PARAM NAME="queryName" VALUE="AuthorNameRetrieve">
26. <PARAM NAME="publishName"VALUE="AuthorData">
27. </APPLET>
28.
29. <APPLET  CODE="xyz.AuthorInputApplet"
30.   NAME="AuthorInputApplet"
31.   HEIGHT=475
32.   WIDTH=475>
33. <PARAM NAME="InfoBusName" VALUE="xyzBus">
34. <PARAM NAME="FontSize" VALUE="10">
35. <PARAM NAME="DataItemName" VALUE="authorName">
36. </APPLET>
37.
38. </CENTER>
39. </BODY>
40. </HTML>
```

The AuthorInputApplet applet accepts from the end user the last name of an author and places the result on the InfoBus. When the user types an author name and clicks the Search button, the AuthorInputApplet applet sends a change notification. Although simple in nature, almost all InfoBus data-producer applets work in this very same fashion. In other words, they simply accept data from some source (such as an end user or a relational database) and once they have data to share, they send a change notification message so that any data consumers that want to know about that specific change event can retrieve the data.

The second applet is a data access component (DAC). It looks for a data item (in this case, the end user's specified author name) from the input applet. Keep in mind that this applet knows nothing about the AuthorInputApplet applet. It simply knows that an author name is going to be placed on the InfoBus. When that data is retrieved, it is used in an SQL query against a database (using JDBC). The result set (containing all the books written by the specified author) is then published on the InfoBus.

As mentioned earlier, a component can be both a data producer and a data consumer. In the case of this applet, both functions are being implemented. Because the author name is being retrieved from the InfoBus, in this step, the applet is a data consumer. However, when the applet uses the author name in a search against a database and publishes the result set on the InfoBus, it is acting as a data producer.

The last part of this demo is a spreadsheet that displays the results of the end user's search. This applet simply looks for information that is being published by the DAC and displays it in rows and columns on a spreadsheet. Therefore, because this applet only retrieves data, it is a data consumer.

In the name of another shameless plug for the use of Java, realize that this entire demo was written in just a few lines of code. Obviously the data access layer (JDBC) is provided and even the spreadsheet that is used in this last applet is a "pre-packaged" Java applet designed specifically to talk to other applications via the InfoBus. The spreadsheet responds to change events from the DAC to display the results of each query.

Now that you've seen the application from a data viewpoint, let's take a different look at the demo. From the point of view of the InfoBus architecture, the application architecture looks a bit different (see Figure 15.2). Notice that the InfoBus is similar to a hardware bus; the three applets are all plugged in to the same bus. In principle, all applets can see the events generated by all other applets. It is then up to the application developer to control which data items will be produced or consumed by which component that is plugged in to the InfoBus. However, there is one restriction to note here: All the applets that are connected to an InfoBus must reside in the same Java Virtual Machine (JVM). This is a current restriction of the InfoBus and brings up an interesting point. What is the difference between the InfoBus and RMI (remote method invocation), and, more specifically, when should you use which technique?

Comparing InfoBus and Java RMI

The InfoBus architecture addresses JavaBeans communicating with one another from within a *single JVM*. In other words, the InfoBus is not intended for cross-JVM communications. RMI, on the other hand, is intended for communication across JVMs across the network. As for IIOP, one can envision a JavaBeans component that uses RMI to talk to something on another JVM and then publishes the data on the InfoBus. However, keep in mind that all of this does not necessarily mean that a local JavaBean cannot retrieve data located on another machine. In fact, in this example, the DAC has a connection to a remote data source and uses JDBC to query it. However, all the JavaBeans that communicated the data between each other using the InfoBus are themselves located in the same JVM.

Additionally, although this example shows one producer for each consumer, and vice versa, multiple consumers can receive and use data published by a producer, and a consumer can easily obtain data from multiple producers. In fact, a request for data can elicit multiple responses. Multiple conversations can occur simultaneously without requiring anything special from the participating components. As you can see, you are bound only by your specific problem domain and your imagination.

15

INFOBUS

Now that you've seen a textual description of how the application works, take a look at Figures 15.1 and 15.2. These figures graphically depict how the data in this application flows from one component to another from a logical standpoint as well as from a architectural standpoint (using the InfoBus).

FIGURE 15.1

From a logical standpoint, the components directly communicate with one another in order to send or retrieve data.

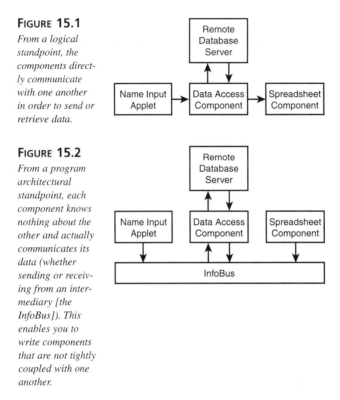

FIGURE 15.2

From a program architectural standpoint, each component knows nothing about the other and actually communicates its data (whether sending or receiving from an intermediary [the InfoBus]). This enables you to write components that are not tightly coupled with one another.

Overview of the InfoBus Process for Data Exchange

The InfoBus supports a stylized protocol for data exchange between InfoBus components that consists of the following major elements:

- *Membership*—Any Java class can join the InfoBus if it implements the InfoBusMember interface. The membership process connects applets to an InfoBus instance in preparation for data exchange.

- *Rendezvous*—An InfoBus application supplies an object that implements InfoBusDataProducer or InfoBusDataConsumer interfaces (or both) to listen for events appropriate to a component's role as a producer or consumer. A producer can also announce the availability of information to all listeners. When a producer gets a request event for information it can supply, it creates an instance of a data item and provides it to the requesting consumer. The consumer can request a particular item by name or ask for a data item in reaction to a producer's announcement of its availability. Remember that the producer doesn't need to know anything about the consumer. Its role is to simply make data available according to the rules of the InfoBus architecture. You will see how this is done shortly.

- *Data access*—InfoBus specifies a number of standard interfaces to provide direct data transfer between a producer and consumer. The interfaces include `ImmediateAccess`, which provides an InfoBus wrapper for a simple data item; `ArrayAccess`, which provides access functions for an array with arbitrary dimensions; and `RowsetAccess`, which provides a row and column interface to support database solutions. In addition to these, InfoBus applications can also use the standard Java collection interfaces defined in JDK 1.2.

- *Change notification*—When a consumer has received a data item from a producer, it can request notifications of all changes to the data by registering a `DataItemChangeListener` on the data item. As the producer detects changes, either because of changes in the external data source or because of modifications made by consumers, it will announce the changes to all listeners.

Let's consider how each of these plays a role in the `AuthorInputApplet`.

Implementing `InfoBusMember` to Get on the Bus

For the demo application, the first need is to connect the components to the InfoBus. The main application class, `SimpleDataProducer`, implements the required `InfoBusMember` interface. The methods required by `InfoBusMember` are designed to support an `InfoBus` property and listeners for changes to the property. An `InfoBusMemberSupport` class is available that encapsulates the required functionality, and the `SimpleDataProducer` uses this by creating an instance of `InfoBusMemberSupport` and delegating all methods to that class.

The following code indicates that `AuthorInputApplet` implements `InfoBusMember` (as well as other interfaces, explained later) in this manner. It declares member data that holds a reference to the `InfoBusMemberSupport` instance, and it defines each method required for `InfoBusMember`, delegating the work to the support instance. In the code snippet, I show only one method implementation; the implementation of the other methods is similar.

```
public class AuthorInputApplet extends Applet implements InfoBusMember,
    InfoBusDataProducer, ActionListener
```

15

INFOBUS

```
{
    // use an InfoBusMemberSupport to hold
    // our InfoBus
    private InfoBusMemberSupport m_IBHolder;

    // put the String to be published in a
    // SimpleDataItem
    private SimpleDataItem m_data;

    // the name of the InfoBus to which we
    // connect
    private String m_busName = null;

    // the name we use to publish our data
    private String m_authorLastName;

    // following used to synchronize
    // Available and Revoke events
    private Object m_AvailRevokeInterlock = new Object();

    // Delegate all calls to our
    // InfoBusMemberSupport
    // object, m_IBHolder

    public InfoBus getInfoBus()
    {
        return m_IBHolder.getInfoBus();
    }

    // other InfoBusMember calls are
    // delegated in the same fashion.
```

The InfoBusMemberSupport instance must be created before any calls are delegated to it, of course. In this example, I do this work in the applet's init() method after calling Applet.init():

```
public void init()
{
        super.init();

        // the "this" in the following
         // constructor tells the
        // support to use this object in the
        // source field of all events
        // it issues.

        m_IBHolder = new InfoBusMemberSupport( this );
```

The init() method also sets up a property change listener so that you know when your own InfoBus property has changed. This is important for creating reusable components; a Java bean will typically have its InfoBus set by its bean container.

```
m_IBHolder.addInfoBusPropertyListener ( this );
```

The "default InfoBus" can be used for communication between applets on the same browser page. A *default InfoBus* is one whose name is created from the DOCBASE provided by applets. Alternatively, an applet or bean can have the name of the InfoBus it should join specified externally. It is good practice to allow the application designer to specify the name of the InfoBus to use. In the code below, the supplied name is used if an InfoBusName parameter is found; otherwise, the default InfoBus is used.

```
m_busName = getParameter( "InfoBusName" ); // leave null if not there
```

Similarly, a data item name should be configurable. Data item names are used in the rendezvous; in the current example the producer will offer the author name as a named data item. The code below gets the data item name and saves it for later.

```
    m_authorLastName = getParameter( "DataItemName" );

    if ( m_authorLastName == null )
    {
        m_authorLastName = "authorName";
    }
```

Notice that InfoBusMemberSupport also provides a convenient, high-level method that can be called to join either a named or default InfoBus. The start() method is a good place to call it. InfoBusMemberSupport.leaveInfoBus() can be called in the stop() method. joinInfoBus can throw an exception; these statements are inside a try...catch block in the source file.

```
if ( m_busName != null )
{
    // gets a named bus using the busName string
    m_IBHolder.joinInfoBus ( m_busName );
}
else
{   //gets default bus for this applet
    m_IBHolder.joinInfoBus( this );
}
```

In the InfoBus model, the rendezvous is asynchronous. Data producers announce the availability of new data as it becomes ready at, say, completion of a URL read or completion of a calculation. Data consumers solicit data from producers as they require that data (at applet initialization, redraw, and so on).

`AuthorInputApplet` listens for requests for data and announces the availability of data by implementing an `InfoBusDataProducer` listener object and adding it to the list of listeners on the InfoBus it joined. For simplicity, our example shows this interface implemented on the main applet class; in a real-world application, I recommend that the listener object be separate from the main class to prevent unwanted introspection because the listener reference can be obtained by any other InfoBus component on the same bus.

`InfoBusDataProducer` defines only one method, which is called each time a consumer on the same bus requests data by name. The producer compares the requested data name to the name received from a parameter and sets the data item if they match.

InfoBus Interface Definitions

`InfoBusMember` is an interface implemented by a Java class in order to become a member of the InfoBus. Its primary purpose is to manage the `InfoBus` property, which keeps a reference to the InfoBus instance the member has joined. `InfoBusMember` also allows an external entity (for example, a bean container) to set the InfoBus it wants a member to talk to so that a bean builder can control the communication between its beans.

`InfoBusDataProducer` is an event listener implemented by data producers to receive request events from consumers.

`InfoBusDataConsumer` is an event listener implemented by data consumers to receive events indicating the availability and revocation of items offered by producers.

`DataItem` is an interface that provides methods used for learning about a data item. Consumers can discover MIME-type information, get a reference to the producer's event listener, or ask for the value associated with a property string.

`DataItemChangeManager` is the interface that provides methods used by a consumer to add or remove a change listener. A producer implements `DataItemChangeManager` on all data items for which it is willing to provide change notification to listeners.

A consumer implements the `DataItemChangeListener` interface and registers the object with the producer's `DataItemChangeManager` to be informed of changes that occur on a data item.

`ImmediateAccess` is implemented by a `DataItem` that needs to retrieve data values directly from calls to methods on this interface. You can get an immediate rendering of the data as a `String` or `Object`. A method can be used to change the value or throw an exception for read-only items.

`ArrayAccess` is implemented by data items that are collections of `DataItems` organized in an *n*-dimensional array. The `ArrayAccess` interface includes methods to determine dimensions, obtain individual elements of the data set, iterate over all elements in the set, and subdivide one `ArrayAccess` object into two (that is, to divide a data set of two columns and five rows into two data sets of one column and five rows).

`RowsetAccess` is an interface for data items that are collections of rows obtained from a data source such as a relational database server. The `RowsetAccess` interface contains methods to discover the number of columns as well as their names and data types, to get the next row, to obtain column values, and to insert, update, and delete rows.

`DbAccess` is a database interface that allows the data consumer to issue retrieval and non-retrieval queries and to optionally have the result announced as a `DataItem`.

InfoBus applications can exchange information using any of the access interfaces described below. The JDK 1.2 Collection interfaces can also be used for accessing structured information in a standard, application-independent fashion.

```
public void dataItemRequested( InfoBusItemRequestedEvent ibe )
{
    if ( m_data == null )
    {      // user hasn't clicked Search
           // yet, so item isn't available.
           return;
    }
    String s = ibe.getDataItemName();
    if ( ( null != s  ) && s.equals( m_authorLastName ) )
    {
        // THREADSAFETY: make our activity
        // on a positive match thread safe

        synchronized (m_data)
        // NEVER USE OUR INFOBUS AS THE
        // LOCK OBJECT
        {
            ibe.setDataItem( m_data );
        }
        }
    }
}
```

The `InfoBusDataProducer` listens for request events. The listener can be registered when `start()` is called, after you join the InfoBus.

```
    if( null !=


    {
       try
       {
       // Add event listening when the
       // applet is started
```

```
                    m_InfoBusHolder.getInfoBus().
                    addDataProducer(this);
            }
            catch ( InfoBusMembershipException e )
            { /* handle exception */ }
    }
```

The data item is created and announced the first time the button is pushed. For the second and each successive time the button is pushed, you just set the new value.

```
private void searchClicked ()
{
    if ( m_data == null )
    { //first click, so create data item
        //and announce
      m_data = new SimpleDataItem( textField1.getText(), this );
        // THREADSAFETY: create a lock to
        // prevent a REVOKE from being sent
        // before the AVAILABLE has
        // completed
        synchronized ( m_AvailRevoke
            Interlock )
        {
            InfoBus ib =
                m_IBHolder.getInfoBus();
                ib.fireItemAvailable(
                m_authorLastName,this );
        }
    }
    else
    {
            m_data.setValue( textField1.
            getText() );
    }
}
```

You revoke the data item when stop() is called and remove your listener from the InfoBus.

```
// revoke our data item
    synchronized ( m_AvailRevokeInterlock )
    {
       InfoBus ib = m_IBHolder.getInfoBus();
       ib.fireItemRevoked( m_authorLastName,
           this );
    }

    // tell the IBMSupport to leave its bus
    try
    {
       m_IBHolder.leaveInfoBus();
```

```
    }
    catch ( PropertyVetoException pve )
    {
        // do nothing - our InfoBus property
        // is managed by external bean
    }
    catch ( InfoBusMembershipException ibme )
    {
        // do nothing - simply means we
        // already had null for IB
    }
```

Different data producers manage different types of data; consumers might want to receive this data in simple or complex ways. To accommodate the needs of both producers and consumers, the InfoBus defines a determinate number of data access interfaces.

AuthorInputApplet uses a separate class, SimpleDataItem, to house the data it publishes. This class is a general-purpose implementation of ImmediateAccess; you'll look at the implementation of the methods required for your application in the following section.

A Cop to Control Heavy Traffic

The role of a data controller is to play traffic cop on the InfoBus. Essentially, a data controller is an optional InfoBus component that lives between any data producer and its consumers in order to regulate or redirect the flow of data. In the presence of a data controller, individual data producers and consumers do not talk to each other directly, but instead communicate through the third-party controller. This requires no programmatic changes to either data producers or consumers: If one or more data controllers are registered on the InfoBus, events arriving on the Bus are distributed only to the controllers. The controllers then assume responsibility for identifying the potential consumers of each event and distributing it to them directly.

Data controllers are potentially quite complex. They might keep track of data producers that have offered particular data items, and of data consumers that have requested data items, to provide late binding of producer to consumer.

ImmediateAccess defines three ways of getting the data. getValueAsString() returns a simple string rendering of the data. getPresentationString() is similar, but can provide a rendering appropriate for a specified locale. For example, if ImmediateAccess is being used to house a monetary value, getValueAsString() might return "1000.00" whereas getPresentationString(), given a locale for the United States, might return "$1,000.00." The other access method is one that provides a reference to the object held by ImmediateAccess.

For our purposes, the following simple implementations will suffice:

```
public String getValueAsString()
{
     return m_value != null ?
        m_value.toString() : new String("");
}

    // Note that getPresentationString() is
    // identical to getValueAsString()
    // for this simple example.

    public Object getValueAsObject()
    {
       return m_value;
    }
```

The DAC provides a row and column interface to the information returned by the query. This can be done using the `ArrayAccess` interface or the database-specific `RowsetAccess` interface. A really flexible DAC might implement both interfaces to support the widest possible audience of consumers, some of which might understand only one or the other.

The `DataItem` interface is used to provide descriptive information for a data item. The methods include `getTransferrable()`, which provides, among other things, access to a MIME type for the item; `getProperty()`, which allows a producer to return an object in response to a property name it recognizes; and `getProducer()`, which returns a reference to the event listener of the producer for identification purposes.

`SimpleDataItem` returns null for the first two and a reference to the `AuthorInputApplet` instance that supplies the item. Notice that this example is vulnerable to unwanted introspection, in that `AuthorInputApplet` has several other interfaces. A security-conscious application could implement `InfoBusDataProducer` in a class with no other functions to avoid giving out such information to nosy consumers.

The `AuthorInputApplet` class allows the user to enter the last name of an author and then click Search to find the books written by that author. The first time Search is clicked, the data item is announced, as you saw earlier. Every succeeding time you send a change notification, the DAC does a query when it gets the item and for each change in value to the data item.

Producers can easily implement the `DataItemChangeManager` interface to support change notification to its listeners using the `DataItemChangeSupport` class. This approach recalls what you did with `InfoBusMemberSupport`: Create an instance of the class and delegate all calls from the interface to the matching calls in the support class.

DataItemChangeSupport also provides methods that can be used to fire change methods of each type. AuthorInputApplet calls SimpleDataItem.setValue when the user clicks Search to set a new author name for look up. SimpleDataItem.setValue sets the new value and then calls a method to fire an event indicating the change in value to all registered listeners:

```
m_DICS.fireItemValueChanged ( this, null );
```

Putting It All Together

The last piece of our example is the HTML code that places the InfoBus components and controls the way they talk to each other. In this example HTML code, notice that all three applications have parameters that specify the name of an InfoBus. Because all three use the same name, they will see each other on the InfoBus.

The first applet is the AuthorInputApplet example examined in this chapter. Its data item name has been specified as authorName.

Remember that the second applet, the data access component, is both a consumer of a lookup string and the producer of a table of data returned by a query. A parameter called queryName specifies the data item name for the lookup string with a value of authorName. Because the value is the same as the parameter AuthorInputApplet produces, they will exchange this data. The data item name for the query result data is specified by the parameter publishName, whose value is specified as AuthorData.

Finally, the sheet component specifies a data item name with its DataName parameter value of AuthorData. Again, because this matches the data item name produced by the DAC, the sheet will be able to display the data from the query (see Figure 15.3).

FIGURE 15.3

Results of multiple components sharing data using the InfoBus.

Summary

As you have seen throughout this chapter, the power of the InfoBus lies in its capability to enable multiple agnostic components to communicate or share data through an intermediary (the InfoBus itself). The results are components that, while needing data from other components, are not so tightly coupled with those components as to make both development and maintenance difficult.

Enterprise and Network Protocols

PART V

CHAPTER 16

Internet Communication Using Sockets (TCP/IP)

In This Chapter

All source code for this chapter can be found on the Sams Publishing Website at
`http://www.mcp.com/info/0-672/0-672-31424-x.`

JavaBeans and Java are designed with networking in mind. The Java language has Internet networking capabilities built into its packages. In this chapter, you learn about the TCP/IP suite of network protocols, learn about network services, use sockets and Internet addresses, and use the User Datagram Protocol (UDP). Next, you learn how to write server and client beans that can be used in Telnet applications. You test these beans using the Beans Development Kit's handy BeanBox tool. The BeanBox is ideal for wiring together your beans and testing them in a sort of prototype application. You run two instances of BeanBox, each in a separate Java Virtual Machine (JVM), and wire together a prototype Telnet server and Telnet client application, and then watch them communicate using TCP. Finally, you hand code a Telnet server and Telnet client application using the Telnet beans you created earlier in the chapter.

Communicating Over Networks

Communicating over networks requires reliable delivery services that can carry information between any two computers in a network as vast as the Internet. The delivery services must work regardless of the computer hardware and software connected to the network. The Internet provides delivery services using a suite of protocols commonly known as TCP/IP. Nearly all networks now provide TCP/IP as one of the protocols you can use for communicating with their resources. You use TCP/IP when you create JavaBeans components that network most of the time.

Using TCP/IP

As mentioned previously, TCP/IP is the common name given to a suite of networking protocols. TCP/IP is a shorthand expression for Transport Control Protocol/Internet Protocol. The name includes the two most commonly used protocols in the suite separated by a slash.

The TCP/IP suite of protocols operates on four levels stacked one on top of the other like four boxes. From bottom to top they are

- Network Access layer
- Network layer
- Transport layer
- Application layer

TCP handles transmission control and error checking at the transport layer, while IP only handles addressing at the network layer.

Internet Communication Using Sockets (TCP/IP)

CHAPTER 16

313

16

INTERNET
COMMUNICATION
USING SOCKETS

The Network Access Layer

Network Access is the bottom layer that sits right next to the physical connection to the network. It provides a large number of specialized network access protocols that interface between the protocols above it in the Network layer and the data link layer and physical network connection below.

> **Note**
>
> The data link layer is part of the Open Systems Integration reference model for a standard network layer structure and is not part of the TCP/IP network protocol suite.

The Network Layer

The next layer up, the Network layer, includes the most important and most heavily used protocol in the TCP/IP suite, the Internet Protocol. All of the higher-level protocols use IP as the transport vehicle for their network communications. Among the functions performed by IP are

- Packaging upper-layer data into datagrams
- Implementing the TCP/IP addressing system
- Routing datagrams between different networks
- Passing data between the Transport and Network Access layers in both directions

> **Note**
>
> A *datagram* is a packet of data created by IP that functions as the fundamental data unit of a TCP/IP network. Each datagram includes a core of data (like a letter) encapsulated by various delivery information such as the destination address and the sender's address (like an envelope).

IP is an unreliable, connectionless protocol. It's an unreliable protocol because it has no mechanisms of its own for error detection and correction. There is no guarantee that datagrams sent using IP by itself will arrive at their destination in the order in which they were sent, or even that they will arrive at all. IP is a connectionless protocol because it sends datagrams without having previously checked the availability of the destination computer.

Even though IP is an unreliable, connectionless protocol, it is used by all TCP/IP delivery services for a variety of functions. One of the Internet Protocol's most important functions is providing IP addresses, the method used for uniquely identifying each machine on a network.

The Transport Layer

Your Java network programming is most likely to deal directly with one of the two protocols that operate in the second layer from the top, the Transport layer. The two protocols are the User Datagram Protocol (UDP) and the Transmission Control Protocol (TCP). Both protocols deliver datagrams to the appropriate port on the destination computer. However, they differ in three important ways: the simplicity of the service, the rapidity of delivery, and the reliability of delivery.

UDP is the simpler service that generally results in faster delivery and does not provide a high degree of reliability. In contrast, TCP is the more complicated service that generally results in slower delivery, but it provides a high degree of reliability.

The Application Layer

Protocols running in the Application layer, the top layer of the TCP/IP protocol suite stack, are closest to the user. In fact, users can directly interact with many of the protocols including FTP and Telnet. All of the protocols in the Application layer make use of the underlying Transport and Network protocols for their transmissions.

> **Note**
>
> Application layer protocols are also known as network services. You will learn more about network services in the next section, "Using Network Services."

Using Network Services

TCP/IP networks provide a variety of network services through their Application layer protocols. Network services include electronic mail, Telnet for remote logon, and File Transfer Protocol (FTP) for transferring files across networks.

Each network service is associated with a port. A *port* is a logical number assigned to a particular service through which the service is requested. Some network services and their common port numbers are listed in Table 16.1.

Table 16.1   Network Services

Service	Port	Description
FTP Data	20	File Transfer Protocol data
FTP Control	21	File Transfer Protocol commands
Telnet	23	Telnet remote logon
SMTP	25	Simple Mail Transfer Protocol
DNS	53	Domain Name Server
TFTP	69	Trivial File Transfer Protocol
Finger	79	Finger

Using Sockets

Use network services on other computers over the Internet by using sockets. A *socket* is the combination of an IP address and a port number. An IP address consists of 32-bits represented by four decimal values. Each decimal value is from 0 to 255 and is separated from the other values by periods. For instance, 204.71.177.66 is the IP address associated with the following computer name, www.yahoo.com. Computer names are also known as *host names*. The combination of the IP address and Telnet port 23 is a socket and looks like 204.71.177.66:23.

> **Note**
>
> You can get the IP address of any computer name with the `ping` command. The `ping` command is a UNIX command that is also supplied with the Microsoft Windows operating systems. For instance, to resolve the www.yahoo.com IP address, type in **ping -a www.yahoo.com** at your DOS window's command prompt while connected with the Internet.

You always make use of sockets in beans that use or provide network services. Java provides a variety of socket classes in the `java.net` package. You will use the `DatagramSocket` class to send and receive datagrams through UDP later in this chapter. Then you'll use the more sophisticated `Socket` and `ServerSocket` classes to implement TCP in Telnet applications.

Using Internet Addresses

Internet addresses, also known as IP addresses, are fundamental to Internet communication. You encapsulate IP addresses in `InetAddress` objects using Java's `InetAddress` class. That is, each `InetAddress` object encapsulates the IP address of a particular host computer. The `InetAddress` class is part of the `java.net` package.

The `InetAddress` class is unusual in that it doesn't provide public constructors. You create `InetAddress` objects by using one of three `InetAddress` class methods: `getByName()`, `getAllByName()`, and `getLocalHost()`.

You will probably find yourself using the `InetAddress` class's `getByName()` method most of the time. The `getByName()` method is declared as follows:

```
public static InetAddress getByName(String host) throws UnknownHostException
```

The method returns an `InetAddress` object encapsulating the IP address of the host computer whose name you pass as a `String` object to the method's `host` parameter. For instance, if you pass `www.yahoo.com` to `getByName()` method's `host` parameter, the method returns an `InetAddress` object encapsulating Yahoo's IP address.

Some computers have more than one IP address. You can get an array of `InetAddress` objects encapsulating all of the IP addresses associated with a particular computer by using the `InetAddress` class's `getAllByName()` method, as shown in the following:

```
public static InetAddress[] getAllByName(String host)
    throws UnknownHostException
```

Pass the `host` parameter a `String` object representing the host computer's name just as you did for the `getByName()` method described previously. The `getAllByName()` method, however, returns an array of `InetAddress` objects, one for each IP address associated with the host computer.

Use the `InetAddress` class's `getLocalHost()` method, shown next, to create the `InetAddress` objects encapsulating the IP address of the local host computer.

```
public static InetAddress getLocalHost() throws UnknownHostException
```

The `getLocalHost()` method has no parameters.

Creating Beans Using UDP

You now know enough about Internet communication to try it out. There are two ends to Internet communication, the sender and the receiver. The sending program sends data to a socket, which is an Internet address and port number. The receiving program waits at

Internet Communication Using Sockets (TCP/IP)

CHAPTER 16

317

16

INTERNET
COMMUNICATION
USING SOCKETS

and periodically checks an Internet address and port number for incoming data. That's all there is to it on one level. The following compares clients to servers:

Client	Server
Operates on a variable port number, assigned at connect time	Nearly always operates on a fixed port
Initiates the connection and the request	Listens for a request but initiates no dialog
Generally only handles one thread for one connection	Generally handles multiple threads for multiple client connections
Relatively simple in design	Relatively complex in design

On another level, there are complicated implementation details. However, Java makes it easy for you. Java provides classes that you've already been introduced to that encapsulate all of the details. You just need to know when to create the particular objects used in UDP transmission. You go through all of the steps while you create UDP send and receive beans in the following sections.

Using UDP

Use UDP if you need a rapid, uncomplicated way to deliver information across a network. UDP is a Transport layer protocol that adds little to the Network layer IP through which it passes its data for network delivery. UDP, like IP, is a connectionless, unreliable protocol. The main thing UDP adds is the port number of the service desired on the destination computer. The result is a simple, fast, network delivery protocol that can lose some of your information.

Java provides two classes that make it easy for you to use UDP in your JavaBeans components: the `DatagramPacket` and `DatagramSocket` classes. Both classes are part of the `java.net` package.

Instances of the `DatagramPacket` class represent datagram packets. The `DatagramPacket` class provides two constructors, one for datagram packets that are sent and one for datagram packets that are received. Details about creating `DatagramPacket` objects are provided in the following sections on sending and receiving datagram packets.

A `DatagramSocket` object represents the process that sends or receives datagram packets. The `DatagramSocket` class provides three constructors. The constructor you use to create a `DatagramSocket` object depends on what computer and port you want it to send and receive datagram packets. Create a `DatagramSocket` object using the constructor that has no parameters, shown next, when you want datagram packets sent and received over any available port on the local host computer.

```
public DatagramSocket() throws SocketException
```

Create a `DatagramSocket` object using the `DatagramSocket` constructor that provides a single parameter, shown next, when you want datagram packets sent and received over a particular port on the local host computer.

```
public DatagramSocket(int port) throws SocketException
```

Pass an integer value representing the port number you want included in the socket to the `port` parameter. For instance, pass `69` to the `port` parameter so that datagram packets are sent and received over port 69 (the port often used for TFTP) on the local host computer.

Finally, create a `DatagramSocket` object using the constructor that provides two parameters, shown next, when you want datagram packets sent and received over a particular port on a particular host computer.

```
public DatagramSocket(int port, InetAddress laddr) throws SocketException
```

The `port` parameter takes an integer value representing the port number you want included in the socket. Pass the `laddr` parameter an `InetAddress` object encapsulating the IP address of the host computer you want included in the socket.

Don't worry if this section seems abstract; you'll put these classes to use shortly. Java's `DatagramPacket` and `DatagramSocket` classes provide the core functionality of the send and receive datagram beans you'll create in the following sections.

Sending Datagram Packets

Sending datagram packets using UDP takes only three steps:

1. Create a `DatagramPacket` object.
2. Create a `DatagramSocket` object.
3. Send a datagram packet.

Write a Java bean named `UDPSend` that sends datagram packets using UDP in the following sections. Follow along by frequently referring to the `UDPSend` bean code in Listing 16.1. You'll write the bean for receiving the datagram packets using UDP, `UDPReceive`, in the "Receiving Datagram Packets" section later this chapter.

> **Note**
>
> The classes you write in this chapter are all part of the sams.net package.

You will design the UDPSend bean so that it has a property that holds a String object representing the Internet address you want to send a datagram packet to and a property that holds a String object encapsulating the message you want to send. You'll name the two properties internetAddress and message respectively. In addition to the property accessor methods, you will add a public sendData() method for sending the message to a remote computer. Both of UDPSend bean's properties will be used by the sendData() method to create DatagramPacket objects. After it creates the DatagramSocket object, the sendData() method will send the object as a datagram packet.

Create the internetAddress property by declaring the internetAddress private String data field, as shown in the following:

```
private String internetAddress = "localhost";
```

The property is set to "localhost" by default. This results in the IP address of the local host computer, the computer that the bean resides on, being encapsulated in the InetAddress object assigned to the ipAddress variable. It's the call to the private encapsulateAddress() method, shown next, in the UDPSend class constructor that creates the InetAddress object.

```
private InetAddress encapsulateAddress( ) {
  try {
    return InetAddress.getByName( internetAddress );
  }
  catch( Exception e ) {
    return null;
  }
}
```

The encapsulateAddress() method passes the internetAddress property to InetAddress class's getByName() method. The internetAddress property is a String object representation of the Internet address to which you want to send a message. As mentioned previously, it's "localhost" by default, but you can change it through the internetAddress property editor during design time. The getByName() method returns an InetAddress object that is passed to the calling statement.

Add the internetAddress property accessor and mutator methods, as shown in the following:

```
public void setInternetAddress( String address ) {
  internetAddress = address;
  ipAddress = encapsulateAddress( );
}

public String getInternetAddress( ) {
  return internetAddress;
}
```

The `setInternetAddress()` mutator method needs to call the `encapuslateAddress()` method after the `internetAddress` property is updated so that the IP address encapsulated by the `InetAddress` object assigned to the `ipAddress` variable is up to date.

Create a message property by declaring the `message` private `String` variable, as shown in the following:

```
private String message = "I traveled the network as a datagram packet.";
```

The `message` variable is set to the default message `"I traveled the network as a datagram packet."` Add the property's accessor methods, as shown in the following:

```
public void setMessage( String message ) {
  this.message = message;
}

public String getMessage( ) {
  return message;
}
```

There's nothing surprising here. The accessor methods are kept simple.

You're finished creating `UDPSend` bean's properties. The main work of creating a `DatagramPacket`, creating a `DatagramSocket`, and sending the datagram is all done in the `sendData()` method.

Creating `DatagramPacket` Objects

The first statement in `UDPSend` bean's `sendData()` method, shown next, creates a `DatagramPacket` object used for sending datagram packets.

```
packet = new DatagramPacket( message.getBytes( ),
    message.length( ), ipAddress, port );
```

The `DatagramPacket` class provides two constructors. One constructor, for creating `DatagramPacket` objects used for receiving datagram packets, is described later in this chapter in the "Receiving Datagram Packets" section. The other constructor is shown in the previous line of code. The following is the signature of this constructor:

```
public DatagramPacket(byte ibuf[], int ilength,
    InetAddress iaddr, int iport)
```

The `DatagramPacket` constructor for creating `DatagramPacket` objects that send datagram packets takes four parameters: `ibuf`, `ilength`, `iaddr`, and `iport`.

The first parameter, `ibuf`, takes a byte array containing the data that is sent as a datagram packet. In the `UDPSend` class, it's the `String` object assigned to the `message` variable that is sent as a datagram packet. Therefore, the program passes a byte array version of the data assigned to the `message` variable to the `DatagramPacket` constructor's `ibuf` parameter by invoking the `String` class's `getBytes()` method.

The second parameter in the DatagramPacket constructor, the ilength parameter, takes an integer value representing the length of the data you're sending. The UDPSend class passes the length of the string being sent by calling the String class's length() method.

The third parameter, iaddr, takes the datagram packet's destination IP address encapsulated by an InetAddress object. The UDPSend class passes the InetAddress object assigned to the ipAddress variable, which encapsulates the destination IP address, to the iaddr parameter.

Finally, the DatagramPacket constructor's fourth parameter, iport, takes the integer value of the destination port. In the UDPSend class, the port variable assigned port number 69 is passed to iport.

> **Note**
>
> Be sure that the sending DatagramPacket object and the receiving DatagramSocket object are set to the same port value.

Creating DatagramSocket Objects

The second statement in UDPSend bean's sendData() method creates a DatagramSocket. UDPSend objects never receive datagram packets, therefore they can use any socket. That is, when a UDPReceive object receives datagram packets, both the IP address that the object resides on and the port it uses must be known. On the other hand, UDPSend objects can send datagram packets using any port (as long as the receiver is expecting that port), so the port number need never be explicitly defined for sockets that only send datagram packets. The IP address is, of course, the local host computer. The DatagramSocket class constructor without parameters automatically creates a DatagramSocket object that uses any available port and the local host computer IP address, which is exactly how the UDPSend class creates its DatagramSocket object. The new DatagramSocket object is assigned to the socket variable.

The third statement in UDPSend bean's sendData() method actually sends the datagram packet using the DatagramSocket class's send() method. The following is the signature of this send() method:

```
public void send(DatagramPacket p) throws IOException
```

Send a datagram packet by passing a DatagramPacket object to the DatagramSocket class's send() method p parameter. This is exactly what the third statement in UDPSend class's sendData() method does, as shown in the following:

```
socket.send( packet );
```

The `DatagramPacket` object assigned to the `packet` variable is passed to the `DatagramSocket` class's `send()` method. The `DatagramSocket` object is assigned to the `socket` variable.

The final statement in the `sendData()` method closes the socket. You should always close a socket after you're finished sending datagrams.

In summary, `UDPSend` bean's `packet` variable represents a datagram packet, and its `socket` variable represents the local UDP socket from which the packet is sent out. The datagram packet is passed to the local UDP socket and is sent on its way, as you can see in Listing 16.1. Another bean must be in place to receive the datagram packet. The receiving bean must create a UDP socket with the same IP address and port number as is carried by the datagram packet created by the sending bean. In the next section you'll create a bean that receives datagram packets from the `UDPSend` bean.

Listing 16.1   Source Code for `UDPSend.java`

```java
package sams.net;

import java.net.DatagramPacket;
import java.net.DatagramSocket;
import java.net.InetAddress;

public class UDPSend {
  private int port = 69;
  private DatagramPacket packet = null;
  private DatagramSocket socket = null;
  private InetAddress ipAddress = null;
  private String internetAddress = "localhost";
  private String message = "I traveled the network as a datagram packet.";

  public UDPSend( ) {
    ipAddress = encapsulateAddress( );
  }

  public void setInternetAddress( String address ) {
    internetAddress = address;
    ipAddress = encapsulateAddress( );
  }

  public String getInternetAddress( ) {
    return internetAddress;
  }

  public void setMessage( String message ) {
    this.message = message;
```

```
  }

  public String getMessage( ) {
    return message;
  }

  public void sendData( ) {
    try {
      packet = new DatagramPacket( message.getBytes( ),
        message.length( ), ipAddress, port );
      socket = new DatagramSocket( );
      socket.send( packet );
      socket.close( );
    }
    catch( Exception e ) {
    }
  }

  private InetAddress encapsulateAddress( ) {
    try {
      return InetAddress.getByName( internetAddress );
    }
    catch( Exception e ) {
      return null;
    }
  }
}
```

Receiving Datagram Packets

Receiving datagram packets using UDP takes only three steps, which are similar to the steps taken to send packets:

1. Create a DatagramPacket object.
2. Create a DatagramSocket object.
3. Receive a datagram packet.

In the following sections, you'll write a Java bean named UDPReceive that uses UDP to receive datagram packets sent by the UDPSend bean. You will write two classes for the UDPReceive bean. The UDPReceive class will provide a graphic interface and start a thread running. The thread will keep a vigilant lookout for datagram packets addressed to its socket. You will write the UDPReceiveThread class, which is the class that the bean instantiates its thread object from and which will do nearly all of the bean's work.

Writing the `UDPReceiveThread` Class

`UDPReceive` bean's `UDPReceiveThread` class, shown in Listing 16.2, is derived from Java's `Thread` class and contains just a constructor and a `run()` method. The constructor, shown next, takes a reference to a `UDPReceive` object through its `window` parameter.

```
public UDPReceiveThread( UDPReceive window ) {
  this.window = window;
}
```

This reference to the bean's graphical interface class is assigned to the `window` class variable. The `UDPReceiveThread` object needs a reference to the graphical interface class so that it can pass messages to the interface. All of the rest of the class's work is done in its `run()` method.

Creating `DatagramPacket` Objects

The first statement in the `UDPReceiveThread` class's `run()` method, shown next, creates a `DatagramPacket` object used for receiving datagram packets.

```
packet = new DatagramPacket( buffer, buffer.length );
```

The `DatagramPacket` object in the receiving bean is simply a receptacle for the incoming datagram packet. The following is the signature of the `DatagramPacket` constructor used for creating `DatagramPacket` objects that receive datagram packets:

```
public DatagramPacket(byte ibuf[], int ilength)
```

This `DatagramPacket` constructor takes two parameters: `ibuf` and `ilength`. The first parameter, `ibuf`, takes an empty byte array large enough to hold the incoming datagram packet. The declaration area in the `UDPReceiveThread` class declares the `buffer` variable as a byte array and assigns the variable an empty array of 2,048 bytes. The second parameter, `ilength`, takes an integer value of the length of the byte array passed to the first parameter. The `UDPReceiveThread` class passes the size of the byte array to the `ilength` parameter using the array's `length` constant.

Creating `DatagramSocket` Objects

The second statement in the `UDPReceiveThread` class's `run()` method creates a `DatagramSocket`. `UDPReceive` beans receive datagram packets, therefore they must explicitly use the same IP address and the port to which the datagram packet is addressed. Of course, the datagram packet must be sent to the receiving bean's local host computer IP address, so the only thing that the receiving bean must do is create a socket for receiving datagram packets on the same port to which the packets are being sent.

The `DatagramSocket` class constructor, with either one or two parameters, creates sockets for receiving datagram packets. The `UDPReceiveThread` class uses the constructor with one parameter, as shown in the following:

```
public DatagramSocket(int port)
```

Pass the `port` parameter an integer value of the port at which the datagram packets will arrive. The `DatagramPacket` object created in the `UDPSend` bean delivers its datagram packet to port number 69. Therefore, the `UDPReceiveThread` class must pass 69 to `DatagramSocket` constructor's `port` parameter to receive the datagram packet. The following statement in the `UDPReceiveThread` class constructor does just that:

```
socket = new DatagramSocket( port );
```

The `port` variable is assigned the integer value 69 in the `UDPReceiveThead` class's declaration area.

Using `DatagramSocket`'s `receive()` Method

After sending a notice to its graphical interface saying that it's waiting to receive a message, the `UDPReceive` bean receives the datagram packet using `DatagramSocket` class's `receive()` method, as shown in the following:

```
public synchronized void receive(DatagramPacket p)
```

Receive a datagram packet by passing the `DatagramPacket` object with an empty byte array to the p parameter in `DatagramSocket` class's `receive()` method. This is exactly what the next statement in `UDPReceiveThread` class's `run()` method does

```
socket.receive( packet );
```

The `UDPReceive` bean waits during execution of this statement until it receives a datagram packet. The waiting is known as *blocking*. When a method blocks, it holds up program execution. The `DatagramPacket` class `receive()` method blocks until a datagram is received. That's why the message before the call to the `receive()` method is handy.

The final two statements in the `run()` method should look familiar (see Listing 16.2). The call to the `setMessage()` method sends the text message in the datagram packet to be displayed in `UDPReceive` bean's graphical interface. The final statement closes `UDPReceive` bean's socket after receiving a message.

Listing 16.2   Source Code for UDPReceiveThread.java

```java
package sams.net;

import java.net.DatagramPacket;
import java.net.DatagramSocket;

class UDPReceiveThread extends Thread {
  private int port = 69;
  private byte buffer[] = new byte[2048];
  private DatagramPacket packet = null;
  private DatagramSocket socket = null;
  private String message = "";
  private UDPReceive window = null;

  public UDPReceiveThread( UDPReceive window ) {
    this.window = window;
  }

  public void run( ) {
    try {
      packet = new DatagramPacket( buffer, buffer.length );
      socket = new DatagramSocket( port );
      window.setMessage( "Waiting to receive message..." );
      socket.receive( packet );
      window.setMessage( new String( buffer, 0, packet.getLength( ) ) );
      socket.close( );
    }
    catch( Exception e ) {
    }
  }
}
```

Writing the UDPReceive Class

UDPReceive bean's UDPReceive class, shown in Listing 16.3, creates the beans graphic user interface and displays messages passed from its thread onto the interface. The class is derived from Java's Canvas class. The bean has no properties, but it has two important public methods: the startRunning() and stopRunning() methods.

You start and stop the UDPReceive bean's thread by calling the startRunning() and stopRunning() methods. When the thread's running, it can receive data; when it's stopped, it can't. You can wire up other beans to these methods, or you can call them directly through code.

The startRunning() method, shown next, first checks to make sure that there is no thread already running. If there isn't, it creates a new UDPReceiveThread object and starts it running. Otherwise, it stops the old thread and then creates and starts a new thread. Finally, it sets the running variable to true.

```
public void startRunning( ) {
  if( thread == null ) {
    thread = new UDPReceiveThread( this );
    thread.start( );
  }
  else {
    thread.stop( );
    thread = null;
    thread = new UDPReceiveThread( this );
    thread.start( );
  }
  running = true;
}
```

The `stopRunning()` method, shown next, first checks to make sure that there is a thread. If there is, it stops the thread and assigns `null` to the `thread` variable. A `false` value is assigned to the `running` variable, and `"The UDPReceive Bean"` is assigned to the `message` variable. Finally, the `repaint()` method is called, as seen in Listing 16.3.

```
public void stopRunning( ) {
  if( thread != null ) {
    thread.stop( );
    thread = null;
  }
  running = false;
  message = "The UDPReceive Bean";
  repaint( );
}
```

You're now ready to test your UDP beans.

Listing 16.3   Source Code for `UDPReceive.java`

```
package sams.net;

import java.awt.Graphics;

public class UDPReceive extends java.awt.Canvas {
  private String message = "";
  private boolean running = false;
  private UDPReceiveThread thread = null;

  public UDPReceive( ) {
    setSize( 300, 30 );
    message = "The UDPReceive Bean";
    repaint( );
  }

  public void stopRunning( ) {
```

continues

Listing 16.3   continued

```
      if( thread != null ) {
        thread.stop( );
        thread = null;
      }
      running = false;
      message = "The UDPReceive Bean";
      repaint( );
    }

    public void startRunning( ) {
      if( thread == null ) {
        thread = new UDPReceiveThread( this );
        thread.start( );
      }
      else {
        thread.stop( );
        thread = null;
        thread = new UDPReceiveThread( this );
        thread.start( );
      }
      running = true;
    }

    public synchronized void setMessage( String message ) {
      this.message = message;
      repaint( );
    }

    public void paint( Graphics g ) {
      g.drawString( message, 20, 20 );
    }
}
```

Using the UDPSend and UDPReceive Beans

Try out the UDP networking Java beans you just wrote. Package the beans into a JAR file using the udp.man manifest file in Listing 16.4. Type the following command at your DOS or console window prompt.

```
jar cmf udp.man udp.jar sams
```

Open two DOS or console windows on your local machine and change their directories so that you're in the BeanBox directory in both windows. Start up the BeanBox in one of the DOS windows and place a UDPReceive bean and in the BeanBox window. The UDPReceive bean should display the message The UDPReceive Bean, as shown in Figure 16.1.

Listing 16.4 Source Code for udp.man

```
Name: sams/net/UDPSend.class
Java-Bean: True

Name: sams/net/UDPReceive.class
Java-Bean: True

Name: sams/net/UDPReceiveThread.class
Java-Bean: False
```

FIGURE 16.1

The UDPReceive *bean displays a default message.*

Add two OurButton beans to the BeanBox window so that you can wire them up as start and stop buttons. Change the label property of one OurButton bean to Start. Wire this bean's actionPerformed event to the UDPReceive bean's startRunning() method. Change the label property of the other OurButton bean to Stop and wire its actionPerformed event to the UDPReceive bean's stopRunning() method.

Disable BeanBox's design mode. Your UDPReceive bean should look something like in Figure 16.2.

FIGURE 16.2

Your simple UDP application for receiving datagram packets is ready to use.

Start up the BeanBox from the other DOS or console window and place a UDPSend bean in the BeanBox window. The UDPSend bean is an invisible runtime bean with two properties and an important public method, the sendData() method. Add an OurButton bean to the BeanBox window and change its label property to Send Data. Then wire the button's actionPerformed event to the UDPSend bean's sendData() method. Disable the BeanBox design mode. This BeanBox window should look similar to the one in Figure 16.3.

FIGURE 16.3

Wire up the UDPSend *bean to a button bean.*

With both BeanBox windows set up and displayed at the same time, you can now try sending a UDP datagram package. First, start the UDPReceive bean's thread running by clicking the Start button in its BeanBox window. The UDPReceive bean should display a waiting to receive message, as shown in Figure 16.4.

FIGURE 16.4

The UDPReceive *bean is ready to receive a message through its socket.*

Send the data by clicking the Send Data button wired up to the UDPSend bean. The UDPReceive bean should receive a datagram package with the default message "I traveled the network as a datagram packet," as shown in Figure 16.5.

FIGURE 16.5

The UDPReceive *bean receives a datagram package over the Internet and displays it to its graphic interface.*

Internet Communication Using Sockets (TCP/IP)

CHAPTER **16**

331

16

INTERNET
COMMUNICATION
USING SOCKETS

Using TCP

Use TCP if you need highly reliable delivery of information across a network. TCP is a Transport layer protocol that is a connection-oriented protocol. It exchanges a series of datagram packets (called a *handshake*) with the destination host computer to establish the availability of the destination host and to let the host know about the sending host before any user data are actually transmitted. Because UDP doesn't have the handshaking overhead, it's faster.

Once the connection between the sending and receiving hosts is established, the fundamental unit of data transmission is no longer considered to be the datagram packet. Each packet is now considered to be a segment in a stream of data flowing between machines. TCP uses a system called positive acknowledgment with retransmission to guarantee the reliable delivery of each segment. Also, each segment carries out a checksum verification routine to make sure that a transmitted segment isn't corrupt. (If it is, it's resent.)

Java provides two classes that make it easy for you to use TCP in your Java beans: the ServerSocket and Socket classes. Both classes are part of the java.net package. Instances of the ServerSocket class represent server sockets that wait for socket requests to come over the network. Instances of the Socket class represent client sockets used to connect with server sockets with create TCP streams. First, you will use the ServerSocket class in the creation of a Telnet server bean. Next you will use the Socket class to create a Telnet client bean.

Creating a Telnet Server Bean

A Telnet server performs two generally defined tasks. It is a process that waits for an incoming request, or handshake, from a remote client to create a TCP stream and, once it's connected with a Telnet client, it receives and responds to commands. It should be able to connect with any number of Telnet clients at the same time. In the next sections you'll create two classes, each class corresponding to one of the previously mentioned tasks. The TelnetServer bean's TelnetServer class waits for incoming requests from remote clients and the TelnetClientService class receives and responds to commands from remote clients. Another bean that you'll create later provides a graphical interface. The TelnetServer bean is designed so you can plug it into any application. You pass messages from the TelnetServer bean to the rest of an application through bound property change events.

> **Note**
>
> The `TelnetServer` and `TelnetClientService` classes are mutually dependent. In other words, the `TelnetServer` class contains variable declarations using the `TelnetClientService` class and the `TelnetClientService` class contain variable declarations using the `TelnetServer` class. If you try to compile either one of these classes by itself, you get a whole lot of errors. You compile mutually dependent classes by referencing both classes after the `javac` command. Get more explicit instructions in the "Compiling the `TelnetServer` Classes" section later in this chapter.

The `TelnetServer` class is the `TelnetServer` bean's namesake. It creates the thread that waits for incoming requests from Telnet clients. When the `TelnetServer` bean receives and accepts a request for a connection with a Telnet client, it creates a `TelnetClientService` object that runs in its own thread. The `TelnetClientService` object runs a continuous loop that receives and responds to commands from its associated Telnet client.

Each time the `TelnetServer` object accepts a new connection with a Telnet client, it spawns a new `TelnetClientService` object that runs in its own separate thread. Each `TelnetClientService` object only communicates with the particular Telnet client that spawned it. Several `TelnetClientService` objects can run at the same time, this is limited only set by the number of clients allowed to be connected at one time by the instance of the `ServerSocket` class.

> **Note**
>
> Each Telnet connection takes computer hardware resources such as memory and processing. There is a practical limit set on the number of Telnet connections that your Telnet server can handle at one time by your computer hardware.

Writing the `TelnetServer` Class

First, write a `TelnetServer` class that does the following three things:

- Creates a `ServerSocket` object
- Listens for Telnet client connection requests
- Creates a `TelnetClientService` object when it accepts a Telnet client connection request

Refer to the `TelnetServer` class code in Listing 16.5 frequently while reading this section.

The `TelnetServer` class implements Java's Runnable interface and provides two properties; the `message` and `serviceMessage` properties. It also provides two important public methods: `start()` and `stop()`. The two properties allow the `TelnetServer` bean to communicate with other beans, applications, and scripting languages. The `start()` and `stop()` methods provide target methods that you can use to start and stop the running of the `TelnetServer` thread.

Creating Bound Properties

You need to add support for sending property change events using Java's `PropertyChangeSupport` class, and you need to add support for registering the event with property change event listeners. Create a `PropertyChangeSupport` variable named `changes` at the beginning of the `TelnetServer` class using the following declaration:

```
private PropertyChangeSupport changes =
    new PropertyChangeSupport( this );
```

Add support for adding and removing property change event listeners to the `TelnetServer` registration list by adding the `addPropertyChangeListener()` and `removePropertyChangeListener()` methods, shown next, to the `TelnetServer` class.

```
public void addPropertyChangeListener(
   PropertyChangeListener listener ) {
  changes.addPropertyChangeListener( listener );
}

public void removePropertyChangeListener(
   PropertyChangeListener listener ) {
  changes.removePropertyChangeListener( listener );
}
```

Note

Learn more about the Java event model in Chapter 6, "Event Model."

The message property holds humanly readable messages from the TelnetServer thread. The thread sends messages to the `message` property after a server socket is created and when the server connects with a new Telnet client. The `message` property is bound, so that every time the `TelnetServer` thread places a new message in the `message` property, a property change event is created. Of course, the event is only created if a property change event listener is registered with the class.

The `message` property mutator method, shown next, assigns the previous contents of the `message` variable to the `oldMessage` local string variable. The new message is then assigned to the `message` variable. And, finally, the `PropertyChangeSupport` class's `firePropertyChange()` method is called.

```
public void setMessage( String newMessage ) {
 String oldMessage = message;
 message = newMessage;
 changes.firePropertyChange( "message", oldMessage, newMessage );
}
```

The `firePropertyChange()` method creates a `PropertyChangeEvent` object if it's registered with a property change event listener. The name of the bound property is passed to the method's first parameter, the variable holding the old message is passed to the second parameter, and the new message is passed to the third parameter. All three pieces of information are available to the event listener that receives the `PropertyChangeEvent` object.

The `message` property accessor method, shown next, is standard and simply returns the value assigned to the `message` variable.

```
public String getMessage( ) {
 return message;
}
```

The `serviceMessage` property is similar to the `message` property except that it receives humanly readable messages from the `TelnetClientService` thread. Commands typed into connected Telnet clients by users are processed by the `TelnetClientService` thread. These commands are also held by the `serviceMessage` property. Like the `message` property, the `serviceMessage` property is bound and creates a property change event every time the property is changed as long as the property change event is registered with an event listener.

The `serviceMessage` property mutator and accessor methods are shown next. They are the same as the `message` property accessor methods except, of course, they use the `serviceMessage` variable rather than the `message` variable.

```
public void setServiceMessage( String newServiceMessage ) {
   String oldServiceMessage = serviceMessage;
   serviceMessage = newServiceMessage;
   changes.firePropertyChange( "serviceMessage",
    oldServiceMessage, newServiceMessage );
}

public String getServiceMessage( ) {
   return serviceMessage;
}
```

Creating Public Methods

When you design a bean, you want to be sure to provide public methods so that other beans, applications, or scripting languages can control important aspects of your bean's functions. You can start and stop the TelnetServer bean through the start() and stop() methods.

You start the TelnetServer running by calling the start() method, shown in the following:

```
public void start( ) {
  if ( thread == null ) {
    thread = new Thread( this );
    try {
      listener = new ServerSocket( TELNET_PORT, 5 );
    }
    catch ( IOException e ) {
    }
    thread.start( );
    setMessage( "Telnet server started" );
  }
}
```

The TelnetServer class runs in a separate thread. Therefore, you first test to see that the TelnetServer thread isn't already running. If it isn't, you create a new thread, create a new ServerSocket object, and start the thread running by calling the Thread class's start() method. You learn more about creating a ServerSocket object shortly in the "Creating ServerSocket Objects" section.

The stop() method, shown next, is a straightforward way to stop the TelnetServer thread.

```
public void stop( ) {
  if ( thread != null ) {
    thread.stop( );
    thread = null;
  }
}
```

The method checks to see that there is, in fact, a thread running. If there is, the thread is stopped by a call to the Thread class's stop() method and null is assigned to the thread variable.

Creating ServerSocket Objects

The following shows again that the start() method contains a statement creating a ServerSocket object:

```
listener = new ServerSocket( TELNET_PORT, 5 );
```

The `ServerSocket` object is assigned to the `listener` variable. The `TelnetServer` object uses the `ServerSocket` object to listen for TCP connection requests from TCP client sockets. The signature of the `ServerSocket` constructor is shown in the following:

```
ServerSocket(int port, int backlog)
```

This `ServerSocket` constructor takes two parameters: `port` and `backlog`. The first parameter, `port`, takes an integer value representing the port number of the server socket. The declaration area in the `ServerSocket` class declares the `TELNET_PORT` integer constant value `23`, the port value typically used for Telnet. The `TelnetServer` class passes the `TELNET_PORT` integer constant to the `port` parameter. The second parameter, `backlog`, takes an integer value representing the maximum number of TCP connections the server socket can accept at one time. The `TelnetServer` class passes the `backlog` parameter the value of `5` so that the `TelnetServer` bean can only accept five simultaneous Telnet sessions. You can experiment with this number. The number of connections that your computer can handle depends on your computer's hardware resources.

Listening for Socket Requests

When someone or something starts the `TelnetServer` bean's thread running by calling its `start()` method, the `ServerSocket` object is created and the `message` property is sent its first message through the following statement:

```
setMessage( "Telnet server started" );
```

Beans, applications, or scripting languages with property change event listeners registered with the TelnetServer bean receive the message and can display or act on it accordingly.

`TelnetServer` thread's `run()` method then begins running and the second message is sent to the message property through the following statement:

```
setMessage( "Waiting for client..." );
```

Any objects registered to listen find out that the `TelnetServer` is waiting for Telnet clients to request connections. Then the `TelnetServer` thread goes into an infinite `while` loop.

The first statement in the infinite `while` loop, shown next, tells the `ServerSocket` object, held by the `listener` variable, to keep a vigilant lookout for client sockets requesting connections.

```
Socket client = listener.accept( );
```

The `ServerSocket` object calls the `ServerSocket` class's `accept()` method, as shown in the following:

```
public Socket accept()
```

The `accept()` method listens for client sockets requesting connections. When it accepts a request, it creates a TCP connection between the client and server sockets. The `accept()` method blocks further program execution until a connection is made. Therefore, the infinite loop is paused on the first statement until the server socket receives a request to make a connection with a client socket. When the connection is made, a reference to the client socket is passed to the `client` variable, and the rest of the statements of the loop are executed until the statement with the `ServerSocket` class's `accept()` method is executed again. The thread pauses again until another client socket requests a connection and the whole process is repeated.

After a TCP connection is formed, the next statement in the loop sends the message to the `message` property that a client socket was accepted. Then, as shown in the following statement, a new `TelnetClientService` object is created.

```
TelnetClientService serviceThread =
    new TelnetClientService( client, this );
```

The `TelnetClientService` object runs a loop for receiving and responding to commands sent from the Telnet client socket. You write the `TelnetClientService` class in the next section, "Writing the `TelnetClientService` Class." Its constructor takes a reference to the `Socket` object of the client socket that the `TelnetClientService` object will service. It also takes a reference to `TelnetServer` bean's `TelnetServer` object so it has access to the `setServiceMessage` method. The new `TelnetClientService` object is assigned to the `clientThread` variable.

After a `TelnetClientService` object is created, the final statement in `TelnetServer` class's infinite loop is executed. The following statement starts the new `TelnetClientService` object's thread running:

```
clientThread.start( );
```

The same loop is executed over and over until something kills the process, as seen in Listing 16.5. In the next section, you write the `TelnetClientService` class, which does most of the work in a TelnetServer session.

> **Note**
>
> Wait to compile the `TelnetServer` class until you can compile the `TelnetClientService` class along with it. More instructions about compiling these mutually dependent classes are in the "Compiling the `TelnetServer` Classes" section that follows.

Listing 16.5 Source Code for `TelnetServer.java`

```java
package sams.net;

import java.beans.PropertyChangeListener;
import java.beans.PropertyChangeSupport;
import java.io.IOException;
import java.net.ServerSocket;
import java.net.Socket;

public class TelnetServer implements Runnable {
  private final int TELNET_PORT = 23;
  private ServerSocket listener = null;
  private String message = "";
  private String serviceMessage = "";
  private Thread thread = null;
  private PropertyChangeSupport changes =
    new PropertyChangeSupport( this );

  public void start( ) {
    if ( thread == null ) {
      thread = new Thread( this );
      try {
        listener = new ServerSocket( TELNET_PORT, 5 );
      }
      catch ( IOException e ) {
      }
      thread.start( );
      setMessage( "Telnet server started" );
    }
  }

  public void stop( ) {
    if ( thread != null ) {
      thread.stop( );
      thread = null;
    }
  }

  public void run() {
    setMessage( "Waiting for client..." );
    while ( true ) {
      try {
        Socket client = listener.accept( );
        setMessage( "Client accepted" );
        TelnetClientService serviceThread =
         new TelnetClientService( client, this );
        serviceThread.start( );
```

```
      }
      catch ( IOException e ) {
      }
    }
  }

  public void setMessage( String newMessage ) {
    String oldMessage = message;
    message = newMessage;
    changes.firePropertyChange( "message", oldMessage, newMessage );
  }

  public String getMessage( ) {
    return message;
  }

  public void setServiceMessage( String newServiceMessage ) {
    String oldServiceMessage = serviceMessage;
    serviceMessage = newServiceMessage;
    changes.firePropertyChange( "serviceMessage",
      oldServiceMessage, newServiceMessage );
  }

  public String getServiceMessage( ) {
    return serviceMessage;
  }

  public void addPropertyChangeListener(
      PropertyChangeListener listener ) {
    changes.addPropertyChangeListener( listener );
  }

  public void removePropertyChangeListener(
      PropertyChangeListener listener ) {
    changes.removePropertyChangeListener( listener );
  }
}
```

Writing the `TelnetClientService` Class

Write a `TelnetClientService` class that does the following three things:

- Creates buffered data input and output streams for communicating with the Telnet client
- Prompts the Telnet client for login and password verification
- Runs an infinite loop for receiving and responding to commands sent from the Telnet client socket

Refer to the `TelnetClientService` class code in Listing 16.6 frequently while reading this section.

The `TelnetClientService` class has a constructor and a `run()` method. This class doesn't provide any properties or public methods. The `TelnetServer` class provides all of the bean's properties and public methods. The `TelnetServer` class provides the `serviceMessage` property that the `TelnetClientService` class uses. The `TelnetClientService` class constructor assigns the `Socket` object passed from a `TelnetClient` bean to the `clientSocket` class variable, and then it creates buffered data input and output streams.

Creating Buffered Data Input and Output

You use two Java classes to create buffered data streams. Create a buffered input data stream using the `BufferedInputStream` class and create a buffered output data stream using the `BufferedOutputStream`. The `BufferedInputStream` class provides two constructors. One constructor, shown next, creates a `BufferedInputStream` object that uses a default buffer size of 512 bytes.

```
public BufferedInputStream(InputStream in)
```

This constructor has one parameter, `in`, that takes an `InputStream` object. `InputStream` is an abstract class, so you actually pass the `in` parameter a subclass of the `InputStream` class. If it seems like you're going in circles here, you're right! The `BufferedInputStream` class is itself a subclass of the `InputStream` class. Java's input and output streams nest. Java's `Socket` class, however, makes it easy to get the TCP input stream and nest it inside the `BufferedInputStream` object so that a buffer is created for the TCP input. You'll see how to do this shortly, but first look at `BufferedInputStream` class's other constructor, shown in the following:

```
public BufferedInputStream(InputStream in, int size)
```

This constructor has two parameters, the `in` parameter that you've seen already and the `size` parameter. The `size` parameter takes an integer value representing the size of the buffer you want created for the `BufferedInputStream` object.

The `TelnetClientService` constructor creates a buffered input data stream from a `TelnetClient` bean with the following line of code:

```
dataInput = new BufferedInputStream( clientSocket.getInputStream( ) );
```

The statement includes the `BufferedInputStream` constructor that takes one parameter. You pass the TCP `InputStream` from the client socket (from the `TelnetClient` bean with which it's connected) to the `BufferedInputStream` object by calling the `Socket` class `getInputStream()` method. (Recall that the `clientSocket` variable holds a

Internet Communication Using Sockets (TCP/IP)

CHAPTER 16

341

16

INTERNET
COMMUNICATION
USING SOCKETS

reference to the `TelnetClient` bean's `Socket` object.) The following shows the signature for `Socket` class's `getInputStream()` method:

```
public InputStream getInputStream()
```

The new `BufferedInputStream` object is assigned to the `dataInput` class variable. The `TelnetServerClientThread` object is ready to receive input from the `TelnetClient` that spawned its creation.

The procedures discussed previously repeat in the next, and final, statement in the `TelnetClientService` constructor, shown next, with two differences. Java's `BufferedOutputStream` class is used instead of the `BufferedInputStream` class and the `Socket` class's `getOutputStream()` method is used instead of its `getInputStream()` method.

```
dataOutput = new BufferedOutputStream( clientSocket.getOutputStream( ) );
```

As you probably suspect, the `BufferedOutputStream` class provides two constructors identical to the `BufferedInputStream` constructors, except that these take an `OutputStream` object as one of the parameters, the `out` parameter. Both constructors are shown next.

```
public BufferedOutputStream(OutputStream out)
public BufferedOutputStream(OutputStream out, int size)
```

Like the `InputStream` class, `OutputStream` is an abstract class. You pass the TCP `OutputStream` from the client socket to the `BufferedOutputStream` object by calling the `Socket` class `getOutputStream()` method. The following is the signature for `Socket` class's `getOutputStream()` method:

```
public OutputStream getOutputStream()
```

The new `BufferedOutputStream` object is assigned to the `dataOutput` class variable. The `TelnetServerClientThread` object is ready to send output to the `TelnetClient` that spawned its creation.

Running `TelnetClientService` Object's Thread

The `TelnetService` object starts the `TelnetClientService` object right after creating it through a call to the `TelnetClientService` class's `start()` method, inherited from Java's `Thread` class. Running the `start()` method results in a call to the `run()` method where most of the work is done. That's where the `TelnetServer` bean prompts the Telnet client for login and password verification. Then the method enters into an infinite loop, which begins receiving and responding to commands sent from the Telnet client socket.

Adding Login and Password Verification

The first part of the `TelnetClientService` class's `run()` method, from the first statement to the `while` statement, processes login and password verification from the Telnet client. This version of Telnet doesn't actually process the login and password verification like they should be processed in a full-blown Telnet server. The code is meant to be instructive.

The first thing that the `TelnetClientService` class's `run()` method does is create a `String` object encapsulating a login prompt, as shown in the first statement of the following three initial statements:

```
String login = "Login";
dataOutput.write( login.getBytes( ) );
dataOutput.flush( );
```

Next, the login prompt is sent through the buffered output stream to the `TelnetClient` bean as a byte array. This is done in the second line of the preceding code. The login prompt is sent to the output stream by using the `write()` method that the `BufferedOutputStream` class inherited from the `FilterOutputStream` class. The following is the `write()` method's signature:

```
public void write(byte b[])
```

The `write()` method takes an array of bytes. Use the `String` class's `getBytes()` method, shown next, to translate the login prompt encapsulated in a `String` object into a byte array.

```
public byte[] getBytes()
```

Finally, the `BufferedOutputStream` class's `flush()` method, shown next, is used to force any bytes that may be left in the output stream's buffer into the output stream.

```
public synchronized void flush()
```

The next segment of code reads the user's response to the login prompt from the buffered input stream and assigns the response to the `serviceMessage` property. Then it sends a password prompt to the `TelnetClient` bean, as shown in the following:

```
int count = 0;
byte buf[] = new byte[255];
count = dataInput.read( buf, 0, 255 );
user = new String( buf, 0, count );
server.setServiceMessage( "User is " + user );
String passwordPrompt = "Enter your password";
dataOutput.write( passwordPrompt.getBytes( ) );
dataOutput.flush( );
```

Internet Communication Using Sockets (TCP/IP)

CHAPTER 16

343

16

INTERNET
COMMUNICATION
USING SOCKETS

The first two lines of code declare variables that are used throughout the run() method. The program uses the count variable to hold the integer value of the length of data, in bytes, read from the buffered input stream. It uses the buf variable as a temporary buffer, 255 bytes long, to hold data read from the buffered input stream.

The third line of code in the preceding code segment reads data sent from the TelnetClient program by using the BufferedInputStream class's read() method, shown in the following:

```
public synchronized int read(byte b[], int off, int len)
```

The read() method has three parameters: the b, off, and len parameters. The b parameter takes an empty byte array large enough to capture the data arriving from the TelnetClient bean through the buffered input stream. The buf variable described previously fills the role. The off parameter takes an integer value representing the number of bytes that should be read from the input stream before bytes begin to be saved. All of TelnetClientService class's invocations of the read() method pass the off parameter a 0 and save all incoming bytes. Finally, the len parameter takes an integer value that represents the maximum number of bytes that can be read. The value of the len parameter should be no larger than the size of the buffer into which the data is being read. All of the calls to the read() method in the TelnetClientService class pass 255, the size of the buf variable, to the len parameter.

The BufferedInputStream class's read() method blocks further execution of the thread until it receives something from the TelnetClient bean. So the Telnet server thread supporting a particular client just sits there until a user responds to the server's prompt. Once the user responds, the server reads the response from the buffered input data stream through the BufferedInputStream class's read() method. Then the server sends a new prompt. This time it's a password prompt, as you can see from the last few lines from the previous code segment.

After the user responds with a password, the login and password verification sequence (without the actual verification) is finished. A welcome message is sent to the TelnetClient bean telling the user to enter commands. Then a String object encapsulating a message to enter commands is created and saved in the prompt variable, and an infinite loop begins executing.

The first five lines in the infinite while loop do almost all of the work, and they're all statements that you've already seen in the TelnetClientService class. Program execution stops and waits at the BufferedInputStream class's read() method for input from the user. When it arrives, it's assigned to the TelnetClient class's serviceMessage property. Then a new prompt to enter a command is sent to the TelnetClient bean. The rest of the lines in the loop check the command to see if any action should be taken.

Processing Telnet Client Commands

The final part of the infinite `while` loop in the `TelnetClientService` class's `run()` method checks the command sent from the `TelnetClient` bean to see if the server should take any one of two actions: Close the current socket or kill the whole `TelnetServer` process.

The `TelnetClientService` class recognizes two commands, `exit` and `quit`, that close the current socket. An `if` statement determines whether the `command` variable, the variable holding the `String` object encapsulating the command received from the `TelnetClient` bean, is equal to either `exit` or `quit`. The program uses the `String` class's `equals()` method, shown next, to determine the equality.

```
public boolean equals(Object anObject)
```

The `String` class's `equals()` method tests to see if the `Object` object passed to the `anObject` parameter is equal to the string encapsulated in the `String` object. If they are equal, the method returns a `true`; otherwise, it returns a `false`. When either case is true, a message that the client is disconnected is assigned to the `TelnetServer` class's `serviceMessage` property, and then the socket is closed using the `Socket` class's `close()` method, as shown in the following:

```
public synchronized void close()
```

One command, `kill`, kills the whole `TelnetServer` process. An `else...if` clause tests to see if the command sent from the `TelnetClient` is a `kill` command. This can be seen in Listing 16.6. If it is a `kill` command, a message that the server is assigned to the `TelnetServer` class's `serviceMessage` property, and the `System` class's `exit()` method is called.

> **Caution**
>
> Beware that a call to the `System` class's `exit()` method results in exiting the whole Java process. In other words, it closes down the JVM in which the `TelnetServer` bean runs.

Listing 16.6   Source Code for `TelnetClientService.java`

```
package sams.net;

import java.io.BufferedInputStream;
import java.io.BufferedOutputStream;
import java.io.IOException;
```

Internet Communication Using Sockets (TCP/IP)

CHAPTER 16

345

16

INTERNET
COMMUNICATION
USING SOCKETS

```java
import java.net.Socket;

class TelnetClientService extends Thread {
  private Socket clientSocket = null;
  private TelnetServer server = null;
  private BufferedInputStream dataInput = null;
  private BufferedOutputStream dataOutput = null;

  public TelnetClientService( Socket client, TelnetServer server ) {
    clientSocket = client;
    this.server = server;
    try {
      dataInput = new BufferedInputStream( client.getInputStream( ) );
      dataOutput = new BufferedOutputStream( client.getOutputStream( ) );
    }
    catch ( IOException e ) {
    }
  }

  public void run( ) {
    String user;
    String password;

    try {
      String login = "Login";
      dataOutput.write( login.getBytes( ) );
      dataOutput.flush( );

      int count = 0;
      byte buf[] = new byte[255];
      count = dataInput.read( buf, 0, 255 );
      user = new String( buf, 0, count );
      server.setServiceMessage( "User is " + user );
      String passwordPrompt = "Enter your password";
      dataOutput.write( passwordPrompt.getBytes( ) );
      dataOutput.flush( );

      count = dataInput.read( buf, 0, 255 );
      password = new String( buf, 0, count );
      server.setServiceMessage( "Password is " + password );
      String welcome = "Welcome! Enter command";
      dataOutput.write( welcome.getBytes( ) );
      dataOutput.flush( );

      String prompt = "Enter a command";
      String command = null;

      while ( true ) {
```

continues

Listing 16.6   continued

```
        count = dataInput.read( buf, 0, 255 );
        command =  new String( buf, 0, count );
        server.setServiceMessage( command );
        dataOutput.write( prompt.getBytes( ) );
        dataOutput.flush( );
        if( command.equals( "exit" ) || command.equals( "quit" ) ) {
          server.setServiceMessage( "Client disconnected" );
          clientSocket.close( );
        }
        else if( command.equals( "kill" ) ) {
          server.setServiceMessage( "Server killed" );
          System.exit( 0 );
        }
      }
    }
    catch ( IOException e ) {
    }
  }
}
```

Compiling the `TelnetServer` Classes

The `TelnetServer` and `TelnetClientService` classes are mutually dependent. The `TelnetServer` class contains variable declarations using the `TelnetClientService` class, and the `TelnetClientService` class contains variable declarations using the `TelnetServer` class. If you try to compile either one of these classes by itself, you get a whole lot of errors. Compile mutually dependent classes by referencing both classes after the `javac` command.

Open a DOS or console window and change to your root class directory, such as `c:\jdk1.2.x\myclasses`. Place the `TelnetServer.java` and `TelnetClientService.java` files in the correct directory, such as the `c:\jdk1.2.x\myclasses\sams\net` directory. Then type in the following command at the DOS or console window prompt:

```
javac sams\net\TelnetServer.java sams\net\TelnetClientService.java
```

You should find the compiled class files in the `c:\jdk1.2.x\myclasses\sams\net` directory when `javac` is done compiling.

Creating a `TelnetClient` Bean

You put a lot of work into writing the `TelnetServer` bean. Luckily, all that work makes writing the `TelnetClient` bean relatively easy. Much of what you learned earlier this chapter applies to writing the `TelnetClient` bean. Users interact remotely with the `TelnetServer` bean through direct interactions with the `TelnetClient` bean.

Internet Communication Using Sockets (TCP/IP)

CHAPTER 16

347

16

INTERNET
COMMUNICATION
USING SOCKETS

The `TelnetClient` bean is composed of three classes: the `TelnetClient`,
`TelnetClientCommands`, and `TelnetClientThread` classes. The `TelnetClient` class is
the bean's namesake and the class that provides the bean's graphic user interface. It
spawns the `TelnetClientThread` that runs in an infinite loop and communicates with
`TelnetServer` beans. The `TelnetClientCommands` class reacts to user input into the
`TelnetClient` bean's graphic user interface.

Writing the `TelnetClient` Class

The `TelnetClient` class, shown in Listing 16.7, is extended from Java's `Panel` class and
contains two graphic user interface components: a label and a text field. The class provides the `internetAddress` property and `start()` and `stop()` public methods. Use the
`internetAddress` property to change the address of the Telnet server with which you
want the `TelnetClient` bean to connect. Use the `start()` and `stop()` methods to start
and stop running the `TelnetClient` bean. All of the code in the `TelnetClient` class
should be familiar to you, but go through it quickly as a review.

Create the `internetAddress` property by declaring the `internetAddress` private `String`
variable, shown next, as you did when you wrote the `UDPSend` bean.

```
private String internetAddress = "localhost";
```

The property is set to `"localhost"` by default. Change the `internetAddress` property
through its mutator method as follows:

```
public void setInternetAddress( String address ) {
  internetAddress = address;
}
```

The `setInternetAddress()` mutator method is very simple. It updates the name of the
Internet address held by the `internetAddress` property. The `internetAddress` property
accessor method is also simple, as you can see from the following code:

```
public String getInternetAddress( ) {
  return internetAddress;
}
```

The `TelnetClient` constructor, shown next, adds a `Label` and a `TextField` component to
the `TelnetClient` container class. Recall that the `TelnetClient` class is derived from
Java's `Panel` class.

```
public TelnetClient( ) {
  clientCommands = new TelnetClientCommands( this );
  add( myLabel = new Label( "Messages from a Telnet server" ) );
  add( myTextField = new TextField( "Messages to server" ) );
  myTextField.addActionListener( clientCommands );
}
```

The constructor also creates a `TelnetClientCommands` object and registers it as an action event listener to the `TextField` component. You write the `TelnetClientCommands` class later this chapter in the "Writing the `TelnetClientCommands` Class" section.

The `TelnetClientThread` class does the main work of the `TelnetClient` bean. The `TelnetClient` class is mainly used to create the bean's graphic user interface. The `TelnetClientThread` class is derived from Java's `Thread` class. You start the `TelnetClient` bean by calling `TelnetClient` class's `start()` method, as shown in the following:

```java
public void start( ) {
  if( clientThread == null ) {
    clientThread = new TelnetClientThread( this );
    clientThread.start( );
    myTextField.setText( "" );
  }
}
```

The `start()` method starts the `TelnetClientThread` object's thread running. First, it checks to see if there is a `TelnetClientThread` thread running already. If there isn't, a new `TelnetClientThread` object is created and its `start()` method is called. The last statement in the `start()` method clears the `TextField` component of any text.

You stop the `TelnetClient` bean running by calling its `stop()` method, as shown in the following:

```java
public void stop( ) {
  if( clientThread != null ) {
    clientThread.stop( );
    clientThread = null;
  }
}
```

The `stop()` method checks to see if a `TelnetClientThread` thread is running. If there is, the thread is stopped and the `clientThread` variable holding the `TelnetClientThread` object is assigned `null`.

The final two methods, shown next in Listing 16.7, set the size of `TelnetClient` bean's panel to 200 pixels wide by 75 pixels high.

```java
public Dimension getMinimumSize() {
  return new Dimension(200, 75);
}

public Dimension getPreferredSize() {
  return minimumSize();
}
```

Listing 16.7 Source Code for `TelnetClient.java`

```java
package sams.net;

import java.awt.Dimension;
import java.awt.Label;
import java.awt.TextField;

public class TelnetClient extends java.awt.Panel {
  private TelnetClientThread clientThread = null;
  private TelnetClientCommands clientCommands = null;
  private String internetAddress = "localhost";

  boolean enter = false;
  TextField myTextField = null;
  Label myLabel = null;

  public TelnetClient( ) {
    clientCommands = new TelnetClientCommands( this );
    add( myLabel = new Label( "Messages from a Telnet server" ) );
    add( myTextField = new TextField( "Messages to server" ) );
    myTextField.addActionListener( clientCommands );
  }

  public void start( ) {
    if( clientThread == null ) {
      clientThread = new TelnetClientThread( this );
      clientThread.start( );
      myTextField.setText( "" );
    }
  }

  public void stop( ) {
    if( clientThread != null ) {
      clientThread.stop( );
      clientThread = null;
    }
  }

  public void setInternetAddress( String address ) {
    internetAddress = address;
  }

  public String getInternetAddress( ) {
    return internetAddress;
  }

  public Dimension minimumSize() {
```

continues

Listing 16.7 continued

```
   return new Dimension(200, 75);
 }

 public Dimension preferredSize() {
   return minimumSize();
 }
}
```

Writing the `TelnetClientThread` Class

The `TelnetClientThread` class, shown in Listing 16.8, does most of `TelnetClient` bean's work. The `TelnetClientThread` class does the following four things:

- Creates an IP address from the `internetAddress` property
- Creates buffered data input, output streams for communicating with `TelnetServer` beans
- Runs an infinite loop for sending and receiving commands through TCP with a `TelnetServer` bean
- Tests user commands to see if an action should be carried out

The `TelnetClientThread` class is extended from Java's `Thread` class and includes a constructor and a `run()` method. The constructor includes code that creates an `InetAddress` object, a `Socket` object, two `BufferedInputStream` objects, and a `BufferedOutputStream` object.

The `TelnetClientThread` constructor calls the private `encapsulateAddress()` method, shown next, after assigning a reference to `TelnetClient` bean's `TelnetClient` object to the `telnetClient` variable. The call results in the IP address of the local host computer, the computer on which the bean resides, being encapsulated in the `InetAddress` object that is assigned to the `ipAddress` variable.

```
private InetAddress encapsulateAddress( ) {
  try {
    return InetAddress.getByName( telnetClient.internetAddress );
  }
  catch( Exception e ) {
    return null;
  }
}
```

The `encapsulateAddress()` method passes the `internetAddress` property to the `InetAddress` class's `getByName()` method. The `internetAddress` property is a `String` object representation of the Internet address to which you want to send a message. The property is set to `"localhost"` by default, but you can change it through the `TelnetClient` bean's `internetAddress` property editor during design time or through the property's mutator method during runtime. The `getByName()` method returns an `InetAddress` object that is passed to the calling statement.

The `TelnetClientThread` constructor creates a `Socket` object after it creates a new `InetAddress` object. You haven't used the `Socket` class before now.

Using Java's `Socket` Class

Instantiating Java's `Socket` class creates a TCP stream socket connected to the specified host computer and port number. The `Socket` class provides a half a dozen constructors. The following are the two most commonly used constructors:

```
public Socket(String host, int port)
public Socket(InetAddress address, int port)
```

The first constructor requires a `String` object representing the name of the TCP connection's host computer passed to its first parameter, `host`, and an integer value representing the port number where the process will be found passed to the second parameter, `port`.

The second constructor requires an `InetAddress` object encapsulating the IP address of the TCP connection's host computer passed to its first parameter, `address`, and, like the first constructor, it takes an integer value representing the port number where the process will be found passed to the second parameter, `port`.

The `TelnetClientThread` class uses the first version of the `Socket` constructor to create `Socket` objects. These are, of course, the very `Socket` objects passed to and manipulated by the `TelnetServer` bean you wrote earlier in this chapter.

The rest of the `TelnetClientThread` class should look familiar to you from writing the `TelnetServer` bean. Most of the work is done in the infinite `while` loop found in the `run()` method. The loop goes through the familiar read data and write data cycle with the one difference that it reads from two sources: the `TelnetServer` with which it's connected and the local user of the `TelnetClient` bean. User input arrives through `TelnetClient` bean's graphic user interface provided by the `TelnetClient` class. Specifically, a user types in commands into the `TelnetClient` bean's text field. You learn more about this in the next section when you write `TelnetClient` bean's `TelnetClientCommands` class.

Finally, the `TelnetClientThread` class's `run()` method, shown in Listing 16.8, includes an `if` statement that tests for all three of the commands that either end the TCP connection by killing the socket or kill the `TelnetServer` bean. Either way, the program breaks out of the infinite loop and the `TelnetClient` bean and its associated program is closed.

Listing 16.8   Source Code for `TelnetClientThread.java`

```java
package sams.net;

import java.io.BufferedInputStream;
import java.io.BufferedOutputStream;
import java.io.IOException;
import java.net.InetAddress;
import java.net.Socket;

class TelnetClientThread extends Thread {
  private final int TELNET_PORT = 23;
  private Socket socket = null;
  private BufferedInputStream dataInput = null;
  private BufferedOutputStream dataOutput = null;
  private TelnetClient telnetClient = null;
  private InetAddress ipAddress = null;

  public TelnetClientThread( TelnetClient telnetClient ) {
    this.telnetClient = telnetClient;
    ipAddress = encapsulateAddress( );
    try {
      socket = new Socket( ipAddress, TELNET_PORT );
      telnetClient.myLabel.setText( "Socket created" );
      Thread.sleep( 500 );
      dataInput = new BufferedInputStream( socket.getInputStream( ) );
      dataOutput = new BufferedOutputStream( socket.getOutputStream( ) );
    }
    catch ( Exception e ) {
    }
  }

  public void run( ) {
    int count = 0;
    byte buf[] = new byte[255];
    String command = null;

    while ( true ) {
      try {
        count = dataInput.read( buf, 0, 255 );
        telnetClient.myLabel.setText( new String( buf, 0, count ) );
        while( !telnetClient.enter ) Thread.sleep( 100 );
        command = telnetClient.myTextField.getText( );
        dataOutput.write( command.getBytes( ) );
        dataOutput.flush( );
        telnetClient.myTextField.setText( "" );
        telnetClient.enter = false;
        if( command.equals( "exit" ) || command.equals( "quit" )
            || command.equals( "kill" ) ) {
```

```
            Thread.sleep( 1000 );
            System.exit( 0 );
            break;
        }
      }
      catch ( Exception e ) {
      }
    }
  }

  private InetAddress encapsulateAddress( ) {
    try {
      return InetAddress.getByName( telnetClient.getInternetAddress( ) );
    }
    catch( Exception e ) {
      return null;
    }
  }
}
```

Writing the `TelnetClientCommands` Class

The `TelnetClientCommands` class, shown in Listing 16.9, is registered to receive action events from the `TextField` object created by the `TelnetClient` class. Pressing your Enter or Return key while a `TextField` object has the focus causes it to fire off an action event. The `TelnetClientCommands` class catches the action event and assigns `true` to the `TelnetClient` class's enter variable. This `enter` variable is central to the proper function of the infinite loop in the `TelnetClientThread` class.

The `enter` variable is `false` by default. This makes the infinite loop in `TelnetClientThread` class's `run()` method pause because of the following code:

```
while( !telnetClient.enter ) Thread.sleep( 100 );
```

The `telnetClient` variable holds a reference to the `TelnetClient` object. This `while` statement keeps looping as long as `TelnetClient` object's enter variable is `false`. Finally, after a user enters text into `TelnetClient` bean's text field and presses the Enter or Return key, the `enter` variable becomes `true`, the `while` loop is broken, and the following statement is executed:

```
command = telnetClient.myTextField.getText( );
```

This statement gathers the text typed into the bean's text field and assigns it to the `command` variable as can be seen in Listing 16.9. The statements that follow send the command to the `TelnetServer`, clear the `TelnetClient` bean's text field, and finally set the `enter` variable back to `false`.

Listing 16.9   Source Code for `TelnetClientCommands.java`

```java
package sams.net;

import java.awt.event.ActionEvent;

class TelnetClientCommands implements java.awt.event.ActionListener {
  TelnetClient telnetClient = null;

  public TelnetClientCommands( TelnetClient telnetClient ) {
    this.telnetClient = telnetClient;
  }

  public void actionPerformed( ActionEvent e ) {
    switch( e.getID( ) ) {
      case ActionEvent.ACTION_PERFORMED:
        telnetClient.enter = true;
        break;
    }
  }
}
```

Creating the TelnetServerInterface Bean

You designed the `TelnetServer` bean as an invisible runtime bean. It's a flexible bean that can be used in nearly any application that needs a Telnet server. You'll test the `TelnetServer` bean by wiring it up with a simple interface that displays the messages held by the `TelnetServer` bean's `message` and `serviceMessage` properties.

Recall that `TelnetServer` bean's `message` property holds messages that originate in the `TelnetServer` bean itself. Its `serviceMessage` property, in contrast, holds messages received from Telnet clients. Also recall that both properties are bound, therefore, they send the `PropertyChangeEvent` objects each time they're set to a new value. Any object that you want to get the contents of `TelnetServer` bean's properties must implement the `PropertyChangeListener` interface. The `PropertyChangeListener` interface is necessary so that the object can be registered with the `TelnetServer` bean as a property change event listener.

In this section, you will create the `TelnetServerInterface` bean for displaying messages processed through the `TelnetServer` bean. The bean is created from the `TelnetServerInterface` class shown in Listing 16.10. The class extends the `TextArea` class from Java's `java.awt` package and implements the `PropertyChangeListener` interface from the `java.beans` package.

Internet Communication Using Sockets (TCP/IP)

CHAPTER 16

355

16

INTERNET
COMMUNICATION
USING SOCKETS

The `PropertyChangeListener` interface provides one abstract method, the `propertyChange()` method, which you must implement. In fact, the `propertyChange()` method, shown next, does almost all of the work in the `TelnetServerInterface` bean.

```
public void propertyChange( PropertyChangeEvent event ) {
  String propertyName = event.getPropertyName( );
  if ( propertyName == "message" ¦¦ propertyName == "serviceMessage" ) {
    append( (String) event.getNewValue( ) + "\n" );
  }
}
```

The `propertyChange()` method is called every time the object that registered the `TelnetServerInterface` bean as a property change event listener creates a `PropertyChangeEvent` object. A reference to the `PropertyChangeEvent` object itself is passed to the `propertyChange()` method through the `event` parameter.

The `PropertyChangeEvent` object encapsulates all of the information you need about the contents of `TelnetServer` bean's properties. It contains the property's name, the property's old value, and the property's new value. You can get these values using the `PropertyChangeEvent` class's accessor methods: `getPropertyName()`, `getOldValue()`, and `getNewValue()`.

The first thing that the `propertyChange()` method in the `TelnetServerInterface` bean does is find out if the `PropertyChangeEvent` object it received encapsulates one of the two `TelnetServer` bean properties. The first statement gets the current `PropertyChangeEvent` object's property name by calling the `getPropertyName()` method. The property name is assigned to the `propertyName` local string variable. The `if` statement then checks to see if the `String` object held by the `propertyName` variable is equal to `"message"` or `"serviceMessage"`. If it is, the statement in the `if` statement block, shown next, is executed.

```
append( (String) event.getNewValue( ) + "\n" );
```

The code calls the `PropertyChangeEvent` class's `getNewValue()` method, which returns the latest `TelnetServer` bean message. The return value is cast as a `String` object because you know that the properties you're checking are strings. The method's return type is `Object` so that the method can return any kind of object that a property can hold. The new line escape character is added to the string returned by the `getNewValue()` method so that each string is put in its own line. Finally, the string is displayed in the `TelnetServerInterface` bean text area by using the `TextArea` class's `append()` method.

That's all there is to displaying `TelnetServer` bean's `message` and `serviceMessage` properties. The two remaining methods in the `TelnetServerInterface` class should look familiar to you. They're the `Component` class's `getMinimumSize()` and `getPreferredSize()` methods that you use to set the size of a graphical user interface object. With the `TelnetServerInterface` bean finished, you are ready to test your Telnet beans.

Listing 16.10   Source Code for `TelnetServerInterface.java`

```java
package sams.net;

import java.awt.Color;
import java.awt.Dimension;
import java.beans.PropertyChangeEvent;

public class TelnetServerInterface extends java.awt.TextArea
   implements java.beans.PropertyChangeListener, java.io.Serializable {

  public void propertyChange( PropertyChangeEvent event ) {
    String propertyName = event.getPropertyName( );
    if ( propertyName == "message" ||
      propertyName == "serviceMessage" ) {
      append( (String) event.getNewValue( ) + "\n" );
    }
  }

  public Dimension getMinimumSize() {
    return new Dimension(150, 150);
  }

  public Dimension getPreferredSize() {
    return getMinimumSize();
  }
}
```

Packaging the Beans into a JAR

Try out the TCP networking Java beans that you've written. Compile all of the six Telnet classes: `TelnetServer`, `TelnetClientService`, `TelnetClient`, `TelnetClientCommands`, `TelnetClientThread`, and `TelnetServerInterface`.

> **Note**
>
> Remember to run the Java compiler `javac` in your DOS or console window from your root class directory `c:\jdk1.2.x\myclasses`. Place the source Java files for the Telnet classes in the `c:\jdk1.2.x\myclasses\sams\net` directory. Finally, recall that the `TelnetServer` and `TelnetClientService` classes are mutually dependent, so you need to place references to both classes in the same `javac` command (see the "Compiling the `TelnetServer` Classes" section earlier in this chapter).

Internet Communication Using Sockets (TCP/IP)

CHAPTER 16

357

16

INTERNET
COMMUNICATION
USING SOCKETS

Once you've compiled the classes, package them up into a JAR file named `telnet.jar` using the `telnet.man` manifest file shown in Listing 16.11. The six classes make up three beans: `TelnetServer`, `TelnetClient`, and `TelnetServerInterface`. Run the following command from your DOS or console window prompt:

```
jar -cmf telnet.man telnet.jar sams
```

Listing 16.11   Source Code for `telnet.man`

```
Name: sams/net/TelnetServer.class
Java-Bean: True

Name: sams/net/TelnetClientService.class
Java-Bean: False

Name: sams/net/TelnetServerInterface.class
Java-Bean: True

Name: sams/net/TelnetClient.class
Java-Bean: True

Name: sams/net/TelnetClientThread.class
Java-Bean: False

Name: sams/net/TelnetClientCommands.class
Java-Bean: False
```

Testing the Telnet Beans

Once the beans are packaged, open two DOS or console windows on your local machine and change their directories so that you're in the same folder as the BeanBox in both windows. You'll run two copies of the BeanBox, one for a Telnet server and one for a Telnet client application.

Assembling the Telnet Server Application

In this section you will assemble a Telnet server application by wiring together various beans in a BeanBox. Run the BeanBox in one of the DOS or console windows then add a `TelnetServer` bean, two `OurButton` beans, and a `TelnetServerInterface` bean to the BeanBox window.

One `OurButton` bean is to start the `TelnetServer` running, and the other `OurButton` bean is to stop it. Change the label property of one `OurButton` bean to `Start` and the other to `Stop`, and then arrange the beans something like Figure 16.6.

FIGURE 16.6

Arrange the beans that you'll wire together into a Telnet server application.

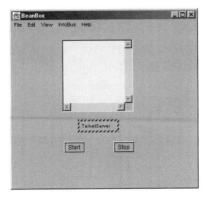

Next, you wire up your Telnet server application. You will begin by connecting the Start button with the TelnetServer bean. Select the OurButton bean with Start as its label property. Open the Events submenu by selecting Events from the BeanBox Edit menu. Then open the Action submenu by selecting Action from the Events submenu. Finally, select the actionPerformed command from the Action submenu. A wire appears from the Start button to the tip of your mouse cursor. Point to the TelnetServer bean and click. The EventTargetDialog dialog box appears (see Figure 16.7).

FIGURE 16.7

Select the target method that you want the event to trigger.

Select the TelnetServer bean's start() method then click the OK button. BeanBox generates the code that wires the beans together properly. Do the same thing to wire together the Stop button's actionPerformed event with the TelnetServer bean's stop() method.

After you're done wiring up the buttons with the TelnetServer bean, wire up the TelnetServer bean with the TelnetServerInterface bean. Connect TelnetServer bean's propertyChange event to TelnetServerInterface bean's propertyChange() method. You do this by going through the same steps you did previously. After you're finished, take the BeanBox out of design mode by selecting the Disable Design Mode command from the View menu.

> **Tip**
>
> You might run into difficulties when you try to click the `TelnetServerInterface` bean to open the EventTargetDialog dialog box. The BeanBox can be fussy about where you click a bean. In this case, you need to click close to the edge of the bean to activate the dialog box.

Assembling the Telnet Client Application

In this section you assemble a Telnet client application. Start another BeanBox running in the other DOS or console window. The Telnet client application consists of three beans: the `TelnetClient` bean and two `OurButton` beans. Add these three beans to the BeanBox window. As in the TelnetServer application, one `OurButton` bean is to start and the other `OurButton` bean is to stop the `TelnetClient` running. Change the label property of one `OurButton` bean to `Start` and the other to `Stop`, and then arrange the beans something like Figure 16.8.

FIGURE 16.8

Arrange the beans that you'll wire together into a Telnet client application.

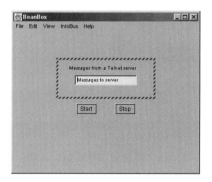

Next, wire up your Telnet client application. All you need to do is wire up the Start and Stop buttons to the `TelnetClient` bean's `start()` and `stop()` methods as you did when you wired up the Telnet server application. For instance, to connect the Start button with the `TelnetClient` bean, select the `OurButton` bean with `Start` as its label property. Open the Events submenu by selecting Events from the BeanBox Edit menu. Then open the Action submenu by selecting Action from the Events submenu. Finally, select the `actionPerformed` command from the Action submenu. A wire appears from the Start button to the tip of your mouse cursor. Point to the `TelnetClient` bean and click. The EventTargetDialog dialog box appears. Select the `TargetClient` bean's `start()` method from the dialog box, and then click the OK button. Repeat these steps to wire together the Stop button's `actionPerformed` event with `TelnetClient` bean's `stop()` method.

You're finished assembling your Telnet client application. Take this BeanBox out of design mode by selecting the `Disable Design Mode` command from the View menu.

Running Your Telnet Applications

Always start Telnet server applications first. A Telnet client application is only useful if it can connect with a Telnet server. Start your Telnet server application by clicking the Start button in the BeanBox window holding the Telnet server application you wired together. When the application starts, it displays a message that the Telnet server has started followed by a message that says that the Telnet server is waiting for a Telnet client request for a connection (see Figure 16.9).

FIGURE 16.9

When you start the Telnet server application, the TelnetServer Interface *bean displays messages from the* TelnetServer *bean.*

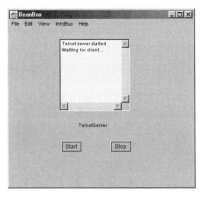

Start the Telnet client application by clicking the Start button in the BeanBox window holding the Telnet client application you assembled. First, you should see the Telnet client display a message that a socket is created followed by a login prompt (see Figure 16.10).

FIGURE 16.10

On starting the Telnet client application, the TelnetClient *bean displays a login prompt.*

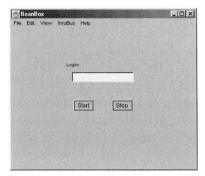

Internet Communication Using Sockets (TCP/IP)

CHAPTER 16

361

16

**INTERNET
COMMUNICATION
USING SOCKETS**

Concurrently, the Telnet server application should display a client accepted message (see Figure 16.11). In fact, the login prompt you see displayed by the Telnet client application was sent from the Telnet server using TCP.

FIGURE 16.11

The Telnet server application displays a message that a connection with a Telnet client has been accepted.

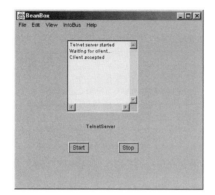

Type a login name into the Telnet client text box. You can use any login name, such as Don, which is shown in Figure 16.12.

FIGURE 16.12

The login name Don is typed into the Telnet client application's text box.

Press your Enter or Return key after entering a login name. The text box in your Telnet client should be cleared. The login name is sent using TCP to the Telnet server application. The Telnet server application displays the login name (see Figure 16.13).

Your Telnet client application should be prompting you to enter a password. The Telnet server sends the password prompt to the Telnet client after it receives the user's login name. Type in any password into the Telnet client's text box (see Figure 16.14).

FIGURE **16.13**

*The login name
Don is sent to and
displayed by the
Telnet server
application.*

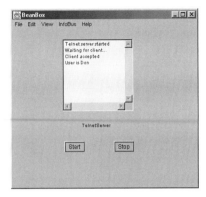

Note

Recall that a true password checking mechanism isn't implemented in the Telnet
server application. Don't type in any of your real passwords at the Telnet client
password prompt.

FIGURE **16.14**

*The Telnet client
application
prompts for a
password after
you enter your
login name.*

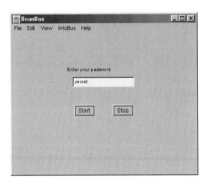

Press your Enter or Return key after entering a dummy password. The text box in your
Telnet client should be cleared. The password is sent using TCP to the Telnet server
application. The Telnet server application displays the password (see Figure 16.15).

Note

Don't display passwords in a release version of the Telnet server application. The
display of passwords here is for pedagogical purposes.

FIGURE 16.15

The password entered into the Telnet client application text box is sent to and displayed by the Telnet server application.

Your Telnet client application should display a welcome message and prompt you to enter a command. The Telnet server sends the welcome message and command prompt to the Telnet client after it receives the user's password. Of course, the Telnet server in a real password-checking situation would only welcome you if you entered a valid password. Type any command into the Telnet client's text box (see Figure 16.16).

FIGURE 16.16

Enter any command, such as testing, *into the Telnet client application text box.*

Press your Enter or Return key after entering a dummy command. The text box in your Telnet client should be cleared. The command is sent using TCP to the Telnet server application. The Telnet server application displays the command (see Figure 16.17).

Your Telnet client application should display a prompt for you to enter a command. The TelnetClient bean has entered into its infinite loop. The Telnet server sends the welcome command prompt to the Telnet client each time it receives input from the Telnet client. Type in any command into the Telnet client's text box and press your Enter or Return key. The Telnet client sends each command to the Telnet server and the server displays the commands (see Figure 16.18).

FIGURE 16.17

The Telnet server application displays the command you entered into the Telnet client application text box.

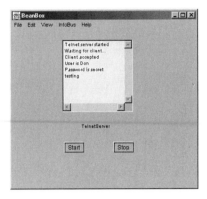

FIGURE 16.18

The Telnet server application displays three commands that were typed in succession into the Telnet client application text box as one, two, *and* three.

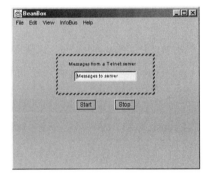

Experiment with your Telnet applications and don't forget to try the built-in commands: quit, exit, and kill. The quit and exit commands close the Telnet client application. The kill command closes both the Telnet client and the Telnet server application. Also, remember that you can connect more than one Telnet client application with a Telnet server application.

Hand Coding Applications Using JavaBeans

You can use Java beans the same way you use classes when you manually write code for an application. In fact, beans are often the same things as a Java class except that they follow the JavaBeans design patterns. The one difference between bean code and a Java class is that a bean can be composed of more than one class. Nevertheless, there is always a primary class that goes by the same name as the bean. It's that primary class you call in your code. In this section, you use the Telnet beans you wrote earlier to hand code a Telnet server and Telnet client application.

Internet Communication Using Sockets (TCP/IP)

CHAPTER 16

365

16

INTERNET
COMMUNICATION
USING SOCKETS

When you hand code applications using beans, you don't get the advantage of automatic introspection. You don't see all of a bean's properties, events, and methods. Instead, it's critical that these are documented so that you know, for instance, that the `TelnetServer` bean has a `start()` method. This is no different than the need for documenting a class library, but it does demonstrate one of the advances made by using component architectures in graphic environments. Another major difference when you hand code applications is that you can't visually set bean properties. In this section, you learn how to set bean properties and register event listeners through hand coding.

Writing the Telnet Server Application

In this section you write a Telnet server application named `MyTelnetServer` based on the Telnet server application you assembled in the BeanBox in the earlier section "Assembling the Telnet Server Application." Use the following five steps to write the `MyTelnetServer` application, shown in Listing 16.12.

1. Create a graphic user interface container.
2. Add beans and other components to the container.
3. Implement an `ActionListener` interface.
4. Register event listeners.
5. Add a `main()` method.

Creating a GUI Container

The `MyTelnetServer` application displays graphic user interface objects that sit inside a panel which sits inside a frame. You usually set up applications that use graphic components in this way because Java's `Panel` class provides a handy container that automatically uses a `BorderLayout` to organize the components. Java's `Frame` class provides a full-featured window to contain and display the nicely laid out components.

Extend the `MyTelnetServer` class from Java's `Frame` class. There are only three steps you need to take after extending the `MyTelnetServer` class from the `Frame` class.

1. Set the title and the size of the frame.
2. Add a `Panel` object to the `Frame` object.
3. Make the frame visible.

Setting the Title and Frame Size

You add the title of the `MyTelnetServer` application to the title bar across the top of the frame in the first statement in the `MyTelnetServer` class constructor, as shown in the following:

```
setTitle( "My Telnet Server" );
```

Next, set the size of the frame using the statement in the next line of code, as shown in the following:

```
setSize( 200, 225 );
```

The first parameter in the `Frame` class's `setSize()` method (inherited from the `Component` class) takes an integer value for the width of the frame in pixels. Its second parameter takes an integer value for the height of the frame in pixels.

Adding the `Panel` Object

The next two lines in the `MyTelnetServer` constructor, shown next, create a new `Panel` object and add it to the `Frame` object.

```
myPanel = new Panel( );
add( myPanel );
```

You add components to the `Frame` object and other containers by using the `Container` class's `add()` method. (Java's `Frame` class inherits the `Container` class.)

Making the Frame Visible

You make a `Frame` object visible by passing `true` to its `setVisible()` method inherited from the `Container` class. The `MyTelnetServer` application `Frame` object is made visible using the following statement:

```
myServer.setVisible( true );
```

The statement forms the second line of the `MyTelnetServer` class's `main()` method. The first line of code creates the `MyTelnetServer` object and assigns it to the `myServer` variable.

Adding the Beans

`MyTelnetServer` uses three different beans: `TelnetServer`, `TelnetServerInterface`, and `Button`. Usually you create an instance of each bean in your application class's constructor. Oftentimes you also set bean properties in the application's constructor.

You import beans just like you import any other class. You import Java's Abstract Windowing Toolkit `Button` class in the usual way with the following line of code at the top of your Java class:

```
import java.awt.Button;
```

Likewise, you would import the `TelnetServer` bean with the following line of code:

```
import sams.net.TelnetServer;
```

Internet Communication Using Sockets (TCP/IP)

CHAPTER 16

367

16

INTERNET
COMMUNICATION
USING SOCKETS

The `TelnetServer` bean actually consists of two classes: `TelnetServer` and `TelnetClientService`. You only import the bean's namesake class and the rest follow. In this case, however, you don't need to import any of the Telnet beans because your applications are part of the same package that the Telnet beans are part of, the `sams.net` package.

You will add four instances of beans to the `MyTelnetServer` application: one instance of the `TelnetServer` bean, one instance of the `TelnetServerInterface` bean, and two instances of the `Button` bean. You create instances of beans in the same way that you create instances of Java classes. You use the `new` keyword.

`MyTelnetServer` application's four beans are created in the following lines of code from the `MyTelnetServer` constructor:

```
telnetServerInterface = new TelnetServerInterface( );
myPanel.add( telnetServerInterface );
startButton = new Button( "Start" );
myPanel.add( startButton );
stopButton = new Button( "Stop" );
myPanel.add( stopButton );
telnetServer = new TelnetServer( );
```

The code follows the addition of the `Panel` object to the application's `Frame` object, and it includes the addition of three of the instantiated beans to the `Panel` object: `TelnetServerInterface` and two `Button` beans.

Implementing the `ActionListener` Interface

The `MyTelnetServer` application connects action events produced by graphical user interface beans (the `Button` objects) with the `TelnetServer` bean's `start()` and `stop()` public methods. To do this, the `MyTelnetServer` class must implement the `ActionListener` interface from Java's `java.awt.event` package.

The `ActionListener` interface declares one abstract method, the `actionPerformed()` method. The `actionPerformed()` method contains the code to connect up component action events with bean public methods. Add the following `actionPerformed()` method to the `MyTelnetServer` class:

```
public void actionPerformed( ActionEvent event ) {
  String command = event.getActionCommand( );
  if( command == "Start" )
    telnetServer.start( );
  else if ( command == "Stop" )
    telnetServer.stop( );
}
```

When a registered component produces an `ActionEvent` object, the object is passed to `actionPerformed()` method's event parameter. The first statement in the `actionPerformed()` method gets the name of the action command encapsulated by the `ActionEvent` object by using the `ActionEvent` class's `getActionCommand()` method.

You are wiring two `Button` objects to public methods in the `TelnetServer` bean. By default, a `Button` object's action command is the string value held by the button's `label` property. Recall that one button's label value is `Start` and the other is `Stop`. Therefore, the `ActionEvent` objects created by these buttons encapsulate the `start` and `stop` commands respectively. This generally works out well, because a button's label usually reflects what action is taken when you click it. Indeed, you're wiring the Start button to the `TelnetServer` bean's `start()` method and the Stop button to its `stop()` method.

After getting the action command, the `actionPerformed()` method tests the command to see if it's equal to `"Start"` or `"Stop"`, the two commands expected from the `Button` beans that you're wiring up to the `TelnetServer` bean. Recall that an instance of the `TelnetServer` bean was created and assigned to the `telnetServer` variable. If the action command is equal to `"Start"`, the `TelnetServer` bean's `start()` method is executed with the following statement:

```
telnetServer.start( );
```

If the action command is equal to `"Stop"`, the `TelnetServer` bean's `stop()` method is executed with the following statement:

```
telnetServer.stop( );
```

You're almost finished wiring the Start and Stop buttons to the `TelnetServer` bean. To finish, you need to register the `MyTelnetServer` object with the `Button` beans.

Registering Event Listeners

The last three lines of code in the `MyTelnetServer` class constructor, shown next, register event listeners.

```
startButton.addActionListener( this );
stopButton.addActionListener( this );
telnetServer.addPropertyChangeListener( telnetServerInterface );
```

You just finished adding an `ActionListener` interface to the `MyTelnetServer` class in the last section so that you can connect the appropriate action commands from the buttons to the appropriate public methods in the `TelnetServer` bean. Register the `MyTelnetServer` object with the Start and Stop buttons by calling each button's `addActionListener()` method and passing the method the `MyTelnetServer` object by using the `this` keyword.

Finally, you need to register `MyTelnetServer` application's `TelnetServerInterface` object with its `TelnetServer` object as a property change listener. Recall that the `TelnetServerInterface` class implements the `PropertyChangeListener` interface. The `TelnetServerInterface` class is designed to listen for and display messages encapsulated in `PropertyChangeEvent` objects created by the `TelnetServer` bean. Register the `TelnetServerInterface` object with the `TelnetServer` bean by calling the `TelnetServer` class's `addPropertyChangeListener()` method.

Adding the `main()` Method

Your final task in writing the `MyTelnetServer` application is to add a `main()` method. You need a `main()` method because `MyTelnetServer` is an application that can run on its own in a JVM. `MyTelnetServer` class's `main()` method, shown next, is simple.

```
public static void main( String args[] ) {
  MyTelnetServer myServer = new MyTelnetServer( );
  myServer.setVisible( true );
}
```

The first statement creates an instance of the `MyTelnetServer` class and the second statement makes it visible. Compile the code and it's ready to run. However, the `MyTelnetServer` application isn't very useful until you can run Telnet client applications that connect with it (see Listing 16.12).

> **Note**
>
> Make sure that all of the Telnet classes are compiled in your `c:\jdk1.2.x\myclasses\sams\net` directory before you try to compile any of the classes you write in this section. The Telnet applications depend on the compiled Telnet classes.

Listing 16.12   Source Code for `MyTelnetServer.java`

```
package sams.net;

import java.awt.Button;
import java.awt.Event;
import java.awt.Panel;
import java.awt.event.ActionEvent;

public class MyTelnetServer extends java.awt.Frame
```

continues

Listing 16.12 continued

```java
  implements java.awt.event.ActionListener {
private Panel myPanel = null;
private TelnetServer telnetServer = null;
private TelnetServerInterface telnetServerInterface = null;
private Button startButton = null;
private Button stopButton = null;

public MyTelnetServer( ) {
  setTitle( "My Telnet Server" );
  setSize( 200, 225 );
  myPanel = new Panel( );
  add( myPanel );
  telnetServerInterface = new TelnetServerInterface( );
  myPanel.add( telnetServerInterface );
  startButton = new Button( "Start" );
  myPanel.add( startButton );
  stopButton = new Button( "Stop" );
  myPanel.add( stopButton );
  telnetServer = new TelnetServer( );

  startButton.addActionListener( this );
  stopButton.addActionListener( this );
  telnetServer.addPropertyChangeListener( telnetServerInterface );
}

public void actionPerformed( ActionEvent event ) {
  String command = event.getActionCommand( );
  if( command == "Start" )
    telnetServer.start( );
  else if ( command == "Stop" )
    telnetServer.stop( );
}

public static void main( String args[] ) {
  MyTelnetServer myServer = new MyTelnetServer( );
  myServer.setVisible( true );
}
}
```

Writing the Telnet Client Application

Write a Telnet client application named MyTelnetClient based on the Telnet client application you assembled in the BeanBox in the earlier section "Assembling the Telnet Client Application." Use the same five steps to write the MyTelnetClient application, shown in Listing 16.13, that you used to write the MyTelnetServer application in the last section.

1. Create a graphic user interface container.

2. Add beans and other components to the container.

3. Implement an `ActionListener` interface.

4. Register event listeners.

5. Add a `main()` method.

> **Note**
>
> In fact, you use similar steps to write any application using beans.

Creating a GUI Container

The `MyTelnetClient` application displays graphical user interface objects that sit inside a panel which sits inside a frame. Extend the `MyTelnetClient` class from Java's `Frame` class, and then go through the following three steps to complete the graphical user interface container.

1. Set the title and the size of the frame.

2. Add a `Panel` object to the `Frame` object.

3. Make the frame visible.

Setting the Title and Frame Size

You add the title of the `MyTelnetClient` application to the title bar across the top of the frame in the first statement in the `MyTelnetClient` class constructor, as shown in the following:

```
setTitle( "My Telnet Client" );
```

Next, set the size of the frame with following line of code:

```
setSize( 200, 225 );
```

The first parameter in the `Frame` class's `setSize()` method (inherited from the `Component` class) takes an integer value for the width of the frame in millimeters. Its second parameter takes an integer value for the height of the frame in millimeters.

Adding the `Panel` Object

The next two lines in the `MyTelnetClient` constructor, shown next, create a new `Panel` object and add it to the `Frame` object.

```
myPanel = new Panel( );
add( myPanel );
```

You add components to the `Frame` object and other containers by using the `Container` class's `add()` method. (Java's `Frame` class inherits the `Container` class.)

Making the Frame Visible

You make a `Frame` object visible by passing `true` to its `setVisible()` method inherited from the `Container` class. The `MyTelnetClient` application `Frame` object is made visible using the following statement:

```
myServer.setVisible( true );
```

This is the second line of code in `MyTelnetClient` class's `main()` method. The first line of code creates the `MyTelnetClient` object and assigns it to the `myClient` variable.

Adding the Beans

`MyTelnetServer` uses two different beans: `TelnetClient` and `Button` beans. You will add three instances of beans to the `MyTelnetClient` application: one instance of the `TelnetClient` bean and two instances of the `Button` bean. As you saw earlier this section, you create instances of beans in the same way that you create instances of Java classes using the `new` keyword.

`MyTelnetClient` application's three beans are created in the following lines of code from the `MyTelnetClient` constructor:

```
telnetClient = new TelnetClient( );
myPanel.add( telnetClient );
startButton = new Button( "Start" );
myPanel.add( startButton );
stopButton = new Button( "Stop" );
myPanel.add( stopButton );
```

The code follows the addition of the `Panel` object to the application's `Frame` object. Each of the three instantiated beans, `TelnetClient` bean and two `Button` beans, are added to the `Panel` object.

Implementing the `ActionListener` Interface

The `MyTelnetClient` application connects action events produced by the `Button` with the `TelnetClient` bean's `start()` and `stop()` public methods. To do this, the `MyTelnetClient` class must implement the `ActionListener` interface from Java's `java.awt.event` package.

As you're well aware now, the `ActionListener` interface declares one abstract method—`actionPerformed()`. You write the `actionPerformed()` method so that it contains the code to connect up component action events with bean public methods. Add the following `actionPerformed()` method to the `MyTelnetClient` class:

```
public void actionPerformed( ActionEvent event ) {
  String command = event.getActionCommand( );
```

Internet Communication Using Sockets (TCP/IP)

CHAPTER 16

373

16

INTERNET
COMMUNICATION
USING SOCKETS

```
    if( command == "Start" )
      telnetClient.start( );
    else if ( command == "Stop" )
      telnetClient.stop( );
}
```

After getting the action command, the `actionPerformed()` method tests the command to see if it's equal to `"Start"` or `"Stop"`, the two commands expected from the `Button` beans that you're wiring up to the `TelnetClient` bean. If the action command is equal to `"Start"`, the `TelnetClient` bean's `start()` method is executed with the following statement:

```
telnetClient.start( );
```

If the action command is equal to `"Stop"`, the `TelnetClient` bean's `stop()` method is executed with the following statement:

```
telnetClient.stop( );
```

You're almost finished wiring the Start and Stop buttons to the `TelnetClient` bean. To finish, you need to register the `MyTelnetClient` object with the `Button` beans.

Registering Event Listeners

The last two lines of code in the `MyTelnetClient` class constructor, shown next, register event listeners.

```
startButton.addActionListener( this );
stopButton.addActionListener( this );
```

You just finished adding an `ActionListener` interface to the `MyTelnetClient` class in the last section. Now connect the appropriate action commands from the buttons to the appropriate public methods in the `TelnetClient` bean. Register the `MyTelnetClient` object with the Start and Stop buttons by calling each button's `addActionListener()` method and passing the method the `MyTelnetClient` object by using the `this` keyword.

Adding the `main()` Method

Your final task in writing the `MyTelnetClient` application is to add a `main()` method. You need a `main()` method because `MyTelnetClient` is an application that can run on its own in a JVM. The following is `MyTelnetClient` class's `main()` method:

```
public static void main( String args[] ) {
  MyTelnetClient myClient = new MyTelnetClient( );
  myClient.setVisible( true );
}
```

The first statement, shown in Listing 16.13, creates an instance of the `MyTelnetClient` class, and the second statement makes it visible. Compile the code. You take your new Telnet applications for a test ride in the next section.

Listing 16.13   Source Code for `MyTelnetClient.java`

```java
package sams.net;

import java.awt.Button;
import java.awt.Panel;
import java.awt.event.ActionEvent;

public class MyTelnetClient extends java.awt.Frame
   implements java.awt.event.ActionListener {
  private Panel myPanel = null;
  private TelnetClient telnetClient = null;
  private Button startButton = null;
  private Button stopButton = null;

  public MyTelnetClient( ) {
    setTitle( "My Telnet Client" );
    setSize( 200, 225 );
    myPanel = new Panel( );
    add( myPanel );
    telnetClient = new TelnetClient( );
    myPanel.add( telnetClient );
    startButton = new Button( "Start" );
    myPanel.add( startButton );
    stopButton = new Button( "Stop" );
    myPanel.add( stopButton );

    startButton.addActionListener( this );
    stopButton.addActionListener( this );
  }

  public void actionPerformed( ActionEvent event ) {
    String command = event.getActionCommand( );
    if( command == "Start" )
      telnetClient.start( );
    else if ( command == "Stop" )
      telnetClient.stop( );
  }

  public static void main( String args[] ) {
    MyTelnetClient myClient = new MyTelnetClient( );
    myClient.setVisible( true );
  }
}
```

Internet Communication Using Sockets (TCP/IP)

CHAPTER 16

375

16

INTERNET
COMMUNICATION
USING SOCKETS

Running Your Telnet Applications

Test the Telnet applications you wrote in the last section. Run them through the same tests you tried on the prototype applications you created in BeanBox windows earlier in this chapter. With the hand coded applications, you don't need to arrange beans in container windows or connect them up. Your applications are complete and ready to distribute.

Open two DOS or console windows on your local computer as you did earlier in this chapter. You open one window for each JVM that you'll run. Always start your Telnet server application, `MyTelnetServer`, first. Start the `MyTelnetServer` application by typing the following command in one of your DOS windows:

```
java sams.net.MyTelnetServer
```

The `MyTelnetServer` application launches and should look something like Figure 16.19.

FIGURE 16.19

The `MyTelnetServer` *application runs from the DOS command prompt.*

The `MyTelnetServer` application looks nearly identical to the Telnet server application you assembled earlier in this chapter. However, start the application by clicking the `Start` button in `MyTelnetServer` application's interface and you'll notice a difference. It displays a message that the Telnet server has started, followed by a message that says that the Telnet server is waiting for a Telnet client request for a connection (see Figure 16.20).

FIGURE 16.20

When you start the `MyTelnetServer` *application, it displays messages from the* `TelnetServer` *bean.*

`MyTelnetServer` should be a lot faster than the prototype applications you assembled in BeanBox windows.

Start the `MyTelnetClient` application by typing the following command in the DOS window you haven't used yet:

```
java sams.net.MyTelnetClient
```

The `MyTelnetClient` application launches and should look something like Figure 16.21.

FIGURE 16.21

The `MyTelnetClient` *application runs from the DOS command prompt.*

Click the `MyTelnetClient` application Start button to start it running. You should see the `MyTelnetClient` application display a message that a socket is created followed by a login prompt (see Figure 16.22).

FIGURE 16.22

The `MyTelnetClient` *application displays a login prompt after you start it.*

Concurrently, the `MyTelnetServer` application displays a client accepted message (see Figure 16.23). The login prompt you see displayed by the `MyTelnetClient` application was sent from the `MyTelnetServer` application using TCP.

FIGURE 16.23

The `MyTelnetServer` *application displays a message that it accepts a connection with a* `MyTelnetClient` *application.*

Internet Communication Using Sockets (TCP/IP)

CHAPTER 16

377

16

INTERNET
COMMUNICATION
USING SOCKETS

Type a login name into the `MyTelnetClient` application text box. You can use any login name, for example, **Don**, as shown in Figure 16.24.

FIGURE 16.24

The login name Don is typed into the `MyTelnetClient` *application text box.*

Press your Enter or Return key after entering a login name. The text box in the `MyTelnetClient` application should be cleared. The login name is sent using TCP to the `MyTelnetServer` application. The `MyTelnetServer` application displays the login name (see Figure 16.25).

FIGURE 16.25

The login name Don is sent to and displayed by the `MyTelnetServer` *application.*

The `MyTelnetClient` application should be prompting you to enter a password. The `MyTelnetServer` application sends the password prompt to the `MyTelnetClient` application after it receives the user's login name. Type in any password into the `MyTelnetClient` application text box (see Figure 16.26).

> **Note**
>
> Recall that a true password checking mechanism isn't implemented. Don't type in any of your real passwords at the `MyTelnetClient` application password prompt.

FIGURE 16.26

The `MyTelnetClient` *application prompts you for a password after your login name is entered.*

Press your Enter or Return key after entering a dummy password. The text box in the MyTelnetClient application should be cleared. The password is sent using TCP to the MyTelnetServer application. The MyTelnetServer application displays the password (see Figure 16.27).

> **Caution**
>
> Don't display passwords in a release version of the MyTelnetServer application. The display of passwords here is for pedagogical purposes.

FIGURE 16.27

The password entered into the MyTelnetClient *application text box is sent to and displayed by the* MyTelnetServer *application.*

The MyTelnetClient application should display a welcome message and prompt you to enter a command. The MyTelnetServer application sends the welcome message and command prompt to the MyTelnetClient application after it receives the user's password. Of course, in a real password-checking situation, the MyTelnetServer application would only welcome you if you entered a valid password. Type any command into the MyTelnetClient application text box (see Figure 16.28).

FIGURE 16.28

Enter any command, such as testing, *into the* MyTelnetClient *application text box.*

Press your Enter or Return key after entering a dummy command. The text box in the MyTelnetClient application should be cleared. The command is sent using TCP to the MyTelnetServer application. The MyTelnetServer application displays the command (see Figure 16.29).

Internet Communication Using Sockets (TCP/IP)

CHAPTER 16

379

16

INTERNET
COMMUNICATION
USING SOCKETS

FIGURE 16.29

The
`MyTelnetServer`
application displays the command you entered into the
`MyTelnetClient`
application text box.

The `MyTelnetClient` application should display a prompt for you to enter a command. The `TelnetClient` bean has entered into its infinite loop. The `MyTelnetServer` application sends the welcome command prompt to the `MyTelnetClient` application each time it receives input from the `MyTelnetClient` application.

Type any command into the `MyTelnetClient` application text box and press your Enter or Return key. The `MyTelnetClient` application sends each command to the `MyTelnetServer` application, which displays the commands (see Figure 16.30).

FIGURE 16.30

The
`MyTelnetServer`
application displays three commands that were typed in succession into the
`MyTelnetClient`
application text box as one, two, *and* three.

Experiment with your Telnet applications and don't forget to try the built-in commands: quit, exit, and kill. The quit and exit commands close the `MyTelnetClient` application. The kill command closes both the `MyTelnetClient` and the `MyTelnetServer` applications. Also, remember that you can connect more than one `MyTelnetClient` application with a `MyTelnetServer` application.

Summary

In this chapter, you sent your first datagram packet with your own beans. You used the same procedures to create beans that communicate all sorts of information across the Internet. You learned about the TCP/IP suite of network protocols. These include the low-level Internet protocol that provides the all-important IP address functionality and datagram packaging. The User Datagram Protocol you used is a simple but relatively unreliable way of sending data across the Internet. You created beans that use the robust Transport Communication Protocol (TCP) and formed the basis for Telnet applications. Finally, you wired up beans using the BeanBox to create prototype Telnet applications, and then you hand-coded Telnet applications that used the same Telnet beans.

Remote Method Invocation (RMI)

All source code for this chapter can be found on the Sams Publishing Website at
`http://www.mcp.com/info/0-672/0-672-31424-x.`

Remote Method Invocation (RMI) is a useful tool that can be used to create applications that communicate over the Internet. Remote Method Invocation provides a way for you to create distributed beans that can invoke methods of remote Java objects running in other Java Virtual Machines on other computers. In this chapter, you learn about the Java Distributed Object Model and Remote Method Invocation, and you create an application that uses RMI.

Java Distributed Object Model

You've probably used sockets to communicate over the Internet, but sockets treat computers as distinct and separate objects. Sockets provide communication between computers by encoding and decoding messages sent between them through the many layers of TCP/IP.

> **Note**
>
> Learn more about sockets and TCP/IP in Chapter 16, "Internet Communication Using Sockets (TCP/IP)."

Now, and even more in the future, computers connected up into networks are being treated as one giant computer—a computing enterprise. Operating systems and applications use distributed models to carry out computations without regard to the particular machine on which the computations are being performed. This is known as *distributed computing*.

You can use the Java Distributed Object Model to create beans that carry out distributed computations. The Java Distributed Object Model is a language-specific, remote-method invocation system. Java's Remote Method Invocation works across Java Virtual Machines and across different computers, but it does not work across different programming languages. Beans that use RMI must run in a 100 percent Java environment.

When you use RMI, you're invoking the method of a remote interface on a remote Java object. Invoking a method on a remote Java object looks just the same to you, the programmer, as invoking a method on a local Java object. All of the work is done through remote interfaces.

Creating an RMI Application

In this section, you create a distributed JVM-to-JVM application by writing a Java application RMI server and JavaBeans components for a RMI client. You can use Rapid Application Development (RAD), such as the BeanBox or hand coding, to pull together the beans into a RMI client.

The RMI application you create in this section is a simple beginning of a chat application. It's simplified to show you the principles of building an RMI application. You can use what you learn and what you already know from developing Telnet applications to create a really cool RMI chat application.

> **Note**
>
> Learn more about developing Telnet applications in Chapter 16.

You will create a chat server that has two methods: the `receiveMessage()` method that receives a message and the `sendMessage()` method that sends a message. The server is a Java application. You also create a chat client. The client is a bean that has two properties, the `message` and `remoteMessage` properties. The `remoteMessage` property is bound. In other words, a property change event is created whenever the content of the `remoteMessage` property is changed. The chat client's `setMessage()` setter method, in addition to setting the contents of the `message` property, calls the chat server's `receiveMessage()` method and passes the message held by the message property to the server. Then the method does a silly thing—it gets the message back by calling the chat server's `sendMessage()` method and passes the message to the `setRemoteMessage()` setter method. This is done for purely demonstration purposes. You wrap up the project by creating a couple of beans to act as user interfaces for your RMI client bean. You write an RMI application in three steps.

1. Write a Java remote interface.
2. Write a Java remote object (the server).
3. Write a Java bean that invokes one or more methods on the remote server.

Defining a Remote Interface

A remote interface is an object that contains a definition of all of the methods contained in its associated remote object. The remote interface sports the same name as the remote object except that `Impl` (standing for implementation) is appended to the remote object's name. For instance, the remote interface you write in this section is named ChatServer. The associated remote object class that you write in the next section is named ChatServerImpl. The Impl portion of the name is appended by the tool. It's a standard convention.

The ChatServer remote interface is shown in Listing 17.1. You can see that ChatServer is declared with the interface keyword, and that it extends Java's Remote interface. All remote interfaces extend Java's Remote interface, found in the java.rmi package. The interface contains a declaration list of the remote object's remotely accessible methods. The remote object always implements its associated Remote interface.

> **Note**
>
> You learn all about the remote object methods in the next section when you write them. However, you may be wondering about the RemoteException object that each method throws. All methods remotely accessible through RMI must throw the RemoteException object found in the java.rmi package.

Listing 17.1   Source Code for ChatServer.java

```
package sams.rmi;

import java.rmi.RemoteException;

public interface ChatServer extends java.rmi.Remote {
   String receiveMessage( ) throws RemoteException;
   void sendMessage( String message ) throws RemoteException;
}
```

Implementing a Remote Object

You wrote an interface that defines all of the remotely accessible methods your remote object must implement. Now implement the class, the ChatServerImpl class shown in Listing 17.2, which defines the remote object itself.

The ChatServerImpl class extends Java's UnicastRemoteObject class and it implements the ChatServer interface that you wrote in the last section. You find the UnicastRemoteObject class in the java.rmi.server package. The UnicastRemoteObject class is a subclass of the RemoteObject class, which is also found in the java.rmi.server package. All remote objects should extend the RemoteObject class, usually by extending the UnicastRemoteObject class. The UnicastRemoteObject class takes care of all the details of connecting objects across networks for you.

The `ChatServerImpl` object runs as a Java application; therefore, the `ChatServerImpl` class has a `main()` method. The first statement in the method, shown next, creates an RMI security manager using the `RMISecurityManager` class found in the `java.rmi` package.

The security manager performs many of the basic security checks that the `ClassLoader` does when you load an applet. It does a basic check against malicious code. RMI is the key feature Microsoft chose to omit in the IE 4.0 browser (adding ammunition to the Sun lawsuit).

```
System.setSecurityManager( new RMISecurityManager( ) );
```

Next, the method creates the `ChatServerImpl` object through a call to the `ChatServerImpl` class constructor in the next statement. The class constructor takes a `String` object with the name of the server. Pass the string `"ChatServer"` to the constructor. The statement assigns the `ChatServerImpl` object to the `remoteObject` variable.

```
ChatServerImpl remoteObject = new ChatServerImpl( "ChatServer" );
```

The third statement in the `ChatServerImpl` class's `main()` method, shown next, associates (binds) the Uniform Resource Locator (URL) reference to the remote object—the `ChatServerImpl` object—by using the `Naming` class's `rebind()` method.

```
Naming.rebind( "/ChatServer", remoteObject );
```

Pass the `rebind()` method's first parameter the URL of the remote object, including its name. Pass the unqualified name of the remote object `"/ChatServer"`. It's a nonqualified name because it doesn't specify the precise host machine on which the object is installed. You don't need to spell out the host machine unless it's a different machine from the client. It's generally easiest to develop and test your RMI applications on the same computer, so use an unqualified name for now.

> **Note**
>
> When you use an RMI application across a network, you would need to include a name in full URL format. The name would need to include the protocol, host, and (optionally) the port number of the location of the remote object.

The last statement in the `main()` method, shown next, prints out the message that the chat server was added to the registry.

```
System.out.println( "ChatServer was just added to the registry..." );
```

A remote object registry must run in the same JVM of each remote object and before the remote object is created. When you create the remote object, the remote object's name is registered with the remote object registry. This is done in the statement that calls the Naming class's rebind() method.

You've finished writing the ChatServer interface and the ChatServerImpl class. You're done writing the RMI server. Next, you write the RMI client bean as shown in Listing 17.2.

Listing 17.2   Source Code for ChatServerImpl.java

```java
package sams.rmi;

import java.rmi.Naming;
import java.rmi.RemoteException;
import java.rmi.RMISecurityManager;

public class ChatServerImpl extends java.rmi.server.UnicastRemoteObject
    implements ChatServer {
  private String serverName;
  private String message;

  public ChatServerImpl( String s ) throws RemoteException {
    super( );
    serverName = s;
  }

  public void sendMessage( String message ) throws RemoteException {
    this.message = message;
  }

  public String receiveMessage( ) throws RemoteException {
    return message;
  }

  public static void main( String args[] ) {
    System.setSecurityManager( new RMISecurityManager( ) );
    try {
      ChatServerImpl remoteObject = new ChatServerImpl( "ChatServer" );
      Naming.rebind( "/ChatServer", remoteObject );
      System.out.println( "ChatServer was just added to the registry..." );
    }
    catch ( Exception e ) {
      System.out.println( e.getMessage( ) );
    }
  }
}
```

Creating a Client

Now, you'll create an RMI client bean that is able to call methods on the ChatServerImpl object. These method calls look just as if you're calling methods in a local object. That's the beauty of using RMI.

Your RMI client bean, named Chat, consists of one object created from the Chat class shown in Listing 17.3. The Chat bean has two properties: message and remoteMessage. It's also an action event listener. It implements the ActionListener interface and the actionPerformed() method.

The Chat bean is created as an action event listener, so you can wire up objects to it, especially interface objects for passing messages. The actionPerformed() method sets the message property equal to the action event object's command. You see how this works later when you create an input bean and wire up the Chat RMI client application.

The other event processing in the Chat bean is provided by the bound remoteMessage property. Each time the setRemoteMessage() setter method is called, a property change event is fired off. Providing the property change event lets you wire an interface bean to the Chat bean that displays messages arriving from a remote object as they're received. You must, of course, add the appropriate addPropertyChangeListener() and removePropertyChangeListener() methods to the Chat class so that the bean can register event listeners.

You've seen all of this before, but the Chat class also has new RMI-specific code, especially in its connect() method, as shown in the following:

```
public void connect( ) {
  try {
    chatServer = ( ChatServer ) Naming.lookup( "/ChatServer" );
    setRemoteMessage( "You're connected!\n" );
  }
  catch ( Exception ex ) {
  }
}
```

The Chat class's connect() method is a public method, so you can wire an object to activate it. A call to the connect() method connects the chat client with the chat server. The first statement in the connect() method uses the Naming class's lookup() method to assign the chat server remote object to the chatServer variable. You pass the lookup() method the name, including the URL, of the remote object. Pass the unqualified name "/ChatServer" while you're developing and performing early tests on your RMI chat application.

17

REMOTE METHOD
INVOCATION
(RMI)

After you have a variable containing a copy of the remote object, you're able to call any of the methods that form a part of the object's remote interface. You call the remote object methods from inside the sentMessage() method with the following two statements:

```
chatServer.sendMessage( message );
setRemoteMessage( chatServer.receiveMessage( ) );
```

You can see that calling the remote ChatServerImpl object's sendMessage() and receiveMessage() methods is just like calling local object methods. You can see this in Listing 17.3.

Listing 17.3 Source Code for Chat.java

```
package sams.rmi;

import java.awt.Dimension;
import java.awt.event.ActionEvent;
import java.beans.PropertyChangeListener;
import java.beans.PropertyChangeSupport;
import java.rmi.Naming;

public class Chat implements java.io.Serializable,
    java.awt.event.ActionListener {
  private String message = "";
  private String remoteMessage = "";
private PropertyChangeSupport changes =
    new PropertyChangeSupport( this );
  private ChatServer chatServer = null;

  public String getMessage( ) {
    return message;
  }

  public void setMessage( String message ) {
    if( chatServer != null ) {
      this.message = message;
      try {
        chatServer.sendMessage( message );
        setRemoteMessage( chatServer.receiveMessage( ) );
      }
      catch ( Exception e ) {
      }
    }
  }

  public String getRemoteMessage( ) {
    return remoteMessage;
  }
```

```
  public void setRemoteMessage( String newRemoteMessage ) {
    String oldRemoteMessage = remoteMessage;
    remoteMessage = newRemoteMessage;
changes.firePropertyChange( "remoteMessage",
      oldRemoteMessage, newRemoteMessage );
  }

  public void connect( ) {
    try {
      chatServer = ( ChatServer ) Naming.lookup( "/ChatServer" );
      setRemoteMessage( "You're connected!\n" );
    }
    catch ( Exception ex ) {
    }
  }

  public void actionPerformed( ActionEvent e ) {
    switch( e.getID( ) ) {
      case ActionEvent.ACTION_PERFORMED:
        setMessage( e.getActionCommand( ) );
        break;
    }
  }

public void addPropertyChangeListener(
    PropertyChangeListener listener ) {
    changes.addPropertyChangeListener( listener );
  }

public void removePropertyChangeListener(
    PropertyChangeListener listener ) {
    changes.removePropertyChangeListener( listener );
  }
}
```

Compiling in Two Steps

Compile the chat application's source code now that you have finished writing the chat
server application and the chat client bean. As usual, you compile the Java code using the
javac compiler (or equivalent). However, there is another compilation step to creating
RMI applications. You need to generate stub and skeleton files.

Generating Stubs and Skeletons

A *stub* is a client-side object that stands-in or substitutes for your remote interface object.
A *skeleton* is a server-side stand-in or substitute. If a RMI client wants to invoke a
method on a RMI server, the client forwards the request to the stub and then the stub forwards the request to the skeleton. Finally, the skeleton forwards the request to the server.

Use `rmic` to create your RMI application's stub and skeleton. Java's `rmic` tool is the RMI compiler. The RMI compiler takes compiled Java class files as input and produces stub and skeleton files. After all of the RMI client and server classes are compiled, run the `rmic` compiler by typing the following command at the DOS command prompt:

```
rmic -d c:\jdk1.2.x\myclasses\ sams.rmi.ChatServerImpl
```

Your root class directory, `c:\jdk1.2.x\myclasses`, follows the `-d` flag, which is followed by the full classname including its package (`sams.rmi.ChatServerImpl`). After the `rmic` compiler is done, you should find a `ChatServerImpl_Stub` and a `ChatServerImpl_Skel` classes in the `c:\jdk1.2.x\myclasses\sams\rmi` directory.

Almost everything is in place for your RMI chat application, but before you package the beans and test the code, you need to create two graphic interface beans for the chat client.

Creating Chat Graphic Interface Beans

You need a way to input and display messages through the chat client, so in this section you will create a pair of graphic interface beans to wire up with your chat client bean. Java's `TextField` class provides a text box for inputting messages. Create a `ChatInput` bean by writing the `ChatInput` class, shown in Listing 17.4, that extends the `TextField` class.

The `ChatInput` class enables the local processing of action events, and it sets its text box to 20 columns wide. The processing of local action events occurs in the `processActionEvent()` method, which simply clears the text box when an action event occurs.

> **Note**
>
> Recall that `TextField` objects produce action events when they have the focus and you press your Enter or Return key.

Listing 17.4 Source Code for `ChatInput.java`

```java
package sams.rmi;

import java.awt.AWTEvent;
import java.awt.event.ActionEvent;

public class ChatInput extends java.awt.TextField
```

```
  implements java.io.Serializable {
public ChatInput( ) {
  enableEvents( AWTEvent.ACTION_EVENT_MASK );
  setColumns( 20 );
}

public void processActionEvent( ActionEvent e ) {
  setText( "" );
  super.processActionEvent( e );
}
}
```

Display messages from the chat client using the `ChatInterface` bean shown in Listing 17.5. The `ChatInterface` class extends Java's `TextArea` class and implements the `PropertyChangeListener` interface. Because it's a listener for property change events, you can wire the `ChatInterface` bean to `Chat` bean's bound `remoteMessage` property. The `ChatInterface` class's (`propertyChange`) method checks to see that the property change event was produced by the `remoteMessage` property. If it was, the string carried by the event is displayed in the bean's text area.

Listing 17.5   Source Code for `ChatInterface.java`

```
package sams.rmi;

import java.awt.Dimension;
import java.beans.PropertyChangeEvent;

public class ChatInterface extends java.awt.TextArea
    implements java.beans.PropertyChangeListener, java.io.Serializable {
  public void propertyChange( PropertyChangeEvent event ) {
    String propertyName = event.getPropertyName( );
    if ( propertyName.equals( "remoteMessage" ) ) {
      append( (String) event.getNewValue( ) + "\n" );
    }
  }

  public Dimension getMinimumSize() {
    return new Dimension(150, 150);
  }

  public Dimension getPreferredSize() {
    return getMinimumSize();
  }
}
```

Packaging Your Beans

Package all the compiled Java classes from your chat client into a JAR file, along with the supporting files for remote calls to the chat server. Your Chat bean needs the ChatServer interface class and the ChatServerImpl_Stub class to run. Use the chat.man manifest file in Listing 17.6 to create the chat.jar file. Run the following command at the DOS or console prompt:

```
jar -cmf chat.man chat.jar sams
```

Listing 17.6 Source Code for chat.man

```
Name: sams/rmi/Chat.class
Java-Bean: True

Name: sams/rmi/ChatInput.class
Java-Bean: True

Name: sams/rmi/ChatInterface.class
Java-Bean: True

Name: sams/rmi/ChatServer.class
Java-Bean: False

Name: sams/rmi/ChatServerImpl_Stub.class
Java-Bean: False
```

Testing Your Chat Application

Test your new chat application. Normally you place the chat.jar JAR file in the c:\bdk\jars directory of the computer on which you want to run the chat client application. You typically place the ChatServerImpl.class along with the supporting ChatServer.class, ChatServerImpl_Skel.class, and ChatServerImpl_Stub.class files on the computer that you want to run the chat server application. In this case, you place all of these files in their appropriate places on the same computer.

Running the Chat Server Application

Begin your test by starting the chat server application. Open a DOS or console window and go to your root Java class directory c:\jdk1.2.x\myclasses. Before starting anything else, you need to create a remote object registry.

Use Java's rmiregistry tool to create a remote object registry. All remote objects need to register themselves with the remote object registry so clients can look them up. Type in the following command at the DOS command prompt:

```
start rmiregistry 1099
```

The RMI registry tool starts up and displays a blank DOS window of its own.

The final step is to start the chat server, which also completes the server's registration with the RMI registry. Type in the following command at the DOS command prompt:

```
java -Djava.rmi.server sams.rmi.ChatServerImpl
```

> **Note**
>
> Run java in your root class directory `c:\jdk1.2.x\myclasses`.

The chat server application is launched and registered with the RMI registry and the `ChatServerImpl` application should tell you so by printing a message to your DOS window.

Assembling and Running a Chat Client Application

Make sure that the `chat.jar` file is in the `c:\bdk\jars` directory and then run the BeanBox. Place a `Chat`, a `ChatInput`, a `ChatInterface`, and an `OurButton` bean in the BeanBox window and arrange them as shown in Figure 17.1. Change the label in the `OurButton` bean to read `Connect`.

FIGURE 17.1

Arrange the chat client application beans in the BeanBox window.

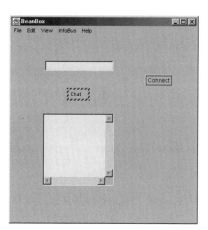

Wire the `ChatInput` bean's `actionPerformed` event with the `Chat` bean's `actionPerformed()` method. Wire the `OurButton` bean's `actionPerformed` event with the `Chat` bean's `connect()` method. Finally, wire the `Chat` bean's `propertyChange` event with the `ChatInterface` bean's `propertyChange()` method.

Disable the design mode and try out your new chat client application. Click the Connect button. Your chat client should connect with your chat server and display a message that it's done so (see Figure 17.2).

FIGURE 17.2

The chat client application connects with the chat server application when you click the Connect button.

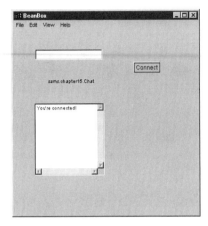

Now you can test the passing of messages between client and server. Type in various messages into the chat client input text box. The messages are sent to the chat server, returned to the chat client, and are finally displayed in the chat client's text area (see Figure 17.3).

FIGURE 17.3

Messages are sent from the chat client's text box to the chat server and back to the chat client's text area.

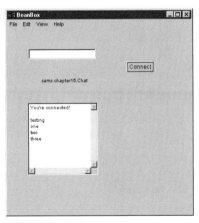

Summary

In this chapter, you created a Java client server application that uses Remote Method Invocation or RMI. RMI is handy because you call methods on local and remote Java objects in the exact same way. In fact, you call methods in the same way that you always call methods in Java. Almost all of the work to achieve this benefit is done by Java and simple tools. You can build distributed beans for distributed applications with relative ease using Java's RMI.

17

REMOTE METHOD
INVOCATION
(RMI)

Java Remote Method Protocol (JRMP)

All source code for this chapter can be found on the Sams Publishing Website at
`http://www.mcp.com/info/0-672/0-672-31424-x.`

Remote Method Invocation (RMI) enables the programmer to create distributed Java-to-Java applications, in which the methods of remote Java objects can be invoked from other Java virtual machines, possibly on different hosts. A Java program can make a call on a remote object once it obtains a reference to the remote object, either by looking up the remote object in the bootstrap naming service provided by RMI or by receiving the reference as an argument or a return value. A client can call a remote object in a server, and that server can also be a client of other remote objects. RMI uses Object Serialization to marshal and unmarshal parameters and does not truncate types, supporting true object-oriented polymorphism. Although we cover CORBA in the next chapter, it's important to point out that this is an advantage of RMI over CORBA.

Network Programming

Network programming has always been a challenge for programmers. Usually a program on a client computer must contact a server and access a database on the server. Thinking back to 1988 when I wrote my first network application that shared data among computers on a Novell network gives me a large headache. Every single step of the process required well-planned, difficult-to-write-and-debug, complicated code.

In the early days, programs that shared data over a network had to use some sort of protocol over which packets of data were sent. Within the packets of data were contained directive codes and data. The directive codes told the receiving program how to handle any data that was contained in the packet, and the data provided the information the remote computer needed.

Sockets

The most common way to send data back and forth between networked computers has been through a metaphor known as sockets. Sockets (which originated with the UNIX operating system) provide endpoints between networked computers, through which blocks of data can be sent.

While sockets provide a great way to transfer data, that's all they provide. It's up to the applications to decide what data to send, how to format it, and when to send it. The receiving application must decide how to use the incoming data, how it's formatted, and what it means.

Remote Procedure Calls

In the not too distant past, a new approach to network programming was introduced—Remote Procedure Calls (RPC). Its purpose was to allow network programs to communicate via a layer of abstraction that shields the developer from the tedious task of formatting and sending packets of data.

Remote procedure calls provide a system that enables an application to call procedures that exist on another machine. This system gives the impression that one is calling standard procedures in a local application. In fact, the RPC system bundles the parameters, ships them off to another machine, passes them to an application running on that machine, takes the results, packages them, and ships them back to the application that made the call in the first place.

This system greatly simplifies marshalling parameters back and forth and relieves the programmer of the task of implementing protocols for packaging and sending parameters, as well as unpacking values returned from the procedure calls.

Enter RMI

RMI is a Java-specific middleware specification that allows client Java programs to invoke server Java objects as if they were local. RMI is tightly coupled with the Java language. Hence, there are no separate IDL mappings that are required to invoke remote object methods. This is different from DCOM or CORBA, where IDL mappings have to be created to invoke remote methods. (More on CORBA in Chapter 20, "CORBA IDL," and Chapter 21, "Java/CORBA Development Using Caffeine.")

Because RMI is tightly coupled with the Java language, RMI can work with true sub-classes. Neither DCOM nor CORBA can work with true subclasses because they are static object models. This is a mixed blessing. While it allows you to work with true subclasses, it eliminates the ability to work with disparate programming languages.

Because of this, parameters passed during method calls between machines can be true Java objects. This is impossible in DCOM or CORBA at present.

If a process in an RMI system receives an object of a class that it has never seen before, it can request that its class information be sent over the network.

Over and above all this, RMI supports Distributed Garbage Collection. The distributed Garbage Collection ties into the local Garbage Collectors in each JVM.

RMI Background

Because both the client and the server may reside on different machines/processes, there needs to be a mechanism that can establish a relationship between the two. Java-RMI uses a network-based registry program called `RMIRegistry` to keep track of the distributed objects.

The server object makes methods available for remote invocation by binding it to a name in the RMI Registry. The client object can check for the availability of a certain server object by looking up its name in the registry. The RMI Registry acts as a central management point for Java-RMI. The RMI Registry is a simple name repository. It does not address the problem of actually invoking remote methods.

Because the two objects may physically reside on different machines, a mechanism is needed to transmit the client's request to invoke a method on the server object to the server object and provide a response. Java-RMI uses an approach similar to RPC in this regard. The code for the server object must be processed by an RMI compiler called rmic, which is part of the JDK.

The rmic compiler generates two files: a stub and a skeleton. The stub resides on the client machine and the skeleton resides on the server machine. When a client invokes a server method, the JVM looks at the stub to do type checking. The request is then routed to the skeleton on the server, which in turn calls the appropriate method on the server object. In other words, the stub acts as a proxy to the skeleton, and the skeleton is a proxy to the actual remote method.

Creating Server and Client Programs Using RMI

Up to this point, you've been presented with a background explanation of RMI and learned about what's behind it. Now you're going to take some time and create an extremely simple program. It's simple because there are a number of steps to create RMI server and client programs. Before the code gets complicated, you need to thoroughly understand the necessary steps.

There are two programs you'll create—a server and a client program. First, you must create an interface that defines the methods that can be accessed via the remote application. Then, you'll write the server program. Next, the client program will be written. The RMIC program is then used to create the stub and skeleton classes. Finally, you'll run everything and watch it work.

> **Note**
>
> The directory in which all of the .java files were created and used was my d:\chapter18 directory. If you decide to use a different directory, make sure all the steps reflect this change. The directory that was used was explicitly given when compiling the code and using the RMIC program. The exact syntax is shown when appropriate in the following explanations.

All of the files for this chapter can be found in the JavaBeans unleashed section on the www.mcp.com Web site.

Writing the Remote Interface—Step 1

Any class that exports objects must implement an interface which defines the methods that can be accessed via a remote application. The class may have methods that are not defined in this interface, but these methods won't be available to remote clients. It's also possible for a single class to implement many remote interfaces so that different methods are available depending on which interface the object is being cast as.

The interface you write must be derived from java.rmi.Remote. In Listing 18.1, you have a single method that takes no arguments and returns a String object.

LISTING 18.1   Source Code for the GetTimeServer Interface

```
package gettimeserver;

public interface GetTimeServer extends java.rmi.Remote
{

  public String getServerTime()
    throws java.rmi.RemoteException;

}
```

Note that the time returned will be that of the server, not the client. For this reason, the client system clock might not be the same as the server time that's returned.

Writing the Server Program—Step 2

Now you have an interface. The next step is to create the server program that implements the interface. The program consists mostly of the main() and the getServerTime() methods.

The getServerTime() method simply returns a String object that's built from the current server time. The main() method creates a new GetTimeServerImpl class and binds it to the registry server. One important thing to note is that the rebind() method is used instead of the bind() method. If the name is already in use by a previously launched copy of the program, bind() will throw an AlreadyBoundException. Using rebind() avoids this possibility. Listing 18.2 shows the server program.

Note that some class names carry Impl as the last four characters of their name. This is a convention used by most Java programmers to denote implementation classes.

LISTING 18.2 Source Code for the `GetTimeServerImpl` Class

```java
package gettimeserver;

import java.rmi.*;
import java.rmi.server.UnicastRemoteObject;

public class GetTimeServerImpl extends UnicastRemoteObject
   implements GetTimeServer
{

  public String getServerTime()
  {

    System.out.println( "Sending data..." );
    return( new java.util.Date().toString() );

  }

  public GetTimeServerImpl()
    throws RemoteException
  {

    System.out.println( "Initializing GetTimeServer" );

  }

  public static void main( String arg[] )
  {

    System.setSecurityManager( new RMISecurityManager() );

    try
    {

      GetTimeServerImpl TSI = new GetTimeServerImpl();
      Naming.rebind( "GetTimeServer", TSI );
      System.out.println( "Registered GetTimeServer with registry" );
    }
    catch( RemoteException re )
    {

      System.out.println( "Error: " + re.getMessage() );

    }
    catch( java.net.MalformedURLException mue )
    {

      System.out.println( "URL Error: " + mue.getMessage() );
```

```
      }

    }

}
```

Writing the Client Program—Step 3

Writing the client program is a piece of cake. All you have to do is create a class, look up the class on the remote server, and call the `getServerTime()` method. A large portion of the code in Listing 18.3 is catching exceptions and outputting debug code.

While I was developing this, I hardwired the IP address. This isn't usually necessary; you can instead use `127.0.0.1`, which is the local loopback.

LISTING 18.3 Source Code for the `TimeClient` Class

```
package gettimeserver;

import java.rmi.*;

public class TimeClient
{

  public static void main( String argc[] )
  {

    String time = null;

    try
    {

      GetTimeServer TS =
        (GetTimeServer) Naming.lookup( "rmi://204.211.184.206/GetTimeServer" );

      time = TS.getServerTime();

    }
    catch( NotBoundException nbe )
    {

      System.out.println( "GetTimeServer was not found in registry" );

    }
    catch( RemoteException re )
```

continues

LISTING 18.3   continued

```
  {

    System.out.println( "Time error: " + re.getMessage() );
    System.exit( 0 );

  }
  catch( java.net.MalformedURLException mue )
  {

    System.out.println( "URL error: " + mue.getMessage() );
    System.exit( 0 );

  }

 if( time != null )
   System.out.println( "The time is: " + time );

 }

}
```

Compiling the Server and Client Programs—Step 4

Before running any of these programs, the .java files must be compiled. I used the compiler from Visual Café, but the same syntax is applicable for Sun's compiler. When I compiled the code, I was in the d:\Chapter18 directory. You can avoid specifying the directory if javac is in your path. The following is the command line:

```
javac -d d:\Chapter18 GetTimeServer.java GetTimeServerImpl.java TimeClient.java
```

The .class files will be created in the same directory as your source files.

Using RMIC—Step 5

Once the class files have been created, the stub and skeleton classes must be generated. The stub file is the client-side proxy to the remote method, and the skeleton is the server-side proxy. All marshalling of data and method access is done through these two objects. The stub and skeleton files can be generated directly from the gettimeserver.GetTimeServer class file that was created by the compiler.

Once again, as with the compile step, I was in the d:\Chapter18 directory when I ran RMIC. The following command line created the stub and skeleton class files (and put them in the gettimeserver directory):

```
rmic -d d:\Chapter18 gettimeserver.GetTimeServerImpl
```

Running the Server and Client Program

All the source code modules have been compiled and the stub and skeleton class files have been created. It's time to run the program. It's not as easy as executing a single program, though. The following steps show you what to do.

Starting the Registry—Run Step 1

The RMI registry server must be running on the server for things to work properly. It's name is `rmiregistry.exe` and it comes with Visual Café, JBuilder, Sun's Java SDK, and most other Java environments.

To run it from an NT command prompt, type the following:

```
start rmiregistry
```

More than likely, your development system has placed it in the path. If not, you'll get a command-line error message. If this happens, check to see where the program is and make sure it's in the path.

When it successfully runs, you won't see much more than a prompt window indicating that the program is running (see Figure 18.1). This is the Symantec version of `rmiregistry.exe`. The Sun version won't give any visual cue of its successful running at all.

FIGURE 18.1

In this figure, you can see that the RMI registry program (named `rmiregistry.exe`) *is running.*

Starting the Server Program—Run Step 2

Once the registry is running, you can start the `GetTimeServerImpl` program. When I ran it, I was in the `d:\Chapter18` directory. Type the following command line:

```
start java gettimeserver.GetTimeServerImpl
```

The program displayed the debug information indicating it initialized, and `GetTimeServer` was registered (see Figure 18.2).

18

JAVA REMOTE
METHOD
PROTOCOL (JRMP)

FIGURE 18.2

In this figure, you can see the `GetTimeServerImpl` *program after it has started.*

Starting the Client Program—Run Step 3

The last thing you need to do is run the client program. The following command line starts the `TimeClient` program:

```
java gettimeserver.TimeClient
```

If you use the start command, the newly-created window won't stay visible long enough to read the time. Instead, simply invoke the JVM to run the `TimeClient` program and you'll see something similar to Figure 18.3. Notice in the window that contains the `GetTimeServerImpl` program that it displays a text string when the time is being retrieved.

FIGURE 18.3

The client program executes quickly as you can see the server program outputting its debug statements.

Recapping the Steps

It's time to recap all the steps you took to create and build this simple program. The following list can be used as a guide:

1. Write a remote interface.
2. Write a server program.
3. Write a client program.
4. Compile the server and client programs.
5. Run RMIC and create the stub and skeleton files.

6. Run the program by doing the following:

    A. Run the RMI registry server.

    B. Run the server program.

    C. Run the client program.

The RMI Classes

For your convenience, the RMI classes are summed up in Table 18.1.

TABLE 18.1   RMI Class Summary

Class	Description
MarshalledObject	A MarshalledObject contains a byte stream with the serialized representation of an object given to its constructor.
Naming	The Naming class provides methods for storing and obtaining references to remote objects in the remote object registry.
RMISecurityManager	RMISecurityManager provides an example security manager for use by RMI applications that use downloaded code.

Creating Another Pair of RMI Server and Client Programs

Now that you've created one pair of programs that use RMI, it's time to create another pair. The server program will read any file from the hard drive and return it to the client program in the form of a String object.

As with the previous programs, the directory in which all the .java files were created and used was my d:\chapter18 directory. If you decide to use a different directory, make sure all the steps reflect this change. The directory that was used was explicitly given when compiling the code and using the RMIC program. The exact syntax is shown when appropriate in the following explanations.

All the files for this chapter can be found in the JavaBeans Unleashed section on the www.mcp.com Web site.

Writing the Remote Interface—Step 1

Since you're exporting an object that must implement an interface that defines the `readFile()` method, you must define an interface. Again, the interface you write must be derived from `java.rmi.Remote`. In Listing 18.4, you have a single method that takes one argument (a `String` object that contains the filename) and returns a `String` object (the file data).

LISTING 18.4   Source Code for the `FileServer` Interface

```
package fileserver;

public interface FileServer extends java.rmi.Remote
{

  public String readFile( String strFilename )
    throws java.rmi.RemoteException;

}
```

Writing the Server Program—Step 2

Now you have an interface. Your next step is to create the server program. The program consists mostly of the `main()` and the `readFile()` methods.

The `readFile()` method returns a `String` object that contains all the data that will be read in from a file on the server's hard drive. The client program specifies the filename to be read—this is the single argument that the `readFile()` method takes. The `main()` method creates a new `FileServerImpl` class and binds it to the registry server. As before, use `rebind()` instead of `bind()`. Listing 18.5 shows the server program.

LISTING 18.5   Source Code for the `FileServerImpl` Class

```
package fileserver;

import java.rmi.*;
import java.rmi.server.UnicastRemoteObject;
import java.io.*;

public class FileServerImpl extends UnicastRemoteObject implements FileServer
{

  public String readFile( String strFilename )
  {
    String strFiledata = "";
```

```
System.out.println( "Reading file..." );

try
{
  FileInputStream inputFile = new FileInputStream( strFilename );
  BufferedInputStream is = new BufferedInputStream( inputFile );

  int i;
  while( ( i = is.read() ) != -1 )
    strFiledata += (char) i;

  is.close();
}
catch( IOException e )
{

  strFiledata = "IOException: " + e.getMessage();

}

System.out.println( "Sending file..." );

return( strFiledata );

}

public FileServerImpl()
  throws RemoteException
{

  System.out.println( "Initializing FileServer" );

}

public static void main( String arg[] )
{

  System.setSecurityManager( new RMISecurityManager() );

  try
  {

    FileServerImpl FSI = new FileServerImpl();
    Naming.rebind( "FileServer", FSI );
    System.out.println( "Registered FileServer with registry" );
  }
  catch( RemoteException re )
  {
```

continues

LISTING **18.5**   continued

```
      System.out.println( "Error: " + re.getMessage() );

    }
    catch( java.net.MalformedURLException mue )
    {

      System.out.println( "URL Error: " + mue.getMessage() );

    }

  }

}
```

Writing the Client Program—Step 3

Writing this client program is just as easy as the first one that retrieved the time from the server. The code is seen in Listing 18.6.

LISTING **18.6**   Source Code for the FileClient Class

```
package fileserver;

import java.rmi.*;

public class FileClient
{
  public static void main( String argc[] )
  {

    String strFiledata = null;

    try
    {

      FileServer FS =
        (FileServer) Naming.lookup( "rmi://199.72.119.68/FileServer" );

      strFiledata = FS.readFile( "C:\\AUTOEXEC.BAT" );

    }
    catch( NotBoundException nbe )
    {
```

```
    System.out.println( "FileServer was not found in registry" );

  }
  catch( RemoteException re )
  {

    System.out.println( "Time error: " + re.getMessage() );
    System.exit( 0 );

  }
  catch( java.net.MalformedURLException mue )
  {

    System.out.println( "URL error: " + mue.getMessage() );
    System.exit( 0 );

  }

  if( strFiledata != null )
    System.out.println( strFiledata );

  }

}
```

Building and Running the Programs

This section describes the build and run process for the two programs.

1. Compile the source code with the following syntax:

   ```
   javac -d d:\Chapter18 FileServer.java FileServerImpl.java FileClient.java
   ```

2. Use RMIC to generate the stub and skeleton files with the following syntax:

   ```
   rmic -d d:\Chapter18\fileserver.FileServerImpl
   ```

3. Run the RMI registry program with the following syntax:

   ```
   start rmiregistry
   ```

4. Run the server program with the following syntax:

   ```
   start java fileserver.FileServerImpl
   ```

5. Run the client program with the following syntax:

   ```
   java fileserver.FileClient
   ```

When the client program runs, you'll see the server program display some debug lines letting you know that it's reading a file and then sending a file. The client program displays the file data once it's received (see Figure 18.4).

FIGURE 18.4

The client program executes quickly and displays the contents of the server's `autoexec.bat` *file.*

RMI Exceptions

You may have noticed that a number of exceptions were caught in the two programs you created. You'll have to be careful in your programming that you catch and handle them correctly. Table 18.2 contains the RMI exceptions and will be a valuable reference when you get down to programming with RMI.

TABLE 18.2 Exception Summary

Exception	Summary
AccessException	An AccessException is thrown by certain methods of the java.rmi.Naming class (specifically bind, rebind, and unbind) and methods of the java.rmi.activation.ActivationSysteminterface to indicate that the caller does not have permission to perform the action requested by the method call.
AlreadyBoundException	An AlreadyBoundException is thrown if an attempt is made to bind an object in the registry to a name that already has an associated binding.
ConnectException	A ConnectException is thrown if a connection is refused to the remote host for a remote method call.
ConnectIOException	A ConnectIOException is thrown if an IOException occurs while making a connection to the remote host for a remote method call.
MarshalException	A MarshalException is thrown if a java.io.IOException occurs while marshalling the remote call header, arguments, or return value for a remote method call.
NoSuchObjectException	A NoSuchObjectException is thrown if an attempt is made to invoke a method on an object that no longer exists in the remote virtual machine.

NotBoundException	A NotBoundException is thrown if an attempt is made to look up or unbind in the registry a name that has no associated binding.
RemoteException	A RemoteException is the common superclass for a number of communication-related exceptions that can occur during the execution of a remote method call.
ServerError	A ServerError is thrown as a result of a remote method call if the execution of the remote method on the server machine throws a java.lang.Error.
ServerException	A ServerException is thrown as a result of a remote method call if the execution of the remote method on the server machine throws a RemoteException.
StubNotFoundException	A StubNotFoundException is thrown if a valid stub class could not be found for a remote object when it is exported, or when a remote object is passed in a remote method call as a parameter or return value.
UnexpectedException	An UnexpectedException is thrown if the client of a remote method call receives, as a result of the call, a checked exception that is not among the checked exception types declared in the throws clause of the method in the remote interface.
UnknownHostException	An UnknownHostException is thrown if a java.net.UnknownHostException occurs while creating a connection to the remote host for a remote method call.
UnmarshalException	An UnmarshalException can be thrown while unmarshalling the parameters or results of a remote method call if any of the following conditions occur: if an exception occurs while unmarshalling the call header, if the protocol for the return value is invalid, or if a java.io.IOException occurs unmarshalling parameters (on the server side) or the return value (on the client side).

18

JAVA REMOTE
METHOD
PROTOCOL (JRMP)

Summary

RMI gives you a powerful tool in your arsenal of network programming. Rather than open sockets and send formatted data, you can actually call methods on the remote computer. In addition, the data marshalling is done for you in the process as an extra bonus.

If you do any network programming with Java, RMI will become part of your projects, and they'll be easier to code, easier to debug, and more robust as a result.

CHAPTER 19

CORBA: Using
Java IDL

All source code for this chapter can be found on the
Sams Publishing Website at
http://www.mcp.com/info/0-672/0-672-31424-x.

The Common Object Request Broker Architecture (CORBA) is a specification that enables distributed software components to work together regardless of the programming language used to develop them, the computer platform they run on, or the computer networks they use. Java IDL is a set of packages and tools that enables you to create CORBA-compliant software in Java. Java IDL is part of the core Java2 (JDK 1.2) runtime environment. Therefore, you know that your CORBA-compliant JavaBeans components can run on any Java platform.

CORBA

Software components written for a variety of computer platforms in a range of programming languages are brought together across the computing enterprise through CORBA, an Open Management Group (OMG) specification. This is made possible through two CORBA technologies: the Object Request Broker (ORB) and the Interface Definition Language (IDL).

For complete information on CORBA, check `http://www.omg.org`. Java IDL is included for the first time with JDK 1.2. It was, however, available as a separate add-on for JDK 1.1.

Other languages, such as C++, support CORBA, and there are different vendors, such as VisiBroker, that offer variations. One variation is discussed in the next chapter.

Object Request Broker (ORB)

The Object Request Broker (ORB) forms the core of CORBA. Client applications find objects and invoke methods anywhere across the computing enterprise through an ORB. The ORB masks the details of the object's location, programming language, or type of platform and passes requests, responses, and exceptions between a client object and a server object. A repository maintains details about server objects such as their location. Objects need to be registered for the ORB to manage them and make them available to client applications. The ORB is the CORBA communication channel.

Interface Definition Language (IDL)

The Interface Definition Language (IDL) is used to create component interfaces that all objects conforming to the CORBA specification can understand. A Java bean's public methods and constants are made available to all CORBA-compliant objects on the enterprise through IDL. OMG IDL is a purely descriptive language used to map an object's interface defined in its own programming language to a language that is understood by all objects within the CORBA universe. In fact, an interface defined in IDL is almost exactly the same as a Java interface. The following sections describe how IDL is mapped onto Java.

> **Note**
>
> IDL syntax is similar to C, C++, and Java.

IDL Modules to Java Packages

A module in IDL is equivalent to a package in Java. A module groups interfaces together into their own namespace. An important point to remember is that IDL compilers actually generate Java code. The following is an example of a sams module, which maps onto a sams package in Java.

```
module sams {
  // IDL code, including interface definitions
};
```

This module is mapped to the following Java code.

```
package sams;
```

> **Note**
>
> Begin a comment on a single line in IDL with two forward slashes (//). Multi-line comments are started using /* and ended with */. These are the same conventions as in C, C++, and Java.

Define a module using the `module` keyword followed by open and closed braces ({}) and ended with a semicolon (;). All interfaces defined between the braces ({}) are part of that module.

You can nest modules in IDL just as you can nest packages in Java. For example, the following IDL code creates a corba module inside the sams module.

```
module sams {
  module corba {
    // IDL code, including interface definitions
  };
};
```

Interfaces added at the remark in this code are in a module equivalent to the `sams.corba` package. These nested modules are mapped to the following Java code:

```
package sams.corba;
```

IDL Data Types to Java Data Types

Java is an almost purely object-oriented language. Almost, because Java includes a set of primitive data types that are not objects. Primitive data types are included in addition to reference data types (objects) for reasons of efficiency. IDL provides equivalent data types for all of the Java primitive data types, as shown in Table 19.1, and only one reference type; objects created from the `java.lang.String` class, as shown in Table 19.2.

> **Note**
>
> See Chapter 24, "Introspection," for more information on primitive and reference data types.

TABLE 19.1 Mapping Primitive Data Types

IDL Data Type	Java Data Type	Size
octet	byte	8-bits
short	short	16-bits
unsigned short	short	16-bits
long	int	32-bits
unsigned long	int	32-bits
long long	long	64-bits
unsigned long long	long	64-bits
float	float	32-bits
double	double	64-bits
boolean	boolean	1-bit
char	char	IDL 8-bits/Java 16-bits
wchar	char	16-bits

Although there are IDL equivalents for all Java primitive data types, they don't always use the same keyword. For instance, the IDL equivalent of a Java `int` data type is the `long` data type. One primitive data type mapping is a bit less straightforward than the rest; the `char` data type mapping.

Java char is a 16-bit data type, but the ASCII characters that you probably use most of the time are based on an 8-bit definition. Java provides 16-bits for characters so that you can use the Unicode character standard. The 16-bit Unicode standard can include up to 65,536 characters compared with the 8-bit ASCII limit of 256 characters. That gives the Unicode character set plenty of room to represent the symbols and characters from nearly all the languages of the world past and present.

ASCII characters are incorporated as part of the Unicode character set. That's why you can use 8-bit ASCII characters with the Java 16-bit char data type. However, in IDL the char data type is 8-bits long, which works with ASCII but not Unicode characters. IDL throws a CORBA::DATA_CONVERSION exception if you try to map the 8-bit IDL char data type onto a Java char data type variable assigned Unicode characters. Use the 16-bit IDL wchar (w for wide) data type when you're mapping onto Java variables assigned Unicode characters.

IDL provides a direct data type mapping to objects created from the java.lang.String class, as shown in Table 19.2. Strings are made up of characters and, as you've just seen, Java characters can be from the Unicode or ASCII character sets. If you're creating your strings using ASCII characters, map the IDL string data type onto the java.lang.String data type. Otherwise, if you're using Unicode, use the IDL wstring data type.

TABLE 19.2 Mapping String Data Types

IDL Data Type	*Java Data Type*	*IDL Exception*
string	java.lang.String	CORBA::MARSHAL, CORBA::DATA_CONVERSION
wstring	java.lang.String	CORBA::MARSHAL

IDL Boolean Constants to Java Boolean Literals

Literals, values typed directly into your code, are mostly the same in IDL and Java. However, the Boolean values in Java are literals defined by the true and false keywords, whereas there are no Boolean literals in IDL. IDL maps the TRUE and FALSE constants to Java's true and false literals, as shown in Table 19.3.

TABLE 19.3 Boolean Constants and Literals

IDL Constant	*Java Literal*
TRUE	true
FALSE	false

IDL Constants to Java Constants

You might think that mapping constants between IDL and Java is a simple matter. It's not as simple as you might think, because IDL allows the definition of constants in modules as well as in interfaces, but Java only allows the definition of constants in classes and interfaces. IDL constants are mapped to Java in two different ways, depending on whether the constant is defined inside or outside an interface.

> **Note**
>
> IDL constants are defined using the `const` keyword, and Java constants are defined using the `static` and `final` keywords.

IDL Constant Defined in an Interface

You can define constants inside an interface in IDL. The IDL example shown next defines a 32-bit integer constant named `MY_CONSTANT` as part of the `MyInterface` interface, which is part of the `corba` module nested inside the `sams` module.

> **Note**
>
> A 32-bit integer is defined using the `long` keyword in IDL and the `int` keyword in Java. Learn more about primitive data type mapping between IDL and Java in the "IDL Data Types to Java Data Types" section earlier in this chapter.

```
module sams {
  module corba {
    interface MyInterface {
      const long MY_CONSTANT = 38;
    };
  };
};
```

This IDL code maps to the following Java code:

```
package sams.corba;

public interface MyInterface extends org.omg.CORBA.Object {
  public static final int MY_CONSTANT = (int) (38L);
}
```

> **Note**
>
> All Java interfaces mapped from interfaces written in IDL extend the
> org.omg.CORBA.object interface, which is part of the core Java platform. Learn
> more about IDL to Java interface mapping in the "IDL Interfaces to Java
> Interfaces" section later in this chapter.

The interface is declared as part of the sams.corba package, and MyInterface is
declared as a public interface. Inside the sams.corba.MyInterface interface signature,
the 32-bit integer constant named MY_CONSTANT is defined.

IDL Constant Defined Outside an Interface

You can define constants outside interfaces and inside modules in IDL. The IDL example
shown next defines a 32-bit integer constant named MY_CONSTANT in the corba module
nested inside the sams module.

```
module sams {
  module corba {
    const long MY_CONSTANT = 38;
  };
};
```

The IDL code above maps to the following Java code.

```
package sams.corba;

public class MY_CONSTANT {
  public static final int value = (int) (38L);
}
```

The constant name is mapped to a class because Java does not allow the definition of
constants outside of classes or interfaces. The new MY_CONSTANT class is declared as part
of the sams.corba package. The value of the IDL constant is assigned to the value constant defined in the sams.corba.MY_CONSTANT class.

IDL Interfaces to Java Interfaces

Writing in IDL, as the name Interface Definition Language implies, is about writing
interfaces. The strong emphasis on interfaces in Java makes it an excellent language for
mapping IDL and using the CORBA specification. All Java interfaces mapped from

19

**CORBA: USING
JAVA IDL**

interfaces written in IDL extend the `org.omg.CORBA.object` interface, which is part of the core Java platform. `MyInterface` is an interface defined in the following IDL code:

```
interface MyInterface {
  // add code here
};
```

This IDL interface code maps to the following Java code:

```
public interface MyInterface extends org.omg.CORBA.Object {
  // add code here
}
```

An IDL interface can include one or more operations, constants, or attributes in any combination. Recall that you write IDL interfaces to define available properties, methods, and constants in JavaBeans components or other objects. You can define operations in IDL that map to Java methods, constants in IDL that map to Java constants, and attributes in IDL that map to Java properties. Mapping constants is explained earlier this chapter in the "IDL Constants to Java Constants" Section. IDL operations to Java methods and IDL attributes to Java properties mapping are explained in the following sections.

IDL Operations to Java Methods

An IDL operation maps directly to a Java method. Unlike in a Java method, all IDL parameters must include one of the three operation parameter modifiers listed in Table 19.4.

TABLE 19.4   IDL Operation Parameter Modifiers

Modifier	*Description*
in	Data is passed through the parameter to the corresponding Java method. IDL operation parameters modified by in are mapped to the normal Java parameter passing mechanisms.
out	An instance of a holder class is passed through the parameter to the method. The value encapsulated by the holder object can be modified and returned.
inout	Specifies a combination of the in and out parameter passing mechanisms.

IDL parameters modified with in are mapped to the familiar Java parameter passing mechanisms. For example, the following IDL code defines the `myMethod()` operation with the `num` parameter modified by in:

```
module sams {
  module corba {
    interface MyInterface {
      void myMethod( in long num );
    };
  };
};
```

The myMethod() operation maps to the following Java myMethod() method definition:

```
package sams.corba;

public interface MyInterface extends org.omg.CORBA.Object {
  void myMethod(int num);
}
```

This method definition looks like the definition of any method that takes an integer parameter. The num parameter is passed by value so that the original variable remains inaccessible to the method and the value assigned to it remains unchanged.

IDL parameters modified with out are mapped to parameters defined using special CORBA holder data types. The holder data types are created from classes included in the org.omg.CORBA package, which is part of the core Java platform. For example, the following IDL code defines the myMethod() operation with the num parameter modified by out.

```
module sams {
  module corba {
    interface MyInterface {
      void myMethod( out long num );
    };
  };
};
```

This myMethod() operation using the out parameter modifier maps to the following Java myMethod() method definition:

```
package sams.corba;

public interface MyInterface extends org.omg.CORBA.Object {
  void myMethod(org.omg.CORBA.IntHolder num);
}
```

The num parameter is defined in IDL as taking a 32-bit integer (long) which maps to int in Java. The IDL to Java mapping specifies that the holder object for int parameters is instantiated from the org.omg.CORBA.IntHolder class. A client object instantiates the org.omg.CORBA.IntHolder class and passes the new IntHolder object to the myMethod() implemented on the server object. The method can assign a new value to a variable encapsulated by the IntHolder object and pass it back to the client object.

19

CORBA: USING JAVA IDL

> **Note**
>
> Java methods can only return one value. What if you want to pass more than one value back to a client object from a server object? IDL solves the problem by allowing data to be passed from the method through method parameters.

CORBA uses holder data types to store "in" and "out" parameters in IDL methods. Let's take, for example, a holder class for an `int`. If an IDL method signature has an IDL long as an "out" or "inout" parameter, the programmer must pass an instance of `IntHolder` as the corresponding parameter in the method invocation; for "inout" parameters, the programmer must also fill the "in" value to be sent to the server. Before the method invocation returns, the ORB will fill in the value corresponding to the "out" value returned from the server.

If `myIntHolder` is an instance of `IntHolder`, the value stored in its value field can be accessed with `myIntHolder.value`.

IDL parameters modified with `inout` are mapped to parameters defined using both value passing and special CORBA holder data types. For example, the following IDL code defines the `myMethod()` operation with the `num` parameter modified by `inout`:

```
module sams {
  module corba {
    interface MyInterface {
      void myMethod( inout long num );
    };
  };
};
```

The `myMethod()` operation using the `inout` parameter modifier maps to the following Java `myMethod()` method definition:

```
package sams.corba;

public interface MyInterface extends org.omg.CORBA.Object {
  void myMethod(org.omg.CORBA.IntHolder num);
}
```

Return values defined in IDL operations map directly to return values defined in Java methods. For example, in the following IDL code the `myMethod()` operation returns a 32-bit integer:

```
module sams {
  module corba {
    interface MyInterface {
      long myMethod( in long num );
    };
  };
};
```

This `myMethod()` operation maps to the following Java `myMethod()` method:

```
package sams.corba;

public interface MyInterface extends org.omg.CORBA.Object {
  int myMethod(int num);
}
```

IDL Attributes to JavaBeans Properties

Use IDL attributes when you need to expose properties through an IDL interface. Define an attribute using the `attribute` keyword such as for the `name` property in the following example:

```
module sams {
  module corba {
    interface MyInterface {
      attribute string name;
    };
  };
};
```

This IDL code maps to the following code in Java:

```
package sams.corba;

public interface MyInterface extends org.omg.CORBA.Object {
  String name();
  void name(String arg);
}
```

You can see that the IDL code maps to a getter method and a setter method. However, these accessor methods do not follow the JavaBeans specification design patterns. To expose bean properties, it's best to add operators to the IDL code with the proper accessor method names. When you follow the JavaBeans specification design patterns, the getter method for the `name` property should be named `getName()`, and the setter method should be named `setName()`. The following IDL code maps to the proper accessor methods:

```
module sams {
  module corba {
    interface MyInterface {
      string getName( );
      void setName( in string name );
    };
  };
};
```

This IDL code maps to the following code in Java:

```
package sams.corba;

public interface MyInterface extends org.omg.CORBA.Object {
  String getName();
  void setName(String name);
}
```

These accessor methods follow the JavaBeans design patterns for a `name` property.

19

CORBA: USING
JAVA IDL

IDL Exceptions to Java Exceptions

Each standard IDL exception has a Java class associated with it in the `org.omg.CORBA` package. For instance, if an attempt is made to assign a Unicode character to an IDL parameter declared as a char data type, a `CORBA::DATA_CONVERSION` exception is thrown. The Java code throws the equivalent exception instantiated from the `org.omg.CORBA.DATA_CONVERSION` class. IDL exceptions and their Java class equivalents are listed in Table 19.5.

TABLE 19.5   IDL to Java Exception Mapping

IDL Exception	*Java Class*
CORBA::BAD_CONTEXT	org.omg.CORBA.BAD_CONTEXT
CORBA::BAD_INV_ORDER	org.omg.CORBA.BAD_INV_ORDER
CORBA::BAD_OPERATION	org.omg.CORBA.BAD_OPERATION
CORBA::BAD_PARAM	org.omg.CORBA.BAD_PARAM
CORBA::BAD_TYPECODE	org.omg.CORBA.BAD_TYPECODE
CORBA::COMM_FAILURE	org.omg.CORBA.COMM_FAILURE
CORBA::DATA_CONVERSION	org.omg.CORBA.DATA_CONVERSION
CORBA::FREE_MEM	org.omg.CORBA.FREE_MEM
CORBA::INITIALIZE	org.omg.CORBA.INITIALIZE
CORBA::IMP_LIMIT	org.omg.CORBA.IMP_LIMIT
CORBA::INTERNAL	org.omg.CORBA.INTERNAL
CORBA::INTF_REPOS	org.omg.CORBA.INTF_REPOS
CORBA::INV_FLAG	org.omg.CORBA.INV_FLAG
CORBA::INV_IDENT	org.omg.CORBA.INV_IDENT
CORBA::INV_OBJREF	org.omg.CORBA.INV_OBJREF
CORBA::INVALIDTRANSACTION	org.omg.CORBA.INVALIDTRANSACTION
CORBA::MARSHAL	org.omg.CORBA.MARSHAL
CORBA::NO_IMPLEMENT	org.omg.CORBA.NO_IMPLEMENT
CORBA::NO_MEMORY	org.omg.CORBA.NO_MEMORY
CORBA::NO_PERMISSION	org.omg.CORBA.NO_PERMISSION
CORBA::NO_RESOURCES	org.omg.CORBA.NO_RESOURCES
CORBA::NO_RESPONSE	org.omg.CORBA.NO_RESPONSE
CORBA::OBJ_ADAPTER	org.omg.CORBA.OBJ_ADAPTER
CORBA::OBJECT_NOT_EXIST	org.omg.CORBA.OBJECT_NOT_EXIST
CORBA::PERSIST_STORE	org.omg.CORBA.PERSIST_STORE

IDL Exception	Java Class
CORBA::TRANSACTIONREQUIRED	org.omg.CORBA.TRANSACTIONREQUIRED
CORBA::TRANSACTIONROLLEDBACK	org.omg.CORBA.TRANSACTIONROLLEDBACK
CORBA::TRANSIENT	org.omg.CORBA.TRANSIENT
CORBA::UNKNOWN	org.omg.CORBA.UNKNOWN

Java IDL

Java IDL stands for a whole set of packages and tools, including the Interface Definition Language (IDL), that is part of the core Java platform. There are four major components that form the Java IDL:

- The idltojava Compiler
- Java IDL ORB
- Java IDL Transient Name Server
- Java IDL Packages

Note

IDL is also known as OMG IDL for the Object Management Group Interface Definition Language. The Object Management Group (OMG) is the organization that developed the CORBA specifications along with IDL. You can visit the OMG Web site at http://www.omg.org/.

The `idltojava` Compiler

The idltojava compiler automatically maps interfaces you wrote in IDL to Java interfaces. You feed the idltojava compiler an IDL file and it creates Java files containing interfaces and support classes.

Note

The idltojava compiler is now included with Java2. If you have an earlier version, the idltojava compiler is the only part of Java IDL that isn't included in the Java Development Kit. You can get the idltojava compiler free from the Java Developer Connection Web site at http://developer.java.sun.com/developer/earlyAccess/jdk12/idltojava.html.

The `idltojava` compiler that's used on Solaris is hard-coded to use Microsoft Visual C++. However, you can set environment variables so that the `idltojava` tool uses a different C++ preprocessor, such as the freely available GNU C++ compiler. Or you can use no preprocessor at all if you add `-fno-cpp` argument to the `idltojava` command. If you use a C++ preprocessor you must be sure that the folder with the compiler is included in your computer's `Path` variable so that the `idltojava` compiler can find it.

Java IDL ORB

The Java platform includes a Java IDL Object Request Broker (ORB). The ORB is CORBA's central communication engine. When a CORBA client object requests an operation or service, the ORB connects it with the CORBA server object that provides it. The Java IDL ORB only supports transient objects, it doesn't support objects that persist beyond the lifetime of the server process.

Java IDL Transient Name Server

The Java IDL Transient Name Server is a naming service provided with the core Java platform. A naming service is a CORBA service that names CORBA objects by binding a name to a reference to that object. The name binding is stored. When a client supplies the name of an object, the naming service is consulted. If the object is registered with the naming service, a reference to the object is returned.

> **Note**
>
> Each object reference and name pair is known as a name binding.

You must start the Java IDL Name Server before starting any program that tries to use its naming services. Start the Java IDL Name Server by typing the following command at the console or DOS window prompt

```
tnameserv
```

By default, the Java IDL Name Server listens on port 900 for binding and reference requests. In case you were wondering, other ORBs can communicate with the Java IDL Name Server using IIOP. You can specify a different port using the `ORBInitialPort` argument, as shown in the following command:

```
tnameserv -ORBInitialPort 1050
```

This command tells the naming service to listen for binding and reference requests on port 1050.

Java IDL Packages

Java IDL includes seven packages that are part of the core Java platform. These packages are listed and described in Table 19.6.

TABLE 19.6   Java IDL Packages

Package	Description
org.omg.CORBA	Provides the mapping of the OMG CORBA APIs to the Java programming language, including the class ORB, which is implemented so that a programmer can use it as a fully-functional Object Request Broker (ORB)
org.omg.CORBA.DynAnyPackage	Provides the exceptions used with the org.omg.CORBA.DynAny interface
org.omg.CORBA.ORBPackage	Provides exceptions thrown by the org.omg.CORBA.ORB class including the InvalidName exception, which is thrown by the org.omg.CORBA.ORB class resolve_initial_references() method
org.omg.CORBA.portable	Provides a set of Object Request Broker (ORB) application programming interfaces (APIs) that makes it possible for code generated by one vendor to run on another vendor's ORB
org.omg.CORBA.TypeCodePackage	Provides the user-defined BadKind and Bounds exceptions, which are thrown by methods in the org.omg.CORBA.TypeCode class
org.omg.CosNaming	Provides the naming service for Java IDL
org.omg.CosNaming. NamingContextPackage	Provides the exceptions used in the org.omg.CosNaming package and the Helper and Holder classes for those exceptions

Create a CORBA Application

CORBA applications work on a client/server model. In this section, you create a CORBA-client application that loads an image file and then sends it across the enterprise to a CORBA server application. The server application displays the image in a separate window upon receiving it. One of the interesting things about this application is that the Interface Definition Language (IDL) does not include an equivalent data type to the java.awt.Image class. In fact, only the Java primitive data types, except for the `java.lang.String` class, are defined in IDL. You get around this potential problem by creating your own data classes that you can completely map to IDL and that map onto the Java data type. Begin writing your CORBA applications by defining the server interfaces using (IDL).

Defining Server Interfaces Using IDL

You need to write two IDL interfaces for the image server: one for an object that encapsulates the image (`IDLImageInterface`) and one for the server itself (`ImageServerInterface`). These interfaces are added to the `corba` module nested in the `sams` module, as shown in Listing 19.1, so that they map to the `sams.corba` package in Java.

Create an interface that represents an object that bridges between IDL and the `java.awt.Image` class by breaking down an `Image` object into smaller pieces. `Image` objects are composed of three properties: a collection of pixels, height, and width. Each pixel in an `Image` object is represented by a 32-bit integer. Therefore, you need to define a sequence of 32-bit integers using the IDL `sequence` keyword and `long` data type. The following line of IDL code defines the `longSequence` data type using the `typedef` keyword:

```
typedef sequence<long> longSequence;
```

Now you can define the interface, named `IDLImageInterface`, that represents an object, the `IDLImage` object. It's the `IDLImage` object that forms a bridge between IDL and the `java.awt.Image` class. The three `Image` object properties, pixels, image height, and image width, are represented within the `IDLImage` object by the `imageData`, `height`, and `width` properties. Write the following `IDLImageInterface` interface definition in IDL with accessor methods for each of the three properties:

```
interface IDLImageInterface {
  long getHeight( );
  long getWidth( );
  longSequence getImageData( );
};
```

With the `IDLImage` class defined, you're ready to define the image server interface. The `ImageServer` object will expose one method through its CORBA interface, which will allow client objects to pass the server an image and have it displayed. The `displayImage()` method is exposed through the `displayImage()` operation in the following IDL code.

```
interface ImageServerInterface {
  void displayImage( in IDLImageInterface image );
};
```

That completes the CORBA interfaces defined in IDL for this project. Your next step is to compile the IDL code using the `idltojava` compiler.

LISTING 19.1 Source code for `ImageServerInterface.idl`

```
module sams {
  module corba {
    typedef sequence<long> longSequence;

    interface IDLImageInterface {
      long getHeight( );
      long getWidth( );
      longSequence getImageData( );
    };

    interface ImageServerInterface {
      void displayImage( in IDLImageInterface image );
    };
  };
};
```

Compiling the IDL File

After you've defined your server object's interface in IDL, you then need to map the IDL to Java. This is done for you by the `idltojava` compiler (see the "The `idltojava` Compiler" section earlier in this chapter).

Place the `ImageServerInterface.idl` file in your root class directory and then enter the following command at your console or DOS window prompt:

```
idltojava -fno-cpp ImageServerInterface.idl
```

The `idltojava` compiler creates twelve new files, which are listed in Table 19.7. Six of the files contain code for final Java classes that can be used by other objects to help map between CORBA and Java. Two of the files, `IDLImageInterface.java` and `ImageServerInterface.java`, contain code for Java versions of the IDL interfaces you wrote in the `ImageServerInterface.idl` file. Each CORBA server object written in Java must implement the Java version of its CORBA interface. The `sams.corba.IDLImage` class must implement the `sams.corba.IDLImageInterface` interface created by the `idltojava` compiler. Likewise, the `sams.corba.ImageServer` class must implement the `sams.corba.ImageServerInterface` interface. These interfaces declare abstract methods that enable your Java language objects to act as CORBA server objects.

19

CORBA: USING JAVA IDL

You could implement the appropriate interface in your server class and then write all of the CORBA support methods yourself. However, the idltojava compiler creates a Java class for each interface that implements the interface and includes the support methods already written for you. The sams.corba._IDLImageInterfaceImplBase class implements the sams.corba.IDLImageInterface interface and the sams.corba._ImageServerInterfaceImplBase class implements the sams.corba.ImageServerInterface interface. You write server classes in the following sections that extend these base classes.

TABLE 19.7 Java Files Created from ImageServerInterface.idl

Java File	*Description*
_IDLImageInterfaceImplBase	An abstract class that implements the sams.corba.IDLImageInterface interface. This class is the server skeleton, which provides basic CORBA functionality for the IDLImage server.
_IDLImageInterfaceStub	A class that implements the sams.corba.IDLImageInterface interface. This class is the client stub, which provides CORBA functionality for the client.
_ImageServerInterfaceImplBase	An abstract class that implements the sams.corba.ImageServerInterface interface. This class is the server skeleton, which provides basic CORBA functionality for the ImageServer server.
_ImageServerInterfaceStub	A class that implements the sams.corba.ImageServerInterface interface. This class is the client stub, which provides CORBA functionality for the client.
IDLImageInterface	Java version of the IDL interface. This interface extends the org.omg.CORBA.Object interface, which provides standard CORBA object functionality to Java objects.
IDLImageInterfaceHelper	A final class that provides helper methods, including the narrow() method required to cast CORBA object references to their proper data types.
IDLImageInterfaceHolder	A final class that holds a public instance member of the sams.corba.IDLImage data type. The class provides operations for out and inout arguments, which CORBA has but which do not map easily to the Java language.

Java File	*Description*
`ImageServerInterface`	Java version of the IDL interface. This interface extends the `org.omg.CORBA.Object` interface, which provides standard CORBA object functionality to Java objects.
`ImageServerInterfaceHelper`	A final class that provides helper methods, including the `narrow()` method required to cast CORBA object references to their proper data types.
`ImageServerInterfaceHolder`	A final class that holds a public instance member of the `sams.corba.ImageServer` data type. The class provides operations for `out` and `inout` arguments, which CORBA has but which do not map easily to the Java language.
`longSequenceHelper`	A final class that provides helper methods, including the `narrow()` method required to cast CORBA object references to their proper types.
`longSequenceHolder`	A final class that holds a public instance member of the `sams.corba.longSequence` data type. The class provides operations for `out` and `inout` arguments, which CORBA has but which do not map easily to the Java language.

Implementing Data Code

The image data itself is encapsulated in its own CORBA server object so that it can be translated between Java and CORBA data types. The `sams.corba.IDLImage` class encapsulates image data and breaks it into three parts: a sequence of 32-bit integers representing the image pixels, a 32-bit integer representing the image height, and a 32-bit integer representing the image width.

The implementation of the `sams.corba.IDLImage` class is shown in Listing 19.2. The collection of pixels is assigned to the `imageData` variable. The height of the image is assigned to the `height` variable and the width of the image is assigned to the `width` variable. These three properties are the key to the class's ability to communicate an image through CORBA interfaces. Otherwise, the only significant code in the `sams.corba.IDLImage` class is in its implementation of the `obtainImageData()` method. The `obtainImageData()` method uses the standard Java classes from the Abstract Windowing Toolkit (AWT) to load images and extract image pixel data.

LISTING 19.2 Source code for `IDLImage.java`

```java
package sams.corba;

import java.awt.Component;
import java.awt.Image;
import java.awt.MediaTracker;
import java.awt.image.ImageObserver;
import java.awt.image.PixelGrabber;

public final class IDLImage extends _IDLImageInterfaceImplBase {
  private Image image = null;
  private int[] imageData = null;
  private Component observer = null;
  private int height = 0;
  private int width = 0;

  public IDLImage( Image image, Component observer ) {
    this.image = image;
    this.observer = observer;
    obtainImageData( );
  }

  public int[] getImageData( ) {
    return imageData;
  }

  public int getHeight( ) {
    return height;;
  }

  public int getWidth( ) {
    return width;
  }

  private void obtainImageData( ) {
    try {
      MediaTracker track = new MediaTracker( observer );
      track.addImage( image, 0 );
      track.waitForAll( );
    }
    catch ( Exception e ) {
      System.out.println( "error at load: " + e );
    }
    height = image.getHeight( observer );
    width = image.getWidth( observer );
    imageData = new int[width * height];
    PixelGrabber grabber = new PixelGrabber( image, 0, 0, width, height,
        imageData, 0, width );
    try {
      grabber.grabPixels( );
```

```
      }
      catch ( InterruptedException e ) {
        System.err.println( "interrupted waiting for pixels!" );
        return;
      }
      if ( ( grabber.getStatus( ) & ImageObserver.ABORT ) != 0 ) {
        System.err.println( "image fetch aborted or errored" );
        return;
      }
    }
  }
}
```

Implementing Server Code

The `ImageServer` application receives images from clients and displays them in a window. The code that displays the images is contained in two classes separate from the server class itself. These are the `sams.corba.ImageServerWindow` and `sams.corba.ImagePanel` classes.

The `sams.corba.ImageServerWindow` class, shown in Listing 19.3, transforms the data encapsulated by the `IDLImage` object into data encapsulated by an `Image` object. The class is extended from the `java.awt.Frame` class, so when it's instantiated a window appears. An `ImagePanel` object is added to the `Frame` object and displayed by the window.

LISTING 19.3 Source code for `ImageServerWindow.java`

```
package sams.corba;

import java.awt.FlowLayout;
import java.awt.Frame;
import java.awt.Image;
import java.awt.Label;
import java.awt.event.WindowAdapter;
import java.awt.event.WindowEvent;
import java.awt.image.MemoryImageSource;

public final class ImageServerWindow extends Frame {
  private Label lableStatus = null;

  public ImageServerWindow( ) {
    super( "Image Server" );
    setLayout( new FlowLayout( ) );
    lableStatus = new Label( );
    setWait( );
```

continues

19

CORBA: USING
JAVA IDL

LISTING 19.3 continued

```java
    add( lableStatus );
    addWindowListener( new WindowEventHandler( ) );
  }

  private void setWait( ) {
    lableStatus.setText( "Waiting For An Image" );
  }

  private void setProcessing( ) {
    lableStatus.setText( "Processing Image" );
  }

  public void displayImage( IDLImageInterface idlImage ) {
    setProcessing( );
    Image image = createImage( new MemoryImageSource( idlImage.getWidth( ),
        idlImage.getHeight( ), idlImage.getImageData( ), 0,
        idlImage.getWidth( ) ) );
    Frame f = new Frame( );
    f.setLayout( new FlowLayout( ) );
    f.add( new ImagePanel( image ) );
    f.pack( );
    f.setVisible( true );
    setWait( );
  }

  class WindowEventHandler extends WindowAdapter {
    public void windowClosing( WindowEvent e ) {
      System.exit( 0 );
    }
  }
}
```

The sams.corba.ImagePanel class, shown in Listing 19.4, is a simple extension of the java.awt.Panel class that draws the image to the Panel object's graphic user interface.

LISTING 19.4 Source code for ImagePanel.java

```java
package sams.corba;

import java.awt.Dimension;
import java.awt.Graphics;
import java.awt.Image;
import java.awt.Panel;

public class ImagePanel extends Panel {
```

```
  private Image image = null;

  public ImagePanel( Image image ) {
    this.image = image;
  }

  public final void paint( Graphics g ) {
    g.drawImage( image, 0, 0, this );
  }

  public final Dimension getMinimumSize( ) {
    return new Dimension( image.getWidth( this ), image.getHeight( this ) );
  }

  public final Dimension getPreferredSize( ) {
    return new Dimension( image.getWidth( this ), image.getHeight( this ) );
  }
}
```

The sams.corba.ImageServer class, shown in Listing 19.5 later in this chapter, extends the sams.corba._ImageServerInterfaceImplBase class created by the idltojava compiler. The sams.corba._ImageServerInterfaceImplBase class implements the sams.corba.ImageServerInterface interface and includes most of the code that enables an ImageServer object to operate as a CORBA server object.

All of the code used to connect the ImageServer object with the CORBA enterprise is in the main() method. The first statement in the main() method, shown next, creates and initializes the Object Request Broker (ORB) and assigns it to the orb variable.

```
ORB orb = ORB.init( args, null );
```

The ImageServer application gains access to the CORBA environment by creating a new instance of an ORB through an init() method. The init() methods are static so they can be called outside of an ORB object. This is important because ORB objects are only created through calls to init() methods. ORBs are not created through class constructors.

The second statement, shown next, creates a new ImageServer object and assigns it to the server variable.

```
ImageServer server = new ImageServer( );
```

CORBA programmers often call the server object the *servant*. The ImageServer object is registered with the ORB by calling the connect() method, as shown in the next statement:

```
orb.connect( server );
```

19

CORBA: USING JAVA IDL

The next statements in the main() method, shown next, get a reference to the transient name server that must be running on the machine for the CORBA server to work.

```
org.omg.CORBA.Object objRef = null;
try {
  objRef = orb.resolve_initial_references( "NameService" );
}
catch ( org.omg.CORBA.ORBPackage.InvalidName ine ) {
}
```

This important code is the call to the ORB object resolve_initial_references() method. The method returns the object reference associated with the service name passed as a string parameter, in this case "NameService", which is the name of the transient name server provided with the Java platform (see the "Java IDL Transient Name Server" section earlier in this chapter). The object reference is assigned to the objRef variable.

The next statement in the main() method, shown next, gets the root naming context through the transient name server.

```
NamingContext ncRef = NamingContextHelper.narrow( objRef );
```

The reference to the transient name server is passed to the org.omg.NamingContextHelper class static narrow() method. Recall that helper classes provide static methods for casting CORBA object references to their proper types. A NamingContext object encapsulating a reference to the transient name server is returned and assigned to the ncRef variable.

The ImageServer object is bound as the "Image Server" to the naming context in the transient name server in the statements shown next.

```
NameComponent nc = new NameComponent( "Image Server", "" );
NameComponent path[] = { nc };
try {
  ncRef.rebind( path, server );
}
catch ( org.omg.CosNaming.NamingContextPackage.InvalidName ine ) {
}
catch ( org.omg.CosNaming.NamingContextPackage.CannotProceed cpe ) {
}
catch ( org.omg.CosNaming.NamingContextPackage.NotFound nfe ) {
}
```

The first statement retrieves the name of the server, "Image Server", encapsulated in an object instantiated from the org.omg.CosNaming.NameComponent class. The NameComponent object is assigned to the nc variable, which is then assigned to the path[] array and passed, along with a reference to the ImageServer object itself, to the transient name server's rebind() method. This completes connecting the ORB with the ImageServer object through the transient name server.

The final statements in the `main()` method, shown next, make the server wait for calls to its methods from client applications.

```
java.lang.Object sync = new java.lang.Object( );
synchronized ( sync ) {
try {
  sync.wait( );
}
catch ( InterruptedException ie ) {
}
```

Compile the classes in this section and then start the transient name server by typing the following command at your console or DOS window prompt:

```
tnameserv
```

You should see transient name server output similar to what you see in Figure 19.1.

FIGURE 19.1

A console window after starting the transient name server.

Open a new console or DOS window, type the following at the prompt in the root class directory:

```
java sams.corba.ImageServer
```

The `ImageServer` application appears, as shown in Figure 19.2, and waits for images sent from client applications, which you build in the next section.

FIGURE 19.2

The `ImageServer` application waits for an image sent from a client application.

The sams.corba.ImageServer class includes most of the code that enables an
ImageServer object to operate as a CORBA server object.

LISTING 19.5   Source code for ImageServer.java

```java
package sams.corba;

import org.omg.CORBA.ORB;
import org.omg.CosNaming.NameComponent;
import org.omg.CosNaming.NamingContext;
import org.omg.CosNaming.NamingContextHelper;

public class ImageServer extends _ImageServerInterfaceImplBase {
  private ImageServerWindow window = null;

  public ImageServer( ) {
    window = new ImageServerWindow( );
    window.pack( );
    window.setVisible( true );
  }

  public void displayImage( IDLImageInterface idlImage ) {
    window.displayImage( idlImage );
  }

  public static void main( String[] args ) {
    ORB orb = ORB.init( args, null );
    ImageServer server = new ImageServer( );
    orb.connect( server );
    // get the root naming context
    org.omg.CORBA.Object objRef = null;
    try {
            objRef = orb.resolve_initial_references( "NameService" );
    }
    catch ( org.omg.CORBA.ORBPackage.InvalidName ine ) {
    }
    NamingContext ncRef = NamingContextHelper.narrow( objRef );
    // bind the Object Reference in Naming
    NameComponent nc = new NameComponent( "Image Server", "" );
    NameComponent path[] = { nc };
    try {
      ncRef.rebind( path, server );
    }
    catch ( org.omg.CosNaming.NamingContextPackage.InvalidName ine ) {
    }
    catch ( org.omg.CosNaming.NamingContextPackage.CannotProceed cpe ) {
    }
    catch ( org.omg.CosNaming.NamingContextPackage.NotFound nfe ) {
    }
    // wait for invocations from clients
```

```
      java.lang.Object sync = new java.lang.Object( );
      synchronized ( sync ) {
        try {
          sync.wait( );
        }
        catch ( InterruptedException ie ) {
        }
      }
    }
}
```

Implementing Client Code

The `sams.corba.ImageClient` class, shown in Listing 19.6, contains typical code utilizing the AWT to display messages, buttons, and dialog boxes for finding and loading image files. CORBA-specific code is found in the `main()` method and is identical to the ORB initialization and ORB binding with the transient name server that is carried out in the `sams.corba.ImageServer` class. The only difference is that the object doesn't go into a wait state. `ImageClient` objects send an image to a server when a user tells them to do so.

Compile the `ImageServer.java` file and then open a new console or DOS window. Type the following command at the prompt in the root class directory:

```
java sams.corba.ImageClient
```

The `ImageClient` application appears, as shown in Figure 19.3.

FIGURE 19.3

The `ImageClient` *application waits for a user to load and send an image.*

19

CORBA: USING JAVA IDL

LISTING 19.6   Source code for `ImageClient.java`

```
package sams.corba;

import java.awt.Button;
import java.awt.FileDialog;
import java.awt.Frame;
import java.awt.GridLayout;
import java.awt.Image;
import java.awt.Label;
```

continues

LISTING 19.6   continued

```java
import java.awt.event.ActionEvent;
import java.awt.event.ActionListener;
import java.awt.event.WindowAdapter;
import java.awt.event.WindowEvent;
import org.omg.CORBA.ORB;
import org.omg.CosNaming.NameComponent;
import org.omg.CosNaming.NamingContext;
import org.omg.CosNaming.NamingContextHelper;

public final class ImageClient extends Frame implements ActionListener {
  private Image imageActive = null;
  private ImageServerInterface imageServer = null;
  private Button buttonLoad = null;
  private Button buttonSendToServer = null;
  private Label lableImageActive = null;
  private String[] arguments = null;

  public ImageClient( String[] args ) {
    arguments = args;
    doBind( );
    buildScreen( );
    addWindowListener( new WindowEventHandler( ) );
  }

  private void doBind( ) {
    ORB orb = ORB.init( arguments, null );
    // get the root naming context
    org.omg.CORBA.Object objRef = null;
    try {
      objRef = orb.resolve_initial_references( "NameService" );
    }
    catch ( org.omg.CORBA.ORBPackage.InvalidName ine ) {
    }
    NamingContext ncRef = NamingContextHelper.narrow( objRef );
    // resolve the Object Reference in Naming
    NameComponent nc = new NameComponent( "Image Server", "" );
    NameComponent path[] = { nc };
    try {
      imageServer = ImageServerInterfaceHelper.narrow( ncRef.resolve( path ) );
    }
    catch ( org.omg.CosNaming.NamingContextPackage.InvalidName ine ) {
    }
    catch ( org.omg.CosNaming.NamingContextPackage.CannotProceed cpe ) {
    }
    catch ( org.omg.CosNaming.NamingContextPackage.NotFound nfe ) {
    }
  }

  private void buildScreen( ) {
```

```
    setLayout( new GridLayout( 2, 2, 10, 10 ) );
    add( new Label( "Active Image" ) );
    add( lableImageActive = new Label( "None Selected" ) );
    add( buttonLoad = new Button( "Load Image" ) );
    add( buttonSendToServer = new Button( "Send Image To Server" ) );
    buttonLoad.addActionListener( this );
    buttonSendToServer.addActionListener( this );
  }

  public void actionPerformed( ActionEvent ae ) {
    Button target = ( Button ) ae.getSource( );
    if( target == buttonLoad )
      doLoad( );
    else
      sendImageToServer( );
  }

  private final void doLoad( ) {
    FileDialog dialogOpen = new FileDialog( this, "Choose An Image",
FileDialog.LOAD );
    dialogOpen.setVisible( true );
    if( dialogOpen.getFile( ) == null )
      return;
    StringBuffer bufFile = new StringBuffer( );
    bufFile.append( dialogOpen.getDirectory( ) );
    bufFile.append( dialogOpen.getFile( ) );
    String sFile = dialogOpen.getFile( );
    if( isValid( sFile ) ) {
      String sFileName = sFile.substring( 0, sFile.indexOf( '.' ) );
      imageActive = getToolkit( ).getImage( bufFile.toString( ) );
      lableImageActive.setText( sFile );
    }
  }

  private boolean isValid( String name ) {
    String extension = name.substring( name.indexOf( '.' ) + 1,
      name.length( ) );
    if( extension.equalsIgnoreCase( "gif" ) )
      return true;
    if( extension.equalsIgnoreCase( "jpg" ) )
      return true;
    if( extension.equalsIgnoreCase( "jpeg" ) )
      return true;
    return false;
  }

  private void sendImageToServer( ) {
```

continues

Listing 19.6   continued

```
    if( imageServer == null )
      return;
    IDLImageInterface idlImage = new IDLImage( imageActive, this );
    imageServer.displayImage( idlImage );
  }

  public static void main( String[] args ) {
    ImageClient client = new ImageClient( args );
    client.pack( );
    client.setVisible( true );
  }

  class WindowEventHandler extends WindowAdapter {
    public void windowClosing( WindowEvent e ) {
      System.exit( 0 );
    }
  }
}
```

Summary

In this chapter, you learned about the Common Object Request Broker Architecture (CORBA), a specification that enables distributed software components to work together regardless of the programming language used to develop them, the computer platform they run on, or the computer networks they use. You learned about the set of packages and tools that enable you to create CORBA-compliant software in Java known as Java IDL. Then you wrote Java applications that transmit image files through CORBA. The core Java platform supports all your enterprise development using CORBA.

Corba IDL

IN THIS CHAPTER

All source code for this chapter can be found on the Sams Publishing Website at
`http://www.mcp.com/info/0-672/0-672-31424-x.`

The next wave in Internet innovation is distributed objects. The Common Object Request Broker Architecture (CORBA), defined by the Object Management Group (OMG), specifies how, without regard to client, server operating systems, or programming, software objects can work together when distributed over a network.

CORBA is a complete distributed object platform that extends applications across networks, languages, component boundaries, and operating systems. A client application is connected with the other objects it wants to use through an Object Request Broker (ORB) of CORBA. The knowledge of whether the object inhabits the same computer or an obscure computer elsewhere on the network is not important for the client application. There are only two pieces of information that are needed by the client application: the object's name and how to use the object's interface. The details of locating the object, routing the request, and returning the request are all taken care of by the ORB.

There were three instrumental trends taking shape as CORBA grew.

First, the significance of a two decade-old program object- oriented approach to programming became increasingly important to the software development community. Second, new application models based on small, task-specific components were being advocated by industry leaders such as Microsoft, IBM, and Apple. Components are now easier to write and update due to the pieces being smaller than the general purpose applications. Only those software parts that are out of date can be effectively, conveniently, and cheaply upgraded, which allows the user to purchase only the parts they need rather than the whole package. Small components can also be more easily distributed over a network than their monolithic ancestors. The goal of having different systems work together seamlessly comes to light with component architectures.

Third, the Java programming language burst forth in early 1995, just after the release of CORBA 2.0 as if it were to endorse the concepts underlying the vision of an object-oriented, component-based future. An object-oriented development environment was created through Java in which small software could run on any operating system. This enabled the components to be used over the Internet, which by then was surging with popularity. CORBA is one of the few platforms that fits both the component-based and Internet-based approaches to building and using software. CORBA provides a way to divide application logic among objects distributed over a network, variety of serves, and some on clients. It also serves as a passageway for those objects to communicate and use each others' services. Through services such as introspection, dynamic discovery, transactions, security, naming, and more, CORBA greatly supplements Java. Java is linked to the mobile code environment and the world of interoperable objects through CORBA.

One of the advantages of using CORBA is that the software component can be shared between applications as well as reused. The well-defined interface of each object, due to the encapsulated details of the inner workings in each object, reduces the complexity of he application. CORBA is also unique in the sense that once an object is implemented and tested, it can be reused, reducing development costs. The platform independence of CORBA allows one to run and invoke the object from any platform; one is able to run the object from the platform that makes the most sense for that object. The language independence also allows you to recycle code while enhancing your existing programming skills. Some examples of other languages that support CORBA are C++, Cobol, and Delphi.

Using CORBA, software objects with defined interfaces can interoperate across corporate intranets and across the Internet. The benefits of this application for information technology (IT) organizations and application developers are extremely significant. One of the first benefits is choice: CORBA is based on an open, published specification and is supported by numerous hardware and operating system platforms. Due to the portability of CORBA Java objects, you can build objects on one platform and send them to any other supported platform. The OMG Web site can be found at `http://www.omg.org`.

CORBA's Main Points

Interoperability. The use of the Internet Inter-ORB Protocol (IIOP) enables CORBA objects to be fully interoperable across different vendors' ORBs. When selecting an ORB, CORBAServices, and software objects (even when they are developed by different vendors), an enterprise IT organization may only need to consider its functional needs. Software bridges are also available from vendors such as Iona and Visigenic (now part of Inprise) that enable communications between CORBA objects and objects developed using Microsoft's DCOM technology.

Modularity. Developers can modify objects without breaking other parts of their application because interface and implementation are separate, and CORBA objects interact via interfaces. The object interface stays the same, which has no effect on other objects or applications when changing an objects implementation.

Compatibility. CORBA enables you to protect your investment in existing systems by encapsulating a legacy application, module, or entry point within a CORBA IDL wrapper that defines the legacy code. You are now able to interoperate with other objects in a distributed environment.

Security. Encryption, authentication, and authorization are all security features provided by CORBA to protect data and to control user access to objects and their services.

20

CORBA IDL

It's envisioned that CORBA and the IIOP (the Internet Inter-ORB Protocol) will be as omnipresent as HTML and HTTP, making Internet-based services as widely available as Internet-based content is today. CORBA has already been implemented by many companies and has been endorsed by the OMG, which consists of 700 plus members, some of which include Sun, IBM, Oracle, Hewlett-Packard, Digital Equipment Corporation, Apple Computer, Novell, and BEA. There are thousands of CORBA applications currently in use and implemented by many organizations. CORBA allows the interaction of virtually all languages because the objects are stored on servers of all types. Rather than large applications, these objects are small software components. Because to this, objects can be updated and distributed far more quickly and easily than the older, traditional software.

The middleware that establishes the client-server relationship between objects is the CORBA Object Request Broker (ORB). By using an ORB, a client object is able to invoke a method on a server object that can be on the same machine or across a network. Intercepting the calls and finding an object that can implement the request, passing it the parameters, invoking its method, and returning the results are all things that are done by the ORB. Like SQL, CORBA provides both dynamic and static interfaces to its services. The client only needs to know the parts of an object's interface and does not need to be concerned if it does not know the object's location, its programming language, its operating system, or any other aspect of the system. Also, the client and server roles are dynamic: An object on the ORB can act as either client or server, depending on the occasion.

Communication is the key. Communication between CORBA objects is made possible through the ORBs and CORBA architecture. The objects are small software components that provide some kind of a service, such as access to a database, account management, or inventory tracking. The ORBs are essential to the architecture. To be part of the CORBA scheme for any client or server, it must include an ORB to help it find and communicate with other CORBA objects. When equipped with an ORB, a client or server can use the services of any CORBA objects on any server or host on the network. When an object provides services to another object, it's a server; when it requests services from another object, it's a client, thereby allowing the object to be both a client and a server.

The CORBA architecture provides a set of services that help objects interact with each other. (In the CORBA world, services means both the functionality provided by the objects themselves and the services provided by the CORBA architecture to help objects communicate.)

The services are among the efficiencies provided by CORBA: You write your object's code, and CORBA takes care of how your object identifies itself, finds other objects, learns of network events, handles object-to-object transactions, and maintains security. The services include the following:

- A CORBA naming service allows a CORBA client to locate a named CORBA object. It maps a human-readable name to a CORBA object reference.

- Enabling objects to dynamically register and unregister interest in specific events is provided by an event service. Both publishers and subscribers each connect to an event channel; publishers send messages (events) to the event channel, and subscribers receive these messages (events asynchronously).

- A transaction service allows transaction contexts between objects to be transparently propagated through IIOP. This service coordinates two-phase commits of transactions (flat or nested) among objects.

- Encryption, authentication, and authorization to protect data and to control user access to objects and their services are all provided by the security service of CORBA. The security service also manages the delegation of credentials between objects.

Among other things, CORBA 2.0 also defines the Internet Inter-ORB Protocol (IIOP) to govern how objects communicate over the network. IIOP allows state data to be preserved across multiple invocations of objects and across multiple connections, unlike HTTP.

A user can access services of objects from a multitude of servers and hosts with an ORB-enabled browser (such as Netscape Navigator 4.5 or later). By using IIOP and the client ORB, a CORBA object can access the services of an object on a Web server (through the server ORB), which then can access one or more objects on relational databases or legacy systems (as long an each system includes an ORB). The services of other objects through an ORB that reside on the client system are requested by the a client object. Using IIOP, the client ORB then reaches across the network, looking for ORBs on other systems and the server objects that can provide the requested services. The CORBA naming system provides each object with a unique name, which identifies it and its services to other objects. When the ORB has found the requested service/object, the client object then communicates with the server object, still using IIOP. Each object's IDL interface tells other objects how to use its services and the results those services generate.

As a practical example, consider a parcel-tracking application. Imagine that an Internet user wants to track delivery of a package. From a browser, the user first enters a URL that points to the delivery company's Web server. The server then uses HTTP to send a Web page to the user; that page contains an embedded Java applet that is the client component of the parcel-tracking system. Note that so far, nothing is different from a

20

CORBA IDL

traditional HTTP Web transaction. Then the user enters a parcel-tracking number into the appropriate field in the Java applet. Using the client-side ORB, the applet then generates and sends an IIOP message across the network, looking for a specifically-named server object that can acquire the status of the parcel. The ORB on the server with the appropriate parcel-tracking object picks up the message and invokes the object's status-finding method. Through the server ORB, the object then generates another IIOP message looking for an object on a legacy system that contains all the parcel company's data. Upon obtaining the last request through its ORB, the mainframe containing the data-tracking object determines that status of the parcel from its database. The mainframe returns an IIOP message with the information to the server object. The server then routes the information—again with IIOP and the ORBs-to the Java applet running on the client, which displays the results to the user.

Objects of CORBA do not have nor do they need information about each other's implementation details. The only way they communicate is through their published interfaces, and the ORB manages these communications transparently to users. For example, the client could be a PC running Windows, a Macintosh, a workstation, a network computer, a handheld personal computer, or even a set-top box. Legacy code can be included in Server objects because they can be programmed in a variety of languages. Clients can access functionality directly, without going through Web server software and without the performance costs of processing a CGI script for each user access, because they communicate with the objects through IIOP.

One may create CORBA objects in one of two general ways:

- Use `java2iiop` (also called Caffeine), provided with Netscape's Enterprise Server. This utility processes Java bytecode and generates files for CORBA objects.
- Write and compile an interface definition language (IDL) specification.

CORBA defines an interface definition language (IDL) that provides a language-neutral way to describe a CORBA object and the services it provides. The IDL is a key component because it lets components written in different languages communicate with each other using IIOP and the rest of the CORBA architecture. Objects of CORBA can inhabit different types of systems, including Windows or UNIX servers and IBM 3090 or DEC VAX mainframes. They can be written in different languages. Objects can communicate and use each others' services to their services through ORBs on clients, servers, database systems, mainframes, and other systems on the network, as long as interfaces to their services are written in IDL.

These are the basic steps:

1. Write a specification for the objects using IDL.

2. Using the appropriate compiler, compile the IDL code into Java or C++ code stubs and skeletons. The stubs are used by the client, and the server skeletons provide the framework that you fill in with the code for the service one's object is to provide.

3. Write the Java or C++ code to implement the service.

4. Compile the code created in the step 3.

The choice of whether to use Java or C++ depends solely on the user's preferences and the solution he or she is trying to develop. Java is probably a bit more flexible in usage, because a Java object will work on any operating system with a Java Virtual Machine (JVM). However, C++ may give better performance, depending on one's server environment.

CORBA provides a path for advancing legacy systems and other existing code bases into the cross-platform, Internet-based present and future. One is able to abridge a legacy application, module, or entry point in a CORBA IDL wrapper that defines an interface to the legacy code. Creating such an object wrapper gives the legacy code a CORBA-compliant interface, thereby enabling it to interoperate with other objects in a distributed computing environment. CORBA bridges the present with the future of distributed Internet-based object computing, unlike many competing schemes.

It is important to divide your legacy code and other code into smaller objects and write an IDL specification for them. By doing this, it will expose the object's services to other CORBA objects across the Internet, making it possible for other CORBA objects to communicate with one's objects. With CORBA, one is able to preserve their current code base and give it an interface (through IDL) that makes it accessible through Internet technology.

Building CORBA Applications

This example is specially designed to walk you through designing and developing a simple pair of interacting Java IDL applications. It begins with an overview of the steps to building a CORBA application in Java IDL. Then it takes you through every step need to produce a running server and client that interact using CORBA.

Java IDL

Java IDL is a reference implementation in Java of an Object Request Broker (ORB) that is compliant with the OMG-approved Java mapping for IDL. It is designed to provide interoperable CORBA support, including ubiquitous thin client Web access to other IIOP-compliant Common Object Request Broker Architecture (CORBA) services, for Java applications.

20

CORBA IDL

Java IDL is designed to work with the Web model of zero-install clients that are down-loaded from the network into a browser. Because the runtime is implemented complete-ly in Java, it can be packaged and downloaded, with any applets that depend on it, to any platform that supports Java. These downloaded applets can then communicate directly with IIOP-compliant enterprise services, thus providing ubiquitous access at low cost. In some cases, the runtime support may already be integrated directly into the Java platform.

Although Java IDL was specifically designed to support the downloaded applet model, it works equally well for applications' Java clients and servers running standalone.

Defining the Interface with IDL

You define the interface for the remote object using the OMG's interface definition lan-guage (IDL). IDL is used instead of the Java language because the idltojava compiler automatically maps from IDL, generating all Java language stub and skeleton source files, along with the infrastructure code for connecting to the ORB. By using IDL, the user makes it possible for developers to implement clients and servers in any other CORBA-compliant language.

It's important to note that you would get the IDL interfaces from the implementer—such as a service provider or vendor—if you were implementing a client for an existing CORBA service, or a server for an existing client. After that, you would run the idltojava compiler over those interfaces and follow the steps for creating the client of server described in this path.

When you run the idltojava compiler over your interface definition file, it generates the Java version of the interface, as well as the class code files for the stubs and skeletons that enable your applications to hook into the ORB.

If you don't have the idltojava compiler, you can go to http://developer. javasoft.com. You'll first have to register and create a login ID and password, and then you can download the idltojava compiler from http://java.sun.com/products/jdk/idl/.

After running the idltojava compiler, you are able to use the skeletons it generates to put together your server application. In addition to implementing the methods of the remote interface, your server code includes a mechanism to start the ORB and wait for invocation from a remote client.

By the same token, you use the stubs generated by the idltojava compiler as the basis of your client application. The stubs to start its ORB are built by the client code, look up the server using the name service provided with Java IDL, obtain a reference for the remote object, and call its method.

Once a server and a client are implemented, one is able to start the name service, start the server, and then run the client.

The basic tasks for building a CORBA-distributed application using Java IDL are taught in this section. Using both applet and application clients, you'll build the classic Hello World program as a distributed application. The Hello World program contains a single operation that returns a string to be printed.

Communication Between the Client and the Server

The following is a summary of how the CORBA client and server interact.

1. The client (application or applet) begins the sayHello operation of the HelloServer.

2. The ORB transfers that invocation to the servant object registered for that IDL interface.

3. The servant's sayHello() method runs, returning a Java string.

4. The ORB transfers that string back to the client.

5. The client prints the value of the string.

Despite its simple design, the Hello World program allows the user to learn and experiment with all the tasks required to develop almost any CORBA program that uses static invocation.

There are two very important things you must have before beginning to work with Java IDL: version 1.2 of the JDK software and the idltojava compiler. The JDK provides the API and ORB needed to enable CORBA-based distributed object interaction. The idltojava compiler uses IDL-to-Java mapping to convert IDL interface definitions to corresponding Java interfaces, classes, and methods, which you can then use to implement your client and server code.

For the Hello World program, you will write a simple IDL interface. The IDL interface is what defines the contract between the client and server parts of your application, specifying what operations and attributes are available. OMG IDL is programming-language–independent. One must first map it to Java before writing any of the implementation code. (Running idltojava on the IDL file does this for you automatically.)

20

CORBA IDL

Writing the IDL File

The IDL for Hello World is extremely simple; its single interface has a single operation. You only need to perform the following three steps.

Declaring the CORBA IDL Module—Step 1

A CORBA module is a namespace that acts as a container for related interfaces and declarations. It corresponds closely to a Java package. Each module statement in an IDL file is mapped to a Java package statement.

1. Create a text file named Hello.idl.

2. In your file, enter the following module statement:

```
module HelloApp
{
  // Add subsequent lines of code here.
};
```

3. Save the file. When you run idltojava on the IDL, this statement will generate a package statement in the Java code.

Declaring the Interface—Step 2

Like Java interfaces, CORBA interfaces declare the API contract that an object has with other objects. Each interface statement in the IDL maps to a Java interface statement when mapped. In your Hello.idl file, enter the following interface statement:

```
module HelloApp
{
  interface Hello // Add
  {               // these
                  // four
  };              // lines.
};
```

When you compile the IDL, this statement will generate an interface statement in the Java code. Your client and server class will implement the Hello interface in different ways.

Declaring the Operations—Step 3

CORBA operations are the behavior that servers promise to perform on behalf of clients that invoke them. Each operation statement in the IDL generates a corresponding method statement in the generated Java interface.

In your Hello.idl file, enter the following operation statement:

```
module HelloApp
{
  interface Hello
  {
```

```
    string sayHello(); //Add this line.
  };
};
```

Because your little `Hello World` application has only a single operation, `Hello.idl` is now complete.

Mapping IDL to Java

The `idltojava` tool reads OMG IDL files and creates the required Java files. `idltojava` defaults are set up so that is you need both client and server files (as you do for your `Hello World` program), you simply enter the tool name and the name of your IDL file:

1. Go to a command line prompt.
2. Change directory to the location of your `Hello.idl` file.
3. Enter the following compiler command:

    ```
    idltojava -fno -cpp Hello.idl
    ```

If you list the contents of the directory, you will see that a directory called `HelloApp` has been created and that is contains five files. Try opening `Hello.java` in your text editor. It looks like the following:

```
/* Hello.java as generated by idltojava */
package HelloApp;
public interface Hello
   extends org.omg. CORBA.Object{
   String say Hello();
}
```

With an interface this simple, it is easy to see how the IDL statements map to the generated Java statements. Table 20.1 shows the mapping of IDL statements to Java statements. You may want to refer back to Chapter 18, "Java Remote Method Protocol (JRMP)," where the mapping between IDL and Java is explained in more detail.

Table 20.1 Mapping of IDL Statements to Java Statements

IDL Statement	Java Statement
`module HelloApp`	`package HelloApp;`
`interface Hello`	`public interface Hello`
`string sayHello();`	`String sayHello();`

The single surprising item is the `extends` statement. All CORBA objects are derived from `org.omg.CORBA.Object` to ensure required CORBA functionality. The required code is generated by `idltojava`—you do not need to do any mapping yourself.

20

CORBA IDL

Understanding the `idltojava` Compiler Output

The `idltojava` compiler generates a number of files based on the options chosen on the command line. Because these provide standard functionality, you can ignore them until it is time to deploy and run your program. The five files generated by the `idltojava` are

- `_HelloImplBase.java` This abstract class is the server skeleton, providing basic CORBA functionality for the server. It implements the `Hello.java` interface.

- `Hello.java` This interface contains the Java version of your IDL interface. It contains the single method `sayHello`. The `Hello.java` interface extends `org.omg.CORBA.Object`, providing standard CORBA object functionality, notably the `narrow` method required to cast CORBA object references to their proper types.

- `HelloHelper.java` The helper file for the program.

- `_HelloStub.java` The generated stub file.

- `HelloHolder.java` This final class holds a public instance member of type `Hello`. It provides operations for out and inout arguments that CORBA has but which do not map easily to Java's semantics. When you write the IDL interface, you do all the programming required to generate all these files for your distributed application. The only additional work required is the actual implementation of client and server classes. In the section that follows, you will create `HelloClient.java` and `HelloApplet.java` client classes and the `HelloServer.java` class.

Troubleshooting

The following are typical error messages that can be emitted from `idltojava`.

- `"idltojava" not found` When trying to run `idltojava` on the file `Hello.idl` and the system cannot find `idltojava`, it is most likely not in your executable path. Make sure that the location of `idltojava` is in your path, and try again.

- `preprocessor failed` `idltojava` uses a C/C++ preprocessor by default. You can change the default by setting two environment variables, CPP and CPPARGS. If you do not want to use a preprocessor, you can turn it off by adding `-fno-cpp` to the `idltojava` command line.

Developing a Client Application

This section introduces the basics of writing a CORBA client application. Many of the steps are identical to those required for writing applets. The major difference is that the applet code appears in the `init()` method rather than in `main()`. The complete code for the applet version follows shortly (`HelloApplet.java`).

The basic shell of a CORBA client is the same as many Java applications: You import required library packages, declare the application class, define a `main()` method, and remember to handle any exceptions.

Start your text editor and save a new file titled `HelloClient.java` to your project directory. Import the packages required for the client class:

```
import HelloApp.*;        //The package containing our stubs.
import org.omg.CosNaming.*; //HelloClient will use the naming
                            //service.
import org.omg.CORBA.*;    // All CORBA applications need these
                            //classes.
```

If you are writing an applet, you also need to import `java.awt.Graphics` and `org.omg.CosmamingContextPackage.*`. The latter package contains special exceptions thrown by the name service.

In `HelloClient.java`, declare the client class:

```
public class HelloClient
{
  // Add the main method here in the next step.
}
```

In the applet version of this code, `HelloApplet.java`, you declare the applet class as shown in the following:

```
public class HelloApplet extends java.applet.Applet
{
  // Put the init() method here in the next step.
}
```

Every Java application needs a `main()` method. Declare it within the scope of the `HelloClient` class, as shown in the following:

```
public static void main( String args[] )
{
  // Put the try-catch block here in the next step.
}
```

Because all CORBA programs can throw CORBA system exceptions at runtime, you will place all of the main functionality within a `try...catch` block. CORBA programs throw system exceptions whenever trouble occurs during any of the processes involved in invoking the server from the client.

Your exception handler prints the name of the exception and its stack trace to standard output, so you can see what kind of thing has gone wrong.

Inside main(), set up a try...catch block:

```
try
{
  // Add the rest of the HelloClient code here.
}
catch( Exception e )
{
  System.out.println( "ERROR : " + e.getMessage() );
  e.printStackTrace( System.out );
}
```

A CORBA client needs a local ORB object to perform all of its marshalling and IIOP work. Every client instantiates an org.omg.CORBA.ORB object and initializes it by passing the object certain information about itself.

InsideHelloClient.java's try...catch block, declare and initialize an ORB variable:

```
ORB orb = ORB.init( args, null );
```

The call to the ORB's init() method passes in your application's command line arguments, allowing you to set certain properties at runtime.

Once the application has an ORB, it can ask the ORB to locate the actual service it needs, in this case the Hello server. There are a number of ways for a CORBA client to get an initial object reference; your client application will use the COS Naming Service specified by OMG and provided with Java IDL.

The first step in using the naming service is to get the initial naming context. In the try...catch block, below your ORB initialization, call orb.resolve_initial_references to get an object reference to the name server:

```
org.omg.CORBA.Object objRef =
  orb.resolve_initial_references( "NameService" );
```

The string "NameService" is defined for all CORBA ORBs. When you pass in that string, the ORB returns the initial naming context, an object reference to the name service.

ObjRef is a generic CORBA object, just as all other CORBA object references. To use it as a NamingContext object, you must narrow it to its proper type. Add the call to narrow just after the previous statement.

```
NamingContext ncRef = NamingContextHelper.narrow( objRef );
```

Here you see the use of an idltojava–generated helper class, similar in function to HelloHelper. The ncRef object is now an org.omg.CosNamingContext, and you can use it to access the naming service and find other services. You will do that in the next step.

Names can have different structures, depending upon the implementation of the naming service. Consequently, CORBA name servers handle complex names by way of `NameComponent` objects. Each `NameComponent` hold a single part, or element, of the name. An array of `NameComponent` objects can hold a fully-specified path to an object on any computer file or disk system. To find the `Hello` server, you first need a `NameComponent` to hold an identifying string for the `Hello` server. Access this code directly after the call to `narrow`.

```
NameComponent nc = new NameComponent( "Hello", "" );
```

This statement sets the ID field of nc, the new `Namecomponent`, to `"Hello"` and the Kind field to an empty string.

Because the path to the `Hello` object has just one element, create a single-element array out of nc. The `NamingContext.resolve` method requires the following array for its work:

```
NameComponent path[] = {nc};
```

Finally, pass `path` to the naming service's `resolve` method to get an object reference to the `Hello` server, and `narrow` it to a `Hello` object:

```
Hello helloRef = HelloHelper.narrow( ncRef.resolve( path ) );
```

Here you see the `HelloHelper` helper class at work. The `resolve` method returns a generic CORBA object, as you saw earlier when locating the name service itself. Therefore, you immediately narrow it to a `Hello` object, which is the object reference you need to perform the rest of your work.

CORBA invocations look like a method call on a local object. The complications of marshalling parameters to the wire, routing them to the server-side ORB, unmarshalling, and placing the upcall to the server method are completely transparent to the client programmer. Because so much is done for you by generated code, invocation is really the easiest part of CORBA programming.

1. Continuing with the `try...catch` block in `HelloClient.java`, enter the following invocation after the call to the name service's `resolve` method:

   ```
   String strHello = helloRef.sayHello();
   ```

2. Finally, add code to print the results of the invocation to standard output:

   ```
   System.out.println( strHello );
   ```

3. Save and close `HelloClient.java`.

20

CORBA IDL

Setting Up the HTML File for Applets

`Sample.html` is provided for displaying your finished applet, but you need to customize a few attributes and parameters.

1. Open `Sample.html` in your text editor.

2. Inside the `<APPLET>` tag, enter the path to your project directory as the value for the `CODEBASE` attribute.

3. In the first `<PARAM>` tag, enter the name of the machine where the CORBA name server runs (most likely your local machine name) as the value for `ORBInitialHost`.

4. Make sure the second `<PARAM>` tag is set to the value of `ORBInitialPort` that you are using to run the name server (it's preset to 1050 to work with the default used in the examples in this trail). In any case, it should be a value above 1028.

Writing the Server Code

This section introduces the basics of writing a CORBA transient server.

The structure of a CORBA server program is the same as most Java applications: You import required library packages, declare the server class, define a `main()` method, and remember to handle any exceptions.

Start your text editor and create a new file titled `HelloServer.java`. Next, important the packages required for the client class:

```
// The Package containing our stubs.
import HelloApp.*;
// HelloServer will use the naming service.
import org.omg.CosNaming.*;
// The package containing special exceptions
// thrown by the name service.
import org.omg.CORBA.*;

public class HelloServer
{
  // Add the main method here in the next step.
}
```

Declare a standard `main()` method:

```
public static void main( String args[] )
{
  // add the try--catch block here in the next step.
}
```

Because all CORBA programs can throw CORBA system exceptions at runtime, you will place all of the main functionality within a try...catch block. CORBA programs throw runtime exceptions whenever trouble occurs during any of the processes (marshalling, unmarshalling, upcall) involved in invocation. The exception handler simply prints the exception and its stack trace to standard output so you can see what kind of thing has gone wrong.

Inside main(), set up a try...catch block:

```
try
{
  // Add the rest of the HelloServer code here.
}
catch( Exception e )
{
  System.err.println( "ERROR: " + e.getMessage() );
  e.printStackTrace( System.out );
}
```

Just like a client, a CORBA server also needs a local ORB object. Every server instantiates an ORB and registers its servant objects so that the ORB can find the server when it receives an invocation for it.

Inside HelloServer.java's try...catch block, declare and initialize an ORB variable:

```
ORB orb = ORB.init( args, null );
```

The call to the ORB's init() method passes in the server's command line arguments, allowing you to set certain properties at runtime.

A server is a process that instantiates one or more servant objects. The servant implements the interface generated by idltojava and actually performs the work of the operations on that interface. Your HelloServer needs a HelloServant.

Inside the try...catch block, just make a call to init(), instantiate the servant object:

```
HelloServant helloRef = new HelloServant();
```

This servant class isn't defined yet; you will do that in a later step. Next, connect the servant to the ORB, so that the ORB can recognize invocation on it and pass it along to the correct servant:

```
orb.connect( helloRef );
```

20

CORBA IDL

At the end of `HelloServer.java`, outside the `HelloServer` class, define the class for the servant objects.

1. Declare the servant class:

```
class Helloservant extends _HelloImplBase
{
    // Add the sayHello method here in the next stop.
}
```

2. The servant is a subclass of `_HelloImplBase` so it inherits the general CORBA functionality generated for it by the compiler.

3. Declare the required `sayHello` method:

```
public String sayHello()
{
    // Add the method implementation here in the next step.
}
```

4. Write the say `Hello` implementation:

```
return( "\nHello World!!\n" );
```

`HelloServer` works with the naming service to make the servant object's operations available to clients. The server needs an object reference to the name service so it can register itself and ensure that invocations on the `Hello` interface are routed to its servant object.

In the `try...catch` block, after instantiation of the servant, call `orb.resolve_initial_references` to get an objects reference to the name server:

```
org.omg.CORBA.Object objRef =
  orb.resolve_initial_references( "NameService" );
```

The string `NameService` is defined for all CORBA ORBs. When you pass in that string, the ORB returns a naming context object that is an object reference for the name service.

As with all CORBA object references, object references, `objRef` is a generic CORBA object. To use it as a `NamingContext` object, you must narrow it to its proper type. Add the call to `narrow` just after the previous statement:

```
NamingContext ncRef = NamingContextHellper.narrow( objRef );
```

Here you see the use of the `idltojava`–generated helper class, similar in function to `HelloHelper`. The `ncRef` object is now an `org.omg.CosNaming.NamingContext` and you can use it to access the naming service and register the server. You will do that in the next step.

1. Just after the call to `narrow`, create a new `Namecomponent` member:

```
NameComponent nc + new NameComponent( "Hello", "" );
```

2. This statement sets the ID field of nc, the new Namecomponent, to "Hello" and the Kind component to the empty string. Because the path to the Hello has a single element, create the single-element array the NamingContext.resolve requires for its work:

```
NameComponent path[] = {nc};
```

3. Finally, pass path and the servant object to the naming service, binding the servant object to the "Hello" ID:

```
ncRef.rebind( path, helloRef );
```

Now, when the client calls resolve("Hello") on the initial naming context, the naming service returns an object reference to the Hello servant.

The server is ready; it simply needs to wait around for a client to request its service. To achieve that, enter the following code at the end of (but within) the try...catch block:

```
java.lang.Object sync = new java.lang.Object();
synchronized( sync )
{
  sync.wait( 90 );
}
```

This form of Object.wait requires HelloServer to remain alive (though quiescent) until an invocation comes from the ORB. Because of its placement in main(), after an invocation completes and sayHello returns, the server will wait again.

Compiling and Running the Hello World Application

At this point, you've written the Hello.idl file, run the idltojava compiler on it, and you've written the code for the client and server.

Compiling the Client Application

Now you'll compile the application. The steps to do this are as follows:

1. Compile HelloClient.java:

```
javac HelloClient.java HelloApp\*.java
```

2. Correct any errors in your file and recompile if necessary.

3. You should see HelloClient.class in the project directory.

20

CORBA IDL

Compile the Server

The following are the steps to compile the server application:

1. Compile `HelloServer.java`:

   `javac HelloServer.java HelloApp\*.java`

2. Correct any errors in your file and recompile if necessary.

3. You should see `HelloServer.class` and `HelloServant.class` in the project directory.

Running the Client/Server Application

Now it's time to run the client and server applications. The steps to do so are as follows:

1. Run `tnameserv`.

2. From a second system prompt or shell, start the `Hello` server:

   `java HelloServer -ORBInitialPort 1050`

3. From a third prompt or shell, run the `Hello` application client:

   `java HelloClient -OrbInitialPort 1050`

4. The client prints the string from the server to the command line;

   `Hello world!!`

Remember to stop both the `NameServer` and the `HelloServer` processes after the client application returns successfully.

Summary

In this chapter, you've learned the basics of CORBA IDL. After working through the examples, you should be able to branch off and do some experimenting.

CHAPTER 21

Java/CORBA Development Using Caffeine

All source code for this chapter can be found on the Sams Publishing Website at
`http://www.mcp.com/info/0-672/0-672-31424-x.`

There is a CORBA product that's easier to use than standard CORBA ORB products. It was developed simultaneously by Netscape and Visigenic and is known as Caffeine. Caffeine includes the following:

- A Java2IIOP code generator that takes Java interface files as input and automatically produces IIOP-compliant stubs and skeletons.

- A Java2IDL compiler that automatically produces CORBA IDL from your Java code.

- A URL-based CORBA Naming Service. For Java programmers, the generation of CORBA IDL is made totally transparent.

Caffeine gives you all the benefits of CORBA from within the Java object model. All you do is simply write ordinary Java classes using RMI-like semantics to make them remote. Your objects are then automatically made CORBA-compliant. How? The Netscape/Visigenic implementation discovers your remote Java classes by reading byte-codes. You can even ask Caffeine to generate the CORBA IDL interfaces from your Java classes. After that you can access the IDL descriptions from an Interface Repository.

In contrast to the Java RMI, Caffeine's underlying VisiBroker for Java ORB lets your Java objects communicate with all the objects in the CORBA/IIOP universe—including C, C++, and Smalltalk objects. Caffeine invokes a default URL-based naming scheme using VisiBroker's OSAgent and CORBA Naming Services. Caffeine runs on CORBA/IIOP. Surprisingly, it gives all the benefits of CORBA transactions, security, introspection, and intergalactic connectivity to your Java objects.

This chapter starts with a brief tutorial on Caffeine. I explain how to use Caffeine to create client and server applications. You'll also write the Caffeinated version of `Hello World`, and then run it.

> **Note**
>
> For this chapter, you need a copy of VisiBroker for Java. You can download a trial version from `http://www.borland.com/visibroker/download/`.

The Basics of Caffeine

In this section I'll go over the highlights of Caffeine development and explain the Caffeine development process, Java2IIOP, and Java2IDL. Then you'll look at some of the ways that Caffeine extends CORBA.

Caffeine uses Java both as an interface definition language and as an implementation language (just as RMI does). And also like RMI, the Caffeine development process starts with a Java interface. The first thing that you do is declare your Java interface to be remote by extending it—either directly or indirectly—from `org.omg.CORBA.Object`. Using javac, you must compile your interfaces and then run the output through Java2IIOP.

For each remote Java interface Java2IIOP comes across, it will create a package with the following four classes:

- A client-side class called `_st_XXX`, where *XXX* is the name of your interface
- A server-side skeleton class called `_XXXImplBase`, where *XXX* is the name of your interface
- Helper classes for your interface
- Holder classes for your interface

These classes are identical to the ones IDL2Java generates (see Chapter 20, "CORBA IDL"). The only difference between the two is that IDL2Java starts with CORBA IDL input and then generates the IIOP stubs and skeletons, while Java2IIOP starts with Java interfaces and then generates the same IIOP stubs and skeletons. In this sense, Caffeine provides a "pure Java" alternative for creating Java CORBA objects.

Using Java2IDL

Caffeine creates CORBA IIOP objects directly from Java. This is good news because you don't have to write a single line of CORBA IDL to create these objects. However, what if you want to tap in to all the good stuff CORBA IDL provides—including self-describing objects, language-neutral interface repositories, and dynamic invocations? Caffeine gives you the best of both worlds.

The other trick in the Caffeine arsenal is called Java2IDL. This precompiler parses your Java code by looking for remote interfaces and then generates CORBA IDL files. You can load this IDL into a CORBA Interface Repository using VisiBroker's IDL2ir utility. For your Java classes, the CORBA IDL serves as a language-neutral specification. If you do not use pass-by-value, your Caffeinated Java objects can be accessed from CORBA/IIOP clients written in a variety of languages, such as C, C++, Ada, Smalltalk, and COBAL. However, in contrast to RMI-over-RMP, these RMI objects can only be called by other Java RMI objects. In addition, your Caffeinated Java clients can call multilingual server objects on a CORBA/IIOP ORB, but RMI objects can only call other RMI Java objects.

Passing CORBA Objects by Value

You might remember from Chapter 18 that RMI lets you pass by value local objects that are in parameters in a remote method invocation. What this means is that the actual state of the object is copied in the call. In contrast, CORBA only supports pass-by-value for non-object types.

CORBA 2.0 lets you specify both object types and non-object types as in, out, and inout arguments of IDL-specified methods (or operations, in CORBA-speak). Non-object types of CORBA can be basic or constructed.

CORBA copies the values of in parameters from the client to the server; it copies the values of out parameters from the server to the client as part of a reply. Finally, it copies inout parameters in both directions—during the invocation and the reply. However, CORBA only passes an object's reference; it does not copy the state of the object. The issue here is that CORBA does not currently copy-by-value the object's state; it only copies by value non-object types.

The idea that all objects are remotable is what CORBA builds on. Consequently, they can be accessed through their object reference. Thus, you just pass object references in a call, not the object itself. You will not have any problems if you create your remote applications starting from CORBA IDL. IDL won't let you pass objects by value. However, if you use Caffeine, you face the following problem: Java interfaces can define method invocations that include parameters that reference local objects. These references to local Java objects are only useful within a single virtual machine. So the ORB must copy these objects across Java virtual machines.

What's the solution to this problem? You have three options. The first is that you can refrain from passing local objects as parameters in remote Java invocations. If you must pass an object, make it remotable. The second option is that you can wait for Caffeine to implement the OMG's new Objects-by-Value standard for objects. In mid-1996, the OMG did issue such an RFP—it's called ORBOS RFP2. Finally, your third option is to use VisiBroker for Java right now. This ORB lets you pass objects by value using a non-standard extension to IIOP; it is the basis for the new OMG standard, but with modifications.

How does VisiBroker pass objects by value without breaking IIOP? The answer is that it does this by using something called *extensible structs*, which are upwardly compatible extensions of CORBA structs (or structures); the new standard calls them *value types*. You can use these structs to pass objects by value with all CORBA language mappings, not just Java. In theory, you should be able to pass an object's state across languages such as OO-COBOL, C++, Smalltalk, and Java.

An extensible struct adds the following functions to an ordinary CORBA struct: support for arbitrary recursive definitions that let you pass graphs of objects; the use of nested encodings; and an outer encoding that can represent the extensible struct as an opaque sequence of octets, which makes the struct transportable on IIOP ORBs that are not struct-aware.

In plain English, what I am trying to say is that an extensible struct is simply a way to flatten the state of an object and all its parent objects. The flattened object can then be transported on any IIOP ORB. VisiBroker for Java uses these structs to flatten a Java object by writing to the extensible struct all the fields of an object—from the first field of the base class to the last field of the most derived class. These fields are stored using normal IIOP encodings. The sender marshals the struct; the receiver must unmarshal it and reconstruct the state of the object field-by-field. VisiBroker stubs and skeletons know exactly how to marshal and unmarshal these extensible structs. It's all done transparently. Note that both the Visigenic implementation and the new standard use a single-inheritance graph. This is good for Java, but it might not be that good for C++.

The Caffeine Development Process

This section shows the steps you must follow to create your Caffeine client and server classes and then run them. Let's go through these steps one-by-one and see what's involved:

1. Define a remote interface. Your server object must declare its services through a remote Java interface. It does this by extending `org.omg.CORBA.Object`. Each method in a remote interface must throw either a CORBA system or user exception.

2. Optionally, generate CORBA IDL. To generate CORBA IDL, run your Java interfaces through Java2IDL. You can also run your Caffeine clients and servers without CORBA IDL.

3. Compile your interface. You must compile your interface using javac.

4. Create the IIOP stubs and skeletons. Run the Caffeine Java2IIOP compiler (or postprocessor) against the (.class) files to generate client stubs and server skeletons for your remote classes. The stubs are what provide IIOP proxies for your server objects. They marshal remote calls and send them to the server skeleton (the `_XXXImplBase` receives the remote call, unmarshals the parameters, and then calls your implementation class). The Java2IIOP compiler also creates Helper and Holder classes for your interface.

5. Implement the remote interface. You must provide a Java server class that implements the interface you published to the outside world. You must derive this class from the _XXXImplBase class.

6. Compile your server class. You must compile your server class using javac.

7. Start the VisiBroker Service. Start OSAgent. You can also use Caffeine's URL-based Naming Service. (Note that Netscape does not use OSAgent.)

8. Start your server objects. You must load your server classes and then create instances of remote objects.

9. Write your client code. The client consists mostly of ordinary Java code. You use a Naming Service to locate a remote object. You then implement its methods through a stub that serves as a proxy for the remote object. These stubs are also generated by Java2IIOP.

10. Compile the client code using javac.

11. Start the client. You must load the client classes and their stubs.

As you can see, Caffeine follows a very RMI-like development process. You develop in Java and then use CORBA/IIOP as your ORB. If you are a Java developer, you get the best of the two worlds. CORBA developers might prefer to start with IDL.

The Caffeine URL Name Service

There are a variety of Naming Services that you can use with Caffeine. Visigenic offers three services: OSAgents (or SmartAgents), CORBA COS Naming Service, and a URL-based name service. Also, Netscape provides its own version of the URL Name Service. Consequently, it does not require the Visigenic OSAgent engine in order to work. In this section, I'll cover the Netscape version of the URL-based naming scheme; it is part of Enterprise Server 3.0c with the WAI patch (or later).

Web Application Interface (WAI) lets you write server-side application extensions to Enterprise Server 3.X functionality. A Web Application Server (WAS) is a WAI application that you write using either Java or C++. It is like a CORBA Servlet.

The Netscape URL-based Naming Service can be used to bind and resolve CORBA object references to URLs. Applications written in Java, JavaScript, or C++ are able to access the Netscape URL Name Server. These applications can be CORBA servers or CORBA clients running in either browsers or standalone mode. Runtimes are available on both the Communicator and Enterprise Server 3.X. The Netscape-defined netscape.WAI.Naming class provides the API to the URL-based Naming Service.

You implement `register`, `registerObject`, or `registerWAS` to associate a CORBA object with a URL string. Using these methods will help you create different URL structures. For example, `register()` automatically inserts a `/NameService` string between the host and the `path/object` name; `registerWAS()` introduces an extra `/WAS` subdirectory. Ordinary CORBA objects map to URLs with the following structure:

```
http://hostAndPort/NameService/Name
```

WAI objects must support an extra subdirectory:

```
http://hostAndPort/NameService/Was/Name
```

To obtain the CORBA object reference associated with URL, you invoke `resolve()` and `resolveURI()`. The `resolve()` call automatically inserts a `/NameService` string between the host and the `path/object` name. With `resolveURI()`, however, you must explicitly put the `/NameService` in your URL string.

The `getRootNaming()` method returns the CORBA root `NamingContext` object. Note that Netscape's URL naming is built on top of the CORBA Naming Service. To get to the underlying CORBA service, you can use this call. By implementing `nameFromString` you can create CORBA Name structure from a string. Table 21.1 contains a more detailed class description.

Table 21.1   Detailed Class Descriptions

Methods	Description
`registerWAS()`	Registers an object implementation with a URL that has the following format: `http://host:port/NameService/WAS/object_name`
`resolveWAS()`	Resolves an object name and returns the corresponding object reference.
`resolveURI()`	Resolves a URL that has the following format: `http://host:port/NameService/WAS/object_name`, and returns the corresponding object reference.
`registerObject()`	Registers an object implementation with a URL of the form `http://hostname:portnumber/NameService/object_name`
`putObject()`	Associates an object with a URL, effectively registering the object with the name service.
`putContext()`	Associates a naming context with a URL. You can register an object under this naming context.

A URL-Naming Scenario

Let's walk through the steps of a URL-naming:

1. The server gives URL names to its objects. The server invokes `register()` for every object reference it wants to associate with a URL name. For each object, the server must pass a URL string and an object reference. Here is an example of the code:

   ```
   // Create CORBA Object
   HelloImpl hi = new HelloImp( "Hello" );
   // Register the URL of this object
   netscape.WAI.Naming.register( "http://rick:80/Hello" , hi );
   ```

2. The client binds to the URL. The client invokes `resolve()` on the Name Server and then passes it the URL of the remote object. This method returns the object reference associated with this URL. You must then typecast the generic CORBA object that is returned to its interface type. Here's a code example:

   ```
   // Find the CORBA object ref for this URL
   String url = http://rick/NameService/Hello;

   //Resolve object
   org.omg.CORBA.Object o = netscape.WAI.Naming.resolve( url );
   ```

3. Invoke methods on the server object. It is business as usual. The client implements methods on the remote server object through its local proxy stub.

The Netscape URL-based Naming Service provides a layer on top of the regular CORBA Naming Service. You use URL strings instead of dealing with CORBA Naming Contexts and generic data structures. After that, the Service then translates these URLs into CORBA name bindings and contexts. These bindings are stored in the Netscape Name Server's database.

OMG is currently working on an Interoperable Naming Service; it was proposed by IBM, SunSoft, Netscape, Oracle, and Visigenic. One of the most essential elements of this new service is a URL-based naming system on top of the CORBA Naming Service. The Netscape URL-based Naming Service might become this standard.

Visigenic also provides a URL-based Naming Service; it's part of the Caffeine URL Naming package. In this package the functions are very similar to the Netscape service. However, there are two differences. The first difference is that VisiBroker uses different API semantics: `register_URL()` instead of `register()`; `locate_URL()` instead of `resolve()`. The second difference is that the implementation is not very scalable. VisiBroker uses an HTTP server for its naming database. It first creates a file with the URL name on an HTTP server. Then it writes to the file the "stringified" IOR for a particular object reference. This practice is very resource intensive: It costs you only one file per object URL on the HTTP server. Consequently, it doesn't scale well. In contrast, Netscape stores the URLs in a regular database. Therefore, it is a more scalable solution.

A Caffeine Version of HelloWorld

Knowing the URL-Naming Service, the only new interface that Caffeine introduces, lets us jump right in and write some code. After all, Caffeine is just another way to develop CORBA code.

The Client

The client program consists of a single Java class: `HelloWorldCaffeineClient` (see Listing 21.1). This class provides a main method that performs the following functions: initializes the ORB; locates and then obtains a reference to a HelloWorld server object; invokes the `getGreeting()` method to get the greeting string; and displays the average Caffeinated Ping performance.

It is important to note that this example uses a URL-based naming scheme to locate a reference to the remote object.

Listing 21.1 `HelloWorldCaffeineClient` Source Code

```
// HelloWorldCaffeineClient.java Static Client, VisiBroker for Java
class HelloWorldCaffeineClient
{
  public static void main( String args [] )
  {
    try{
      //Initialize the ORB
      System.out.println( "Initializing the ORB" );
      org.omg.CORBA.Object obj =
        netscapeWAI.Naming.resolve( "http://www.infinitevision.net/
➥HelloWorldCaffeine" );
      HelloWorldCaffeine.HelloWorldCaffeine greeting =
➥HelloWorldCaffeine.HelloWorldCaffeineHelper.narrow( obj );

      // Setting initial greeting
      greeting.setGreeting( "Hello There World!" );

      // Calculate Start time
      long starttime = System.currentTimeMillis();

      for( int i=0; i<100; i++ )
```

continues

Listing 21.1   continued

```
    strGreeting = greeting.getGreeting();

   // Calculate stop time; print out statistics
   long stopTime = System.currentTimeMillis();
   System.out.println( "Avg Ping =" + ( ( stopTime - startTime )
➥/ 100f ) + "msecs" );

   System.outprintln( "Greeting = " + greeting.getGreeting() );
  }
  catch( org.omg.CORBA.SystemException e )
  {
    System.err.println( "System Exception" );
    System.err.println( e );
  }
 }
}
```

The Caffeinated HelloWorld Server

Consisting of one Java interface and two classes is the server side of the Caffeine HelloWorld. The `HelloWorldCaffeineImpl` class implements the `HelloWorldCaffeine` remote interface. The `HelloWorldCaffeineServer` class provides a main method that initializes the server and then instantiates a single `HelloWorldCaffeineImpl` object (see Listing 21.2). In Listing 21.3 you'll see the `HelloWorldCaffeineImplClass` source code, and in Listing 21.4 you'll see the `HelloWorldCaffeineServer` source code.

Listing 21.2   The `HelloWorldCaffeine` Interface

```
package HelloWorldCaffeine;
public interface HelloWorldCaffeine extends org.omg.CORBA.Object
{
  public int getGreeting();
  public void setGreeting( String strNewGreeting );
}
```

Listing 21.3   The `HelloWorldCaffeineImplClass`

```
// HelloWorldCaffeineImpl.java: the HelloWorldCaffeine Implementation
class HelloWorldCaffeineImpl extends
➥HelloWorldCaffeine._HelloWorldCaffeineImplBase
{
```

```java
    private String strGreeting;

    HelloWorldCaffeineImpl( String name )
    {
      super( name );
      System.out.println( "HelloWorldCaffeine Object Created" );
      strGreeting = "Hello World!";
    }

    public String getGreeting()
    {
      return( strGreeting );
    }
    public void setSum( String strNewGreeting )
    {
      strGreeting = strNewGreeting;
    }
}
```

Listing 21.4 The HelloWorldCaffeineServer Source Code

```java
// HelloWorldCaffeineServer.java
import netscape.WAI.Naming;
class HelloWorldCaffeineServer
{
  static public void main( String [] args )
  {
    try
    {
      // Initialize the ORB
      org.omg.CORBA.ORB orb = org.omg.CORBA.ORB.init( argus, null );

      // Create the HelloWorldCaffeine object.
      HelloWorldCaffeineImpl greeting = new HelloWorldCaffeineImple (
➥"My HelloWorldCaffeine" );

      // Export to the ORB the newly created object
      orb.connect( greeting );

      // register the server with the Web Naming Service
      String host = java.net.InetAddress.getLocalHost().getHostName();
      String url = "http://" = host = "/HelloWorldCaffeine";
      System.out.println( "URL = " + url );
      Naming.register( url, greeting );
      System.out.println( "HelloWorldCaffeine registered" );

      // wait forever for current thread to die
      Thread.current Thread().join();
    }
```

continues

Listing 21.4 continued

```
   catch( Exception e )
   {
     System.err.println( e );
   }
  }
}
```

The HelloWorldCaffeine interface shown in Listing 21.3 extends org.omg.CORBA, as shown in the code. The HelloWorldCaffeineImpl class implements these methods and extends the skeleton class, _HelloWorldCaffeineImplBase. Also, HelloWorldCaffeineImpl invokes a constructor that registers the newly created object's name with CORBA through its super.

The Java interface file is called HelloWorldCaffeine. The Java2IIOP compiler places all the classes it generates in this package, including the stub, skeleton, Helper, and Holder classes.

The server's main method is provided by the HelloWorldCaffeineServer. The class provides the following functions: initializes the ORB; creates a new HelloWorldCaffeineImpl object; connects to the ORB; invokes register() to associate the IOR of the HelloWorld object with a URL-based name; and waits for requests.

Compiling the Client and Server Programs

You are now ready to compile the CORBA Caffeine client and server programs. Be sure that you have installed VisiBroker for Java 3.4, the Symantec Visual Café compiler, and the Java JDK. You also need to have Netscape Enterprise Server 3.0c or later installed, and you must include the nisb.zip file in your CLASSPATH.

To compile the Java interface, you must first go to the appropriate directory and enter the following command at the prompt:

```
javac HelloWorldCaffeine.java
```

Next, you must generate the stubs and skeletons using Java2IIOP. To do this, enter the following command at the prompt:

```
java2iiop HelloWorldCaffeine -no_comments
```

Java/CORBA Development Using Caffeine

CHAPTER 21

477

21

JAVA/CORBA
DEVELOPMENT
USING CAFFEINE

You can optionally generate CORBA IDL. To do this, enter the following command at the prompt:

```
Java2IDL HelloWorldCaffeine > HelloWorldCaffeine.idl
```

Next, you must compile the code for the client and server. To do this, you can either run the make file provided in the subdirectory or enter the following commands at the prompt:

```
javac -d \Chapter21\classes HelloWorldCaffeineClient.java

javac -d \Chapter21\classes HelloWorldCaffeineServer.java

javac -d \Chapter21\classes HelloWorldCaffeineImpl.java
```

The `-d` option tells the compiler to put the (.class) files it creates into the directory you specify, in this case, the `\Chapter21\classes` subdirectory.

If everything goes according to plan, you should have some compiled Java code—including a stub and skeleton—that you can now run.

Running the Client and Server Programs

You must have Enterprise Server 3.0 running and your server program must have the authority to make updates to Web Naming to run the Caffeine client/server programs.

First, you must start the server. Enter the following command at the prompt to run the server program:

```
start java HelloWorldCaffeineServer
```

Now you can finally start the client. Enter the following command at the prompt:

```
java HelloWorldCaffeineClient
```

You should see a screen output that looks like this:

```
Initializing the ORB
Resolving the HelloWorldCaffeine Name
Setting greeting to "Hello There World!"
Avg Ping = 3.612 msecs
Greeting = "Hello There World!"
```

Summary

Caffeine provides three main innovations that make CORBA more friendly to Java developers. It lets you pass local objects by value; it lets you use Java both as an interface definition language and as an implementation language; and it supports a persistent URL-based naming scheme. In contrast, the RMI URL Name Server is volatile; you lose all your name bindings when the Name Server process terminates.

Caffeine provides an excellent pure Java solution on top of CORBA/IIOP today. It is a CORBA alternative to RMI-over-RMP. Eventually, Caffeine and RMI will converge when they both implement the new CORBA RMI-over-IIOP semantics.

Enterprise Client/Server Computing

PART
VI

IN THIS PART

Developing Multitier Applications Using Java

The purpose of this chapter is to give you a high-level understanding of distributed programming options for Java programmers. This understanding will provide you with a solid foundation upon which you can base your design decisions in the future.

Multitier Application Architecture

Multitier Application Architecture was designed to provide an environment that is suitable for the development of fully portable, Java technology-based, enterprise-class application systems using the Enterprise Java platform. Often the true measure of an enterprise application system comes down to system scalability and total throughput. How many users can concurrently use the system? How many objects can by instantiated in a given time frame? And how many transactions can be processed per second?

Enterprise application systems support high scalability by using a multitier, distributed application architecture. A *multitier application* is an application that has been partitioned into multiple application components. There are a number of significant advantages provided by multitier applications over traditional client/server architectures, including improvements in scalability, performance, reliability, manageability, reusability, and flexibility.

Application Partitioning

In a traditional client/server application, the client application contains presentation logic (window and control manipulation), business logic (algorithms and business rules), and data manipulation logic (database connections and SQL queries)—a "fat client." Generally, a relational database management system (which is actually not a part of the application) is the server.

In a multitier architecture, however, the client application contains only presentation logic—a "thin client."

Partitioned into separate components and deployed on one or more servers are the business logic and data access logic.

Increased Scalability and Performance

Moving the business and data manipulation logic to a server allows an application to take advantage of the power of multithreaded and multiprocessing systems. Server components can pool and share scarce resources, such as processors, threads, database connections, and network sessions.

Highly active components can be replicated and distributed across multiple systems as system demands increase. Although modern client/server systems can easily support hundreds of concurrent users, their scalability has limits. More or bigger servers can be added to the environment to boost performance and to support additional users if the design is efficient. Multitier systems can scale to support hundreds of thousands or millions of concurrent users.

Increased Reliability

A multitier environment can also support many levels of redundancy. A multitier architecture eliminates bottlenecks or single points of failure via replication and distribution. High reliability and consistent system availability to support critical business operations are supported by the multitier approach.

Increased Manageability

A thin client application is easier to manage than a traditional client/server application. Very little code is actually deployed on the client systems. Most of the application logic is deployed, managed, and maintained on the servers. Through a centralized management environment, fixes, upgrades, new versions, and extensions can all be administered.

Increased Flexibility

The multitier application architecture supports extremely flexible application systems. The majority of the application logic is invoked or implemented in small modular components. The actual business logic in the components is encapsulated behind an abstract, well-defined interface. Without requiring a change to the interface, the code within an individual component can be modified. Therefore, a component can be changed without affecting the other components within the application. Multitier applications can easily adapt to reflect changing business requirements.

Reusability and Integration

By the nature of its interface, a server component is a reusable software building block. Each component performs a specific set of functions that are published and accessible to any other application through the interface. For example, a particular business function can be implemented once and then reused in another application that requires the function. Application development becomes a matter of assembling the proper components into a configuration that performs the required application functions if an organization maintains comprehensive functions.

Multi-Client Support

Any number of client environments can access the same server component through its interface. A variety of client devices, including traditional desktop workstations, Web clients, or more esoteric clients such as information appliances, smartcards, or personal data assistants, can all be supported by a single multitier application.

Although server components and multitier concepts have been around for nearly a decade, relatively few organizations have put them to use. Until recently, most organizations did not feel the scalability pressures that require a multitier architecture. But the impetus of Web-based computing is driving a growing interest in the multitier approach. Web-based business applications require a thin-client application architecture to support massive scalability and to support browser-based clients and rapid applet downloads.

More Difficult Development

Unfortunately, building multitier applications isn't quite as easy as building client/server applications. Multitier applications have to interact with a variety of middleware services. The applications must support multithreading, resource sharing, replication, and load balancing in order to attain the scalability, performance, and reliability characteristics of multitier computing.

Application Servers

An application server automates some of the more complex features of multitier computing.

An application server manages and recycles scarce system resources, such as processes, threads, memory, database connections, and network sessions, on behalf of the applications. Some of the more sophisticated application servers offer load-balancing services that can distribute application processing across multiple systems.

Access to infrastructure services, such as naming, directory, transactions, persistence, and security, are provided by an application server. Until recently, though, every application server used a proprietary set of interfaces. Each enterprise application had to be implemented with a specific runtime environment in mind, and applications were not portable across application servers—not even Java applications.

Enterprise JavaBeans Specification

The Enterprise JavaBeans specification defines a standard model for a Java application server that supports complete portability. The model to invoke support for Enterprise JavaBeans components can be used by any vendor. Systems such as TP monitors, CORBA runtime systems, COM runtime systems, database systems, Web server systems, or other server-based runtime systems can be adapted to support portable Enterprise JavaBeans components.

Two-Tier Client/Server

In a two-tier client/server system there are two systems invoked—the client and the server—and they communicate through middleware of some kind. The slash in client/server is sometimes referred to as the middleware. It is a vague term that covers all the distributed software needed to support interactions between clients and servers. An example might start with the TCP/IP stacks running on client and server machines on the World Wide Web. The server normally includes the persistence domain and, finally, probably includes a database management system (DBMS). Alternatively, it might be a simple file server. Normally, the client will include the user interface (often a GUI).

Frequently there will be many clients talking to a single server. Where the core domain software resides in a two-tier client/server system varies. In some systems it might be on the client. These are sometimes called fat client systems and are the more traditional systems. In such systems, the server simply serves up data to the client when asked and stores data given to it by clients. On the client all the processing of the data is done.

The alternative, as you might have guessed, is the fat server or thin client system, in which most of the core domain code runs on the server. This is often achieved by the DBMS using stored procedures, procedures that are stored in the database and implemented remotely by the client. The advantage is that less data has to be transferred across the network (so network traffic is reduced). Most two-tier systems share the core domain code between the client and the server. An example of a two-tier system would be a Visual Basic client on your PC talking to an database on an Alpha2 machine.

Middleware

Middleware probably has the biggest share of acronyms in the computing industry. Here are a few. Some you will recognize, many you probably won't.

DCE	*ONC+*	*Netware*	*Named Pipes*
LAN Server	LAN Manager	Vines	TCP/IP
APPC	NetBIOS	MOM	ODBC
DRDA	EDA/SQL	SAG/CLI	Oracle Glue
ATMI	TxRPC	XATMI	MAPI
VIM	VIC	SMTP	CORBA
DCOM	HTTP	S-HTTP	SSL
SNMP	CMIP	ORBs	

22

DEVELOPING
MULTITIER
APPLICATIONS

Middleware is used to invoke a service with the API on the client that is used. It covers the transmission of the request over the network (and all the layers it has to go through before and after the transmission) and the response. If you think of a mail order business as a client/server system, the middleware would be everything that happens between you posting your order and it arriving on someone's desk at the mail order company—the sorting and so on. It also covers everything that happens to the goods on their way from the company warehouse to your letter box. It does not cover what happens at the company in the processing of your order: That is in the server's domain.

Designing Thin Java Client Applications for Network Computers

It's tough to write large Java applets for use over the Internet. The reason is that large Java applets take time to download. For those of us with T1 connections, we have plenty of bandwidth and the download time isn't too bad. But if you're dialed up, the situation can be aggravating. If your applet is too large, the application will be so annoying to use that it'll throw a wet blanket on users' perceptions. Thin client applications solve this to a large degree because what gets downloaded is much smaller than a fat applet that has all of the business logic as well as the user interface.

The Java Application

There is one example application in this chapter. It is a hypothetical for discussion and is an order entry application that allows Internet users to order items over the Web. The client contains an interactive order form that lists order items and allows the user to enter quantities, calculate line item and total costs, and submit the order to a database for processing.

Model View Controller (MVC) Design Patterns

To design thin Java clients, your Java application must have a clear separation between the presentation of your application and the application logic, which is the essence of Model View Controller application design patterns. In the Model View Controller paradigm, the View is the presentation component of your application. This includes the rendering of windows, panels, text fields, and other GUI widgets. The Model component consists of all the application domain specific objects and behaviors, otherwise known as the application or business logic. For the order entry application, the model consists of two Java classes, the `Order` and `Order Item` classes. The `Order` object is a collection of

Order Items and quantities. It knows how to calculate a total price for the order and submit an order to the database. The order item contains an item number and price. The Controller interprets action inputs from the user, directing the model and/or the view to change as appropriate. For the order entry application, a controller is needed to handle the mouse click on the Submit Order button GUI widget. Many GUI frameworks implement pure or variations of MVC design patterns. For instance, the Java Foundation Classes (JFC) implement a MVC variation where the View and Controller components are combined into one component to optimize object usage.

The Heavy Client

Most Java applets on the Web today fall into the heavyweight Java client category. One reason is that they are easiest to design and implement because there is little or no server application supporting the client except for the possibility of a data base server. These are one- or two-tier applications where most, if not all, of the application or business logic is downloaded to the client and requires no server application to service client requests.

The two-tier Java application architecture leads to heavyweight client implementation because all of the MVC components live on the client, with only the persistent domain data residing on the server. The heavy client includes

- *Views*—All of the application's graphical user interface (GUI) widgets needed to present the application to the user.
- *Controllers*—All of the controllers needed to handle user input direct the view/model to change when appropriate.
- *Model*—All of the application domain objects and logic.
- *JDBC*—All of the JDBC classes to support the data base access.
- *JDBC Driver*—A native-protocol, all-Java database driver that communicates with the database directly using a propriety database protocol.

Applying this two-tier design for the heavyweight version of the order application, the following Java classes are necessary:

Java Class	Description
OrderApplet	The Java applet for the order application. Initializes and destroys the applet. Instantiates OrderView and OrderController.
OrderView	The screen panel for the order entry form. Includes all the creation and layout for the GUI widgets in the order form panel.

continues

22

DEVELOPING
MULTITIER
APPLICATIONS

Java Class	Description
OrderController	Handles the GUI events for the widgets in the OrderView. Dispatches messages to the Order and OrderItem domain objects.
Order	Domain object that represents the order. Includes APIs to add items to the order, calculate total cost, and submit the order.
OrderItem	Domain object for one item in an order. There is one order item for each possible item a user can order. An order item has a unique item number and price.

The order application is a simple one. In a more realistic scenario, networked applications might have hundreds of screens, controllers, and domain objects. The heavyweight implementation would result in several megabytes of Java code being downloaded to the network client computer.

The Thin Client

The thin client architecture distributes much of the design to the server, leaving as little code as possible on the client. This multitier client/server design limits the client to include only View components and moves the Controller component from the client to the server. In addition, the entire Model (the application domain objects and logic) is moved to the server, including all the database-supporting code (JDBC) and the database driver. As a result, thin client applications are always two-tier or three-tier applications (three-tier if a database is involved).

Thin Client Protocol Framework (TCPF)

TCPF was developed by Avitek, a company specializing in Java client/server solutions. They've managed to make a success story of the Java Web server, and they developed the Thin Client Protocol Framework as a client/server tool for developers. You can visit their Web site at http://www.Avatek.com for more information. Distributing the View and Controller components to different networked client/server computers requires a protocol framework that transports client view information to server controllers and transports server controller responses back to the client view.

Existing distributed protocols, such as RMI and CORBA/IIOP, can be used as a solution in the thin client architecture to distribute the View and Controller components across a network of machines. However, using HTTP is an interesting protocol solution for the thin client design and it's the solution discussed in this chapter, called the Thin Client Protocol Framework (TCPF). HTTP provides a lighter weight and much simpler mechanism for communicating between the distributed View and Controller components than do CORBA or RMI. Also, the HTTP solution tends to have fewer firewall

Developing Multitier Applications Using Java

CHAPTER 22

489

22

DEVELOPING
MULTITIER
APPLICATIONS

issues than CORBA and RMI solutions although these now include HTTP tunneling features as well.

On the client, the TCPF is responsible for providing the View components of an application with a mechanism to send GUI events and associated data as HTTP requests to a server application and handle the server response to the request. The client component of the TCPF includes

- Widget adapters
- Component Registry
- Request/response data objects
- TCPF (request/response) adapter

Each GUI widget in a view, such as a Java Panel, is associated with a type of widget adapter that corresponds to the GUI widget's type. For instance, there is a `TextAdapter` for `TextField` widgets and a `ListAdapter` for `List` widgets. Widget adapters know how to handle events for their associated widget and know how to get and set values for the widget.

The Component Registry is a dictionary of GUI widget names and widget adapters. Each GUI widget in a view has a unique name prefixed by its controller's name, for example, `'OrderController.submitBtn'`. When instantiated, each GUI widget registers its unique name and widget adapter instance with the Component Registry. When a GUI event of interest is fired, the TCPF calls on the Component Registry to retrieve the data from the widget associated with the event and constructs a data object for the widget. This data object includes the widget's unique name and the data associated with the event. Other data objects can be constructed from other widgets in the client that are needed to process the event on the server.

The TCPF Request Adapter is responsible for packaging and serializing the data objects being sent to the server, making the HTTP connection to the server application, and writing the HTTP server request. After the server application handles the request, the TCPF Response Adapter on the client deserializes the HTTP response from the server application back into data objects and calls on the Component Registry to update the values in the GUI widgets associated with these data objects.

On the server, the TCPF's job is to dispatch these client HTTP requests to server-side controllers and handle packaging of the server controller responses back to the client. The server components of the TCPF are

- TCPF Request Servlet
- Service (request/response) Manager
- Request/response data objects
- Controller Registry

During server initialization, all the controllers required for the application are instantiated and registered with the server application's Controller Registry. The Controller Registry is a dictionary of instantiated controller objects keyed by controller name.

The TCPF server component also includes a Java Servlet, referred to as the TCPF Request Servlet. This Java Servlet receives the HTTP request sent by the client's TCPF Request Adapter and dispatches it to the Service Request Manager. The Service Request Manager de-serializes the HTTP content into request data objects, which contain a client widget's name (prefixed with its controller's name) and its data. Using the controller name in a request data object, the Service Request Manager accesses the Controller Registry to find the controller associated with the data object. Next, the Service Request Manager sends a message to the controller to process the event information in the data object. For example, if the data object contains data about an action event for an order submit button widget, the controller would ask the order domain object to perform a submit, which would insert the domain object into a database.

After the controller has finished processing the data sent to it, it sends a response message back to the Service Request Manager. A response is always directed to a widget or set of widgets in the client. The Service Manager packages up the response into the same data object format used in the request and serializes the response. The TCPF Request Servlet then takes the serialized data and sends it back to the client in the content of an HTTP request. When the client's TCPF Response Adapter receives the HTTP response, it de-serializes the HTTP contents into response data objects that have the same object structure as the request data objects. For each data object, the Service Response Adapter retrieves the widget name and data from the data object and uses the Component Registry to find the associated widget adapter. Then the Response Adapter sets the widget's value by sending a message to the widget adapter.

Applying this thin client framework protocol to the thin version of the order application, the following Java classes are necessary:

Client Java Class	Description
OrderApplet	The Java Applet for the order application. Initializes and destroys the applet. Instantiates the OrderView and ComponentRegistry.
OrderView	The screen panel for the order entry form. Includes all the creation and layout for the GUI widgets in the order form panel. Creates the widget adapters.
TextFieldAdapter	The widget adapter that handles getting and setting text in a text field widget.
ButtonAdapter	The widget adapter that handles getting and setting push button states.

Client Java Class	Description
ComponentRegistry	Dictionary of GUI component names and widget adapters.
TCPFAdapter	Handles packaging of the GUI events in a request to the server. Handles the dispatching of the server response to the widget adapters.

Server Java Class	Description
TCPFServlet	The Java Servlet that receives thin client HTTP requests and generates thin client HTTP responses back to the client.
ServiceManager	Dispatches thin client requests to the appropriate server controller. Packages the response that will be sent back to the thin client.
ControllerRegistry	Dictionary of controller names and controller instances.
OrderController	Handles the event data sent to it by ServiceManager. Dispatches messages to the Order and OrderItem domain.
Order	Domain object that represents the order. Includes APIs to add items to the order, calculate total cost, and submit the order.
OrderItem	Domain object for one item in an order. There is one order item for each possible item a user can order. An order item has a unique item number and price.

Because the order application only has one screen, the download savings provided by the thin client architecture is not easily seen. If this application had 20 screens with 50 domain objects, the savings would be large over the heavyweight client because the 20 controllers and 50 domain objects would not be downloaded.

Summary

The heavyweight Java client architecture is much simpler and easier to implement because all three components of the Model View Controller design pattern reside on the client machine. However, you pay the price in download times and the amount of memory needed on the client to run the application. Also, if the heavy client application requires database access, the database driver needs to be downloaded to the client as well. Applications using database drivers residing on the client might also have to deal with firewall issues because most database drivers use a socket-based database protocol to access the database server.

The thin Java client requires a more complex architecture because the View component resides on the client and the Controller and Model components reside on the server. This distribution requires a thin client protocol framework that assists in transporting GUI events and associated data from the client to the server. However, this design can result in smaller but more frequent network traffic because all GUI events are dispatched to the server. An enhancement to this design would be to reduce the number of trips to the server by identifying which events do not require a trip to the server and processing those on the client.

Although more challenging to build, the thin client design payoff is big, resulting in applications with much smaller client downloads, much less client machine memory needed to run the application, no firewall concerns, and more scalable applications—all of which are necessary for building successful networked applications.

Using Enterprise JavaBeans

CHAPTER 23

The original JavaBeans specification characterizes the standard properties and behavior of Java components that essentially function on the client side of a client/server system. This sole focus on the client is altered by the introduction of Enterprise JavaBeans Specification Version 1.0. As a component architecture for building scalable, multitier, distributed applications, Enterprise JavaBeans enable you to create dynamically extensible application servers.

The initial Enterprise JavaBeans Specification has led to an explosion of interest in Enterprise JavaBeans (EJB) by companies such as Oracle, Borland, Tandem, Symantec, Sybase, and Visigenic. These companies, as well as many others, deliver and/or advertise products that are compliant to the EJB specification. This chapter takes an in-depth look at the new and improved Enterprise JavaBeans. We'll discuss the contrasting elements that exist between EJB and the original JavaBeans component model as well as why EJB has kindled such a flame of interest. But one advisory first: We'll not be looking at how-to topics or source code. This chapter is an architectural overview; it's not a tutorial. A lot of territory is covered by EJB. If you don't have an understanding of the basic concepts involved, the code snippets and programming tricks are meaningless.

It's necessary to obtain some historical background in order to understand why EJB is so attractive to developers. First, we'll look at the history of client/server systems as well as the current state of affairs. Next, we'll discuss the various parts of an EJB system. These parts include EJB components, which live on an EJB container running inside an EJB server. Also, you'll learn about EJB objects, which are used as a kind of remote control of EJB components by the client. We'll review the two types of EJBs: session and entity objects. You'll also read about remote and home interfaces, which respectively create EJB instances and provide access to the EJB's business methods. Additionally, you'll learn how extensible servers can be built using Enterprise JavaBeans. First, however, let's take a step back in time.

Client/Server History

The mainframe computer was the first born into the new age of computer technology. It was considered to be the best of what was available. Big, expensive machines that were used by large organizations to support their daily business operations were state-of-the-art in information processing through the 1960s. In the 1970s, minicomputers and timesharing increased the accessibility of computing power. However, information and processing were still centralized on individual machines.

In contrast, the first personal computers evolved in the 1980s. These computers were like thousands of tiny information islands that quickly cluttered the corporate landscape. They produced reports of variable quality, lost critical data when they crashed, and quickly became inconsistent with each other due to the multitude of vendors manufacturing them.

Client/Server to the Rescue

Client/server architecture solves the problem of how to handle the need for both centralized data control and widespread data accessibility. The information stored in the client/server systems is kept relatively centralized (or is partitioned and/or replicated among distributed servers). The centrally stored information facilitates the control and consistency of data while still providing access to the data user's need.

Now, client/server systems are commonly composed of various numbers of tiers. The standard old mainframe or timesharing system is known as single tier. In this system the user interface runs on the same computer (or a remote terminal) as the database and business applications. These easy-to-manage systems have a simple data consistency because the data is stored in only one place. Single-tier systems, unfortunately, have limited scalability and are prone to availability hazards (if one computer's down, your whole business goes down)—especially if communication is involved.

The first client/server systems were two-tier. In these systems, which are still common today, the user interface ran on the client and the database lived on the server. Most of the business logic is performed by a garden-variety type of two-tier server that updates shared data by sending streams of SQL to the server. Because the client/server conversation occurs at the level of the server's database language, this is a flexible solution. In such a system, a properly designed client can be modified to reflect new business conditions and rules without modifying the server. This proves to be true as long as the server has access to the database schema (tables, views, and so forth) needed to perform the transactions. The server in this type of two-tier system is known as a database server.

Database servers do have some liabilities. In many cases, the SQL for a certain business function, such as adding an item to an order, is identical except for the data that is being inserted or updated from call to call. Nearly identical SQL for each business function is parsed and re-parsed by the database server. For example, all SQL statements for finding a customer in the database are most likely very similar. This fact also holds true to the SQL statements for adding an item to an order. The time this parsing takes would be more useful spent actually processing data. Remedies to this problem include SQL parse caches and stored procedures. Versioning the clients and the database at the same time is another problem. All machines must shut down for upgrades, and clients or servers that fall behind in their software version usually are not usable until they have been upgraded.

23

USING ENTERPRISE
JAVABEANS

Application Servers

An application server is a popular alternative to the database server architecture. This particular type of server has the ability to solve some of the problems common to database servers.

The environment of a database server uses the server mostly for persistence and enforcing data integrity, and usually executes business methods on the client. In an application server, business methods run on the server and the client requests that the server executes these methods. In this sequence of events, the client and server will generally use a protocol that symbolizes a conversation at the level of business transactions, instead of at the level of tables and rows. Such application servers suffer from versioning problems, but they often perform better than their database counterparts. These application servers function as a layer in between the database and client. For more information about tiered client/server programming, refer to Chapter 22, "Developing Multitier Applications Using Java."

By adding additional tiers to the architecture, both database and application systems can be enhanced. An intermediate component between the client and the server is placed by so-called three-tier systems. The liabilities of two-tier systems have been addressed by an entire industry: middleware. One type of middleware is a transaction-processing monitor that receives streams of requests from many clients, and might balance the weight between multiple servers, provide failover when a server fails, and manage transactions on behalf of a client. Other types of middleware provide three layers of service. These types provide communications protocol translation, consolidate requests and responses between clients and multiple heterogeneous servers (this is particularly popular in dealing with legacy systems in business process reengineering), and/or provide service metering and network traffic information. Systems with more than these three layers of service have resulted in multiple tiers which lead to more flexibility and interoperability. For example, n-tier systems are generalizations of three-tier systems, with each layer of software providing a different level of service to the layers above and beneath it. The n-tier perspective does not consider the network a simple means for a client to access a single server. Instead, it views the network as a pool of distributed services.

Client/server systems have increasingly moved toward object-orientation just as object-oriented languages and techniques have become vogue. The CORBA architecture (see Chapters 20 and 21) allows objects within applications—even those written in different languages—to run on separate machines, depending on the needs of a given application. Applications written years ago can be packaged as CORBA services and inter-operate with all new systems. The design of Enterprise JavaBeans—which allows it to be compatible with CORBA—is another entry into the object-oriented, application-server ring.

Enterprise JavaBeans and Extensible Application Servers

Our step back in history has given us an understanding of application servers. Now, let's see what Enterprise JavaBeans has to offer in that context.

The basic idea behind Enterprise JavaBeans is that a framework is created for components that may be plugged in to a server. This allows that particular server's functionality to be extended. The only similarity between standard JavaBeans and Enterprise JavaBeans is that similar concepts are used. EJB technology is governed by Enterprise JavaBeans Specification. This governing force is very different and much larger than the JavaBeans component specification. The EJB Spec calls out the various players in the EJB client/server system, describes how EJB inter-operates with the client and with existing systems, spells out EJB's compatibility with CORBA, and defines the responsibilities for the various components in the system.

Enterprise JavaBeans Goals

The EJB Spec attempts to meet several goals at once:

The design of EJB makes it easy for developers to create applications that free them from low-level system details of managing transactions, load balancing, threads, and so on. This enables application developers to concentrate on business logic, leaving the details of managing the data processing to the framework. However, it's possible to customize these lower-level services for specialized applications.

The EJB Spec defines the major structures of the EJB framework, then specifically defines the contracts between those major structures. The client, the server, and the individual components have responsibilities that are all clearly explained. (We'll review what these structures are momentarily.) The job of a developer creating an Enterprise JavaBean component contrasts greatly with the job of one creating an EJB-compliant server, and the responsibilities of each developer is described by the specification.

The goal of EJB is to become the standard way for client/server applications to be built in the Java language. EJB server components from various vendors can be combined to produce a custom server just as the original JavaBeans or Delphi components from different vendors can be combined to produce a custom client. EJB components, being Java classes, enable those components to run in any EJB-compliant server without recompilation. Platform-specific solutions could never offer this unique benefit.

Finally, Enterprise JavaBeans can inter-operate with non-Java apps, are compatible with CORBA, and are compatible with other Java APIs.

How an EJB Client/Server System Operates

To understand how an EJB client/server system operates, you must first understand the basic parts of an EJB system:

- The EJB component
- The EJB container
- The EJB object

The Enterprise JavaBeans Component

Just like a traditional JavaBean, an Enterprise JavaBean is a component. Enterprise JavaBeans execute within an EJB container, which in turn executes within an EJB server. An EJB server can be any server that can host an EJB container and provide it with the necessary services. (This means that many existing servers may be extended to be EJB servers. In fact, many vendors have achieved this, or intend to do so.)

An EJB component is the type of EJB class most likely to be considered an Enterprise JavaBean. It's simply a Java class that was written by an EJB developer to implement business logic. In the EJB system, all the other classes either support client access to, or provide services (like persistence) to, EJB component classes.

The Enterprise JavaBeans Container

The EJB component actually lives inside the EJB container. The EJB container provides services such as transaction and resource management, versioning, scalability, mobility, persistence, and security to the EJB components it contains. The EJB component developer can concentrate on business rules and leave database manipulation and other such fine details to the container because the EJB container handles all the functions listed above. For example, if the decision is made by a single EJB component to abort the current transaction, the component tells its container (in a manner defined by the EJB Spec), and the container is responsible for taking all necessary steps to cancel or abort the transaction in progress. Multiple EJB component instances usually exist inside one EJB container.

The EJB Object and the Remote Interface

The EJB object serves as the means by which client programs execute methods on remote EJBs. The EJB object implements the remote interface of the EJB component on the server. The "business" methods of the EJB component are represented by the remote interface. The remote interface does useful work, such as deferring a patient to a specialist or creating an order form. The remote interface will be discussed in more detail later.

By looking at their interfaces, EJB objects and EJB components look identical. However, they are separate classes. Both the EJB objects and EJB components implement the same interface (the EJB components' remote interface), but they have very different tasks. The EJB object runs on the client and remotely executes the EJB component's methods. An EJB component runs on the server in an EJB container and implements the business logic.

For a moment, pretend that your VCR is an EJB component. The EJB object is then analogous to your remote control: Both the VCR and the remote control have the same buttons on the front, but they perform different functions. Pushing the Rewind button on the VCR itself is equivalent to pushing the Rewind button on your VCR's remote control. This is true even though it's the VCR, and not the remote, that actually rewinds a tape.

On a similar note, if you call the `addEmployee()` method on an EJB object, it calls (indirectly, through the network) the `addEmployee()` method on the remote EJB component. (In reality, the call travels through the EJB container, but that's an implementation detail.) Enterprise JavaBeans also has the interface (described below) that helps you find your "remote control"—even if it has found its way between the cushions of your couch.

The EJB Object Class

A code generation tool that comes with the EJB container is responsible for the actual implementation of an EJB object. The EJB object's interface is the EJB component's remote interface. The same remote interface is implemented by the EJB component object (created by the container and tools associated with the container) and the EJB object (created by the EJB developer). To the client, an EJB object looks just like an object from the application domain, such as an order form. But the EJB object, which runs on the server inside an EJB container, is just a stand-in for the actual EJB. When the client calls a method on an EJB object, the EJB object method communicates with the remote EJB container, requesting that the same method be called (on the correct remote EJB) with the same arguments (on behalf of the client). This is the core concept behind how an EJB client/server system actually works.

Types of Enterprise JavaBeans

Session beans and entity beans are the two basic types of Enterprise JavaBeans. In a distributed EJB application, these two types of beans play different roles.

A session bean is an EJB instance associated with a single client. Usually session beans are not persistent—although they have the potential to be persistent—and they may or may not take part in transactions. Session objects, in particular, do not generally survive server crashes. A session object might be, for example, an EJB living inside a Web server that serves HTML pages to a user on a browser and tracks that user's path through the site. The session object will be destroyed after a specified idle time or when the user leaves the site. Although the session object stores information to the database, its purpose is not to represent or update existing database contents; rather, it corresponds to one client performing some actions on the server EJBs.

An entity bean represents information persistently stored in a database. Entity beans may provide data access to multiple users because they are associated with database transactions. The data represented by the entity bean is persistent, enabling entity beans to survive server crashes (this is because when the server comes back online, it can reconstruct the bean from the underlying data.) An entity bean might represent an underlying database row, or a single SELECT result row, in relational terms. An entity bean may represent a single object, with its associated attributes and relationships, in an object-oriented database (OODB). (For example, an entity bean might be an Employee object for a particular employee in a company's Human Resources database.)

EJB objects are created on the server (we'll see how momentarily); Enterprise JavaBeans clients manipulate them as if they were local objects. This makes the development of EJB clients almost as easy as writing a client that runs locally. The developer has the task of creating, using, and destroying objects. However, these objects have counterparts executing on a server that do the actual work. Entity beans represent and manipulate persistent application domain data, while session beans manage information relating to a conversation between the client and the server. One way to conceptualize this is that entity beans replace the various sorts of queries used in a traditional two or three-tiered system; session beans cover everything else.

Every EJB includes a unique identifier, which forms the identity of the information for entity beans. For example, an Employee object might be uniquely identified by an EmployeeIDNumber. The concept of a primary key in a relational database system is analogous to this scenario. A session bean's unique identifier is whatever may distinguish it from other beans of its type. It may be the port number and host name of a remote connection, or simply a randomly generated key that the client uses to uniquely identify a given bean.

As you can see, there's more than one way to provide a unique identifier to a bean. The method is almost always determined by the developer based on what's best for the situation.

Creating Server-Side Beans: The Home Interface

A client program contacts a server and requests that the server create an Enterprise JavaBean to do data processing on its behalf. The server then creates the server-side object (the EJB component instance) in response, returning a proxy object (the EJB object) whose interface is the same as the EJB components and whose implementation performs remote method invocations on the client's behalf. Then the client uses the EJB object as if it were a local object, oblivious to the fact that all the work is actually being done by a remote object.

How are objects on a server created by a client program? The EJB container is responsible for the operations involving the lifecycle of server-side beans. The container is actually contacted by the client program, which requests that a particular type of object be created. The container responds with an EJB object that can be used to manipulate the new EJB component.

Every EJB component class includes a home interface, which defines the methods for creating, initializing, destroying, and (in the case of entity beans) finding EJB instances on the server. The home interface serves as a contract between an EJB component class and its container, which defines construction, destruction, and lookup of EJB instances.

An EJB home interface extends the interface `javax.ejb.EJBHome`, which defines base-level functionality for a home interface. In this interface, all methods must be Java RMI-compatible. This means that every method must be usable by the `java.rmi` package. (An in-depth discussion of "RMI-compatible" is beyond the scope of this chapter.) The EJB home interface also defines one or more `create()` methods, whose signatures are distinct and whose names are all created. The remote interface for the EJB is the return value of these object create methods. The remote interface consists of the business methods the EJB provides, as previously stated. (We'll look at the remote interface shortly.)

The Java Naming and Directory Interface (JNDI)—see Chapter 13, "Java Naming and Directory Interface (JNDI)"—is used to locate the home interface for the desirable class of bean when a client wants to create a server-side bean. As a standard extension to the Java core, the JNDI provides a global service to any Java environment. This allows Java programs to locate and use resources by name, to find out information about those resources, and to traverse structures of resources. The use of JNDI by EJB is an indication that EJB is meeting its goal of compatibility with other Java APIs. For the details of how to use JNDI to locate a home interface, see Chapter 13.

23

USING ENTERPRISE
JAVABEANS

Once the client has the home interface for the EJB class it wants to create, it calls one of the `create()` methods on the home interface to create a server-side object. A remote method call is made by the client-side home interface to the EJB container on the server. This then creates the EJB object's methods, which are forwarded to the container. The container typically defers the implementation of the method to the EJB component. However, the container is also responsible for detecting some error conditions, such as nonexistence of the EJB component, and throwing appropriate exceptions. Entity beans use additional home interface finder methods to locate individual persistent JavaBeans. This is done on the basis of the bean's primary key. For example, the home interface might be used to create an instance of a `ProductionFacility` object, then the `ProductionFacilityCode` number could be given to the finder method to locate the object representing a specific facility.

A method telling the container to remove a server-side instance of an EJB component is also included in the home interface. The server-side instance is destroyed by this method. Attempting to use the EJB object corresponding to a removed EJB causes an exception to be thrown.

Using Server-Side Beans: The Remote Interface

As soon as the client has an EJB object, it can call that object's methods. These methods are simply implementations of the remote interface of the EJB component class. An EJB remote interface extends the interface `javax.ejb.EJBObject` and can define any method it wishes. However, the argument and return types for each method must be RMI-compatible, and each method must contain `java.rmi.RemoteException` in its throws clause. In addition, each method in an EJB remote interface must correspond exactly (in name, argument number and type, return type, and throws clause) to a matching method in the Enterprise JavaBean component class the interface represents.

Summary

A server component technology's fundamental goal is this: to create a server whose methods, at runtime, are extensible. For example, how can someone purchase an accounting package, drop it into a running server, and use the client software that came with the package to access the server functionality—all without shutting the server down, or even recompiling it?

Enterprise JavaBeans' answer is to create the client in terms of remote interfaces. These remote interfaces are implemented on the client as remote method invocations and the exact same interface is implemented as domain functionality on the server side. JNDI is used by the EJB server to publish these services and their availability. The client uses JNDI to find the home interface of a new class by name, and then uses the home interface to create objects with the remote interface that provides the service. The late binding between available interfaces on a server and the interface names is what makes an EJB server runtime-extensible.

The surface of this technology is barely scratched by this introduction to Enterprise JavaBeans. Issues such as scalability, replication, distributed processing, deployment, security, or transactions are not even addressed. These topics will have to be left for another day. Now that you have a basic understanding of the Enterprise JavaBeans framework, you're ready to begin exploring how to create EJB applications in Java code.

For years, Java developers have had to choose between two distributed object technologies—Java's Remote Method Invocation (RMI) and CORBA. RMI's simplicity has made it a popular choice. Unlike CORBA, it doesn't require that you learn a new interface definition language. However, RMI lacks the portability and power of CORBA. The first draft of Enterprise JavaBeans (EJB) promised to unify the easy programmability of Java RMI with the cross-language support of CORBA. It promised to set standards for server-side programming using Java. The new version of EJB has delivered on that promise.

EJB differs from an RMI service. To develop an RMI/CORBA service, you write an interface that lists the services provided. In client/server programs, you include some API-specific calls. As a result, these RMI services will not run in a CORBA environment, and vice versa. In addition, these services have to independently handle database connections, transactions, and so on.

In the EJB environment, the container plays an important role. The client makes a call to the container to get an instance of `EJBHome`. Then it constructs the `EJBObject` by calling the `create()` method on `EJBHome`. `EJBObject` sits between the client and the EJB components, and it implements middleware interfaces. (In the Java environment the `EJBObject` implements RMI interfaces, and in the CORBA environment, it implements CORBA interfaces.)

23

USING ENTERPRISE JAVABEANS

Deploying Beans to the Enterprise

PART
VII

IN THIS PART

Introspection

24

CHAPTER

JavaBeans introspection is when a bean reflects on its own internal state or the internal state of other beans. The analogy with your own kind of introspection, when you examine your own internal state or feelings, is clearly made by the designers of JavaBeans introspection. The classes and methods that make introspection on a bean possible are implemented in the Reflection Application Programming Interface (Reflection API).

Beans presumably don't have emotions, but they can reflect on their internal states; the constructors, methods, and data fields (variables) that they implement, how they are implemented, and what, if anything is currently assigned to them. Introspection is a critical part of the JavaBeans specification. Tools, and sometimes beans or other applications, must be able to dynamically analyze a bean's class to build a picture of the bean's public interface. Finding out the properties, events, and methods supported by a bean, and presenting the current state of its properties, is critical for the ability to treat beans as independent software components and to use beans in rapid application development environments (RAD). In this chapter, you learn about the Java Reflection API and how it works. Then you learn how to use the `java.beans.Introspector` class, which provides the standard methods for allowing your Java beans to support introspection.

Reflection API

Introspection is possible due to the support of the Reflection API provided in the `java.lang.reflect` package. Your objects can get instances, descriptions, and interfaces of other objects through the Reflection API. You can determine all the methods and variables in an object, and you can determine all the exceptions and events thrown by an object. For reflection to work, all data types must be represented as objects. No problem, because Java is an object-oriented programming language, right? Actually, it is somewhat of a problem, because Java is a hybrid object-oriented programming language.

A Hybrid Object-Oriented Language

Strictly speaking, Java doesn't qualify as a pure object-oriented language because, in addition to objects (reference types), Java supports primitive types. Java is what is known as a hybrid object-oriented language. Java supports the following two language data types:

- Primitive types (`boolean`, `char`, `byte`, `short`, `int`, `long`, `float`, and `double`)
- Reference types (all classes and interfaces)

This hybrid approach might be considered a blemish on the Java language to object-oriented language purists. However, the approach provides the advantage of the superior performance of primitive data types over objects. For instance, if array indexing used integer objects as indices, or if `java.lang.String` objects were made up of character objects, Java would be a much slower and memory resource-hungry language. Whenever possible, Java uses primitive types for time and memory critical processes.

The disadvantage of a hybrid object-oriented language is that the different data types are incompatible. There must be a way to convert data from one type to another. Most of the time a primitive `boolean` data type is all that is needed. However, sometimes Java needs to act on the primitive `boolean` data type as if it were an object, as is the case during reflection or introspection of the object encapsulating the `boolean` data type.

The answer is to provide type wrappers, listed in Table 24.1, which provide class equivalents to primitive types. Each wrapper class provides constructors and methods that transform primitive data types into objects and objects into primitive data types.

TABLE 24.1   Primitive Type Wrappers

Class	*Primitive Type*
java.lang.Boolean	boolean
java.lang.Byte	byte
java.lang.Character	char
java.lang.Double	double
java.lang.Float	float
java.lang.Integer	int
java.lang.Long	long
java.lang.Short	short

Note

There is also a `java.lang.Void` class that is used to act as a placeholder for `void` return types.

24

INTROSPECTION

The `java.lang.Class` Object

Each object running in a Java Virtual Machine (JVM) has an associated `java.lang.Class` super object. The `java.lang.Class` object encapsulates all the information about an instantiated class or interface and gives you the ability to locate and reflect into inner classes, which are classes contained within another class.

> **Note**
>
> Java Reflection must be able to represent the primitive type values as objects so that it can retrieve its associated java.lang.Class object. The classes discussed in the last section and listed in Table 24.1 make this possible.

Getting `java.lang.Class` Objects

There are many ways to retrieve java.lang.Class objects. These include using the following:

- The java.lang.Object class's getClass() method
- The java.lang.Class class's getSuperClass() and forName() methods
- Primitive type constants
- Class literals

The way you retrieve a java.lang.Class object in any particular piece of code depends on factors, such as if it will be retrieved from a primitive data type. The following sections present the different ways to retrieve a java.lang.Class object, and when you should use them.

Using the `java.lang.Object` Class's `getClass()` Method

Since the java.lang.Object class is the base class for all Java classes, you can use the java.lang.Object class's getClass() method to get the java.lang.Class object associated with any Java object. The following example uses the getClass() method to get the java.lang.Class object associated with the object assigned to the myButton variable.

```
Class class = myButton.getClass();
```

The object assigned to the myButton variable could be any kind of button, including a button instantiated from the java.awt.Button or javax.swing.JButton classes. The call to the getClass() method returns a java.lang.Class object encapsulating the information that tells you exactly from which class it is instantiated.

Using the `java.lang.Class` Class's `getSuperClass()` and `forName()` Methods

Suppose that you want to know if the java.lang.Class object associated with the object assigned to the myButton variable, used as an example in the previous section, is instantiated from the `java.awt.Button` or `javax.swing.JButton` class. And suppose that you called the `getClass()` method that the object inherited from the `java.lang.Object` class and the returned `java.lang.Class` object tells you that the object assigned to the `myButton` variable is instantiated from the `mypackage.MySpecialButton` class. You still don't know from which button class this class is extended.

Use the `java.lang.Class` class's `getSuperClass()` method to find out the class from which the `mypackage.MySpecialButton` class is extended. Once you get the `java.lang.Class` object, as in the example in the previous section, you call the `getSuperClass()` method on that object, as shown in the following example:

```
Class superclass = class.getSuperClass();
```

The `java.lang.Class` object returned and assigned to the `superclass` variable encapsulates the name and other information about the superclass of the object assigned to the `myButton` variable in the previous section.

The `java.lang.Class` class includes another method useful for getting the `java.lang.Class` object associated with a particular object, the `forName()` method. The `forName()` method is static, so you can use it without obtaining an instance of the `java.lang.Class` class. For instance, get the `java.lang.Class` object for the `javax.swing.JButton` object using the following expression:

```
Class.forName("javax.swing.JButton")
```

The `forName()` method actually loads and links the class whose class name is passed to it. Use this method for getting `java.lang.Class` objects from classes that aren't yet instantiated.

Prefetching classes before you're ready to instantiate them can reduce wait time. If you load a class before it is instantiated when something else is going on, users won't have to wait because it's already loaded.

One trick many application developers use is to display a splash screen. Users get used to seeing to copyright information and don't think about the fact that stuff is loading in the background. When the preloaded data and classes are called for, they don't have to be loaded and users don't need to wait.

Using Primitive Type Constants

For primitive types, there is another way to get an object's associated `java.lang.Class` object. Each of the primitive type wrapper classes in Table 24.1 provides a public class

24

INTROSPECTION

constant named `TYPE` that represents the `java.lang.Class` object of the particular class. You can represent the `java.lang.Class` object for the `java.lang.Integer` class, for instance, with the following literal:

```
Integer.TYPE
```

The `TYPE` constant is only available for the primitive types.

Using Class Literals

Class literals provide another way to get the `java.lang.Class` object associated with any type value, including primitive types. You form a class literal by appending `.class` to any type name. For instance, you can obtain the `java.lang.Class` object associated with a `java.lang.Integer` object using the following syntax:

```
Integer.class
```

You can also get the `java.lang.Class` object associated with an integer primitive data type (`int`) using the following syntax:

```
int.class
```

You use the same syntax to get the `java.lang.Class` object associated with objects of your own creation. For instance, get the `java.lang.Class` object associated with `mypackage.MyObject` by using the following syntax:

```
MyObject.class
```

The class literal always evaluates to a `java.lang.Class` object.

Implementing Reflection

Reflection is a low-level API and is only recommended for those programmers creating developer tools. Most programmers should use introspection through the `java.beans.Introspector` class that you learn about in the "Introspection" section later this chapter. Nevertheless, it is instructive to see how JavaBeans introspection works through reflection. In this section, you implement a bean, the `Reflective` bean, that uses the Reflection API to expose the properties of other beans.

Reflective Bean

You type the complete name of a Java bean into the `Reflective` bean's text field and the `Reflective` bean displays the reflected bean's properties in a list. You can click an item in the list and its value is displayed. The `Reflective` bean is shown in Figure 24.1 displaying information about the `javax.swing.JButton` class.

FIGURE 24.1

The Reflective
*bean is displayed
in the BeanBox.*

The Reflective bean is composed of one class: the sams.introspect.Reflective class
in the Reflective.java file. In the following sections you go through the source code
for the Reflective bean, which is shown in Listing 24.1.

Creating the Interface

The Reflective bean contains three controls and is extended from the java.awt.Panel
class. The first statement in the sams.introspect.Reflective class constructor, shown
next, sets up the Reflective bean's layout manager.

```
setLayout( new BorderLayout( ) );
```

The java.awt.Panel class inherits the setLayout() method from the
java.awt.Container class. The BorderLayout object created from the
java.awt.BorderLayout class arranges and resizes the components it contains so that
they fit into five regions: NORTH, SOUTH, EAST, WEST, and CENTER. When you add the three
other controls to the Reflective bean, two text fields and a list control, you specify the
region to which you want the control added.

The three controls that you add to the Reflective bean interface are created and
assigned to sams.introspect.Reflective class variables. The following are the variable
declarations:

```
private TextField className = new TextField( );
private List propertyList = new List( );
private TextField propertyValue = new TextField( );
```

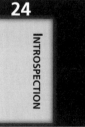

24

INTROSPECTION

A `TextField` object is created and assigned to the `className` variable. You type the name of the bean encapsulating the properties that you want to expose into this text field. A `List` object, which displays the reflected bean's properties, is created and assigned to the `propertyList` variable. A `TextField` object that displays the value of the property that you click in the property list is assigned to the `propertyValue` variable.

The `sams.introspect.Reflective` class constructor sets the default size of these three controls through the following statements:

```
className.setSize( 130, 40 );
propertyList.setSize( 130, 600 );
propertyValue.setSize( 130, 40 );
```

You want the name of a bean processed after you're finished typing it into the class name text field. You can set this up by requiring the user to press the Enter key when the name is entered. `TextField` objects generate an `ActionEvent` object when the Enter key is pressed. Add an action listener to the classname text field with the following statement, so that processing can be carried out when an Enter key is pressed while the class name text field has the focus.

```
className.addActionListener( this );
```

This statement is added to the `sams.introspect.Reflective` class constructor. The `Reflective` object is passed as the action listener. This is why the `sams.introspect.Reflective` class implements the `java.awt.event.ActionListener` interface, and why you must add the `actionPerformed()` method to the class. The `actionPerformed()` method is called when the action event listener receives an `ActionEvent` object.

> **Note**
>
> Recall that the `actionPerformed()` method is declared as an abstract method in the `java.awt.event.ActionListener` interface. Learn more about the Java Event Model in Chapter 6, "Event Model."

The classname text field is added to the `North` area of the `Reflective` bean interface through the following statement added to the `sams.introspect.Reflective` class constructor that calls the `add()` method.

```
add( className, BorderLayout.NORTH );
```

The `Reflective` bean's property list control displays the bean's properties. You can display the value of any property that you click in the bean's property value text field. Because the property value text field can only display one value at a time, you need to set the property list control so that users can select only one item at a time. You can do this by adding the following statement to the `sams.introspect.Reflective` class constructor:

```
propertyList.setMultipleMode( false );
```

Pass `false` to the `java.awt.List` class `setMultipleMode()` method to set the control to so that only single selections are allowed.

Making a selection in the property list won't cause anything to happen in the `Reflective` bean until you add an item event listener to listen for selections made in the `List` object. Add an item listener to the property list by including the following statement in the `sams.introspect.Reflective` class constructor:

```
propertyList.addItemListener( this );
```

This statement is added to the `sams.introspect.Reflective` class constructor. The Reflective object is passed as the action listener. This is why the `sams.introspect.Reflective` class implements the `java.awt.event. ItemListener` interface, and why you must add the `itemStateChanged()` method to the class. The `itemStateChanged()` method is called when the item event listener receives an `ItemEvent` object.

> **Note**
>
> The `itemStateChanged()` method is declared as an abstract method in the `java.awt.event.ItemListener` interface. Learn more about the Java Event Model in Chapter 6.

The property list control is added to the central area of the `Reflective` bean interface through the following statement added to the `sams.introspect.Reflective` class constructor:

```
add( propertyList, BorderLayout.CENTER );
```

The `Reflective` bean interface includes a property value text field that displays the value of the currently selected property in the property list control. The property value text

24

INTROSPECTION

field is not editable. The following statement added to the `sams.introspect.Reflective` class constructor sets the property value text field so that it's not editable:

```
propertyValue.setEditable( false );
```

The property value control is added to the southern area of the `Reflective` bean interface through the following statement added to the `sams.introspect.Reflective` class constructor:

```
add( propertyValue, BorderLayout.SOUTH );
```

Exposing Properties

Reflective bean's `findProperties()` method carries out the work of exposing a bean's properties. After the name of the bean that you want investigated is entered into the classname text field and you've pressed the Enter key, the `actionPerformed()` method is called. A reference to the instantiated bean that you want to investigate is passed to the `theObject` parameter of the `actionPerformed()` method.

The bean's associated `Class` object is retrieved in the `findProperties()` method in the following the statement by calling the `getClass()` method inherited from the `java.lang.Object` class:

```
target = theObject.getClass( );
```

With the bean's associated `Class` object assigned to the target variable, you can use the various methods provided by the `java.lang.Class` class that you learned about in earlier sections of this chapter to expose the bean's internal information. There are no methods to directly retrieve the properties encapsulated by a bean, so the `findProperties()` method retrieves the bean's properties indirectly by getting the bean's getter and setter methods using the `java.lang.Class` class's `getMethods()` method. The following statement retrieves the bean's methods:

```
Method[] publicMethods = target.getMethods( );
```

An array of methods encapsulated by the investigated bean is assigned to the `publicMethods` variable. The rest of the logic in the `findProperties()` method, which is almost all inside a `for` loop, extracts the property names from the retrieved getter and setter methods. The first part of the `if...else if...else` statement in the `for` loop, shown next, checks if the current method in the array is a setter method.

```
if ( methodName.startsWith( "set" ) ) {
  propertyName = Character.toLowerCase( methodName.charAt( 3 ) ) +
methodName.substring( 4 );
  writeProperties.put( propertyName, methodName );
  if ( readProperties.get( propertyName ) != null )
    continue;
}
```

If the method is a setter method, the property name is extracted from the method name and assigned to the `propertyName` variable. Recall that the JavaBeans design patterns specify that all setter methods are named after the property they set with `set` added as a prefix.

Properties that have associated setter methods are writable, so the next statement adds the property name and method name to the write properties array assigned to the `writeProperties` variable.

Finally, you check if the same property has already been extracted from a getter method and added to the read properties array assigned to the `readProperties` variable. If it has, the property has already been added to the properties array assigned to the properties variable through the following statement, which is after the `if...else if...else` statement.

```
properties.addElement( propertyName );
```

You don't want to add the property to the list more than once, so the `continue` keyword is invoked and the program continues the `for` loop.

The second part of the `if...else if...else` statement, the `else...if` part, is nearly identical to the first, except that it checks to see if the current method in the array is a getter method. This part of the statement is shown in the following:

```
else if ( methodName.startsWith( "get" ) ) {
  propertyName = Character.toLowerCase( methodName.charAt( 3 ) ) +
methodName.substring( 4 );
  readProperties.put( propertyName, methodName );
  if ( writeProperties.get( propertyName ) != null )
    continue;
}
```

The third part of the `if...else if...else` statement, the `else` part, simply invokes the `continue` keyword when the `current` method is neither a setter nor a getter method. This is important so that the statement that adds a property name to the properties array isn't executed. Once the entire array of methods has been sifted through, a vector of property names is passed back to the calling code.

24

INTROSPECTION

LISTING 24.1 Source Code for `Reflective.java`

```
package sams.introspect;

import java.awt.BorderLayout;
import java.awt.List;
import java.awt.Panel;
import java.awt.TextField;
```

continues

LISTING 24.1   continued

```java
import java.awt.event.ActionEvent;
import java.awt.event.ActionListener;
import java.awt.event.ItemEvent;
import java.awt.event.ItemListener;
import java.beans.Beans;
import java.io.IOException;
import java.lang.reflect.InvocationTargetException;
import java.lang.reflect.Method;
import java.util.Enumeration;
import java.util.Hashtable;
import java.util.Vector;

public class Reflective extends Panel implements ActionListener, ItemListener {
  private Vector properties = null;
  private List propertyList = new List( );
  private TextField propertyValue = new TextField( );
  private TextField className = new TextField( );
  private Class target = null;
  private Hashtable readProperties = new Hashtable( );
  private Hashtable writeProperties = new Hashtable( );
  private Object bean = null;

  public Reflective( ) {
    setLayout( new BorderLayout( ) );
    className.setSize( 130, 40 );
    propertyList.setSize( 130, 600 );
    propertyList.setMultipleMode( false );
    propertyValue.setSize( 130, 40 );
    propertyValue.setEditable( false );
    className.addActionListener( this );
    propertyList.addItemListener( this );
    add( className, BorderLayout.NORTH );
    add( propertyList, BorderLayout.CENTER );
    add( propertyValue, BorderLayout.SOUTH );
  }

  private Vector findProperties( Object theObject ) {
    Vector properties = new Vector( );
    String methodName = null;
    String propertyName = null;
    target = theObject.getClass( );
    Method[] publicMethods = target.getMethods( );
    for ( int i = 0; i < publicMethods.length; i++ ) {
      methodName = publicMethods[i].getName( );
      if ( methodName.startsWith( "set" ) ) {
        propertyName =
          Character.toLowerCase( methodName.charAt( 3 ) ) +
            methodName.substring( 4 );
```

```
          writeProperties.put( propertyName, methodName );
          if ( readProperties.get( propertyName ) != null )
            continue;
      }
      else if ( methodName.startsWith( "get" ) ) {
        propertyName =
            Character.toLowerCase( methodName.charAt( 3 ) ) +
                methodName.substring( 4 );
        readProperties.put( propertyName, methodName );
        if ( writeProperties.get( propertyName ) != null )
          continue;
      }
      else
        continue;
      properties.addElement( propertyName );
    }
    return properties;
}

private void buildList( Vector listItems ) {
    propertyList.removeAll( );
    Enumeration vectorIterator = listItems.elements( );
    while ( vectorIterator.hasMoreElements( ) ) {
      String item = ( String ) vectorIterator.nextElement( );
      propertyList.add( item );
    }
}

public void actionPerformed( ActionEvent actionEvent ) {
    String targetName = className.getText( );
    try {
      bean = Beans.instantiate( null, targetName );
    }
    catch ( ClassNotFoundException noBean ) {
      System.out.println( "Bean instantiation error: " + noBean );
      bean = null;
    }
    catch ( IOException ioError ) {
      System.out.println( "Bean instantiation I/O error: " + ioError );
      bean = null;
    }
    if ( bean != null ) {
      properties = findProperties( bean );
      buildList( properties );
    }
    else
      propertyList.removeAll( );
```

24

INTROSPECTION

continues

LISTING 24.1 continued

```java
  }

  public void itemStateChanged( ItemEvent itemEvent ) {
    String propertyValueText = null;
    String methodName = null;
    Method getter = null;
    Object value = "! ERROR !";
    Class[] argsList = {};
    String property = ( ( List ) ( itemEvent.getSource( ) ) ).getSelectedItem(
);
    if ( readProperties.get( property ) == null )
      propertyValueText = "not a read property";
    else {
      methodName = ( String ) ( readProperties.get( property ) );
      try {
        getter = target.getMethod( methodName, argsList );
      }
      catch ( NoSuchMethodException ouch ) {
        System.out.println( "" );
        System.out.println( "We don't support indexed getters" + ouch );
      }
      System.out.println(
          "Invoking '" + methodName + "()' to obtain property value" );
      try {
        value = getter.invoke( bean, argsList );
      }
      catch ( IllegalArgumentException badArgs ) {
        System.out.println( badArgs );
        System.exit( 10 );
      }
      catch ( IllegalAccessException noAccess ) {
        System.out.println( noAccess );
        System.exit( 10 );
      }
      catch ( InvocationTargetException wrongTarget ) {
        System.out.println( wrongTarget );
        System.exit( 10 );
      }
      if ( value == null )
        value = "null";
      propertyValueText = value.toString( );
    }
    propertyValue.setText( propertyValueText );
  }
}
```

The `reflective.man` Manifest File

Package the `Reflective` bean into the `reflective.jar` file by creating the manifest file shown in Listing 24.2 and then by typing the following command at a command prompt in your root class directory:

```
jar -cmf reflective.man reflective.jar sams\introspect
```

LISTING 24.2 Source Code for `reflective.man`

```
Name: sams/introspect/Reflective.class
Java-Bean: True
```

Introspection

Introspection is central to the JavaBeans software component specification since it makes rapid application development (RAD) possible using standard software components. It is imperative that introspection is carried out the same way by all development environments and other JavaBeans containers. For this reason, all applications that use introspection should use the `java.beans.Introspector` class.

The `java.beans.Introspector` Class

The `java.beans.Introspector` class sets the JavaBeans introspection standard. Its main function is to return a `BeanInfo` object encapsulating the information for the bean in which you're interested. Use one of the three `getBeanInfo()` methods for this purpose. The following are the signatures of these three methods:

```
getBeanInfo( Class beanClass )
getBeanInfo( Class beanClass, Class stopClass )
getBeanInfo(Class beanClass, int flags )
```

24

INTROSPECTION

Note

All of the `java.beans.Introspector` class methods are declared with the `static` keyword, so you never need to create `Introspector` objects.

The first of the three `getBeanInfo()` methods has one parameter that you pass the `Class` object of the bean that you want to introspect. The returned `BeanInfo` object encapsulates all of the introspected bean's properties, exposed methods, and events, including all of the properties, exposed methods, and events inherited from classes that the bean extends.

The second of the three getBeanInfo() methods has two parameters. Pass the first parameter, beanClass, the Class object associated with the bean that you want to introspect. Pass the second parameter, stopClass, the Class object of the base class at which you want to stop the introspection. The returned BeanInfo object encapsulates the properties, exposed methods, and events found in the classes that make up the introspected bean up to the stop class. The properties, exposed methods, and events of the stop class itself, and classes above the stop class in the bean's member class hierarchy, are not included in the BeanInfo object returned by the getBeanInfo() method.

The third and final getBeanInfo() method has two parameters. Pass the first parameter, beanClass, the Class object associated with the bean that you want to introspect. Pass the second parameter, flags, the flags that control how introspection is carried out. There are three valid flags that you can use, which are defined as java.beans.Introspector class constants (see Table 24.2). The properties, exposed methods, and events encapsulated in the BeanInfo object returned by the getBeanInfo() method depend on the flag passed to the flags parameter.

TABLE 24.2   Flags Defined as java.beans.Introspector Class Constants

Class Constant	*Description*
IGNORE_ALL_BEANINFO	Ignore all bean information associated with the specified bean class and all of its parent classes.
IGNORE_IMMEDIATE_BEANINFO	Ignore all bean information associated with the specified bean class.
USE_ALL_BEANINFO	Expose all bean information associated with the specified bean class and all of its parent classes.

Implementing Introspection

Introspection using the java.beans.Introspector class is straightforward. Get a BeanInfo object encapsulating a bean's internal information by using one of the three java.beans.Introspector class getBeanInfo() methods described in the previous section, and then use methods found in the java.beans.BeanInfo interface to get the bean's properties, exposed methods, and events. In this section, you implement the Introspection bean, which uses java.beans.Introspector class's getBeanInfo() methods to expose properties, methods, and events of other beans.

Introspection **Bean**

Expose a bean's properties, methods, and events by typing its complete name into the `Introspection` bean's text field. The introspected bean's information is displayed in a text area displayed by the `Introspection` bean. Check the Bean Only check box if you want to display only the bean's immediate information, or make sure that the check box is cleared if you want all of its information displayed, including all of the properties, methods, and events that it inherits from its parent classes. The `Introspection` bean displaying information about the `javax.swing.JButton` class with the Bean Only check box checked is shown in Figure 24.2.

FIGURE 24.2

The `Introspection` *bean is displayed in the BeanBox.*

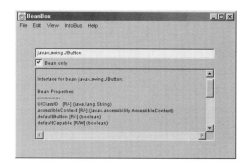

The Introspection bean is composed of one class, the `sams.introspect.Introspection` class in the `Introspection.java` file. The source code is shown in Listing 24.3.

When a user presses the Enter key after entering the name of a bean into the classname text field, the `Introspection` bean's `actionPerformed()` method is executed. The bean is instantiated, and then one of the two `java.beans.Introspector` class's `getBeanInfo()` methods is executed, depending on the state of the `beanOnly` variable. If the Bean Only check box is checked, `true` is assigned to the `beanOnly` variable; otherwise, `false` is assigned.

If `true` is assigned to the `beanOnly` variable, only the properties, methods, and events declared in the introspected bean's class are exposed. The following statement fetches the bean's superclass, the class just above the bean's class in the bean's class hierarchy:

```
Class stopClass = beanClass.getSuperclass( );
```

The `Class` object associated with the bean's superclass is assigned to the `stopClass` variable, which is used by the following statement to keep from introspecting any of the bean's parent classes:

```
beanInformation = Introspector.getBeanInfo( beanClass, stopClass );
```

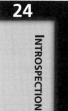

24

INTROSPECTION

Otherwise, if the `beanOnly` variable is assigned `false`, all of the bean's properties, methods, and events are exposed, including those inherited from the bean's parent classes by executing the following statement:

```
beanInformation = Introspector.getBeanInfo( beanClass );
```

The rest of the code in the `Introspection.java` source file utilizes the bean's various properties, methods, and events encapsulated by the `BeanInfo` object returned by the `getBeanInfo()` method and assigned to the `beanInformation` variable. Get the properties, methods, and events by using `java.beans.BeanInfo` class getter methods, and then print them out to the `Introspection` bean's text area.

LISTING 24.3 Source Code for `Introspection.java`

```java
package sams.introspect;

import java.awt.BorderLayout;
import java.awt.Checkbox;
import java.awt.Panel;
import java.awt.TextArea;
import java.awt.TextField;
import java.awt.event.ActionEvent;
import java.awt.event.ActionListener;
import java.awt.event.ItemEvent;
import java.awt.event.ItemListener;
import java.beans.BeanInfo;
import java.beans.Beans;
import java.beans.EventSetDescriptor;
import java.beans.IntrospectionException;
import java.beans.Introspector;
import java.beans.MethodDescriptor;
import java.beans.PropertyDescriptor;
import java.io.IOException;
import java.lang.reflect.Method;

public class Introspection extends Panel implements ActionListener,
        ItemListener {
  private TextField className = new TextField( );
  private TextArea displayInfo = new TextArea( );
  private Checkbox beanOnlyCheckbox = new Checkbox( "Bean only", true );
  private Object bean = null;
  private BeanInfo beanInformation = null;
  private boolean beanOnly = true;

  public Introspection( ) {
    setLayout( new BorderLayout( ) );
    className.setSize( 130, 40 );
    displayInfo.setSize( 130, 600 );
    displayInfo.setEditable( false );
```

```
    className.addActionListener( this );
    beanOnlyCheckbox.addItemListener( this );
    add( className, BorderLayout.NORTH );
    add( beanOnlyCheckbox, BorderLayout.CENTER );
    add( displayInfo, BorderLayout.SOUTH );
  }

  public void actionPerformed( ActionEvent actionEvent ) {
    String beanName = className.getText( );
    try {
      bean = Beans.instantiate( null, beanName );
    }
    catch ( ClassNotFoundException noBean ) {
      System.out.println( "Bean instantiation error: " + noBean );
      bean = null;
    }
    catch ( IOException ioError ) {
      System.out.println( "Bean instantiation I/O error: " + ioError );
      bean = null;
    }
    if ( bean != null ) {
      try {
        Class beanClass = bean.getClass( );
        if ( beanOnly ) {
          Class stopClass = beanClass.getSuperclass( );
          beanInformation = Introspector.getBeanInfo( beanClass, stopClass );
        }
        else
          beanInformation = Introspector.getBeanInfo( beanClass );
      }
      catch ( IntrospectionException obscureBean ) {
        System.out.println( "ERROR: Introspector failed to X-ray your bean." );
        System.exit( 10 );
      }
      displayInfo.append( "\n" );
      displayInfo.append( "\n" );
      displayInfo.append( "Interface for bean " + beanName + ":\n" );
      displayBeanProperties( beanInformation );
      displayBeanFiredEvents( beanInformation );
      displayBeanPublicMethods( beanInformation );
    }
  }

  protected void displayBeanProperties( BeanInfo beanInfo ) {
    PropertyDescriptor[] props = beanInfo.getPropertyDescriptors( );
    displayInfo.append( "\n" );
    displayInfo.append( "Bean Properties: \n" );
    if ( props == null || props.length == 0 ) {
```

24

INTROSPECTION

continues

LISTING 24.3   continued

```
      displayInfo.append( "(none)\n" );
      return;
    }
    displayInfo.append( "----------------\n" );
    for ( int i = 0; i < props.length; i++ ) {
      PropertyDescriptor propertyDescriptor = props[i];
      Method getter = propertyDescriptor.getReadMethod( );
      Method setter = propertyDescriptor.getWriteMethod( );
      String readWrite = ( getter == null ) ? "-" : "R";
      readWrite += "/";
      readWrite += ( setter == null ) ? "-" : "W";
      String propertyName = propertyDescriptor.getName( );
      String propertyType = propertyDescriptor.getPropertyType( ).getName( );
      String columnPadding = columnPadding( 12, propertyName );
      String propertyInfo =
          propertyName + columnPadding + "[" + readWrite + "] " +
              "(" + propertyType + ")\n";
      displayInfo.append( propertyInfo );
    }
  }

  private static String spaces = "                                            \
                       ";

  public String columnPadding( int columnWidth, String string ) {
    int numberOfPaddingSpaces = columnWidth - string.length( );
    if( numberOfPaddingSpaces < 1 )
      numberOfPaddingSpaces = 1;
    return spaces.substring( 0, numberOfPaddingSpaces );
  }

  public void shrinkStringBufferBy( int numChars, StringBuffer sb ) {
    int currentStringLength = sb.length( );
    int newLength = Math.max( 0, currentStringLength - numChars );
    sb.setLength( newLength );
  }

  protected void displayBeanFiredEvents( BeanInfo beanInfo ) {
    EventSetDescriptor[] events = beanInfo.getEventSetDescriptors( );
    displayInfo.append( "\n" );
    displayInfo.append( "Bean fired event sets: \n" );
    if ( events == null || events.length == 0 ) {
      displayInfo.append( "(none)\n" );
      return;
    }
    displayInfo.append( "----------------\n" );
    for ( int i = 0; i < events.length; i++ ) {
```

```
        EventSetDescriptor eventSetDescriptor = events[i];
        Class listenerType = eventSetDescriptor.getListenerType( );
        String eventSetInfo = listenerType.getName( );
        displayInfo.append( "All events for interface: " + eventSetInfo + "\n" );
    }
  }

  protected void displayBeanPublicMethods( BeanInfo beanInfo ) {
    MethodDescriptor[] methods = beanInfo.getMethodDescriptors( );
    displayInfo.append( "\n" );
    displayInfo.append( "Bean public methods: \n" );
    if ( methods == null || methods.length == 0 ) {
      displayInfo.append( "(none)\n" );
      return;
    }
    displayInfo.append( "----------------\n" );
    for ( int i = 0; i < methods.length; i++ ) {
      MethodDescriptor methodDescriptor = methods[i];
      String methodName = methodDescriptor.getName( );
      Method aMethod = methodDescriptor.getMethod( );
      Class[] parameterTypes = aMethod.getParameterTypes( );
      String returnTypeName = aMethod.getReturnType( ).getName( );
      String parameterList = genParameterList( parameterTypes );
      String column1Padding = columnPadding( 19, returnTypeName );
      String column2Padding = columnPadding( 16, methodName );
      String methodInfo =
          returnTypeName + column1Padding + methodName + column2Padding +
          "(" + parameterList + ")" + ";\n";
      displayInfo.append( methodInfo );
    }
  }

  protected String genParameterList( Class[] types ) {
    StringBuffer sb = new StringBuffer( );
    if ( types != null ) {
      for ( int i = 0; i < types.length; i++ ) {
        String typeName = types[i].getName( );
        sb.append( typeName + ", " );
      }
      shrinkStringBufferBy( 2, sb );
    }
    return sb.toString( );
  }

  public void itemStateChanged( ItemEvent itemEvent ) {
    beanOnly = beanOnlyCheckbox.getState( );
  }
}
```

24

INTROSPECTION

The `introspection.man` Manifest File

Package the `Introspection` bean into the `introspection.jar` file by creating the manifest file shown in Listing 24.4, and then by typing the following command at a command prompt in your root class directory:

```
jar –cmf introspection.man introspection.jar sams\introspect
```

LISTING 24.4   Source Code for `introspection.man`.

```
Name: sams/introspect/Introspection.class
Java-Bean: True
```

Summary

Introspection, which relies on reflection and the Reflection API, is an essential mechanism that makes JavaBeans possible. Beans are independent software components that rely on their ability to communicate with other beans to get jobs done. In addition, JavaBeans-compatible application builder environments must be able to expose the properties, methods, and events encapsulated by beans to enable rapid application development (RAD). In this chapter, you explored the Java Reflection API and introspection using the `java.beans.Introspector` class. Now that you understand reflection and introspection, you can create bean container classes or JavaBeans development tools.

Customization

25

CHAPTER

All source code for this chapter can be found on the Sams Publishing Website at
`http://www.mcp.com/info/0-672/0-672-31424-x.`

You can provide special tools, such as customized property editors, with your bean so that various visual testing and development environments display them after the introspection of the bean. JavaBeans-compatible application builders (such as Visual Café and JBuilder) perform introspection on your beans and display your bean's properties, events, and public methods according to the rules set down by the JavaBeans design patterns. You can customize your bean to control the information gathered by other software components or applications about the bean through introspection.

In this chapter we're going to talk about customization. First you'll learn about displaying bean icons. Following this, the chapter works through the process of controlling visible properties. The next section covers providing custom text-based property editors. Lastly, the chapter talks about providing a bean customizer, including creating beans that can be customized and then creating the bean's customizer object.

Displaying a Bean Icon

You can add support for displaying tool palette icons to your bean. When you do, application builders can display an icon to represent your bean. The way an icon is displayed, its resolution, or even if an icon is displayed at all, is up to the application builder itself. You can provide the icons for those builders that use them. For example, your bean's icon can show up in the icon palette in Symantec's Visual Café tool or in the BeanBox.

You will now add 16×16 pixel and 32×32 pixel color icon support to the `PictureButton` bean from Chapter 7, "Beans as Graphical User Interface Components," Listing 7.4. The icons are held in the `PictureButtonIcon16.gif` and `PictureButtonIcon32.gif` files provided in the JavaBeans Unleashed section of the `www.mcp.com` Web site and are shown in Figure 25.1.

FIGURE 25.1

The bean informa-
tion icons for the
`PictureButton`
bean.

Add graphic icon support to a bean through an instance of the `java.beans.SimpleBeanInfo` class, which is a special class that implements the `java.beans.BeanInfo` interface. Both the `java.beans.SimpleBeanInfo` class and the `java.beans.BeanInfo` interface are used for providing explicit information about your bean. However, using the `java.beans.SimpleBeanInfo` class is easier than using the `java.beans.BeanInfo` interface, because the class implements all the interface's abstract methods for you so that you only need to override the methods that you want to use.

Extend the `sams.customize.PictureButtonBeanInfo` class from the `java.beans.SimpleBeanInfo` class, and name the source file **PictureButtonBeanInfo.java**, as shown in Listing 25.1.

Override the `java.beans.SimpleBeanInfo` class's `getIcon()` method to provide information on the `PictureButton` bean's icons. The following is the method's signature:

```
public Image getIcon(int iconKind)
```

Application builders and other tools that display bean icons (such as the BeanBox provided with the Bean Development Kit (BDK)) indicate the kind of icon they're looking for by passing the `getIcon()` method an integer constant through the method's `iconKind` parameter. The integer constant can be any one of the following four, which are defined in the `java.beans.BeanInfo` interface:

- `ICON_COLOR_16x16` A 16×16-bit color icon
- `ICON_MONO_16x16` A 16×16-bit monochrome icon
- `ICON_COLOR_32x32` A 32×32-bit color icon
- `ICON_MONO_32x32` A 32×32-bit monochrome icon

Your task in the overridden `getIcon()` method is to test for requests for icon types that you're providing with your bean. If an icon you provide is requested, you load the icon using the `java.beans.SimpleBeanInfo` class's `loadImage()` method, whose signature is shown in the following:

```
public Image loadImage(String resourceName)
```

The `loadImage()` method assumes that the icon file is in the bean's JAR. All you do is pass the icon's filename as a string to the `loadImage()` method's `resourceName` parameter.

The `getIcon()` method, in Listing 25.1, first declares a local variable named `image` that can be assigned an `Image` object. The `image` variable is initially assigned `null`. Then the `iconKind` parameter is tested to see if it requests a 16×16-bit color icon. If it does, the `PictureButtonIcon16.gif` file is loaded using the `loadImage()` method, and the image is assigned to the `image` variable. Otherwise, `iconKind` is tested to see if it requests a 32×32-bit color icon. If yes, the `PictureButtonIcon32.gif` file is loaded using the `loadImage()` method, and the image is assigned to the `image` variable. Finally, the contents of the `image` variable is returned by the `getIcon()` method to the calling object. If none of the icons that you provided were requested, the `null` value is passed. Otherwise, one of the icons is passed as an `Image` object.

25

CUSTOMIZATION

LISTING 25.1   Source Code for `PictureButtonBeanInfo.java`

```java
package sams.customize;

import java.awt.Image;
import java.beans.BeanInfo;
import java.beans.SimpleBeanInfo;

public class PictureButtonBeanInfo extends SimpleBeanInfo {
  public Image getIcon( int iconKind ) {
    Image image = null;
    if( iconKind == BeanInfo.ICON_COLOR_16x16 )
      image = loadImage( "PictureButtonIcon16.gif" );
    else if( iconKind == BeanInfo.ICON_COLOR_32x32 )
      image = loadImage( "PictureButtonIcon32.gif" );
    return image;
  }
}
```

That's all there is to adding icon support to your bean. Compile the
`sams.customize.PictureButtonBeanInfo` class and add it to a JAR file, along with the
`sams.customize.PictureButton` class and all the image files—including the icon image
files. For instance, use the manifest file shown in Listing 25.2 to create a
`picturebutton.jar` file containing five image files: `teddy0.jpg`, `stop.gif`, `go.gif`,
`PictureButtonIcon16.gif`, and `PictureButtonIcon32.gif`. Type the following command at your console or MS-DOS window prompt:

```
jar -cmf picturebutton.man picturebutton.jar sams\customize
```

When you add the JAR file to your BeanBox, you should see the 16×16-bit color icon
displayed to the left of `PictureButton` bean's name in the ToolBox window like, as
shown in Figure 25.2.

LISTING 25.2   Source Code for `picturebutton.man`

```
Name: sams/customize/PictureButton.class
Java-Bean: True

Name: sams/customize/PictureButtonBeanInfo.class
Java-Bean: False

Name: sams/customize/teddy0.jpg
Java-Bean: False

Name: sams/customize/stop.gif
Java-Bean: False

Name: sams/customize/go.gif
```

```
Java-Bean: False

Name: sams/customize/PictureButtonIcon16.gif
Java-Bean: False

Name: sams/customize/PictureButtonIcon32.gif
Java-Bean: False
```

FIGURE 25.2

The BeanBox displays 16×16-bit color icons.

You can add icon support to any of your beans by using these same methods. Just keep a couple of things in mind. Only GIF files are supported for icons, and it's recommended that you support the 16×16-bit color icon format if you support only one icon type. It's also recommended that you use icons with transparent backgrounds. The preceding icons don't have transparent backgrounds, but you can easily convert them so they do in many of the tools that manipulate GIF files. Usually you pick a single color, like gray, that will be transparent. Then, when the icon is displayed, the existing background color is rendered rather than the background color of the icon itself.

Controlling Visible Properties

The next step in making your `PictureButton` bean polished and professional for use in rapid application development (RAD) is to hide properties inherited from parent classes that don't make sense in your bean. Without any modifications, the Properties window for the `PictureButton` bean displays six properties, as shown in Figure 25.3.

25

CUSTOMIZATION

FIGURE 25.3

The
`PictureButton`
*bean displays six
properties in
BeanBox's
Properties win-
dow, including
four properties
inherited from the*
`Canvas` *class.*

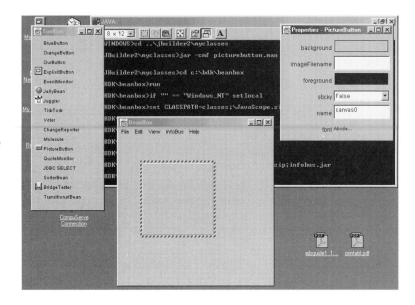

The `PictureButton` bean inherited the font property, but you haven't provided any provision for displaying text. Therefore, it doesn't make any sense to provide a font property. The `PictureButton` bean has also inherited foreground, background, and name properties. Hide all of them, except the name property and the two properties—`imageFilename` and `sticky`—that you added yourself to the `sams.customize.PictureButton` class.

Use the `java.beans.SimpleBeanInfo` class again to control the properties that are visible and those that aren't. Add a new overridden method, the `getPropertyDescriptors()` method, to the `sams.customize.PictureButtonBeanInfo` class you extended from the `java.beans.SimpleBeanInfo` class in the last section. The modified `sams.customize.PictureButtonBeanInfo` class is shown in Listing 25.3.

Override automatic analysis of your bean's properties by implementing the `java.beans.SimpleBeanInfo` class's `getPropertyDescriptor()` method. The following is the method's signature:

```
public PropertyDescriptor[] getPropertyDescriptors()
```

When you override property introspection, you must create `PropertyDescriptor` objects from the `java.beans.PropertyDescriptor` class for every property that the bean has. The following is the signature of the `java.beans.PropertyDescriptor` class constructor:

```
public PropertyDescriptor(String propertyName, Class beanClass)
    throws IntrospectionException
```

You pass the property's name to the `propertyName` parameter as a `String` object, and you pass the name of the bean's class file to the `beanClass` parameter.

Explicitly set all the properties that you want hidden after you create `PropertyDescriptor` objects for them. You use the `setHidden()` method inherited by the `java.beans.PropertyDescriptor` class from the `java.beans.FeatureDescriptor` class to hide a property. The following is the `setHidden()` method signature:

```
public void setHidden(boolean hidden)
```

Pass `true` to its `hidden` Boolean parameter, and the `setHidden()` method hides the property encapsulated by the `PropertyDescriptor` object. The following three statements reproduced from the `sams.customize.PictureButtonBeanInfo` class's `getPropertyDescriptors()` method hides `PictureButton` bean's foreground, background, and font properties.

```
foreground.setHidden( true );
background.setHidden( true );
font.setHidden( true );
```

Finally, all six `PropertyDescriptor` objects are added to a `PropertyDescriptor` array named `pd` and returned or passed to the calling object. If `null` is returned for some reason, automatic introspection of the bean's properties kicks in.

LISTING 25.3   Source Code for `PictureButtonBeanInfo.java` (Modified)

```java
package sams.customize;

import java.awt.Image;
import java.beans.BeanInfo;
import java.beans.IntrospectionException;
import java.beans.PropertyDescriptor;
import java.beans.SimpleBeanInfo;

public class PictureButtonBeanInfo extends SimpleBeanInfo {
  public Image getIcon( int iconKind) {
    Image image = null;
    if( iconKind == BeanInfo.ICON_COLOR_16x16 )
      image = loadImage( "PictureButtonIcon16.gif" );
    else if( iconKind == BeanInfo.ICON_COLOR_32x32 )
      image = loadImage( "PictureButtonIcon16.gif" );
    return image;
  }

  public PropertyDescriptor[] getPropertyDescriptors( ) {
    try {
```

continues

LISTING 25.3   continued

```
PropertyDescriptor
  foreground =
    new PropertyDescriptor( "foreground", PictureButton.class ),
  background =
    new PropertyDescriptor( "background", PictureButton.class ),
  font = new PropertyDescriptor( "font", PictureButton.class ),
  name = new PropertyDescriptor( "name", PictureButton.class ),
  imageFilename  =
    new PropertyDescriptor( "imageFilename", PictureButton.class ),
  sticky = new PropertyDescriptor( "sticky", PictureButton.class );
foreground.setHidden( true );
background.setHidden( true );
font.setHidden( true );
PropertyDescriptor[] pd =
  { foreground, background, font, name, imageFilename, sticky };
return pd;
    }
  catch( IntrospectionException e ) {
    return null;
    }
  }
}
```

Recompile the `sams.customize.PictureButtonBeanInfo` class, and add it to a JAR file as you did in the last section. You should see three properties when you select the `PictureButton` bean in the BeanBox window and see its properties listed in the Properties window, as shown in Figure 25.4.

FIGURE 25.4

The `PictureButton` *bean displays three properties in BeanBox's Properties window after you hide three other properties using the* `sams.customize. PictureButtonBean Info` *class.*

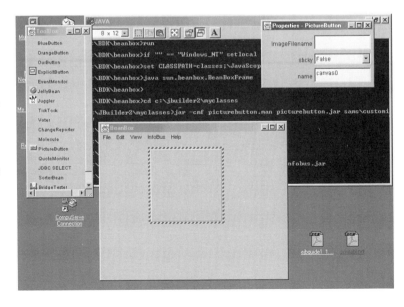

Providing Custom Text-Based Property Editors

Your `PictureButton` bean is looking slick. However, how will your users know what images are available for them to display on the face of the button? The `imageFilename` property editor is a blank text box. It requires that users know the full filename of the image file that they want to load from `PictureButton` bean's JAR file. Your users shouldn't need to work so hard, and you shouldn't need to provide outside documentation so that they can know such things. Instead, add a custom property editor to the `PictureButton` bean that lists the available files. Now all users need to do is select the file they want.

You need to do two things to provide the `PictureButton` bean with a custom property editor. You need to write a class file for the property editor, and you need to add a statement to `sams.customize.PictureButtonBeanInfo` class's `getPropertyDescriptors()` method.

Write a class for the `imageFilename` property editor named `sams.customize.ImageFilenameEditor`, as shown in Listing 25.4. The `sams.customize.ImageFilenameEditor` class extends the `java.beans.PropertyEditorSupport` class. The `java.beans.PropertyEditorSupport` class is a convenience class that implements all the abstract methods in the `java.beans.PropertyEditor` interface, so you only need to override those methods that you want to use. In this case, you want to implement a property editor that lists the three image files available to the image button. Use `java.beans.PropertyEditorSupport` class's `getTags()` method for this purpose. The following is the method's signature:

```
public String[] getTags()
```

Use the `getTags()` method to return an array of strings when an application builder or other visual design tool inquires as to the type of property editor the `imageFilename` property has. These tools display the array of strings in a drop-down list. The `getTags()` method in Listing 25.4 creates a string array of the three image files available to the `PictureButton` bean and then passes the array to the calling object.

LISTING 25.4 Source Code for `ImageFilenameEditor.java`

```
package sams.customize;

import java.beans.PropertyEditorSupport;
```

continues

25

CUSTOMIZATION

LISTING 25.4 continued

```
public class ImageFilenameEditor extends PropertyEditorSupport {
  public String[] getTags( ) {
    String result[] = {"go.gif", "stop.gif", "teddy0.jpg"};
    return result;
  }
}
```

After you write imageFilename property's sams.customize.ImageFilenameEditor class, you need to add the following line of code to the getPropertyDescriptors() method in the sams.customize.PictureButtonBeanInfo class:

```
imageFilename.setPropertyEditorClass( ImageFilenameEditor.class );
```

Place this statement after you declare the imageFilename variable, and assign a PropertyDescriptor object to it. The new statement is highlighted in bold type in Listing 25.5. The statement calls the java.beans.PropertyDescriptor class's setPropertyEditorClass() method. The class passed to this method is set as defining the property editor for the property encapsulated by the PropertyDescriptor object. In this case, the sams.customize.ImageFilenameEditor class you just wrote is set as the property editor for the imageFilename property.

LISTING 25.5 Source Code for PictureButtonBeanInfo.java (Modified Again)

```
package sams.customize;

import java.awt.Image;
import java.beans.BeanInfo;
import java.beans.IntrospectionException;
import java.beans.PropertyDescriptor;
import java.beans.SimpleBeanInfo;

public class PictureButtonBeanInfo extends SimpleBeanInfo {
  public Image getIcon( int iconKind) {
    Image image = null;
    if( iconKind == BeanInfo.ICON_COLOR_16x16 )
      image = loadImage( "PictureButtonIcon16.gif" );
    else if( iconKind == BeanInfo.ICON_COLOR_32x32 )
      image = loadImage( "PictureButtonIcon16.gif" );
    return image;
  }

  public PropertyDescriptor[] getPropertyDescriptors( ) {
    try {
      PropertyDescriptor
        foreground =
```

```
        new PropertyDescriptor( "foreground", PictureButton.class ),
      background =
        new PropertyDescriptor( "background", PictureButton.class ),
      font = new PropertyDescriptor( "font", PictureButton.class ),
      name = new PropertyDescriptor( "name", PictureButton.class ),
      imageFilename  =
        new PropertyDescriptor( "imageFilename", PictureButton.class ),
      sticky = new PropertyDescriptor( "sticky", PictureButton.class );
      imageFilename.setPropertyEditorClass( ImageFilenameEditor.class );
      foreground.setHidden( true );
      background.setHidden( true );
      font.setHidden( true );
      PropertyDescriptor[] pd = { foreground, background, font, name,
➥imageFilename, sticky };
      return pd;
    }
    catch( IntrospectionException e ) {
      return null;
    }
  }
}
```

Compile the `sams.customize.ImageFilenameEditor` and
`sams.customize.PictureButtonBeanInfo` classes, and then package them into a JAR
using the modified `picturebutton.man` manifest file in Listing 25.6.

Place the `PictureButton` bean into the BeanBox window and, while the bean is still
highlighted, check out its `imageFilename` property editor displayed in the Properties window. You should see the three image files listed in a drop-down list like the one shown in
Figure 25.5. Select any filename from the list and it will be loaded and displayed by the
`PictureButton` bean.

LISTING 25.6 Source Code for `picturebutton.man` (Modified)

```
Name: sams/customize/PictureButton.class
Java-Bean: True

Name: sams/customize/PictureButtonBeanInfo.class
Java-Bean: False

Name: sams/customize/ImageFilenameEditor.class
Java-Bean: False

Name: sams/customize/teddy0.jpg
Java-Bean: False
```

25

CUSTOMIZATION

continues

LISTING 25.6   continued

```
Name: sams/customize/stop.gif
Java-Bean: False

Name: sams/customize/go.gif
Java-Bean: False

Name: sams/customize/PictureButtonIcon16.gif
Java-Bean: False

Name: sams/customize/PictureButtonIcon32.gif
Java-Bean: False
```

FIGURE 25.5

The
PictureButton
bean displays the
three image file-
names in a new
imageFilename
property editor.

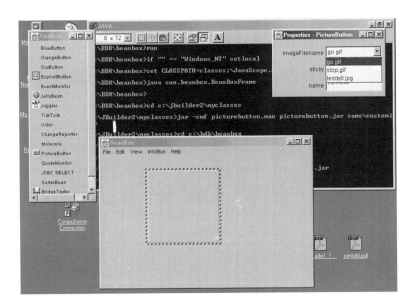

Providing a Bean Customizer

Provide beans with graphical user interfaces for easy configuration by creating an associated object implementing the java.beans.Customizer interface. A bean customizer goes beyond property editors by providing an easy-to-use graphic interface for changing a wide range of bean options. Create your own customizer interfaces, or use some of the standard interfaces provided by the Java platform. In this section, you write a simple bean that supplies a customizer interface for choosing its background colors using the standard javax.swing.JColorChooser class.

Creating a Bean

You can associate a customizer with any Java bean. For this example, create a bean that displays the word "Hello" on a small piece of canvas. The source code for this simple bean, named `Hello`, is shown in Listing 25.7.

LISTING 25.7 Source Code for `Hello.java`

```java
package sams.customize;

import java.awt.Canvas;
import java.awt.Dimension;
import java.awt.Graphics;

public class Hello extends Canvas {
  public Hello( ) {
    setSize( 75, 40 );
  }

  public void paint( Graphics g ) {
    Dimension dimension = getSize( );
    g.drawString( "Hello", dimension.width/3, dimension.height/2 );
  }
}
```

The code for the `Hello` bean is straightforward. If you package the `Hello.class` file into a JAR file right now, the result would look like the screen shown in Figure 25.6.

FIGURE 25.6

The Hello bean displays a simple hello.

Creating the Bean's `Customizer` Object

The `Hello` bean is simple, but you want users to have ultimate control over the background color displayed by the bean. The property editor provided by the BeanBox tool for the background property, shown in Figure 25.7, provides a minimal interface for choosing a color.

Editors vary among application builder tool vendors. In contrast, the Java platform provides a standard color chooser with an advanced interface through the `javax.swing.JColorChooser` class. Displaying a `JColorChooser` object in the customizer interface will give users the fine control that you want over the `Hello` bean's background color.

There is no standard naming convention for customizer objects. However, it's a good idea to name the class after its associated bean class—in this case, the `sams.customize.Hello.java` class—with `Customizer` appended to it, so the customizer class associated with the `Hello` bean should be named `sams.customize.HelloCustomizer.java`. Listing 25.8 shows the source code written to the `HelloCustomizer.java` file.

The `java.beans.Customizer` Interface

All customizer classes must implement the `java.beans.Customizer` interface. This interface defines one abstract method that is required in the customizer class, the `setObject()` method. The `setObject()` method is called by application builder environments and other programs that take advantage of customizer interfaces. The customizer object's associated bean is passed to the `setObject()` method's `bean` parameter. You should always declare a private class variable with the customizer's associated bean class declared as its data type as shown in the following:

```
private Hello theBean = null;
```

In the `setObject()` method, assign the bean passed through the `bean` parameter to the `theBean` variable. The `bean` parameter is defined using the `java.lang.Object` class data type, so you need to perform type casting to assign the reference to the `theBean` variable. Type cast the reference assigned to the bean parameter to the `sams.customize.Help.java` class as shown in the following:

```
theBean = ( Hello ) bean;
```

With these simple statements, the associated bean's public methods are available to the customizer. You'll see how this becomes useful in the next section when you create a `JColorChooser` object with the current background color of the `Hello` bean selected by default.

The `javax.swing.JColorChooser` Class

In this section, you add code so that the `Help` bean's customizer creates a `JColorChooser` object in the `setObject()` method. Declare a private class variable named `colorChooser` with the `java.swing.JColorChooser` class data type, as shown in the following:

```
private JColorChooser colorChooser = null;
```

Next, add the following statement to create a `JColorChooser` object with the current background color of the `Hello` bean selected by default.

```
colorChooser = new JColorChooser( theBean.getBackground( ) );
```

You call the `Hello` bean's `getBackground()` method (a reference to the `Hello` bean is assigned to the `theBean` variable), which returns the bean's current background color and passes it, encapsulated in a `Color` object, to the newly created `JColorChooser` object. The new JColorChooser object is assigned to the `colorChooser` variable.

The `java.beans.PropertyChangeListener` Interface

The `Hello` bean customizer will react to property change events produced by the `JColorChooser` object. Whenever the color property changes, the `Hello` bean's `setBackground()` method will be called to set its background to the new color.

Add the `java.beans.PropertyChangeListener` interface to the interfaces implemented by the `sams.customize.HelloCustomizer` class. You must also add the `propertyChange()` method, shown next, defined as an abstract method in the `java.beans.PropertyChangeListener` interface to the `sams.customize.HelloCustomizer` class.

```
public void propertyChange( PropertyChangeEvent event ) {
    theBean.setBackground( colorChooser.getColor( ) );
  }
```

Whenever the `JColorChooser` object produces a `PropertyChangeEvent` object the `Hello` bean's `setBackground()` method is called. The code gets the currently selected color in the `JColorChooser` object through the object's `getColor()` method. The color, encapsulated in a `Color` object, is passed to the `Hello` bean `setBackground()` method. The result is that the bean's background color is set to the color selected in the `JColorChooser` object.

These mechanisms only work if you register the property change event listener, the `HelloCustomizer` object, with the property change event source, the `JColorChooser` object. Register the `sams.customize.HelloCustomizer` class as a property change listener to the `JColorChooser` object by adding the following statement to the `sams.customize.HelloCustomizer` class's `setObject()` method:

```
colorChooser.addPropertyChangeListener( this );
```

Finally, add the `JColorChooser` object to the `HelloCustomizer` object, so that the customizer displays the color chooser. The `sams.customize.HelloCustomizer` class is extended from the `java.awt.Panel` class. Add the following statement to the `sams. customize.HelloCustomizer` class's `setObject()` method:

```
add( colorChooser );
```

You've completed most of the `Hello` bean example. There is one more step. You must associate a bean's customizer object through a `BeanInfo` object because beans are not automatically associated with their customizer objects. You do this using a `java.beans.BeanInfo` class.

LISTING 25.8   Source Code for `HelloCustomizer.java`

```java
package sams.customize;

import java.awt.Panel;
import java.beans.Customizer;
import java.beans.PropertyChangeEvent;
import java.beans.PropertyChangeListener;
import javax.swing.JColorChooser;

public class HelloCustomizer extends Panel
    implements Customizer, PropertyChangeListener {
  private Hello theBean = null;
  private JColorChooser colorChooser = null;

  public void setObject( Object bean ) {
    theBean = ( Hello ) bean;
    colorChooser = new JColorChooser( theBean.getBackground( ) );
    colorChooser.addPropertyChangeListener( this );
    add( colorChooser );
  }

  public void propertyChange( PropertyChangeEvent event ) {
    theBean.setBackground( colorChooser.getColor( ) );
  }
}
```

Creating the Bean's `BeanInfo` Object

You associate a bean's customizer object through a `BeanInfo` object. Recall that a bean is automatically associated with an object with that bean's name and `BeanInfo` appended to it. For instance, an object named `HelloBeanInfo` is automatically associated with the `Hello` bean and is considered by the Java platform to be the `BeanInfo` object for the `Hello` bean.

Associating a customizer object with a bean is a matter of adding just one method with one statement to a bean's associated bean information class. Override the `getBeanDescriptor()` method in a bean information class extended from the `java.beans.SimpleBeanInfo` class, shown in the `sams.customize.HelloBeanInfo` class in Listing 25.9. Bean environments call the `getBeanDescriptor()` method to check for an associated customizer. Add the following statement to this method to associate a customizer class with the bean:

```java
return new BeanDescriptor( Hello.class, HelloCustomizer.class );
```

The method returns a new `BeanDescriptor` object that is passed the bean class and the customizer class.

LISTING 25.9 Source Code for `HelloBeanInfo.java`

```
package sams.customize;

import java.beans.BeanDescriptor;
import java.beans.SimpleBeanInfo;

public class HelloBeanInfo extends SimpleBeanInfo {
  public BeanDescriptor getBeanDescriptor( ) {
    return new BeanDescriptor( Hello.class, HelloCustomizer.class );
  }
}
```

Packaging and Running the Bean

The `Hello` bean with its customizer is nearly ready to be tested. Package all the bean's classes, the `Hello.class`, `HelloBeanInfo.class`, and `HelloCustomizer.class` files into a JAR file using the `hello.man` manifest file shown in Listing 25.10.

LISTING 25.10 Source Code for `hello.man`

```
Name: sams/customize/Hello.class
Java-Bean: True

Name: sams/customize/HelloBeanInfo.class
Java-Bean: False

Name: sams/customize/HelloCustomizer.class
Java-Bean: False
```

Type the following command from the root class directory in your console or DOS window prompt.

```
jar -cmf hello.man hello.jar sams\customize
```

Place the `hello.jar` file in the jar folder inside the `Bdk` folder, and then run your BeanBox tool. When you place the `Hello` bean in the BeanBox window and the `Hello` bean remains selected, the `customize` command appears on the Edit menu. Select the `customize` command from the BeanBox tool's Edit menu, and the `Hello` bean customizer should appear, as shown in Figure 25.8.

FIGURE 25.8

The BeanBox tool displays Hello *bean's customizer.*

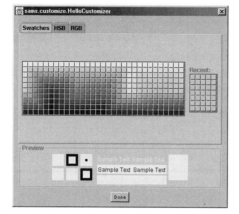

Summary

Application developers who use your beans will usually depend entirely on the graphic representation of your bean presented by an application builder. Therefore, it's usually beneficial to go beyond the default automatic introspection provided for beans and customize the way visual application builder environments present your bean's properties, events, and methods. In this chapter, you learned how to polish up beans and make them ready to use in application builders. You learned how to make beans more professional looking and easier to use by adding graphic icons, controlling the visibility of their properties, and adding custom property editors. You also learned how to add customizers to your beans to make it easy for users to perform detailed configurations of your Java beans.

CHAPTER 26

International Beans

All source code for this chapter can be found on the Sams Publishing Website at
`http://www.mcp.com/info/0-672/0-672-31424-x`.

Introduction

You can create beans that can be used globally by internationalizing your JavaBeans code. Internationalization is the process of isolating all of the language-dependent and customs-dependent code in your bean from the language- and customs-independent code. Customs dependencies include date and number formats. Java provides classes and interfaces to internationalize your beans so they can be used anywhere in the world. In this chapter, you will create a global bean, use Java's `Locale` and `ListResourceBundle` classes, and support the display of different languages.

Creating Global Beans

There are about five billion people on earth, and you want as many of them as possible to use your beans. You can create global beans: beans that display information to users in their preferred language and according to their customs.

Programs are often written with one language and one culture or set of customs in mind. In fact, this is usually done without any planning. Program developers use their own favorite language and adopt their own customs. This was fine when software was distributed locally for the most part, but now software is released and distributed over the Internet and used globally.

The pool of potential users or buyers of your software component or application is expanded through Internet access. However, the Internet's global reach necessarily means that there are users of many different native languages, and these users follow a wide range of different customs. If only your software component or application could adapt to whatever language or custom its user preferred, a lot more people might use it. Java provides the tools so that you can create beans that adapt to preferred languages and customs. They're able to *localize*.

You can create beans that localize to any locale. A *locale* is a geographic, political, or culturally cohesive region that shares the same language and customs. Countries or states do not define locales. Canada is a country that has at least two locales—English Canada and French Canada. The native population in Canada probably adds several other locales to the country. In fact, you'll probably never be able to create a bean that covers all locales, even if they could be clearly defined. For instance, if you were to include Navaho, Cajun, Gaelic-speaking Ireland, and all locales of this size across the world, you'd spend a lifetime.

Choose the locales you support carefully. Support the people that are most likely to use your bean. You can always add support for more locales, so you might start by supporting only North American English, for instance. After the bean is distributed, you might find that a large number of Russians use it. At that point you can add support for the Russian language and customs. In other words, you can localize the bean for Russia. As your bean matures, you might find that you've added support for locales all over the world.

You're able to incrementally add locale support to your beans because they support internationalization or the isolation of language- and customs-dependent code. You can write your beans so that the language- and customs-dependent data are packaged in their own separate objects. The object that's instantiated at any one time depends on the user's locale. Furthermore, you can represent each locale by a `Locale` object.

Localizing Objects

Internationalize your beans by isolating locale-specific code and data.

- Represent a locale using Java's `Locale` class.
- Encapsulate locale-specific data in resource bundles.

Using Java's `Locale` Class

Java's `Locale` class represents a specific geographic, political, or cultural region. Create a `Locale` object for each locale you want represented. `Locale` objects do not encapsulate any data related to the locale represented.

The `Locale` class is part of the `java.util` package. Create a `Locale` object using one of the `Locale` class's two constructors.

```
Locale(String language, String country)
Locale(String language, String country, String variant)
```

Pass a `String` object encapsulating a special code representing the language you want encapsulated in the `Locale` object you're creating to the first parameter of either constructor. You use an international standard code set developed by the International Standards Organization (ISO) named the ISO Language Code. For example, `en` is the ISO Language Code for the English language.

Pass a `String` object encapsulating a special code representing the country you want encapsulated in the `Locale` object you're creating to the second parameter of either constructor. You use the ISO Country Code. For example, `US` is the ISO Country Code for the United States of America.

Java supports a long list of ISO Language Code and Country Code combinations. These are listed in Table 26.1.

The second constructor takes one more parameter in addition to ISO Language and Country Codes. It takes a String object containing a variant code. Java supports just one variant code, shown in parentheses in Table 26.1. The variant code is B for the Bokmal variant, listed in parentheses next to a listing of the Norway country code. The reason the Bokmal variant is needed is that there are two versions of the Norwegian language: Nynorsk and Bokmal. By default Nynorsk is assumed unless this variant indicates the Bokmal variation of the language.

TABLE 26.1   Valid Java Locales

Language Code	Country Code	Language	Country
da	DK	Danish	Denmark
de	AT	German	Austria
de	CH	German	Switzerland
de	DE	German	Germany
el	GR	Greek	Greece
en	CA	English	Canada
en	GB	English	United Kingdom
en	IE	English	Ireland
en	US	English	United States
es	ES	Spanish	Spain
fi	FI	Finish	Finland
fr	BE	French	Belgium
fr	CA	French	Canada

Language Code	Country Code	Language	Country
fr	CH	French	Switzerland
fr	FR	French	France
it	CH	Italian	Switzerland
it	IT	Italian	Italy
ja	JP	Japanese	Japan
ko	KR	Korean	Korea
nl	BE	Dutch	Belgium
nl	NL	Dutch	Netherlands
no	NO	Norwegian (Nynorsk)	Norway
no	NO (B)	Norwegian (Bokmal)	Norway
pt	PT	Portuguese	Portugal
sv	SE	Swedish	Sweden
tr	TR	Turkish	Turkey
zh	CN	Chinese (simplified)	China
zh	TW	Chinese (traditional)	Taiwan

The Locale class provides class constants, listed in Table 26.2, to make it easier to create Locale objects. You don't need to look up the ISO Language and ISO Country Codes. For instance, you can create a Locale object representing the United States using the following line of code.

```
Locale localeUS = new Locale.US;
```

This line of code is equivalent to the following line of code that creates a Locale object using a Locale class constructor.

```
Locale localeUS = new Locale( "en", "US" );
```

There is one other way that your bean can create a Locale object. All of your JavaBeans components that are children of Java's Component class inherit Component class's getLocale() method. The following is this method's signature:

```
public Locale getLocale()
```

The getLocale() method returns the current locale of the component. If the component doesn't have a locale, the locale of the component's parent is returned. You can use this method for setting your bean's locale based on the container application.

TABLE 26.2 Locale Class Constants

Constant	Language Code	Country Code
CANADA	en	CA
CANADA_FRENCH	fr	CA
CHINA	zh	CN
CHINESE	zh	CN
ENGLISH	en	GB
FRANCE	fr	FR
FRENCH	fr	FR
GERMAN	de	DE
GERMANY	de	DE
ITALIAN	it	IT
ITALY	it	IT
JAPAN	ja	JP
JAPANESE	ja	JP
KOREA	ko	KR
KOREAN	ko	KR
PRC	zh	CN
SIMPLIFIED_CHINESE	zh	CN
TAIWAN	zh	TW
TRADITIONAL_CHINESE	zh	TW
UK	en	GB
US	en	US

Using `Locale` Objects

Once a bean creates a `Locale` object, it can do two things with the object:

- Get information about the locale encapsulated in the object.
- Pass the `Locale` object to other objects that perform locale-sensitive operations.

Getting Locale Information

Use the Locale class's many methods to get information on a locale. When you're displaying the information to users, be sure to get the information using one of `Locale` class's several getter methods that return information in human readable form. These

methods take the form `getDisplayXXX()` where *XXX* is the label for the information type, such as `Language` for the name of the language encapsulated by the `Locale` object.

Using Locale-Sensitive Objects

A locale-sensitive object is an instance of a Java class written so that the state of the object depends on the locale of the object. For instance, an object that displays numbers is locale-sensitive if the format of the number displayed depends on the object's locale. You will create a bean later that includes a locale-sensitive object. If your bean doesn't have any locale-sensitive objects, there's no reason for you to provide it locale information.

Bundling Resources

Isolate locale-sensitive data by putting it into resource bundles. All sorts of data can be locale-sensitive including labels, dates, time, numbers, error messages, sounds, and images. Your bean should provide a version of data for each locale that it supports.

Java provides three classes for creating resource bundles: the `ResourceBundle`, `ListResourceBundle`, and `PropertyResourceBundle` classes. All the resource bundle classes are part of the `java.util` package. Use Java's `ResourceBundle` class to encapsulate locale-specific data. The `ListResourceBundle` and `PropertyResourceBundle` classes are convenience subclasses of the `ResourceBundle` class. The `ListResourceBundle` class lets you manage locale-specific resources using a list that's designed for easy use, and the `PropertyResourceBundle` class gives you a convenient way to manage resources that are referenced through property files.

Writing the `GlobalBean` Bean

We will now write an internationalized bean, named `GlobalBean`, shown in Listing 26.6. `GlobalBean` is subclassed from Java's `Panel` class. It displays a list of locales in a `List` object and a greeting in a `Label` object. Its default locale is `English (United States)`. Double-click any of the five locales in the list that `GlobalBean` supports and the greeting for the appropriate locale displays in the `Label` object.

Write the `GlobalBean` class so that it implements the `ActionListener` interface. You register the `GlobalBean` object as an action event listener with the `Label` object so users can select the locale through the list displayed in the `Label` object. You do this in the `GlobalBean` class constructor. All the bean's code is in the class constructor, and the `GlobalBean` class's only method, the `actionPerformed()` method that you must add when you implement the `ActionListener` interface.

Creating Locale Objects

Declare and create Locale and ListResourceBundle objects before you write the class constructor. The GlobalBean bean supports five locales: English (United States), Dutch (Netherlands), French (France), German (Germany), and Italian (Italy). Declare a Locale variable named supportedLocales using the following line of code:

```
private Locale supportedLocales[] = { Locale.US,
                                      new Locale( "nl", "NL" ), // Dutch
                                      Locale.FRENCH,
                                      Locale.GERMAN,
                                      Locale.ITALIAN };
```

The supportedLocales variable holds an array of Locale objects. The variable is declared with empty brackets, which means that the array will be the same length as the number of Locale objects created at the time the variable is declared.

Five Locale objects are created and assigned to the supportedLocales variable. Create all but one Locale object by using one of the Locale constants listed in Table 26.2. There is no constant for creating the Dutch (Netherlands) locale, so you get to try using one of the Locale class constructors to create it yourself. Pass the ISO Language Code for Dutch (nl) and the ISO Country Code for the Netherlands (NL) to the first and second parameters in the Locale class constructor.

> **Note**
>
> You can look up the ISO Language Code for Dutch and the ISO Country Code for the Netherlands in Table 26.1, earlier in this chapter.

Writing the LabelsBundle Classes

The GlobalBean bean resources are encapsulated in five LabelsBundle classes, one for each of the five locales that the bean supports. All five of the classes are identical except for their data, which consists of a single greeting. They're all extended from the ListResourceBundle class. The default class that encapsulates data for the English (United States) locale is named LabelsBundle. Each of the other classes has the same root name with a two letter suffix attached that represents the locale of the data that the class encapsulates (see Table 26.3 earlier this chapter).

Java's ListResourceBundle class declares one abstract method, getContents(), that you must implement. Objects access data encapsulated in objects created from the ListResourceBundle class by calling the getContents() method, which returns a two-dimensional array Object object. This object contains a key and the key's locale data.

Look at the default `LabelsBundle` class code in Listing 26.1. You create a two-dimensional Object, named `contents`. You only want a greeting, therefore there is only one key and one piece of data entered into the array. Give the data a meaningful key that you use to access the same kind of data across classes for different locales. For instance, the key for the greetings data can be named `GreetingsLabel` after the `Label` object that displays the data. The greetings data itself is `Hello` because this class contains the data for the English (United States) locale. The class's `getContents()` method simply returns the contents of the `contents` variable you created.

LISTING 26.1 Source Code for `LabelsBundle.java`

```
package sams.global;

// English

class LabelsBundle extends java.util.ListResourceBundle {
  private static final Object[][] contents = { {"GreetingsLabel", "Hello" } };

  public Object[][] getContents( ) {
    return contents;
  }
}
```

As already mentioned, the only difference between the `LabelsBundle` class and the four other classes is the greetings data. For instance, the `LabelsBundle` class named `LabelsBundle_nl` for the Dutch (Netherlands) locale, shown in Listing 26.2, contains the greeting "Hoe Gaat Het Met Jou?" The greeting for French in Listing 26.3 is "Bonjour." The greeting for German in Listing 26.4 is "Guten Tag." And the greeting for Italian in Listing 26.5 is "Ciao! Come va?"

LISTING 26.2 Source Code for `LabelsBundle_nl.java`

```
package sams.global;

// Dutch

class LabelsBundle_nl extends java.util.ListResourceBundle {
  private static final Object[][] contents =
    { {"GreetingsLabel", "Hoe Gaat Het Met Jou?" } };

  public Object[][] getContents( ) {
    return contents;
  }
}
```

LISTING 26.3 Source Code for `LabelsBundle_fr.java`

```java
package sams.global;

// French

class LabelsBundle_fr extends java.util.ListResourceBundle {
  private static final Object[][] contents = { {"GreetingsLabel", "Bonjour" } };

  public Object[][] getContents( ) {
    return contents;
  }
}
```

LISTING 26.4 Source Code for `LabelsBundle_de.java`

```java
package sams.global;

// German

class LabelsBundle_de extends java.util.ListResourceBundle {
  private static final Object[][] contents =
    { {"GreetingsLabel", "Guten Tag" } };

  public Object[][] getContents( ) {
    return contents;
  }
}
```

LISTING 26.5 Source Code for `LabelsBundle_it.java`

```java
package sams.global;

// Italian

class LabelsBundle_it extends java.util.ListResourceBundle {
  private static final Object[][] contents = { {"GreetingsLabel", "Ciao! Come
va?" } };

  public Object[][] getContents( ) {
    return contents;
  }
}
```

Creating `ListResourceBundle` Objects

Declare and create an array of `ListResourceBundle` objects by writing the following line of code:

```
private ListResourceBundle labels[] = { new LabelsBundle( ),
                                         new LabelsBundle_nl( ),
                                         new LabelsBundle_fr( ),
                                         new LabelsBundle_de( ),
                                         new LabelsBundle_it( ) };
```

The `labels` variable holds an array of `LabelsBundle` objects. The five `LabelsBundle` objects are created and assigned to the `labels` variable. You write the five varieties of `LabelsBundle` classes later in this chapter.

The `LabelsBundle` classes are extended from `ListResourceBundle` class. The default class is named `LabelsBundle`, and it encapsulates the resource string for the English (United States) locale. Each of the other classes uses the `LabelsBundle` classname, but with a two letter suffix that indicates the locale encapsulated by the class. The name of each class and the locale of the data encapsulated by the object created from the class are listed in Table 26.3.

TABLE 26.3   `ListResourceBundle` Class Names and Locale

Class Name	Locale
LabelsBundle	English (United States)
LabelsBundle_nl	Dutch (Netherlands)
LabelsBundle_fr	French (France)
LabelsBundle_de	German (Germany)
LabelsBundle_it	Italian (Italy)

Adding the `GlobalBean` Class Constructor

The `GlobalBean` class constructor creates the `List` and `Label` objects, adds them to the `GlobalBean` panel, and, finally, makes the panel and its contents visible. Create the `List` object for holding the list of supported locales using the following code:

```
localeList = new List( );
```

After you create the `List` object, loop through the `supportedLocales` array and add the supported locale names to the `List` object, as shown in the following:

```
for ( int i = 0; i < supportedLocales.length; i++ ) {
  localeList.add( supportedLocales[i].getDisplayName( ) );
}
```

Use a `for` loop to loop through the array of supported locales. The `supportedLocales.length` statement returns the number of `Locale` objects assigned to the `supportedLocales` array, which provides the number of locales supported by the `GlobalBean` bean. The name of each locale is accessed from each `List` object held in the `localeList` variable by calling the `Locale` class's `getDisplayName()` method. The `getDisplayName()` method passes each locale name, encapsulated in a `String` object, to the `List` class's `add()` method, which adds the locale name to the `List` object held by the `localeList` variable.

The next step is to register an action listener object with the `List` object held by the `localeList` variable. The user selects the locale he or she wants from the locale list presented in the `List` object. To work, the `GlobalBean` bean needs to detect action events created by the `List` object and act on them. You register the `GlobalBean` object with the `List` object using the following code:

```
localeList.addActionListener( this );
```

Finally, add the `List` object assigned to the `localeList` variable to the `GlobalBean` panel with the following statement:

```
add( localeList );
```

Create the `Label` object that displays greetings and assign it to the `greetingLabel` variable with the following statement:

```
greetingsLabel = new Label( );
```

Then add the `Label` object to the `GlobalBean` panel using the `add()` method:

```
add( greetingsLabel );
```

Finally, display the default greeting in the label. Call the `ListResourceBundle` class's `getString()` method on the first `ListResourceBundle` object in the `labels` array. The first object in the array holds the English (United States) resource. You pass the `getString()` method the key to the resource that you want displayed. You will practice using keys to resources later in this chapter when you write the `LabelsBundle` classes. For now, it's enough to know that the `GreetingLabel` key gets the greetings from any one of the `LabelsBundle` classes and returns it as a `String` object. The language of the greetings returned depends on the locale of the `LabelsBundle` class that the `getString()`

method is called on. The greeting is added to the `Label` object assigned to the `greetingsLabel` variable using the `setText()` method, as shown in the following:

```
greetingsLabel.setText( labels[0].getString( "GreetingsLabel" ) );
```

The final statement in the `GlobalBean` class constructor, shown next, makes the panel and its contents visible.

```
setVisible( true );
```

Adding the `actionPerformed()` Method

You must add an `actionPerformed()` method because it's an abstract method defined in the `ActionListener` interface. The `List` object created in the `GlobalBean` class constructor registered the `GlobalBean` object as its action event listener. The `actionPerformed()` method is called and passed an `ActionEvent` object whenever a user double-clicks the left mouse button on a command in the `List` object.

Get the action command encapsulated by the `ActionEvent` object and assign it to the `command` variable, as shown in the first statement in the `actionPerformed()`:

```
String command = e.getActionCommand( );
```

Next, loop through the supported locales using a `for` loop, and check to see if the command held in the `command` variable equals a supported locale using the following code:

```
int selectedLocale = 0;
for ( int i = 0; i < supportedLocales.length; i++ ) {
  if ( command.equals( supportedLocales[i].getDisplayName( ) ) ) {
    selectedLocale = i;
    break;
  }
}
```

If the command equals one of the supported locales, the current index is assigned to the `selectedLocale` local variable, and the `for` loop is exited. Otherwise, the default index of 0 for the English (United State) locale is used. Text appropriate to the current locale is displayed in the greetings label when the `selectedLocale` variable is used as the labels array index, as shown in the following:

```
greetingsLabel.setText( labels[selectedLocale].getString( "GreetingsLabel" ) );
```

Pass the same resource key, `GreetingsLabel`, to the `getString()` method of a `LabelsBundle` object in the `labels` array to get the appropriate greeting.

Your `GlobalBean` class is complete as shown in Listing 26.6. Now you need to write five `LabelsBundle` classes, one for each locale that the `GlobalBean` bean supports.

LISTING 26.6 Source Code for `GlobalBean.java`

```java
package sams.global;

import java.awt.Dimension;
import java.awt.Label;
import java.awt.List;
import java.awt.event.ActionEvent;
import java.util.ListResourceBundle;
import java.util.Locale;

public class GlobalBean extends java.awt.Panel
    implements java.awt.event.ActionListener {
  private Locale supportedLocales[] = { Locale.US,
                                        new Locale( "nl", "NL" ), // Dutch
                                        Locale.FRENCH,
                                        Locale.GERMAN,
                                        Locale.ITALIAN };

  private ListResourceBundle labels[] = { new LabelsBundle( ),
                                          new LabelsBundle_nl( ),
                                          new LabelsBundle_fr( ),
                                          new LabelsBundle_de( ),
                                          new LabelsBundle_it( ) };

  private List localeList = null;
  private Label greetingsLabel = null;

  public GlobalBean( ) {
    localeList = new List( );
    for ( int i = 0; i < supportedLocales.length; i++ ) {
      localeList.add( supportedLocales[i].getDisplayName( ) );
    }
    localeList.addActionListener( this );
    add( localeList );
    greetingsLabel = new Label( );
    add( greetingsLabel );
    greetingsLabel.setText( labels[0].getString( "GreetingsLabel" ) );
    setVisible( true );
  }

  public void actionPerformed( ActionEvent e ) {
    String command = e.getActionCommand( );
    int selectedLocale = 0;
    for ( int i = 0; i < supportedLocales.length; i++ ) {
      if ( command.equals( supportedLocales[i].getDisplayName( ) ) ) {
        selectedLocale = i;
        break;
      }
    }
```

26

```
    greetingsLabel.setText( labels[selectedLocale].getString( "GreetingsLabel" )
);
    }
}
```

Using the `GlobalBean` Bean

Compile your `GlobalBean` class and the five `LabelsBundle` classes, and then package them into a `globalbean.jar` file by using the `globalbean.man` manifest file in Listing 26.7. Run the following command at the DOS or console prompt.

```
jar -cmf globalbean.man globalbean.jar sams
```

LISTING 26.7   Source Code for `globalbean.man`

```
Name: sams/global/GlobalBean.class
Java-Bean: True

Name: sams/global/LabelsBundle.class
Java-Bean: False

Name: sams/global/LabelsBundle_de.class
Java-Bean: False

Name: sams/global/LabelsBundle_fr.class
Java-Bean: False

Name: sams/global/LabelsBundle_it.class
Java-Bean: False

Name: sams/global/LabelsBundle_nl.class
Java-Bean: False
```

Add the `globalbean.jar` file to your BeanBox tool's `jar` folder and start up the BeanBox. Add a `GlobalBean` bean to the BeanBox window. The `GlobalBean` bean displaying its default English (United States) locale method should look like Figure 26.1.

FIGURE 26.1

The default `GlobalBean` *bean locale displays the* `Hello` *greeting.*

Point to any one of the five locales listed in `GlobalBean` bean's list and double-click your left mouse button. The greeting is displayed in the appropriate language for the locale you selected. For instance, if you select the French locale, the bean displays the greeting `Bonjour` seen in Figure 26.2.

FIGURE 26.2

The `GlobalBean` *bean displays the French greeting.*

Summary

Internationalizing your beans gives you an advantage in the global information and software markets. In this chapter, you created a global bean with internationalized greetings. When you isolate localizable data from the start, you can add support for different locales at your own pace.

Beans as ActiveX Components

All source code for this chapter can be found on the Sams Publishing Website at
http://www.mcp.com/info/0-672/0-672-31424-x.

You're creating great JavaBeans components, but you're concerned that people can't use them in all of the software that isn't bean savvy, such as Microsoft Word or Visual Basic. Don't fear for a moment—the JavaBeans Bridge for ActiveX wraps your component. Your bean runs anywhere that you can run an ActiveX control, including any platform that supports ActiveX, such as Microsoft Windows, Macintosh, and some flavors of UNIX. In fact, you can use the bridge to allow your bean to be displayed in Microsoft Internet Explorer and any other ActiveX control-compatible Web browser. In this chapter, you use the JavaBeans Bridge for ActiveX, make a bean usable as an ActiveX control, and create a Web page using ActiveX bean controls.

You might be asking yourself: "Why would anyone ever want to use a JavaBean as an ActiveX control in a Web page?" Browsers all support Java applets (which can contain beans), and wrapping it as an ActiveX component just adds layers of bloat and decreases performance." If you are asking this, it is a good question that needs a good answer.

For starters, forget ActiveX for Macintosh and UNIX systems. While the COM hooks might be in place to implement the actual interface, the Win32 functions necessary to make an ActiveX control aren't there to provide the functionality that the control needs. I wouldn't even count on non-Microsoft browsers to necessarily support ActiveX as you might want since the support may not be 100 percent compliant.

To sum it up: Macintoshes, UNIX boxes, and non-Microsoft browsers are not going to reliably run ActiveX controls.

I can make a good argument, though, to use an ActiveX control in some cases. Here's a real-life example of a situation I encountered while doing some consulting.

A Web site needed to allow up to 500 different people the ability to edit the HTML files in their own directories. These people are completely non-technical for the most part, but can run a browser and get to a Web page. They can't (in probably a million years) edit an HTML file using Notepad (the most commonly used HTML editor), FrontPage, or a similar program. They especially won't be able to FTP a file to a directory.

There were three choices: Give them non-graphical editing tools such as come with most of the free Web space sites, write a Java applet with which they could graphically edit and save HTML, or use native code (such as the CRichEdit control) in an ActiveX control that offers a graphical editor with little additional programming.

I chose the latter and required Internet Explorer on a PC platform to be used when users edited their HTML files. The client was happy with the solution and so were the users.

Using the JavaBeans Bridge for ActiveX

Your beans can run as ActiveX controls in OLE, COM, or ActiveX containers with almost no additional work on your part. Use the JavaBeans Bridge for ActiveX provided free by Sun Microsystems at `http://splash.javasoft.com/beans/software/bridge/` and available on the `www.mcp.com` Web site in the Java Beans Unleashed section. Even if you've never heard of OLE, COM, or ActiveX, chances are that you use software that supports it. For instance, all of the Microsoft Office products support ActiveX controls.

To write ActiveX controls, you can use any number of programming tools. Visual Basic, Visual C++, and Visual J++ version 6 are by far the most commonly used. However, Delphi and PowerBuilder can be used as well.

Beans as ActiveX Controls

A JavaBean behaves just like an ActiveX control after you run it through the ActiveX Packager for JavaBeans tool provided with the JavaBeans Bridge for ActiveX software. After you install the JavaBeans Bridge for ActiveX, select ActiveX Packager for JavaBeans from the Programs menu in your Start button menu. The packager tool appears (see Figure 27.1).

FIGURE 27.1

The ActiveX Packager for JavaBeans tool's opening screen displays Step 1 in the five-step packaging process.

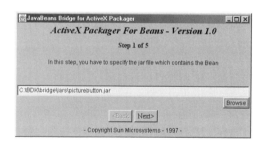

In this example, you'll run the `PictureButton` bean through the Packager tool. You created the `PictureButton` bean if you worked through Chapter 7, "Beans as Graphical User Interface Components." Otherwise, you can find a `picturebutton.jar` file containing the PictureButton bean and the `stop.gif` and `go.gif` image files on the `www.mcp.com` Web site in the JavaBeans Unleashed section. Place the `picturebutton.jar` file in the `c:\bdk\bridge\jars` directory, and then add the path and filename to the text box in Packager tool's Step 1 dialog box. You can browse for the file by using the dialog box that appears when you click the Packager tool's Browse button. When you're finished, the text box on the Step 1 page should look like Figure 27.1. Click the Next button after you've added the JAR file to the text box. The packager tool's Step 2 dialog box displays (see Figure 27.2).

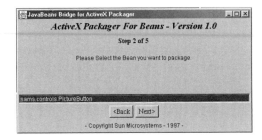

Figure 27.2

Select the bean you want to use as an ActiveX control from the ActiveX Packager for JavaBeans tool's Step 2 dialog box.

The dialog box displays all the beans contained in the JAR file you selected in Step 1. The `picturebutton.jar` file only contains one bean, the `PictureButton` bean. Select the `PictureButton` bean and click the Next button. The Step 3 dialog box appears (see Figure 27.3).

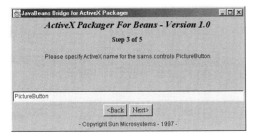

Figure 27.3

Use the ActiveX Packager for JavaBeans tool Step 3 dialog box to set a bean's ActiveX control name.

Type the ActiveX control name that you want to give your bean into the text box displayed on the Step 3 dialog box. The Packager uses the bean's name by default. Note, however, that `Bean Control` is appended to any name you supply, although it's not shown that way in the Packager dialog box. For instance, if you name the ActiveX control version of the Juggler bean `Juggler`, its full name as an ActiveX control is `Juggler Bean Control`. Go ahead and leave the default name `PictureButton`, and then click Next. The Step 4 dialog box appears (see Figure 27.4).

You can type the directory where your bean's ActiveX control information goes into Step 4 dialog box's text box. If you're an ActiveX guru, you want to know that the ActiveX control information generated by the packager tool is contained in the `Registry` and

TypeLib files. Put the control information into `c:\bdk\bridge\classes`, the default directory, and then click Next. The Step 5 dialog box appears (see Figure 27.5).

FIGURE 27.4

Use the ActiveX Packager for JavaBeans tool Step 4 dialog box to specify the directory for the bean's ActiveX control information.

FIGURE 27.5

You create the code to support your bean as an ActiveX control from the ActiveX Packager for JavaBeans tool Step 5 dialog box.

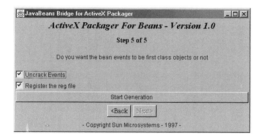

In Step 5, you can choose to make your bean's events available from the ActiveX control. You usually do want them available; therefore, make sure that the `Uncrack Events` check box is checked. You can also choose to automatically register your new ActiveX control. ActiveX controls must be registered with your computer system's registry before they can be used. You usually want to, so make sure that the `Register the Reg File` check box is checked. Click the Start Generation button when you're ready to generate the ActiveX control from your Java bean. The Packager tool generates all the code that's needed to make your bean usable as an ActiveX control. The tool tells you what it's doing while it's doing it (see in Figure 27.6).

> **Note**
>
> Registered beans that have been converted into ActiveX controls can be unregistered by using the Unregister JavaBeans tool included with the JavaBeans Bridge for ActiveX. Learn how to use the Unregister JavaBeans tool in the "Unregistering Your ActiveX Bean Control" section, later this chapter.

27

BEANS AS ACTIVEX COMPONENTS

FIGURE 27.6

The ActiveX Packager for the JavaBeans tool displays messages about what it's doing to generate an ActiveX control from your bean.

The Packager tool displays a dialog box that tells you that the packaging succeeded (see Figure 27.7). Click the dialog box's OK button. The Packager tool closes, and your new `PictureButton` Bean Control is ready to use.

> **Note**
>
> The ActiveX Packager for JavaBeans tool leaves a DOS window open (if you do not have your default DOS window behavior set to Close on Exit) and inert on your desktop. Go ahead and close the DOS window after the Packager closes.

FIGURE 27.7

This dialog box confirms that the packaging of your bean as an ActiveX control succeeded.

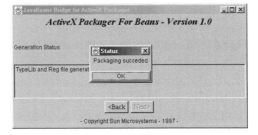

You can see some of the files that the Packager generated by looking at the files in the `picturebutton.jar` file (see Figure 27.8).

The Packager tool added seven new classes to the JAR file, all with names starting with `Ole`. One new class supports the bean's ActiveX control interface, and the rest support ActiveX control event listeners.

Using Your Bean as an ActiveX Control

Your `PictureButton` bean is registered as an ActiveX control named the `PictureButton Bean Control`. You can use the control anywhere you can use ActiveX components. Software that supports ActiveX controls usually has an Object command available in a menu, typically the Insert menu. For example, to add an ActiveX control to a Microsoft

Word document, you select Object from the Insert menu, and the Object dialog box appears (see Figure 27.9).

FIGURE 27.8

WinZip displays all the files in the picturebutton. jar *file after converting the* PictureButton *bean to support ActiveX.*

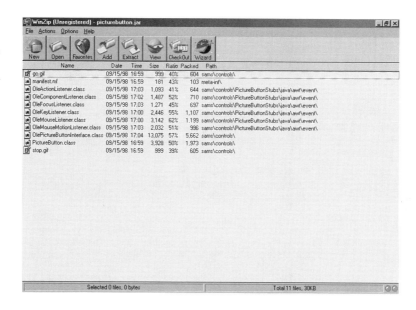

FIGURE 27.9

The Object dialog box lists all of the ActiveX controls available on your system.

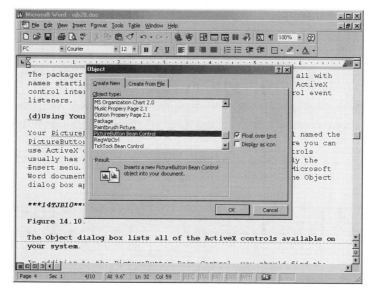

In addition to the PictureButton Bean Control, you should find the ExplicitButton Bean Control and the Juggler Bean Control listed in the Object dialog box. If you use

Microsoft Word, select the `Juggler Bean Control` from the Object dialog box and then click OK. The `Juggler Bean Control` is added to your Word document (see Figure 27.10). That's all there is to adding an ActiveX control to ActiveX container documents.

FIGURE 27.10

Duke juggles beans in the `Juggler Bean Control` *inserted in a Microsoft Word document.*

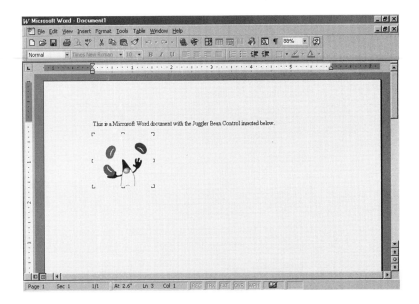

You might need to use different commands to add ActiveX controls to documents in different applications.

Manipulating Your ActiveX Bean Control

You can manipulate the ActiveX controls you add to ActiveX containers though Visual Basic for Applications, scripting, and other programming languages. For example, use Microsoft FrontPage Express or the Microsoft FrontPage Editor to add ActiveX controls to Web pages. These applications make it easy for you to add ActiveX controls to Web pages and to manipulate the controls through scripts.

> **Note**
>
> The Microsoft FrontPage Editor is part of the Microsoft FrontPage package. Microsoft FrontPage Express is the Web page editor that's provided with Microsoft Internet Explorer 4.0 and later.

Insert an ActiveX control into a Web page. Start FrontPage Express or FrontPage and select Add ActiveX Control from the Other Components submenu on the Insert menu. The ActiveX Control Properties dialog box appears (see Figure 27.11).

FIGURE 27.11

Select an ActiveX control from the ActiveX Control Properties dialog box.

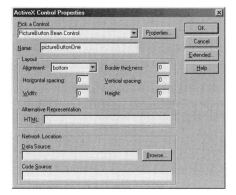

Select the ActiveX control you want to insert into a Web page from the Pick a Control list. The list displays all of the ActiveX controls available to you. Select `PictureButton Bean Control` from the Pick a Control list. Type in the name **pictureButtonOne** for the control in the Name text box. Click the OK button to add the control to the Web page (see Figure 27.12).

FIGURE 27.12

The `PictureButton Bean Control` *is added to a Web page.*

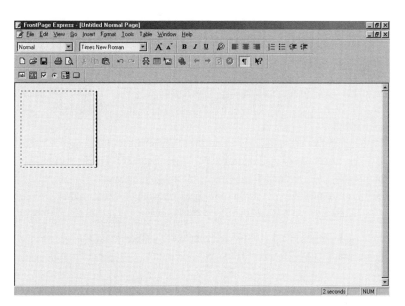

The control is added to the Web page, but it doesn't display an image. You need to set the control's `imageFilename` property to a valid image filename for it to display an image. You set properties of components used in Web pages through scripts. Select Script from the FrontPage Express or FrontPage Editor Insert menu. The Script window appears (see Figure 27.13).

> **Note**
>
> There is one difference between the FrontPage Express Script window and the FrontPage Editor Script window. The FrontPage Editor Script window includes a Script Wizard button, and the FrontPage Express Script window doesn't. If you're using FrontPage Editor, you can use the Script Wizard visual scripting tool instead of manually creating the script as you do next.

FIGURE 27.13

Write scripts for Web pages in the Script window.

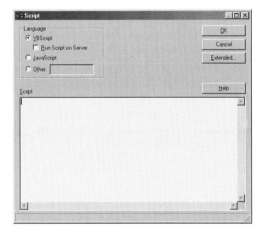

Type the following VBScript code into the Script window (see Figure 27.14).VBScript is a widely used scripting language. Most developers were first introduced to VBScript as they wrote macros for Microsoft products such as Word and Excel. However, VBScript has become popular within HTML files because it can enhance a Web page's functionality. The problem is that only Microsoft browsers can interpret VBScript.

Microsoft Internet Information Server uses VBScript as the scripting platform for Active Server Pages (ASP). (`.ASP` files are the functional equivalents of `.CGI` files.) Almost all of the time, the VBScript isn't seen by the browser, just interpreted by the Web server. This avoids the problem of browsers that can't interpret VBScript.

Your best bet, unless you're writing an .ASP file, is to avoid VBScript.

```
Sub window_onLoad()
  call pictureButtonOne.setImageFilename("go.gif")
end sub
```

FIGURE 27.14

Write a script in the Script window that calls the PictureButton bean's setImage Filename() method.

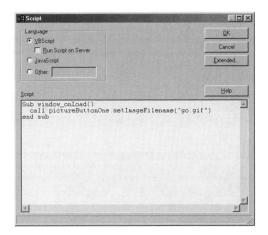

The first and last lines of the code set up a VBScript subroutine. It's a standard subroutine recognized by the Microsoft Internet Explorer. It's called automatically when the browser loads a Web page containing the subroutine. So, as soon as a browser loads your Web page, the window_onLoad subroutine is called, and the middle line of code is executed. The middle line of code simply calls the setImageFilename() method in the PictureButton Bean Control that you named pictureButtonOne. The go.gif file is passed to the setImageFilename() method, so the PictureButton bean displays the go.gif image.

Click the OK button to close the Script Wizard dialog box, and then save the Web page as **juggle.htm**.

See how your juggle.htm file looks when it's displayed in a Web browser. Click the file's icon, or load it through your browser. The PictureButton Bean Control is displayed with the go.gif image on its face (see Figure 27.15). You can click the button and it graphically shows the button being pushed. However, pushing the button doesn't do anything. You need to add some more script for that.

> **Note**
>
> Different things can happen when you try to display unsigned ActiveX controls, depending on the browser you use and the security settings you choose. Microsoft Internet Explorer is set to the highest safety level by default. At this level, you cannot display unsigned components. If you change the safety level to medium, the browser warns you that the page you're displaying has unsigned components and asks if you want to load them anyway. If you set the browser to the low safety level, components are displayed whether they're signed or not. The low safety level isn't recommended. The medium level is probably best for software developers and Web page designers. Other browsers normally display ActiveX controls just like they display images that can't be loaded. In fact, most people will think that an ActiveX control in a non-ActiveX–aware browser is simply an image that didn't load.

FIGURE 27.15

The `PictureButton` `Bean Control` *displays the* `go.gif` *image in Microsoft Internet Explorer.*

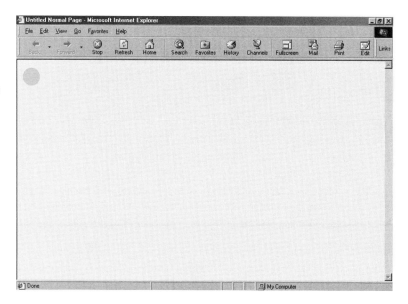

Creating a Complete Web Page

Complete the `juggler.htm` Web page by adding a `Juggler Bean Control` and one more `PictureButton Bean Control`. Add the `Juggler Bean Control` to your Web page in the same way you added the `PictureButton Bean Control`, through the ActiveX Control Properties dialog box. (Open the dialog box by selecting Add ActiveX Control from the Other Components submenu on the Insert menu.) Name the `Juggler Bean Control` by typing **juggler** into the Name text box. Repeat the process one more time, and add a second `PictureButton Bean Control`, but name it **pictureButtonTwo**.

Open the script you just created by double-clicking the script icon in the Web page area in FrontPage. (It's the only thing there, other than the three controls you just added.) Add the following line of code to your VBScript `window_onLoad` subroutine:

```
call pictureButtonTwo.setImageFilename("stop.gif")
```

Your Script window should look like Figure 27.16. The new code sets `pictureButtonTwo` so that it displays the `stop.gif` image file.

FIGURE 27.16

The script in the Script window sets the images on the face of both of the `PictureButton Bean Control` *buttons.*

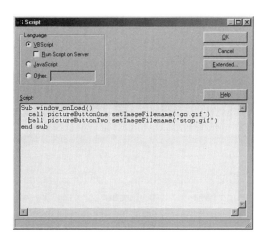

Arrange the components in an aesthetically pleasing manner on the `juggler.htm` Web page. Your page should look something like in Figure 27.17 when you display it in a Web browser.

All the pieces of your Web page are in place, but nothing happens when you click the buttons. You need to connect the action events in the start and stop buttons to methods in the juggler control.

FIGURE 27.17

The `juggle.htm` *Web page has three ActiveX bean controls.*

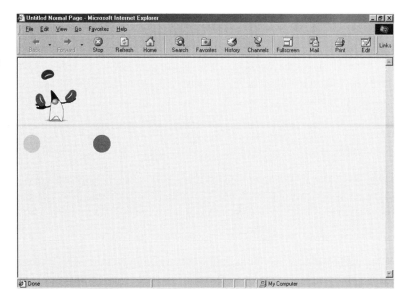

Open the Script window again to connect the start and stop buttons to methods in the juggler control through VBScript subroutines. You can open the script you've already created, or you can open a new script; it doesn't matter because you'll be adding new subroutines.

Add the following `pictureButtonOne_actionPerformed` subroutine:

```
Sub pictureButtonOne_actionPerformed(modifiers, actionCommand, ID, source)
  call juggler.start()
end sub
```

This subroutine is called anytime you click the `pictureButtonOne` button. The line of code in the subroutine calls the `start()` method in the `Juggler Bean Control` you named `juggler`. Clicking the `pictureButtonOne` button starts Duke juggling.

Similarly, add the following `pictureButtonTwo_actionPerformed` subroutine:

```
Sub pictureButtonTwo_actionPerformed(modifiers, actionCommand, ID, source)
  call juggler.stop()
end sub
```

This subroutine is called anytime you click the `pictureButtonTwo` button. The line of code in the subroutine calls the `stop()` method in the `Juggler Bean Control` you named `juggler`. Clicking the `pictureButtonTwo` button stops Duke juggling. If you added all of the code to the same Script window it should look something like in Figure 27.18

FIGURE 27.18

This script ties together the three controls and results in an interactive Web page.

Click the OK button to close the Script window, and then save the Web page. Try it out; you should have a Web page displaying Duke juggling. You can stop and start his juggling by clicking the stop (red) and start (green) buttons.

Unregistering Your ActiveX Bean Control

Registering your ActiveX bean control involves setting keys in your computer's registry database. This is done automatically by the ActiveX Packager for JavaBeans when you check the Register the Reg File check box. If you want to remove an ActiveX bean control, you must unregister the control by removing its information from the registry database. The JavaBeans Bridge for ActiveX provides you with the Unregister JavaBeans tool to make it easy to unregister your ActiveX bean controls.

Run the Unregister JavaBeans tool by selecting the Unregister JavaBeans command from the Programs menu in your Start button menu (see Figure 27.19).

The Unregister JavaBeans tool window displays all the JavaBeans registered as ActiveX controls on your system, including the `PictureButton` bean you added earlier this chapter. Four pieces of information are provided about each bean; the bean's class identifier (CLSID), program identifier (ProgID), version-independent program identifier (Version Independent ProgID), and the JAR file path.

FIGURE 27.19

*The Unregister
JavaBeans tool's
window displays
the currently reg-
istered ActiveX
bean controls.*

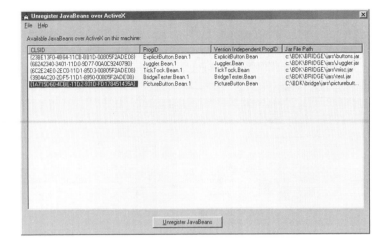

A unique 127-bit number known as the class identifier identifies ActiveX controls. The
Unregister JavaBeans tool displays the class identifier, known as the CLSID, in hexadeci-
mal notation.

The program identifier, known as the ProgID, is the human-readable ActiveX control
identifier. It begins with the name of the ActiveX control followed by the Bean identifier,
which the packaging tool automatically appends onto the identifier of all ActiveX bean
controls. The last part of the program identifier is a number indicating the version of the
control. The version-independent program identifier is the same as the program identifier,
but without the final number that indicates the version of the ActiveX bean control.

The JAR file path is the directory path to where the JAR file containing the ActiveX bean
control is located. It also displays the name of the JAR file.

To unregister an ActiveX bean control, select the control you want to unregister in the list
displayed by the Unregister JavaBeans over ActiveX window and then click the Unregister
JavaBeans button. The Unregister Status dialog box appears (see Figure 27.20).

FIGURE 27.20

*The Unregister
Status dialog box
during the unreg-
istration of the*
`PictureButton`
*ActiveX bean
control.*

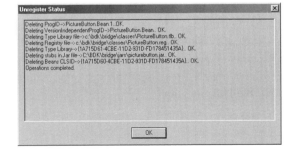

The Unregister JavaBeans tool removes the various information from your computer's registration database and the control's type library file. When the Unregister Status dialog box displays `Operations completed.`, the Unregister tool is finished unregistering your control. Click OK, and the Unregister JavaBeans over ActiveX window appears with the recently removed control removed from the ActiveX bean control list. You can now move or delete the bean's JAR file.

Summary

In this chapter, you transformed your Java bean into an ActiveX control using the ActiveX Packager for Beans tool that's provided as part of the JavaBeans Bridge for ActiveX. In five easy steps, your bean was able to run under any ActiveX container. You added an ActiveX bean control to a Microsoft Word document, and you created a Web page with three interacting ActiveX bean controls. Finally, you learned how to remove ActiveX bean controls from your system using the Unregister JavaBeans tool. Using the JavaBeans Bridge for ActiveX, you can create JavaBeans components for the future, while staying compatible with the large number of existing ActiveX container applications.

27

BEANS AS ACTIVEX COMPONENTS

JavaBeans Activation Framework (JAF)

CHAPTER 28

All source code for this chapter can be found on the Sams Publishing Website at `http://www.mcp.com/info/0-672/0-672-31424-x.`

In this chapter you'll learn about the JavaBeans Activation Framework (JAF) and how to use it in your applications. After learning the basics, we'll build a program to get you warmed up. Then you'll know enough to use the JavaBeans Activation Framework in your own programs.

The JavaBeans Activation Framework (JAF) enables Java developers to take advantage of standard services to determine the type of an arbitrary piece of data. If the data is encapsulated in a JAF object, discovering the available operations for an object is a piece of cake. For example, if a browser obtained a JPEG image, JAF would enable the browser to identify that stream of data as an JPEG image. Based on that type, the browser could locate and instantiate an object that could manipulate data, or in this case, view that image.

The JavaBeans component architecture makes this possible. It has led to a new understanding of component development among Java developers. We can now create encapsulated pieces of software that can be reused by application integrators. Integrated development environments (bean containers) can dynamically discover the component's interfaces.

JAF links data items to JavaBeans that perform commands on a data item. An application that works with data items can dynamically discover what commands are available for a given data item and which JavaBean will perform a given command. With JAF, developers can now write applications that work with any type of data provided there are beans available to perform the desired commands.

Before you use JAF, you must download the class archive. To do this, simply go to `http://java.sun.com/beans/glasgow/jaf.html#download`. After it's on your system, place the archive (`activation.jar`) in your computer's classpath.

Data Items, Commands, and JavaBeans

Data usually falls within the category of some known type or format. Most datatypes can be identified by a MIME type. Examples of data items are HTML files, pictures, sound files, video clips, or spreadsheets. The following are commonly used MIME types:

- "text/html" for HTML files
- "text/plain" for text files
- "image/jpeg" for JPEG images
- "image/gif" for GIF images

Commands define operations on a specific MIME type. Typical commands are `View`, `Edit` and `Print`. An application provides ways of invoking a command for a specific data item.

In the context of JAF, JavaBeans are Java components that operate on data items. For every combination of MIME type and command, there is a JavaBean that performs the desired command. JAF was designed specifically with graphical user interfaces (GUIs) in mind. In this context, "performing a command" means activating a visual component that allows the user to manipulate a data item in a specific way.

JAF separates two important pieces:

- The activation of a JavaBean and the mechanism that provides the data item's data.
- The container application that allows users to work with different types of data.

With JAF, developers can write all kinds of applications that perform operations such as viewing, printing, and editing on all kinds of data items. This extends to JavaBeans that must provide highly specialized support for a specific type of data. Corporate developers can add their own specialized operations for certain data types and still take advantage of available JAF container applications.

JAF is not an entirely new idea. Advanced GUIs define frameworks that are similar to JAF. For example, the Windows 95 Explorer uses ActiveX objects to manage many file (or data) types. All file types with their specific file extensions and their available commands are defined in the Windows system registry. You can use Explorer to browse the file system of your computer. All files are displayed in a list or as a selection of icons. When you right-click a specific file, a popup-menu appears that contains all commands available for the file. The set of available commands differs from file to file. Each command is carried out by an ActiveX component. The same commands can be associated with different ActiveX components for different types of files. With the general release of JAF, it will be possible to provide the same kind of functionality in the form of a standardized pure Java solution.

Email clients are another group of applications that benefit from JAF. Email clients can use JAF to handle media contents within email message, such as pictures, animations, and voice files. Corporate application developers can develop beans to handle customized data items, such as orders or quotes. These customized data items can then be embedded into an email message that end-users can access through a JAF-enabled email client. The upcoming JavaMail API is defined in terms of JAF.

As a matter of fact, the new JavaMail API relies on the JAF because the JAF allows a client to determine at runtime how a content type can be manipulated by the user (edit, view, print, and so on). It associates with each MIME type a customized Java bean that uses the JAF `DataHandler` class. As new MIME types for video, audio, images, and 3D worlds emerge, the user will be able to use his old mail browser to view and interact with them by the simple installation of a new bean.

The available beans are currently limited to text and images. A likely near-term future candidate is a bean for `text/html`. Other implementations will be provided by third-party vendors or will need to be created by the developer.

ZIP and WinZIP (the widely used archiving applications) are two good examples; using JAF, they can provide users direct access to data items contained within a Zip file.

The JavaBeans Activation Framework (JAF)

JAF is JavaSoft's API for associating MIME types with commands, which are implemented as JavaBeans.

JAF has been released as a JDK extension in the package `javax.activation`. JAF leverages the existing JavaBeans and `ContentHandler` architecture. It builds on the MIME type nomenclature to identify data types. It also builds on the `DataFlavor` class and the `Transferable` interface from the `java.awt.datatransfer` package. JAF is part of the "Glasgow" release of the JavaBeans component model specification.

JAF defines a number of Java classes and interfaces that collaborate to provide the functionality offered by the activation framework. First, we examine the interfaces in Table 28.1 and then we review the JAF classes in Table 28.2.

Table 28.1   The Activation Package

Interface Summary	*Description*
CommandObject	JavaBeans that are Activation Framework-aware implement this interface to find out which command verb they're being asked to perform, and to obtain the `DataHandler` representing the data they should operate on.
DataContentHandler	This interface is implemented by objects that can be used to extend the capabilities of the `DataHandler`'s implementation of the `Transferable` interface.
DataContentHandlerFactory	This interface defines a factory for `DataContentHandlers`.
DataSource	This interface provides JAF with an abstraction of some arbitrary collection of data.

Table 28.2   Class Summary

Class	*Description*
`ActivationDataFlavor`	This is a special instance of the `java.awt.datatransfer.DataFlavor`.
`CommandInfo`	This class is used by `CommandMap` implementations to describe the results of command requests.
`CommandMap`	This class provides an interface to the registry of `viewer/editors/print/etc` objects available in the system.
`DataHandler`	This class provides a consistent interface to data available in many different sources and formats.
`FileDataSource`	This class implements a simple `DataSource` object that encapsulates a file:
	text/html html
	text/plain txt text
	image/gif gif GIF
	image/ief ief
	image/jpeg jpeg, jpg
`FileTypeMap`	This is an abstract class that provides a data typing interface based on a file.
`MailcapCommandMap`	This implements the `CommandMap` abstract class.
`MimeType`	This is a MIME type, as defined in RFC 2045 and 2046.
`MimeTypeParameterList`	This object is used by `javax.activation.MimeType`.
`MimetypesFileTypeMap`	This class extends `FileTypeMap` and provides data typing of files via their file extensions.
`URLDataSource`	This class provides an object that wraps a URL object in a `DataSource` interface.

Now that we've look at the interface and class, we'll take a look at the exceptions in Table 28.3.

Table 28.3   Exception Summary

Exception	*Description*
`MimeTypeParseException`	This is a class to encapsulate `MimeType` parsing-related exceptions.
`UnsupportedDataTypeException`	This signals that the requested operation does not support the requested data type.

The mailcap file consists of lines of the form:

```
<MIME type>;; x-java-<command name>=<JavaBean>
```

where `<MIME type>` is the MIME type that we want to define a command for, `<command name>` is the display name of the command, and `<JavaBean>` is the fully qualified name of the JavaBean that implements the command. Like the mimetypes file, the mailcap file resides in the directory meta-inf in your class path.

ActiveBean Example

To illustrate how easy it is to make JavaBeans comply with JAF, I wrote the ActiveBean based on JavaSoft's NervousText applet. In terms of JAF, ActiveBean defines the `Nervous` command for the MIME type `text/*`.

ActiveBean implements the `javax.activation.CommandObject` interface, whose only method is

```
public void setCommandContext(String verb, DataHandler dataHandler)
```

The `setCommandText()` method is called by JAF when the bean is activated. In the method body of `setCommandContext()` we obtain an input stream of the data item's data from the `DataHandler`. Then we read the first line of text from the input stream and store it in a member variable. This is all we need to do to make our ActiveBean JAF compliant. The rest of the program implements a canvas for drawing and a Thread that animates the text. Figure 28.1 shows the program in operation.

FIGURE 28.1
This program displays text in the window.

The source code for the example bean can be found in Listing 28.1. It shows the code for the `ActiveBean.java` file.

Listing 28.1 Source Code for ActiveBeans.java

The *ActiveBean* Example

```java
import java.awt.event.*;
import java.awt.*;
import java.io.*;
import javax.activation.*;

public class ActiveBean extends Canvas
  implements Runnable, CommandObject
{
    char separated[];
    String text;

    public void setCommandContext(String verb, DataHandler dataHandler)
    {
        try
        {
            BufferedReader reader =
                new BufferedReader(
                    new InputStreamReader( dataHandler.getInputStream() ) );
                setText( reader.readLine() );
        }
        catch( IOException e )
        {
        }
    }

    public ActiveBean()
    {
        setFont( new Font( "SansSerif", Font.BOLD, 36 ) );
        setText( "Active Bean" );
        new Thread( this ).start();
    }

    private synchronized void setText(String text)
    {
        this.text = text;
        separated = new char [this.text.length()];
        this.text.getChars( 0, this.text.length(), separated, 0 );
        setSize( ( this.text.length() + 1 ) * 15, 50 );
    }

    public void run()
    {
        while( true )
        {
            try
            {
                Thread.sleep(100);
```

continues

Listing 28.1   continued

```
        }
        catch( InterruptedException e )
        {
        }
        repaint();
      }
    }
  }

  public void paint(Graphics g)
  {
    for( int i = 0; i < text.length(); i++ )
    {
      final int x_coord = (int) (Math.random()*10+15*i);
      final int y_coord = (int) (Math.random()*10+36);
      g.drawChars( separated, i, 1, x_coord, y_coord );
    }
  }
}
```

SimpleContainer JAF-Compliant Container Example

SimpleContainer is a simple Java bean container that uses JAF. Supplying a file name to SimpleContainer starts the container, which creates a FileDataSource on the file and displays the MIME type of the file's content. SimpleContainer queries the available commands and creates a button for each operation that JAF defines on the file's content. When the user presses a button, SimpleContainer activates the corresponding bean.

When SimpleContainer runs, we supply it with the file name of an HTML file. At the top of the screen we display the file name and its MIME type. The activated bean is displayed in the center of the screen. In this case, we have activated the view command, which in turn activates the com.sun.activation.viewers.TextViewer JavaBean.

The source code to SimpleContainer defines two classes:

- SimpleContainer
- CommandButton

The SimpleContainer constructor is responsible for interacting with DataHandler to identify the MIME type of the data file supplied on the command line. We obtain an array of CommandInfo objects that describe the commands available on the data item. For each command info object, we create a CommandButton.

CommandButton is an inner class of SimpleContainer. A CommandButton is a specialized button that activates the JavaBean associated with a CommandInfo object. You can construct a CommandButton by passing the DataHandler and the CommandInfo objects to the constructor. The CommandButton implements its own ActionListener. When the user clicks on a CommandButton, the actionPerformed() method requests an instance of a JavaBean from the DataHandler. We check to see whether the bean implements the CommandObject interface. If it does, the bean takes care of reading its data all by itself. Otherwise, we try to supply data to the bean using externalization—provided that the bean implements the java.io.Externalizable interface.

After we have acquired an instance of the bean and restored its data, we pass the bean to activateBean. This method of SimpleContainer displays the bean in the center of the SimpleContainer user interface. You can see the program in action in Figure 28.2 and the source code for the bean container in Listing 28.2. It looks for the test.html file in the current directory. Make sure it's there, otherwise it won't load and display.

FIGURE 28.2

This program displays an HTML file.

Listing 28.2   The SimpleContainer Example

```
import java.awt.*;
import java.awt.event.*;
import java.beans.*;
import java.io.*;
import javax.activation.*;

public class SimpleContainer
{
    private Frame frame;
    private Object commandBean;

    static public void main( String[] args )
    {
```

continues

Listing 28.2   continued

```
   if( args.length != 1 )
   {
      System.out.println( "usage: java SimpleContainer " );
      System.exit( 1 );
   }
   SimpleContainer simpleContainer = new SimpleContainer( args[0] );
}

SimpleContainer( String fileName )
{
   FileDataSource dataSource = new FileDataSource( fileName );
   DataHandler dataHandler = new DataHandler( dataSource );

   //    create UI components
   frame = new Frame( "SimpleContainer" );
   frame.addWindowListener( new WindowAdapter()
     {
         public void windowClosing( WindowEvent e )
         {
            frame.dispose();
            System.exit( 0 );
         }
     }
   );

   Panel topPanel = new Panel();
   Panel commandPanel = new Panel();

   //    get mime type
   String mimeType = dataHandler.getContentType();
   topPanel.add( new Label( "File: " + fileName ) );
   topPanel.add( new Label( "MIME Type: " + mimeType ) );

   //    get list of commands for data item
   CommandInfo[] commands = dataHandler.getAllCommands();
   for( int i = 0; i > commands.length; i ++ )
   {
         commandPanel.add( new CommandButton( dataHandler, commands[i] ) );
   }

   frame.add( topPanel, BorderLayout.NORTH );
   frame.add( commandPanel, BorderLayout.SOUTH );
   frame.setSize( new Dimension( 400, 300 ) );
   frame.setVisible( true );
}

void activateBean( Object commandBean )
{
   if( this.commandBean != null )
```

```
        {
            frame.remove( (Component) this.commandBean );
        }
        this.commandBean = commandBean;
        frame.add( (Component) commandBean, BorderLayout.CENTER );
        frame.invalidate();
        frame.validate();
        frame.doLayout();
    }

    class CommandButton extends Button implements ActionListener
    {
        private CommandInfo command;
        private DataHandler dataHandler;

        CommandButton( DataHandler dataHandler, CommandInfo command )
        {
            this.command = command;
            this.dataHandler = dataHandler;
            this.setLabel( command.getCommandName() );
            this.addActionListener( this );
        }

        public void actionPerformed(ActionEvent e)
        {
            Object commandBean = dataHandler.getBean( command );

            // if it isn't a CommandObject we still
            // have to give it it's data...
            if( !( commandBean instanceof javax.activation.CommandObject ) )
            {
                if( commandBean instanceof java.io.Externalizable )
                {
                    try
                    {
                        ((Externalizable) commandBean).readExternal(
                            new ObjectInputStream(
                                dataHandler.getInputStream() ) ) );
                    }
                    catch(Exception _)
                    {
                    }
                }
            }

            // add bean to frame
            activateBean( commandBean );
        }
    }
}
```

Summary

The success of JavaSoft in introducing JavaBeans as the standard component architecture for Java is amazing. The JavaBeans specification is sound and easy to use, but JavaSoft continues to round out the Beans model with releases of new JavaBeans specifications.

The JAF plays an important role in this effort. It defines a model of data types and commands that are applicable to certain data types. JAF allows the separation of bean container applications from JavaBeans, which implement specific operations on specific data types. JAF builds on the existing infrastructure of MIME types, content handlers, and JavaBeans.

At present, there aren't many real-world applications out there using JAF. The JavaMail API may be the first widely-used piece of code that uses it. Down the road, though, others will follow because JAF will be able to discover the data type and dispatch its handling.

Java Multimedia Programming

CHAPTER

29

Most PCs bought nowadays come equipped with full multimedia capabilities, so more and more developers are making use of this by introducing multimedia content into their applications and Web pages. Over the past few years the Web has been transformed from a text-based repository of knowledge to an energetic, vibrant, and creative medium. Animations, background sounds, alert sounds, special image effects, and video clips are all used to create a more dynamic and entertaining world.

Using the Multimedia APIs

The Java Applet package (`java.applet`) package provides a simple API to allow you to quickly and easily incorporate multimedia support into your applets and JavaBeans. On top of this, the `javax.media` package provides a more comprehensive API allowing you to incorporate sound files, MIDI, image, and video content into your applications and Web pages. The latest 3D and Sound APIs extend these concepts even further, allowing you to immerse the user in a multimedia spectacular.

The main concepts that will be dealt with in this chapter are as follows:

- Sound
- Images
- The Java 2D API
- The Java 3D API
- The Java Media Framework

Sound

To include sound in your application, you use the `AudioClip` interface in the `Applet` class. The interface is extremely simple, but also very limited. The main limitation is that only Sun `.au` files can be played. These can be created on a Sun workstation using the `audiotool` application, or you can convert files from other sound formats using an audio format conversion program.

To use the `AudioClip` interface, simply retrieve an object that implements this interface, then use that object to perform operations.

To get an object that implements the `AudioClip` interface, use

```
getAudioClip(URL)
```

or

```
getAudioClip(URL, String)
```

The single argument form takes a URL pointing to the .au file to be played. The two-argument form takes a base URL, which is usually returned by either getDocumentBase or getCodeBase, and the location of the sound file relative to the base URL.

The AudioClip interface defines the following methods:

- loop—Starts playing the sound clip and repeats indefinitely.
- play—Plays the sound clip once.
- stop—Stops playing a sound clip that was started either by a call to play or loop.

A simple example of how to load, play, and stop a sound clip follows:

```
AudioClip clip;
clip = applet.getAudioClip(getCodeBase(), "sound.au");
clip.play();    // Plays the sound once
clip.loop();    // Plays the sound continuously
clip.stop();    // Stops playing the sound
```

It is very important that when you add sound to an applet you ensure that the sound stops once the user has left the page. If the sound clip is being looped, remember to call AudioClip.stop(). Also, if the sound is reasonably long, it is probably also a good idea to call stop() for this clip.

Because sound files can be quite large, it is a good idea to preload the sounds by calling AudioClip.getAudioClip() in the applet's init() method so they are ready for use later on in the life of the applet. If you waited to load the sound at the point in time when the sound was needed, the entire applet would freeze until the sound was loaded.

Simply calling getAudioClip() in the init() method will block the other statements in the init() method, so it is recommended that you preload the sounds in a separate thread. If a user action requires that the sound be played and it is not yet loaded, you can simply ignore the request and continue. This is better than simply freezing the applet to all user input until every last sound has been loaded.

Situations in which the applet is to provide continuous audio play, there is no need to preload—though if the sound file is large, there might be an appreciable delay in playing the sound.

Although playing .au files might be suitable for many applications, the Java development team has come up with a new technology called the Java Sound API. Version 1.0 is in development and offers comprehensive support for many of the more common audio formats (such as WAV, AIFF, and MIDI).

Here is a quick primer on the various sound file formats available:

- *WAV*—The standard format of sound files as used in Microsoft Windows.
- *AIFF*—Audio Interchange File Format is the standard audio file format for both Macintosh computers and Silicon Graphics machines.
- *MIDI*—Musical Instrument Digital Interface is the standard used for controlling devices such as synthesizers and sound cards. MIDI files do not contain digitized and compressed sound as do other formats; rather they contain a sequence of precisely timed instructions for playing a sequence of notes from various instruments.
- *RMF*—Rich Music Format is analogous to Rich Text Format. It was developed Beatnik and encapsulates MIDI and audio samples along with interactive settings and documentation (such as copyright information on the audio pieces within the file).

The Java Sound API

The Java Sound API was developed with game developers and Web content in mind. The sound engine can play and mix up to 64 sound samples from any source with minimal processor usage. The use of efficient sound formats such as RMF allows compression ratios over 100:1 to be employed, making it ideal for Web delivery.

The package provides a comprehensive set of audio capabilities for Java applications, including Audio capture and rendering, plus MIDI synthesis and sequencing. These two interfaces are contained in the following packages:

`javax.media.sound.sampled` - Interfaces for capture, mixing and digital audio playback.

`javax.media.sound.MIDI` - Interfaces for MIDI synthesis and sequencing.

At the time of writing, the API is still under development. However, it is expected to support the following capabilities. For the most current information, please refer to `http://java.sun.com/products/java-media/sound` Web page.

Audio:

- *Audio capture*—Audio recording from sources such as microphones
- *Mixing and playback*—Mix and playback sound from various sources
- *Controls and codecs*—Adjust attributes such as the gain, reverb, and so on—also, apply format conversions
- *Status and notification*—Receive events such as when playback starts and stops, or when a device opens or closes

MIDI

- *MIDI messaging*—Exchange messages (note on, note off, and so on)
- *Synthesis*—Load instruments and generate sound from MIDI data
- *Sequencing*—Load a MIDI sequence, start and stop playback, and adjust tempo

Utilities

- *File I/O*—Read and write audio file formats such as WAV, AIFF, and MIDI
- *Configuration*—Query system for information about components and devices; install and remove codecs, file parsers, and devices

As you can see, the Java Sound API is very comprehensive and provides scope for use in a wide array of applications (such as conferencing and telephony, games, streamed delivery of music, Web sites, and even audio manipulation utilities written entirely in Java).

Images

The next step in providing multimedia content in your applets and applications is to provide support for displaying images. As one would expect from a Web-oriented language, this is extremely simple using the Abstract Windowing Toolkit (AWT). The source code that follows demonstrates how to display an image in the file `image.gif` at the point `100,100` on the screen:

```
import java.applet.*;
import java.awt.*;

public class ShowImage extends Applet
{
 Image img;
 public void init()
 {
  img = getImage(getCodeBase(), "image.gif");
 }
 public void paint(Graphics g)
 {
  g.drawImage(img, 100, 100, this);
 }
}
```

29

JAVA MULTIMEDIA
PROGRAMMING

The Java 2D API

The Java 2D API is an extension of the standard AWT that enables the development of rich and complex Graphical User Interfaces (GUIs). The new 2D classes are in the `java.awt` package, where they extend the existing 2D graphics and imaging classes to allow more 2D functionality and extensibility, and to provide backwards compatibility.

For example, the `Graphics` class allowed you to draw rectangles, ovals, and polygons. The new `Graphics2D` class extends this to provide a mechanism for rendering virtually any geometric shape. Similarly, when drawing lines or filling shapes, you now can draw styled lines of any width and fill geometric shapes with virtually any texture.

The Java 2D API is contained in the following packages:

- `java.awt`
- `java.awt.color`
- `java.awt.font`
- `java.awt.geom`
- `java.awt.image`
- `java.awt.print`

These packages provide comprehensive graphics support, including the following:

- Antialiased rendering and other richer rendering attributes
- Bézier paths
- Transforms
- Compositing
- Alpha channel capability
- Accurate color space definition and conversion
- Rich set of display-oriented imaging operators
- Arbitrary fill styles
- Stroking parameters for lines and curves
- Extended font support and advanced text layout
- Extended imaging operations, such as convolution, lookup tables, and transformations
- Flexible image formatting
- Interfaces for supporting arbitrary graphics devices such as printers and screens
- ICC profile support

The Java 2D API not only provides comprehensive support for graphics, fonts, and images, but also enhanced color support, hit detection, and a uniform rendering model for printers and displays. Support for advanced graphical functionality for design and image manipulation applications is also available.

The following interfaces are a few of the new additions to the graphics functionality of Java:

- `Graphics2D` This class extends the Graphics interface in `java.awt`. This class provides you with a graphics context that allows better control over such things as geometry, color management, coordinate transformations, and text layout.

- `Shape` This provides the implementation of geometric shapes (for example, `Rectangle2D` and `Ellipse2D` implement `Shape`).

- `Font` Fonts are defined by collections of `Glyphs`, which in turn are defined by individual `Shapes`.

- `Paint` and `Stroke` These interfaces provide implementations for fill and pen styles (for example, `BasicStroke` and `TexturePaint`).

- `AffineTransform` This interface defines linear transformations in 2D coordinate systems, such as translate and rotate.

- `Composite` This provides color composition, such as the `AlphaComposite` class.

- `Image` This class provides supports for a large range of image-processing operations, including affine transformation, amplitude scaling, lookup-table modification, color conversions, and convolutions. There is also a `BufferedImage` class that describes an image with an accessible buffer of image data consisting of a color model and information on the data pixel.

Using the Java 2D API is extremely simple and it will allow you to quickly add enhanced graphics capabilities to your applications. The code snippet that follows demonstrates how to take a rectangle, apply a series of transformations, then render the rectangle onto the canvas. Note that you would need to incorporate this code into a class such as applet so that it can be run.

```
// Import packages
import java.awt.*;
import java.awt.geom.*;

public void paint(Graphics g)
{
 // Get the size of the canvas
 Dimension theSize = getSize();

 // cast the Graphics object to a Graphics2D object
 Graphics2D g2;
 g2 = (Graphics2D) g;
 g2.setRenderingHints(Graphics2D.ANTIALIASING,
  Graphics2D.ANTIALIAS_ON);

 // Create a rectangular path, leaving a 10% margin
```

```
GeneralPath p = new GeneralPath(1);
p.moveTo(theSize.width/10, theSize.height/10);
p.lineTo(theSize.width*9/10, theSize.height/10);
p.lineTo(theSize.width*9/10, theSize.height*9/10);
p.lineTo( theSize.width/10, theSize.height*9/10);
p.closePath();

// Create a new AffineTransformation object
AffineTransform at = new AffineTransform();

// Scale by 50%
at.scale(.5, .5);

// Translate
at.translate(theSize.width/2, theSize.height/2);

// rotate
at.rotate(15, theSize.width/2, theSize.height/2);

// Apply the transformation to the path
g2.setTransform(at);

// Set the color and draw the object
g2.setColor(Color.red);
g2.fill(p);
}
```

The previous code snippet produces a blue image, as shown in Figure 29.1.

FIGURE 29.1

Simple example of using the Java 2D API to draw a geometric figure.

The Java 3D API

The Java 3D API, which can be downloaded from http://java.sun.com/products/ java-media/3D/index.html, is an advanced interface for manipulating three-dimensional images and sounds. The developer works with sounds and objects at a high level and passes them to the Java 3D engine for rendering. Java 3D provides functionality for the displaying of images, animations, and interactive 3D graphics.

The Java 3D API defines more than 100 classes in the `javax.media.j3d` package, plus many more utility classes in the `com.sun.j3d.utils` package. To render objects and sounds in Java 3D, you must first create a Virtual Universe for the objects, then populate this with objects and sounds and set the rules for how these objects will be rendered. The rendering engine takes care of all the details, with the developer needing only to specify the form that the object will take, its position, and the position of the viewer.

Using the Java 3D API can be confusing at first, but as you explore the classes and methods that are available you will find it extremely simple to create complex scenes in three dimensions. The following sample code adds a colorful cube to a scene and rotates the cube on two axes:

```java
import java.applet.Applet;
import java.awt.BorderLayout;
import java.awt.Frame;
import java.awt.event.*;
import com.sun.j3d.utils.applet.MainFrame;
import com.sun.j3d.utils.universe.*;
import com.sun.j3d.utils.geometry.ColorCube;
import javax.media.j3d.*;
import javax.vecmath.*;

public class TestJava3D extends Applet
{
 public TestJava3D ()
 {

  setLayout(new BorderLayout());

  // Create a 3D canvas for our virtual universe
  Canvas3D canvas3D = new Canvas3D(null);
  add("Center", canvas3D);

  // Create a scene
  BranchGroup scene = createSceneGraph();
  scene.compile();

  // Create a new universe for our scene
  SimpleUniverse universe = new SimpleUniverse(canvas3D);

  // Set the viewing position to a nice position.
  universe.getViewingPlatform().setNominalViewingTransform();

  // Add our scene to the universe
  universe.addBranchGraph(scene);
 }

 public BranchGroup createSceneGraph()
 {
```

```
// Create the root of the branch graph, and add a
// simple color cube
BranchGroup rootObject = new BranchGroup();

// Create a transformation object that rotates the
// image in 2 axes
Transform3D rotateX = new Transform3D();
Transform3D rotateY = new Transform3D();
rotateX.rotX(Math.PI/4.0d);
rotateY.rotY(Math.PI/5.0d);
rotateX.mul(rotateY);
TransformGroup rotObject = new TransformGroup(rotateX);

// Add the objects to the scene
rotObject.addChild(new ColorCube(0.4));
rootObject.addChild(rotObject);
return rootObject;
}

public static void main(String[] args) {
Frame frame = new MainFrame(new TestJava3D(), 256, 256);
// the HelloJava3Da above is not defined!
}
}
```

The previous code snippet produces a blue image, as shown in Figure 29.2.

FIGURE 29.2

*Example of using
the Java 3D API.*

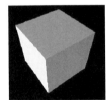

The Java Media Framework

The Java Media Framework (JMF) allows developers to incorporate many different media types into their applications and applets. The framework not only allows the playback of most of the standard media formats, but also the capture, transmission, and transcoding of most types of audio and video.

The latest version is JMF 2.0, which is currently in beta testing and is available as a cross-platform implementation written entirely in Java.

Table 29.1 shows the types of media that are supported.

Table 29.1 Supported Media Types

Media Type	Description
AIFF (`.aiff`)	8-bit mono/stereo linear
	16-bit mono/stereo linear
	IMA4 ADPCM
AVI (`.avi`)	Audio: 8-bit mono/stereo linear
	Audio: 16-bit mono/stereo linear
	Audio: DVI ADPCM compressed
	Audio: G.711 (U-law)
	Audio: A-law
	Audio: GSM mono
	Audio: ACM (A-law, GSM610, MSNAudio, MSADPCM)
	Video: Cinepak
	Video: Indeo (iv31 and iv32)
	Video: JPEG (411, 422, 111)
	Video: RGB
	Video: YUV
	Video: VCM (IV41, IV51, VGPX, WINX, YV12, I263, CRAM, MPG4)
Flash (`.swf`, `.spl`)	Macromedia Flash 2
GSM (`.gsm`)	GSM mono audio
HotMedia (`.mvr`)	IBM HotMedia
MPEG-1 Video (`.mpg`)	Multiplexed System stream
	Video-only stream
MPEG Layer II Audio (`.mp2`)	MPEG layer 1, 2 audio
MPEG Layer III Audio (`.mp3`)	MPEG layer 1, 2, or 3 audio
QuickTime (`.mov`)	Audio: 8-bit mono/stereo linear
	Audio: 16-bit mono/stereo linear
	Audio: G.711 (U-law)
	Audio: A-law
	Audio: GSM mono
	Audio: IMA4 ADPCM
	Video: Cinepak
	Video: H.261
	Video: H.263
	Video: Indeo (iv31 and iv32)
	Video: JPEG (411, 422, 111)
	Video: RGB

29

JAVA MULTIMEDIA PROGRAMMING

continues

Table 29.1   continued

Media Type	Description
Sun Audio (.au)	8-bit mono/stereo linear
	16-bit mono/stereo linear
	G.711 (U-law)
	A-law
Wave (.wav)	8-bit mono/stereo linear
	16-bit mono/stereo linear
	G.711 (U-law)
	A-law
	GSM mono
	DVI ADPCM
	MS ADPCM
	ACM**

JMF 2.0 also supports various Capture devices, Real-time Transport Protocol (RTP) formats, and RTP Client and Servers.

To use JMF to display an animation or movie in your applet, you need to the
javax.media.Manager package to create a PlayerFactory.

```
Player player = Manager.createPlayer("animation.mov");
```

The player must be "realized" and "prefetched" before it can be started. Realization causes the player to find all resources the player needs, and prefetching loads these resources and initializes the player so it is ready for playing.

The call to Realize is non-blocking, but the player must be realized before any of its methods can be called. The following example uses a blocking realize to ensure that the player will not be used until it is realized:

```
boolean realized = false;

public synchronized void blockingRealize()
{
 player.realize();
 while (!realized)
 {
  try
  {
   wait();
  } catch (java.lang.InterruptedException e)
  {
   status.setText("Interrupted...exiting.");
   System.exit(1);
```

```
  }
 }
}

public synchronized void controllerUpdate (ControllerEvent event)
{
 if (event instanceof RealizeCompleteEvent)
 {
  realized = true;
  notify();
 } else if (event instanceof EndOfMediaEvent)
 {
  eomReached = true;
 }
}
```

A call to `player.start()` will now start the animation.

The previous example merely scratches the surface of what is possible with JMF, but it does demonstrate how quick and easy it is to incorporate almost any media type into your applications and applets.

Summary

This chapter has shown you how quick and easy it is to add full multimedia support to your applets and JavaBeans. Anything from a simple sound loop to full image manipulation is possible. With the advent of fast JVMs and with multimedia support on PCs almost a standard, adding multimedia components to your applications and Web pages can enhance the effectiveness immensely. Beyond simply adding a little spice to an otherwise dull Web page, multimedia can provide valuable feedback; also, it can both attract and retain the attention of the viewer.

With many companies now providing an almost endless supply of third-party multimedia JavaBeans, the possibilities are limited only by your imagination. Java beans are simple to integrate, which makes them the quickest and simplest way to increase the impact of your applications and Web pages with a minimum of effort.

29

JAVA MULTIMEDIA
PROGRAMMING

3D Beans

Java 3D provides you with a 100 percent Java application programming interface that allows you to bring three-dimensional graphics and virtual realities to the computing enterprise. Recreational computer users demand exciting multimedia effects, and professional computer users search for software features that provide an edge over their competition. Use the Java 3D packages to incorporate three-dimensional graphics and sound into your JavaBeans components and satisfy both types of user.

Java 3D is an official Java extension. You must install Java 3D onto your computer before you can develop or run beans that use the Java 3D API. Java 3D includes two core packages, native code, and a set of utility packages.

Many of the newer Java development products have the 3D API included. The version of Visual Café that I have does. But your development tool may not. If that's the case you'll have to download it.

You can either get the standard OpenGL Java 3D 1.1.2 package or a beta of an enhanced package that is optimized for the Windows DirectX 6.1 platform (results in faster operation/rendering). Go to `http://java.sun.com/products/java-media/3D/` and make sure the `.jar` files are put into a directory in your classpath.

Using Java 3D

When you use Java 3D in your beans, the object composing the area that displays three-dimensional graphics must be instantiated from the `javax.media.j3d.Canvas3D` class, resulting in a heavyweight component. Heavyweight components execute native code. The tight coupling of the `javax.media.j3d.Canvas3D` class with native code allows optimization of the computationally expensive rendering of three-dimensional graphics. 3D graphics created using Java 3D can be impressively fast.

The down side of the Java 3D API's reliance on native code is that each computer platform needs its own implementation of Java 3D. In fact, sometimes there are different Java 3D implementations for the same platform. For instance, on Windows platforms, you might install an implementation of Java 3D that uses OpenGL or DirectX to render its graphics. The good news is that the particular implementation doesn't affect the way you write your program. The Java 3D API is the same across all implementations.

> **Note**
>
> OpenGL is probably the most popular low-level graphics library and is used across a wide range of computer platforms, including several flavors of UNIX and Windows. Microsoft licensed OpenGL from Silicon Graphics, the developer

of OpenGL, to include the package with its NT operating systems. Microsoft also supplies an OpenGL package for Windows 95 that you can download from the Microsoft Web site. OpenGL is supplied with Windows 98 and later and all of the Windows NT operating systems.

> **Note**
>
> DirectX is an application programming interface designed by Microsoft to boost multimedia performance on Windows platforms.

> **Note**
>
> Java 3D native code is supplied to Windows platforms in a dynamic link library (DLL), the j3d.dll file.

The two core Java 3D package names begin with the standard extension name `javax`. One package, the `javax.media.j3d` package, includes all the core geometry and audio classes. The contents of this package are contained in the `j3dcore.jar` and `j3daudio.jar` files placed, during setup (see the next section, "Installing the Java 3D SDK"), in the `..\jre\lib\ext` directory. The other package, the `javax.vecmath` package, includes classes designed to support using linear algebra in your Beans displaying 3D graphics. The contents of this package are contained in the `vecmath.jar` file, which is also placed in the `jre\lib\ext` directory.

Installing the Java 3D SDK

Browse through the available implementations of Java 3D and decide on the best implementation for your platform and needs. The current implementation list is on the Sun Web site.

After you decide on the implementation, download and install the Java 3D Software Development Kit (SDK). Four JAR files are installed as standard extensions to the core Java platform: the `j3dcore.jar`, `j3daudio.jar`, `j3dutils.jar`, and `vecmath.jar` files. There is also a `j3d.dll` file that must be in the path of your Java 3D beans.

30

3D BEANS

Building a Java 3D Bean

All Java 3D projects involve carrying out at least three steps:

- Creating a `Canvas3D` object
- Creating a universe
- Creating objects or sounds

The `Canvas3D` object forms the canvas that your three-dimensional universe is painted on. The universe is an object that contains all of your three-dimensional objects and sounds. Of course, you must design, create, or record the objects and sounds that will populate your universe. In this section you will build a simple Java 3D bean, the `WindowOnMyUniverse` bean, to get a feel for these three basic steps. This bean displays only one side of a cube, like the one shown in Figure 30.1.

FIGURE 30.1

The `WindowOnMy`
`Universe` *bean,*
which shows one
side of a virtual
cube.

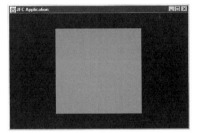

The cube in the first version of the `WindowOnMyUniverse` bean (as shown in Listing 30.1) doesn't look any different than a square. To make matters worse, the cube doesn't move and you can't move around the cube. Don't despair! This is, after all, your first Java 3D bean. At the end of this section you try moving the cube and allowing the user to move around the cube.

Listing 30.1   Source Code for `WindowOnMyUniverse.java`

```
package sams.java3d;

import com.sun.j3d.utils.geometry.ColorCube;
import com.sun.j3d.utils.universe.SimpleUniverse;
import java.awt.BorderLayout;
import javax.media.j3d.BranchGroup;
import javax.media.j3d.Canvas3D;
import javax.swing.JPanel;

public class WindowOnMyUniverse extends JPanel {
  public WindowOnMyUniverse( ) {
```

```
      super( );
      setLayout( new BorderLayout( ) );
      Canvas3D canvas = new Canvas3D( null );
      add( "Center", canvas );
      SimpleUniverse myUniverse = new SimpleUniverse( canvas );
      myUniverse.getViewingPlatform( ).setNominalViewingTransform( );
      myUniverse.addBranchGraph( createSceneGraph( ) );
      setSize( 400, 400 );
      setVisible( true );
   }

  private BranchGroup createSceneGraph( ) {
    BranchGroup root = new BranchGroup( );
    ColorCube cube = new ColorCube( 0.4 );
    root.addChild( cube );
    return root;
  }
}
```

An explanation of the previous code can be found in the next section.

Creating a `Canvas3D` Object

All Java 3D virtual universes and the objects and sounds contained in them must be displayed on a `Canvas3D` object instantiated from the `javax.media.j3d.Canvas3D` class. `javax.media.j3d.Canvas3D` is a heavyweight class extended from the `java.awt.Canvas` class.

`Canvas3D` objects encapsulate code that communicates with the graphics hardware on the computer it finds itself running on. This is done through the Java Native Interface (JNI) application programming interface.

> **Note**
>
> Heavyweight components refer to Java objects that encapsulate code that have native peers.

The `javax.media.j3d.Canvas3D` class has only one constructor with the signature shown here.

```
public Canvas3D(java.awt.GraphicsConfiguration graphicsConfiguration)
```

The constructor takes one parameter: a `GraphicsConfiguration` object created from the `java.awt.GraphicsConfiguration` class. A `GraphicsConfiguration` object encapsulates information about the graphics destination characteristics of the computer hardware on which the bean is currently running.

Typically when you create a Java 3D bean, the bean is extended from a `java.awt.Panel` or `javax.swing.JPanel` class. The `WindowOnMyUniverse` bean is extended from the `javax.swing.JPanel` class. The canvas on which your universe is rendered is added to the panel.

> **Note**
>
> `JPanel` objects are lightweight. `Canvas3D` objects are heavyweight.

Make sure the container that you want to hold a `Canvas3D` object is using the border layout by calling the `java.awt.Container` class `setLayout()` method and passing the method a `BorderLayout` object instantiated from the `java.awt.BorderLayout` class.

The first statement in the `sams.java3d.WindowOnMyUniverse` class constructor is a call to the parent constructor with no arguments. As shown below, this first statement is followed by a call to the `setLayout()` method, which is inherited from the `java.awt.Container` class by the `javax.swing.JPanel` class.

```
super( );
setLayout( new BorderLayout( ) );
```

When the canvas container is using the border layout, you're ready to create a `Canvas3D` object. The next statement in the `sams.java3d.WindowOnMyUniverse` class constructor, shown below, creates a `Canvas3D` object.

```
Canvas3D canvas = new Canvas3D( null );
```

Under many circumstances, you can simply pass `null` to the `javax.media.j3d.Canvas3D` class constructor and the current graphic destination characteristics are used. Finally, add the canvas to the center of the panel with a call to the `add()` method inherited from the `java.awt.Container` class.

```
add( "Center", canvas );
```

This completes the canvas creation process for displaying Java 3D universes. Under some circumstances you will want to get the current graphics configuration explicitly in your code. Usually this is done when you want to customize the configuration. Various classes provide methods for retrieving `GraphicConfiguration` objects. For instance, the `com.sun.j3d.utils.universe.SimpleUniverse` class provides the `getPreferred Configuration()` method.

Creating a Universe

All three-dimensional objects and sounds created using Java 3D exist within a three-dimensional space known as a universe. You create a "bare bones" virtual universe by instantiating the Java 3D API's `javax.j3d.VirtualUniverse` class. However, if want to take an easier approach, use the `com.sun.j3d.utils.universe.SimpleUniverse` class supplied with the Java 3D utility classes. The `WindowOnMyUniverse` bean creates a `SimpleUniverse` object.

Using the `SimpleUniverse` class sounds easier than using the `VirtualUniverse` class when you're first getting started. It's not, though, at that stage. They're both just as easy to use when the code is simple. But the `VirtualUniverse` class has quite a bit more horsepower with additional capabilities and will load slower. If you don't need the additional capabilities, stick with the `SimpleUniverse` class.

Using the `SimpleUniverse` Class

The `com.sun.j3d.utils.universe.SimpleUniverse` class extends `javax.j3d.VirtualUniverse` and adds enough features to its parent class to provide a simple but fully functional user environment when the class is instantiated. The main thing that the `com.sun.j3d.utils.universe.SimpleUniverse` class takes care of for you is setting up the viewer side of the Java 3D bean. The viewer connects the canvas to the universe, thereby providing a view of the universe.

The `com.sun.j3d.utils.universe.SimpleUniverse` class has four class constructors, which are listed with their parameters in Table 30.1. The no argument class constructor creates a default canvas along with default `Viewer` and `ViewerPlatform` objects that connect the default `Canvas3D` object with the universe. This option results in the canvas being displayed within its own frame. The code in Listing 30.2 demonstrates the use of the no argument class constructor in an application.

Table 30.1   `com.sun.j3d.utils.universe.SimpleUniverse` Class Constructors

Signature	*Parameter Descriptions*
`SimpleUniverse( )`	The no argument constructor. The default canvas is used to draw on.
`SimpleUniverse (Canvas3D canvas)`	canvas: The canvas to draw on. Pass `null` and the default canvas is used.

continues

30

3D BEANS

Table 30.1 continued

Signature	Parameter Descriptions
SimpleUniverse(HiRes Coordorigin, int numTransforms, Canvas3D canvas, java.net. URL userConfig	origin: The location, in three-dimensions, of the Locale object. Pass null to set the origin to (0, 0, 0). numTransforms: The number of transforms to be in the MultiTransformGroup object. canvas: The canvas to draw on. Pass null and the default canvas is used. userConfig
SimpleUniverse ViewingPlatform (ViewingPlatform viewingPlatform, Viewer viewer)	viewingPlatform: The object to use. viewer: The Viewer object to use.

Listing 30.2 Source Code for Minimalist.java

```java
package sams.java3d;

import com.sun.j3d.utils.geometry.ColorCube;
import com.sun.j3d.utils.universe.SimpleUniverse;
import javax.media.j3d.BranchGroup;
import javax.media.j3d.Canvas3D;

public class Minimalist {
  public Minimalist( ) {
    SimpleUniverse myUniverse = new SimpleUniverse( );
    myUniverse.getViewingPlatform( ).setNominalViewingTransform( );
    myUniverse.addBranchGraph( createSceneGraph( ) );
  }

  private BranchGroup createSceneGraph( ) {
    BranchGroup root = new BranchGroup( );
    ColorCube cube = new ColorCube( 0.4 );
    root.addChild( cube );
    return root;
  }

  public static void main( String[] args ) {
    new Minimalist( );
  }
}
```

Probably the most commonly used class constructor is the one that takes a single parameter, a `Canvas3D` object. This is the class constructor used by the `WindowOnMyUniverse` Bean. The `Canvas3D` object created by the bean and assigned to the `canvas` variable is passed to the `com.sun.j3d.utils.universe.SimpleUniverse` class constructor, as shown in the following line of code.

```
SimpleUniverse myUniverse = new SimpleUniverse( canvas );
```

This statement creates a universe and connects it to the `Canvas3D` object to draw on. This connection is made through a `ViewingPlatform` and a `Viewer` object created by the `SimpleUniverse` object. One of the remaining two `com.sun.j3d.utils.universe.` `SimpleUniverse` class constructors provides a way for you to assign custom `ViewingPlatform` or `Viewer` objects to your universe. Learn more about these objects in the next section "Displaying a Typical View of Your Universe". The other class constructor enables you to assign a custom origin to your universe.

Displaying a Typical View of Your Universe

A `SimpleUniverse` object sets up the viewer for you, which attaches a universe to a canvas where views of the universe are drawn. Nevertheless, typically you'll want to customize the view of your universe. For a simple universe with a simple set of objects, like in the `WindowOnMyUniverse` bean, the `com.sun.j3d.utils.ViewingPlatform` class's `setNominalViewingTransform()` method provides a good view of the universe's origin.

Access your `SimpleUniverse` object's `ViewingPlatform` object through the `com.sun.j3d.utils.universe.SimpleUniverse` class `getViewingPlatform()` method. The complete statement for setting up a nominal view in `WindowOnMyUniverse` bean is reproduced below.

```
myUniverse.getViewingPlatform( ).setNominalViewingTransform( );
```

Now that you've set up a good view of your universe's origin, you might be wondering where in the universe that origin is and how it's defined. A universe can be quite large, so Java 3D provides markers, known as `Locale` objects, to help you keep track of where you are. By default, a `SimpleUniverse` object has a `Locale` object at its origin, which is defined as the point in three-dimensional space where the x, y, and z axes are all zero (0). You add your visible (or aural) objects to a `Locale` object. Therefore, by default, your objects are attached to your `SimpleUniverse` object at its origin.

> **Note**
>
> Learn more about the `Locale` object in the section "Using the `VirtualUniverse` Class" later in this chapter.

30

3D Beans

At this point, you don't need detailed information on the `Locale` object because the `com.sun.j3d.utils.universe.SimpleUniverse` class takes care of the details for you. The last statement in the `sams.java3d.WindowOnMyUniverse` class constructor adds an object (a colored cube) to the universe. This is accomplished by calling the `com.sun.j3d.utils.universe.SimpleUniverse` class `addBranchGraph()` method and passing the method a scene graph, as shown in the statement below.

```
myUniverse.addBranchGraph( createSceneGraph( ) );
```

The scene graph is a technical term for the collection of objects along with their attributes and behaviors that make up part of your universe. The scene graph in the `WindowOnMyUniverse` bean is created in the `createSceneGraph()` method, which you will cover in detail in the next section, "Creating Objects or Sounds." The `addBranchGraph()` method gets its name from the fact that the root object in any scene graph is always a `BranchGroup` object. The `createSceneGraph()` method returns a reference to the `BranchGroup` object attached to the scene graph and passes it to the `addBranchGraph()` method, which adds the `BranchGroup` object to a `Locale` object through a call to the `javax.media.j3d.Locale` class `addBranchGraph()` method.

Creating Objects or Sounds

The `WindowOnMyUniverse` bean is nearly complete except that the universe is empty. No objects or sounds exist in the simple universe. The `sams.java3d.WindowOnMyUniverse` class `createSceneGraph()` method creates an object, a colored cube, to populate your universe. This simple scene graph takes four steps to make. First, create a root `BranchGroup` object, as shown in the following statement.

```
BranchGroup root = new BranchGroup( );
```

A scene graph is a collection of objects along with their attributes and behaviors that make up a scene in a universe. Each scene graph must have at its root a `BranchGroup` object created from the `javax.media.j3d.BranchGroup` class. `BranchGroup` objects are the only objects that can be added to a `Locale` object, which is the only possible attachment point for a scene graph in a universe.

You can add any number of geometric or sound objects to a `BranchGroup` object. This simple Java 3D bean uses a utility class provided with the Java 3D API, the `com.sun.j3d.utils.geometry.ColorCube` class, which creates a color cube when instantiated. The second statement in the `createSceneGraph()` method reproduced below creates a color cube.

```
ColorCube cube = new ColorCube( 0.4 );
```

The `com.sun.j3d.utils.geometry.ColorCube` class provides two class constructors: one no argument constructor and the other with a single double parameter that sets the scale of the cube with respect to the universe. Use the no argument constructor to create a `ColorCube` object with the length of each edge equal to one. When you use the other constructor, the length of each edge is equal to the number you passed to its double parameter multiplied by one unit in length. For instance, the cube created by the `WindowOnMyUniverse` bean is 0.4 times 1 units long on each edge; 0.4 units deep, 0.4 units wide, and 0.4 units tall.

> **Note**
>
> One unit in length in Java 3D is equal to one meter by convention.

After the cube has been created, it is added to the `BranchGroup` object assigned to the root variable. This is done in the following statement:

```
root.addChild( cube );
```

Finally, the `createSceneGraph()` method returns the `BranchGroup` object through its last statement, reproduced below, so that it can be passed to an `addBranchGraph()` method.

```
return root;
```

The `SimpleUniverse` object created by the `WindowOnMyUniverse` bean provides an `addBranchGraph()` method that, when called, adds the scene graph attached to the passed `BranchGroup` object to a universe.

The `sams.java3d.WindowOnMyUniverse` class, shown in Listing 30.1, is complete. The finished bean should look similar to the one shown in Figure 30.1 (which is run inside of an application) after you compile the class, package it into a JAR file, and then run the bean in the BeanBox. Wow! You can see the blue side of a cube. Okay, it's not so exciting. In fact, you can't even tell that you're looking at a cube. The universe might as well contain a red square. Modify the `WindowOnMyUniverse` bean in the following sections to get a better view of the cube.

Moving the Cube Around

A universe created using Java 3D only really becomes interesting when you are able to see objects from different perspectives. You might do this by moving through the universe around an object, as you will in the next section "Moving As Transformation."

30

3D BEANS

There are two ways to get an object to move in a Java 3D universe. One way is to enable users to manipulate objects through user interfaces such as a mouse. You learn how to enable object manipulation in the "Manipulating the Cube" section later in this chapter. The other way to move an object is to program it to move by itself. In this section you enable the colored cube to spin around its vertical axis (y-axis).

The MoveCube bean displays a rotating cube. The source code for creating this bean is shown in Listing 30.3, and you can see the bean itself, displayed in an application window, in Figure 30.2.

FIGURE 30.2

A cube spins around its y-axis in the MoveCube *Bean.*

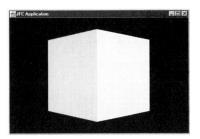

Listing 30.3   Source Code for MoveCube.java

```java
package sams.java3d;

import com.sun.j3d.utils.geometry.ColorCube;
import com.sun.j3d.utils.universe.SimpleUniverse;
import java.awt.BorderLayout;
import javax.media.j3d.Alpha;
import javax.media.j3d.BoundingSphere;
import javax.media.j3d.BranchGroup;
import javax.media.j3d.Canvas3D;
import javax.media.j3d.RotationInterpolator;
import javax.media.j3d.Transform3D;
import javax.media.j3d.TransformGroup;
import javax.swing.JPanel;
import javax.vecmath.Point3d;

public class MoveCube extends JPanel {
  public MoveCube( ) {
    super( );
    setLayout( new BorderLayout( ) );
    Canvas3D canvas = new Canvas3D( null );
    add( "Center", canvas );
    SimpleUniverse myUniverse = new SimpleUniverse( canvas );
    myUniverse.getViewingPlatform( ).setNominalViewingTransform( );
    myUniverse.addBranchGraph( createSceneGraph( ) );
    setSize( 400, 400 );
```

```
    setVisible( true );
  }

  private BranchGroup createSceneGraph( ) {
    BranchGroup root = new BranchGroup( );
    ColorCube cube = new ColorCube( 0.4 );
    TransformGroup rotate = createRotatingBehavior( );
    rotate.addChild( cube );
    root.addChild( rotate );
    return root;
  }

  private TransformGroup createRotatingBehavior( ) {
    TransformGroup rotate = new TransformGroup( );
    rotate.setCapability( TransformGroup.ALLOW_TRANSFORM_WRITE );
    Alpha rotationAlpha = new Alpha( -1, 5000 );
    RotationInterpolator rotator = new RotationInterpolator(
➥rotationAlpha, rotate );
    BoundingSphere bounds = new BoundingSphere( new
➥Point3d( 0.0,0.0,0.0 ), 100.0 );
    rotator.setSchedulingBounds( bounds );
    rotate.addChild( rotator );
    return rotate;
  }
}
```

Moving as Transformation

Java 3D provides a convenient interface for programming your objects to move. Change in a Java 3D universe is accomplished through transformation. Transforming an object's location in the universe to another location creates movement.

> **Note**
>
> You can also use the Java 3D API to change an object's color, size, or any of many other object attributes. Make an attribute change by transforming it.

Transform object attributes such as location through Java 3D transform and interpolator classes. A transform object encapsulates a description of the change that you want an object to go through. The description is not made, of course, in everyday language but is laid out as an algorithm using the Java language. Interpolator objects set a change defined by a transform object into motion. Interpolators bring time into your universe.

30

3D BEANS

> **Note**
>
> An *algorithm* is a finite group of steps that is carried out to solve a problem.

The `sams.java3d.MoveCube` class, shown in Listing 30.3, is almost identical to the `sams.java3d.WindowOnMyUniverse` class described in earlier sections of this chapter and shown in Listing 30.1, except for the `createRotatingBehavior()` method and a couple of statements added to the `createSceneGraph()` method. These are the places that the transform and interpolator objects are created and used.

Using the `TransformGroup` Class

Any object that goes through changes must be attached to a `TransformGroup` object. An object instantiated from the `javax.media.j3d.TransformGroup` class encapsulates a transform matrix, which is encapsulated by an object instantiated from the `javax.media.j3d.Transform3D` class. The no argument `javax.media.j3d.TransformGroup` class constructor creates a default identity matrix that results in no changes in the object.

> **Note**
>
> Think of an object's identity being retained when it is transformed through an identity matrix. The object is the same before the transform as it is after the transform.
>
> A generalized transform object is represented internally as a 4×4 double precision floating point matrix. The mathematical representation is row major, as in traditional matrix mathematics (think way back to Algebra 2). A transform has an associated type, and all type classification is left to the `Transform3D` object.

The other `javax.media.j3d.TransformGroup` class constructor takes one parameter, a `Transform3D` object. Through this constructor you can create a `TransformGroup` object that carries out any type of transform you're able to encode in the 4x4 double-precision floating-point matrix encapsulated by a `Transform3D` object.

You might be a linear algebra guru, in which case you can create transformation matrices and use them to create `TransformGroup` objects. More typically, `TransformGroup` objects are instantiated using the no argument constructor and then other objects, such as interpolators, are attached to the group. These other objects figure out the appropriate transform matrix for you and pass it to the `TransformGroup` object. This is the approach taken by the `MoveCube` bean. The `sams.java3d.MoveCube` class `createRotatingBehavior()` method creates a `TransformGroup` object using the no argument class constructor, as shown in the code reproduced below.

```
TransformGroup rotate = new TransformGroup( );
```

The `TransformGroup` object assigned to the `rotate` variable encapsulates an identity matrix. Other objects that are added to this branch of the scene graph later in the `createRotatingBehavior()` method modify the identity matrix so that it produces the desired transforms. The modification of `TransformGroup` object data isn't allowed, however, unless you explicitly tell the object that it's allowed. Telling an object what it can and cannot do is known as setting its capabilities.

Setting Capabilities

Objects in a Java 3D scene graph are protected from modification unless you tell the object to allow modification. This is known as setting the object's capabilities. The `MoveCube` bean `TransformGroup` object begins with the default identity transform. The transform matrix is changed by an interpolator object, which is added so that the cube shown by the bean is rotated. Cube rotation is accomplished through changes in the matrix encapsulated by the `TransformGroup` object. The `TransformGroup` object's `setCapability()` method, inherited from the `javax.media.j3d.SceneGraphObject` class, must be called to allow the object's `Transform3D` object to be modified. The second statement in the `sams.java3d.MoveCube` class `createRotatingBehavior()` method, reproduced below, sets the capability to write new transformation matrices to its `TransformGroup` object.

```
rotate.setCapability( TransformGroup.ALLOW_TRANSFORM_WRITE );
```

The integer constant passed to the `setCapability()` method determines the kind of capability that's set. The `javax.media.j3d.TransformGroup` class provides several integer constants; the two listed in Table 30.2 are defined in the class itself and the rest are inherited from its parent classes.

Table 30.2   `javax.media.j3d.TransformGroup` Class Capability Integer Constants

Constant	Description
ALLOW_TRANSFORM_READ	Allows reading the object's transform matrix.
ALLOW_TRANSFORM_WRITE	Allows writing to the object's transform matrix.

30

3D BEANS

Capability integer constants are all static and public, so they're accessible without creating a class instance. That is, to access the `ALLOW_TRANSFORM_WRITE` constant, simply write `TransformGroup.ALLOW_TRANSFORM_WRITE` as shown in the `MoveCube` bean statement.

> **Note**
>
> The capability constants are declared as `public static final int`. Recall that all statically defined constants, variables, methods, or inner classes belong to the class that they're declared in and not any particular object instantiated from the class. Also recall that data fields declared as `final` in Java are constants.

After access to write to a transform matrix is granted, as it is in the `MoveCube` bean, the appropriate transform matrix must be created and written to the `TransformGroup` object.

There are two kinds of transforms that will typically be applied to your Java 3D objects: spatial and temporal transforms. Examples of spatial transforms include transforming the scale or location of a cube. Temporal transforms have to do with time and might involve the change of a 3D shape over time. Often, spatial transforms are carried out in conjunction with temporal transforms. A cube, for instance, might change in size and location over time.

The cube in the `MoveCube` bean changes its orientation in space over time. The cube stays at the same location in the universe but it spins around its y-axis. At a detailed level you could say that all of the points through the center of the cube along its y-axis remain at the same location across time. They are static. However, all of the other points in the cube move in a circle around the y-axis. They change their locations across time. You don't need to worry about each individual point in a cube when you set it spinning using the Java 3D API. Java 3D provides the `javax.media.j3d.Alpha` class used for defining time's influence on virtual objects. The API also provides interpolator classes that define how an object's shape, color, location, or other attribute changes with time. Interpolator classes are set into action by `Alpha` objects.

Using the `Alpha` Class

Time's influence on an object in a Java 3D universe is defined by objects instantiated from the `javax.media.j3d.Alpha` class. The general task of an `Alpha` object is to generate a floating-point value between 0.0 and 1.0 (inclusive) that reflects some function of time. In this way, an `Alpha` object provides the way an object changes over time. An attribute of an object might smoothly change over 10 seconds, 10 minutes, or 10 hours. Or it might change continuously as long as the universe exists. An `Alpha` object defines how the change proceeds over time.

The cube in the MoveCube bean spins continuously around its y-axis. In addition to specifying continuous rotation, the Alpha object created by the sams.java3d.MoveCube class specifies the rate of rotation. The statement in the createRotatingBehavior() method reproduced below creates an Alpha object and assigns it to the rotationAlpha variable.

```
Alpha rotationAlpha = new Alpha( -1, 5000 );
```

The Alpha object is created using one of the four class constructors listed in Table 30.3; the constructor takes two parameters. The first parameter takes an integer value that tells the Alpha object the number of times to run the alpha loop. Passing -1 to the loop count parameter results in a continuously running alpha loop. The second parameter takes a long integer value that defines the number of milliseconds that it takes for the alpha value to go from 0.0 to 1.0. In the MoveCube bean, this value, set to 5000 milliseconds or 5 seconds, determines the speed of cube rotation. The rest of the Alpha object parameters are set to the default values listed in Table 30.4.

Table 30.3 javax.media.j3d.Alpha Class Constructors

Signature	*Parameter Descriptions*
Alpha( )	The no argument constructor. Results in the creation of an Alpha object with default parameter values.
Alpha(int loopCount, long increasingAlpha Duration)	loopCount: The number of times to run this alpha loop. Pass a -1 to continuously run this alpha loop.
	increasingAlphaDuration: The period of time in milliseconds that the alpha takes to go from 0.0 to 1.0.
Alpha(int loopCount, long triggerTime, long phaseDelayDuration, long increasing AlphaDuration, long increasing phaseDelayDuration AlphaRamp Duration, long alphaAtOneDuration)	loopCount: The number of times to run this alpha loop. Pass a -1 to continuously run this alpha loop.
	triggerTime: The time, in milliseconds, to set off this Alpha object's trigger. The alpha loop begins running when the trigger goes off unless a phase delay is set (see the parameter).
	phaseDelayDuration: The number of milliseconds to wait after this Alpha object's trigger goes off to begin running the alpha loop.
	increasingAlphaDuration: The period of time in milliseconds that the alpha loop takes to go from 0.0 to 1.0.

continues

30

3D BEANS

Table 30.3 continued

Signature	Parameter Descriptions
	increasingAlphaRampDuration: The period of time in milliseconds that the alpha loop takes to complete.
	alphaAtOneDuration: The period of time in milliseconds that the alpha loop value remains at 1.0.

`Alpha( int loopCount,`
`int mode, long`
`triggerTime, long`
`phaseDelayDuration, long`
`increasingAlphaDuration,`
`long increasingAlphaRamp`
`Duration, long`
`alphaAtOneDuration, long`
`decreasingAlphaDuration,`
`long decreasingAlphaRamp`
`Duration, long`
`alphaAtZeroDuration )`
	loopCount: The number of times to run this alpha loop. Pass a -1 to continuously run this alpha loop.

	triggerTime: This Alpha object's trigger. The alpha loop begins running when the trigger goes off unless a phase delay is set (see the phaseDelayDuration parameter).
	phaseDelayDuration: The number of milliseconds to wait after his Alpha object's trigger goes off to begin running the alpha loop.
	increasingAlphaDuration: The period of time in milliseconds that the alpha loop takes to go from 0.0 to 1.0.
	increasingAlphaRampDuration: The period of time in milliseconds that the alpha loop takes to complete.
	alphaAtOneDuration: The period of time in milliseconds that the alpha loop value remains at 1.0.
	decreasingAlphaDuration: The period of time in milliseconds that the alpha loop takes to go from 1.0 to 0.0.
	decreasingAlphaRampDuration: The period of time in milliseconds that the alpha loop takes to complete.
	alphaAtZeroDuration: The period of time in milliseconds that the alpha loop value remains at 0.0.

Table 30.4 will give you the default parameters for the Alpha class.

Table 30.4   `javax.media.j3d.Alpha` Class Default Parameter Values

Parameter	*Default Value*
`loopCount`	`-1`
`mode`	`INCREASING_ENABLE`
`triggerTime`	`0`
`phaseDelayDuration`	`0`
`increasingAlphaDuration`	`1000`
`increasingAlphaRampDuration`	`0`
`alphaAtOneDuration`	`0`
`decreasingAlphaDuration`	`0`
`decreasingAlphaRampDuration`	`0`
`alphaAtZeroDuration`	`0`

The parameter values for the `MoveCube` bean result in a continuously rotating cube at slow or modest speed. Try changing the value passed to the `increasingAlphaDuration` parameter from `5000` to `2000`. The cube's spin will increase in speed; it'll complete one rotation every two seconds (2000 milliseconds) rather than complete one rotation every five seconds (5000 milliseconds). The `Alpha` object by itself doesn't carry out the rotation. An `Alpha` object must feed its alpha value to an interpolator that determines the kind of transform carried out.

Using the `RotationInterpolator` Class

The `MoveCube` bean uses the `javax.media.j3d.RotationInterpolator` class to rotate the cube around its y-axis. The speed of rotation is dependent on how quickly the supplied alpha value changes. The `MoveCube` bean creates a `RotationInterpolator` object by executing the following statement:

```
RotationInterpolator rotator = new RotationInterpolator( rotationAlpha, rotate );
```

This statement includes one of two `javax.media.j3d.RotationInterpolator` class constructors, which are listed in Table 30.5. This class constructor takes two parameters, an `Alpha` object and a `TransformGroup` object. You created each of these in previous sections. The resulting `RotationInterpolator` object uses the alpha value produced by the `Alpha` object to smoothly move the cube attached to the `TransformGroup` object around the y-axis between two angles, which is set by default to 0 and 360 degrees (or 0 and 2PI radians). In other words, the cube smoothly rotates in a complete circle around its central axis.

Table 30.5   `javax.media.j3d.RotationInterpolator` Class Constructors

Signature	*Parameter Descriptions*

`RotationInterpolator`
`(Alpha alpha,`
`TransformGroup target)`
	alpha: The `Alpha` object used by this interpolator.
	
	target: The target `TransformGroup` object for this interpolator.

`RotationInterpolator`
`(Alpha alpha,`
`TransformGroup target,`
`Transform3D axisOfRotation,`
`float minimumAngle, float`
`maximumAngle )`
	alpha: The `Alpha` object used by this interpolator.
	
	target: The target `TransformGroup` object for this interpolator.
	
	axisOfRotation: The `Transform3D` object that defines the local coordinate system in which this interpolator operates. The rotation is around the y-axis of this local coordinate system.
	
	minimumAngle: The starting angle in radians.
	
	maximumAngle: The ending angle in radians.

You can set the start and stop angle of rotation through the other
`javax.media.j3d.RotationInterpolator` class constructor listed in Table 30.5. For
instance, creating a `RotationInterpolator` object using the following statement results
in a cube that rotates half way and then suddenly jumps back to where it started from and
rotates half way again.

```
RotationInterpolator rotator = new RotationInterpolator( rotationAlpha, rotate,
➥new Transform3D, 0.0f, ( float ) Math.PI );
```

The constructor takes angles in radians. 0 degrees is equivalent to 0 radians and 360
degrees (a complete circle) is equivalent to 2PI radians. The example above rotates from
0 degrees (0 radians) to 180 degrees (PI radians).

> **Note**
>
> The only way you can tell that the cube jumps from half way turned back to the
> beginning is by following the colors. Notice the progression of colors as the
> cube rotates when it rotates a complete 360 degrees (2PI radians). Then com-
> pare the color progression when the cube is rotating only half way.

Setting Scheduling Bounds

The final step in creating a bean that displays a rotating cube is to define the boundaries within which the bean is scheduled to rotate. This step is essential but not very interesting in the case of a universe that you don't move around in, which is the case here. You watch the cube spin in the MoveCube bean but you cannot move around the cube. You will learn how to move around the cube in the "Manipulating the Cube" next section in this chapter.

A scheduling bound is the volume within which the particular transform is valid and is executed. If you move outside this bound, the transform stops. This makes sense when you move around a universe because when you get a certain distance away from a particular object you might no longer see it. Why pay the computational price for rotating a cube if you can't see it?

You must set scheduling bounds in a universe that users don't move through. Simply set the bounds so that they encompass the objects that are displayed. The following statement creates a BoundingSphere object that encompasses the colored cube in the MoveCube bean.

```
BoundingSphere bounds = new BoundingSphere( new Point3d( 0.0,0.0,0.0 ), 100.0 );
```

The class constructor used creates a BoundingSphere object with a given center point and radius length. This is one of four javax.media.j3d.BoundingSphere class constructors, which are listed in Table 30.6. The first of the two parameters takes a Point3d object encapsulating the position of the center of the bounding sphere within the universe. The point of origin in the universe is {0.0, 0.0, 0.0}, or 0.0 units in the direction of the x-axis, 0.0 units in the direction of the y-axis, and 0.0 units in the direction of the z-axis. The second parameter takes a double value that defines the radius of the sphere. An arbitrarily large value, 100.0, is passed because users don't move around in this universe.

Note

Point3d objects are instantiated from the javax.vecmath.Point3d class included with the Java 3D API. The javax.vecmath package includes several classes useful for using linear algebra in your calculations. Linear algebra, primarily meaning vector and matrix math, is particularly useful for computations involving three-dimensional graphics. Details, however, are beyond the scope of this book. For more information, consult a book on programming three-dimensional graphics.

30

3D BEANS

Table 30.6 `javax.media.j3d.BoundingSphere` Class Constructors

Signature	Parameter Descriptions
`BoundingSphere( )`	The no argument constructor. Results in the creation of a `BoundingSphere` object with default parameter values, its center at {0, 0, 0} and a radius of 1.
`BoundingSphere( Bounds boundsObject )`	`boundsObject`: The `Bounds` object used to construct and initialize this `BoundingSphere` object.
`BoundingSphere( Bounds[] boundsObjects )`	`boundsObjects`: An array of `Bounds` objects used to construct and initialize this `BoundingSphere` object.
`BoundingSphere( Point3d center, double radius )`	`center`: The center of the bounding sphere.
	`radius`: The radius of the bounding sphere.

After a `BoundingSphere` object is created and assigned to the `bounds` variable, you can set the bounds within which the `RotatorInterpolator` object carries out its interpolation. The `javax.media.j3d.RotatorInterpolator` class has a `setSchedulingBounds()` method that you pass a scheduling bounds object. The `MoveCube` bean includes the following statement in its `createRotatingBehavior()` method to set the interpolator's scheduling boundary:

```
rotator.setSchedulingBounds( bounds );
```

With the scheduling bounds set, the interpolator will transform the colored cube over time. All of the objects that encapsulate the cube's rotating behavior must be attached to a `TransformGroup` object that will also be attached to the cube. The following statement adds the `RotatorInterpolator` object to the `TransformGroup` object assigned to the `rotate` variable.

```
rotate.addChild( rotator );
```

At this point, the `createRotatingBehavior()` method has packaged together all the objects necessary for rotating the colored cube. The final statement in the method, reproduced below, returns the `TransformGroup` object with all of the rotating behavior machinery attached.

```
return rotate;
```

The returned `TransformGroup` object is assigned to the `rotate` variable in the `createSceneGraph()` method. The colored cube is added to the `TransformGroup` object, which is then added to a `BranchGroup` object. The `BranchGroup` object, as you saw in previous sections, is the only object you can attach to a universe. Once the `BranchGroup` object is attached to the universe, the scene graph is live.

Manipulating the Cube

Objects can move themselves, but they can also move through manipulation. You might, for instance, pick up a coffee mug, move it around, and hold it to get a better look at its design. The ability to manipulate objects in a virtual universe provides a natural environment for users to explore. Rather than simply watching a cube rotate, a user is able to grab hold of the cube and move it around to look at it from any angle he wants. In this section, you write a bean that displays a colored cube that you're able to spin around its point of origin.

Drag the color cube displayed by the `ManipulateCube` bean by holding down your left mouse button while pointing to the cube and moving your mouse. The cube spins in any direction you want around its point of origin. The source code for creating the `ManipulateCube` bean is shown in Listing 30.4, and the bean is pictured in an application window shown in Figure 30.3.

FIGURE 30.3

Manipulate a cube by dragging it in the `ManipulateCube` *bean.*

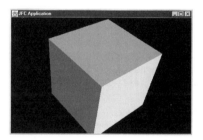

Listing 30.4   Source Code for `ManipulateCube.java`

```
package sams.java3d;

import com.sun.j3d.utils.behaviors.mouse.MouseRotate;
import com.sun.j3d.utils.geometry.ColorCube;
import com.sun.j3d.utils.universe.SimpleUniverse;
import java.awt.BorderLayout;
import javax.media.j3d.BoundingSphere;
import javax.media.j3d.BranchGroup;
import javax.media.j3d.Canvas3D;
import javax.media.j3d.Transform3D;
import javax.media.j3d.TransformGroup;
import javax.swing.JPanel;
import javax.vecmath.Point3d;

public class ManipulateCube extends JPanel {
  public ManipulateCube( ) {
    super( );
```

continues

Listing 30.4   continued

```
      setLayout( new BorderLayout( ) );
      Canvas3D canvas = new Canvas3D( null );
      add( "Center", canvas );
      SimpleUniverse myUniverse = new SimpleUniverse( canvas );
      myUniverse.getViewingPlatform( ).setNominalViewingTransform( );
      myUniverse.addBranchGraph( createSceneGraph( ) );
      setSize( 400, 400 );
      setVisible( true );
   }

   private BranchGroup createSceneGraph( ) {
      BranchGroup root = new BranchGroup( );
      ColorCube cube = new ColorCube( 0.4 );
      TransformGroup manipulate = createManipulationBehavior( );
      manipulate.addChild( cube );
      root.addChild( manipulate );
      return root;
   }

   private TransformGroup createManipulationBehavior( ) {
      TransformGroup manipulate = new TransformGroup( );
      manipulate.setCapability( TransformGroup.ALLOW_TRANSFORM_READ );
      manipulate.setCapability( TransformGroup.ALLOW_TRANSFORM_WRITE );
      MouseRotate mouseRotate = new MouseRotate( manipulate );
      BoundingSphere bounds = new BoundingSphere(
➥new Point3d( 0.0,0.0,0.0 ), 100.0 );
      mouseRotate.setSchedulingBounds( bounds );
      manipulate.addChild( mouseRotate );
      return manipulate;
   }
}
```

The `sams.java3d.ManipulateCube` class shown in Listing 30.4 is nearly identical to the `sams.java3d.MoveCube` class shown in Listing 30.3. There is one statement in the `createSceneGraph()` method that is different between these classes. A `ManipulateCube` object has a `createManipulationBehavior()` method rather than the `createRotatingBehavior()` method encapsulated by the `MoveCube` object. This difference is reflected in the third statement reproduced below from the `sams.java3d.ManipulateCube` class's `createSceneGraph()` method.

```
TransformGroup manipulate = createManipulationBehavior( );
```

This statement calls the `createManipulationBehavior()` method rather than the `createRotationBehavior()` method. Both methods return `TransformGroup` objects. The differences of importance between these classes are between these two methods, which implement the two different behaviors displayed by these beans.

An Object Moving or Moving An Object?

The ManipulateCube bean demonstrates the way to code for moving an object, as opposed to the MoveCube bean, which demonstrates the way to write code for an object moving on its own through a universe. The createManipulationBehavior() method, reproduced in full below, creates all of the appropriate machinery to enable users to manipulate a cube using their mouse.

```
private TransformGroup createManipulationBehavior( ) {
  TransformGroup manipulate = new TransformGroup( );
  manipulate.setCapability( TransformGroup.ALLOW_TRANSFORM_READ );
  manipulate.setCapability( TransformGroup.ALLOW_TRANSFORM_WRITE );
  MouseRotate mouseRotate = new MouseRotate( manipulate );
  BoundingSphere bounds = new BoundingSphere( new Point3d( 0.0,0.0,0.0 ),100.0 );
  mouseRotate.setSchedulingBounds( bounds );
  manipulate.addChild( mouseRotate );
  return manipulate;
}
```

Compare this new method with the createRotatingBehavior() method, reproduced below, developed in earlier sections for the MoveCube bean.

```
private TransformGroup createRotatingBehavior( ) {
  TransformGroup rotate = new TransformGroup( );
  rotate.setCapability( TransformGroup.ALLOW_TRANSFORM_WRITE );
  Alpha rotationAlpha = new Alpha( -1, 5000 );
  RotationInterpolator rotator = new RotationInterpolator(
➥rotationAlpha, rotate );
  BoundingSphere bounds = new BoundingSphere( new Point3d( 0.0,0.0,0.0 ),
➥100.0 );
  rotator.setSchedulingBounds( bounds );
  rotate.addChild( rotator );
  return rotate;
}
```

The major differences are that in the createManipulationBehavior() method you are

- Setting the capability to read, in addition to write, a transform from the TransformGroup object.

- Creating a MouseRotate object, which is used rather than the RotationInterpolator object.

- Interacting with the cube using a mouse provides input to the MouseRotate object, rather than using an Alpha object to provide alpha values to the interpolator.

30

3D BEANS

Setting the `ALLOW_TRANSFORM_READ` Capability

Setting capabilities is always straightforward. Look up the scene graph object in the Java 3D API documentation, which lists all of the class's capability constants in the field summary section. You can spot a capability constant by the `ALLOW` that is prepended to the constant name, such as `ALLOW_TRANSFORM_READ`.

The `TransformGroup` object assigned to the `manipulate` variable is set to allow other objects to both read and write to its encapsulated transform information. The following two statements copied from the `createManipulationBehavior()` method set these capabilities by using the `setCapability()` method inherited by the `javax.media.j3d.TransformGroup` class from the `javax.media.j3d.SceneGraphObject` class.

```
manipulate.setCapability( TransformGroup.ALLOW_TRANSFORM_READ );
manipulate.setCapability( TransformGroup.ALLOW_TRANSFORM_WRITE );
```

> **Note**
>
> Only children of the `javax.media.j3d.SceneGraphObject` class have capabilities that can be set.

Setting these capabilities allows a two-way interaction between the `TransformGroup` object that sets the current cube position and the `MouseRotate` object that reads user mouse input, which it transforms into new cube positions.

Using the `MouseRotate` Class

The Java 3D API provides a class that does all of the work to allow users to rotate an object by dragging their mouse. The `com.sun.j3d.behaviors.mouse.MouseRotate` class polls for mouse input and uses the results to determine the transform of the dragged object's orientation in virtual space.

The `ManipulateCube` bean uses a `MouseRotate` object to enable users to manipulate the color cube. All it takes to add this behavior to a scene graph is to create the `MouseRotate` object and attach it to a `TransformGroup` object. The following statement accomplishes this task in the `createManipulationBehavior()` method of the `sams.java3d.ManipulateCube` class:

```
MouseRotate mouseRotate = new MouseRotate( manipulate );
```

The bean's `TransformGroup` object assigned to the `manipulate` variable is passed to the `com.sun.j3d.behaviors.mouse.MouseRotate` class constructor. This is one of three class constructors, which are listed in Table 30.7. If you use one of the other two constructors, you need to call the `com.sun.j3d.behaviors.mouse.MouseRotate` class `setTransformGroup()` method and pass it the `TransformGroup` object you want the `MouseRotate` object on which to operate.

Table 30.7 `com.sun.j3d.behaviors.mouse.MouseRotate` Class Constructors

Signature	Parameter Descriptions
`MouseRotate( )`	The no argument constructor. Results in the creation of a `MouseRotate` object with default wakeup and invert flags (automatic and off, respectively). The object must be associated with a `TransformGroup` object through the `setTransformGroup()` method.
`MouseRotate( int flags )`	`flags`: Passes constants to set wakeup and invert flags. The object must be associated with a `TransformGroup` object through the `setTransformGroup()` method.
`MouseRotate( TransformGroup transformGroup )`	`transformGroup`: The transform group that this object will operate on. The `MouseRotate` object is created with default wakeup and invert flags (automatic and off, respectively).

Moving Around the Cube

You can provide users the opportunity to "step inside" the virtual universe and move around the colored cube, in addition to manipulating it. The Java 3D API provides utility classes to enable full interaction with a virtual universe. One of these classes, the `com.sun.j3d.behaviors.mouse.MouseRotate` class, was described in the previous section "Using the `Mouse Rotate` Class." Use two other classes, the `com.sun.j3d.behaviors. mouse.MouseTranslate` and `com.sun.j3d.behaviors.mouse.MouseZoom` classes, in your bean to allow complete interaction with your virtual universe. In this section, you create the `ExploreCube` bean using these classes and the color cube. The completed running bean is shown in Figure 30.4 and the source code for the `sams.java3d.ExploreCube` class is shown in Listing 30.5.

FIGURE 30.4

Manipulate, zoom, and pan through a virtual universe displaying a color cube in the `ExploreCube` *bean.*

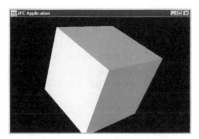

30

3D BEANS

Listing 30.5   Source Code for ExploreCube.java

```java
package sams.java3d;

import com.sun.j3d.utils.behaviors.mouse.MouseRotate;
import com.sun.j3d.utils.behaviors.mouse.MouseTranslate;
import com.sun.j3d.utils.behaviors.mouse.MouseZoom;
import com.sun.j3d.utils.geometry.ColorCube;
import com.sun.j3d.utils.universe.SimpleUniverse;
import java.awt.BorderLayout;
import javax.media.j3d.BoundingSphere;
import javax.media.j3d.BranchGroup;
import javax.media.j3d.Canvas3D;
import javax.media.j3d.Transform3D;
import javax.media.j3d.TransformGroup;
import javax.swing.JPanel;
import javax.vecmath.Point3d;

public class ExploreCube extends JPanel /*implements Externalizable*/ {
  public ExploreCube( ) {
    super( );
    setLayout( new BorderLayout( ) );
    Canvas3D canvas = new Canvas3D( null );
    add( "Center", canvas );
    SimpleUniverse myUniverse = new SimpleUniverse( canvas );
    myUniverse.getViewingPlatform( ).setNominalViewingTransform( );
    myUniverse.addBranchGraph( createSceneGraph( ) );
    setSize( 400, 400 );
    setVisible( true );
  }

  private BranchGroup createSceneGraph( ) {
    BranchGroup root = new BranchGroup( );
    ColorCube cube = new ColorCube( 0.4 );
    TransformGroup manipulate = createManipulationBehavior( );
    manipulate.addChild( cube );
    root.addChild( manipulate );
    return root;
  }

  private TransformGroup createManipulationBehavior( ) {
    TransformGroup manipulate = new TransformGroup( );
    manipulate.setCapability( TransformGroup.ALLOW_TRANSFORM_READ );
    manipulate.setCapability( TransformGroup.ALLOW_TRANSFORM_WRITE );
    MouseRotate mouseRotate = new MouseRotate( manipulate );
    MouseTranslate mouseTranslate = new MouseTranslate( manipulate );
    MouseZoom mouseZoom = new MouseZoom( manipulate );
    BoundingSphere bounds = new BoundingSphere( new Point3d( 0.0,0.0,0.0 ),
➥100.0 );
    mouseRotate.setSchedulingBounds( bounds );
    mouseTranslate.setSchedulingBounds( bounds );
```

```
        mouseZoom.setSchedulingBounds( bounds );
        manipulate.addChild( mouseRotate );
        manipulate.addChild( mouseTranslate );
        manipulate.addChild( mouseZoom );
        return manipulate;
    }
}
```

The `sams.java3d.ExploreCube` class is similar to the `sams.java3d.ManipulateCube` class shown in Listing 30.4. The only difference is that the `createManipulationBehavior()` creates two new objects, the `MouseTranslate` and `MouseZoom` objects.

Using the `MouseTranslate` Class

The Java 3D API provides a class that does all the work to allow users to pan an object across their view by dragging their mouse. The `com.sun.j3d.behaviors.mouse.` `MouseTranslate` class polls for mouse input and uses the results to determine the transform of the dragged object's orientation in virtual space.

> **Note**
>
> Pan through a universe by holding down your right mouse button while moving your mouse.

The `ExploreCube` bean uses a `MouseTranslate` object to enable users to slide by the cube to its left, right, up, or down. All it takes to add this behavior to a scene graph is to create the `MouseTranslate` object and attach it to a `TransformGroup` object. The following statement accomplishes this task in the `createManipulationBehavior()` method of the `sams.java3d.ManipulateCube` class:

```
MouseTranslate mouseTranslate = new MouseTranslate( manipulate );
```

The bean's `TransformGroup` object assigned to the `manipulate` variable is passed to the `com.sun.j3d.behaviors.mouse.MouseTranslate` class constructor. This is one of three class constructors, which are listed in Table 30.8. If you use one of the other two constructors, you need to call the `com.sun.j3d.behaviors.mouse.MouseTranslate` class `setTransformGroup()` method and pass it the `TransformGroup` object you want the `MouseTranslate` object to operate on.

Table 30.8 `com.sun.j3d.behaviors.mouse.MouseTranslate` Class Constructors

Signature	*Parameter Descriptions*
`MouseTranslate( )`	The no argument constructor. Results in the creation of a `MouseTranslate` object with default wakeup and invert flags (automatic and off, respectively). The object must be associated with a `TransformGroup` object through the `setTransformGroup()` method.
`MouseTranslate ( int flags )`	`flags`: Passes constants to set wakeup and invert flags. The object must be associated with a `TransformGroup` object through the `setTransformGroup()` method.
`MouseTranslate ( TransformGroup transformGroup )`	`transformGroup`: The transform group that this object will operate on. The `MouseTranslate` object is created with default wakeup and invert flags (automatic and off, respectively).

Using the `MouseZoom` Class

The Java 3D API provides a class that does all the work to allow users to zoom an object by dragging their mouse. The `com.sun.j3d.behaviors.mouse.MouseZoom` class polls for mouse input and uses the results to determine the transform of the dragged object's orientation in virtual space.

> **Note**
>
> Zoom through a universe by holding down your middle mouse button (if you have one) while moving your mouse. You can also zoom by holding down your Alt button (on the Windows platform, check the Java 3D documentation for other platforms) while you move your mouse. Use this latter method if you don't have a middle mouse button.

The `ExploreCube` bean uses a `MouseZoom` object to enable users to move close up or far away from the color cube. All it takes to add this behavior to a scene graph is to create the `MouseZoom` object and attach it to a `TransformGroup` object. The following statement accomplishes this task in the `createManipulationBehavior()` method of the `sams.java3d.ExploreCube` class:

```
MouseZoom mouseZoom = new MouseZoom( manipulate );
```

The Bean's `TransformGroup` object assigned to the `manipulate` variable is passed to the `com.sun.j3d.behaviors.mouse.MouseZoom` class constructor. This is one of three class constructors, which are listed in Table 30.9. If you use one of the other two constructors, you need to call the `com.sun.j3d.behaviors.mouse.MouseZoom` class `setTransformGroup()` method and pass it the `TransformGroup` object you want the `MouseZoom` object to operate on.

Table 30.9 `com.sun.j3d.behaviors.mouse.MouseZoom` Class Constructors

Signature	*Parameter Descriptions*
`MouseZoom( )`	The no argument constructor. Results in the creation of a `MouseZoom` object with default wakeup and invert flags (automatic and off, respectively). The object must be associated with a `TransformGroup` object through the `setTransformGroup()` method.
`MouseZoom` `( int flags )`	`flags`: Passes constants to set wakeup and invert flags. The object must be associated with a `TransformGroup` object through the `setTransformGroup()` method.
`MouseZoom( TransformGroup` `transformGroup )`	`transformGroup`: The transform group that this object will operate on. The `MouseZoom` object is created with default wakeup and invert flags (automatic and off, respectively).

Summary

In this chapter you created Beans that displayed three-dimensional graphics that could be animated, manipulated, and explored. The Java 3D API provides a high-level interface for writing Beans with 3D graphics and virtual universes and insulates you from low-level hardware specific programming. Write the 3D graphics code once and let the various Java 3D implementations, for instance the OpenGL and DirectX implementations, take care of the platform-specific details. With Java 3D, your Beans take advantage of the latest and most advanced multimedia technology resulting in virtual universes that users can explore, see, and listen to in three dimensions.

30

3D BEANS

INDEX

Get **FREE** books and more...when you register this book online for our Personal Bookshelf Program

http://register.samspublishing.com/

SAMS

Register online and you can sign up for our *FREE Personal Bookshelf Program...*unlimited access to the electronic version of more than 200 complete computer books—immediately! That means you'll have 100,000 pages of valuable information onscreen, at your fingertips!

Plus, you can access product support, including complimentary downloads, technical support files, book-focused links, companion Web sites, author sites, and more!

And you'll be automatically registered to receive a *FREE subscription to a weekly email newsletter* to help you stay current with news, announcements, sample book chapters, and special events, including sweepstakes, contests, and various product giveaways!

We value your comments! Best of all, the entire registration process takes only a few minutes to complete, so go online and get the greatest value going—absolutely FREE!

Don't Miss Out On This Great Opportunity!

Sams is a brand of Macmillan Computer Publishing USA.

For more information, please visit *www.mcp.com*